Educational Psychology

A Developmental Approach

Second Edition

ADDISON-WESLEY PUBLISHING
COMPANY
Reading, Massachusetts
Menlo Park, California
London
Amsterdam ·
Don Mills, Ontario
Sydney

Educational Psychology

A Developmental Approach

Richard C. Sprinthall
American International College

Norman A. Sprinthall
University of Minnesota

This book is in the
ADDISON-WESLEY SERIES IN EDUCATION

To children

Ye are better than all the ballads
That ever were sung or said
For ye are living poems
And all the rest are dead.

H. W. LONGFELLOW

Preface to the second edition

The decision to revise an introductory textbook is always difficult. On the one hand, there is a strong feeling that we shouldn't do too much tampering. Many a good original product has been spoiled by later modifications, so we questioned whether or not to look under the hood when the engine's already running. On the other hand, there is an even stronger sense that improvement is always possible, especially when an author examines his own work carefully. Our decision to revise, however, was not simply an attempt to pay lip service to our general developmental orientation. After all, authors who value growth and development could hardly take a stand in favor of the status quo. Beyond that was our firm view that some important changes were necessary to fill in the gaps in current chapters, add additional material in new chapters, provide more synthesis throughout the work, and build an extensive glossary of key concepts as a reading guide.

These areas of improvement were selected after extensive field testing, reviews, and interviews. Also, we received many unsolicited letters from educators throughout the country offering significant suggestions. As a result, two completely new chapters—on language development and special education—were added. We had originally misjudged the need for an entire chapter on language growth and development and have now rectified that omission. As is obvious, language growth represents a parallel sequence to the other domains of pupil development, such as physical, physiological, intellectual, personal, moral, and ethical growth. Therefore, a thorough examination of this aspect of child development can help to consolidate and strengthen the practicing educator's knowledge base.

The chapter on special education was prompted largely by the enormous shift in school policy in this area. We noted in the first edition that mainstream education was likely to become (pardon the metaphor) the wave of the future. We didn't realize how rapidly that wave would break. In the last few years, forty-nine of the fifty states have passed laws mandating so-called mainstream classes for mildly retarded and handicapped children. The doctrine of the least-restrictive environment for pupils in previously segregated special classes has literally inundated regular classrooms. In the fall of 1975, 25,000 pupils were so mainstreamed in one state alone, California. Such a shift obviously creates a dilemma for regular school teachers and other support personnel, as well as for the entire field of educational psychology. In one sense, such a change almost forces educational psychology itself into a new mainstream. The topic of special education has not traditionally been covered in most texts, largely because special educators themselves were not trained in regular, teacher-education classes. All that must now change. The new chapter is our first attempt to help regular classroom teachers understand the problem itself and (since we continually stress thinking and doing) to provide some practical suggestions for classroom teaching techniques designed to accommodate this increased range of individual differences.

In the other chapters, we have followed a process of adding and pruning. Thus, there is a good deal of general updating to include important new theory and practice. Chapter 5 contains expanded material on the newly emerging field of behavior genetics, and in Chapter 6 we have added Burton "Bud" White's theory and data on the importance of early experience on the development of competent children. We have extended the section on adolescent development in the Erikson chapter (8) in order to provide a more complete picture of that important stage. The changes in Chapter 9 include a broader series of suggestions for teaching divergent creative thinking. Chapter 10, on moral development, has been substantially revised by providing more detailed and balanced descriptions of each stage of moral growth. In Chapter 12, a description and analysis of Skinner's schedules of reinforcement are now included, and in Chapter 13 we have added a fairly comprehensive coverage of Albert Bandura's social-learning theory.

The discussion of teaching-learning, Chapter 14, has also undergone a major revision. We have added a synthesis of developmental perspectives in two areas, intellectual and ethical. Intellectual growth is represented by a combination of the views of Bloom, Piaget, Perry, and David Hunt, while ethical growth is covered in the works of Larry Kohlberg. Our goal in this section is to show how the objectives of educational development encompass both areas, and how the curriculum materials, teachers' conceptions, and pupils' stages are all interrelated.

In Chapter 18 we have updated the section on intelligence and intelligence testing, and have also included new material and evidence regarding the Jensen argument. In addition, this chapter includes the recent findings of Zajonc on the relationship between family size, birth order, and intelligence. In Chapter 20, the major addition is a new section covering the phenomenon of aggression, and the effects of the mass media on the aggressive behavior of the audience. This chapter also contains new material on sex roles in the schools and the "risky shift."

In Chapter 21 we have expanded the information on recent assessments of psychological/affective education programs and suggestions for practice. Chapter 23, on contemporary educational policy issues, includes a series of new topics, such as competency-based teacher education, *Sesame Street* (the impact of televised programming), specific language disability (or "dyslexia"), and a complete rewrite of the section on woman's development by Professor V. Lois Erickson.

Finally, a comprehensive glossary has been added as a ready reference for the beginning reader. The glossary and new chapter summaries were included to provide more structure, both for initial reading and as a means of review.

There are, of course, many to thank for their help in compiling this edition. In Minneapolis, particular thanks go to Professors Stan Deno and Maynard Reynolds for their work on Chapter 22. Carla Hill has been immensely helpful in correcting drafts.

In Springfield, Bob MacLachlan, an expert in clinical and child psychology, provided us with the highly readable and detailed chapter on language acquisition. We also wish to thank Professors Art Bertrand, Joe Cebula, and Phil Faticanti for their many valuable comments and suggestions. George Grosser, the "friendly critic," smoothed out some of the rough details of the early drafts, and we certainly wish to thank Mari Tarpinian for both her typing skills and her many suggestions on wording. Finally, since no book can be completed without the full cooperation of the "home office," we wish to extend our thanks and gratitude to our Addison-Wesley team.

We hope the reader will enjoy and profit from the new edition. We have tried to present major issues clearly, yet without pedantry. We also have presented hard evidence for our positions.

This results in our continuing to have to walk a tightrope between readability and the substantive evidence. Perhaps we can illustrate the basic paradox of a work such as this, which seeks to teach significant ideas, rooted in legitimate knowledge, and yet do it with maximum positive effect. In the classic movie *My Little Chickadee*, Mae West saunters into a school classroom and reads on the blackboard, "I am a good boy. I am a good girl." She turns to the class, eyes the young chargers and says, "What is this, propaganda?" Also, we are reminded of Paul Tillich's dictum, "Most books and most teaching is like throwing stones at the heads of those who haven't yet asked the question." In this regard, we hope we have both stimulated the reader to ask and aided by providing some tentative answers.

Our goal has really been to seek greater excellence within the present purpose of the book. We must leave the final judgment to the reader. We hope you feel neither assaulted by propaganda nor stoned (in the original meaning of that word, of course).

Springfield, Massachusetts   RCS
Minneapolis, Minnesota   NAS
December 1976

Preface to the first edition

Educational psychology has for too many years been like a rejected child, with neither parent willing to either take credit for its birth or take the responsibility for its rearing. Professional educators were suspicious of the field of educational psychology, for they thought it was too theoretical and impractical. The learning theories, though perhaps often elegantly contrived, seemed incapable of translation to classroom practice. The psychology side of educational psychology was often seen as being led by fuzzy-headed theorists who, though able to create new theoretical positions at the drop of a hat, hadn't the vaguest notion of what was going on in the classroom. The psychologists were seen as armchair speculators, eccentric and timid, who kept a lofty distance between themselves and the working teacher, and the psychologist's own attitude often didn't help. It was as though teachers were being insulting and mundane by daring to ask how a certain theory might help children to learn how to spell. The psychologist felt that his or her mission was far too cosmic to be rudely interrupted by such trivialities.

On the other side, many psychologists viewed the educators with equal suspicion and distrust. The educators were seen as somehow unable to grasp the significance of certain theoretical positions, just not quite bright enough to appreciate the pearls of wisdom being offered. Public school teachers and the colleges that trained them were often seen as rising to new heights of mediocrity. The only busy person in a college of education was the mimeograph operator, grinding away at producing sterile hand-outs, full of sound and fury and signifying nothing.

To the educators, thus, the psychologist was a Don Quixote, harebrained, impractical, and virtually useless. To the psychologist, the educator was treated with patronizing condescension, as one not quite ready for admittance to the "club."

And so, with its parents in combat, the fledgling discipline of educational psychology often found itself directionless, willing to be shunted from in-law to in-law, from position to position, with little sense of coherent purpose or unity. There came to be many educational psychologies, so diverse in some instances that the only common feature was the name they shared. Educational psychology was sometimes taught as a thorough course in straight learning theory, with weeks devoted to a topic like Hull's constitution of reaction potential (the reaction potential is determined by the habit strength, sHr, multiplied by the drive, D, the stimulus intensity dynamism, V, and the incentive motivation, K). Prospective teachers often wondered openly at the relevance of this discovery. Educational psychology might in another instance be taught as a thorough course in measurement, where students learned to calculate sophisticated statistical procedures and spent the semester silently and anxiously wondering how this might be of use to them in the classroom. Or, a course in educational psychology might be a chatty, anecdotal, group-discussion coverage of a series of unrelated classroom situations, many hilariously funny, others pathetically depressing. The student was often hard pressed at the end of the semester to find one fact or bit of insight that wasn't already known to him or her when the semester started.

Our goal in this book is to present educational psychology as a legitimate discipline, with its own body of knowledge and its own self-identity. Despite its stormy childhood, educational psychology has matured over the years and has developed a body of literature and a sense of direction. We plan to outline the major contributions from psychology *for* educational practice and present these ideas in a manner that can be both understood and *used* by educators. Our focus will be on the learner in the learning situation, how the learner is changed by and changes those stimulus conditions known as the learning situation.

Since it's the whole child who goes to school, we will spotlight in Unit II the total growth and development of that child, physically, emotionally, intellectually, and morally. Our story of growth and development will begin at the beginning, at conception, for to understand the child who is entering school we must have some understanding of that child's past, of what took place before that point in time when he or she first walks through the classroom door. We will pay special attention to the child's first few years of life, pointing out the crucial importance of early experience in shaping human destiny. The developing child will be followed from the point of view of physical growth, cognitive growth, emotional growth and, in a special section, moral growth—an area too long overlooked by psychologists and educators.

In Unit III we will look at the learning theorists, especially Skinner and Bruner, and will stress those aspects of the various learning positions that have relevance for the working teacher, for example, behavior modification. In these chapters, the learning theorists *will* talk to teachers. Nor will the teacher be overlooked as a person.

We will discuss the human qualities of the teacher in Unit IV, as well as the strategies and goals of effective teaching. We also look at the question of discipline in the classroom and how various techniques may reflect an implicit philosophy on the part of the teacher.

The theme of growth, development, and individual differences will also be looked at from the point of view of assessment, and in Unit V we will present a brief introduction to statistical description and inference. Since educational psychology is a maturing, changing, dynamic field, we will also present a special chapter on reading and understanding research. This is aimed at helping the teacher become equipped to keep abreast of current research developments in the field long after the present course is over. The complex question of intelligence is covered next, the nature of intelligence, intelligence testing, and the social issues that have been generated by the use and abuse of intelligence testing. Learning styles in the classroom will also be covered, and in this context, we will look at the questions of creativity, impulsivity, reflectivity, and deductive and inductive thinking.

The classroom as a social unit is discussed in Unit VI, which points out the pervasive classroom effects of seemingly subtle social stimuli.

In the final unit, we attempt to point out the new directions that are appearing in the field, and we make a prediction or two regarding the future.

Our general view, of course, is that there is no more important issue confronting education and psychology than the need for effective and informed practice in the real world of schools, communities, children, and adolescents. Crisis is probably too strong a word to connote our sense of urgency. Also, the problems that we face are long-standing, indeed almost endemic. The city schools of the nation are in worse shape than they were five years ago. In 1973 a recent follow-up study to the Kerner Commission report indicated that the "schools are more tedious and turbulent" and that racial isolation in the cities was increasing. In general, the quality of instruction and learning in all schools has not appreciably changed in this era. We noted in Chapter 2 that studies done from 1912 to the 1960s indicated that most teaching was really talking. Yet as we go to press, the recent work of Adams and Biddle in 1970 indicates that not only do teachers still do almost all the talking, but that the small amount of pupil talk is all done by the pupils who sit in the six seats down the middle aisle in a typical classroom.

Also, we discern what might be called a morale problem for education and psychology. The wave of optimism that typified the 1950s and early '60s has given way to moods of despair and pessimism. The apparent futility of attempting to reduce educational inequality through the rapid expenditures of vast sums of money has added to the lack of optimism. It is not the time to return to privatism, however we may feel about the failure of recent educational innovations. In fact, now is the time to learn from past mistakes. Educational problems will not be solved by proclamation but by good ideas and wise practice. Our hope is that this volume will help those who are in education now or who may wish to enter in the future to become wise and informed educators. They, in the long run, will make the difference.

We wish to thank our colleagues for their help and guidance on this project. At the Springfield end we especially appreciate Dr. George S. Grosser, the friendly critic, and Dr. Paul Anastasiou, Dr. Arthur Bertrand, Dr. Robert MacLachlan, and Professor Lee Sirois. We also wish to express our deep thanks to Miss Lorraine Rovelli, Miss Brenda Ramsey, and Mrs. Janis Aamodt, who tirelessly transcribed our sometimes baffling hand-written pages and "creative" spelling into the final manuscript.

We also wish to thank those in Cambridge and Minneapolis who generously helped us. Professor Ralph Mosher at Boston University provided much help on the questions of teaching models. Professor Maurice Belanger, now at the University of Quebec, painstakingly reviewed the Piaget chapter and made many helpful suggestions. Professor Larry Kohlberg, as always, provided much aid with the chapters on moral development and discipline. Dr. Delores Gallo at the University of Massachusetts in Boston was the guiding and creative light for the chapter on creativity. Doctors Chris Dowell, Victor Atkins, Barbara Meyer Greenspan, and Raymond Almeida helped with the sections on psychological education in Chapter 20. Professor Peter Kuriloff at the University of Pennsylvania was also very helpful on that chapter. Dr. Bernard Seiderman provided some examples for the teaching chapters.

In Minneapolis, we were helped substantially by Professor Jim Resti's work in cognitive-developmental psychology and by strong conceptual as well as personal support by Professor Roger Wilk. We also appreciate the work of Professor Lois Erickson, especially for writing the section on women's development. Her perspective was invaluable.

It is clear that this volume is the work of many. We gratefully acknowledge their help and support.

Springfield, Massachusetts   RCS
Minneapolis, Minnesota   NAS
January 1974

P.S. We should add as postscript that we have never worked with such a helpful and productive publishing crew as we found at Addison-Wesley. We greatly appreciate their continual positive contributions toward completing a difficult task. Our thanks, again!

Contents

UNIT III

THE NATURE OF LEARNING

UNIT VI

SOCIAL PSYCHOLOGY AND MENTAL HEALTH

UNIT VII

EDUCATIONAL PSYCHOLOGY AND PUBLIC POLICY

Biographies

UNIT I

Introduction

1

Understanding human behavior

Of all the most human tendencies, none is more human than wondering about other human beings. "What makes that person tick?" is a question we find ourselves asking in almost every human situation. When we watch children play we note almost unconsciously the many differences that are so obvious—one child strides confidently around the playground while another moves shyly, almost secretively, from place to place, and a third dashes hurriedly from one activity to the next. The differences immediately strike us and almost as immediately we find ourselves wondering, "Why does Johnny act one way, while Mary acts so completely differently?" This line of questioning, a kind of natural curiosity, helps us notice and explore the wide range of human activity we perceive every day. In fact, only very young children (under three months) are an exception, and then only in special circumstances. We can almost say that from the time a person enters this world to the time the person leaves it, he or she will ask questions and be most curious about other human beings.

Certainly, it was this basic human tendency that gave rise to the field we call psychology, and the tendency to ask questions about learning in particular that gave rise to the subject of educational psychology. "Why and how do humans learn anything?" we ask. "What conditions promote learning?" "Do people learn differently at different ages?" "What are the best ways to teach?" And on and on. Evidence that such questions are not new can be found as far back as the fifth century B.C., in the writings of the first Greek historian, Herodotus. In his description of the ancient civilization of Phrygia, Herodotus describes at length an elaborate experiment in educational psychology. The people of that ancient civilization (1200 B.C.) were curious to find out what language infants

3

The differences among and between children are fascinating in themselves. Children are naturally curious about the world they live in and about the people they meet.

would first speak if they didn't have anyone around to talk to as they grew up. The outcome of the experiment was somewhat farcical,* but the fact that the experiment was undertaken shows that humans have wanted to find out or have "needed to know about" the why and how of learning and human behavior for a very long time.

MISUNDERSTANDING BEHAVIOR

Although we humans have a long history of being curious about behavior, we also have a long history of making absurd statements about the meaning of behavior, especially in education. For whatever reason, we seem to pay lip service to the idea that learning and behavior are highly complicated. Just think for a moment about the amazing array of activities, ideas, feelings, and relationships you can experience. Yet in spite of this great diversity, we seem to have an incurable habit of reducing everything to simple generalizations. Too often we assume that human behavior has one *single cause.* Before you dismiss this statement itself as a generalization, think for a moment about the number of times during the day you hear people making authoritative statements describ-

A simple view: all behavior has a single cause

---

*
To control for outside influences, the Phrygian "educational psychologists" removed newborn infants from their mothers and had them suckle goats and then waited breathlessly to hear the children's first words. The word reportedly was "beekos." If you will sound this out, you will realize the children, far from speaking some "natural" language, copied their bleating goat mothers.

ing why people behave or act the way they do. The currently popular radio and TV "talk" shows are obvious examples. Listeners call the station and, one after the other, make conclusive judgments based on the assumption that a single cause explains other people's actions. "All unions want is more money for themselves." "You can't trust New Yorkers." "All people on welfare are lazy." "All industrialists are robber barons."

If we turn for a moment to the field of education, the same tendency to generalize is apparent. Parents, teachers, and counselors all too often fall into the trap of claiming to know *the reason* a pupil misbehaves in class: "He is not bright." "He's an underachiever because he's lazy." "She has emotional problems because she comes from a broken home." "What can you expect from kids who live in that part of town? They don't want to learn." If you were to read some of the comments in school records, you would find many such examples of authoritative conclusions based on a single cause. You would also see how categorically and with what finality the statements are phrased. We spent a morning looking through student records and copied down the following comments:

10-year-old boy	"Doesn't do well—parents too permissive."
12-year-old girl	"Afraid to learn—parents too strict."
9-year-old boy	"This is the fourth Jones boy I've had; they are all alike. They hate school."
13-year-old girl	"Not like her sisters and brothers, poor student—lazy."
15-year-old boy	"A discipline problem, watch him carefully . . . ."
14-year-old-girl	"A terrible student—boy crazy."
12-year-old boy	"Can't learn a thing because he can't sit still."

Even if you don't have access to school records, you can hear teachers talking in these same terms. Just sit quietly in the corner of a lunch or faculty room sometime and pretend to read while you listen carefully and count the number of single-cause-and-effect statements you hear.

It has also been shown that teachers and supervisors (experienced teachers who should know better) fall into this same trap in supervisory sessions—explaining classroom difficulties by conclusive generalizations: "He has a discipline problem." "She is a behavior problem." "He has a short attention span." If we look carefully at such statements one characteristic stands out: learning difficulties are isolated safely and exclusively within the child or within the child's home. As a last resort educators say, with a feeling of self-righteousness, "After all, his parents don't care whether or not he learns anything. If they don't care, what can we do!" Such a view conveniently overlooks the fact that children spend more time in school than in any other place from their fifth to their sixteenth year. If we decide that nothing can be done with certain children, then indeed nothing will be done.

Such thinking about children's behavior affects much more than the teachers' treatment of them. When teachers limit their thinking to stereotypes, they pass the same kind of thinking on to their students. Ralph Ojemann, one of the pioneers in classroom mental health, has shown that elementary school children

The danger: teaching children to think in stereotyped ways

develop progressively more arbitrary, more stereotyped ways of thinking the longer they remain in school. "It appears that we have a culture which is 'infected' with the arbitrary judgmental or non-understanding approach to behavior and that this infection is being transmitted from one generation to another."[1]

"Psychologizing" about children is part of a natural human tendency to question and be curious about the causes of behavior. However, educators must be particularly careful not to fall into the habit of explaining behavior in terms of a single cause and must guard against locating the blame for upsetting or "bad" behavior exclusively within the child's personality or within his home. If we take a hard and careful look at this problem, we will find that too often we teachers and counselors want our pupils to conform to our view of how they should behave. We should mention, of course, that parents often do exactly the same thing: "My son had a terrible time in the first grade because his teacher was mean." "With a teacher like that—what can you expect!" So parents can play precisely the same game and place all the blame for educational difficulties safely on someone else. It's almost like a basketball game. When the referee calls a foul on one team, there is an immediate and stormy reaction from the offending player, "Who me! I never touched him. He ran into me. With that kind of acting he ought to be in Hollywood!" When, a few moments later, the referee calls a foul on someone on the other team, the roles are suddenly reversed, "Who me! I never touched him. . . ." In the classroom, as in a basketball game, it's always someone else's fault. The teacher may say it's the children, the parents may blame the teacher, while the children may say it's both teachers and parents. We all nominate someone else and use the "psychology" of a single cause and effect to support our views.

Always placing the blame on someone else

THE BILLIARD BALL THEORY OF HUMAN BEHAVIOR

There is often, then, just one reason why Johnny doesn't learn, and that reason is always beyond our control. This kind of illogic serves as a convenient rationalization or "copout" to avoid the necessity of really trying to understand the problems of learning. To explain human behavior in terms of a single cause is to make a billiard ball out of people. In billiards, if we strike the cue ball precisely, we can *cause* the other ball to move in a predictable direction. A single cause has a single effect. Transferring this idea to human behavior is of course completely out of the question. People will freely admit that human beings are more complicated than billiard balls and that their behavior is less predictable, and yet in the same breath they often go on to make a statement that uses single-cause-and-effect reasoning: "We must have a dress code in this school *because* otherwise the kids will go wild." "You gotta keep your eyes on those long-haired, sleazy hippies." It is the convenience of such thinking that makes the billiard ball theory so enduring. If we can find a single cause we don't have to think further or try to understand. The problem is solved and it's the other person's fault. We ask, "Why does Johnny act that way in school?" and as soon as we think we have the reason, we are apt to go no further. If we do this, we may become good billiards players, but we will surely be poor educators.

People and billiard balls: one cause and one effect

THE VOLCANIC THEORY OF HUMAN BEHAVIOR

Often, however, we err in the opposite direction—that is, we view behavior, especially children's behavior in school, as so complex and so contradictory that we would be much better off forgetting about causes entirely. Instead, we assume that the situation will determine what happens. We just float along, behaving in random and unpredictable ways and then, like a volcano, we suddenly erupt. Think for a moment of a long line of cars waiting at a red light on a hot summer's day. The light changes; the first car in line stalls. In no time an explosion occurs—horns blare, red faces shout obscenities—all because of a few moments of delay. The reaction is completely out of proportion to the event itself and disappears almost as quickly as it erupted. The moment the cars start moving again, those faces that were so red they looked like they were about to explode are suddenly transformed into kind, thoughtful faces once again.

Our problem as educators, according to this view, is not to spend a lot of time trying to find out what makes people tick or what causes children to behave in certain ways; that's just wasting time, "psychologizing." Instead, we should figure out ways to keep the pupils busy and working and not worry about understanding their behavior. Behavior is too complicated for us to understand, and, besides, people usually are controlled by situations (traffic jams).

There is no Right Answer, no Final Truth, no Perfect Lesson Plan, and experts often will disagree about what method is best and how the classroom teacher should proceed.

Behavior as impulsive and situational

So let's assume no causes at all for behavior and find ways to control situations —then we don't have to worry about individuals. To avid being overwhelmed by the prospect of really understanding children and teenagers, it's simply a lot easier to assume that behavior is unpredictable and random—"volcanic."

BILLIARD BALLS VERSUS VOLCANOES

If we carefully consider the two major theories many people use for understanding behavior in general, and the behavior of schoolchildren in particular, we will realize the obvious deficiencies of both. However, it is also important to face the fact that these views are commonly shared. The single-cause-and-effect position is the most popular, perhaps because of the tendency of Hollywood movies and daytime TV serials to portray human behavior in terms of a single dramatic cause: "The turning point in young Dr. Malone's childhood came when a neighbor gave him a stethoscope to play with," or, "The youngster listened intently to those prophetic words, 'Some day, young fellow, if you work hard enough you could be president.' The words echoed in his heart that day as young Harry Truman set out . . . ." Such reasoning may make for a dramatic story or gripping personal history, but it is of rather doubtful credibility and can become genuinely dangerous for an educator. If we let a single dramatic incident explain behavior, the illusion of understanding allows us to avoid the hard thinking we must do to understand the whole complex of events that determine how a young person grows up.* However, if we don't take this line of least resistance, we still are not justified in leaping to the other extreme and saying that behavior just happens. We cannot give up trying to explain behavior simply because the single-cause theory is questionable.

The illusion of understanding behavior

A SUPERTHEORY FOR EDUCATION

If we can't reduce human behavior to a single-cause-and-effect relationship or assume that behavior just happens, and if we can't just invent contrived explanations for behavior, in what direction should we head? Where does this leave

---

*

Psychoanalytically inspired movies are the biggest culprits in this regard because of the seemingly scientific method (dream analysis, hypnosis) that leads the patient to disclose the single traumatic childhood event that forever molded his character.

us? It leaves us with one further paradox. We can say, "OK, I'll give up looking for a single cause for each behavior, I'll agree that people are neither billiard balls nor volcanoes, and I'll also agree not to create made-up theories that are just rationalizations. Now what? You've taken away my usual ways of thinking about pupils; what will you replace it with? What do I stand on as a basis for a theory?" In such a vacuum there is one further tendency that we must acknowledge before we can answer the question. We might be tempted to assume that somewhere the theory does exist—a complete, comprehensive, and authoritative answer to all the questions we have about human behavior, especially behavior relating to classrooms and children. There is a deep-rooted tendency in all of us to look for answers that are either totally Right or totally Wrong, and this may leave in us the traces of desire to find the "compleat" theory of behavior, a series of unequivocal, total, and conclusive statements. Then we could simply memorize all the Right Answers, walk into a classroom, and teach the perfect lesson every time. Each class would be a peak experience of maximum learning. Each child would enter the room filled with curiosity, optimally ready to learn, breathlessly awaiting the beginning of an adventure. The air would crackle with the electricity of excitement. The pupils would figuratively grab the teacher by the lapels and ask, in voices choking with anticipation— "Please Teach Us!"

Thus it may be something of a letdown to have to admit that the Right Answer, the Final Truth, and the Perfect Lesson Plan are illusions. As understandable as our desire for certainty is, it is nonetheless unlikely to ever be satisfied: not only are the final answers not in, but it is likely that we will never have all the answers.

Philosophers of science tell us that science offers no final answers, no ultimate truths, that science provides constantly more accurate predictions, not Eternal Truth. The history of science abounds in examples of theoretical positions that were seen as Final Truths, only to be later replaced by other Final Truths. The Flat Earth Society insisted that Columbus would fall off the edge. Phrenologists insisted they could predict behavior by feeling the bumps on a person's head. Scientific thinking in one era is the prescientific thinking of the next, as new and more comprehensive theoretical explanations emerge. We can strive for increasing precision, but ultimate truth, if it exists at all, will be known only when the last fact has been recorded on Judgment Day.

One of the genuine difficulties that a field like educational psychology has created for itself is a tendency to advertise itself falsely. On the one hand there is a tendency to sloganize about our field, to claim, for example, that educational psychology provides all the answers to questions about learning, motivation, and effective teaching. "Using scientific principles derived from psychology and applied to education, we can systematically and faultlessly guide pupil learning in optimal conditions." Such phrases create an expectation in the reader that here at last the Truth will be found. On the other hand, as the reader proceeds gradually it begins to seem as if the so-called laws of human behavior in education are not always clear-cut. Contradictions and inconsistencies do arise. In fact, the advice some psychologists offer seems to contradict the advice of other experts in the field. One theorist will say that programed instruction is the

Theory as a tentative explanation

The search for a perfect lesson plan

best way to individualize learning. Another equally honored theorist will say that programed learning is an educationally dangerous technique because it teaches convergent thinking. Similar controversies occur in great educational debates concerning reading, assessment, open education, team teaching, intelligence, the very nature of learning—in fact, in just about every significant aspect of teaching and learning.

WHAT DO WE DO WHEN EXPERTS DISAGREE?

The difficulty we face, then, is a real one. We may have to teach tomorrow. We can't very well wait for the experts to come to consensus; that might take years, or even generations. What to do? It's a difficult question and one we cannot avoid. To begin, we think it important to restate an earlier point: there is not now, nor is there ever likely to be, a Right Answer, or Supertheory, that will completely explain human behavior. A theory, or a set of assumptions, can at

The educators' paradox

best explain only part of human behavior. Thus the paradox: we can't find all the answers, and we can't give up the search for a better and more adequate understanding of how and why we behave as we do. We may object to the concept of ultimate truth in education, but that is no reason to close the patent office. The paradox is perhaps best summed up by the following aphorism (a saying that contains a general truth for all humans):

In some ways *all* people are the same.

In some ways *some* people are the same.

In some ways *no* people are the same.

There is an entire psychology of individual differences based on the message contained in the last point, "In some ways *no* people are the same." There is an entire psychology of group behavior based on the first point, "In some ways *all* people are the same." And social psychology attempts to come to grips with the content of the middle statement, "In some ways *some* people are the same." This is when it gets bewildering, unless we can expect the premise that *the educator should not look on the field of psychology as a repository for ultimate truth.* Instead, the informed educator should view psychology as a *resource,* as *sets of ideas, suggestions,* and *educated guesses.* He or she should view the field of educational psychology as an ever-changing field that gradually accumulates useful information, not as a fixed body of knowledge or of immutable laws.

Educational psychology does have information, ideas, theories, and practices to offer the educator, whether teacher, counselor, or principal. However, the educator's point of view, the way he or she views educational psychology, is the most critical dimension in this entire volume. This volume contains important concepts and implications for education, but none more important than the attitude toward the field we outlined above, especially if you plan to be actively involved in educating. If you have merely a superficial interest in the field, this perspective is not so important. But if you plan to get involved in teaching,

Psychology as a resource for practice

counseling, or administering, where you will have to put your ideas into practice, then this perspective is crucial. The real danger comes from rigidly applying a few principles of educational psychology and missing the context. We should not underestimate the difficulties of being an educator in the real world. The situation compels us to get down to it—to *do*. We cannot, like the philosopher George Berkeley, take a problem under advisement, retire to a cave, and think about it for a year or so. Education is doing. George Bernard Shaw once said, "Those who can, do, those who can't, teach!" We should revise this quote to, "Those who can do, teach!"

From the start, then, we must accept the view that educational psychology is a special body of resource information. Note, please, that we do not want to promote the phony division between the science and the practice of education that says

Psychology = Science + Truth
  Education = Practice + A few ideas borrowed from the truth

We need to reverse this view so that as educators we use psychology to *inform* our practice. This volume is organized around this perspective. We view the field of psychology from the perspective of educators, those who teach and counsel and administer to children and teenagers. From this position we carefully examine the body of information available from psychology, and we cull and select information. In doing this we find that there is no one right view. Instead, we find some important ideas and elements from one area of psychol-

We should not underestimate the difficulties of being an educator in the real world. The situation compels us to get down to it—to *do*.

ogy, and other ideas from a completely different realm of psychology. We explain why we have selected the material we have and analyze the important and general implications of our choice. We hope in this way to help you become comfortable with the notion that in the future you, too, will carefully examine, cull, and select from the resources of educational psychology in order to improve your practice. With a basis in practice the educator has the valuable perspective of experience in the natural setting. It's like the different perspective and understanding that come from studying animals in zoos rather than in their natural environment: we learn only about the behavior of zoo animals. The same can be said if we study children exclusively in laboratories.

The importance of a perspective

The classroom as a natural environment

The best way to view resources available from educational and general psychology is from the perspective of the natural setting, the classroom. The teacher is obviously not a robot who gets reprogramed with each new research finding. At the same time, the teacher, counselor, or administrator does start by asking questions about individual pupils and groups of pupils—questions about how to manage the learning process, how to maximize motivation, and how to help each child develop. Given the need to act, to do, to teach, the educator can then turn to particular resources to help him or her do an effective job. It is certainly our view that educational psychology provides significant, potential resources as long as we don't assume that these resources are an established body of fixed truth. Too often, people in education accept this view in theory and then go right ahead and write a book, teach a class, or give a lecture implying that there is a single best way.

We ask the reader to beware, then, of both dimensions of this problem—be prepared to take proper measure of the search for a supertheory on one hand and to recognize the tendency to pay only lip service to the concept of multiple perspectives on the other. The second trend is the more difficult to cope with because the reader of the book or the pupil in the classroom feels uneasy and suspects that sooner or later the teacher will drop the pretense of multiple perspectives, come clean, and reveal the single truth. But, as we have

No single theory has all the answers

already pointed out, in human studies there is no single theory. We are much too complicated. Our capacity to reflect on experience, search for meaning, seek stimulation, creates an almost infinite complexity. Add to this such factors as individual variability, the influence of development, change, growth, and evolution, and we can realize the importance of being tentative and relative, in order to build an open perspective. The educators' problem, as we have noted, is the need to act even though the answers will never all be in.

For our part, we will present the components, the ideas and theories from psychology, that provide real insights into the teaching and learning processes. The material will be selective but not necessarily additive. In other words, the parts will not always fit together precisely. For example, it is absolutely critical for educators to be familiar with parts of reinforcement theory—namely, how to arrange reinforcements that will enhance rather than inhibit learning. At the same time, parts of that theory are incompatible with the theory of developmental stages, and yet developmental theory contains the material that educators must know or they will not understand why pupils so often haven't the slightest idea of what is going on in class.

Resources available from educational and general psychology are best viewed from the perspective of
the natural setting, the classroom.

We hope to present a series of ideas from a variety of perspectives so that
you can select just the information you need to practice more effectively. You
will find salient ideas. You will find theories and ideas to inform your practice.
But you will find no one answer.

Some educators and psychologists will say quite openly, "It doesn't really
make much difference what we do as long as we are consistent. Pick a view
(e.g., operant conditioning, discovery teaching, whatever) that is compatible
with your own style and stick to it." Some say it another way, "Feel free to
switch around and see if something works." Or "Do your own thing in the
classroom." Recently, such ideas have been elevated to the status of a theory,
called "spontaneous schooling."[2] Since "hard" evidence from empirical research
has often been inconclusive in educational psychology, this view suggests that
we follow our intuition and ignore the research. This approach resembles the
volcanic theory of behavior and is just about as helpful.

The educator's problem—the need to act even though the answers will never all be in.

Avoid the extremes of impulse and of narrow-minded psychologizing

In our view the educator has more to offer than spontaneous impulse or narrow-minded psychologizing. We see the educator using a guided and examined basis for deciding how to act in the classroom. We also see the educator as capable of comprehending and using a series of perspectives, components of theories, and aspects of the best thinking on the subject of educational practice. An educator cannot rely on a single theory or on a single practice any more than anyone else can. He or she would be as useful as a baseball player who could hit but could not run, throw, or field.

THE PLAN FOR THIS BOOK

Given our objective of providing the future educator with a multidimensional framework for the complex issues of teaching and learning, we have divided the book into units, or categories, that focus on specific educational issues. In this way we hope to keep a constant focus on our dual objectives of theory and practice for the future teacher, counselor, administrator, or parent. To help you know more and be more effective: these are our learning goals.

Chapter 2 takes a brief historical look at education and psychology so that the troubled past can help us understand the present challenge. The philosopher Santayana said that those who are blind to history will be condemned to repeat it. Certainly one of educational psychology's major problems has been this tendency to reinvent the wheel, so to speak. Chapter 2 presents in rather broad strokes some of the major historical trends over roughly the past 70 years.

Unit II (Chapters 3 to 10) focuses on the major issues of child and adolescent development. The perspectives are multiple: physical, cognitive, personal, linguistic, and moral growth and development. We stress the interactive nature of developmental growth, the equal importance of heredity and environment on an individual's behavior. Such an understanding should inoculate us against the simplistic single-cause-and-effect view. This unit also stresses significant learning periods or stages of growth as critical points for effective teaching. This will give you a feeling for the most appropriate learning experience for children and teenagers at each stage of their psychological development. Thus you will be able to base your teaching strategies on an understanding of "where the learner is."

Unit III (Chapters 11 to 13) presents information on techniques and methods of teaching derived from the major learning theories. To some degree the focus is almost opposite that of Unit II. Rather than child and adolescent development, we discuss Bruner's and Skinner's views of instructional strategies, both their major theoretical differences and their educational implications.

Unit IV (Chapters 14 and 15) really focuses on you as a teacher. We examine what has been called the hidden agenda of schooling, the teacher as a person. We try to get at some of the subjective or personal dimensions of teaching,

your own attitudes about knowledge, children, and equally important, about yourself. In some ways this unit could be called a framework for self-examination.

Unit V (Chapters 16 to 19) presents the basic framework of measurement and educational assessment. The design is to help you understand the concepts of measurement, to help you read educational research reports and know the difference between phony claims and genuinely significant outcomes. We pay particular attention to the controversy raging over the meaning and measurement of intelligence. This section concludes with a chapter on creativity, an area almost as controversial as IQ itself.

Unit VI (Chapters 20 to 22) focuses on the psychology of the classroom, the concern for education as a means of producing mentally healthy human beings and mainstream special education. Here you will find some of the newest material on the classroom as a social arena and on problems of educational motivation. We also discuss some of the recently developed programs called either "affective education" or "curriculum in deliberate psychological education." Rather than leaving the problems of mental growth as a specialty for the mental-health clinic, these programs stress the importance of what you as a teacher can do in regular classrooms to promote healthy growth. The chapter on special education and mainstreaming reflects one of the newest directions for classroom practice. The chapter outlines the reasons for mainstreaming, as well as detailing techniques to increase the accommodative capacity of classrooms for all pupils.

Unit VII (Chapter 23) discusses some of the current trends in education. The context is deliberately broad and is meant to provide only a brief exposure to current controversy, especially on educational policy—reading (the great debate), equality or inequality of educational opportunity, dyslexia, children and television, the open classroom, competency-based teacher education, women's development—these are a few of the topics that may take on great significance in the next decade. Hopefully, these issues will give you a background for understanding the past, examining the present, and thinking about the future—a tall order. Before you lose heart contemplating this complexity of ideas and practices, let us close this introduction with a comment from one of this country's first and greatest thinkers in education, William James. James had a gift for reducing complexity to clarity without oversimplifying, and, at the conclusion of his *Talks with Teachers,* he said:

> *I have now ended these talks. If to some of you the things I have said*
> *seem obvious or trivial, it is possible that they may appear less so when,*
> *in the course of a year or two, you find yourselves noticing and apperceiving*
> *events in the schoolroom a little differently, in consequence of some of the*
> *conceptions I have tried to make more clear. I cannot but think that to*
> *apperceive your pupil as a little sensitive, impulsive, associative, and reactive*
> *organism, partly fated and partly free, will lead to a better intelligence of*
> *all his ways. Understand him, then, as such a subtle little piece of machinery.*
> *And if, in addition, you can also see him and love him as well, you will be*
> *in the best possible position for becoming perfect teachers.*[3]

Summary

Teachers, counselors, and administrators often tend to "psychologize" about children. Perhaps this is because, if one can pin a single-cause explanation on a child's behavior, it is much easier to decide the matter is beyond one's control—especially if the single cause is felt to be within the child or within the home. Such stereotyped thinking not only affects the teacher's treatment of students, it ultimately encourages arbitrary ways of thinking in the students themselves.

This "billiard ball" explanation of behavior reduces the complexities of human motivation to simple cause and effect: if we strike the cue ball precisely, we can *cause* a predictable pattern of movement. Such a notion is, of course, misleading. Behavior has multiple causes, and an effort must be made to understand them.

The "volcanic theory" of behavior errs in the opposite direction. Behavior is seen as being so complex and contradictory that one can never hope to understand it. This is equally misleading, for while behavior is complex, its causes are not infinite.

In the field of educational psychology there is no supertheory that can account for all aspects of behavior. The knowledge we possess does not come in the form of ultimate truth or absolute rights and wrongs. Knowledge consists of evaluating possibilities that are relative to time and space. Nevertheless, education looks to psychology to supply scientific answers concerning the nature of the optimal learning environment. What is the perfect lesson plan? What is the correct teaching style? How can we increase student motivation? Experts disagree as to the most effective approaches to these problems. Should the educator therefore ignore the recommendations of psychologists? What perspective should he or she adopt?

Educational psychology offers multiple perspectives regarding the causes of behavior and the most effective methods of teaching and counseling. By being faithful to only one viewpoint, or by ignoring all theories, the educator is bound to lose much valuable insight. Educational psychology should be viewed as a body of resource information that can be used *selectively* to inform one's practice. If applied judiciously, the various theoretical viewpoints can be helpful in sorting out the causes of child behavior, and as a basis for selecting activities to promote growth.

REFERENCES

1
R. H. Ojemann, *New Insights in Health Behavior* (Cleveland: Educational Research Council of America, 1969).

2
J. M. Stevens, *The Process of Schooling* (New York: Holt, Rinehart and Winston, 1967).

3
W. James, *Talks with Teachers* (New York: Norton, 1958).

2

Educational psychology yesterday and today

YESTERDAY: TRIVIA IN THE CLASSROOM

In the late nineteenth century, a visitor to the public schools concluded that most classroom activity consisted of what he called a game of recitation. The pupils and the teacher followed a systematic question-and-answer exercise. The teacher would ask a series of short, factual questions with the rapidity of a machine gunner: "Now class, pay attention. . . . Tell me, who discovered America? ——. What year? ——. How many ships were there? ——. What were their names? ——. How long was the voyage? ——." Each question was followed by a brief pause, and then students with hands raised were called on, again with the speed of light, until one student said the correct answer. At this point the teacher would fire the next question and skip around the class calling on pupils with hands raised until the next right answer was called out. The observer in the nineteenth-century classroom noted that the interaction between teacher and pupil seemed exclusively mechanical. The process seemed to emphasize rote learning, the repetition of facts memorized from the teacher and the textbook. Inquiry was unknown. "In several instances when a pupil stopped for a moment's reflection, the teacher remarked abruptly, 'Don't stop to think, but tell me what you know.' "[1]

These impressions of what we might call trivia in the classroom were given further credence by other observers. An English educator in 1908 noted the "time-honoured" tradition in American classrooms of question-and-answer recitation in distinct contrast to the lecture method used on the continent of Europe. A study of classroom interaction further substantiated question-and-answer as the predominant approach to teaching in this country. Using stenographic

21

notes of actual classroom discussions (this was in the days before tape recorders) a researcher in 1912 found that over 80 percent of all classroom talk consisted of asking and answering brief factual questions—questions that called for a good rote memory and an ability to phrase the answer in the same terms the teacher used. The teacher asked between one and four questions per minute, much like today's TV quiz games where contestants (pupils) are given a few seconds to come up with the right answer; if they don't have the answer at the tip of their tongue, they lose their turn, and the quiz master (teacher) moves on. The researcher noted:

> The fact that one history teacher attempts to realize his educational aims through the process of "hearing" the textbook, day after day, is unfortunate but pardonable; that history, science, mathematics, foreign language and English teachers, collectively are following in the same groove, is a matter for theorists and practitioners to reckon with.[2]

William James, one of this country's first and perhaps greatest commentators on the problems of teaching and learning, provided the following example of the recitation quiz game in the classroom.

> A friend of mine, visiting a school, was asked to examine a young class in geography. Glancing at the book, she said, "Suppose you should dig a hole in the ground, hundreds of feet deep, how should you find it at the bottom —warmer or colder than on top?" None of the class replying, the teacher said: "I'm sure they know, but I think you don't ask the question quite rightly. Let me try." So, taking the book, she said: "In what condition is the interior of the globe?" and received the immediate answer from half the class at once: "The interior of the globe is in a condition of igneous fusion."[3]

TODAY: TRIVIA IN THE CLASSROOM

In the 1960s, fully one-half century after the above observations were made, educational researchers studying classroom interactions between teachers and pupils made the following comments: (1) The teachers tend to do about 70 percent of all talking in the classroom. (2) Most of this talk is in the form of asking questions. (3) Between 80 and 88 percent of all these questions call for rote memory responses. (4) The teachers typically ask two questions per minute. (5) Pupil talk is almost exclusively a short response to the teacher's question. (6) Inquiries and suggestions from pupils are virtually nonexistent.[4]

In a most recent study of 156 randomly selected elementary-school classrooms, these same results reappeared from grades K to 6. The authors noted of their 1974 study: "At all grade levels, the teacher-to-child pattern of interaction overwhelmingly prevailed. This was one of the most monotonously recurring pieces of data. The teacher asked questions and the children responded, usually in a few words and phrases. . . . It is fair to say that this teacher-to-child interaction was the mode in all but about 5 percent of the classes."[5]

Eighty percent of all classroom talk consists of brief, factual, rote responses: the year, 1912

Teachers ask for brief, factual, rote responses in all but 5 percent of classrooms studied: the year, 1974

One researcher at the turn of the century found that over 80% of classroom talk consisted of asking and answering brief, factual questions.

You may be struck by the remarkable similarity in the results of these three sets of studies—after sixty years the same mode persists. The state of affairs raises two questions: Is question-and-answer trivia an effective educational method? If it isn't, then why does it persist?

YOU ARE THERE: TRIVIA IN THE CLASSROOM

Perhaps the best way to begin understanding the effect of rapid-fire question-and-answer procedures would be to ask you to remember such a situation in your own experience. You are in the third grade, sitting in a class of 30 children. The teacher towers over you physically, a difference exaggerated when she stands in front of the seated class. The class has been studying a unit on the American Indian. After a series of questions on Indian lore and myths which you know but didn't get called on for (she had scolded you sternly, saying that you were to remain seated when you raised your hand), the teacher suddenly wheels around and looks directly at you: "What did the Navaho call their houses?" In the confusion, for you are still thinking about a previous question, you don't have the answer. The class falls silent. Twenty-nine children turn toward you. The teacher waits a few seconds that seem like years, and then says, "Well?" "Tepee?" you say, hoping that it's right, but mostly wishing there were a place to hide. "Hogan," the teacher replies. "Hogan—oh, that's what I meant to say," you add in a near-whisper. The moment does pass as the girl two seats away from you expertly fields the next question about how a hogan is constructed. A

What it's like—a first-person account of classroom trivia

few minutes later recess mercifully arrives, and you manage to sneak out as unobtrusively as possible. So much for the question-and-answer quiz and the promotion of learning.

Factual answers and
inquiry teaching: the
paradox

A series of studies has shown, perhaps not as dramatically or as personally as the above incident, that the classroom trivia quiz does not promote learning unless we really think that the recitation of textbook facts is equivalent to learning. If we view the objectives of teaching and learning more broadly (and we shall consider objectives in detail in Chapter 14), then we can only conclude that a form of "Button, button, who has the button?" or "Hogan, hogan, what's a hogan?" does not help students learn except in a negative way. You do learn to play the game after a while; that is, you learn to say the right thing and to act out of reflex. You do remember the acceptable phrases and terms, whether they concern the method of transportation used by the Phoenicians, the kind of a house a Navaho lived in, or the state of igneous fusion in the center of the earth. But is this the process of inquiry we consider desirable? Is this the goal of human thinking? Is this the excitement of seeing new relationships among ideas? Is this the process through which we learn about ourselves?

EDUCATIONAL PSYCHOLOGY: WHERE HAS IT BEEN?

By now you must be asking yourself some pretty fundamental questions: Where has educational psychology been for the past 75 years? If we have been applying even the most rudimentary ideas from psychology to the classroom, shouldn't there have been some significant and dramatic changes between 1900 and 1975? By attempting to answer these important questions, we can begin to understand more clearly the problems that we educators must face. Teaching and learning are complicated processes, indeed almost unmanageably so. The process of interaction between twenty-five or so pupils and an adult is almost a paradox, with so many dimensions that it is almost impossible to describe. William James was one of the first psychologists to grapple directly with the paradox of classroom teaching and learning. The scope and depth of his vision provided initial and brilliant insights. Unfortunately, the field did not follow up on his suggestions until very recently, some fifty to sixty years later. Because of his importance, we will describe his early promise to educational psychology, some of the reasons for the long eclipse of his thinking, and his relevance today.

WILLIAM JAMES: THE EARLY PROMISE

William James exerted tremendous early influence on the whole field of psychology and was probably this country's most significant educational psychologist. In the nineteenth century psychology was considered part of philosophy, not a separate discipline. It was William James at Harvard in the 1890s who began to give systematic attention to psychology as a discipline in its own right and, more importantly for us, began to consider most seriously the question of applying psychology to the problem of the real world rather than leaving it in the laboratory.

James was concerned that the so-called scientific tradition would capture psychology and turn it away from its important purpose of helping us understand more about the processes of teaching and learning. He delivered a series of famous lectures (*Talks with Teachers*) which are as relevant today as when they were originally delivered. At that time "scientific" experiments were thought to be able to give us all the answers, including all the laws that govern human behavior. James feared the dangers of such an exclusive dependence on science. He warned that laboratory scientists . . . "would go off by themselves and use apparatus and consult sources in such a way as to grind out in the requisite number of months some little peppercorn of new truth worthy of being added to the store of extant information on the subject."[6] Such efforts might produce a mound of peppercorns but not necessarily truth.

James wisely saw that psychology had to look to the natural environment for much of its information. Laboratory studies, especially animal studies, might not be such a great help when it came to teaching children. He therefore launched the effort to examine and understand the process of teaching and learning in the classroom. He observed classrooms (remember his igneous fusion anecdote) and also suggested positive alternatives to the state of affairs he observed. For example, he pointed to the central importance of starting lessons at a point just beyond the pupils' present comprehension. The famous dictum "Start where the learner is and proceed" was derived from this insight of William James.

James: start with the pupil

> If the teacher is to explain the distance of the sun from the earth, let him ask . . . "If anyone there in the sun fired off a cannon straight at you, what should you do?" "Get out of the way," would be the answer. "No need of that," the teacher might reply. "You may quietly go to sleep in your room, and get up again, you may wait until your confirmation-day, you may learn a trade, and grow as old as I am—then only will the cannon-ball be getting near, then you may jump to one side! See, so great as that is the sun's distance!"[7]

James's most important effort was to try to convince educators that the observations, thoughts, and questions they brought out of their work with pupils would be a significant source of "scientific" feedback. He was particularly concerned to retain the human mind, or as he called it, "mental life," as a proper object for psychology; in fact, he deliberately defined psychology as the "science of mental life." What goes on "inside" a person's head—thoughts, feelings, interests, values, sentiments—these were what James thought psychologists should study in order to shed light on human strivings and motivations.

Importance of "mental" life—motives, values, feelings

James was the first to warn teachers and educators not to depend on psychology to provide all the answers; and to warn psychology not to present itself as a mirror-image of physical science. He saw psychology as a natural science, filled with uncertainty, an "open system" of questions concerning that most complex of all "systems," the human being. That was the problem, but also it was the challenge.

The difficulties of James's view were many. For example, to say that teaching is a process that we can never fully understand is unsettling to those in search of the truth, as we noted in the previous chapter. To say that we will have to be content with a series of approximations, of good ideas and practices but not perfect ideas or perfect practices, is likewise unsettling.

William James

Born in 1842 in New York City, William James showed litle evidence of academic brilliance during his school years. In fact, his early education was meandering and informal. He attended several private schools in this country and abroad. The only consistent educational experience he had was with his family at the dinner table. Conversation abounded there on every conceivable topic. Each member had the opportunity to test his wits against the others. His multiple talents seemingly prevented him from settling on any one career. His brother, Henry James, became a famous novelist. William in the meantime, studied art for awhile in Newport, Rhode Island, then decided to drop art and attend Harvard College and specialize in chemistry. After two years he switched his field again and transferred to comparative anatomy and physiology. At this point James wrote to a friend that the problem of career choice was limited to four alternatives, "Natural History, Medicine, Printing, and Beggary." He chose medicine but found, once again, some lack of meaning and so interrupted his studies first to collect specimens up the Amazon River and later to spend time recuperating from illness by a trip to Europe. Finally he did complete his medical studies in 1869 and was awarded the only academic degree he ever earned, an M.D. A scholar commented that it "seems a strange one for a man who was to make his mark as a psychologist and philosopher." But the real education of William James was not received in universities and did not lead to degrees. It had been in his home with his family.

When offered a position as instructor at Harvard at the age of 30, James jumped at the chance to drop the sheer drudgery of medicine. He moved from the practice of medicine into the classroom. For James this was an important step; for psychology it turned out to be momentous. He thrived on academic life, worked hard at the craft of college teaching, and very early displayed a talent for both inquiry and teaching. Once again, however, his enormous and restless talent stretched beyond the conventional and past the then recognized academic disciplines. In 1876 he created and began teaching the first psychology course ever taught in this country. His originality and creativity burst forth now, and he poured out lectures which increased in popularity. Essentially he was creating a field of study, shaping the content, and outlining the sequence of topics all simultaneously. He wrote a monumental two-volume basic text for these courses simply titled *Principles of Psychology*. These outlined the basic tenets of psychology, the general themes. He started the first psychological laboratory and anticipated the theory of conditioning later demonstrated by Pavlov, as well as the importance of critical stages of learning, the so-called "Field" theory, and the principles of Gestalt psychology. His original book can provide a modern reader with a relatively up-to-date version of psychology, so substantial was his vision.

For educational psychology James became both an educator and a philosopher. He saw the importance of tailoring educational material to fit the learner's true condition, not the condition that the teacher assumed he should be in. His pride in his own teaching meant that he could model effective instruction as well as tell others how to do it, a talent that few academic scholars can manage even today. In this way James was devoted to the idea of improving all teaching. Education, then

as now, tended to be classed as slightly less respectable than the five "sacred" disciplines. James's independence of mind and his ability to go beyond the conventional once again were in evidence. As a Harvard professor, renowned scholar, and originator of the field of psychology, he devoted much effort and energy to improve the quality of classroom education. His famous lectures, *Talks with Teachers*, are very briefly quoted in the text to give you some feel for his flair with concepts as well as the significance of his thinking. His major point was that the entire enterprise of education is determined by the actual classroom teacher.

In these days of national curriculum projects and technological prescriptions for the classroom, we need to recall the central Jamesian theme: "Psychology is a science—teaching is an art; and sciences never generate arts directly out of themselves. An intermediary inventive mind must make the application, by use of its originality." James was convinced that the future of education depended directly on the quality of the intermediary inventive minds of the teachers. It was they who would do the job in the classroom and they who needed to apply psychological principles humanely. By understanding the nature of children and adolescents as behaving organisms, James was convinced teaching could be improved.

An educational theorist, Paul Woodring, probably

summed up James's significance to education most succinctly. He noted that if James had been read carefully by teachers and teacher educators over the past fifty years, many of our educational difficulties might have been avoided.

James's long and productive life ended in 1910 after some thirty-five years of teaching. The world lost that rare combination of talents that is so infrequent: teacher, scholar, leader, and the ability to go well beyond current thinking. With all this he had a personality so vivid that his sister described him as "born afresh every morning."

Obviously it was, and still is, extraordinarily difficult to consider educational problems in such a broad perspective. James wanted educational psychology to study teaching and learning in the classroom in order to view educational problems in their real, or natural, environment. James wanted to focus both on the objective and on the subjective nature of educational problems. For example, when he spoke of teaching methods, he discussed the teacher and his or her objectives on the one hand, and the pupils and their objectives on the other hand. He compared teaching to warfare:

Teaching as a paradox

The teacher as an army commander

The pupil counter-attacks

In war, all you have to do is to work your enemy into a position in which the natural obstacles prevent him from escaping if he tries to; then to fall on him in numbers superior to his own. . . . Just so in teaching, you must simply work your pupil into such a state of interest—with every other object of attention banished from his mind; then reveal it to him so impressively that he will remember it to his dying day; and finally fill him with devouring curiosity to know what the next steps are . . . ."[8]

So, from the teacher's perspective nothing could be plainer or simpler. The science of general pedagogics couldn't be clearer. Then James mentioned the other side of the classroom equation, schooling from the pupil's point of view. He reminded teachers:

The mind of your own enemy, the pupil, is working away from you as keenly and eagerly as is the mind of the commander on the other side from the scientific general. Just what the respective enemies want and think and what they know and do not know are as hard things for the teacher as for the general to find out."[9]

This clash, between what the teacher wants and what the pupils want, clearly is a difficult problem for science. In an attempt to develop answers, educational psychology moved into an era of laboratory investigations. That emphasis, however, has been something of a mixed blessing.

In rejecting James's views as too unwieldy, educational psychology headed in a logical direction. It seemed sensible when confronted with complexity to narrow the focus, to examine the effect of one variable at a time. And to add strength to this tendency, there was, at the time, an almost passionate desire for psychology to pattern itself after the physical sciences and search for the "molecules" of human behavior. This meant that the emphasis shifted away from naturalistic studies of pupil and teacher behaviors in classrooms. There were too many uncontrolled variables operating in such settings; the open system of a classroom was not a scientifically researchable problem. The desire for precision in measurement and research design forced educational psychology into the laboratory. The era produced many useful pieces of information, especially about some aspects of learning. On balance, however, the focus was too narrow. Too much was left untouched. The classroom, as we noted at the beginning of this chapter, remained tragically similar to its early twentieth-century antecedent. To

Scientific research moves toward the laboratory

understand the impact of the new focus, and its limitations, we will turn to the researcher whose name became synonymous with educational psychology, Edward L. Thorndike.

E. L. THORNDIKE: SCIENTIFIC EDUCATION

The person most responsible for channeling education toward an emphasis on measurement was E. L. Thorndike, a famous professor at Teachers College at Columbia University. Thorndike sought to eliminate speculation, opinion, and naturalistic investigation. In fact, he considered visiting a classroom an extraordinary waste of time. It was much more "scientific" to understand the learning process by experimenting on cats in a laboratory than by observing children in a classroom. And experiment he did. Thorndike studied the behavior of his famous cats in specially designed puzzle boxes. He was interested in how long it took the cats to solve the puzzles (which usually involved getting out of the box) and in learning what rewards were the most effective in achieving the objective (Will a hungry cat learn faster than a "fat" cat—or, in more scientific language, "an organism deprived of nutrition for 48 hours"—if food is the reward?). This procedure led to an almost endless number of empirical studies documenting how many trial-and-error sequences took place before the cat finally "learned" to stick a paw through the grating, lift up the latch to open the cage, and then stroll triumphantly over to the food.[10] As you can see, Thorndike was focusing on one aspect of learning, learning by trial and error. By putting a cat through this sequence often enough, a bond would be formed, a stimulus-response connection in the nervous system, so that the cat would "remember" what to do.

Trial-and-error learning: the law of effect

It has been said that Thorndike was so influential that all subsequent research in education was merely a footnote to his work. His critics noted humorously of his influence that if one of Thorndike's cats behaved unpredictably, it would affect the curriculum for an entire nation.

On the positive side it should be stressed that Thorndike was an important influence because he exploded many of the educational myths of the day. The classical curriculum of the secondary school (four years of Greek, four years of Latin, and so on) had been justified on the grounds that such exercise would "train" the mind: spending time and effort on Latin, for example, made it easier to learn French, while Greek would improve our English. Using precise measurement procedures, Thorndike was able to show that little, if any, disciplining of the mind could be transferred from one subject to the other. In an almost singular way he could proclaim, "If you want to improve your English, study English, not Latin or Greek." Thorndike believed that transfer occurred only when elements in a situation were identical or at least similar to elements in a second situation. Many a subsequent generation had Thorndike and his empirical research to thank for disposing of the mythical justification for the study of Latin and Greek. So Thorndike's contribution cannot be dismissed. However, his importance and influence were so great that educational psychology became almost preoccupied by trial-and-error learning and measurement techniques. All

Exploding some educational myths

Edward L. Thorndike

Born in 1874 as the son of a Protestant minister and brought up in the mill towns of Massachusetts, E. L. Thorndike completed his undergraduate studies in classics at Wesleyan University. A somewhat singular and solitary person, he demonstrated early in his life a capacity for hard work, long hours, and precision. Almost a classic example of the protestant work ethic, Thorndike simply abhorred making even the slightest error and consequently was always striving for perfection in his work. He had enormous amounts of mental energy and virtually threw himself into the task of defining a scientific base for psychology.

At Columbia's Teachers College, he completed his doctorate in the department of philosophy, psychology, anthropology, and education in the late 1890s. At that time, departmental specialization was not yet established. The field of educational psychology was amorphous and resisted a generic definition. Academic psychology and the so-called brass-instrument laboratories and physical measurements represented one stance. At the other end William James at Harvard was lecturing on the art of teaching, separate from the science of psychology. In be-

tween there was a range of philosophers, educators, and psychologists all attempting to give definition and coherence to the field. This was educational psychology's moment of a "cultural revolution." A hundred flowers were blooming when the youthful but dedicated E. L. Thorndike appeared on the scene. Apparently he was not at all intimidated by the first-generation psychologists and educators. As a brand new assistant professor at Teachers College in 1898, he took pleasure in attacking his elders. He referred to this period as his early assertive years. "It is fun to write all the stuff up and smite all the hoary scientists hip and thigh. . . . My thesis is a beauty. . . . I've got some theories which knock the old authorities into a grease spot." For such a fledgling, still in his twenties, to have the inner strength to attack the heroes of the day both in print and in association meetings was most unusual. Possibly within himself Thorndike transformed the protestant ethic into a messianic vision not of religion but of scientific logical positivism. In other words, the dedication that a person might feel toward a religious mission was apparently shifted so that science became his religion.

For the entire 41 years of his professional life, Thorndike remained at Columbia Teachers College. He defined educational psychology as essentially the psychology of laboratory experimentation. His life work was to create a base of scientific knowledge through careful experiments, changing one variable at a time and using precise measures. He insisted that the operational definition was the only definition for science. If you couldn't see, measure, and directly record the phenomenon under investigation, then it was not scientific or even worthwhile. Look, see, and collect data were his bywords for investigators. In fact, he really viewed himself more as an investigator than a scholar. He once noted that he had probably spent over 10,000 hours in reading and studying scientific books and journals, but he devoted more time to his own experiments and writing. His bibliography runs to a prodigious 500 items. Science, he would say, was to be built by research, not proclamation.

When Thorndike finished his classic work on measurement for educational psychology, he sent a copy to William James. The amusing dialogue that resulted went as follows:

Thorndike, to James with academic modesty: "I am sending you a dreadful book which I have written which is in no end scientific but devoid of any spark of human interest."

James's replay: "I opened your new book with full feelings of awe and admiration for your unexampled energy. It was just the thing I had hoped for when I was teaching psychology. . . . I am glad I have graduated from the necessity of using that kind of thing any longer. I shall stick to 'qualitative' work as more congruous with old age!"[11]

His work, as we have noted in the text, became almost an endless series of studies on trial-and-error learning. His famous cats in the puzzle-box represented his observable data. He persuaded his university to create a psychological laboratory for him and there he remained, building the wall of scientific knowledge brick by brick. Thorndike reached the pinnacle of his career in 1934, when he was elected president of the American Association for the Advancement of Science. No psychologist had ever been so honored. In fact, only one

social scientist had ever been elected to head the professional organization that represented the entire scientific community. For Thorndike, then, this was truly the moment of glory. The years of hard work, the struggle to create a scientifically respectable basis for educational psychology, had at last achieved the ultimate recognition. His biographer Geraldine Jonçich has noted that an editorial in the *New York Times* in January 1934 pleased him above all else when it said of him, "But first and last, he is a scientist."

other ideas, perspectives, and theories were practically abandoned. The field grew more narrowly scientific, objective, and empirical. We began to be able to measure educational problems more effectively, but the problems we were measuring were increasingly less significant. In a word, we developed more precise ways of measuring increasingly insignificant educational problems. The range of what we could know was limited to what we could measure.

The single most significant effect of this emphasis on empirical measurement was that it was more suited to showing what was wrong than what was right. This is not to say that educational psychology does not need rigorous measurement procedures and evaluation systems, but it cannot progress as a field if that is its only focus. The movement was more and more to the laboratory, for more and more replications and refinements of essentially the same studies over and over again. When William James warned of grinding out peppercorns, he was predicting the direction the field actually took. Literally thousands of studies have been produced which have had little influence on learning and the practice of teaching. In the careful words of a contemporary educational theorist, "the fruits of this scholarship must appear quite disappointing."[12] Instead of a narrow focus, educational psychology needs to broaden its view to include again studies in the natural environment.*

The research problem: grinding out peppercorns

JOHN DEWEY AND HUMAN ECOLOGY

One of this country's most important theorists, John Dewey, always used the phrase "some organism in some environment."[13] This was his way of emphasizing that you could not study learning in the abstract and ignore the broader context—the environment in which that learning took place. Here is one of his sardonic comments on traditional education.

> The entire range of the universe is first subdivided into sections called studies; then each one of these studies is broken up into bits, and some one bit assigned to a certain year of the course. No order of development is recognized—it is enough that the earlier part were made easier than the later. To use the pertinent illustration of Mr. W. S. Jackman in stating the absurdity of this sort of curriculum: "It must seem to geography teachers that Heaven smiled on them when it ordained but four or five continents, because starting in far enough along the course it was so easy, that it really seemed natural, to give one continent to each grade and then come out right in the eight years."[14]

---

*
The hope and promise of a scientific base tends to promote a narrow professional orthodoxy. Joncich, in her article on Thorndike (*American Psychologist*, 1968, *23*, 434–446), has noted that, "Before scientists cut themselves off from one another by specialization, priority went to cutting themselves off from the public (through) . . . the erection of a series of barriers—specialized graduate degree programs, the development of an esoteric knowledge base and the creation of an unintelligible language." The spawning of countless schools of psychological thought, each with its own training program, its own "Bible" of knowledge, and its own language is testimony to the growth of narrow professionalism and pedantry.

Unfortunately, Dewey's important ideas were misinterpreted. He was thought to be advocating the so-called child-centered curriculum rather than the significant ecological concept of person-in-environment. Cafeteria-style education—where a child was free to choose anything, even to play all day if he or she wanted—was supposedly the result of Dewey's work. However, these "progressive" views on education clearly missed Dewey's point. What he advocated was careful, guided experience for children, arranged according to their interests and capacities. The importance of these concepts for educational psychology should not be missed.

Misunderstanding of Dewey

The central idea of Dewey's work was that the child was not an empty vessel waiting patiently and quietly to be filled up with knowledge. In fact, Dewey's best writing took these traditional assumptions of education to task. For example, he tells of visiting a manufacturer of school furniture one day and having a difficult time finding what he wanted for his school. One dealer, apparently more intelligent than the rest, commented, "I am afraid we have not what you want. You want something at which the children may work; these are all for listening."[15]

The child: not an empty organism

In addition to the concept of active learning, Dewey also stressed the idea of stages of growth and development. In this he foreshadowed the now classic work of Piaget. Dewey noted that the child was often assumed to be a small version of an adult. "The boy was a little man and his mind was a little mind—in everything but size the same as that of the adult. . . . Now we believe in the mind as a growing affair, and hence as essentially changing, presenting distinctive phases of capacity and interest at different periods."[16]

Active learning

Finally, Dewey's most significant assertion was that teaching and learning interacted, that the pupil was as much a part of the learning environment as the

Dewey developed learning environments that ensured children would actively engage in learning. His famous dictum of "learning by doing" became a byword.

John Dewey

Without question one of this country's major educational theorists, John Dewey has had a long and significant influence on the actual practice of edution. Born in 1859, his life spanned almost a century, from the Civil War to 1952. Certainly this period was one of the most eventful for the country as a whole. The United States emerged from a predominantly rural and isolation-ist era to one in which we were the major industrialized power of the globe. The education of American pupils went through a transformation that was almost parallel to these world-shaking changes, in large part because of John Dewey's ideas and his practice.

In some ways Dewey was a true product of nineteenth-century America. Naturally intelligent and serious about his educational mission, he wanted most of all to develop an educational philosophy that could be put into practice. The concepts had to be tested in the real world of schools and in the classrooms. Many philosophers were content to theorize about education and write learned essays. For Dewey, this was not enough. If the ideas were not translated and tested, then the practice of education would forever remain random or at a craft level. An American pragmatist, he had little patience with glossy educational rhetoric. He clearly was a doer.

Born in the heartland of New England, his early years as a Vermont Yankee fostered in him a great respect for natural growth and the critical relationship between person and environment. These themes recur throughout his educational writings. After graduating from the University of Vermont at the age of twenty, he completed his Ph.D. at Johns Hopkins some five years later.

His first professorship was at the University of Minnesota, followed quickly by moves to the University of Michigan and then on to the University of Chicago in 1894. He served as chairman of the department of philosophy and pedagogy. It was at Chicago that he established the first major educational laboratory school in the country. Here at last he had the natural learning environment he needed to test and revise his unique educational ideas. At that time the country's educators were convinced that children were to sit quietly in a classroom and learn by rote a classical curriculum. Instead of strengthening the mind, of course, such a learning environment placed the students in an exceptionally passive role. Anticipating the ideas of Piaget and the open classroom, Dewey developed learning environments which ensured that children would actively engage in learning. His famous dictum of learning through doing became a byword. Experience should precede or at least be concurrent with educational concepts and ideas. This was a revolutionary stance to the educators of the day, because it turned the educational process inside out. An experience-based curriculum to promote both more effective learning and greater competence in living were his dual objectives

By this time in his career he was easily the most widely known educator of his day. It came as no surprise then for Dewey to move in 1904 to the center of educational thought in this continent, the famous Teachers College at Columbia University. He remained there until his formal retirement, twenty-six years later. He produced a multitude of books and lectured throughout the land. An innovator, he was one of those very rare educators who lived to see his ideas put into practice and become an educational doctrine.

Unfortunately, however, his most significant idea was also the most easily misunderstood. His concept of child-centered education was distorted in many instances into a laissez-faire curriculum, and in the late forties and early fifties it became quite fashionable to criticize Dewey as soft-headed. Fortunately for the country's children, this misunderstanding has now been cleared up. The importance of learning by doing finds expression in today's schools in a multitude of ways. Learning laboratories and centers, workshops, lesson units, and school programs devoted to all aspects of human growth are reflections of his views in action. Perhaps Dewey's most important idea, or indeed vision, was the democratic ideal which always remained his goal. By developing significant education for all children, the American dream of free people in a free country might be realized. In his ninety-third year John Dewey died, the vision intact and the country closer to the goal.

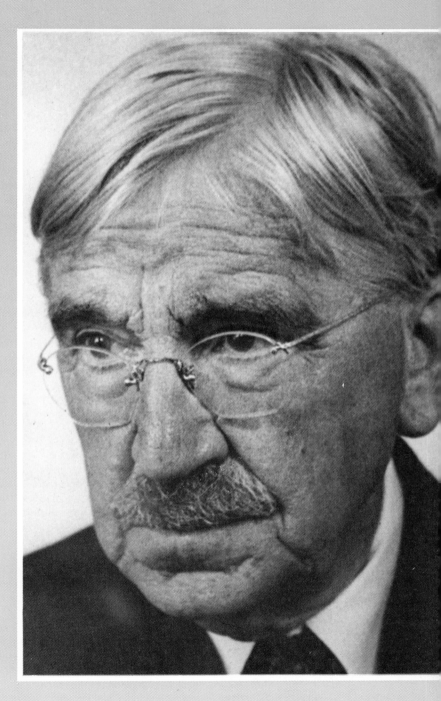

Stages of
development

teacher. He constantly battled against what he saw as the artificial separation between learning and the pupil.

Dewey's central view, then, was to promote a balanced curriculum between experiential learning and careful rational examination. He did not want pupils simply to experience in a vacuum. Supposedly, a teacher, in seeking employment at Dewey's laboratory school, said that he had ten years of teaching experience. Dewey quickly asked, "Was it really ten years or was it one year ten times!" In other words, what had the person learned from the experience? How much reflection, examination, and analysis of the experience had occurred? Thus learning through experience includes what is commonly called "intellectual analysis." Dewey viewed this process as a means of promoting cognitive thought structures. In this area, he essentially anticipated a second Piagetian concept of cognitive structure or schema as the framework for understanding how children come to know and think. The classroom should be a natural environment in which living and learning occur together. In this way Dewey pioneered today's emphasis on education as an ecological process.

EDUCATIONAL PSYCHOLOGY AND THE PROMISE OF ECOLOGY

Today's interest in ecology, a legacy from Dewey, represents a clear and promising direction for the field. The word itself means, literally, the "environment," or the "home." For our purposes the concept brings together "an organism" and "some environment." It considers pupils and teachers individually and together in the environment they share, whether it is a formal classroom or an informal discussion after class.

The individual and
the environment: a
dual perspective

The older disciplines, such as psychology and sociology, have specialized in only half of this whole system. Psychology has traditionally been the study of behavior, while sociology has focused on the environment—those groups, classes, cultures, subcultures, and societies to which we belong. Neither view is really broad enough for our purposes. The sociologist says, "If you want to know what individuals will do (how they will behave), find out what their reference group will do; they will conform to that norm or standard." This view implies, for example, that if your two closest friends vote Republican, then it's almost certain that you, too, will vote Republican. We don't need to know anything about you as an individual.

The psychologist, on the other hand, says that we need to understand people's basic personality structure, their interests, attitudes, values (the so-called noncognitive aspects) as well as the level of intelligence and learning style (the cognitive aspects). If we know this we can explain what makes a person "tick." As you can see, educational psychology has, to a significant degree, followed the view of psychology. This is one of the reasons we know so little about how to promote learning, growth, and development in the natural environment, the classroom. The movement toward ecology, then, is truly a significant new direction. It means that educational psychology can begin to understand the whole system of individual behavior in an environment. We don't have to decide which is more important.

The movement toward ecology is truly a significant new direction. Educational psychology can now begin to understand the whole system of individual behavior in an environment.

Obviously, from our point of view, a position that ignores or gives low priority to either the psychological or the sociological variables is too limited. Unfortunately, however, the traditions separating educational psychology from psychology and from sociology continue. More lip service is paid today to what is sometimes called interaction theory—the study of an individual interacting with the environment—but in most cases, a systematic bias toward one or the other aspect of the situation reveals itself.

Organisms and environments: the two-way street for teaching and learning

ACTION AND REFLECTION: PUPILS AND ENVIRONMENTS
Our purpose is to create, through psychology *in* education, a framework for understanding human beings in their environment. However, we will not be content with mere understanding; the real challenge, we feel, is acting on the basis of that understanding. In the first chapter we talked of education as "doing"

To explain and predict behavior,
the sociologist looks at the group
itself; the psychologist concentrates on how the group influences
the individual as a separate entity.

and of the need to build a basis for informed action. An educator needs to act and to reflect. Focusing exclusively on one or the other process is not possible. Reflective theoreticians are virtually useless in the heat of battle. They prefer to remain on the sidelines and think about what is happening in order to understand. By the time they understand, that battle may have long since concluded. On the other hand, unthinking activists, ready to participate in any activity at the drop of a hat, are equally useless. You probably know people in both categories. In both cases a critical element is missing: reflection and action must go together.

EDUCATIONAL PSYCHOLOGY TODAY: TOWARD A RESOLUTION OF THE IDENTITY CRISIS

From an ecological perspective, the classroom, the school building itself, the school, and the surrounding community function as an open human system. This systems-analysis perspective reminds us that the overall educational environment is extremely broad and, in some ways, overwhelming and intimidating. The sheer number of interactions within a given classroom, multiplied by a number of classrooms, and between schools and communities reaches astronomical proportions. Each aspect of this ecological system represent a series of human interactions: how a teacher responds to a pupil and vice versa; how teachers, counselors, and principals interact; how the professional staff interacts with parents. All these connections form a human ecological network. The open-system concept means quite simply that each aspect of the system, or each person, impacts and is impacted by every other person.

Ecology, then, is an extremely useful concept because it allows us to consider the learning process as a whole system—teacher and pupil behavior individually and together. Too much research in the discipline has been restricted to the splendid isolation of the laboratory; this tells us nothing about pupils in the natural setting of a school. The promise of educational psychology today is that the field will develop as a basis for inquiry and practice (thinking and doing) focused on individuals (pupils and teachers) in their *environments*. We see such ideas as the basis for resolving the identity crisis.

Ecology allows us to
consider the learning
process as
a whole system

In some important ways the field of educational psychology is at a crossroads. We have reviewed the major difficulty for the field, namely, that many school practices remain virtually untouched by findings and research from the field. To say that the practice of education and the field of educational psychology have been like ships that pass in the night is an overstatement—yet it is true to some extent. The results of laboratory studies often cannot be directly applied to the regular classroom and thus to some degree miss the point. In some ways animals are not like pupils, laboratories are not like classrooms, and experimenters are not like teachers.

We have noted William James's important contributions to educational psychology. It may be apparent that managing the learning process is a difficult task, yet James indicated a number of promising directions. We could, for a start, learn to match instructional methods to the particular stage of development of the pupil. A learning atmosphere or environment that takes into account the pupils' capacities and interests addresses both sides of the educational fence: the pupils' needs and the teaching method and subject matter. If educational psychology can become a means for promoting human development, it will resolve its own identity crisis. Such a broad focus is necessary to produce the personnel, teachers, counselors, administrators, and educational interventions to enhance the overall growth and development of pupils.

Even though we are advocating a broad, open-human-systems framework, our intent is not to overwhelm you with an educational enterprise that seems staggeringly complex. While there is little solace in the phrase, "but we never promised you a rose garden," you may find John Dewey's insightful outlook more encouraging. He noted that the educational process in this country is and always will be in the hands of ordinary men and women. Dewey, a firm believer in democracy, equality, and the integrity of each individual, was opposed to elitism and in this sense viewed all humans as fundamentally ordinary. Remember, however, that ordinary humans can perform extraordinary feats given the necessary tools.

Summary

The issues and problems of teaching and learning are described to the prospective educator in real and concrete terms. By comparing classroom interaction studies over a seventy-year span, the difficulties of the recitation mode and the need to change teaching styles are obvious. The case study depicts in a first-hand way why "trivia" in the classroom is just that.

The historical and present relevance of William James as an educational psychologist is detailed. James pointed to the importance of starting lessons at a point just beyond the pupil's present comprehension. Also, he stressed the need to work more in natural environments as opposed to an exclusive focus on the findings from laboratory studies.

By contrast, Thorndike's work illustrates both the gains and losses marked by educational psychology's move to the laboratory and the search for the equivalent of the "molecules" of human behavior. A balanced perspective is needed to understand the need for measurement/assessment as well as for classroom studies.

Dewey, a theorist-practitioner, stressed the notion of an organism interacting in some environment. Dewey's view on active learning (the experience-based curriculum) and the need for careful reflection is critical. It is still too easy today to find educators equating Dewey with a laissez-faire, cafeteria-style education rather than with disciplined inquiry.

In general, there is a need for a view of educational psychology that includes psychology, social psychology, and sociology—or more simply, the organism and the environment. Educational psychology is a field of psychology *in* education—action and reflection, process and content, doing and thinking as ways of promoting human growth and development.

REFERENCES

1
J. M. Rice, *The Public School System of the United States* (New York: Century, 1893).

2
R. Stevens, *The Question as a Measure of Efficiency in Instruction* (New York: Columbia University, Contributions to Education No. 48, 1912).

3
William James, *Talks with Teachers* (New York: Norton, 1958), p. 106.

4
A. Bellack, *et al.*, *Language of the Classroom* (New York: Teachers College Press, 1966).

5
J. I. Goodlad, and M. F. Klein, *Looking Behind the Classroom Door* (Worthington, Ohio: Jones, 1974), p. 51.

6
William James, *Talks with Teachers*, p. 38.

7
William James, *Psychology* (New York: Collier MacMillan, 1968), p. 333.

8
William James, *Talks with Teachers*, p. 25.

9
Ibid.

10
Edward L. Thorndike, *The Fundamentals of Learning* (New York: Teachers College Press, 1932); see also Thorndike's *Educational Psychology*, vol. 2 (New York: Teachers College Press, 1913); and his "Animal Intelligence," *Psychological Review,* Monograph No. 2, 1898.

11
G. Jonçich, "E. L. Thorndike: The Psychologist as Professional Man of Science," *American Psychologist* 23, no. 6 (1968):444.

12
L. S. Shulman, "Reconstruction of Educational Research," *Review of Educational Research* 40 (1970):371–396.

13
J. Dewey, *Logic: The Theory of Inquiry* (New York: Holt, 1938); see also *Democracy and Education* (New York: Macmillan, 1916).

14
J. Dewey, *The Child and the Curriculum: The School and Society* (Chicago: University of Chicago Press, 1956), p. 103.

15
Ibid., p. 31.

16
Ibid., p. 102.

The effects of development on behavior

3

Fundamentals of growth and development

Of all the species that inhabit the earth, the one whose growth and development is the slowest is *Homo sapiens*. The human being spends many long years in a state of physical immaturity, depending on the care and protection of others in order to survive. During the months the child is learning to walk and run with consistent steadiness, to communicate fears, joys, and needs, other species grow to full maturity. A two-year-old rhesus monkey has already attained sexual maturity, and a two-year-old rat may already be senile. "In the development of large muscles and the achievement of mobility, the typical child of two years is comparable to the chimpanzee of two months, the rabbit of two weeks, and the colt of two hours."[1]

Several years ago a study dramatically illustrated the difference in growth rates between species: a husband and wife psychologist team raised their infant son, Donald, along with a baby chimpanzee named Gua. Donald and Gua were treated as much alike as possible. They wore the same clothes, were fed the same food in the same way, and in general were given the same tender, loving care. They were also taught in the same way and given the same amount of practice in such things as standing, walking, eating with a spoon, and even toilet training.[2]

The whole situation must have been a competitive nightmare for poor little Donald, because Gua outstripped him at everything. When Donald was barely able to pull himself into an erect position, Gua was walking, running, and pirouetting around with the grace of a ballet dancer. When Donald still had difficulty even picking up a spoon, Gua was using the spoon to feed herself easily and

Chimpanzees and language development

Donald and Gua—a human baby raised with a chimp

Gua wins round one

45

with little spilling. When Donald was propped up and strapped to the seat of a swing, where he hung limply and loosely, Gua was performing like a trapeze artist on another swing.

The enormous difference in heredity and rate of maturation obviously allowed Gua to reach her genetic potential far sooner than Donald. Eventually, when Donald was nine months old (and the study was ended) he was beginning to catch up to Gua in certain areas, such as following verbal instructions, and to surpass Gua in others, such as speech development. But as for achieving physical mobility, Donald was still far behind.

In another attempt to find out whether environmental stimulation can compensate for heredity, another husband and wife team, with no children of their own, took a chimpanzee, Vicki, into their home and raised her as they would have raised a baby.[3] Above all else they wanted to see whether they could teach Vicki to talk. Despite their efforts, and despite the fact that Vicki did learn to respond to verbal commands, the attempt to teach her to speak ultimately proved to be futile. After three years, Vicki could occasionally utter words like "cup," "mama," and "papa," in an appropriate context, but that was as far as her language skills ever developed. By three years of age the typical human infant has a vocabulary of almost 900 words.

You may be wondering at this point why studies such as these were ever performed—they may seem as absurd as raising a human baby and an eagle together in a nest to see which one would be the first to fly. It may be obvious to you that different species mature at different rates and that chimpanzees achieve physical maturity more rapidly than humans. You may even wonder why anyone would bother trying to train chimps to talk, for if it were possible, it seems likely that someone, somewhere would have observed chimps talking to one another.*

The best way to appreciate why these studies were conducted is to know something about psychology's brief but often stormy history. Our purpose is not to take you on a guided tour of dusty museum oddities, but to give you a general historical background against which the present state of our knowledge will be more meaningful and, hopefully, more appreciated.

THE NATURE-NURTURE CONTROVERSY

Of all the great debates in the history of psychology—and there have been many —the one that has generated the most heat and caused the greatest division in the field is the controversy over nature and nurture. More words have been written and more voices have been raised in anger over this issue than over any other. The warring camps made their positions clear. The hereditarians,

Margin note: Donald catches up

Margin note: Hereditarians minimize the importance of environment

---

*

It is believed that chimps do communicate with each other, not verbally, but through a kind of sign language. Recently a chimpanzee has been trained in the use of the American sign language of the deaf, and the chimp's performance compares favorably with that of a three-year-old child who was deaf from birth. (B. T. Gardner and R. A. Gardner, "Two-way Communication with an Infant Chimpanzee," in A. Schrier and F. Stollnitz, *Behavior of Nonhuman Primates*, New York: Academic Press, 1970.)

Environmentalists claimed that the individual was shaped by how and in what circumstances he or she was raised, or "nurtured."

who favored nature, stridently claimed that all psychological traits were transmitted directly through the genes from generation to generation. Environment was of little consequence. If your father was a horse thief, you will be a horse thief, and if your mother's IQ is only 90, then you shouldn't make plans to go to medical school.

On the other side, the environmentalists as rigidly and shrilly claimed that a person's whole being was shaped by how and in what circumstances one was raised or "nurtured." Genetic endowment was a romantic myth, used to keep kings on their thrones, but of no use to science. The environmentalists held that all people were born genetically equal and that later differences among them were only a result of different environmental opportunities. Any baby could be molded into any kind of adult, provided the appropriate stimulus conditions were provided.

Environmentalists minimize genetic differences

THE HEREDITARIANS SPEAK: HENRY E. GODDARD AND THE "BAD SEED"

In 1912 Henry E. Goddard published an account of the horrible effects of an inferior genetic endowment, a "bad seed," on generation after generation of a family named Kallikak.[1] According to Goddard, who gleaned this material from books, newspapers, personal interviews, and other records, Martin Kallikak (a pseudonym chosen by Goddard to protect the family) was an American Revolutionary War soldier who was responsible for developing two completely different family strains. The "good" Kallikaks (and Goddard traced this strain through 496 descendants) resulted from Kallikak's marriage to a "worthy

The "good" Kallikaks

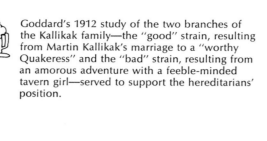

Goddard's 1912 study of the two branches of the Kallikak family—the "good" strain, resulting from Martin Kallikak's marriage to a "worthy Quakeress" and the "bad" strain, resulting from an amorous adventure with a feeble-minded tavern girl—served to support the hereditarians' position.

Quakeress." She bore him "seven upright, worthy children," and from these seven children came "hundreds of the highest types of human beings" . . . doctors, lawyers, businessmen, and even college presidents. Only two of the nearly 500 "good" Kallikaks were of below average intelligence.

Goddard also traced the descendants of an amorous adventure that Martin Kallikak had with a feeble-minded tavern girl. The result of this affair was an illegitimate son, later known to his friends and neighbors as "Old Horror." Fortunately for Goddard's story, even "Old Horror" apparently wasn't considered horrible by everyone, for he went on to father ten children of his own. Goddard identified 480 of these descendants, the "bad" Kallikaks, and found nothing but the lowest form of humanity—horse thieves, prostitutes, alcoholics, and so on. Also, of the bad Kallikaks, he found only 46 who were of normal or near-normal intelligence. The rest, of course were well below average.

Goddard wasted no time worrying about details, such as the dramatic environmental differences that existed between Kallikak's legitimate children and "Old Horror." The explanation was simple: the difference was hereditary.

Goddard's evidence, which was still seriously cited in many psychology texts as late as the 1950s, is considered truly fantastic by modern geneticists. Even if intelligence were as directly and simply related to genotype as eye color (which it isn't), there would still have to be far greater numbers of intelligent members of the "bad" Kallikaks, and vice versa. After all, Martin Kallikak was himself half responsible for "Old Horror." But this was Goddard's point of view, and a cherished belief clouded scientific vision. Charles Davenport, one of America's leading geneticists at the time (1911), even went so far as to argue that human behavioral characteristics had straight Mendelian explanations, laziness being inherited through dominant genes and ambition through recessive genes, for example. Thus, according to Davenport, the genes we inherit from our parents account not only for how intelligent we are, but also for how motivated we are.

THE ENVIRONMENTALISTS SPEAK: JOHN B. WATSON AND "GIVE ME THE BABY"

The strict environmentalists argued against the position of Goddard and the hereditarians. This group allied itself with philosopher John Locke (1691) who said that the mind was a blank slate upon which experience writes. As far as the environmentalist is concerned, the baby is nothing more than a lump of clay

© 1955 United Feature Syndicate, Inc.

that can be molded and fashioned into any shape by the hands of that master craftsman, the environment.

Perhaps the most eloquent spokesman for the environmental position was the early behaviorist, John B. Watson. It was Watson's belief that people are made, not born; that a baby can be shaped into any adult form—trapeze artist, musician, master criminal—through the judicious use of conditioning techniques. Watson began writing about the time (1913) that Pavlov's work in Russia on the conditioning of dogs was beginning to be recognized in the United States. Watson reasoned that if a dog could be conditioned, so too could a baby. In a now classic study, Watson tested this theory by conditioning a nine-month-old baby named Albert to fear a whole variety of objects (stimuli). By the time the study was completed, poor little Albert was intensely afraid of white rats, rabbits, dogs, fur coats, Santa Claus masks, cotton, wool, and anything else that remotely resembled animal fur. All this was accomplished in a mere two months by presenting Albert with a certain stimulus (such as a white rat) and then banging loudly with a hammer on a steel bar a few inches behind Albert's head. Albert soon associated the rat with the terrific din and thus learned to fear the rat. Watson also checked babies for other fear responses and found, for example, that if they are dropped they exhibit a fear response.

Watson conditions Albert

John Broadus Watson

American psychology's most vocal and possibly most influential environmentalist, John B. Watson, was born near Greenville, South Carolina, in 1878. As a student in public school, the young John Watson was something less than spectacular.

He later attributed his lack of early school success to his own "laziness," a rather subjective explanation from the man who demanded objectivity from everyone else. He later attended Furman University, where he studied such diverse topics as

mathematics, Greek, Latin, philosophy, and chemistry. In 1900 he left Furman, having received a master's degree, and headed for the University of Chicago to study under the philosopher John Dewey. He soon found that Dewey was "incomprehensible" to him, and so he changed majors and began studying with James R. Angell, a psychologist, and H. H. Donaldson, a man of many talents: psychologist, biologist, and neurologist.

In 1903 Watson received the first Ph.D. degree in psychology ever conferred at the University of Chicago. For the next five years he taught psychology at the University of Chicago. During this period he taught straight Jamesian psychology in the classroom, but in the basement after class, he conducted numerous animal experiments on both white rats and monkeys.

In 1908 he left Chicago and went to Johns Hopkins University in Baltimore as a full professor. He immediately set up an animal laboratory at Johns Hopkins, and in 1913 he shook the world of psychology with the publication of a paper entitled "Psychology as the Behaviorist Views It." In this paper Watson attacked the orthodox psychology of the day, and he inaugurated a new school of psychological thought —behaviorism. He said that the only valid data in psychology was the behavior of the organism. He saw no room in psychology for mentalistic concepts

like "mind" or "consciousness." The data of psychology should be the observable response, and the best approach to this, in order to rule out any mentalistic overtones, was to study the responses of animals. To be scientifically respectable, psychology must be behavioristic, objective, deterministic, mechanistic, and materialistic.

Watson then acquired a powerful ally. He had read of the work of I. P. Pavlov and the conditioned reflex, and Watson pounced on this concept and made it a central theme of his own behaviorism. In 1919 Watson began his now famous study on the conditioning of the baby Albert B. He conducted this study in collaboration with Rosalie Raynor. Together, Watson and Raynor showed how an apparently normal, healthy baby could be conditioned to fear virtually anything in the observable environment.

In 1920 Watson's career at Johns Hopkins suddenly ended. Amid great notoriety Watson was divorced by his wife and

then asked by Johns Hopkins to resign his professorship. Later that year Watson married his research collaborator, Rosalie Raynor, and then in 1921, entered the advertising business. He began by working in New York City for the advertising agency of J. Walter Thompson. By 1924 he had become vice president of the agency, and he remained in that post for the next twelve years. In 1936 he joined the William Esty agency.

Despite leaving the academic world in 1920, Watson continued to write books and articles which advanced his views on child-rearing and teaching. It wasn't until 1927 that Watson thundered forth his famous words, "Give me the baby and I'll make it climb and use its hands in construction of buildings of stone or wood. . . . I'll make it a thief, a gunman or a dope fiend. . . . Make him a deaf mute, and I will build you a Helen Keller. Men are built, not born."

Watson retired from the business world in 1946 and died in 1958, having exerted great influence on the fields of psychology and education. He made educational psychology more behavioristic, and he emphasized the role of conditioning in the classroom. The study of Albert caused him to believe that human behavior could be minutely controlled. It was Watson who set the stage for the work of B. F. Skinner and the proponents of behavior modification in the classroom.

In order to "cure" Albert of these conditioned fears, Watson proposed, though never actually tried, presenting him with the fear-provoking object again, while "stimulating the erogenous zones (tactual). . . . We should try first the lips, then the nipples and as a final resort the sex organs."[5]

Watson believed that he had come upon ultimate truth in psychology, that, no matter what the genetic background, environmental stimulation in the form of conditioning could produce any behavior. Watson later said wryly, "The Freudians twenty years from now, unless their hypotheses change, when they come to analyze Albert's fear of a seal skin coat . . . will probably tease from him the recital of a dream which upon their analysis will show that Albert at three years of age attempted to play with the pubic hair of the mother and was scolded violently for it."[6]

"Give me the baby . . ."

A few years later, Watson thundered his now famous words, "Give me the baby," and this became the battle cry of environmentalists everywhere. "Give me me the baby and I'll make it climb and use its hands in construction of buildings of stone or wood. . . . I'll make it a thief, a gunman or a dope fiend. The possibilities of shaping it in any direction are almost endless. Even gross anatomical differences limit us far less than you may think. . . . Make him a deaf mute, and I will build you a Helen Keller. Men are built, not born."[7]

After reading about how Albert had been scared half to death by the sound of a steel bar being pounded behind his head and by being dropped, and how it was proposed to "cure" him by manipulating his genitals, the mothers of America did not line up to give Watson their babies.

Watson was striving to provide psychology with hard, scientific facts. His behaviorism was definitely not based on any humanistic view of human behavior or of society in general. Rather, he saw his mission as that of fact finder and cared little if his audience like or disliked the facts. His approach was clinically aseptic and detached.

Even today, behaviorists exhibit a similar disinterest. They often see their ultimate goal as far too cosmic to be constrained by any feelings of sympathy for a particular child. B. F. Skinner, today's leading exponent of behaviorism, was recently criticized for having allegedly said that if given a choice he would rather burn his children than his books. Skinner's self-righteous answer was that he had not used the word "burn." "The word was *bury* . . . much as I admire my children and grandchildren and as dearly as I love them, I still believe that my contribution though my books will prove to be greater than that through my genes. How could a thorough-going environmentalist say otherwise?"[8]

EDUCATIONAL PSYCHOLOGY: THE BATTLEGROUND

Nowhere were the lines between hereditarians and environmentalists more sharply drawn than in the field of educational psychology. The reason for this was that the measurement practitioners and the learning theorists were the major influences on the field from psychology. The measurement practitioners (the IQ and achievement testers) were, by and large, hereditarians. The learning theorists, with very few exceptions, were behaviorists, and behaviorists were environmentalists. Thus it was inevitable that these two groups, both solidly en-

G. Stanley Hall was the foremost American advocate of intelligence as an inherited trait.

Lewis Terman, Hall's student, revised Binet's original scale and introduced the Stanford-Binet tests in 1916.

trenched in the field of educational psychology, and with diametrically opposed views in the nature-nurture debate, would be in constant conflict.

THE IQ TESTERS

The testers had traditionally emphasized heredity, at least on the subject of intelligence. The history of the testing movement goes back to England and Sir Francis Galton, Darwin's cousin. During the later part of the nineteenth century Galton created the first tests designed to measure intellectual potential. Galton believed that intellectual potential was a function of one's sensory equipment, one's power to discriminate among stimuli. He believed that sensory equipment was inherited. Parents who could detect slight differences among stimuli (could discriminate among subtle differences in tonal pitch, for example), were apt to have children with similarly keen powers. Furthermore, Galton believed, these sensory powers had survival value for the species. Cavemen who could detect the slight hiss of a rattlesnake were more likely to stay alive. James McKeen Cattell, who spent some time in Europe studying with Galton, brought this point of view back to the United States and, as Galton had done earlier, devised a series of sensory-motor tests (auditory range, visual range, reaction time, etc.) designed to measure a human's intellectual potential. It was Cattell in 1890 who first used the term "mental test."

Galton devised a sensory-motor test of intelligence; he believed intelligence to be largely inherited

Cattell and Hall bring Galton's message to America

G. Stanley Hall, a distinguished psychologist and the first president of Clark University, had also studied in Europe and had also concluded that intelligence was primarily inherited. Hall became enormously influential among the testers in America both because of the students he influenced (Goddard, Terman, and Gessell) and because he was the first to translate the Binet intelligence tests into English. Hall, perhaps more than any other American psychologist, influenced the testers in America to adopt a heredity posture.

The Stanford-Binet IQ test, which the testers used to obtain much of their data, was introduced by one of Hall's students, L. M. Terman. Starting with the original 1905 Binet scale, Terman created new norms based on American standardizing groups and revised so many of the original items as to practically create a new test (1916). The data collected in his later studies of gifted children seemed to support a genetic explanation of intelligence.

Thus the testers, whose influence on educational psychology was enormous, spread the hereditarian position they had "inherited" from Europe.

THE LEARNING THEORISTS

The learning theorists, mostly Americans, were bound to be a strong influence on educational psychology. After all, what better contribution could psychology make to education than a more thorough understanding of the principles of learning? However, the major force among American learning theorists was behaviorism, and behaviorism was definitely an environmentalist position. John B. Watson, the father of American behaviorism, sounded the clarion call when he wrote, "The data of psychology is behavior."[9] And we have already seen ("Give me the baby") Watson's extreme environmental stance. The behaviorists —Watson, Thorndike, Guthrie, Hull, and Skinner—spread a kind of mechanical-man gospel. They spent little time studying the organism's growth and development. The emphasis was on how the organism learns, regardless of its inherited potential, regardless of its stage of physical or psychological development, and often regardless of its species. In brief, they saw learning as a result of associations formed between stimuli and actions, or impulses to act. These simple associations would accumulate and form larger groups of learned associations. Learning was seen largely as a result of conditioning, similar to Pavlov's dogs learning to salivate at the sound of a certain tone. From his command post at Columbia Teacher's College, E. L. Thorndike issued basic laws of learning that dominated the field of educational psychology, not to mention classroom practices, for over 50 years. As we noted in Chapter 2, it was even suggested that if one of Thorndike's cats acted at all unpredictably in the laboratory, it might change educational practices all over the United States.

Few American learning theorists ever studied children in the classroom, or, in fact, ever studied any children at all. Thorndike and Guthrie worked primarily with cats, Hull with rats, and Skinner with rats and pigeons, but the principles of learning derived from these studies were generalized to human beings. Not that these generalizations were always invalid. They weren't! A child in a classroom can be conditioned to remain in his seat, just as a rat can be conditioned to press a lever. But it is the solid contention of this book that there is much more to human learning than mere conditioning.

The learning theorists certainly had their day, and from 1920 to well past the Second World War the learning theorists with their environmental bias were calling many of the shots in educational psychology in this country.

WHY WAS AN ENVIRONMENTAL POSITION SO ATTRACTIVE IN AMERICA?

There are at least six ways to answer this question.

1

American psychology was dominated by liberals and, almost without exception, they lined up on the side of environmentalism. To their way of thinking heredity doomed humans to a tooth-and-claw world, a racist society where social change was impossible. The nature-nurture argument was rephrased in more "democratic" language as "instinct versus learning," or even "beast versus man." An ideology, a cherished tradition, was getting between the psychologist and his or her data.

American psychologists line up on the side of environmentalism

2

Even though they recognized the importance of genetic influences, psychologists felt that heredity was fixed at conception and that there was no point in studying something that couldn't be changed. Environmental influences, on the other hand, could be manipulated, and heredity became unimportant simply because of its inaccessibility.

3

Genetics, as a discipline, is a relatively new field, and some of the major breakthroughs have occurred only recently. For example, it was only in 1962 that Watson and Crick won the Nobel Prize for their pioneering work on genetic composition.

4

Very few psychologists were familiar with the information that was accumulating about genetics. Psychologists were more familiar with the related fields of sociology and cultural anthropology than they were with genetics. For example, Margaret Mead and Ruth Benedict were better known to students majoring in psychology than Thomas Hunt Morgan or even Charles Davenport.

5

The special field of behavior genetics is of very recent origin. Although foreshadowed by a study published in 1924,[10] it was only in 1940 that Robert Choate Tryon of the University of California at Berkeley published a classic study that set the stage for the current work in this area.[11] Tryon had a large group of rats learn a maze, and then removed those animals that learned the maze quickly from those that learned slowly. By breeding the fast learners only with other fast learners, and the slow learners only with other slow learners, Tryon demonstrated that after seven generations he had created two significantly different groups of rats: maze-bright animals and maze-dull animals. Breeding experiments like this came *after* many of the behaviorists had already made their strong environmental statements.

6

The final reason for neglecting heredity was the long-term damage done by the instinct theorists at the turn of the century. Now thoroughly discredited, instinct theory attempted to explain behavior by describing it in other terms.

Do people have an inborn aggressive tendency that makes them fight? Yes, claimed the instinct theorists, who confused description for explanation, a nominal fallacy.

Why do people fight? Obviously they have an aggressive instinct. Why do people get together in groups? They have a gregarious instinct. And, of course, the reason people twiddle their thumbs is because they have a thumb-twiddling instinct. This kind of reasoning commits what is called the nominal fallacy; it confuses description with explanation. As B. F. Skinner has pointed out, this tactic is extremely dangerous—if we assume that a redescription is an explanation, we may feel we have answers when in fact we don't; and we may give up the search.[12]

ETHOLOGY

Although it was easy for American psychologists to dismiss the naive views of instinct theorists as unworthy of serious consideration, they could not ignore the carefully detailed work of the European ethologists. Ethology is the study of behavior, especially animal behavior, in the natural setting (as opposed to a laboratory setting). Ethologists are primarily interested in discovering innate behavior patterns or, as they call them, innate releasing mechanisms (IRM's)—patterns many American psychologists overlooked, partly because they insisted on studying animals in aseptic, artificial laboratory situations. Releasers are those

Ethologists study behavior in natural settings rather than in the laboratory

stimuli in an organism's environment that trigger unlearned behavior patterns. For example, if the male stickleback fish sees the color red, a rather violent attack response is released. During the breeding season all stickleback males develop bright red bellies, and if one red-bellied fish happens on another's nesting site, the intruder is roundly attacked and driven out of the nesting area.

The following story, possibly apocryphal, nevertheless makes the point. It seems that a graduate student in experimental psychology, unable to obtain a group of specially bred gentle, white Sprague-Dawley rats, undauntedly captured some wild rats from the local dump. To the dismay of the student, rather than learning the route through the complicated maze, these rats simply ate their way through the wooden sides of the maze and quickly devoured the entire sack of food pellets. By the same token, it is highly improbable that a Sprague-Dawley rat, his IRM's bred out of him hundreds of generations ago, could stay alive for five minutes at the city dump. We can imagine this rat sitting passively trying to find a lever to push.

IMPRINTING

Perhaps the ethologists' most important findings—important from the point of view of forcing American psychologists to reevaluate their position on instincts and the role of heredity in determining behavior—came as a result of the work of Konrad Lorenz. Although it was noted as far back as 1873 that newly hatched chicks seem to follow the first moving stimulus they see, it was not until 1935 that Lorenz revived the term *imprinting* to describe this form of learning. He also discovered that this phenomenon could occur only during one critical period

Lorenz and imprinting in a natural setting

Konrad Lorenz, the imprinted "mother" to these goslings, leads his charges on a morning stroll. Imprinted behavior depends on both inheritance and an environmental event early in the life of the organism that has lasting effects.

Konrad Lorenz

If King Solomon had indeed "spake to the animals" in their own language, then it can truly be said that Konrad Lorenz has the wisdom of a Solomon. Ever since he was a child, Lorenz has been observing, studying, and learning to understand the ways of the wildlife, especially Austrian wildlife. During these many years Lorenz has learned to understand the "signal code," or language, of various animal species and has even learned to imitate this code in order to establish two-way communication.

Konrad Lorenz was born in Vienna, Austria, in 1903. His father, Adolph, was a world-famous orthopedic surgeon and a professor at the University of Vienna. His brother, Albert, followed in his father's footsteps and also became a professor of orthopedic surgery at the University of Vienna. During Konrad's childhood, the family spent the summer months at a country home in Altenberg. It was there that Lorenz became fascinated by the fauna of his native country. He explored the woods and ponds, and by age nine had set up his own microscope for studying the tiny wonderworld of the freshwater pond. Says Lorenz, "for he who has once seen the intimate beauty of nature cannot tear himself away from it again. He must become either a poet or a naturalist . . . he may well become both."

His family merely tolerated young Lorenz's avid curiosity about animals. Lorenz brought into his home pet after pet, each more destructive than the last. The tolerance of his parents often wore thin.

Due to his father's insistence, Lorenz became a medical student at the University of Vienna. In 1928 he received his M.D. degree, but his love of animals continued and so did his studies. In 1933 he received his Ph.D. degree in zoology, and for the next four years he continued his research on the behavior of animals in their natural habitats.

In 1937 he began his teaching career, receiving an appointment to teach comparative anatomy and animal psychology at his beloved University of Vienna. In 1937 he also published his now-famous article in the journal, *Auk*, titled "The Companion in the Bird's World." In this article Lorenz described the intricate biological mechanism of imprinting. During their first few hours of life certain organisms will become imprinted on the first moving stimulus object in their visual field. They will then fol-

low this object, usually, of course, their mother, with devotion and marching-band precision. This is how young organisms, especially birds, know which species they belong to, and it also accounts for their flocking behavior. Lorenz had revived the long discredited instinct theory and made it scientifically respectable.

In 1940 he became professor of psychology at the University of Konigsberg in Germany. By this time World War II was raging through Europe, and Germany was at the eye of the storm. The following year, Lorenz was called into the German army and later fought on the eastern front. In 1944 he was captured by the Russians, and after a long and arduous ordeal was released in 1948, three years after the war had officially ended. He immediately resumed his duties at the University of Vienna, but in 1950 he went to Germany again, this time as the assistant director of the Max Planck Institute for Behavioral Physiology. Lorenz is still at the Max Planck Institute, now as director. In October 1973 Lorenz and two other pioneers in behavioral science won the Nobel Prize in Medicine for their work in the comparative study of behavior.

Among his numerous publications are the following books: *King Solomon's Ring* (1952), *Man Meets Dog* (1954), *Evolution and Modification of Behavior* (1965), *On Aggression* (1966), and *Studies in Animal and Human Behavior* (1970).

Lorenz has established ethology, the study of animal behavior in the natural setting, as a serious and respectable discipline. Due in large measure to his careful work, ethology no longer suffers from the early damage done by the naive instinct theorists. The message from Lorenz is: If you want to understand animal behavior, study the animal in its own environment, not in the artificial confines of the laboratory. And perhaps in educational psychology this message translates to the following: If you want to understand school children, study them in the classroom.

in the chick's life. Lorenz noted that goslings would follow not only their mother but any moving stimulus that presented itself within the first few hours of their life. If Lorenz presented himself during this critical period, he found that the goslings would parade after him with a devotion usually reserved for their mother and that this habit would continue throughout the birds' lifetime.[13]

Imprinting also demonstrated in the laboratory

Although imprinting was first noted in the organism's natural environment, it has also been demonstrated in the artificial world of the laboratory, proving that psychology and ethology are not at odds.[14] In fact, under laboratory conditions it was possible to show the exact point in time when imprinting had the most impact—imprinting in ducks, for example, can occur up to 32 hours after hatching, although the optimal time is between 13 and 16 hours of age.

Imprinting provided the perfect example of the careful blending of heredity and environment in producing behavioral change.

CHERISHED BELIEFS AND SCIENTIFIC FACTS

As we have now seen, psychology in general and educational psychology in particular have battled for years over the question of the relative contribution of heredity and environment to behavior. Each side felt that it had the answer. As often happens when narrow or even single causes are sought to explain anything, the search for this single cause results more in the creation of controversy than in the accumulation of knowledge. Each side becomes rigid and dogmatic, and cherished beliefs begin to cloud scientific vision. If Watson had been less zealous in the cause of environmentalism, he could not possibly have over looked the importance of heredity. Nor could Goddard have overlooked the obvious environmental differences between the "good" and "bad" Kallikaks, had not his cherished opinion, his "pride of authorship," clouded his vision.

The search for the single cause

Cherished beliefs cloud scientific vision

This problem is not confined to psychology or to education. In our long quest to gain knowledge about our environment and ourselves, we have often been blinded by cherished beliefs. Advances in astronomy were thwarted for centuries by our egocentric view that the earth, our habitat, must be at the center of the universe. Only slowly and grudgingly did we give up this notion and then only on the understanding that if the earth is not at the center, surely the sun, at the center of our solar system, is at the core of a revolving universe. Ptolemy's heliocentric view of the universe went virtually unchallenged for over a thousand years. Even today it is still for some a sore point to realize that the earth is only a dust spot in this vast and expanding universe. And if we struggled to preserve our special place in the cosmos, it was only a dress rehearsal for the real drama of preserving our glorified role on earth.

Despite our reluctance, we finally accepted our place in the universe—in the sixteenth century. Ptolemy gave way to Copernicus, the earth was put in its proper place, and the ground was prepared for the later theories of Newton and Einstein.

In other areas, however, we were even more backward: physiology as a discipline did not really come into its own until the nineteenth century (it seemed even more threatening to our ego to learn that our bodies were open to the objective scrutiny of science). But the "most unkindest cut of all" was the thrust of the newest scientific discipline, psychology; it insisted on probing our very inner being.

It is, thus, no accident that our search to understand ourselves has only recently come under scientific observation. In the evolution of scientific disciplines there has been a fairly orderly sequence based on the degree to which each science has threatened our self-esteem. As we have seen, and will continue to see, cherished beliefs are hard to give up; this is certainly true of educational psychology in the twentieth century.

NATURE-NURTURE: A MODERN SOLUTION TO AN OLD PROBLEM

It is now clear, in the last quarter of the twentieth century, that the old question of heredity versus environment is unanswerable because it is meaningless. Behavior is not the result of a single cause, but of multiple causes. It is the result of heredity interacting with environment interacting with time (see Fig. 3.1). Our hereditary potential can be nourished or stifled depending on the type, amount, and quality of our environmental encounters and depending on when these encounters occur (they can occur too early or too late to be of optimum benefit).

Behavior has multiple causes

In the chapters that follow we outline some of the major considerations that have moved educational psychology beyond the nature-nurture controversy. Since human behavior is determined by the interaction of both (recall Dewey's phrase, "an organism in some environment"), we need to look at nature and nurture simultaneously. We can then begin to consider, not in a single- or narrow-minded way, but within a broad context, how to educate children and adolescents. We need to know both how to strike and when the iron is hot. In Chapter 5 we present some of the central ideas about the significance and lasting effects of initial experience. In Chapters 6–8 we present the stages of cognitive and personal development to show, in our metaphor, just when the iron is hot. We can then shift our attention to arranging the environment for learning and teaching, to be discussed in the later chapters.

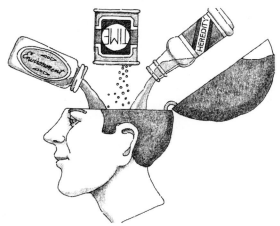

Fig. 3.1 Behavior is the result of heredity interacting with environment interacting with time.

Summary

The causes of behavior are multiple and complex, and it is dangerous to build a psychology of human behavior on the basis of animal studies alone. Growth rates differ markedly among species, and the rate of growth and development among humans is comparatively slow. Studies that compared the rate of maturation between humans and lower species found humans to lag behind.

The nature-nurture controversy created a great division in the field of psychology. Henry Goddard's study of the Kallikaks attempted to "prove" that heredity was the most important factor in determining a person's psychological make-up. John B. Watson argued that environmental influences, through the process of conditioning, were paramount in determining psychological traits.

In the field of educational psychology, the measurement practitioners (IQ testers) were typically strong believers in heredity, whereas the learning theorists were environmentalists. American psychology as a whole, however, tended to believe that environmental influences were more important than hereditary influences.

Ethology, the study of animal behavior in the natural setting as opposed to the laboratory, made the study of instinctive behavior (IRM's) more respectable as a legitimate scientific pursuit. The ethologists demonstrated a special form of learning called imprinting, which could occur only during a critical time period in an organism's life.

Scentific objectivity has historically suffered as a result of the cherished beliefs and strong attitudes held by the scientists themselves or by society in general. Psychology has perhaps been the most affected by this, for it is the discipline concerned with probing our inner being and motivation.

The modern solution to the age-old nature-nurture controversy is that neither heredity nor environment are the sole causes of behavior. Behavior is the result of heredity interacting with environment interacting with time. This final point is critical to an understanding of the rest of the book, and is considered one of psychology's most basic principles.

REFERENCES

1
J. A. R. Wilson, M. C. Robeck, and W. B. Michael, *Psychological Fundations of Learning and Teaching* (New York: McGraw-Hill, 1969), p. 165.

2
W. N. Kellogg and L. A. Kellogg, *The Ape and the Child* (New York: McGraw-Hill, 1963).

3
K. G. Hayes and C. Hayes, "The Intellectual Development of a Home-Raised Chimpanzee," *Proceedings: American Philosophical Society* 95 (1951):105–109.

4
H. E. Goddard, *The Kallikak Family* (New York: Macmillan, 1912).

5
J. B. Watson and R. Raynor, "Conditioned Emotional Reactions," *Journal of Experimental Psychology* 3, no. 8 (1921).

6
Ibid., p. 14.

7
J. B. Watson, "The Behaviorist Looks at Instincts," *Harper's Magazine,* no. 155 (July 1927):233. Reprinted by special permission of *Harper's Magazine.*

8
B. F. Skinner, "Bury Not Burn," *A.P.A. Monitor* 6, no. 11 (November 1975):2.

9
J. B. Watson, "Psychology as the Behaviorist Views It," *Psychological Review* 20 (1913): 158–177.

10
E. C. Tolman, "The Inheritance of Maze Learning Ability in Rats," *Journal of Comparative Psychology* 4 (1924):1–18.

11
R. C. Tryon, "Genetic Differences in Maze-Learning Ability in Rats," *Yearbook Nat. Soc. Stud. Educ.* 39 (1940):111–119.

12
B. F. Skinner, *Science and Human Behavior* (New York: Macmillan, 1953).

13
K. Lorenz, "The Companion in the Bird's World," *Auk* 54 (1937):245–273.

14
E. H. Hess, "Imprinting," *Science* 130 (1959):133–141.

SUGGESTIONS FOR FURTHER READING

Glass, D. C., ed. *Genetics.* New York: Rockefeller University Press, 1968.

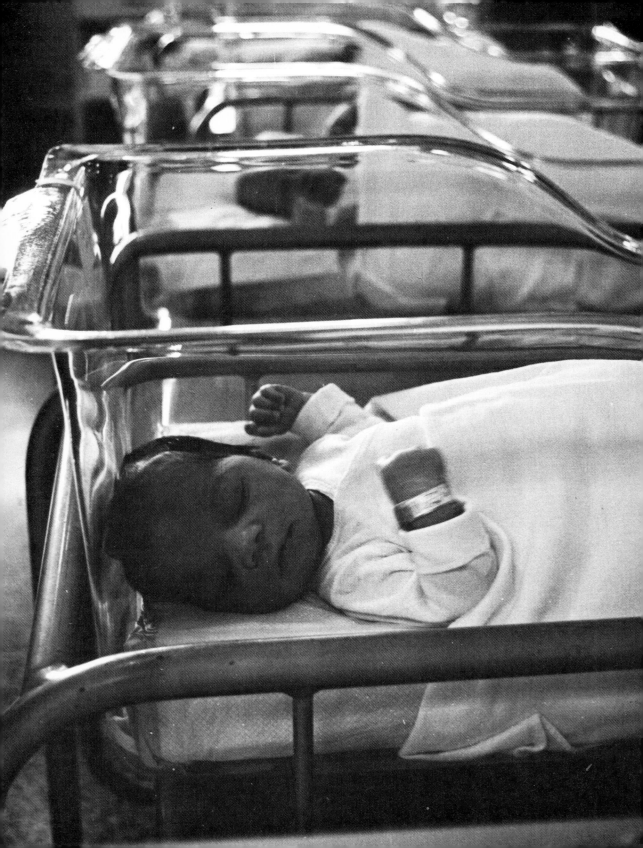

4

Physical growth and development

Each of us begins life as a tiny, watery speck smaller than the period at the end of this sentence. This speck, technically called a zygote, contains the genetic background that will shape and direct our development for the rest of our lives. The zygote is formed at the moment of conception, when the sperm cell of the male fertilizes the egg cell of the female. Half of the genetic background contained in the zygote comes from the father, half from the mother, so that the baby will be like both parents, but not exactly like either one. Thus the zygote contains the hereditary component that will be constantly molded and modified through environmental interactions. And these interactions begin immediately. If the zygote were to be surgically removed from the uterus and placed in a foreign environment, like a glass of water, it would soon perish. If the zygote remains in the uterus and the uterine environment remains healthy, then growth and development continue, and some nine months later the baby is born. It is important to recognize that all during the nine months environmental encounters are occurring. To be sure, the uterine environment is relatively constant, but not totally so. Toxic agents in the mother's uterus can modify, damage, or even halt the development of the zygote. One study even suggests that learning can occur in the uterus.[1] In short, our basic axiom that behavior is a result of the interaction of heredity, environment, and time covers one's entire life, from the moment of conception.

In the beginning—the zygote

Environmental encounters precede birth

THE ABC's OF GENETICS
Our knowledge of genetics is of very recent origin. The science of genetics is based on the study of heredity, the biological transmittal of characteristics from

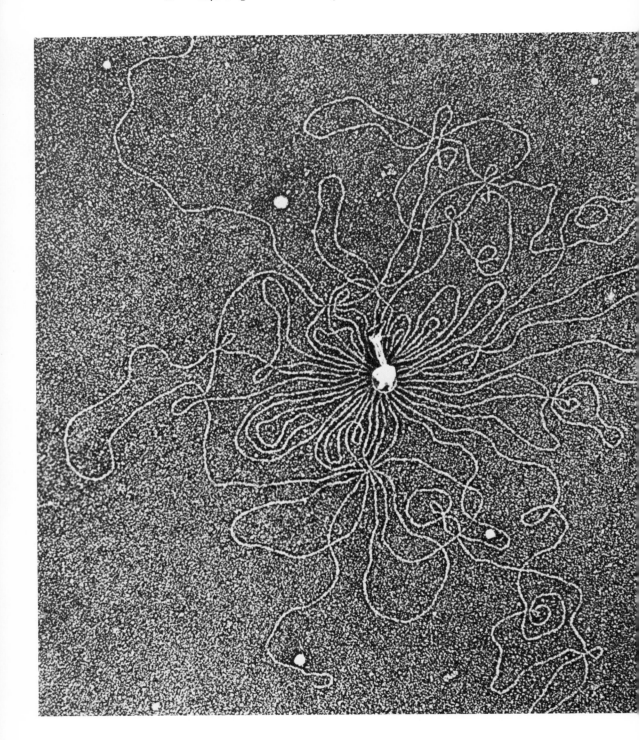

parent to offspring. The nature-nurture argument was based in large part on the fact that not enough was known about nature, and what was known about heredity wasn't fully understood by many psychologists, especially in America.

The fundamental unit of analysis in genetics is the gene. Genes are tiny particles that carry the hereditary characteristics. They are located in the nucleus of each of the body's cells, where they occur in pairs, one from each parent. Estimates of the total number of genes in any single human (the human genome) run anywhere from five to ten million. Since at conception each parent contributes from this vast number of genes, there is obviously room for great genetic variation in the resulting offspring. Except for identical twins, every individual is genetically unique.

Genes are composed of the rather large organic molecules: DNA (deoxyribonucleic acid) and RNA (ribonucleic acid) (see Fig. 4.1). These nucleic acids (DNA and RNA) are located in the chromosomes, which lie in the nucleus of every cell in the body. Chromosomes are fairly long, threadlike bits of protein, and each of the cells in the human body contains 23 pairs of these chromosomes (see Fig. 4.2). However, the germ cells (sperm cells in the male and egg cells in the female) carry only 23 chromosomes, or half the number that exist in the body cells. At conception, then, the zygote receives half of its chromosomes from each parent, 23 from each, and thus achieves its full complement of 23 pairs.

The DNA and RNA molecules are located within the nucleus of each cell, where the chromosomes are arranged. The DNA molecule contains chains of atoms and simpler molecules that code and store information about growth

Genes carry the hereditary message

◀ **Fig. 4.1** DNA and RNA.

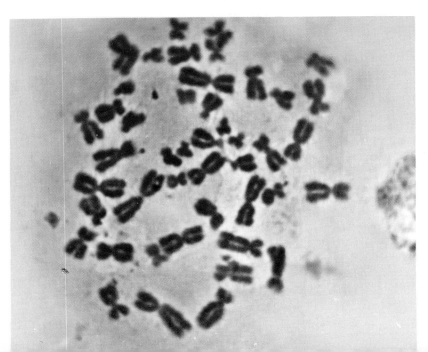

Fig. 4.2 Human chromosomes.

and development. Their arrangement allows the DNA molecule to reproduce itself exactly, that is, to achieve precise self-duplication. For this to occur, the chemical environment must be appropriate. DNA acts as a blueprint or, as it is called by the geneticists, a template, for the formation of certain enzymes that help to guide the development of the organism. The coded information contained in the DNA molecule is transmitted to other parts of the cell by the RNA molecules. DNA may be thought of as the architect's blueprint, while the RNA would be the builder translating this blueprint into a finished home. It must be remembered, however, that these reactions do not occur in a vacuum. The chemical environment must be appropriate for the DNA "architect" and the RNA "builder" to work effectively.

*DNA—the architect
RNA—the builder*

From the moment of conception, then, the individual is a product of the interaction among heredity, environment, and time.

DOMINANTS AND RECESSIVES

Mendel's discoveries

One of the first discoveries in the field of genetics occurred over a hundred years ago when the Austrian monk Gregor Mendel (1822–1884) learned an important fact about inheritance. In his study of the flower color of garden peas, Mendel discovered that some genes are dominant and some recessive. Mendel found that if he crossed a red-flowered pea with another red-flowered pea, the resulting plant would have red flowers. Similarly, if he crossed a white-flowered pea with another white-flowered pea, the resulting plant would have white flowers. But if he crossed a red-flowered pea with a white-flowered pea, the resulting plant would have red flowers. Thus the genes that determine flower color can be dominant or recessive, and in this case, red is dominant over white. Crossing a red with a red, or a white with a white, produces a pure offspring, whereas crossing a red with a white produces a hybrid. When a dominant gene is paired with a recessive gene, the resulting hybrid always exhibits the dominant trait.

Among the human traits that follow this rule, perhaps the best example is eye color. Brown eyes are dominant over blue eyes. Thus if both parents have blue eyes, their children must have blue eyes. This is because, for individuals to have blue eyes, they must be carrying only the recessive genes for eye color. If they were to have a dominant brown-eyed gene and a recessive blue-eyed gene, their eyes would have to be brown. If, however, both parents are brown-eyed, but both are carrying both recessives, their children still might have blue eyes. Chances are greater, however, that they will have brown eyes.

Phenotype—the observed trait

Genotype—the inferred reason for the trait

Two hybrid parents, each with brown eyes, have only a one-in-four chance of producing a blue-eyed child. The trait that shows up is called the phenotype, whereas the one that remains hidden is called the genotype. A person with a phenotype of brown eyes may have a genotype of two brown-eyed genes or a genotype of one brown-eyed and one blue-eyed gene.

A trait like eye color, in which a single pair of genes determines the phenotype, is a fairly rare case in genetics. Most behavioral traits, such as measured intelligence, result from the combination of large numbers of genes. This is called polygenic inheritance, and again dramatizes the enormous potential for genetic differences among individuals.[2]

We can see from even this simplified excursion into genetics that heredity has lawful relationships, and it is certain that future discoveries in this field will uncover many more definite patterns and laws that influence physical traits and behavior. Studies have already shown that, in addition to motor skills and intelligence, schizophrenia and manic-depression have rather strong hereditary components. This is not to deny that environmental influences are important; they are! But the genes do carry constitutional predispositions toward various behaviors which the environment may stifle or nourish.

Diversity—the name of the game in genetics

BEHAVIOR GENETICS

Psychologists are able to examine the possible effects of genetic endowment through both animal and human research. Though the results of animal studies cannot be directly generalized to humans, the animal data may be at least suggestive of hypotheses that might later be pursued when attempting to understand the results of human studies. The studies in behavior genetics, both animal and human, have as their goal the discovery of lawful relationships between genetic endowment and observed behavior.

Animal studies

The genetic studies of animals are typically of two types: inbreeding and selective breeding. Inbreeding studies usually involve the mating of brothers and sisters in order to obtain as much *homozygosity* in the population as possible. Homozygosity means that the gene pairs are identical. When animals are inbred, the like-sexed members come to have the same, or almost the same, genotype. Inbreeding experiments are commonly carried out on such organisms as mice and fruitflies (Drosophila). In one study, for example, fifteen different inbred strains of mice were compared on a number of characteristics.[3] Significant differences were found among the various strains on the behavioral characteristic of exploratory behavior. This tends to indicate that, among mice, willingness to explore new areas is at least partly genetically determined.

Two types of animal studies: inbreeding and selection

In selective-breeding studies, animals of a given strain are tested on some behavioral criterion, such as ability to run a maze. Then, the animals demonstrating extremes of this behavior are selectively mated for generation after generation—that is, the animals with the best performance on the maze, for example, are mated with one another as are the animals with the lowest maze performance. In the previous chapter it was pointed out that one study of this type, carried out by R. C. Tryon, established that after seven generations two significantly different groups of rats had been created: maze-bright animals and maze-dull animals.[4]

In another study, white mice were separated according to the amount of aggressiveness they exhibited. The most- and least-aggressive mice were identified and then selectively bred. Again, after seven generations, dramatic differences in the aggressiveness displayed by the offspring became apparent.[5] In studies such as these, the pure effects of genetic endowment can be examined, since the animals' environments can be carefully controlled.

Human studies

Human studies rely on after-the-fact data

Since social taboos would argue against breeding experiments at the human level (not that there would be a shortage of student volunteers), psychologists must rely on after-the-fact, or *post hoc,* data in studying human genetic endowment. In some studies lineage records are traced backward in an attempt to establish the possibility of direct ancestry, a method used by Henry Goddard (Chapter 3) in his study of the Kallikaks. The problem with this kind of research is that genetic background and environmental influences are easily confounded: Martin Kallikak's "good seed" descendants were subjected to different environmental conditions than were the descendants of "Old Horror." Sir Francis Galton, the father of intelligence testing, was the first to use this lineage technique when he compared the achievements of successive generations of his own brilliant family with those of a less-fortunate family.

In another type of human research in genetics, adopted or foster children are compared with both their biological and foster parents. If the children are behaviorally more similar to their biological parents (whose influence on the child's environment is presumed to be zero) than to their foster parents, the similarity is attributed to heredity.

Perhaps the most popular technique at the human level is to examine for behavioral similarities identical twins who have been reared apart. Since identical (MZ) twins reared separately still have precisely the same genetic endowment, any remaining behavioral similarities are presumed to result from genetic causes. In one study, an attempt was made to discover whether or not there is a genetic component in schizophrenia.[6] In this study, members of MZ twin pairs (called the probands) who had been diagnosed as schizophrenic were located, and their co-twins then searched out. The percentage of co-twins of probands who are also schizophrenic is called the *concordance rate.* When this concordance rate was compared with the concordance rate among fraternal (DZ) twins, researchers found the MZ concordance rate to be substantially higher. Also, in the case of MZ twins reared apart, the concordance rate was roughly 60 percent, a figure that certainly lends some support to the author's genetic interpretation.

PSYCHOLOGY'S FIRST PRINCIPLE

Psychology's first principle and most fundamental axiom is that the organism is a product of heredity, interacting with environment, interacting with time.

$$O = H \leftrightarrow E \leftrightarrow T$$

It is meaningless to ask whether intelligence, or introversion, or any other psychological trait is inherited or learned. It's like asking which is more important in running a car, the engine or the gasoline. Or which is more important in determining the area of a rectangle, the height or the width.

Even something as seemingly directly inherited as physical height is profoundly influenced by environment and time. Even with the inherited potential for tallness, an individual will still be short if the environment prevents physical exercise or proper vitamin intake, especially if this deprivation occurs in early childhood (time).

Keep this first principle constantly in mind during the rest of this chapter. When we discuss developmental stages we will give various age norms. However, it is crucial to remember that these are only averages, that there are large discrepancies between the averages and any individual case. For example, the averages show that children usually utter their first word at twelve months. But, in fact, some children say their first word at eight months, some at twenty-four months. A great deal depends on the amount and quality of environmental stimulation.

Age norms are only averages—deviations from the average are common

Environmental influences in the form of nutrition are also of great importance. The undernourished child may lag in both physiological and psychological growth. In one review of the work in this area, it was concluded that the nine months of prenatal life and the two or three years following birth are "most critical in the growth of brain tissue and are the periods of greatest vulnerability to malnutrition."[7] Mental deficiency was seen as one possible result of an inadequate diet during this critical period of life.

Though the time factor is given great importance in the following discussion, it must be remembered that time is only one factor. While it is a convenient factor to utilize in discussing physical development, it is only part of the total equation. The organism is a product of heredity, environment, and time in constant interaction.

LIFE BEFORE BIRTH

At birth the human baby is already about nine months of age. As a matter of fact, during that first nine months, from conception to birth, more growth occurs than will ever occur again: that tiny speck, the zygote, has grown into a seven- or eight-pound baby by the time it emerges into what William James calls the "blooming, buzzing confusion" of the external environnment.

The zygote

The zygote floats freely in the fluid inside the uterus. After about two weeks it attaches itself to the wall of the uterus and becomes a parasite, receiving all its oxygen and nourishment from the mother's body. By the time the zygote attaches itself to the wall of the uterus, it has already begun to differentiate into three parts: the outer layer, or ectoderm, which will form the brain; the middle layer, or mesoderm, which will form the heart; and the inner layer, or endoderm, which will form the liver.

Prenatal development: Stage I—the zygote

The embryo

The second stage of prenatal development, called the embryonic stage, begins two weeks after conception, at the time the zygote attaches itself to the uterus. At this point the developing organism is called an embryo. The embryonic stage

Prenatal development: Stage II—the embryo

lasts until about eight weeks after conception, and during this stage the organism increases its weight by two million percent. Also during this period the heart begins beating, sex organs are formed, hands and feet are formed and can be flexed, and all the internal organs are formed. By the end of the embryonic period, the organism is clearly identifiable as human.

The fetus

Prenatal development: Stage III—the fetus

From eight weeks after conception until birth the organism is called a fetus. Though the growth rate of the fetus is not as spectacular as the zygote's or embryo's, it is still extremely rapid by postnatal standards. The fetus is definitely a behaving organism, and its behavior can be studied.

Reactions to stimuli. It is known, for example, that the fetus can react to stimuli as early as eight weeks after conception. At this time it is sensitive to stimulation of the nose, lips, and chin. The area of sensitivity gradually increases, and by the fourteenth week, the whole body is sensitive, except for the top and back of the head. The top of the head doesn't respond to stimulation until after birth.

Spontaneous actions. Along with the ability to react to stimuli, the fetus can also act spontaneously. Certainly after the fourth month the mother is aware of fetal activity. This activity is quite diffuse; that is, movements are slow and involve several parts of the body at once.

Prenatal development extremely rapid

All the preceding stages, from conception to birth, are collectively called the prenatal stage of development. Prenatal development is characterized by its rapidity and by a maturation rate that enables the fetus to perform certain functions well before they are actually needed. For example, the fetus can make breathing movements by the fourth month, walking movements by the fifth month, and sucking movements by the sixth month. These activities are not needed until birth, yet they are ready months ahead of time.

PHYSICAL DEVELOPMENT IN CHILDHOOD

The newborn baby, called a neonate, is certainly not a miniature adult. The baby's head and trunk are much larger, proportionally, than they will be at adulthood. For example, the head will only double in size from birth to adulthood, whereas the arms and legs may grow to five times their original length.

The nervous system

In one sense the nervous system is complete at birth; that is, the number of typical nerve cells never increases after birth, but the size of these cells does increase. Also, although the neonate comes equipped with a fully structured nervous system, it is many years before this system can function efficiently.

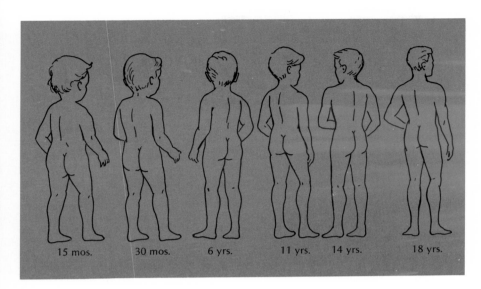

Changes in body proportions as a function of
age. The figures are adjusted to the same height.[8]

Each nerve cell, or neuron, has two basic parts: fibers and cell bodies. Think of the neuron as a fiber with branches at both ends and a bulge (cell body) in the middle. The function of the neuron is to transmit messages (neural impulses) to and from all parts of the body. The branches, or fibers, pick up the messages and send them on their way. The receiving end of a neuron is called a dendrite and the transmitting end is called the axon. In order not to short-circuit the electrically charged neural impulses, most of these fibers are insulated with a white sheath called myelin. The gray-colored cell body does not have this covering. Therefore, the myelin-covered neural pathways are called white matter and the uncovered cell bodies are called gray matter. The myelinization of the nervous system is not complete at birth, so that a great deal of short-circuiting among the baby's neural impulses does indeed occur. This, in part, accounts for the mass activity that is characteristic of a baby's physical reactions. Touching a baby's foot doesn't result in just a foot response, but is usually followed by gross movements of both feet, both arms, and even the trunk. It's as though you had no insulation on the wires leading to your electrical appliances, so that when you turned on the TV, the radio and stereo would go on, the alarm clock would buzz, the dishwasher would start, the coffeepot would begin percolating, and the doorbell would ring. Although the nervous system is structurally complete at birth, it is nowhere near functionally mature. The cerebral cortex, which is crucial for learning and complex behavior, doesn't become functionally mature until about age two, and some maturation continues until about age twelve or fifteen.

The nerve cell, or neuron, transmits the message

The baby's typical response pattern—mass activity

Sleep

Newborn babies spend most of their days asleep, averaging about sixteen hours a day. This time decreases rapidly until by age one year they are sleeping only a little over ten hours a day.

Motor development

One of the most dramatic features of infancy is the development of motor skills. Compared to the neonate, the two-year-old child is a study in grace and physical coordination. One psychologist, M. M. Shirley, studied the development of infants on a week-to-week basis. As can be seen from Table 4.1, Shirley's data

TABLE 4.1 Stages in motor development. The skills listed here illustrate the progressive development of control over different groups of muscles. This development proceeds in an orderly fashion from the head region down the body and out to the ends of the limbs.

Description of stage	Number of cases	Age, weeks Median
First order skills (control of the neck muscles)		
On stomach, chin up	22	3
On stomach, chest up	22	9
Held erect, stepping	19	13
On back, tense for lifting	19	15
Held erect, knees straight	18	15
Sit on lap, support at lower ribs and complete head control	22	19
Second-order skills (control of trunk and upper-limb muscles)		
Sit alone momentarily	22	25
On stomach, knee push or swim	22	25
On back, rolling	19	29
Held erect, stand firmly with help	20	30
Sit alone one minute	20	31
Third-order skills (beginning of body-limb coordination in prone position)		
On stomach, some progress	17	37
On stomach, scoot backward	16	40
Fourth-order skills (balance in upright position with support; locomotion in prone position)		
Stand holding to furniture	22	42
Creep	22	45
Walk when led	21	45
Pull to stand by furniture	17	47
Fifth-order skills (unsupported locomotion in upright position)		
Stand alone	21	62
Walk alone	21	64

Adapted from M. M. Shirley, *The First Two Years, A Study of Twenty-five Babies,* vol. 1, Postural and Locomotor Development (Minneapolis: University of Minnesota Press, 1931), p. 99.

The sequence of motor development.

Although motor development is heavily influenced by biological maturation, practice is necessary to realize full development of potential.

suggest that there is a definite pattern to motor development. Infants can hold up their heads before they can sit alone, sit before they crawl, and crawl before they walk. This pattern of development is almost exactly the same for every human baby, and each child passes through each of these physical stages at almost the same age.[9]

Studies have shown that motor development occurs according to at least three general rules.

1
Cephalocaudal progression—meaning that motor ability develops from the head on down to the toes. The neonate's head is closer to its eventual adult size than is the rest of its body. Also, the infant has more motor control of the head than of the muscles lower down the body. The progression of motor control follows this pattern: first the head; then the shoulders, arms, and abdomen; and finally the legs and feet.

2
Proximodistal progression—meaning that growth and motor ability develop from the central axis of the body on outward. Trunk and shoulder movements occur earlier than separate arm movements. Control of the hands and fingers comes last.[10]

3
Mass to specific-action progression—indicating that the baby's first actions are global and undifferentiated. Slowly, the infant's ability to make specific responses emerges. Refined activity of the fingers and thumb usually don't occur until the baby is about a year old.

Motor development is thus heavily influenced by biological maturation, though practice is certainly necessary for full development of the biological potential.

Sensory development

Many studies have been done to determine what infants are able to receive through their sensory equipment. Since infants obviously cannot give verbal answers to questions, research in this area is much like animal research. If a researcher is trying to find out whether a rat can sense the difference between the colors red and green, the rat can be presented with a red light and food in one goal box and a green light with no food in the other. After a number of trials, if the rat goes consistently to the red light, even when it is randomly switched to the goal box that has no food in it, the researcher would know that the rat can discriminate between red and green. (Studies have shown that rats, in fact, cannot make this discrimination between red and green colors when the amount of illumination is held constant.)

Newborn babies have been shown capable of discriminating between sweet and sour tastes, taste being the most highly developed of all the senses at birth. Responses to different smells have been observed within a few hours of birth.

Newborn babies can discriminate among various tastes, sounds, and smells

Babies as young as six months old can perceive depth.

Some babies respond to sound almost immediately after birth, whereas others may take a few days to gain this sense. This difference is a result of the time it may take for the amniotic fluid to drain out of the hearing mechanism.

Vision develops more slowly

Vision develops more slowly than many of the other senses. Response to light and darkness (the pupillary reflex) is functional within two days after birth, and by ten days infants can follow moving objects with their eyes. By six months of age, infants can discriminate between colors, between such shapes as circles and triangles, and between the faces of parents and strangers.

One classic study has demonstrated that six-month-old infants have the ability to perceive depth and, thus, avoid situations in which they might fall.[11] In this study the babies were placed on a plate of glass which extended from a tabletop across a three-foot drop in space. When the babies reached what they perceived as the edge of the table, they refused to crawl across the rest of the glass. This perceived drop-off is called the visual cliff, and it has been demonstrated not only with infants but with lower organisms such as cats and rats, as well. The ability to perceive a visual cliff obviously has value for survival.

The visual cliff

Speech development

At birth, speech is restricted to general, undifferentiated crying, yet by the second month the baby can communicate both discomfort and contentment through the use of loud crying or gentle cooing. Of all the developmental fac-

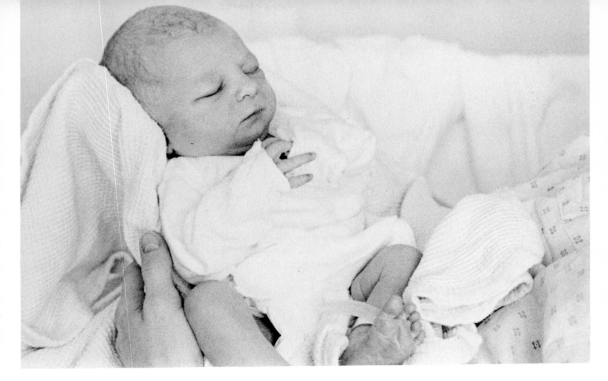

Newborn babies spend most of their days
asleep, averaging about sixteen hours a day.

tors covered so far, speech is obviously the one most influenced by learning.
Yet even speech is built on a biological foundation. In studies of the various
sounds made by infants throughout the world, it has been found that certain
sounds occur at about the same time and in about the same order in all infants.
By listening to the sounds of a baby lying contentedly nearby, one can hear the
basic sounds of all languages throughout the world, from the German gutteral
"r" to the singsong intonation of Chinese.

Learning theorists, such as B. F. Skinner, believe that babies keep some of
these sounds—those reinforced by their parents—and slowly discard those that
are not encouraged. By the ninth or tenth month they are able to imitate some
of the sounds made by others around them.

Other theorists, such as Noam Chomsky, believe there is a heavy genetic
component in language acquisition. Rather than learning language solely on the
basis of reinforcement and imitation, Chomsky argues that language acquisition
may be the result of an inborn "language acquisition device," which directs the
infant's ability to learn.[12]

By about one year of age, babies can associate the sounds they make with
specific objects and thus they begin to utter their first words, words such as
"dada," "mama," or "bye-bye." The young mother is often depressed over the
fact that she's been through an uncomfortable pregnancy and has spent sleep-
less nights feeding, changing, and comforting the baby, only to hear her baby's
first word—"dada."

After the first word, the infant's vocabulary increases slowly for the next few months. This may be due to the total attention the infant is devoting to learning the intricacies of walking. Once walking has been mastered, usually at about eighteen months, language development speeds up. In one study, 154 children below two years of age were tested on the ability to speak or understand certain test words. At twelve months of age, the average vocabulary was three words; by fifteen months it was nineteen words; by eighteen months, twenty-two words. Then came a tremendous spurt, for by twenty-one months of age the average was 118 words, and by twenty-four months, 272 words.[13]

Once walking is mastered, speech develops quickly

These figures are, of course, only averages, and there are great individual differences from one child to the next. For example, children with high IQ's begin talking, on the average, as much as four months earlier than the average child. Also, girls begin talking sooner than boys, use more words in each sentence, and have larger vocabularies.[14]

Girls talk sooner than boys

PHYSICAL DEVELOPMENT IN ADOLESCENCE

Although physical growth proceeds in fits and starts from two years of age to adolescence, it is not until adolescence that another really dramatic growth spurt occurs, and it occurs earlier in girls than in boys (see Fig. 4.3). Though boys are typically taller and heavier than girls at age ten, by age thirteen the girls are taller and heavier than the boys. By age sixteen, the situation returns to the way it had been before the onset of adolescence, with the boys again taller and heavier.

Adolescent growth spurt

In girls, adolescence is signaled by the occurrence of the menarche, or first menstruation. This happens concurrently with breast development, usually by age thirteen, though it is not uncommon for some girls to reach menarche as early as age ten or as late as age sixteen.

Adolescence in boys does not have such clear-cut criteria. If we use such indices as the appearance of pubic hair, the first seminal ejaculation, or increase in the size of the penis and testes, adolescence in boys usually begins between the ages of eleven and seventeen. Again, there is great variation in age among boys reaching puberty.

Special problems for girls

Menarche

Menarche can be a traumatic event in the life of a young girl who is psychologically unprepared. This is especially true for the EM (early-maturing) girl. However, the girl who is secure in her sex identification and who has had adult support and guidance may regard her first menstruation with pride, as a sign that she is "grown up" and is no longer a child. The girl whose parents have prepared her for this new experience is less likely to be anxious about her menarche.

Breast development

Breast development has special psychological overtones in Western culture. America has been described as a breast-oriented nation, and certainly the popularity of the Playmate of the Month, the billboard ads for suntan lotion, the TV adds for "the slightly padded bra," and the direct stares of males of all ages

Fig. 4.3 The adolescent growth spurt typically occurs earlier in girls than in boys.

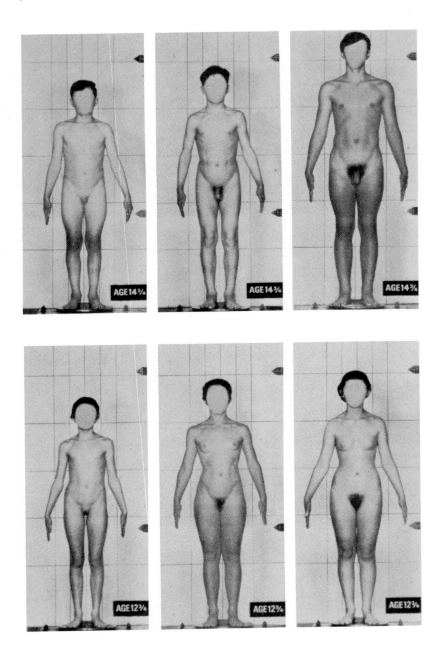

do much to validate this description. During adolescence, then, breast development becomes a psychological symbol of approaching womanhood and sexuality. Typically, physical development of the breast from bud to full size occurs in about three years, from about eleven to about fourteen years of age. The bud-stage almost always precedes menarche and the first signs of pubic hair.

Special problems for boys

Boys who begin puberty relatively late suffer psychological distress for a variety of reasons. LM (late-maturing) boys are apt to be shorter and physically weaker than the early maturers and are thus less apt to become outstanding athletes. Because this and other social reinforcements are fewer, the late-maturing boy more often turns psychologically inward, becoming introverted.

The size of the penis is also of great concern to the adolescent boy. In the shower room after gym classes the adolescent quickly glances from boy to boy, to see whether he "measures up." The boy with the small penis is often openly ridiculed and his masculinity challenged. He worries that he will be an unsuccessful lover. The facts, however, as reported by Masters and Johnson, are that the size of the penis is not highly correlated with a he-man physique or with great physical size. The largest penis they measured (without erection or stretching) was 5½ inches and belonged to a man only 5'7" tall. The shortest penis, just over 2⅓ inches, was found on a man almost 6' tall.[15]

Adolescent boys are often concerned with penis size. According to researchers Masters and Johnson, the size of the penis is not highly correlated with physical size.

Further, Masters and Johnson found little evidence for the widely held myth that the larger the penis the greater the potential for giving sexual satisfaction. Because the vagina distends when excited in order to permit entry and then contracts around the penis in a snug grip, the size of the penis is of little import.

MALE AND FEMALE SEXUALITY

In his classic study on sexuality Alfred Kinsey reached a series of conclusions concerning sexual behavior. Kinsey gathered his data in two major studies during the 1940s and 1950s. He reported:

The Kinsey reports

1
Men reach their period of greatest sexual activity (defined as sexual arousals leading to orgasm) between sixteen and seventeen years of age.

2
Women tend to be less easily sexually aroused at any age, compared to men, and seem less preoccupied by sex than men.

3
Fifty percent of women and 85 percent of men had intercourse before marriage.

4
Forty percent of women and 95 percent of men masturbated to orgasm.[16]

A more recent series of studies of human sexuality has been conducted by Masters and Johnson. Masters and Johnson's results are more up-to-date than Kinsey's and more comprehensive as well, since they studied both the psychological and the physiological aspects of sexuality. Also, while Kinsey depended almost exclusively on in-depth interviewing for his data, Masters and Johnson combined interviewing with direct observation and measurement of sexual activity. In general, their conclusions supported and extended Kinsey's position. They found, for example, that masturbation is a common sexual practice and that it is not harmful. Fears of "going crazy," ruining your complexion, becoming impotent, weakening physical capacity, and so on are all myths. In addition, they found that women are capable of numerous climaxes in a relatively short time and that female orgasms occur in the clitoris not in the vagina, as had been previously suggested.

Masters and Johnson study human sexuality

Probably their most significant conclusions were that humans can remain sexually active throughout their entire life and that at least half of married adults suffer from sexual inadequacy.[17] Masters and Johnson point to the need for effective educational programs to help reduce feelings of sexual inadequacy and to eliminate some of the popular misconceptions about human sexuality. There is no question but that part of the so-called hidden agenda of education during the junior- and senior-high-school years is a concern about human sexuality. Accurate information alone, of course, will not solve the complex issues of sexual inadequacy, but it could be an effective first step.

Educational programs may reduce sexual problems

EARLY AND LATE MATURATION

Much research has gone into discovering what differences exist between early-maturing (EM) and late-maturing (LM) adolescents, differences other than the rate of physical maturity. One must be careful, in interpreting these studies, not to leap to the conclusion that these other differences beween EM and LM adolescents are due only to the adolescent's changing biology. Personality variables, for example, are especially influenced by the way others perceive and, accordingly, treat us. A boy of seventeen whose voice hasn't changed yet, whose body proportions are still as they were when he was twelve, is all too often treated by those around him as though he were, in fact, still only twelve years old. Similarly, the twelve-year-old boy who is speaking in a rich baritone, whose shoulders have broadened, and who shaves daily, is more apt to be treated with dignity and respect. Social psychologists tell us that the way people respond often depends on how others treat them. People who are treated like children very often respond in childlike ways, and those who are treated like adults respond with more maturity. Therefore, if teachers and parents see early maturity as a negative characteristic, the adolescent can be adversely affected. This topic

The rate of adolescent physical maturity may have psychological consequences

will be covered in more detail in Chapter 20. Keeping these interactions in mind, however, we observe that studies on early maturers and late maturers reveal the following.

1

There are almost no differences in IQ, grade placement, or socio-economic status between EM and LM adolescents. There is some evidence, however, that children with extremely high IQ's tend to be early maturers.

2

EM boys were rated by their peers as being physically more attractive and better athletes, and they were more often elected to student office.

3

On personality tests EM boys showed more self-control, more interest in girls, more extroversion, and were more apt to support cultural norms.

4

EM girls were rated by adults as below average on social and personality traits, whereas LM girls were rated above average.

5

In comparing the peer ratings of EM boys and EM girls, EM girls were perceived in a less-favorable way.

Thus, early maturity is more apt to be an advantage to the boy, but may be a disadvantage to the girl in our society.[18]

GROWTH PERIODS AND EDUCATIONAL PROBLEMS

At each age and stage of development children and adolescents need continued assurance from adults in order to accommodate themselves to and assimilate the effects of constant change. During adolescence, diversity and change are at peak intensity, and the differences between the sexes and within the sexes are at a maximum. The junior-high-school years, especially, represent diversity in such areas as physical growth, glandular-sexual changes, social changes, and cognitive shifts. Each individual student and each subgroup of students needs extra support during this critical period. For example, the late-maturing boy needs help in developing confidence, and assurance that before long he too will develop into full maturity. Similarly, the early-maturing girl needs special support to withstand some of the intense pressures she is under from both adults and peers. Handling this situation can be extremely delicate. Class discussions may often do more harm than good, especially when they focus attention on specific students in the class. A public discussion of a particular student's problem may be a humiliating and destructive experience for the individual on whom the spotlight falls. Teachers need to develop an extra awareness of and sensitivity to these aspects of this often-hidden classroom agenda. Careful listening to student concerns and some judicious reading between the lines will provide the teacher with more than a few cues as to possible reasons for a student's sudden "unexplainable" upset, mood change, or rapid attention shift.

In physical education and health classes, posting pictures and charts showing growth curves during adolescence may indeed be a case where a picture is worth a thousand words. It should also be helpful to present the students with some facts of sexual growth and maturation. A few facts in this area may remove the mystery and correct some of the blatant untruths that students often pass on to one another. Information of this sort may often be followed by an audible and collective sigh of relief from the class. This is not to suggest that the teacher should deluge the seventh grader with graphic illustrations from Masters and Johnson, for the student may confuse sex education with sexual encouragement. If a teacher overreacts to this information deficit, the students can be overstimulated. The object is to present information in a style that will help the pupils to become comfortable with their own and their peers' physical, emotional, and sexual growth and less preoccupied by it. The goal is anxiety reduction, not sexual trauma.

Summary

An understanding of the biological basis of behavior is important to understanding developmental psychology. American psychology for too long ignored this important aspect of its own discipline. Little attention, for example, was paid to the emerging field of genetics.

Genetics is a relatively new discipline. It is the study of how characteristics are biologically transmitted from parent to offspring.

The basic unit of analysis in genetics is the gene, a tiny particle of heredity located in the nucleus of each of the body's cells. Genes are composed of DNA and RNA molecules. The DNA acts as a blueprint—or template—and contains the coded genetic information within the nucleus of the cell. RNA transmits this information to other parts of the cell. One of biology's most spectacular recent achievements was the deciphering of this genetic code.

Since each offspring receives large numbers of genes from each parent, the new individual is genetically unique, except in the case of identical twins who begin life as only one cell. Psychologists are able to examine the effects of genetic endowment through both animal and human research.

Psychology's basic principle is that behavior is a result of heredity interacting with environment interacting with time.

Before birth, the human organism goes through three basic stages of development: (1) zygote, (2) embryo, and (3) fetus. Tremendous changes occur during the prenatal period. The organism increases its size dramatically, from a tiny speck 1/175 inch in diameter to a seven- or eight-pound baby in a period of nine months.

Maturation both before and immediately after birth occurs on a time schedule that is fairly consistent for all members of a given species. The maturation of various organs occurs safely ahead of the time when they must be used.

Reflex and motor development, such as holding the head erect, sitting, crawling, and walking, are heavily influenced by biological maturation, though environmental encounters at the appropriate time are important for full development of the biological potential.

Sensory maturation shows functional development either at birth or within a few days of birth. Touch, smell, taste, and hearing develop slightly before vision.

Speech develops from the grunts and cries of birth to a recognizable word by the age of one year. Once the child masters the intricate details of walking, the verbal repertoire increases dramatically.

Adolescence marks the beginning of another growth spurt, a spurt that occurs earlier in girls than boys. The early-maturing girl and the late-maturing boy may have special problems in our culture. Adolescents need extra support and understanding during this critical period of development.

Sex education must be handled sensitively and with compassion. If a teacher spends too much time attempting to detail the intricacies of sex education, the adolescent may feel overstimulated. He or she may confuse education with encouragement, and thus increase rather than decrease his or her psychological problems.

REFERENCES

1
D. K. Spelt, "The Conditioning of the Human Fetus in Utero," *J. of Exp. Psychol.* 38 (1948):338–346.

2
M. I. Lerner, *Heredity, Evolution and Society* (San Francisco: Freeman, 1968), p. 137.

3
W. R. Thompson, "The Inheritance of Behaviour: Behavioural Differences in Fifteen Mouse Strains," *Canadian Journal of Psychology* 7 (1953):145–155.

4
R. C. Tryon, "Genetic Differences in Maze-Learning Ability in Rats, *Yearbook Nat. Soc. Stud. Educ.* 39 (1940):111–119.

5
K. Lagerspetz, *Studies on the Aggressive Behavior of Mice* (Helsinki: Suomalainen Tiedeakatemia, 1964).

6
I. I. Gottesman and J. Shields, *Schizophrenia and Genetics: A Twin Study Vantage Point* (New York: Academic Press, 1972).

7
B. J. Kaplan, "Malnutrition and Mental Deficiency," *Psychology Bulletin* 78 (1972): 321–334.

8
N. Bayley, "Individual Patterns of Development," *Child Development* 27 (1956):45–74.

9
M. M. Shirley, *The First Two Years,* vol. III, *Personality Manifestations,* Inst. Child Welfare Monograph 8 (Minneapolis: University of Minnesota Press, 1933).

10
H. Munsinger, *Fundamentals of Child Development* (New York: Holt, Rinehart and Winston, 1975).

11
E. J. Gibson and R. D. Walk, "The Visual Cliff," *Scientific American* 202 (1960):2–9.

12

N. Chomsky, "A Review of *Verbal Behavior* by B. F. Skinner," *Language* 35 (1959):26–58.

13

M. E. Smith, "An Investigation of the Development of the Sentence and the Extent of Vocabulary in Young Children, *Univ. Iowa Stud. Child Welf.* 3, no. 5 (1926).

14

P. H. Mussen and J. J. Conger, *Child Development and Personality* (New York: Harper & Row, 1969).

15

W. H. Masters and F. E. Johnson, *Human Sexual Response* (Boston: Little, Brown, 1966).

16

A. C. Kinsey *et al., Sexual Behavior in the Human Male* (Philadelphia: W. B. Saunders, 1948); see also *Sexual Behavior in the Human Female* (Philadelphia: W. B. Saunders, 1953).

17

W. H. Masters and F. E. Johnson, *Human Sexual Response,* 1966.

18

J. A. R. Wilson, M. C. Robeck, and W. B. Michael, *Psychological Foundations of Learning and Teaching* (New York: McGraw-Hill, 1969), pp. 188–189.

SUGGESTIONS FOR FURTHER READING

Munsinger, H. *Fundamentals of Child Development.* New York: Holt, Rinehart and Winston, 1975.

5

Early experience

"As the twig is bent, so grows the tree." "You can't teach an old dog new tricks." "Train them during their formative years." These statements and others like them attest to the fact that we have long recognized the importance of early experience on growth and development. Yet it is only within this century that we have come to appreciate how enormously important early experience really is. It is also only very recently that we have begun to recognize in how many ways our psychological and physical beings are affected by the amount and quality of our early experience.

It is true that psychologists have for some time recognized the importance of early experience on emotional growth. Freud, for example, wrote many papers at the turn of the century indicating that personality development is a product of one's childhood. Many educators agreed with this, and special schools were designed to enhance emotional and personal growth during these crucial years. In England, A. S. Neill established Summerhill, a boarding school where the major emphasis was on encouraging healthy emotional adjustment.[1] At Summerhill every student participates in school and curriculum decisions. No classes, books, or exams are required. Free expression of ideas and talent are encouraged, and only minimal restraints are placed on the children in all areas of their lives. There are many schools like Summerhill throughout the world, and it is safe to say that most schools today, not just the Summerhills, have been influenced to some degree by this alternative to the traditional, more authoritarian approach to education.

The point is that as psychologists learn more about human development, educators do respond accordingly—and sometimes too zealously. An indiscriminate embracing of new theory may produce a curriculum that emphasizes one

Summerhill: a school for free expression

particular area at the expense of other important areas. For example, it has been seriously argued that the Summerhills may be nurturing emotional growth at the expense of intellectual growth.

Despite the fact that for many years now early experience has been considered critical in shaping emotional development, psychologists have only recently come to recognize the importance of these same years to intellectual development.

EARLY EXPERIENCE: THE KEY TO THE NATURE-NURTURE PUZZLE

The nature-nurture question remained unresolved for so many years because the issue was stated as an either/or proposition: the hereditarians emphasized heredity at the expense of environment, and the environmentalists emphasized environment at the expense of heredity. Neither side fully recognized the importance of the third dimension, time. Development is a result of heredity interact-

Critical period ing with environment, but a key question remains: Is there a critical—or a best —time for the interaction to take place?

With regard to imprinting, it must be remembered that goslings learn to follow the moving stimulus only if the stimulus is presented during a certain critical time of their lives: from about ten to thirty hours after hatching. Presenting the stimulus thirty-five or forty hours after hatching is no good—no learning occurs. It is obvious that this form of learning, called imprinting, requires a hereditary potential as well as an environmental encounter. But which is more important? In fact, neither matters at all until we mix in the third ingredient, the time at which the encounter occurs. If it happens too soon, no learning or minimal learning occurs, and the same is true if the encounter is too late.

THE TWINS: JOHNNY AND JIMMY

Many years ago, a forward-looking psychologist, Myrtle McGraw, did a comprehensive study of human development, using a pair of twin boys as subjects.[2] One of the twins, Johnny, was given a great amount of early training in a wide variety of activities. The other twin, Jimmy, was given no practice in these activities until months later.

McGraw found that special, early practice had little or no effect on some behaviors, such as creeping, hanging by the hands, grasping objects, or even walking. Though Johnny was given stepping practice almost from birth, both twins took their first halting steps alone at 9 months and both learned to walk almost simultaneously at 12 months. McGraw called behaviors such as these *phylogenetic activities,* and concluded that they are not influenced very much by the environment or special practice. However, with regard to certain special skills, which McGraw called *ontogenetic activities,* the trained twin, Johnny, learned faster than his brother. Johnny began learning to roller-skate when he was twelve months old, just when he was learning to walk, and by fourteen months he was both skating and walking with considerable grace. Jimmy did not begin skating lessons until he was 22 months old, and he did not profit

Early experience aids the development of certain skills

There are critical, optimal periods when children can most easily be taught certain motor skills. For example, it is best to teach a child to roller skate at the same time he or she is learning to walk. However, development of some motor skills is actually retarded by early training.

Early experience hin-
ders the development
of other skills

nearly as much from this late training. McGraw found that delaying the training
made it more difficult to learn this skill. The development of other motor skills,
however, was actually damaged by early training. Johnny was given special training in tricycling when he was 11 months old and displayed little progress until
he was about 19 or 20 months old, when he suddenly improved rather dramatically. Jimmy began tricycling when he was 22 months old, learned the skill
quickly and efficiently, and became superior to his pretrained brother. The twin
with the early training formed poor habits and was unable to develop the skill as
well as the twin whose training was delayed.

McGraw concluded that there are optimal time periods during development
when special training will assure the full acquisition of various motor skills. Said
McGraw, "there are critical periods when any given activity is most susceptible to
modification through repetition of performance."[3]

Despite the fact that her research was carried out more than thirty years ago,
McGraw's conclusions were definitely ahead of their time. She was the first psychologist to speak of "critical periods" in human development, and although
her views were not widely accepted during the heyday of American behaviorism, they now have a very modern ring. In child rearing she urged a middle road
between constantly urging the child to practice new activities and just sitting
back, relaxing, and allowing nature to take its own sweet time. Forcing children
into activities before the critical period, when their nerves and muscles are
simply not ready, is not only useless but, more importantly, may even be damaging.

Critical period
defined

A great deal of research remains to be done in this important area. At this
point there is little hard data to indicate precisely when the various critical periods occur. We do know, however, that critical periods generally coincide with
periods of most rapid growth. John P. Scott has defined the critical period as a
"time when a large effect can be produced by a smaller change in conditions
than in any later or earlier period in life."[4] Scott further states that "there must
be changes taking place within the animal which are correlated with time and
hence account for the existence of critical periods." Thus the concept of critical
periods has profound importance in education. We must hope to catch the
child at exactly that time when environmental encounters will most effectively
allow his or her hereditary potential to flourish. Damage can be done, impair-
ment can occur, if we are either too early or too late.

THE BERKELEY GROWTH STUDY

Beginning in 1929, Nancy Bayley and her colleagues at the University of California, Berkeley, began a long-term study of human growth and development.[5]
This was a longitudinal research study in that the same subjects were followed
and continually tested over the years. Actually, data is still being collected on
the original group of subjects, all of whom are now approximately fifty years of
age. Although the study has contributed vast amounts of new data and fresh
insights on the flow of human development, we will focus on only four specific
observations at this time.

1

IQ's are not constant.   Bayley's results have challenged the belief cherished by some psychologists that one's IQ score is immutable. Bayley finds considerable variation in measured intelligence over long periods of time; in other words, one's IQ score is not indelibly carved in the brain at birth, but is instead a human quality that ebbs and flows as a result of environmental circumstances.[6]

2

IQ variability is greatest during the first few years of life.   By comparing correlations between IQ's measured at various ages, Bayley found that the older the child the greater the IQ stability. This evidence foreshadowed the main thrust of Benjamin Bloom's hypothesis, to be discussed in the next section.

3

Intellectual ability may continue to grow throughout life.   Bayley's data also indicates that intellectual ability does not top out in the late teens or early twenties, but may continue to increase at least up to age fifty. Again, whether an adult's intellect grows or declines seems to be a function of environmental stimulation. The high-school drop-out who spends all his working life bagging groceries in a supermarket is less apt to experience intellectual growth than someone who works in areas requiring more strenuous mental exercise.

4

The components of intellect change with age level.   Perhaps Nancy Bayley's most provocative contribution is her suggestion that intellectual development in childhood occurs in qualitatively different stages. In her view, the fact that a child's growth score gradually shifts in strength from area to area supports the notion that changes occur in the organization of intellectual factors from one age to another. This view is consistent with that of Jean Piaget, to be presented in the next chapter.

BLOOM'S HYPOTHESIS

Benjamin S. Bloom (1964) in an already classic book has analyzed, sorted, and sifted through virtually all the studies on intellectual growth.[7] Bloom plots a negatively accelerated growth curve for intellectual development: that is, with increasing age, there is a decreasingly positive effect from a beneficial environment. Three-year-old children profit far more from enriching experiences than seven- or eight-year-old children. Bloom argues that beneficial early experience is absolutely essential for cognitive growth. Almost two-thirds of our ultimate cognitive ability is formed by the time we are six years old, the age, incidentally, when most children are just entering school. By the time formal education begins, the child's potential for further intellectual development is beginning to top out. Earlier intervention is required, especially among the disadvantaged groups. Experience has its most profound effect very early in life, during the period of most rapid growth.

Two-thirds of our intellectual growth occurs by age six

Nancy Bayley

Nancy Bayley was the first woman ever to win the American Psychological Association's prestigious "Distinguished Scientific Contribution" award. Dr. Bayley received this recognition in 1966, and her citation included the following: "For the enterprise, pertinacity and insight with which she has studied human growth over long segments of the life cycle. ... Her studies have enriched psychology with enduring contributions to the measurement and meaning of intelligence ... her participation in a number of major programs of developmental research is a paradigm of the conjoint efforts which are essential in a field whose problems span the generations" (*American Psychologist* 21, December 1966:1191).

Nancy Bayley was born in 1899 in a small town called "the Dallas" near the northern border of Oregon. She attended local schools there and went on to earn her B.S. and M.A. degrees from the University of Washington. She received her Ph.D. in psychology from Iowa State in 1926, just two years after completing her M.A. degree. For the next two years, she taught at the University of Wyoming, and in 1928 began teaching at the University of California at Berkeley. During the following year she began her famous longitudinal Berkeley Growth Study, starting with sixty-one healthy newborn infants. Testing and retesting this group over the years, both psychologically and physically, she has produced many fresh and startling insights into the complex phenomenon of human growth.

In 1954 Dr. Bayley left Berkeley to become chief of the Child Development section at the National Institute of Mental Health in Bethesda, Maryland, but periodically returned to Berkeley to locate and test her sample subjects for the Berkeley Growth Study. In 1964 she returned to Berkeley to serve both as the Administrator of the newly formed Harold E. Jones Child Study Center and as a research psychologist at the University of California. She retired in 1971.

In addition to being selected as the American Psychological Association's "Distinguished Scientist," Nancy Bayley also won the G. Stanley Hall award in 1971, a special award presented by the A.P.A.'s Division of Developmental Psychology. Though formally retired, Dr. Bayley continues her productive professional career. She has contributed nearly one hundred scientific publications so far, and it is clear that as her 1929 sample continues to ripen and mature, Nancy Bayley will continue to enrich psychology's book of knowledge.

The initial phases of a social relationship are the most critical, and most new relationships are formed during early childhood.

Intellectual abilities are developed and nurtured by stimulus variety.

This is consistent with Scott's argument regarding critical periods. Scott feels that critical periods occur when rapid organization of some kind is going on within the individual. Those changes that take place during a period of rapid change often occur easily and accidentally, and then become a fixed and fairly permanent feature of the newly stabilized organization. Scott also reasons that any time we form new relationships, especially social relationships, can be a critical period for that relationship. Since most new relationships occur in early childhood, this is when most critical periods should occur. However, major new relationships also occur in adolescence and in adulthood. One of the most important critical periods occurs during adolescence, when we form our first sexual relationships. The sexual problems an adult suffers are probably the result of events occurring during adolescence. Another major critical period occurs during adulthood, when a woman bears her first child; and this may be a critical period for both parents.

Black children moving from South to North

Bloom, citing the evidence from Lee's study (1951) of blacks moving from the South to the North, shows that on the question of enriched early environments, the younger the child the better the chances for improvement. Of the black children who moved to Northern schools, the younger they were at the time of the move, the more pronounced was the effect on their IQ scores, For example, if the child was four years old at the time of the move, the average gain was 2½ IQ points per year, whereas if the child was eight or more years old, the average gain from the improved environment was less than ½ an IQ point per year.[8]

Bloom concludes that not only does lack of an enriched environment itself hinder a child's intellectual development, but the loss of precious time is especially harmful because there is no way to compensate for it later on. Just as in the case of Lorenz's goslings, there may be critical periods for intellectual development—once the period is over, new stimuli have less and less effect.

STIMULUS VARIETY: THE BASIC INGREDIENT

J. McV. Hunt reviewed the literature on early experience and reported that early stimulus deprivation is more likely to prevent normal motor development than early motor restriction.[9] For example, Hopi children who are reared on cradleboards, which almost completely inhibit their movements, walk as early as Hopi children reared with full use of their legs. Both groups of Hopi children, cradle-reared and freely reared, walk at about the same age. Thus, as far as walking is concerned, early motor restriction does not seem seriously to affect later motor development. However, the effect of early stimulus restriction is, as Hunt points out, dramatically different. Not only is early stimulus deprivation damaging to later intellectual development, but it also appears to impair later motor development. Wayne Dennis discovered an orphanage in Teheran where the children were kept in a condition of extreme isolation, each one living in a separate, almost soundproof, white cubicle.[10] The result of this severe sensory restriction was that virtually all the children were mentally retarded, and this

Hopi children raised on cradleboards

The orphanage in Teheran

Early motor restriction does not impede later motor development, although early stimulus deprivation does retard later development of both intellectual and motor skills.

despite the fact that they came almost exclusively from the literate population of Iran. This, of course, is further evidence that intellectual development
is a function of both environment and heredity. But perhaps the most remarkable finding of the Dennis study is that these stimulus-deprived children, who
had complete motor freedom, were also physically retarded. Sixty percent of the
children were unable to sit up alone when they were two years old, and 85 percent could not walk when they were four years old. Compare this with the
cradleboard-reared Hopi children. Hunt points out that "these Hopi children
reared on cradleboards were often carried about on their mothers' backs. Thus,
while their arms and legs might be restricted, their eyes and ears could feast
upon a rich variety of inputs."[11]

As Hunt has been insisting for over ten years, the crucial ingredient in intellectual development is stimulus variety. The more the child hears, sees, and
touches, the more the child will want to hear, see, and touch, and the more
intellectual growth will occur. On the other hand, Hunt is careful to advocate
that the child should not suddenly be overwhelmed with stimulus variety. In
what he calls "the problem of the match," he points out that the variety of inputs must somehow be matched with the child's present growth. Too much
stimulus heterogeneity, and the child withdraws in frustration; too little, and the
child withdraws in boredom. Hunt insists that there is a point of optimum stimulus variety which children naturally seek; when this is reached, children display
a joy, a spontaneous interest in learning, and continuous cognitive growth.

The problem of
the match

It is important to emphasize that Hunt and others are not implying that intelligence is fixed, nor that stimulus variety must be matched with innate potential. Quite the contrary! Intellectual abilities grow and are nourished by stimulus variety. The match is between stimulus inputs and the child's present
position on the growth continuum, a position which itself results in large measure from the child's own past experiences and environmental encounters. These
encounters begin at birth. There is even evidence that some learning takes place
before birth, while the child is still in the womb.[12] But certainly during early
infancy, stimulus encounters—for example, in the game of peek-a-boo, which
always seems to entertain—the baby is gathering experience for encounters in
later childhood.

PIAGET AND BRUNER ON EARLY EXPERIENCE

For over forty years at the University of Geneva, Switzerland, Jean Piaget has
been studying human development, especially the development of concept
formation. Through carefully detailed, hour-by-hour observation of the developing child, Piaget has formulated a theory of how children go about the business
of learning to know, learning concept formation. A more detailed account of
Piaget's position is presented in Chapter 6. It is enough now to say that Piaget
describes the child's attempts to develop concepts—such as a concept of self as
an entity separate from the environment, and concepts of time, cause and effect,
conservation, and number.

Piaget's concept of
conservation

Perhaps the most famous of the concepts Piaget has described is that of conservation, which he illustrates in the following manner. He shows a child a short,

wide glass of water, and then pours the water into a tall, thin beaker. The water level is much higher in the thin container than it was in the wide one. The child who recognizes that the amount of water has remained constant regardless of the height is said to have developed the concept of conservation of volume. However, the child who says that the taller beaker contains more water is assumed to have not yet reached this stage of concept formation.

According to Piaget, children can form concepts such as conservation or number only after they have gone through a series of developmental stages that are sequential in nature. Certain cognitive structures, or as Piaget calls them, *schemata*, must be formed before children can understand mathematics, for example. If they have not discovered certain logical relationships, such as that seven large blocks are equal numerically to seven small blocks, then their later understanding of geometrical concepts or even of number itself will be arrested to some extent.

Jerome Bruner fills in more of the details. Bruner, like Piaget, maintains that cognitive growth depends on a process of model formation: the formation of rules, or strategies, for coping with the environment. As they develop, children

Bruner also insists that a variety of stimuli and a changing environment are necessary for proper cognitive growth.

learn various techniques that enable them to make maximum use of the information their environment provides.

It is also important to note that Bruner insists that, for proper cognitive growth to occur, the young child must be exposed to a variety of stimuli, a shifting environment. Stimulus heterogeneity at an early age is a crucial ingredient in intellectual growth. The cognitive growth of children who have been deprived of sensory stimulation for any reason will be arrested, possibly irreversibly so.

Sensory stimulation

Bruner supports his case for environmental encounters by citing the physiological work of Pribram, Magoun, and others.[13] Bruner's interest in the developing organism results not only in the formulation of an explanatory model, but also in a search for physiological correlates. It is now known that the traditional concept of sensory-neural impulses connecting in the nervous system with the motor-neural impulses was an oversimplification. The new evidence, from the organism itself, shows us that when the receptor is stimulated, there is a flow of impulses toward the central nervous system and a simultaneous neural flow back to the receptor. The receptor is not a mere passive recipient of any and all stimulation, but a kind of filter through which only certain stimuli pass. Bruner has maintained that the organism cannot take in all the information the environment contains. Physiological evidence now backs this up, and Bruner sees this as an adaptive phenomenon, the ability to minimize environmental surprises aiding the organism in its quest for survival.

Bruner on model formation

The receptor acts as a filter

THE BIOLOGICAL BASIS OF EARLY EXPERIENCE

Now that we have seen that psychologists such as Scott, Bloom, Hunt, Piaget, and Bruner have pointed to the importance of early experience in determining intellectual level, the next questions might logically be, "What is the biological basis for this argument? Are there corresponding physiological changes taking place as a result of a beneficial early environment?"

The eminent physiological psychologist D.O. Hebb has outlined a theoretical model of the organization of neural activity in the brain.[14] Hebb contends that this organization depends on environmental stimulation, that proper development of the neural arrangements in the brain will not occur unless the developing organism has the opportunity to experience environmental changes.

THE A/S RATIO

Hebb noted that there were significant differences among organisms in the proportion of association and sensory areas within the brain. Compared to the human, a lower organism such as a rat has fewer association areas and more sensory areas. Thus the rat, that workhorse of American psychology, is more sensory-bound, more responsive to the stimuli in its environment than the human. The human brain, with its greater number of association areas, is capable of far more and probably many different varieties of learning than the rat brain. Also, the relatively small sensory area makes the human less a creature of the moment, less apt to respond impulsively to every minute environmental change. It also means that as we go up the phylogenetic continuum, as the ratio of association areas to sensory areas (A/S ratio) increases, the developmental importance of pronounced stimulus heterogeneity also increases. Humans, after all, cannot perceive subtle changes in odor as well as some of the lower primates are able to.

Hebb emphasized the critical importance of early experience on later development, especially on cognitive development. Hebb sees the human brain as unorganized and capable of only relatively simple forms of learning during infancy and early childhood. As the child experiences more and more environmental stimulation, the brain slowly becomes organized. A group of neurons begins to work as a unit. Hebb calls this organized pattern of brain cells a cell assembly. With the formation of a variety of cell assemblies, new learning takes place more quickly. As this process continues, as more cell assemblies are formed, a larger organization takes place: a series of cell assemblies, called phase sequences, are formed. Finally, as the phase sequences begin acting in concert, widespread organization of the brain results, and the child is now capable of extremely rapid learning. The difference between a young child in the cell-assembly stage, slowly and painstakingly learning a simple task, and an older child, with a series of smooth-functioning, integrated phase sequences already formed, quickly learning complex relationships and concepts, is similar to the difference between a do-it-yourself carpenter and an experienced prefab team. The do-it-yourself carpenter, to borrow an analogy,[15] could take months constructing a home that the professional prefab crew could complete in days.

Based on Hebb's hypothesis of cell assemblies and phase sequences, researchers at McGill University compared the performance of animals of enriched early experience with animals of impoverished early experience. The McGill researchers wanted to determine whether organisms provided with stimulus variety during the early period of cell assemblies would reflect this early enrichment in their performance as adults. The researchers found what they were looking for.

Using the Hebb-Williams maze, a kind of animal IQ test, Hebb compared rats raised in the impoverished environment of laboratory cages with rats raised in the home as pets, and found the home-reared animals superior. Other investigations found an even greater difference when they performed the same experiment using dog litter-mates.[16] The results of this study also favored the home-reared pets, lending further support to the suggestion that as we go up the phylogenetic continuum (as we select species with higher A/S ratios) the beneficial effects of an enriched early environment increase.

Perhaps even more significant is the work of Hymovitch.[17] This investigation was conducted entirely within the controlled conditions of the laboratory and showed that stimulus variety during early life was more effective than the same experience in later life. Hymovitch also showed that early stimulus variety was more beneficial to later maze-learning ability than early response variety. Animals with enriched response experience failed to benefit as much, measured by their later performance on the Hebb-Williams maze, as animals with enriched stimulus experience.

Brain organization: cell assemblies and phase sequences

The Hymovitch study: early stimulus variety more important than early motor variety

KRECH PROVIDES MORE EVIDENCE

More direct, and even more startling evidence supporting the early-experience position has been supplied by the exciting and innovative research of Krech.[18] It had been shown that certain drugs, such as Metrazol, may increase an organism's ability to learn, and other drugs, such as Magnesium Pemoline, may increase the organism's ability to retain what has been learned.[19] Krech reasoned, however, that the reverse might also be true; that is, if chemical agents could effect changes in the learning process, then environmental manipulation might effect changes in the chemistry of the brain. By selecting twelve pairs of rat twins and randomly assigning them to two groups, Krech was able to control for possible genetic differences. One group of rats was raised in a stimulating environment, in a cage equipped with ladders, running wheels, and other "rat toys." These animals were let out of their cages for thirty minutes each day and allowed to explore new territory. They were also trained on numerous learning tasks and in general received a rich and varied array of stimulus inputs. The other group of rats was raised in a condition of rather extreme stimulus homogeneity. They lived alone in dimly lit cages, were rarely handled, and were never allowed to explore areas outside the cage. All animals, however, received exactly the same diet.

The structure and chemistry of the brain as a function of early experience

After about three months all the animals were sacrificed and their brains analyzed morphologically and chemically. If Hebb's theory is valid, the brains of the stimulated animals, the animals that had been exposed to a large variety of learning situations, should be anatomically different from the brains of the deprived animals. That is, if the act of learning does indeed form neural cell assemblies and phase sequences, there might be some physical evidence for this in the brains of the stimulated rats. In fact, Krech may have supplied the evidence! The brains of the enriched rats were chemically and structurally different from the brains of their siblings. The cortex (gray matter) was larger, deeper, and heavier in the stimulated rats. Three components have been identified as contributing to this increase in brain size: (1) an increased number of glia cells (possible repositories of memory traces), (2) increased size of the cell bodies and their nuclei, and (3) an increase in the diameter of the blood vessels supplying the cortex.

Chemically, the brains also differed. The brains of the enriched animals showed greater quantities of an important enzyme—acetylcholinesterase—an enzyme that readies a synapse for further neural transmissions. Krech has thus demonstrated that providing stimulus and response variety during the early life of these animals caused chemical and structural changes in their brains and increased their ability to learn and to solve problems. In a very real sense he may have identified some of the physiological correlates of Hebb's constructs.

PHYSIOLOGICAL DEVELOPMENT REQUIRES ENVIRONMENTAL STIMULATION

It is now clear that for proper physiological development to occur, environmental stimulation is necessary; the nervous system and the perceptual apparatus do not mature automatically according to some preset internal clock.

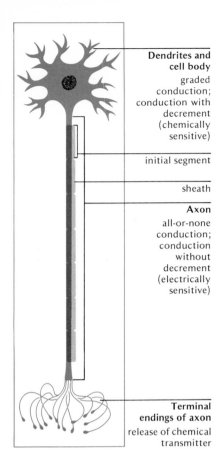

Dendrites and cell body
graded conduction; conduction with decrement (chemically sensitive)

initial segment

sheath

Axon
all-or-none conduction; conduction without decrement (electrically sensitive)

Terminal endings of axon
release of chemical transmitter

Fig. 5.1 Neural impulses travel from one neuron to the next along the branches of the neuron—axons and dendrites.

Critics of the early-experience position often fall back on the neurological argument that, since no new brain cells are added after birth, the central nervous system must remain unchanged, with or without environmental stimulation. They argue that the baby comes into the world with a full complement of typical brain cells and that, since no new cells are added, the baby must make do with the original equipment. However, as Krech has shown, the way this original equipment is organized and modified is definitely a function of environmental interactions. Krech proved that structural and chemical changes within the brain resulted from the type of early experience provided.

Further evidence comes from the exciting research of Joseph Altman.[20] Altman is now challenging the traditional view that newborn children have all the brain cells they will ever get. Altman has found that tiny nerve cells (microneurons) do arise in the brains of young animals after birth. These newly discovered tiny neurons apparently provide interconnections for some of the larger, more typical brain cells.

Neurons send out branches—axons and dendrites—in order that the neural impulse can travel from one neuron to the next (see Fig. 5.1). The junction between the axon of one neuron and the dendrite of the next is called the syn-

Microneurons in the brain develop after birth

apse. The neuron sends a message out along one axon and the dendrite of the next neuron picks the message up at the synapse. Often, the dendrite, the receiving branch, sends out a physical projection called a dendritic spine. This is something like adding another length to your TV antenna in order to get a better picture. Neurologists have found, however, that if these synapses are not used, the dendritic spines wither away and finally disappear. If a synapse is used frequently, new dendritic spines appear. It's as though the size and complexity of the antenna were a function of how often the TV set was used.

It has also been found that sensory apparatus must be stimulated by the environment in order to develop properly. Neurons on the retina of the eye may become damaged unless they are given visual stimulation.

Riesen reared chimpanzees in complete darkness and found that permanent damage was done to their visual apparatus.[21] Degeneration of the ganglion cells of the retina was noted in all animals, but if the period of darkness was twelve weeks or less, a physiological recovery was possible. One animal, kept in darkness for a year, showed more extensive damage and suffered a permanent loss of ganglion cells. Visual stimulation is therefore necessary for the proper development of nervous tissue. It is also necessary because, as Riesen has made clear, we really have to "learn" how to see. Using a similar design, Riesen raised cats in darkness, and although the resulting retinal degeneration was less severe than with the chimpanzees, it did occur.[22] Thus we see that stimulation is more important as we progress up the phylogenetic ladder.

A CAUSE FOR OPTIMISM: THE MILWAUKEE PROJECT

You may be wondering what all these studies of children raised on cradleboards, rats raised in enriched environments, chimps raised in darkness, and so on have to do with the intellectual growth of children. What proof do we have that these theories and studies have any validity in the real world of the schoolchild? Hasn't the early-experience theory been tested, for example in the Head Start program, and been found wanting? The critics of early experience have been quick to point out that Head Start was not an overwhelming success. In fact, however, Head Start was hardly a test of the early-experience position. In most cases, Head Start simply took disadvantaged youngsters of about 5½ years of age and attempted to teach them how to get along in school six months before they entered first grade. Therefore, the early-experience school of thought would also criticize Head Start, but for a different reason: the intervention was too late and it was the wrong kind of intervention.

The Milwaukee Project, the brainchild of F. Rick Heber, shows what can be accomplished when children are trained early enough and when the training is fairly systematic and structured.[23] Studies had previously shown that an IQ that is below average when a child is just starting school tends to get progressively lower as the years go on. It was Heber's hope that by giving children special training at an early enough age he might be able to prevent this deterioration of intelligence. The results of the project have exceeded Heber's original, rather modest expectations.

The first study, begun in 1964, was conducted in an area of Milwaukee which had the lowest income, the highest population density, and the worst living

(margin notes: Nerve cells must be used in order to develop fully; We have to learn how to see; Head Start not a valid test of early-experience position; Structured preschool education)

The children shown here are participants in the Milwaukee Project, directed by F. Rick Heber. From birth through early childhood, children from an urban ghetto were given a special program of individualized and small-group instruction and a variety of experiences, stimuli, and environments. At age two, each child was placed in a nursery school for a well-planned, highly structured educational program. Although it is still too early to draw any definite conclusions, the results seem impressive and underscore the importance of early experience as a major ingredient in cognitive growth.

Ambassador College Photos

conditions in the entire city. Heber deliberately chose an urban slum, since it was known that mental retardation occurs at a far higher rate in urban and rural slums than in other areas. In fact, mental retardation occurs so often in slum environments that some have felt that the inferior living conditions actually cause the retardation. This view ignores the fact that the majority of slum residents are not retarded, and so Heber determined to identify those specific conditions in the lives of retarded children that are unique to them and are not a result of general slum conditions. The most important finding from that first survey is that there is a dependable relationship between the IQ of a retarded child and that of the mother.

Mothers with IQ's 80 and below made up less than half of the group under study, but they had produced 80 percent of the children with IQ's of below 80. It is obvious, on reflection, that retarded mothers hardly have the resources to provide a stimulating and enriched environment for their children. It is also obvious that the mother, who generally spends more time with the children than does the father, should be more significant in shaping the child's intellect. Mental retardation in children is, therefore, more a function of the impaired intellect of the mother than a function of the slum conditions.

The Milwaukee Project actually was begun in 1966 when Heber selected forty mothers with IQ's of 70 or less. By random assignment, their newborn babies were placed either in the experimental group, where intervention took place almost at birth, or in the control group, where the mothers continued to care for their children on their own. Using an organized and fairly structured program, Heber and his staff began working with the experimental group as soon as mother and child returned from the hospital. Staff members visited the homes daily, and after a few months the babies were brought to the Infant Education Center. Here the babies were treated to a rich variety of teaching techniques and materials, all designed to stimulate cognitive growth. Most of the teaching techniques and materials used at the Center had been developed by Heber over the previous several years.[24]

The goal of the project, it must be recalled, was to provide enough stimulation during the critical years of cognitive development so that intellectual deterioration would not occur. The results far surpassed the goal. At 42 months of age the average IQ in the experimental group was 33 points higher than the average in the control group. Some of the trained group registered IQ's of 135—and these were children of mothers whose IQ's were 70 or less! Further, the children in the program were learning faster than the norms for their age group in general.

Since his first publication, Heber now reports that the mean difference between experimental and control children was 30 points at age three, 31 points at age four, and 26 points at age five.[25]

Not only does the child training at the Infant Education Center result in increased IQ test scores on the part of the children, it seems to have the added benefit of inducing positive changes in the mother's interactions with the child.[26]

Heber's Milwaukee Project has provided some extremely promising data, but it is too soon to consider his findings conclusive. Other projects, begun with great promise and fanfare, have ultimately led to disappointment. We must await further evidence from Heber. For example, will the IQ gains of the experimental group be sustained over time? It's hardly enough to establish that a child's IQ at age 42 months is 135 if, when that child is tested years later, that IQ score has dropped to 80. It seems unlikely that this kind of failure will occur in Heber's project, but more time is needed before any conclusive evaluation of the data can be made.

A critical evaluation of the Milwaukee Project was published by Ellis Page.[27] Page raises three major questions about the validity of Heber's study: (1) Were the experimental and control groups really assigned on the basis of random selection? (2) Were the IQ measures really unbiased? and (3) Were the treatments specified in enough detail?

Some doubts about the Milwaukee Project

Page is not convinced that random assignment was indeed utilized. He finds that the two groups, control and experimental, differ significantly on certain physical measurements—measurements, incidentally, which favor the control group. On point two, Page insists that the IQ measures were biased, that perhaps inadvertently Heber's training procedure may have sensitized the experimental children to the testing procedure. On point three, Page is not satisfied with Heber's reporting regarding the treatment received by the experimental children.

As we have said earlier, and as Page himself has said, more time and evidence are needed before a conclusive analysis of Heber's efforts can be made. Though Heber's data seem consistent with the theoretical expectations of the early-experience position, the history of science has shown many times that what ought to be isn't always what is.

THE FIRST THREE YEARS

One of today's most influential members of the early-experience school of thought is Harvard psychologist Burton White. White contends that intellectual and psychological competence are largely determined during a very brief time in the individual's life span, the first three years.[28] Even the first three years is too broad an age-range category, since White is convinced the critical period for psychological growth actually occurs during the eight to eighteen month age period. Growth during the first eight months of life seems to take care of itself, for early development is so heavily influenced by biological factors that little can be done either to arrest or facilitate the growth process. From ages eight to eighteen months, however, environmental encounters become crucial, and here White focuses on the role of the mother. Mothers of competent children are alert and responsive to their childs' needs, without being overly instrusive. The competent mother provides reassurance, guidance, and attention when the child needs this kind of encouragement, but does not needlessly intervene just to prove to herself that she's a good mother. Although White suggests that the child be provided with suitable toys and materials, he believes the real key to sound growth is the quality of the child's interpersonal exchanges. Finally, White suggests that the mother encourage her child to adopt a certain amount of competitiveness, and that this is best done in a nonthreatening context.

THE BEEP EXPERIMENT (Brookline Early Education Project)

Largely as a result of Burton White's research findings, the superintendent of schools in Brookline, Massachusetts, Dr. Robert Sperber, recently introduced the Brookline Early Education Project, BEEP.[29] Working with White, and funded by private sources, Sperber set up a training program to teach parents the skills

BEEP's basic premise   believed necessary for raising competent children. The basic premise of BEEP is that intervention must begin right after birth and in the babies' homes. Teacher-consultants visit the homes on a regular basis and are always on call during the periods between visits. The parents are prodded and gently guided into the use of the BEEP system. The teacher-consultants are never authoritarian—they train by example and the use of skillful questioning. Rather than telling the parent, "Do this," the teacher-consultant will ask, "Have you tried this?".

Along with the training program, BEEP also provides for a thorough series of medical and psychological examinations. Each baby is checked and rechecked for possible sensory impairments and psychological problems that might impede development. Great care is also taken to ensure the babies are on nutritionally sound diets.

Currently, about 300 children are enrolled in BEEP (38 percent from minority groups) and, although the oldest is now only three years of age, the children will be closely monitored throughout their lives.

Using BEEP as a model, other home-centered intervention programs are being set up in various cities throughout the United States. Burton White's main message is that, in order to raise psychologically competent children, mothers must be trained to excel in three key roles during the critical eight-to-eighteen-month period: "(1) as designers and organizers of their children's physical environment; (2) as authorities who set limits to dangerous or annoying behavior; and (3) as consultants to their children in brief episodes, according to need."[30]

It is now fairly certain that early experience is one of the key ingredients in cognitive growth. Had we known this years ago, the disparity between the "good" and "bad" Kallikaks might have been avoided.

THE CRITICS SPEAK

Critics of the early-experience school of thought have fired two recent shots. Herrnstein argued that if we do provide a uniformly beneficial environment for a number of children, we will simply make intelligence more susceptible to hereditary influence than it would otherwise be.[31] Thus, according to Herrnstein, society should not expend either its funds or its energy in attempting to improve the lot of its poor or black citizenry. As one incredulous reader of Herrnstein's account phrased it:

Herrnstein objects

> It is this present, imperfect society that Herrnstein, in the end, urges upon his black fellow citizens. They should abandon their agitation for equality lest they win the self-defeating victory that would expose the poverty of their genetic endowment. In sum, they should stop reminding us of their accusing presence.[32]

Admittedly, individual differences could in no way be caused by a uniform environment; whatever individual differences do arise have to be due to heredity. It should be added, however, that a uniform bad environment would do exactly the same, make all the individual differences in intelligence the outcome of hereditary influences. But in the first instance, the IQ's would fluctuate around a high average value, while in the second, the IQ's would scatter around a low average value. Surely it would be more pleasant for the children themselves, and more beneficial to society in general, to let heredity decide differences among high IQ's than among low ones.[33]

A related theory argues that the "bottom half is always below average."[34] Thus, or so the theory proclaims, if all intelligence quotients are raised by improved educational techniques, the lower class would still be at the bottom of the social order, and nobody's social status would be changed. This argument implies that society need not try to help the lower class by improving educational opportunities, for the result would only be to freeze present social arrangements. This requires comment.

A large factor in social status is occupation. Limitations of intelligence disqualify an individual from ever becoming a good engineer, physician, or attorney, for example. We might think of a threshold IQ for each occupation. With a very high intelligence one has all the intellectual requirements for being everything from a ditch-digger to an engineer. With a very low intelligence one cannot qualify for high- or middle-status occupations. Therefore, the higher the IQ, the more occupations the individual is qualified to fill. But here we arrive at an interesting point. When we consider IQ, the sheer ability to perform a given task, as an occupational requirement, it is the absolute level of intelligence that matters, not the relative level. If the whole IQ scale were lifted above the threshold for the job of power lineman, those jobs requiring less intelligence would all share the same low IQ status, but social-class standing might not seem as important. Many occupational differences would no longer be due to limitations of intelligence, but to a difference of preference and interest, surely a more satisfying arrangement.

A WORD OF CAUTION

With all the recent evidence accumulating on the importance of early experience to cognitive growth, a word of caution to educators is in order. Although it now seems fairly conclusive that stimulus conditions can be provided which will allow for maximum intellectual development, the importance of providing conditions designed to promote emotional growth must not be overlooked. To encourage children to develop their IQ's to 135, only to discover that they are now guilt-ridden and wracked by self-doubt, would not be a great contribution to humankind.

A FINAL COMMENT

You may be wondering whether, if early experience is so significant in determining intellectual ability, there will be anything left for you to accomplish by the time the child reaches school age. Remember: the cognitive growth that takes place during those first critical six years simply provides the base for the intellectual structure the classroom teacher must build. The child should be allowed to begin formal schooling with the necessary background of cognitive skills to be able to take full advantage of the formal educational process. The goal of the early-experience theorists and practitioners is to prepare the child to profit fully from the educational experience. The job of the teacher, then, becomes more challenging, more stimulating, and less frustrating when the child enters school equipped with the necessary tools to learn.

Summary

Though psychologists have for some time pointed to the importance of early experience on emotional growth, only recently has the same attention been paid to cognitive or intellectual growth. It was known, even as long ago as the 1930s, that early in a child's life certain activities could best be learned during certain critical periods. The work of Myrtle McGraw on the twins, Johnny and Jimmy, made this point clear. Also, Nancy Bayley's Berkeley Growth Study was aimed at ferreting out some of the facts regarding changes that occur during the process of intellectual growth. A more recent attempt is the work of Benjamin Bloom.

Bloom states that with increasing age there is less and less effect on intellectual growth from environmental influences. Children at age three, for example, profit more from enriching experiences than children of age nine or ten. Almost two-thirds of one's ultimate cognitive growth occurs by age six.

Hunt sees stimulus variety as the crucial ingredient in cognitive growth. In the "problem of the match," Hunt points to the importance of matching up the proper amount of stimulus variety with the child's present position on the cognitive-growth continuum.

Piaget and Bruner have developed explanatory systems on how and when cognitive growth occurs. Both indicate the importance of sensory inputs and environmental encounters during the child's early years.

Hebb stresses the internal, physiological changes that occur during cognitive growth and development. He cites the neural organization occurring within the brain as the child's ability to learn increases. At birth the brain cells are relatively unorganized, and the cellular organization occurs as a result of the child's own series of learning experiences.

The Krech study on rats shows that the structure and chemical composition of the brain results in part from the quality and quantity of an organism's early experience. Physiological development requires early environmental stimulation.

Rick Heber's Milwaukee Project was started as an attempt to prevent intellectual deterioration among slum children whose mothers were of below-average intelligence. Heber developed a program of early childhood education which may have succeeded in preventing the usually expected cognitive deterioration. The evidence, such as Heber's Milwaukee Project and White's Brookline Early Education Project (BEEP), has provided cautious hope that intellectual growth can be maximized through the use of innovative educational interventions during the early childhood years.

The early-experience school of thought contends that by providing a more beneficial environment during a child's preschool years, higher levels of intellectual functioning can be expected, especially from culturally deprived youngsters. Though providing more uniform environments does make hereditary effects more pronounced, the early-experience position is that the intellectual differences among adults will still be lessened, and people will thus have more occupational choices available to them.

The job of the teacher is in no way minimized by the efforts of the early-experience specialists. Hopefully, children will be more able to reach their intellectual potentials and thus be better able to profit from the educational experiences provided in the classroom. The teacher's job should, accordingly, be more challenging and less frustrating.

REFERENCES

1
A. S. Neill, "The Idea of Summerhill," in R. C. Sprinthall and N. A. Sprinthall, *Educational Psychology: Selected Readings* (New York: Van Nostrand-Reinhold, 1969), pp. 194–198.

2
M. B. McGraw, *Growth: A Study of Johnny and Jimmy* (New York: Appleton-Century, 1935).

3
M. B. McGraw, "Later Development of Children Specially Trained during Infancy," *Child Development,* 1939.

4
J. P. Scott, *Early Experience and the Organization of Behavior* (Belmont, Calif.: Wadsworth, 1968), p. 68.

5

Nancy Bayley, *Studies in the Development of Young Children* (Berkeley: University of California Press, 1940).

6

M. C. Jones, N. Bayley, J. W. MacFarlane, and M. P. Honzik, eds., *The Course of Human Development* (Waltham, Mass.: Xerox, 1971).

7

B. S. Bloom, *Stability and Change in Human Characteristics* (New York: Wiley, 1964).

8

E. S. Lee, "Negro Intelligence and Selective Migration: A Philadelphia Test of the Klineberg Hypothesis," *American Sociological Review* 16 (1951):227–233.

9

J. McV. Hunt, "Revisiting Montessori," in Sprinthall and Sprinthall, *Educational Psychology: Selected Readings,* pp. 45–55.

10

W. Dennis, "Causes of Retardation among Institutional Children: Iran," *Journal of Genetic Psychology* 96 (1960):47–59.

11

J. McV. Hunt, "Revisiting Montessori," p. 52.

12

D. K. Spelt, "The Conditioning of the Human Fetus in Utero," *Journal of Experimental Psychology* 38 (1948):338–346.

13

J. S. Bruner, "Cognitive Consequences of Early Sensory Deprivation," in Sprinthall and Sprinthall, *Educational Psychology: Selected Readings,* pp. 34–36.

14

D. O. Hebb, *The Organization of Behavior* (New York: Wiley, 1949).

15

R. Bugelski, *The Psychology of Learning Applied to Teaching* (Indianapolis-New York: Bobbs-Merrill, 1964).

16

W. R. Thompson and W. Heron, "The Effects of Restricting Early Experience on the Problem Solving Capacity of Dogs," *Canadian Journal of Psychology* 8 (1954):17–31.

17

B. Hymovitch, "The Effect of Experimental Variations on Problem-Solving in the Rat," *Journal of Comparative and Physiological Psychology* 45 (1952):313–321.

18

D. Krech, "The Chemistry of Learning," in Sprinthall and Sprinthall, *Educational Psychology,* pp. 152–156.

19

G. S. Grosser, R. C. Sprinthall, and L. Sirois, "Magnesium Pemoline: Activation of Extinction Responding after Continuous Reinforcement," *Psychological Reports* 21 (1967):11–14.

20

J. Altman, "Postnatal Growth and Differentiation of the Mammalian Brain," in G. C. Quarton, T. Melnechuk, and F. O. Schmitt, *The Neurosciences* (New York: Rockefeller University Press, 1967).

21

A. H. Riesen, "Stimulation as a Requirement for Growth and Function in Behavioral Development," in D. W. Fiske and S. R. Maddi, *Functions of Varied Experience* (Homewood, Ill.: Dorsey, 1961), pp. 57–80.

22
A. H. Riesen, "Studying Perceptual Development Using the Technique of Sensory Deprivation," *Journal of Nervous and Mental Disease* 132 (1961):21–25.

23
R. Heber and H. Garber, "An Experiment in the Prevention of Cultural-Familial Mental Retardation," *Proceedings Second Congress of the International Assoc. for the Scientific Study of Mental Deficiency*, Aug. 25–Sept. 2, 1970.

24
S. P. Strickland, "Can Slum Children Learn?" *American Education*, July 1970, pp. 3–7.

25
R. Heber, "Rehabilitation of Families at Risk for Mental Retardation, Progress Report," University of Wisconsin, Madison, 1972.

26
C. A. Falender and R. Heber, "Mother-Child Interaction and Participation in a Longitudinal Intervention Program," *Developmental Psych.* 11, no. 6 (1975):830–836.

27
E. B. Page, "Miracle in Milwaukee: Raising the IQ," *Educational Researcher* 1 (1972):8–16.

28
B. L. White, *The First Three Years* (Englewood Cliffs, N.J.: Prentice-Hall, 1975).

29
M. Pines, "Head Head Start." *The New York Times,* 26 October 1975.

30
Ibid., p. 58.

31
R. Herrnstein, "I.Q.," *The Atlantic Monthly,* September 1971, pp. 43–64.

32
G. Piel, "The New Hereditarians," *The Nation,* 19 April 1975, p. 458.

33
G. S. Grosser and R. C. Sprinthall, "A Rejoinder to Herrnstein," *The Atlantic Monthly,* February 1972, pp. 38–39.

34
R. F. Biehler, *Psychology Applied to Teaching* (Boston: Houghton Mifflin, 1971), pp. 470–471.

SUGGESTIONS FOR FURTHER READING

Bloom, B. S. *Stability and Change in Human Characteristics.* New York: Wiley, 1964.

Newton, G., and S. Levine, eds. *Early Experience and Behavior.* Springfield, Illinois: C. C. Thomas, 1968.

Scott, J. P. *Early Experience and the Organization of Behavior.* Belmont City, Calif.: Wadsworth, 1968.

6

Cognitive growth

One of the newest and most significant areas of knowledge in educational psychology is cognitive development. In Chapter 3 we introduced the tremendously important concept of stages of growth; that is, a sequence of plateaus, each one distinctively different from the previous one. As children grow and develop they present us with unique opportunities to respond to them in ways that will either facilitate or deter their growth. In a sense, children are maximally responsive at certain sensitive periods, when just the right touch, so to speak, will help them learn. This is most obvious in physical or motor development. Myrtle McGraw's study showing that the best time to teach children to roller-skate was precisely the same time they are learning to walk (12 months) demonstrated vividly and dramatically the importance of matching a child's readiness to learn with the most appropriate teaching. It is neither effective nor efficient to teach roller-skating before, or much after, the child has learned to walk.[1] Everything in the right time and the right season might be the motto for child and adolescent growth and development.

This chapter takes a special look at cognitive development, particularly at the kinds of cognitive stages or plateaus of development that occur during childhood and adolescence. Since cognitive development depends on interaction between the child and the learning environment, we will examine the problems of matching the child to the most appropriate learning tasks. This is another way of saying that we must have some informed basis for what we choose to present to pupils as well as how we present the material. Just as we would not expect children to roller-skate before they can stand up, we must also know when we can expect them to be ready to learn the various intellectual or cognitive tasks. If we understand how the cognitive systems develop, we can avoid both teaching children something before they are ready to learn it and missing a golden opportunity by waiting until well past the most sensitive moment.

STAGES OF COGNITIVE GROWTH

A revolution: the importance of early learning

The fallacy of categorizing children as slow, medium, or fast learners

Our understanding of the growth of brain power has changed so enormously in the past decade that a veritable "revolution in learning" has taken place.[2] Previously the general view was that intelligence was, for all practical purposes, determined prior to birth. This meant that there was nothing to do but accept those inborn differences as natural and provide different educational experiences depending on whether the child was a fast or a slow learner. In other words, the erroneous assumption of innate differences in intelligence produced an unfortunate educational assumption. We assumed that the differences in intelligence were largely differences in the speed of thinking. In fact "mentally retarded" was almost always translated as "slow learner." This meant that the differences in learning were seen as differences in degree, or more precisely, as quantitative differences. Pupils could be rated—much as if they were on a track team—from slow, to moderately fast, to superfast learners.

By understanding how and when cognitive systems develop, we can avoid, on the one hand, teaching children something before they are ready to learn it and, on the other hand, missing a golden opportunity by waiting to well past the most sensitive moment.

The most damaging effect of viewing learning differences as being fixed at birth and as being quantitative (slow to fast) was its effect on educational programs. In general the educational curriculum reflected this idea—the same material or the same curriculum was given to all students only the pace was different, since the "slower" children would not be expected to learn as much or to go as far as the "faster" children.* Starting from a standard curriculum, we would water it down for the "slow learners" and enrich it for the "accelerated learners." The "slow" children would cover, say, half the material the "fast" children would cover in any given period. For example, the "slow" children would only memorize half as much poetry as the "fast" children, or learn fewer spelling words, less arithmetic, or hand in shorter compositions in English. Since there was little or no recognition of major stages of cognitive growth, the differences between a first-grade pupil and a twelfth-grade pupil were largely differences in how much they knew and how fast they learned it. In the same way, differences among first graders (as among twelfth graders) were also quantitative—how much material they learned and how fast they learned it. It has, unfortunately, taken us a long time to get away from these ideas.

Arnold Gesell, who established the famous Institute of Child Development at Yale University during the 1930s, was the first to try to convince educators that growth and development occurred in an unvarying sequence. Many of his ideas and theories were later discarded because they were oversimplifications, but this one concept lasted. Growth stages are major periods of change. Each

Gesell and the concept of developmental stages

---

*
The word curriculum, by the way, comes from a Latin word meaning a course to be run!

Arnold Gesell was one of the first to
advocate that growth and development
occur in an unvarying sequence.

child goes through periods of major reorganization followed by periods of integration when a new stage is reached and the changes are assimilated. While
Gesell made a significant contribution with his idea of developmental growth
stages, he erred in the details of his stages. He made the mistake of overgeneralizing from studying only a few children and he presented an overly detailed
"map" of development. For example, he made hard and fast statements about
all two-year-olds, all two-and-a-half-year-olds, all three-year-olds, and so on.
this created much confusion in the 1930s and 1940s. Parents were literally measuring their children every six months or so against Gesell's developmental
graphs. Gross generalizations resulted: "All twos are terrible," "The threes are
terrific," "At four and a half all children . . . ." For a time, parental demand for
Gesell's truths outran his ability to produce books: *The First Five Years of Life*
was followed by *The Child From Five to Ten*. One mother was heard to comment despairingly, "I don't know what to do with my children anymore. They
are 11 and 13, and Gesell stopped at 10!" You are invited to read some of these
now historical books. They may help you understand some of the influences on
your grandparents as they raised your parents.[3]

The idea of sequential levels of development was most important in all the work of Gesell's institute. He illustrated that growth took place in stages and that the stages themselves were like great leaps forward followed by periods of integration. Therefore, in order to understand cognitive development, you will have to understand more about the process of growth. At what ages do the major breakthroughs occur and when are the periods of consolidation?

Development: great leaps forward and periods of slow growth

PIAGET: A LATE DISCOVERY

Throughout the period 1930–1960, while efforts to break away from the idea of fixed and quantitative intelligence were singularly unsuccessful (with the exception of Gesell's general concept of growth), Jean Piaget was working quietly and almost unnoticed at the J. J. Rousseau Institute for Child Study in Geneva. Using direct, careful, and systematic observation of children (including his own, the now famous Jacqueline, Laurent, and Lucienne), Piaget began to form a view that would revolutionize our understanding of intellectual growth. Although there was brief interest in Piaget's work in this country in the early 1930s, it was really not understood here until quite recently. However, it is no understatement to say that he is now the single most influential contemporary theorist in the area of cognitive development. In fact, one of his rare visits to this country triggered a reception worthy of an astronaut's return from space. Thousands flocked to see him arrive at the airport.

> It was a memorable occasion. With his fringe of long, straight white hair down the sides and back of his balding head, his high forehead, horn-rimmed glasses, gold watch chain and well-worn leather briefcase, he looked like a stock character—The Professor. On the platform, he commanded instant respect. Speaking in a booming voice, in French, he began by describing some of the key stages of children's intellectual development.[4]

PIAGET: THE CONCEPT OF COGNITIVE GROWTH

Piaget's contribution to our understanding of mental growth as a process of interaction, not his Hollywood appearance, accounts for his significance. Through an intensive study of children over long periods of time—a painstaking process of almost endless observation—Piaget began to chart the unexplored territory of the human mind and to produce a map of the stages of cognitive growth. He proposed, first of all, that cognitive growth takes place in developmental stages. This means that the nature and makeup of intelligence changes significantly over time. The differences are not of degree ("slow learners" and "fast learners") but of kind (quality). The transformation of the human mind as it develops can be compared to the transformation of an egg—to caterpillar—to butterfly. The stages of growth are distinctively different from one another, and the content of each stage is a major system that determines the way we understand and make sense of our experiences (particularly the experience of learning from someone else). Obviously, if we wish to provide experiences that will nurture and facilitate growth, we must take into account the intellectual system

Piaget and qualitative differences during stages

"Keep an eye on the kids for awhile, will you, Jean?"

From *APA Monitor,* September–October, 1974.
Copyright © 1974 by the American Psychological
Association. Reprinted by permission.

the child is using at the time. Piaget's work provides us with the broad outlines of the different cognitive systems children use at different periods in their lives. Each new, evolving system is a major qualitative transformation.

PIAGET'S RESEARCH METHOD: REPEATED OBSERVATIONS

It is important to know something about the way Piaget worked, how he was able to propose a system explaining such a highly complex problem as intellectual development. You might think, in these days of supertechnology, that he may have used a complicated computer-based program and enormous research teams. But you would be mistaken. As we have already mentioned, Piaget's work was based on careful and detailed observation of children in natural settings, like homes and schools. From a research-methodology point of view, he was using repeated naturalistic observations. Thus, in some ways, his method is most like the kind of research a teacher or school counselor might do.

Starting almost like that other great "clinical" scientist, Sigmund Freud, Piaget very carefully examined the functioning of intelligence in a few children. On the basis of these subjective impressions, he began to ask himself some questions. Why, for example, did children become confused over family relationships? A child could readily acknowledge, "I have a brother," but would still not understand that the brother also had a brother (or sister). He also found that children at certain ages seem to have great difficulty in understanding "simple" ideas.

It seems hard to imagine that children don't understand that when they pour beans from a short, fat glass to a tall, thin glass, the number of beans remains constant. In one of his classic experiments, Piaget found that if he took two piles of beans, had a child actually count both piles to be sure they had

Careful observations of children in natural environments

A Piagetian question: can a brother have a brother? can a sister have a sister?

Fig. 6.1 A child's drawings of a half-filled glass of water—right side up and upside down.

the same number, and then left one pile spread out on the table, and bunched the second pile together, that—well, see if you can guess what the child will say. Remember, the child goes by what seems biggest. For example, if you ask children of four or five whether they would rather have a nickel or a dime, they are likely to name the nickel, "because it's bigger."

In yet another observation, Piaget asked preschool children to draw a picture of a glass, half-filled with water. He then asked the child to draw the glass upside down. Figure 6.1 shows what one child drew.

At each point in each successive experiment Piaget would carefully reexamine his own questions (hypotheses), and then develop some further ways of testing them. As a result, it has taken almost an entire lifetime to convince skeptical researchers of his scheme. At first his studies were dismissed out of hand because he would try problems out on a single child, or on three or four children. Also, because his sample was so small, he often did without statistics (in this way he joined hands with such theoretically disparate researchers as Freud and Skinner). To make matters even worse, he didn't follow a standard interview format: he wouldn't necessarily ask the same questions of each child, so that no two interviews were exactly comparable. It was almost too easy to criticize and dismiss his work on the grounds that his research designs were not standard. It was common to hear critics refer to his methods as being "as full of holes as a piece of Swiss cheese." Finally, since his work was written in French, there was always the problem of translation. Until recently there were few American psychologists with a sufficiently fluent command of French to communicate the essence of his ideas. Happily, this is no longer the case.

Thus, partly because Piaget did not follow a standard research model and partly because his ideas, if understood, would have necessitated a major revision in our theories of cognitive growth, his work remained largely confined to

Piaget's theory: the product of a lifetime of study

Piaget's first major stage: the sensorimotor. During this stage, cognitive activity is based primarily on immediate experience through the senses.

The rediscovery of Piaget in the past 15 years

Geneva. However, his findings were eventually noticed and have been widely accepted in the past ten to fifteen years. Scientific skeptics began to take notice of his work. Piaget continues to direct a series of studies, including some that use large samples. Essentially, however, it wasn't the sheer number of subjects that mattered, but the emergence, over and over again, of the same principles of intellectual transformation. Through repetition, rather than the single critical experiment, Piaget accumulated sufficient evidence to become the major theoretician of intellectual development today.

PIAGET: THE STAGES OF COGNITIVE GROWTH

After examining the thinking patterns that children use from birth through adolescence, Piaget began to find consistent systems within certain broad age ranges. There are four major stages (see Table 6.1).

TABLE 6.1   Stages of cognitive growth.

Age	Stage
0–2	Sensorimotor
2–7	Intuitive or preoperational
7–11	Concrete operations
11–16	Formal operations

Since the four major stages are quite broad, each stage has subcategories. The important thing to remember, however, is that each major stage is a system of thinking that is qualitatively different from the preceding stage. Each stage is a major transformation in thought processes, compared to the preceding stage —a quantum leap forward, a breakthrough. It is also important to remember that the child must go through each stage in a regular sequence. It is impossible to skip or miss a stage or to by-pass a stage: the stages of cognitive growth are sequential and follow an invariant sequence. Children cannot overcome a developmental lag or speed up their movement from one stage to the next. They need to have sufficient experience in each stage and sufficient time to internalize that experience before they can move on.

Our main concern as educators is to understand the major substance of each stage. Only then can we begin to consider what to teach and how to teach. Although the major substance of each stage is the main structure or scheme for the age span specified, these stages never exist in a pure form. There will always be some elements of the preceding and future stages mixed in. In other words, while a major intellectual activity does define each stage, bits and pieces of other stages will also be present.

SENSORIMOTOR EXPERIENCE (BIRTH TO TWO YEARS)

Cognitive activity during the sensorimotor stage is based primarily on immediate experience through the senses. The major intellectual activity of the stage is the interaction of the senses and the environment. Activity is practical. Without language to label experiences, or to symbolize and hence remember events and ideas, children are dramatically bound to immediate experience—they see what is happening and feel it, but they have no way of categorizing their experience. Responses are almost completely determined by the situation. For example, a hungry child will literally scream the house down for food. It does no good to "tell" a six-month-old, "Now just wait a minute; I'm warming your bottle." The child has no way to represent the idea that in one or two minutes a nice warm bottle of milk will appear, and obviously doesn't know what a minute is, or for that matter, what any of those other words mean. It's like speaking in English to someone who only understands Armenian. The child cannot, so to speak, go to the mental equivalent of an instant replay and say, "Oh, when she says that, it means something good is coming, so I won't be hungry much longer, and my yelling isn't going to make it come faster."

Being tied to immediate experience during this stage also means that there is almost nothing between the child and the environment. The mental organization lives in the raw, so to speak, so that the quality of experience is unusually significant. Thus, what and how the child learns will remain an immediate experience, as vivid as any first experience. It would be fair to say that learning in the sensorimotor stage is a continuous peak experience. It is something like experiencing each day as if it were the first day of school, the opening night of a play, your first final exam, your first date, your first encounter with death, the first time you found yourself completely alone, and so on—all in the same day.

To give you some idea of how easily children at this age are bound by experience and can be victimized by it, we need only think of six-month-olds. This is the age at which children begin to be able to follow an object with their eyes ("visual pursuit"). Their eyes swing back and forth, following the path of a shiny object, fifty to a hundred times. They literally can't take their eyes off the moving object. Because this is the "first" time they have seen an object move from side to side, they will follow its visual path almost indefinitely unless we wisely choose to change the environment.

Visual pursuit

The development of visual pursuit (a sensori-motor behavior) is critical to mental development. Visual pursuit has to be learned before a very important concept, called "object permanence," can be learned. As children begin to grow intellectually, they understand that when an object disappears from view, it still exists even though they can't see it. Whether it's a button hidden under a pillow, a person leaving the room, or a boy or girl hiding behind a door, children who have developed the concept of object permanence know the disappearance is only temporary and they are liberated from endless visual pursuit.

Object permanence: the beginning of the separation of self and the environment

The ability to notice and follow objects might be likened to a first stage of recognition. The growth of object permanence is almost like the beginning of an elementary memory. Children can "hold" in their minds a picture of the missing object; no longer is out of sight, out of mind. The experience of seeing things in the first few months of life and then of seeing those same things disappear and reappear plays an important role in mental development. Piaget has compared sighted babies with those born blind: "The inadequacy of the initial schemata [a complex word meaning mental organization] leads to a lag in development of three to four years and more . . . ."[5] Lacking visual experience during the critical period of sensorimotor learning (birth to two years) prevents the growth of mental structures.

The effects of early blindness on sensori-motor learning

An old adage, "There's no substitute for experience," best summarizes the sensorimotor period of cognitive development. This is so true of the zero- to two-year-olds that it accounts for the recent trend of providing babies with interesting crib mobiles and is also responsible for bringing back the popularity of some of the old-fashioned baby toys like rattles to shake and suck and blankets to hug. Linus, from the Peanuts cartoon, learning with his blanket in tow, stands as the prototype of sensori-motor. A rich and responsive sensory environment is the best means of developing the young child's intelligence.* Note how this relates directly to some of the research findings mentioned in Chapter 5 concerning the development of "intelligent" animals by exposing them to "creative" toys and "interesting" cages. The quality of experience during this first stage prepares the child to move to the next stage, the intuitive or preoperational stage.

INTUITIVE OR PREOPERATIONAL THOUGHT (TWO TO SEVEN YEARS)

During this period the quality of thinking is transformed. Children are no longer bound to their immediate sensory environment. They start developing some mental images in the preceding stage (object permanence, for example) and in this stage they expand that ability by leaps and bounds. Their capacity to store images (words and the grammatical structures of language, for example) in-

Language development: a phenomenal growth

---

*
The implications for the recent growth of day care centers in this regard are obvious. Failure to operate quality programs—rich and responsive sensory environments—will induce, at a critical juncture, serious developmental lags.

Piaget's second stage: intuitive, or preoperational, thought (two to seven years). Vocabulary development is especially significant during this stage.

creases dramatically. Vocabulary development, including the ability to understand and use words, is especially noteworthy. The average two-year-old understands between 200 and 300 words, while the average five-year-old understands 2000 words—a huge percent increase. At two years the child talks in sentences of one or two words. One year later sentences of eight to ten words are not uncommon and the sentences themselves are grammatically correct.[6] Table 6.2 summarizes speech development from two to eight years of age.

TABLE 6.2 Language development.

Two-year-olds	Three- to five-year-olds	Seven- and eight-year-olds
1. One- or two-word sentences	1. Eight- to ten-word sentences	Pronunciation equivalent of adult speech
2. No grammatical form	2. Grammatically correct	
3. Average vocabulary 200 words	3. Average vocabulary 2000 words	
Example: "Ba-Ba"	Examples: "Constantinople" and "Timbuctoo"	

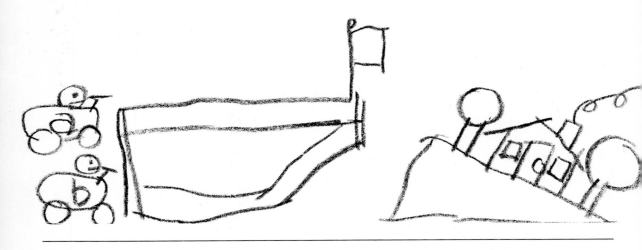

Intuitive: preoperational reasoning. "If Cars A and B get to the finish together, they go at the same speed" is one example of intuitive preoperational reasoning.

A child's drawing of a house on a hill.

During this stage, then, there is a major breakthrough in the use of language. Since this is the time when children are maximally ready to learn language, adults who talk a great deal to children, read to them, teach them songs and nursery rhymes—in other words, use language to communicate with them —have a significant effect on the children's language development.

The importance of practice in language

The predominant learning mode at this stage is intuitive; preoperational children are not overly concerned with precision, but delight in imitating sounds and trying out lots of different words. They are also unconcerned about the consequences of language. This is the time, for example, when preschoolers are hysterically funny over "bathroom" language, taking great glee in using choice expressions such as "poop face."

Obviously, the richer the verbal environment at this time, the more likely it is that language will develop. This is not to suggest that we should force-feed language teaching. In fact, teaching is almost unnecessary. The advantage of the intuitive mode is that children are capable of free associations, fantasies, and unique illogical meanings. They can pretend that stuffed toys are real, they can have imaginary friends, tell wild stories about their parentage, have whole conversations with themselves as well as with inanimate objects—these are all ways children have of trying language out, of teaching themselves. Intuition frees them to be experimental regardless of reality.

Promoting the use of free associations and fantasy thinking

From the adults' point of view the spontaneous nature of a child's language may have its drawbacks. Since the child doesn't worry about logic or reality, if it "feels" OK to talk to a tree, a dog, or a stranger in the street, you can be sure the child will be heard. How many stories have you heard about children who

A child asked to draw an upright pencil falling usually cannot do so. If asked to draw a picture of someone dropping a ball, he will draw the beginning and the end, but not the ball in the process of falling, as pictured here.

suddenly say something like, "Hey Daddy, look at that fat lady standing next to you." We have to remember that such comments are for the good of practice. The more extensive the practice, in spite of embarrassing moments, the greater the future verbal facility and competency. Studies have shown that children who are deprived of speech to any significant degree during this period suffer a developmental lag that may be irreversible.

Piaget, in studying the use of language during this period, found that children seem to talk at rather than with others. We have all had the experience of realizing that the other person wasn't really listening to us; that they were talking over, around, and through us, mostly to hear themselves talk, as the old saying goes. With three- to seven-year-old children this is the predominant mode. Piaget has called it "collective monologue." If you ask a group of children to tell you a story, together, you will find as many different stories as there are children. Their speech patterns are egocentric; they bear little relationship to what others are saying. However, in terms of practice, the collective monologue is another means children have of trying out words without having to wait their turn.

Promoting collective monologues

The intuitive period is truly a golden opportunity for facilitating language development. But we should also make it clear that preoperational thought is a general mode during this time. This is why a child at this level would choose a tall, thin glass of water, rather than a short, wide one. Intuitively it looks like more because it's taller. "Let's not worry that it's thinner," the child might say, "because being taller is enough. It looks bigger to me!" You may think this is a cavalier disregard of the facts, and that's just the point—it is. And it will do absolutely no educational good to tell a child of this age the "real" reasons why the amount of water is the same in both glasses. All you would accomplish would to be to get the child to parrot back what you say, without the slightest understanding. There are literally thousands of uproariously funny stories that illustrate how children understand abstract concepts. Ask a six-year-old to say, and then explain, the pledge of allegiance to the flag ("the Republic of Richard Stands and One Naked Individual") or some biblical references ("Pontius the Pilot on the Flight to Egypt"; "The Father, The Son, and Holy Smoke!"). These will remind us of another aphorism, "The child is not a midget-sized adult." A child's understanding is qualitatively different from an adult's.

The inability to understand proverbs

We can say, then, that the mental structures at the preoperational stage are largely intuitive, freewheeling, and highly imaginative. Do not assume, however, that because the process seems illogical it is necessarily inferior as a mode of thought. Indeed, much work in the area of creativity (see Chapter 19) suggests that intuition and free association are an important aspect of creative or original problem solving. Intuition allows us to break out of the constraints imposed by reality. Inventors, artists, and other creative people commonly find that many of their ideas come to them intuitively or, as it is sometimes called, preconsciously. When we say, "From the mouths of babes . . . ," we are testifying to the importance of intuitive thinking.

Preoperational thinking and creativity

CONCRETE OPERATIONS OR OPERATIONAL THINKING (SEVEN TO ELEVEN YEARS)

Piaget's next stage represents another major reorganization of mental structure. In the preoperational stage children are dreamers, with magical thoughts and fantasies in abundance. Now, in the operational stage, they are young logical positivists who understand functional relationships because they are specific,

The youthful logical positivist

"To the adult mind this room appears disorganized, but to the mind of a child everything is logically arranged for use."

"You said we could paint anything we wanted to!"

Piaget's third stage: concrete operations (seven to eleven years). Activities now can have rules, and schooling at this age should emphasize skills and concrete activity.

because they can test the problems out. For example, if we show children at this age the pile of beans or the water-glass experiment, they will tell us there is no change in volume. This time around they understand the specific, or concrete, aspects of the problem. Now they can measure, weigh, and calculate the amount of water or number of beans so that an apparent difference won't "fool" them.

However, in their wholehearted abandonment of magical thinking, fantasies, and imaginary "friends," they become almost too literal-minded. Their ability to understand the world is now as "logical" as it once was "illogical." For example, they can easily distinguish between dreams and facts, but they cannot separate hypothesis from fact. Five-year-olds usually describe a dream as something that happens in their bedroom, that they watch like a movie, while nine-year-olds describe dreams as mental images inside their heads.[7] Also, once a nine-year-old's mind is made up on a question, new information will not easily change that point of view. In one study, seven- to ten-year-old children were presented with a number of reasons why Stonehenge (a prehistoric site in England) was a fort rather than a religious center. When the rival hypothesis was presented, with new facts, they refused to change their minds. This indicated that they confused facts and theories.[8] The concept of a theory was beyond their mental organization or system and thus their responses were limited to the facts as presented initially. "Just gimme the facts," a child might say.

In humor we also find evidence of the literal-mindednesss of this stage. This is the time when children delight in using explicitness and literalness as a basis for their jokes. Slapstick and pie-throwing reach their zenith during this period. "When am I going to get my just desserts?" asks the fall-guy comedian plaintively. "Are you sure you want it now?" says the partner, holding a cream pie behind his back. You can fill in the balance of the dialogue and imagine the screams of delight from an elementary-age audience.

Literal-minded and concrete thought

If, during the previous stage, children play around with fantasies, during concrete operations they play around with literal-mindedness. One researcher illustrates this juvenile sophistry with the following story (again a favorite at this age): An eight-year-old boy comes to the table with his hands dripping wet. When his mother asks him why he didn't dry his hands, he replies, "But you told me not to wipe my hands on the clean towels." His mother throws up her hands and replies, "I said not to wipe your *dirty* hands on the towels."[9] Another researcher reported the following as a most popular story, "A mother loses her child named Heine. She asks a policeman, 'Have you seen my Heine?' "[10] Usually by this time children are laughing so hard we never hear the punch line. And we must admit, compared to the previous period where the simple phrase "poop face" was considered hilarious, concrete-stage humor is more sophisticated, if not more appealing to adult tastes.

Low comedy: a favorite during concrete operations

SCHOOLING AND CONCRETE OPERATIONS

In many ways schooling at the elementary age seems to fit the pupils' cognitive stage rather well. Where school emphasizes skills and activities as counting, sorting, building, and manipulating, cognitive growth will be nurtured. Field trips to historical sites or science through "kitchen" physics are additional examples. Activities can now have rules. In fact, you could almost say during this time that making the rules for a game, or classroom activity, is more significant than the activity itself. Whereas preschool children will obey rules without understanding why we have them, elementary-school children understand rules because of their functional value. You cannot play real baseball without following the rules. However, we must also remember that they have a literal understanding of the concept of rules—rules are given laws that cannot be changed. Adults understand that rules are a system of regulations that can be replaced by another system, but children see them as fixed, necessary, and arbitrary. The danger, then, is that we will exploit their literal-mindedness in order to manipulate rather than educate them.

Positive and negative aspects of concrete thinking

Thus, while schooling at this age is generally successful where it emphasizes skills and concrete activities, certain other aspects are not useful. For example, there is increasing interest in teaching elementary-age children the structure of knowledge in the various disciplines—math, English, history, science—throughout the entire school sequence. For example, we no longer teach history as facts or events, but as a way of thinking. How does a historian think? What is the process whereby he or she knows (in our earlier example) that Stonehenge was a religious site? How does the historian examine artifacts? Given this broad objective, to teach structure, we then try to develop a spiraling curriculum. At each grade we present the concepts in a more-sophisticated manner.

The spiral curriculum too abstract

Where this process breaks down is precisely at the pupils' level of cognitive understanding. Since their mode of thinking is concrete and they don't have the mental equipment to grasp the cognitive abstractions, they translate the abstractions into concrete and highly specific terms. Boys and girls at this stage develop their own way of understanding the subjects in accord with specific everyday experience. They learn to add in the first grade, take away in the second grade, fractions in the fifth . . . and so on for each subject and each teacher. In the case of subjects in the new curriculum the same situation prevails, but the words have changed; for example, in the "new" math they learn set theory in the second grade, rational and irrational numbers in the fourth, and so on. In other words, the compartments the children use are a reflection of the concrete operations they learn to perform everyday in school. All they have learned, in the meantime, is a new set of rote responses. Mary Alice White, a renowned school psychologist, observed the same situation when it came to the question of what parts of the curriculum are considered most important by the children.[11] You can guess by now that they chose the subjects having the most tests and the most homework. Obviously, from a concrete point of view, that is the way to judge the importance or value of a subject. Even though teachers may say that all the subjects are important, actions speak louder than words, especially during this stage.

Parents of these children also get caught in the trap of the literal-minded thinker. Many parents report being upset and frustrated when they try to help their children with schoolwork. Children comment, "But that's not the way the teacher wants us to do it! She wants us to make the plus sign this way, not that way." "Teacher says we have to do spelling first, then arithmetic." "Fractions

Literal mindedness, or how to create problems between teachers and parents come before decimals." Usually neither the parent nor the teacher realize that the difficulty lies in their child's cognitive level. Instead, parents frequently get mad at their children for not realizing, for example, that decimals and fractions are equivalent. And they get annoyed at the teacher for teaching in such simplistic black-and-white terms. The teacher, on the other hand, gets equally annoyed at reports of such literal-minded parents. The children are caught in the middle between two equally arbitrary systems, neither of which they understand.

FORMAL OPERATIONS (ELEVEN TO SIXTEEN YEARS)

During this final stage, which more or less coincides with adolescence, children can develop full formal patterns of thinking. They are now able to attain logical, rational, abstract strategies. The pendulum problem is one of Piaget's tests for formal operations. Symbolic meanings, metaphors, and similes can now be understood. Stories with a moral can be generalized. Games and simulations can be presented so that pupils understand their implications. For example, if we want to teach something about economic theories and principles we can use a game like *Monopoly,* as long as we ask questions that point to the general principles. If we try this at the elementary age, we would find that the children could understand the game only as a game; they could not generalize from it.

Stimulating abstract thinking

Other powerful means of stimulating abstract thinking are viewing movies and film clips, and participating in art forms such as painting, drama, dance, and music. There are many sources of symbolic material besides that contained in the traditional school subjects. And the more active the symbolic process, the more it enhances cognitive growth during this stage writing poems is more

Piaget's fourth stage: formal operations (eleven to sixteen years). During this stage, children can develop formal patterns of thinking and are able to attain logical, rational strategies.

The pendulum problem   (a Piaget test of formal operations)

Materials: A length of string
             A series of different size weights

1. Demonstrate the swing of a pendulum by attaching one weight to the string and letting it swing.

2. Ask class to predict which is more important in determining how fast or slow the pendulum swings—the *length* of the string or the size of the *weight*.

3. Demonstrate different lengths and different weights and repeat question 2.

Even though it will be clear that the size of the weight has no influence on how fast or slow the pendulum swings, you may be surprised to find how many pupils still insist that weight does make a difference.

effective than reading poems, making films more than viewing, taking part in an improvisational drama more than observing. Probably the most creative and significant task confronting secondary-school teachers is the challenge that this theory of growth presents to build new approaches to curriculum materials.

EDUCATIONAL IMPLICATIONS OF PIAGET'S THEORY OF COGNITIVE DEVELOPMENT

Intelligence and activity

A significant educational implication of cognitive development is that growth in any one stage depends on activity. In other words, the development of brain power is not fixed at birth but is a function of appropriate activity during any particular stage. Children must engage in appropriate activities to learn. This does not mean they should sit and listen to or observe others. In speaking of development in the first two years, Piaget has said, "Sensorimotor causality does not derive from perceptive causality; to the contrary, visual perceptive causality is based upon a tactico-kinesthetic causality that is itself dependent upon the activity proper. . . ."[12] This quote, while demonstrating how difficult it can be to understand a passage from Piaget, also indicates the significance of his equation: Intelligence = Activity. We may recall that anthropological studies, especially studies of prehistoric humans, have indicated that our brainpower increased after the invention of tools. The manipulation of tools, acting or "operating" on axes, knives, and primitive shovels induced the brain to grow. In a sense, primitive men and women, as they began to use tools, were almost challenged to come up with new uses for tools and to invent more efficient and effective tools. The effect of rising to the challenge posed by this activity, the manipulation of tools, itself increased our capacity to understand and become more sophisticated cognitively—the activity developed our "mind." The critical point for us is the key phrase in all of Piaget's writings, that activity produces cognitive growth. Thus, over and over in his writings to educators, Piaget calls for the active school.

The American question: Can we speed up growth?

Inevitably in a technologically oriented society someone asks Piaget what he now calls the American question, "How can we speed up development?" "The first question which I am always asked in the United States is, 'Can one accelerate these stages?'" The answer obviously is "no." Given all that Piaget has shown, we cannot speed up the process of intellectual growth. But there is really more to the question than this. There may be a tendency for us to say, in effect, "Since we can't speed up growth, let's just sit back and wait for it to happen spontaneously." Unfortunately, we cannot assume that cognitive growth will unfold magically (some hopelessly romantic teachers say, "My job is just to stay out of the way while kids learn"). Instead, it is most important to remind ourselves of Piaget's call for an environment that will maximally respond to the child. "Present the subject to be taught in forms assimilable to children of different ages in accordance with their mental structure. . . ."[13]

Stages of growth: the process of accommodation and assimilation

The broad outline of the stages of cognitive growth—sensorimotor, intuitive or preoperational, concrete, and formal—represent major transformations of mental organization. Each stage is qualitatively different from the preceding and is a new means of dealing cognitively with the world. The important thing for educators in all this, however, is to understand how cognitive growth occurs. We have already noted the critical importance of activity. Equally significant is Piaget's concept of accommodation and assimilation. This is a dual process. Children at particular stages are maximally able to assimilate particular kinds of experiences. This means, for example, that sensorimotor experiences can be most fully taken in from birth to two years, preoperational from two to seven, and so on. And it also means the opposite, that it is impossible to assimilate experiences beyond the level of mental development. Thus, as teachers, we can get children to say they know, or force them to memorize, but we should not be fooled into believing that they really understand. Piaget might say, "To know by heart is not to know."

According to Piaget, the activity of assimilating certain experiences from the environment forces the child to accommodate, or internalize, those experiences. Internalizing experiences is critical to cognitive growth and cannot take place if experiences are allowed, literally, to go in one ear and out the other. Piaget suggests that the most complete development takes place when children assimilate experiences from their environment since only then will they be able to accommodate, or internalize, those learnings. As we have indicated, this is the major new challenge facing educators—to develop an array of such experiences to provide maximal cognitive development.

Equilibration and new learning

In addition to the close relationship between intellectual development and activity, Piaget's concept of equilibration is a critical factor in his theory of growth and is important to our discussion of developmental education. We have noted that each person swings back and forth between assimilating new learning material and accommodating that new experience or internalizing the new concepts. This overall dual process of assimilation and accommodation, or as it's sometimes called, differentiation or integration, can be represented by the concept of equilibration.

An illustration may be helpful. Suppose you have just confronted and solved a problem. You are an elementary-age pupil and you believe that the best way to fill an ice-cube tray is to use hot water. (This is a common misconception among children as well as some adults.) Then you conduct an experiment and see that a tray with cold water does freeze faster. If you have had enough experience and you are far enough along in the stage of concrete thinking, you will be ready to "equilibrate"—namely, to accept the new information and the new solution to the ice-cube-tray problem. Thus equilibration gradually moves a person to a more comprehensive and complex mode of functioning. In other words, it's like the process of cognitive conflict resolution. When our cognitive assumption (hot water for ice cubes) becomes "jammed," how do we reconcile the new information with our old theory? Our previous method of thinking is obviously faulty. A new and better solution is embedded in a theory of temperature change. We equilibrate and accept the fact that our old theory was prelogical or prescientific. Thus we can define equilibration as an emerging cognitive structure that reconciles the thinking conflicts of a prior stage.

Perhaps an easier way to remember equilibration is to consider what we experience when we begin to feel that our solution to a problem doesn't quite make it. We sense that a new explanation, or intuitively begin to feel that a new level of understanding, is better. We are not quite sure and in fact may be a bit apprehensive about exploring an unknown; part of us may be attracted toward the change, while another part (our old and comfortable way of thinking) resists. The feelings from cognitive dissonance, or jamming, gradually have to be worked through during equilibration. Some of the old must be relinquished to make room for the new, a process that does involve anxiety.

As a teacher introducing new concepts, slightly better problem-solving methods, or somewhat-more-comprehensive theories, remember that you are inducing some equilibration within the pupils. They will need extra psychological and personal support during such transition periods.

In addition to the extra personal support during new learning, also remember that we cannot speed up growth. There is little sense in teaching preoperational or early concrete thinkers to learn to think abstractly. If for the sake of equilibration we present information clearly over the heads of the pupils, new learning will not take place—there will be no reconciliation of new ideas. In fact, the only notable increases may be in pupil frustration, anxiety, and perhaps rote memorization.

Teaching to facilitate cognitive development

Certainly the major implication of Piaget's framework is that the curriculum should not take cognitive development for granted. To the contrary, the curriculum should provide specific educational experiences, based on the children's

Jean
Piaget

Jean Piaget was born in Neuchatel, Switzerland, in 1896. Piaget was a curious, alert, studious, and extremely bright child. By age ten he had published his first scientific paper, a description of an albino sparrow he had observed in a local park. Between ages eleven and fifteen Piaget worked after school as a laboratory assistant to the director of a natural history museum and in the process became an expert on mollusks and other zoological topics. When he was fifteen, he was offered the job of curator of the mollusk section at a Geneva museum. He received his degree from the University of Neuchatel at age eighteen, and his Ph.D. in natural sciences three years later. Piaget had published more than twenty papers in the field of zoology before reaching his twenty-first birthday. In short, Piaget demonstrated a rare intellectual precocity during his childhood and adolescent years.

Despite his early interest in natural science, the young Piaget read widely in sociology, religion, and philosophy. While studying philosophy he became especially interested in epistemology, the study of how knowledge is obtained. With his background in zoology, Piaget became convinced that biological principles could be utilized in understanding epistemological problems. His search for a bridge between biology and epistemology brought him finally into the world of psychology.

After receiving his doctorate, Piaget sought training in psychology and so left Switzerland to study and gain experience at a number of European laboratories, clinics, and universities. During this time he worked for awhile at Binet's laboratory school in Paris, where he did intelligence testing on French school children. He became fascinated, not by a child's correct answer to a test item, but by a child's incorrect responses. He doggedly pursued the incorrect answers in the hope of learning more about the depth and extent of children's ideas and mental processes. His goal was to understand how children of various ages came upon their knowledge of the world around them. This became Piaget's lifework, to find out how children go about the business of obtaining knowledge.

Later Piaget took detailed, minute-by-minute notes of the mental growth of his own three children, Jacqueline, Lucienne, and Laurent.

In 1929 Piaget went to the University of Geneva, where he became the assistant director of the J. J. Rousseau Institute, and in 1940 he assumed the duties of director at Geneva's Psychology Laboratory.

Piaget has written a tremendous number of books and articles on cognitive growth in children. He believes that intellectual growth is a direct continuation of inborn biological growth. The child is born biologically equipped to make a variety of motor responses, which then provide the framework for the thought processes that follow. The biological givens impose on the developing child an invariant direction to the development of cognitive processes. The ability to think springs from the physiological base. Clearly, Piaget has kept his early training in natural science clearly in mind as he has gone on to develop his system of cognitive growth.

Now in his twilight years, Piaget still is actively seeking answers to some of psychology's most fundamental questions. According to his biographer, friend, and former student, David Elkind, Piaget still rises early, about 4 A.M., and writes at least four publishable pages before teaching his morning classes. His afternoons are devoted to taking long walks and thinking about his current studies and research, and his evenings are spent reading. As soon as his classes are over for the summer, Piaget goes to his mountain retreat in the Alps. As fall approaches, the mountain air turns crisp, the leaves begin to change color, and Piaget comes down the mountain, laden with new material for several articles and books. Piaget has been coming down that mountain for over fifty autumns, and the volume of his writing has been enormous. Just as Freud's name has become synonymous with the study of emotional growth, Piaget is psychology's foremost expert on cognitive growth.

developmental level, to foster growth. This is particularly true for the final stage: formal operations. Just because adolescents are ready to develop formal logical thought processes does not necessarily mean they will think logically. A recent study indicated that almost half the people between sixteen and twenty years of age never completely achieve formal operations.[14] Yet, if you examine many of the curriculum materials at the secondary-school level, you will soon realize that much of the instruction assumes, rather than attempts to develop, formal operational thought.* This is not starting where the learner is developmentally. Nor does this help the pupils learn to use their capacities for formal thought. In fact, it is far too easy for a complex, abstract curriculum to go in one ear and out the other in secondary school.

Each cognitive stage is like a switching station, where the pupil has the option of moving on to the next stage or staying in place. Whether movement occurs depends on the pupil's educational experience at that time. It is our view that much of the difficulty of teaching and learning, especially at the secondary level, arises from a lack of understanding of the process of cognitive development. If teenage pupils cannot understand the curriculum materials they face day after day, we cannot blame them for losing interest completely. We would urge a careful examination of the cognitive assumptions of the curriculum materials. Further, we would urge an examination of the errors pupils make to see whether the material is clearly over their heads or beyond their present comprehension. It may be appropriate to revise lesson plans and use materials that are more within the pupils' level of understanding. Rather than assuming that high-school pupils are all competent in formal operational thought, we should provide experiences and activities to stimulate that development. A careful analysis of student "error" is highly recommended for development assessment.

CHILDREN ARE NOT LIKE ADULTS

Piaget makes it clear that cognitive growth is a continuation of inborn motor processes—that is, the child comes into the world genetically equipped to make certain motor responses and these form the foundation on which later mental structures will be built. Thus, the biological givens inescapably direct cognitive growth. Further, Piaget considers the difference among his three major stages to be based on differences in how the child interacts with his or her environment and the child's own reality. Finally, though Piaget feels that in general the stages of development cannot be speeded up, he does concede that they may be retarded under conditions of low environmental stimulation. Thus, though the onset of the stages are, in a sense, predetermined, environmental stimulation is needed at the right time for the bud of each stage to come to full flower on schedule.

Piaget's theory of cognitive growth, in contrast to earlier views, shows how our thinking processes take dramatically different forms during different periods

---

*
See particularly some of the new social-studies and history materials. The attempt is to teach the concept of an academic discipline as a structure, a tall order even in college or graduate school.

of growth. It also indicates the role of experience and active learning in generating growth and change. Above all, it stresses the importance of assessing the stage to which the pupil as a learner has developed, within the framework of developmental cognitive growth. It is extraordinarily easy to assume that children think almost like adults. For an educator, such a view is both simple-minded and somewhat dangerous.

PIAGETIAN TASKS*

The following Piagetian measurement items may prove helpful in your own classroom. The first series of questions (items 1–11) call for concrete operations including the ability to conserve. Items 12 and 13 require formal operations including the ability to abstract or theorize about the causal relationships that best explain the observed occurrences. Remember to inquire carefully and extensively as to the children's reasons for their answers—i.e., how do they justify their responses.

Instructions

1. Read each item carefully.
2. Answer all the items.
3. Mark the correct answer.
4. Explain your answer.

Practice item: Before you begin, look at the practice item below. Study it carefully to see how you are to find the right answer.

Shown below are two sets of fruit.
Set A has oranges. Set B has apples.

Set A:

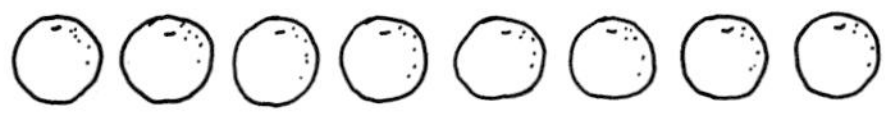

Set B:

A. Of the two sets, which set has the most fruit?

☐ a. Set A has the most fruit.
☐ b. Set B has the most fruit.
☐ c. They have the same number of fruit.
☐ d. None of the above answers is correct.

B. Explain your answer. *Set A has 8 oranges. Set B has 8 apples. Therefore, both sets have the same number of fruit. (or) Set A = 8. Set B = 8. Therefore, Set A = Set B.*

These items were developed by Priscilia Taufer'langke, a doctoral student at the University of Minnesota specializing in tests and measurements.

1. Shown below are two groups of marbles. Each circle represents a marble.

   Group A: 0 0 0 0 0 0 0 0 0

   Group B: 000000000

A. Of the two groups, which group has more marbles?

☐ a. Group A has more marbles.

☐ b. Group B has more marbles.

☐ c. Both groups have the same number of marbles.

☐ d. None of the above answers is correct.

B. Explain your answer. _____

2. Shown below are nine wooden blocks.

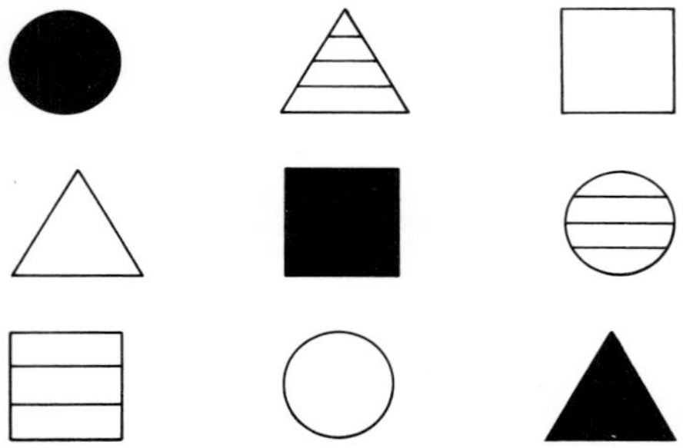

A. Two ways to sort the blocks into groups that are alike would be.

☐ a. By color and by groups of two blocks.

☐ b. By shape and by groups of four blocks.

☐ c. By color and by shape.

☐ d. None of the above answers is correct.

B. Explain your answer. _____

3, 4. Shown below in Picture A is a bottle half full of water.

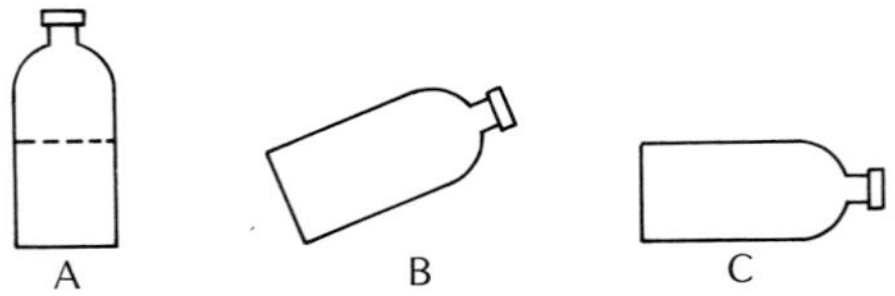

A. Suppose the bottle is tilted as shown in Picture B, and then is placed flat as shown in Picture C. Draw the water levels on the bottles in Picture B and in Picture C.

B. Explain your answers. _____

5. Shown below is a bowl half full of water. Beside it is an iron ball.

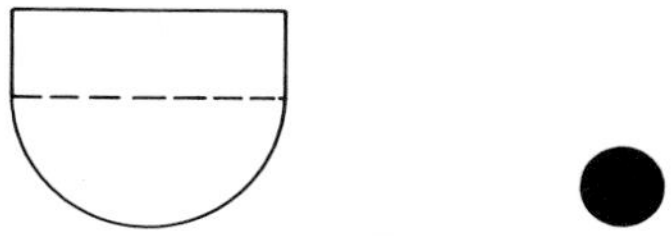

A. Suppose the iron ball is placed into the bowl of water. Will the water in the bowl go up or down, or will the water level remain the same?

☐ a. Remain the same.

☐ b. Go up.

☐ c. Go down.

☐ d. None of the above answers is correct.

B. Explain your answer. _____

_____

_____

6. There are three girls named Jane, Mary, and Susan. Suppose Jane is taller than Mary and Mary is taller than Susan. Is Jane taller than Susan?

☐ a. Yes.

☐ b. No.

☐ c. Both are the same height.

☐ d. Not enough information is given.

Explain your answer. _____

_____

_____

7. Shown below are wooden blocks of different colors and shapes.

A. Are there more black blocks or square blocks?

☐ a. More black blocks.

☐ b. More square blocks.

☐ c. They are equal.

☐ d. None of the above.

B. Are there more white blocks or triangle blocks?

☐ a. More white blocks.

☐ b. More triangle blocks.

☐ c. They are equal.

☐ d. None of the above.

C. Are there more triangle blocks or black
    blocks?

☐ a. More black blocks.

☐ b. More triangle blocks.

☐ c. They are equal.

☐ d. None of the above.

D. Explain your answers to A, B and C. _____

_____

_____

_____

8. Shown below are two sets of glasses. Set I
   has two large glasses which contain equal
   amounts of water. Set II has two small glasses
   which are empty. Each small glass is half the
   size of a large glass.

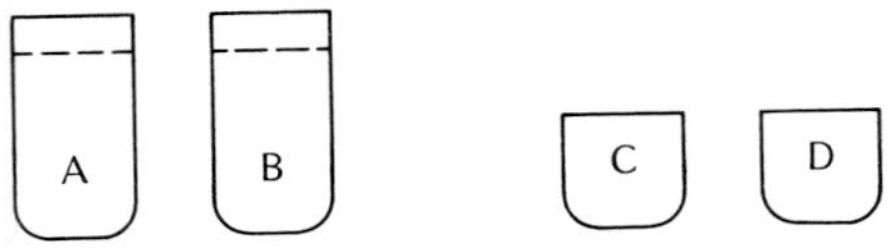

Set I   *Set II*

A. Suppose the water in glass A in Set I is
    poured into glasses C and D in Set II. Which
    set will then have more water?

☐ a. Set I.

☐ b. Set II.

☐ c. Not enough information is given.

☐ d. None of the above.

B. Explain your answer. _____

_____

_____

_____

9. There are three girls whose names are Ann, Elizabeth, and Mary. Suppose Ann is not as heavy as
   Elizabeth and Ann is heavier than Mary. Who is the heaviest of the three?

☐ a. Ann.

☐ b. Elizabeth.

☐ c. Mary.

☐ d. Not enough information is given.

Explain your answer. _____

_____

_____

_____

10. Imagine that a snail is placed on one end of a small board on a table. As the snail starts moving to the other end of the board, the board is being moved at the same speed in the opposite direction. As the snail arrives at the end of the board, how far will it have moved in relation to the table.

- [ ] a. End of the table.
- [ ] b. Same place.
- [ ] c. As far as the length of the board.
- [ ] d. Not enough information is given.

Explain your answer. _____

11. Shown below are two bowls half full of water, and two clay balls. The amounts of water in the two bowls are equal. The two clay balls are equal.

A. Suppose clay ball C is shaped into a block as shown in E, and then ball D is placed in bowl A and block E is placed in bowl B. What will happen to the water level in the bowls?

- [ ] a. Go up to the same level.
- [ ] b. Go down to the same level.
- [ ] c. Go up to different levels.
- [ ] d. Go down to different levels.

B. Explain your answer. _____

12. The diagram below represents a scale. Beside it are several rings representing balls of different weights for balancing the bar of the scale.

A. Suppose a four ounce ring was placed on the scale as shown at point 4 in the diagram. By using one of the weights below, show how the bar could be balanced.

- [ ] a. Place the 8 ounce ring on 2.
- [ ] b. Place the 4 ounce ring on 5.
- [ ] c. Place the 2 ounce ring on 2.
- [ ] d. None of the above.

B. Explain your answer. _____

13. Shown below is a pendulum made in the form of an object hanging from a string. Also shown are pendulums with different string lengths and different weights.

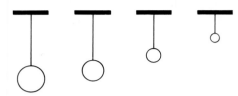

A. A science class made some trials to see if the pupils could find out what made the pendulum swing faster or slower. The following is a record of the class observations of swing.

Length	Weight	Rate	Comment
short	light	slow	false
short	heavy	fast	true
long	light	fast	false
long	light	slow	true
short	heavy	slow	false
short	light	fast	true
long	heavy	fast	false
long	heavy	slow	true

By studying the above table of observations, select the choice which seems best.

☐ a. It is the weight.

☐ b. It is the length.

☐ c. It is the combination of both.

☐ d. None of the above.

B. Explain your answer. _____

Answers: 1. c; 2. c; 3, 4. B C ⊏----⊐ ; 5. b; 6. a; 7. A a, B a, C c; 8. d; 9. b; 10. b; 11. a; 12. a; 13. b.

Summary

The definition of cognitive developmental stages is presented in contrast to the quantitative view of growth and change. Development is qualitative—great leaps forward followed by periods of integration rather than linear, step-by-step changes in degree.

Piaget's work, background, research procedures, and findings created a new and significant theory regarding the process of cognitive growth stages. The stages are defined by system of thinking employed and by modal age—sensorimotor, 0–24 months; preoperational/intuitive, 2–7 years; concrete operations, 7–11 years; formal-abstract, 11 years.

A basic Piagetian concept denotes the importance of activity as a central ingredient of intelligence. Active learning experiences tend to promote cognitive growth while passive and vicarious experiences tend to have minimal effects. "To know by heart is not to know."

The so-called "matching" question is presented in a more complex way than the old "readiness" principle. It is critical to understand the Piaget equation: Activity = Intelligence. The old readiness notion implied waiting around and then checking to see if the child was ready to learn—whether the so-called teachable moment had arrived. In the Piaget sense of the active school, it is inappropriate to wait. Instead, the learning environment is set to maximally interact with children. The active process gets the child "ready" for the next stage. Also, this is a way for an educator to answer the famous "American question"—i.e., Can we accelerate development? Curriculum materials and teaching should seek to promote rather than assume development.

A major goal of the chapter is to convey the notion that intelligence is not simply an in-born trait. Your role as educators is to battle that commonly held assumption. Also critical is the effect that such assumptions have on our attitudes toward the children we may someday teach. If you can realize that the activity channel is too often neglected as a major mode of learning, you may find an additional way to reach children and teenagers. Certainly the need to set up active school experiences to promote formal logical thinking in high school is obvious. The "hands on" approach is highly recommended, whereas the passive watching of plays, listening to orchestras, visiting museums, etc., is not viewed as having as much educational merit, beyond momentarily raising consciousness.

REFERENCES

1
M. B. McGraw, *Growth: A Study of Johnny and Jimmy* (New York: Appleton, 1935).

2
M. Pines, *A Revolution in Learning* (New York: Harper & Row, 1970).

3
A. Gesell, *The First Five Years of Life* (New York: Harper & Row, 1940).

4
M. Pines, *A Revolution in Learning*, p. 58.

5
J. Piaget, *Science of Education and the Psychology of the Child* (New York: Viking, 1970), p. 30.

6
J. Kagan and E. Haverman, *Psychology: An Introduction* (New York: Harcourt, 1968), p. 549.

7
J. Piaget, *Science of Education*, p. 30.

8
D. Elkind, *Children and Adolescents* (New York: Oxford Press, 1970), p. 54.

9
D. Elkind, *Children and Adolescents*, p. 59.

10
M. Wolfenstein, *Children's Humor* (Glencoe, Ill.: Free Press, 1954).

11
M. A. White, "The View from the Pupil's Desk," *Urban Review* 2 (1968):5–7.

12
J. Piaget, *Science and Education*, p. 34.

13
J. Piaget, *Science and Education*, p. 153.

14
L. Kohlberg and R. DeVries, "Relations between Piaget and Psychometric Assessments of Intelligence," in C. Lavatelli, ed., *The Natural Curriculum* (Urbana: University of Illinois Press, 1971).

7

Languge development

Learning to talk and to understand other people are among the most complex skills children acquire.* While language ability is, at least to some extent, biologically determined, humans are nevertheless the only animals to acquire a highly developed system of communication. Other animals communicate, to be sure. Many birds, for example, have elaborate songs, which both attract mates and announce an established breeding territory to other birds of the same species. Bees are able to communicate to other members of their hive both the direction and the relative distance of food sources. These forms, however, are extremely primitive when compared to human systems of communication.

Recently, psychologists have been engaged in rather extensive research to investigate the language potential of our closest relatives in the animal world, the great apes. Because chimpanzees are not physically able to produce the sounds used in human language, Gardner and Gardner taught a young female chimpanzee named Washoe the American Sign Language used by deaf persons. After four years of intensive training in a highly enriched environment, Washoe was able to understand several hundred signs and used over 130 of them, in many combinations.[1] In another study, Premack was able to teach a chimpanzee named Sarah to use plastic shapes of various colors for words. Some symbols represented objects, but others stood for action words like "give," or for rela-

The language potential of apes

*

This section was written especially for this volume by Dr. Robert F. MacLachlan, Professor of Psychology and Director of the Dexter Counseling Center, American International College.

149

tional words like "on." In earlier experiments, many primates had learned to associate symbols with objects. But Sarah went far beyond the previous accomplishments of other chimps. Not only was she able to understand and follow directions "written" for her, she also used the symbols to make up sentences of her own. Thus Sarah showed that chimpanzees have the capacity to utilize grammar, at least on a primitive level.[2]

Other studies are now in progress. To approximate as closely as possible the language experience of human infants, very young gorillas and chimpanzees are being raised by deaf persons, for whom the American Sign Language is a "native" language. We soon may find that the differences we have so long assumed to exist between apes and humans are not as great as we once believed. Yet it is only human beings who are capable of using language in an infinite fashion. The wide range of ideas and feelings we can relate to others, the subtle shades of meaning we are able to communicate, and the huge and varied written literature we have produced all are the results of a highly complex system of behaviors which only humans seem able to master.

In this chapter we shall consider what the field of psychology has learned about how children acquire speech. We examine some of the current theories of language to see what they have to offer the classroom teacher, and spend some time exploring the notion that children's language is different from that of adults. Children do *not* speak incorrect adult language; they speak child language, which follows the general principles of development discussed in earlier chapters of this book. The nature of child language and the changes that occur in child language at different levels of development are topics of considerable importance to the teacher.

PREVERBAL BEHAVIOR

Children do not usually begin to speak meaningful language before they are a year old. Yet during this first year, babies engage in a wide range of vocalizations. Crying is the first sound. By three months, most babies are *cooing*, a

Three infant cries: the pain cry, the hunger cry, the pleasure cry.

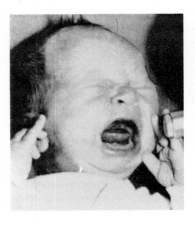 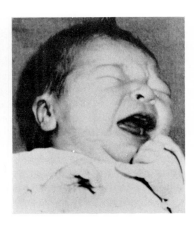 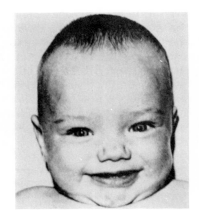

series of soft, primarily vowel sounds that seem to be produced when the baby is relaxed and content. Babies at this age also *gurgle*, speech which involves consonant as well as vowel sounds. In addition, babies become aware of the speech of others during these early months, and will stop their own vocalizing to listen to other people talking.

By six months, a new phase—*babbling*—occurs. Babbling may continue until the child is more than a year old and differs from cooing in several ways. First, the child spends much more time making sounds. Often he or she will babble while lying in the crib, before going to sleep or upon awakening. Secondly, new combinations of sounds appear. Where cooing seems to be highly unstructured, babbling usually consists of consonant and vowel sounds combined in syllables like *ka* and *di*. Lastly, at about eight or nine months of age, the child begins to string sounds together, repeating the same syllable patterns, such as "mi-mi-mi-mi-mi-mi-mi." Shirley, in her observations of babies, recorded babblings such as "bah-bah-bah" and "erdah-erdah." During this period babies also begin to vary the pitch and volume of the vocalizations, much in the manner of real speech.[3]

By six months of age, babbling occurs

Eric Lenneberg is a psychologist who has done extensive research on language development in children of different countries. Using a device called a sound spectrograph, which transforms sounds to wave patterns that can then be transcribed on paper, he obtained records of many sample infant vocalizations. These records show that there are distinct differences among the components of sounds made when a child is crying, cooing, or babbling. Furthermore, these sounds are different still from those made by a mother who tries to copy her child by responding with cooing or babbling sounds of her own. Because of the precision of such analyses, we know that infants make many more sounds while cooing and babbling than are used in the production of any one language.[4]

All children make prelinguistic sounds. Even deaf children babble, a fact that strongly suggests that early vocalizing may be innately biologically determined. Yet a study done a number of years ago showed that the rate at which three-month-old infants produce sounds can be increased by certain types of reinforcement, such as smiling or touching the infant whenever he or she makes a sound. When these reinforcements are no longer forthcoming, the rate of sound production returns to its original level.[5] Thus, environmental variables also contribute to the acquisition of language—and the nature-nurture phenomenon emerges again.

Environmetal variables contribute to language acquisition

THE BEGINNINGS OF CONVENTIONAL SPEECH

The sounds that infants produce while babbling are the basic units of spoken language. They are called *phonemes*. The number of phonemes used in the world's languages varies from under twenty to over eighty. In English, there are about forty-five phonemes.

The basic unit of meaning is called a *morpheme*. Many morphemes are words, like "boy" or "good" or "run." But when we add an *s* to "boy," we change the meaning of the word. "Boy" + *s* = more than one boy, i.e., "boys." Since it adds the concept of more than one to the original morpheme, plural *s* is also a morpheme. In similar fashion, we put "pre" before the word "pay"—

The sounds children most frequently hear adults use are not always those they speak first.

prepay—to convey the notion of an action that occurs before a given point in time. Morphemes, then, may be root words, prefixes, or suffixes. Morphemes consist of one or more phonemes.

During the early decades of the study of child development, most psychologists assumed that when basic speech sounds were practiced and learned well enough, children would combine them in imitation of the language they heard and would begin to speak words. Early psychologists assumed that language is a continuous process of imitation, beginning with phonemes, progressing onward to morphemes and words, and finally to combinations of words, phrases, and sentences. Yet current research indicates that this continuous theory of language is almost certainly wrong.

Babbling has little to do with the development of complex language

Several facts lead us to believe that babbling has very little to do with the development of more complex language. First, although deaf children babble in very similar fashion to hearing children, they do not progress on to conventional speech without much effort and special training.

Second, the sounds children most frequently hear adults use are not always those they speak first. For example, while s is one of the phonemes used most by adults, it is one of the last phonemes to emerge in children's speech. Prelinguistic consonant sounds tend to be ones like g and k, which are made at the back of the mouth. In early speech, however, these consonants do not occur. Rather, children use consonants like p and m, sounds formed at the front of the mouth. It seems evident, therefore, that children use different sounds in early speech than they have been practicing while babbling.[6]

LENNEBERG: THE BIOLOGICAL FOUNDATIONS OF LANGUAGE

Eric Lenneberg, in the process of studying language acquisition in children all over the world, has given us a cogent explanation for the apparent discontinuity in language development. He has discovered consistent, regular, and fixed developmental patterns of language in all normal children, language "milestones," as he calls them, that occur in the same sequences and at the same time the world over, regardless of the cultural environment of the child. A Chinese child, a central African child, and a child growing up in London have nearly identical patterns of speech development. Furthermore, these language milestones parallel a sequence of milestones in motor development.

Table 7.1 Lenneberg's description of language development showing how it is synchronized with motor development.

At the completion of:	Motor development	Vocalization and Language
12 weeks	Supports head when in prone position; weight is on elbows; hands mostly open; no grasp reflex.	Markedly less crying than at 8 weeks; when talked to and nodded at, smiles, followed by squealing-gurgling sounds usually called *cooing*, which is vowel-like in character and pitch-modulated; sustains cooing for 15–20 seconds.
16 weeks	Plays with a rattle placed in hands (by shaking it and staring at it), head self-supported; tonic neck reflex subsiding.	Responds to human sounds more definitely; turns head; eyes seem to search for speaker; occasionally some chuckling sounds.
20 weeks	Sits with props.	The vowel-like cooing sounds begin to be interspersed with more consonantal sounds; labial fricatives, spirants and nasals are common; acoustically, all vocalizations are very different from the sounds of the mature language of the environment.
6 months	Sitting: bends forward and uses hands for support; can bear weight when put into standing position, but cannot yet stand without holding on; reaching: unilateral; grasp: no thumb apposition yet; releases cube when given another.	Cooing changing into babbling resembling one-syllable utterances; neither vowels nor consonants have very fixed recurrences; most common utterances sound somewhat like ma, mu, da, or di.
8 months	Stands holding on; grasps with thumb apposition; picks up pellet with thumb and finger tips.	Reduplication (or more continuous repetitions) becomes frequent; intonation patterns become distinct; utterances can signal emphasis and emotions.

At the comple-tion of:	Motor development	Vocalization and Language
10 months	Creeps efficiently; takes side-steps, holding on; pulls to standing position.	Vocalizations are mixed with sound-play such as gurgling or bubble-blowing; appears to wish to imitate sounds, but the imitations are never quite successful; beginning to differentiate between words heard by making differential adjustment.
12 months	Walks when held by one hand; walks on feet and hands—knees in air; mouthing of objects almost stopped; seats self on floor.	Identical sound sequences are replicated with higher relative frequency of occurrence and words (mamma or dadda) are emerging; definite signs of understanding some words and simple commands (show me your eyes).
18 months	Grasp, prehension, and release fully developed; gait stiff, propulsive, and precipitated; sits on child's chair with only fair aim; creeps downstairs backward; has difficulty building tower of three cubes.	Has a definite repertoire of words —more than three, but less than fifty; still much babbling but now of several syllables with intricate intonation pattern; no attempt at communicating information and no frustration for not being understood; words may include items such as thank you or come here, but there is little ability to join any of the lexical items into spontaneous two-item phrases; understanding is progressing rapidly.
24 months	Runs, but falls in sudden turns; can quickly alternate between sitting and stance; walks stairs up or down, one foot forward only.	Vocabulary of more than fifty items (some children seem to be able to name everything in environment); begins spontaneously to join vocabulary items into two-word phrases; all phrases appear to be own creations; definite increase in communicative behavior and interest in language.
30 months	Jumps up into air with both feet; stands on one foot for about two seconds; takes few steps on tiptoe; jumps from chair; good hand and finger coordination; can move	Fastest increase in vocabulary with many new additions every day; no babbling at all; utterances have communicative intent; frustrated if not understood by adults;

At the comple-tion of:	Motor development	Vocalization and Language
	digits independently; manipulation of objects much improved; builds tower of six cubes.	utterances consist of at least two words, many have three or even five words; sentences and phrases have characteristic child grammar, that is, they are rarely verbatim repetitions of an adult utterance; intelligibility is not very good yet, though there is great variation among children; seems to understand everything that is said to him or her.
3 years	Tiptoes three yards; runs smoothly with acceleration and deceleration; negotiates sharp and fast curves without difficulty; walks stairs by alternating feet; jumps 12 inches; can operate tricycle.	Vocabulary of some 1000 words; about 80% of utterances are intelligible even to strangers; grammatical complexity of utterances is roughly that of colloquial adult language, although mistakes still occur.
4 years	Jumps over rope; hops on right foot; catches ball in arms; walks line.	Language is well-established; deviations from the adult norm tend to be more in style than in grammar.

For example, the typical six-month-old baby can sit alone and can bear weight when put in a standing position, but cannot stand holding on to support. At this same point in development, the infant's language is changing from cooing to a form of babbling which is principally one syllable in nature. Lenneberg considers this progression of development to be genetically determined and maturational in nature. Consequently, practice is of little importance. Because it has great functional importance, Lenneberg feels that the biological language system is highly resistant to disruption. Deaf children, for example, can learn written language even though they have never heard spoken language. Even children who are severely neglected, or otherwise deprived, learn language. Furthermore, children with unusually slow maturational processes, such as those with Downs' syndrome (or mongolism, as it is sometimes called) develop language in the same *order* as normal children, but at a lower rate, parallel to their physical maturation.[7]

Lenneberg also argues that there appears to be a critical period for language development between infancy and adolescence. Children up to the age of puberty can learn to speak more than one language, or even several languages, fluently and with relative ease. Adolescents and adults, on the other hand, usually must study a language to learn it and rarely acquire the fluency of a native-born speaker. The children of families living in a foreign country usually learn the language of the country much faster than their parents, and often serve as family interpreters. In addition to having difficulty learning a new language, adults rarely can overcome a "foreign accent," as Cary Grant and Henry Kissinger illustrate. Such a critical-periods hypothesis lends support to teaching foreign languages in elementary schools, or even earlier, particularly when a conversational approach is used.

While it does not seem probable that all language acquisition is innate, Lenneberg's research has provided a substantial amount of data indicating that underlying biological determinants permit human beings to acquire language. His contribution is particularly important because it gives considerable support to the work of others, notably Noam Chomsky, who have, in other contexts, postulated such biological determinants of language development.

Underlying biological determinants permit humans to acquire language

SOME THEORIES OF LANGUAGE DEVELOPMENT

Until quite recently, the study of language development was relatively simple and straightforward. Psychologists gauged a child's progress in language by such observable measures as the increasing number of words used and the length and complexity of the sentences produced. In an early study, M. E. Smith assessed the vocabulary of children of different ages. She found that the typical one-year-old can speak three words; an average two-year-old, 272 words; and a six-year-old, about 2500 words.[8] To measure a child's growth in other aspects of language, sentences were analyzed into grammatical parts. The use of complex sentences with clauses, for example, was considered more mature language than the use of simple compound sentences.

Until about twenty years ago, psychologists, in the American behaviorist tradition, were generally interested only in what children did, rather than in what they seemed to understand. Yet while a year-old infant may speak only three words, the child understands a great many more. The child can respond to a large number of statements and requests, and clearly is much more knowledgeable about language than a three-word vocabulary would indicate. But psychologists, under the influence of J. B. Watson's dictum to study only what can be directly observed, did not concern themselves with trying to understand what was going on within the child.

The principal explanation of the behaviorists for language development was that language, like almost every other human behavior, conformed to the laws of associative learning. Psychologists used such concepts as classical conditioning, discrimination learning, association, and generalization to explain the various aspects of learning to talk. Perhaps the most influential of the learning theorists to study language acquisition is B. F. Skinner, whose book *Verbal Behavior* was published in 1957.[9] We will discuss Skinner in great detail in Chapters 12 and 13; at this point, only those aspects of his theories which pertain to language acquisition will be examined.

Behaviorists view language development as conforming to the laws of associative learning

LANGUAGE DEVELOPMENT: A BEHAVIORIST VIEW

Skinner had earlier postulated a powerful theory of learning. A large number of human behaviors or responses are spontaneous—they are not elicited by particular stimuli. Skinner terms such behaviors *operants,* and calls their rather consistent rates of occurrence, *operant levels.* The rate at which a particular operant is produced may be increased if the behavior is followed immediately by a stimulus like food, called a *reinforcing stimulus.* Many different stimuli may have reinforcing properties. For an infant, his or her bottle, the presence of mother, or pleasant, soothing sounds all may be reinforcing.

Skinner has shown that reinforcing stimuli, when consistently presented immediately following operant behavior, will substantially increase that behavior's frequency of occurrence. As long as the reinforcement is continued, a high level of responding is maintained. Whenever the reinforcement is discontinued, however, the rate of responding decreases, ultimately falling back to the original operant level. Such a process of decreasing response level is called *extinction.*

According to Skinner, the babbling behavior of babies is an operant. He feels that parents selectively reinforce those sounds that are most like the sounds of adult language, thereby causing the baby to make these particular sounds more frequently. At first, parents reinforce sounds that barely resemble words. For example, when a baby babbles "deh-deh," parents may sponteneously react with pleasure at the prospect of the child saying "Daddy." Their pleasure is reinforcing and the baby begins to make the sounds more frequently. Increasingly, parental reinforcement is elicited only as the sounds the child emits more closely

According to Skinner, the babbling behavior of babies is an operant. Parents selectively reinforce those sounds that are most like the sounds of adult language, and the baby therefore repeats those sounds more frequently.

approximate the real word. "Dah-dah" rather than "deh-deh" may next be re-inforced, and later, only "dah-di," and so on.

Skinner calls this process of reinforcing by increasingly precise approxima-tions *shaping*. Not only do parents shape words, they also shape sentences. Furthermore, Skinner believes children are able to recognize when their own sounds resemble those of their parents. This awareness is satisfying and therefore reinforcing. Thus, according to Skinner, language can be acquired by self-rein-forcement, as well as by reinforcement from others.

Autoclitic frame permits child to expand language by generalizing

As development continues, the child acquires other verbal devices that in-crease the level of verbal skills. One such device is a partial sentence, called an autoclitic frame, which permits children to expand their ability to talk by the process of generalization. For example, a child may say, "Me want candy." When this response is reinforced, perhaps by receiving a piece of candy, "me want" becomes an autoclitic frame. By substituting, the child can now say "Me want water" or "Me want ball." Shaping also continues to be effective in helping the child acquire more precise language; "Me want ball" will ultimately, according to Skinner, be shaped to "I want the ball." The child also learns to associate particular environmental cues or situations with certain speech re-sponses. "Mommy" is early associated with one particular person; "bye-bye" may be associated with people leaving, or perhaps with riding in a car. Later, the child begins to say "please" when he or she wants something and "thank you" when it is provided. Such associations are usually taught by others, but children also learn such relationships by observing and imitating the adults around them.

Other behavioristic learning theorists have modified Skinner's ideas to a cer-tain extent, using more complex learning models to explain certain kinds of verbal behavior. Yet all these theorists share a common approach to language: each sees the child as passively responding to environmental stimuli and re-gards language acquisition as primarily the result of reinforcements initiated by other people, not the product of the child's own pursuit and active intention.

Learning theory does not deal with the question of language growth

Learning theory offers us a rather useful explanation of how vocabulary and some spoken aspects of language are acquired. It does not, however, seem able to deal with many of the questions that arise in our attempts to understand language growth. For answers to such problems as how the child comes to use new combinations of words never before heard, we must turn to another theo-retical approach.

PSYCHOLINGUISTIC THEORIES

Psychologists have not had a monopoly on the study of language. Linguists for many years have been interested in both the structure of language and in seman-tics, the study of the meaning of words and word groups. As psychologists and linguists became more aware of their parallel interests, they began to combine efforts, and ultimately created the field of psycholinguistics. As a discipline, psy-cholinguistics attempts to study both the structure of language and the ways in which language is acquired and used.

The partnership of psychology and linguistics has been a lively one. Psycholinguists have asked many searching questions challenging some of the basic assumptions of psychology, and psychologists have had to reassess their thinking on a number of fundamental issues. In particular, those notions of the learning theorists regarding language acquisition have been seriously attacked.

Psycholoinguistics is a highly technical discipline. It has developed complex theoretical systems and workers within the field have gathered extensive amounts of data. To summarize such findings and theories would be nearly impossible. Yet in order to understand the impact of psycholinguistics, it is necessary to look at some of the most powerful concepts which psycholinguists have developed. We then can attempt to see why these notions have made such an impact on our attempts to understand how children acquire language.

The partnership of psychology and linguistics

THE CONCEPT OF INFINITE GENERATIVITY

In every language, established rules govern how words are put together. The ways in which we make sentences, ask questions, or change the tenses of verbs are all prescribed by rules of grammar and syntax. Grammatical rules are generally both complex and subtle. Yet all children come to use them with astonishing ease and speed, not only to understand the communications of others, but also to create language of their own. Linguists feel that knowing a language means first of all being able to use its grammatical rules. Without rules, a person can only imitate what he or she hears. Being able to use the rules allows a person to create, to speak, and to understand an unlimited number of sentences.

Most of the sentences we hear or speak, read or write, are sentences we have never seen before. You, the reader, are able to understand this particular sentence even though it is new to you. And you are able to put together sentences you have never heard or seen, enabling you to communicate a new idea or experience to others. Thus, in a manner of speaking, language is a continuous process of creativity. By using a relatively small, finite set of rules, a person is able to create and produce a nearly limitless number of meaningful sentences. Linguists call this quality of language *infinite generativity*.

A finite set of rules can generate a limitless number of meaningful sentences

PERFORMANCE AND COMPETENCE

For a number of years, linguists, Noam Chomsky in particular,[10] have distinguished between language *performance* and language *competence*. Language performance is what people do when they speak. For small children, performance is often only a poorly articulated word, or perhaps a combination of words such as "Me good," or "allgone bottle." Even adults often use imperfect speech: sentences are left unfinished, words are omitted, subjects do not agree with verbs, word order or form varies from what the rules of grammar dictate. Furthermore, when one is tired, upset, or under the influence of alcohol or other drugs, one's language may become even more inexact and ambiguous.

Because of the imperfections of spoken speech, psycholinguists feel that explanations for the growth of language skills which are based primarily on the process of imitation are not very substantial. Children have a bewildering number of highly variable and inexact models to imitate. If such models were our principal source of learning language, no one would ever learn to speak correctly. A recent study has shown that children apparently learn to speak more quickly when their parents respond to the content of their speech, rather than when parents attempt to correct or enlarge children's imperfect speech efforts.[11] For example, when a small girl asks a question like, "What you doed last morning?" it seems more helpful to tell her about what you did yesterday morning than to correct the errors in her question. The most telling argument against the influence of imitation, however, is that most of children's speech appears to be original, not imitative.

Because language performance is overt behavior, it is the aspect of language growth most studied by American psychologists. Linguists, however, maintain that the essential measure of language growth is not observable language behavior, but rather the nonobservable phenomenon of language competence— i.e., the underlying knowledge of the structure and rules of language. According to linguistic theory, language competence is what makes language performance possible. Competence includes such things as a person's judgment about which sentences are grammatical and which are not; or the ability to decide which sentences are ambiguous and which ones have a clear meaning. Competence also includes knowledge of how language should sound, and knowledge of the meaning of words and sentences.

Language perfor-mance versus language competence

Piaget has theorized about one aspect of language competence, the knowledge of meaning. He feels that language and thinking are closely related; for him, language is an outgrowth of the child's development of general cognitive abilities, of the ability to think. At first, words do not stand for anything; sound is merely an aspect of a whole situation, much as shape and color are for the child. At some point during the latter half of the first year, however, the infant discovers that words stand for something else—he or she acquires an understanding of the symbolic nature of words.[12] Bruner suggests a similar notion when he talks about symbolic representation (see Chapter 12).

Piaget and Bruner, however, are notable exceptions. Because language competence is not directly observable, it has not been studied extensively by psychologists. Psycholinguists, on the other hand, have persuasively argued that only by attempting to study competence will we acquire real knowledge of how the growth of language proceeds. Increasingly, researchers are focusing on methods to study this underlying aspect of language development.

STRUCTURE

In the same way that phonemes can be grouped into morphemes and words, words can be grouped into phrases. Linguists often describe a sentence by its *phrase structure,* an analysis of how the various phrases in the sentence are organized. Phrase structure can be represented by diagrams called phrase markers.

In Fig. 7.1, two sentences are analyzed into their phrase structures. The phrase markings show how the words are related to each other and what part each plays in the sentence.

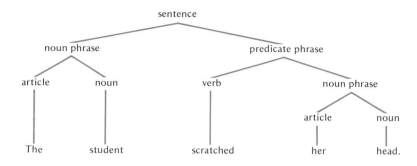

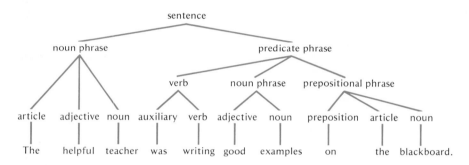

Fig. 7.1 Two sentences analyzed into their phrase structures.

According to Noam Chomsky, there are rules for combining words into phrases and phrases into sentences. One such rule is that a sentence (S) consists of a noun phrase (NP) and a predicate phrase (PredP). Such a rule may be expressed by S ⟶ NP + PredP. Because this rule is an instruction to rewrite the left-hand symbol with those on the right-hand side, it is called a *rewrite rule*. Another rewrite rule might be that a noun phrase (NP) consists of an article (Art) plus a noun (N): NP ⟶ Art + N; and a predicate phrase (PredP) consists of a verb (V) and a noun phrase (NP): PredP ⟶ V + NP. By using a relatively small series of rewrite rules, we can generate an infinite series of sentences, merely substituting different words or phrases into the appropriate part of the rule. Because these rules focus on phrases, they are called *phrase-structure rules.*

Phrase structures also show us how words in a sentence are grouped, and where we should pause as we talk. Using the first phrase structure diagram in Fig. 7.1, we would say: (The student) (scratched) (her head). (The student) (scratched her) (head) or (The) (student scratched) (her head) would both be rejected as not meaningful or illogical. Even when we speak without pausing correctly, there is evidence that people listening tend to hear the pauses where they should occur. The results of one study suggest that in ordinary conversation a listener does not perceive each word separately. A person hears each phrase rather than each word as a primary unit of meaning, including the pauses oc- curring at either side of each phrase, whether or not they were spoken in that fashion.[13] The effects of phrase structure are also seen in the way we store in- formation in our memories. In another study subjects were given a word from a sentence they had memorized and were asked to recall the word that followed. When the second word was in the same phrase as the cue word, it was recalled more quickly than when it was in the following phrase. This suggests that sen- tences are remembered with their phrase structures intact.[14]

TRANSFORMATIONAL GRAMMAR

As we have seen, by determining the phrase structure of a spoken sentence, we can analyze the actual sound sequence of that sentence. But consider these two sentences: "Emily asked the teacher a question"; and, "A question was asked of the teacher by Emily." Although the phrase structures of these two sentences are quite different, they obviously mean the same thing. According to Chomsky, every sentence has two levels of linguistic structure. The *surface structure* is the precise order in which the words are spoken; the *deep structure* is the mean- ing or underlying abstract concept of the sentence. The two sentences above have different surface structures but the same deep structure. Now consider this example: "Entertaining friends can be a pleasure." This is an ambiguous sen- tence. One possible meaning is that it may be pleasurable to have friends who entertain us. Or, it may mean that it can be rewarding to entertain friends. In the first, we are *being* entertained; in the second we are *doing* the entertaining. Here, then, we have one surface structure with two deep structures. Two sep- arate ideas have been formulated in the same manner.

Chomsky postulates that in order to communicate an idea, or deep struc- ture, we change or transform the deep structure to a surface structure by apply- ing a set of rewrite rules called *transformational rules.* These rules allow us to translate into precise spoken or written language (surface structure) ideas that exist only in our minds and are thus unknowable to others (deep structure) until they are translated into language (surface structure).

Transformational rules apply to the relationships among the possible sen- tences that can be generated by an idea or deep structure in the same way that phrase-structure rules apply to relationships among words. These two sets of rules comprise what Chomsky calls *transformational grammar.* They are the rules by which people change their own ideas into spoken language, and by which they also understand the meaning of other people's spoken or written communication.

Despite the complexities of the underlying grammatical structure of a lan- guage, children seem to acquire the use of grammar in nearly adult fashion by the time they are four.[15] In a famous review of B. F. Skinner's book *Verbal*

Surface structure is the order in which words are spoken; deep structure is the underlying meaning of the sentence

Behavior, Chomsky clashed strongly not only with Skinner but with the whole learning-theory approach to language. Chomsky argues that the ability to convey and understand meaning, which, as we have seen, he calls deep structure is the essential feature of language use. Deep structure is never directly spoken or heard—only the transformations of deep structure into surface structure are spoken and heard. Consequently, deep structure can never be imitated or reinforced. Yet the child still manages to acquire the rules of transformational grammar before beginning school. In addition, Chomsky points out that to acquire sufficient stimulus-response connections to explain human language proficiency would require more time than the average lifespan would allow.[16] Chomsky proposes instead that the human nervous system contains innate mechanisms that make it possible for the child to construct the rules of language. Since these mechanisms are innate, the same rules should appear in the same sequence for every child initially, later being modified to fit the particular rules of his or her own language. Thus, according to Chomsky, all children acquire language in a biologically determined, maturational manner, much as they learn to walk.[17]

Deep structure can never be imitated or reinforced

While he does not specify the neurological mechanisms by which such development takes place, Chomsky's hypothesis has been strengthened by other researchers, who have been more specific. Lenneberg, creator of the language-milestones concept, has probably given the most important support to Chomsky's position. Lenneberg feels that language ability is an inherited characteristic specific to the species *Homo sapiens.* On the basis of the considerable universality of patterns of language growth in children around the world, he proposes that particular brain centers exist which enable human beings to acquire language. He points out that only humans have the vocal apparatus to produce so many sounds. Furthermore, he notes that we have a specialized auditory system to process speech sounds—nonspeech sounds are processed differently.

Lenneberg supports Chomsky—language ability is an inherited characteristic of Homo sapiens

Alvin Liberman, a psychologist who has extensively investigated ways in which we both construct and perceive speech sounds, has shown that we can process many more phonemes than nonspeech sounds in the same interval of time. He has also shown that we perceive and classify phonemes quite differently than we perceive nonspeech sounds, even when the phonemes are electronically synthesized and thus are not part of normal speech.[18] Other research indicates that infants as young as one month of age appear to distinguish between the human voice and other sounds in their environments[19] and can also tell the difference between *p* and *b.*[20] It is common observation that young children acquire rules for making plurals and past tenses. That the child is using rules becomes obvious when he or she applies them to words that are irregularly inflected; that is, words whose plurals or past tenses do not follow the rules. Children often say "goed" for "went," "runned" for "ran," or "gooses" for "geese." Sometimes a child will use both a correct form and an incorrect one in the same sentence, as "I did it yesterday, and I doed it before, too."

Children acquire rules for making plurals and past tenses

The application of a grammatical rule in such an overgeneralized fashion also occurs among children who speak German, Russian, and other languages.[21] Since words like "gooses" or "runned" are made up by the child and do not occur in the language, neither the theory of imitation nor that of reinforcement can explain why such speech should be universal. In other words, children from a variety of cultures make the same cultural mistakes in language usage at particular stages of development. These "errors" are not random and are not modeled by adults.

Studies of this sort, and others like them, have given considerable credence to Chomsky's notion that many aspects of language development are innately determined and maturational in nature. Such support, at the same time, has tended to diminish the influence of learning theory as the principal explanation of how children acquire language. In one study Roger Brown and his co-workers at Harvard recorded many verbal interchanges between parents and children and observed that parents tend to respond to the content of a child's communication, rather than to its form.[22] Much of a child's early speech tends to be incorrect grammatically. Therefore, by responding, parents often reinforce ungrammatical speech. If the child says, "Sister not a boy, he a girl," a parent might reply, "That's right," because sister is, in fact, a girl. If, on the other hand, the child speaks a perfect grammatical sentence like "The snow is warm," a parent would probably disagree. Yet despite the reinforcement of ungrammatical speech, the child still learns to speak correctly. Parents tend to respond to deep structure rather than to surface structure, thereby, without realizing it, supporting Chomsky and reducing the influence of Skinner in this particular area.

The evidence at this point clearly implies that *early* language development is primarily innately determined. On the other hand, vocabulary and many of the spoken aspects of language seem to be influenced considerably by learning.

The evidence at this point clearly implies that *early* language development is primarily innately determined. While the exact mechanisms by which this development occurs have yet to be specified, the insights of the psycholinguists and the studies their theories have prompted give strong support to the role of biological determination. Yet all children do not learn to speak the same language. A Russian child learns Russian and an American child learns English. Obviously, therefore, the language one hears influences the acquisition of speech.

The role of learning seems important in other ways, too. Regional differences in speech are undoubtedly a result of imitation, perhaps reinforced by social factors. John Kennedy's broad Boston accent or the soft drawl of Dinah Shore are well-known examples of how speech varies from location to location. People who move from one area of the country to another often acquire the speech patterns of their new region. The ideas of learning theory can also help us in teaching language. One successful method for improving language performance in preschool children relies heavily on imitation, repetition, and reinforcement.[23,24]

The role of learning in language development

We do not, of course, have all the answers about how children learn language. Probably the best way to assess the data thus far accummulated is to say that grammar and those aspects of language related to structure seem to be primarily the product of heredity, while vocabulary and many of the spoken aspects of language seem to be considerably influenced by learning.

SPEECH DEVELOPMENT

The first word

The child's first meaningful word is generally spoken around the age of one year. Some children begin talking as early as nine months, while others may not begin using words until they are eighteen months. First words are not always recognizable, for infants frequently use unique and novel combinations of sounds to represent some idea. The context and the intonation help to convey meaning. For example, a baby girl who sees a bottle and says in a straightforward manner "bah-bah" seems to be identifying or labelling her bottle. If on another occasion her voice rises as she says "bah-bah?", we may guess that she is asking for her bottle. If she bangs her hands on the tray of her highchair and yells "bah-bah!" in a complaining voice, it seems pretty clear that she's hungry for her milk. Even though the child is using only one word, she is able to convey a whole sentence of meaning. Such one-word sentences are known as *holophrases*, and are common forms of early speech.

Holophrase: child's one-word sentence

The first sentence

For several months after speaking a first word, the child acquires only a few new words. Speech is still not an extensive part of general behavior. Some children say their first words before they have learned to walk. These children often cease talking altogether while mastering walking, almost as though they are unable to concentrate on two such complex endeavors at the same time.

Around the age of eighteen months, children begin to learn to speak a great many more words, and by two years they are combining two words together in a sentence. For a while, the total language output consists of one-word and two-word sentences. Later, words in combination appear and the length of sentences increases. Observations of this sort were among the earliest made in the study of language. Those studies that described increasing language competence in the form of charts and tables, such as the one by M. E. Smith mentioned on page 156, have been called *count studies,* and obviously are relatively unsophisticated.[25]

Under the increasing influence of psycholinguistic theories, psychologists in the past decade have been looking at the development of speech patterns in a new way. Rather than merely assessing vocabulary size and sentence length in the manner of the early counters, researchers have begun to look at children's language as if it were a foreign language. This new outlook assumes that the child is not speaking imperfect adult language, but rather is speaking qualitatively valid child language. How the child puts words together and what rules he or she uses are as important as which words are actually employed. To put it another way, the child's developing grammar is of as much concern as is his or her vocabulary. Operating within a qualitative-developmental-stage framework, psychologists studying language growth no longer view children as midget-sized adults. To understand the child, we need to understand his or her unique system of language.

Child speaks child language, not imperfect adult language

PIVOT GRAMMAR

One of the first people to notice the structure of children's early speech was Martin Braine. He studied the early word combinations of three children: Gregory, Andrew, and Steven. In analyzing the two-word combinations of these children, Braine discovered that there were a few words the children used very frequently. These *pivot words,* as Braine called them, were combined with many other words to make a large number of two-word sentences. One child, Gregory, used "my," "see," and "allgone" as pivot words, forming sentences like "see boy," "see boat," "my mommy," "my daddy," "allgone shoe," "allgone egg."[26] Children always use pivot words in the same position. Usually they come first, although a pivot word like "it" is used last—"push it," or "do it." By using a pivot word and another open-class word, termed an *X-word,* a child can construct a wide range of sentences. Given the rule "Pivot word—X word," the child can also create sentences adults never use. Gregory, for example, said "byebye hot." This sentence communicates an idea effectively in a manner quite alien to adult speech. Braine's study demonstrated that children at a very early age are using rules of grammar. Some of these rules will continue to be used as the child's speech patterns mature; others are used only when the child is young. Braine also demonstrated how pivot grammar enables children to create word combinations they have not previously heard.

Using only two words, a child is able to communicate a variety of ideas. He or she can locate or name something, "there book"; ask for something, "want gum"; or describe an event, "hit ball." Before long, the child can ask a question, "where ball?" and express negation, "no wash." Cross-cultural studies show that children's speech is remarkably similar the world over, in form and sequence as well as in the functions it serves.[27]

Table 7.2 Functions of two-word sentences in child speech, with examples from several languages.

Function of utterance	English	German	Russian	Samoan
Locate, name	there book that car see doggie	buch da [book there] gukuk wauwau [see doggie]	Tosya tam [Tosya there]	Keith lea [Keith there]
Demand, desire	want gum more milk give candy	mehr milch [more milk] bitte apfel [please apple]	yeshchë moloko [more milk] day chasy [give watch]	mai pepe [give doll] fia moe [want sleep]
Negate	no wet no wash not hungry allgone milk	nicht blasen [not blow] kaffee nein [coffee no]	vody net [water no] gus' tyu-tyu [goose gone]	le 'ai [not eat] uma mea [allgone thing]
Describe event or situation	Bambi go mail come hit ball block fall baby highchair	puppe kommt [doll comes] tiktak hängt [clock hangs] sofa sitzen [sofa sit] messer schneiden [cut knife]	mama prua [mama walk] papa bay-bay [papa sleep] korka upala [crust fell] nashia yaichko [found egg] baba kreslo [grandma armchair]	pa'u pepe [fall doll] tapale 'oe [hit you] tu'u lalo [put down]
Indicate possesion	my shoe mama dress	mein ball [my ball] mamas hut [mama's hat]	mami chashka [mama's cup] pup moya [navel my]	lole a'u [candy my] polo 'oe [ball your] paluni mama [balloon mama]
Modify, qualify	pretty dress big boat	milch heiss [milk hot] armer wauwau [poor dog]	mama khoroshaya [mama good] papa bol'shoy [papa big]	fa'ali'i pepe [headstrong baby]
Question	where ball	wo ball [where ball]	gde papa [where papa]	fea Punafu [where Punafu]

Source: D. I. Slobin, *Psycholinguistics* (Glenview, Illinois: Scott, Foresman, 1971). Reprinted by permission.

> While most of the child's acquisition of grammar
> seems to occur in the early years, some complex
> syntax patterns are acquired only in middle childhood.

TELEGRAPHIC SPEECH

Roger Brown studied the language of three children—Adam, Sarah, and Eve—over an extended period of time.[28] As would be expected, the length and complexity of the children's speech increased as they grew older. One of the most interesting facts to emerge from his study, however, was that children often omit words that would be found in adult speech. Such omissions do not seem to be random. Children leave out words like "of" or "the," as well as word endings like "ed" or "s," which are not very important to the meaning of the sentence. They emphasize, however, words that are important to the meaning they want to express. Such words are called *content words*. Even when they are imitating the speech of their parents, children make these omissions. A child who hears his father ask, "Where is Daddy's coat?" may repeat "Where Daddy coat?" Such abbreviated speech, often called *telegraphic speech,* has been found to be remarkably similar among children from many different cultures.[29]

Children omit words unimportant to the message they want to convey

While children can produce a large variety of word combinations in their early language, because of its telegraphic nature, early speech is often ambiguous. "Mommy, shoe" might mean "Mommy, give me my shoe" or "Mommy is putting on my shoe" or "That's Mommy's shoe." To fully understand the child's meaning, we often need to know the context in which the speech is occurring. Researchers are currently recording children's language by means of videotape, thus preserving such nonauditory cues as the situation, the child's facial expression, and the intonation of his or her voice.

COMPLEX SENTENCES

By age three, sentences are longer and more grammatically complex

By the time children are three years of age, they are constructing sentences that are both longer and grammatically more sophisticated than the two-year-old's pivot sentences. "My dress" is expanded to "my pretty dress" by adding a modifier. Next, children begin to use phrases within a sentence: "I want to do it" or "When Daddy come to home?" The complex process of transforming a simple declarative sentence into a question is mastered. At first children simply add a question word, "Where my ball?" Then they begin to use auxiliary verbs, "Where my ball is?" Finally, they transform the word order, "Where is my ball?"

While most of the child's acquisition of grammar seems to occur in the early years, some complex syntax patterns are acquired only in middle childhood. In one recent study, five-year-old children were given a blindfolded doll and asked, "Is the doll easy to see or hard to see?" Most of them did not understand the question and replied that the doll was hard to see. When the children were asked to make the doll easy to see, they removed the blindfold. Nine-year-old children, on the other hand, understood the first question and typically responded that the doll was easy to see. When asked to make the doll hard to see, they blocked their own eyes.[30]

SEMANTICS AND COGNITIVE DEVELOPMENT

As the above discussion indicates, there has been increasing and valuable emphasis on trying to assess the meaning of a child's language. The term linguists give to that aspect of language which involves meaning and understanding is *semantics,* a particularly complex area to categorize. While it is obviously a part of language, what a child means is also a product of his or her thought processes.

At present, cognitive theorists are extending their research into the area of language development. We have already mentioned Piaget's notion that language development is a part of a broader general cognitive development and semantic development. In a recent study, rather than analyzing vocabulary into the parts of speech traditionally used to describe adult language—such as nouns, verbs, and adjectives—the vocabularies of eighteen children between ages one and two were analyzed into categories representing different functions. While a small percentage of their words were action words or modifiers, about two-thirds of their vocabulary consisted of words naming things and people. These children did not seem to acquire words simply by hearing them. Rather, they learned words related to things they could play with or manipulate. Furthermore, children who had more experiences with other people or more experiences outside their homes developed vocabulary more quickly. Piaget believes that children develop concepts in just this manner—by interacting with their environments. Each child seemed to have a specialty area where he or she knew a number of words: Paul knew the names of several animals, even though his total vocabulary was only thirty words; Jane knew the names of different types of food, although she had mastered only fifty words. No child, however, had any words to represent higher-level concepts, words called *superordinate words.* Paul did not use the word "animal," nor did Jane use "food." We know that superordinate concepts do not develop in children until they are close to school age. This study seems to indicate that the kinds of experiences a child has may influence not only the growth of specific concepts, but also the development of language.[31]

Piaget was one of the first psychologists to be aware of differences between children's thought processes and those of adults. Since he believes that language is an aspect of thoughts, it is not surprising that Piaget also noticed parallel differences in language development as well. Piaget observed that while language is primarily used to communicate with others, all language does not seem communicative. Even adults sometimes talk aloud when no one is present, and children, Piaget has observed, often seem to use language for reasons other than communication. He called such noncommunicative language *egocentric speech.*

The term "egocentric" does not here denote selfish or conceited; rather, Piaget means that the child is focused on himself or herself because cognitive development has not proceeded sufficiently far for the child to understand someone else's point of view. As noted in Chapter 6, such modes of thinking are characteristic of preoperational children.

In studying the speech habits of a number of children from ages four to seven, Piaget found that approximately one-third of their language was noncommunicative or egocentric in nature. He observed three types of egocentric

Piaget: children develop concepts by interacting with their environments

Egocentric speech—noncommunicative language

speech. The first, *repetition,* involves a child repeating something he or she has just heard. For example, one child might say to another, "You have a red shirt on," and the other repeats, "I have a red shirt on, not a blue one." The child is unaware that he is repeating what the other child has said. Piaget postulates that such speech is not communicative—it is often spoken to no one in particular. Rather, it may be the child is practicing a concept he or she already knows in order to strengthen it. Piaget also feels children sometimes talk for the sheer enjoyment of using words.

The second type of egocentric speech, *monologue,* occurs when the child is alone yet talks out loud, frequently for long periods of time. "Now let's see, first I take this little block and put it on that big block. No, that's not the right one. . . . I'll use this one instead. . . . This is going to be a nice tower." Piaget hypothesizes that, in small children, words and actions are not yet fully differentiated. Words are still as much a part of events as actions are, and the child reproduces both. Piaget also speculates that monologue may represent wish fulfillment—that is, the child creates in words what he or she may not be able to do in action. If Sarah's tower of blocks collapses, at least she created it in words.

Two types of egocentric speech: monologue and collective monologue

The most frequent type of egocentric speech, *collective monologue,* occurs when several children are together. Although one of them speaks for a long period of time, the others do not listen. The speaker often wants the other children to listen and is not conscious of their inattention. Even if they wanted to, however, the other children could not understand the speech because it is egocentric—it makes sense only to the speaker and he or she is simply not aware of the difficulty. Such communication is common in imaginative play, as when a child playing at being a car driver utters a constant flow of sentences interspersed with car noises, horn beepings, and so forth, while the children around pay little or no attention. Piaget speculates that collective monologues can be explained in the same manner as monologues.[32]

It is quite important for teachers to become familiar with the concept of egocentric speech, especially teachers of preschool and elementary children, for they will encounter such speech more frequently. The teacher should understand that children's speech is not always intended as communicative; rather, the child may be, in a manner of speaking, thinking out loud. But even when children are attempting to communicate, they are not always successful and do not always understand that they are not making themselves clear. One child, after several frustrating attempts to be understood by an adult, finally asked, "Do you have a deaf ear?" Such responses must be expected and dealt with patiently. Only by asking questions and attempting to clarify the child's communication can the teacher finally understand and respond appropriately. It is crucial to remember that such speech is *not* the product of ignorant, slow, or uncooperative children. Indeed, to the child, the teacher at such times is the one who appears ignorant or impaired.

Teachers must understand that a child's speech is not always intended as communicative

Irene Alschuler, like Piaget, feels that language development is related to overall cognitive development. She is currently attempting a variation on earlier research. By teaching parents to provide an enriched language environment for their young children, she hopes to find increased cognitive development. A number of eighteen-month-old children were divided into three groups: in the first, a control group, mother and child received no special treatment; in the second group, the partial-treatment group, mothers received a curriculum guide containing a series of activities that would provide a variety of verbal interactions between mother and child; and, in the third group, the full-treatment group, mothers received the curriculum guide as well as periodic visits from Alschuler. During these visist, she would interact with the child and answer questions and offer suggestions to mothers. She thus served as a model to the mothers in this group and provided the added support of personal contact as well. In addition, all the mothers of children in the third group met together twice during the six-month experimental period.

At the end of the six months, no differences in language development were apparent between the first two groups. The children in the third group, however, were significantly more advanced in their language behavior.[33] Alschuler's study indicated that mothers can significantly influence the rate at which their children acquire language skills, with appropriate consultation from a specialist. She feels that while the benefits of modeling may have been of some importance, parents noted that the opportunities provided by the group meetings to share experiences were of particular value in motivating them to consistently provide verbal experiences for their children.

From data gathered during the prekindergarten evaluation by the various school systems in which most of her subjects are enrolled, Alschuler has been able to determine that the differences she found in her study when the children were two years of age have been maintained up to the age of five.[34] She is currently engaged in the second half of the study, which will attempt to correlate early language development with measures of later cognitive development. If she is able to establish such a correlation, it will be a significant contribution to our knowledge of the relationship between language and cognitive abilities.

BLACK ENGLISH

Recently, linguists have focused increasing attention on dialects, a variant of a language which differs in terms of vocabulary, grammar, and pronunciation. Some dialects vary so markedly that they are scarcely recognizable as derivatives of one common language. In certain countries, in fact, speakers of one regional dialect may not understand a word spoken by someone using the dialect of another region.

One of the dialects used in the United States is Black English. Until recently, this dialect was generally viewed as low-class, sloppy, or "poor people's talk." Children who speak Black English often accept and adopt this point of view about themselves. Their consequent feelings of inadequacy and lowered self-esteem often lead them to become discouraged, defeatist, or belligerent in school, often in self-defense.[35]

Recent studies by linguists, however, have shown that notions of the inferiority of Black English are incorrect. Black English has its own structure and grammar, as complex and complete as those of Standard English.[36] Differences in grammar and pronunciation have been traced to the West African languages that most black immigrants spoke when they came to America. Much in

Mothers can significantly influence the rate of their children's language acquisition

Black English has its own structure and grammar

Recent studies have shown that notions of the inferiority of Black English are incorrect. Black English has its own structure and grammar, as complex and complete as that of Standard English.

Ambassador College Photo

the same way that a German immigrant says "dis" for "this," because there is no *th* sound in German, a speaker of Black English says "tin" for "thin," or "raht" for "right." Table 7.3 compares some phrases in the two dialects, illustrating grammatical differences.

Some Black English words have been assimilated into Standard English. "Tote," meaning to carry, and "dig," to understand or to admire, are examples.

Table 7.3

Standard English	Black English
He's working (regularly)	He be working
He's working (at the moment)	He working
He said he's coming	He say he coming
Those boys	Them boy
Nobody knows it	Nobody don't know it

Adapted from D. Seymour, "Black Children, Black Speech," *Commonweal*, 19 November 1971.

Children who speak Black English also learn Standard English, usually when they get to school. But like most people who learn a second language, their level of proficiency may not be as great as it is in their native language. Standard English is often used by lower-class black children when speaking with persons in authority. At such times, they use short sentences, simplified grammar, and speak without much expressiveness. In contrast, when they speak with their friends, their language is highly expressive and as grammatically complex as that used by any children their age.[37]

Poor school achievement among black students for many years was felt to be a product of inadequate language acquisition. We know now that although such students have usually developed quite normally in their original language, they are being taught and evaluated in a second language, with which most of them are not as familiar. Several alternatives have been suggested to deal with this problem. Proponents of the first, currently prevailing approach feel that black students, like those from any minority group, must learn the main language of the country. Another suggestion is that black children be taught in Black English, much as many Spanish-speaking children are being taught in Spanish. This proposal has been put forth by some black leaders, yet has been opposed by many middle-class black parents. It seems highly likely that changing attitudes and values in the classroom about Black English would promote an atmosphere more conducive to learning and personal growth. Dorothy Seymour, in a fascinating and highly informative article, suggests that an official policy of bidialectalism represents an ideal solution. She thinks black students should learn enough Standard English to use it when necessary, and that teachers should learn enough about Black English to appreciate and understand its complexity and legitimacy.[38]

Some favor a policy of bidialectalism

Such problems are not easily solved, given that value systems and attitudes of prejudice are often long enduring and highly resistant to change. Furthermore, recent speculation on differences in intelligence between whites and blacks has added another highly volatile issue to an already difficult problem. Yet it is important that we do not become discouraged, that we continue to press for additional enlightenment in our search to provide the best possible education for each student.

IMPLICATIONS OF LANGUAGE DEVELOPMENT FOR TEACHERS

We have stressed the point of view that children's language is qualitatively distinct from the language used by adults. Such language is *not* incorrect adult language; it is child language. Particularly during preschool and elementary-school grades, it is important for the teacher to listen to the language children actually employ. It seems neither necessary nor appropriate for young children to practice adult speech.

It is also essential that teachers understand that speakers of any of the dialects of English are not speaking "bad English." Rather, several dialects, and Black English in particular, operate according to different rules of grammar. Yet such dialects are also complex and legitimate modes of language.

Some rules of thumb for teachers:

1
Listen carefully, yet not judgmentally, to children's language in order to understand what they are trying to say. Remember: their words may not convey exactly what they intend you to understand.

2
Respond to the content of the message, without necessarily correcting the form of children's phrases. You do not need to repeat their "incorrect" phrases, but do not make a point of implying a comparison between your speech and theirs. Remember: you help children to develop their language best by responding to the content, not the form of their language. When a child says to you, "My fadder and me goed to the park yesterday," it is most helpful to respond with something like, "That sounds like it must have been fun. Tell me about it," rather than, "You mean your father and you went to the park yesterday."

3
Encourage children to verbalize their feelings, ideas, and descriptions of things they hear, feel, taste, and see.

4
Ask open-ended questions, rather than questions that can be answered in a brief word or two. Such an approach encourages children to use their own language, makes them less inhibited, and allows them to be more creative.

Summary

Language is a skill that only human beings acquire. Recent research, however, is demonstrating that chimpanzees and other apes, while they cannot speak, have the capacity to acquire sign vocabularies and to utilize grammar.

Before they begin to talk, all children, even those who are born deaf, coo and babble. These universal patterns of development strongly suggest biological determinants for language acquisition. Yet preverbal behavior can also be modified by appropriate interaction with the environment. So, both heredity and environment contribute to language growth.

During the babbling stage, children produce speech sounds called phonemes, the basic units of spoken language. Later on, children use combinations of phonemes to produce morphemes, basic units of meaningful speech. Lenneberg has found that children all over the world show nearly identical patterns of speech development, and believes there must be strong biological determinants to language which are very difficult to disrupt. He also suggests that there is a critical period for language development.

B. F. Skinner has used learning theory to explain how language is acquired. He believes that babblings are operants, and that they are conditioned by adult reinforcements. By shaping, parents produce increasingly precise speech in children. Ultimately, he argues, children come to reinforce their own correct speech patterns. Such a point of view offers an explanation of how vocabulary is acquired and how certain other aspects of spoken language, such as regional accents, occur. But a major problem for learning theory is its inability to explain how children can create original speech, and how they acquire grammar at a very early age.

Psycholinguistics is a field that combines the knowledge and points of view of both psychologists and linguists. It attempts to understand both the structure of language and how language is acquired. Psycholinguists have strongly disagreed with the notions of learning theorists like Skinner. They reject the concepts of imitation and reinforcement as primary in the acquisition of language. Instead, they feel that people use a relatively small series of rules to produce an infinite variety of language. The ability to acquire and use such rules gives children language competence, even though their language performance—the way they speak—may not reveal the extent of their language abilities.

Chomsky has proposed that certain rules, called rewrite rules, allow us to combine words into phrases, and phrases into sentences. He also has proposed another set of rules that allows us to translate our thoughts and ideas into spoken language. The level of ideas is termed deep structure, and spoken language is referred to as surface structure. Chomsky calls the rules that allow us to change deep structure to surface structure transformational rules. He believes that our nervous systems contain built-in mechanisms that enable each child to construct the rules of language. A number of recent research studies tend to support Chomsky's view of language development.

The psycholinguists are particularly convincing in their explanation of the early aspects of language development. Yet children obviously learn the particular language of their native environment. Thus, learning is also an important process in language acquisition.

Children begin to talk around the age of a year, using one-word sentences called holophrases. By the age of two, children are combining two words into a sentence. Children's language is different from adult language, and proceeds through a number of developmental changes as children grow older. Using pivot grammar, for instance, a two-year-old can combine many words into two-word sentences, many of which may be original. As children become older, they combine more words together into telegraphic speech. Such speech is found in similar form all over the world among preschool children. More complex grammatical forms continue to be acquired into middle childhood.

Piaget feels that children's language is an aspect of their ability to think. As they interact with their environments and acquire increasing knowledge, their language ability grows in parallel fashion. Some language, Piaget says, is not intended to be communication. Children from ages four to seven often talk when alone, or when other children present are not listening to them. Piaget calls such language egocentric speech, and feels that children at this age have not completely separated talking from thinking. Egocentric speech may help a child strengthen new knowledge and also may involve wish fulfillment by using fantasy achievements when reality achievements are not possible. Children during this age period do not always understand that they are not expressing themselves clearly.

Children who are bilingual, or who speak a dialect of English like Black English, have special problems dealing with Standard English. It is important for teachers to understand that such language is not substandard or inferior, but involves different rules of grammar. The problems of providing for the needs of children who are bidialectical are complex. Teachers of such students may need to become familiar with the specific dialect involved, must recognize the legitimacy of such language, and must strive to maintain the self-esteem of children who use it. In fact, such an attitude is helpful in dealing with all children, since child language is different from all adult language. The insightful teacher will listen to students' language, respond to its content rather than its form, and encourage students to use their own language extensively.

REFERENCES

1
B. T. Gardner and R. A. Gardner, "Two-Way Communication with an Infant Chimpanzee," in A. Schrier and F. Stollnitz, eds., *Behavior of Non-Human Primates,* IV (New York: Academic Press, 1971).

2
D. Premack, "A Functional Analysis of Language," *Journal of the Experimental Analysis of Behavior* 14 (1970):107–125.

3
M. M. Shirley, *The First Two Years: A Study of Twenty-Five Babies,* vol. II, *Intellectual Development* (Minneapolis: University of Minnesota Press, 1933, 1961).

4
E. Lenneberg, *Biological Foundations of Language* (New York, Wiley, 1967).

5
H. L. Rheingold, J. L. Gerwirtz, and H. W. Ross, "Social Conditioning of Vocalizations in the Infant," *Journal of Comparative and Physiological Psychology* 52 (1959)68–73.

6
D. McNeill, "The Development of Language," in P. H. Mussen, ed., *Carmichael's Manual of Child Psychology,* 3d ed., vol. 1 (New York, Wiley, 1970).

7
E. Lenneberg, *Biological Foundations of Language.*

8
M. E. Smith, "An Investigation of the Development of the Sentence and the Extent of Vocabulary in Young Children," *University of Iowa Studies in Child Welfare* 3 (1926):5.

9
B. F. Skinner, *Verbal Behavior* (New York: Appleton-Century-Crofts, 1957).

10
N. Chomsky, *Syntactic Structures* (The Hague: Mouton, 1957).

11
C. Cazden, "Environmental Assistance to the Child's Acquisition of Grammar" (Ph.D. dissertation, Graduate School of Education, Harvard University, 1965).

12
J. Piaget, "Le langage et la pensee du point de vue genetique," *Acta Psychol.* 10 (1954):51–60.

13
T. G. Bever, J. R. Lackner, and R. Kirk, "The Underlying Structures of Sentences Are the Primary Units of Immediate Speech Processing," *Perception and Psychophysics* 5 (1969):225–31.

14
A. L. Wilkes and R. A. Kennedy, "Relationship between Pausing and Retrieval Latency in Sentences of Varying Grammatical Form," *Journal of Experimental Psychology* 79 (1969):241–45.

15
E. Lenneberg, *Biological Foundations of Language.*

16
N. Chomsky, "Review of *Verbal Behavior* by B. F. Skinner," *Language* 35 (1959):26–58.

17
N. Chomsky, *Reflections on Language* (New York: Pantheon, 1975).

18
A. M. Liberman, F. S. Cooper, D. P. Shankweiler, and M. Studder-Kennedy, "Perception of the Speech Code," *Psychological Review* 74 (1967):431–461.

19
P. H. Wolff, "The Natural History of Crying and Other Vocalizations in Early Infancy," in B. M. Foss, ed., *Determinants of Infant Behavior*, vol. 4 (London: Methuen, 1966), pp. 81–109.

20
P. Eimas, E. R. Siqueland, P. Jusczyk, and J. Vigorito, "Speech Perception in Infants," *Science* 171 (1971)303–306.

21
D. I. Slobin, *Psycholinguistics* (Glenview, Illinois: Scott Foresman, 1971).

22
R. Brown, *A First Language* (Cambridge, Mass.: Harvard University Press, 1973).

23
C. Bereiter and S. Engelmann, *Teaching Disadvantaged Children in the Preschool* (Englewood Cliffs, N.J.: Prentice-Hall, 1966).

24
J. Osborn, "Teaching a Language to Disadvantaged Children," in M. A. Brottman, ed., *Language Remediation for the Disadvantaged Preschool Child. Monographs of the Society for Research in Child Development* 33, no. 8 (1968):36–48.

25
L. Bloom, "Language Development Review," in F. Horowitz, ed., *Review of Child Development Research*, vol. 4 (New York: Russell Sage, 1975).

26
M. D. Braine, "The Ontogeny of English Phrase Structure; the First Phrase," *Language* 39 (1963):1–13.

27
D. I. Slobin, *Psycholinguistics.*

28
R. Brown, *A First Language.*

29
D. I. Slobin, "Cognitive Prerequisities for the Development of Grammar," in C. A. Ferguson, ed., *Studies of Child Language Development* (New York: Holt, 1973).

30
C. Chomsky, *The Acquisition of Syntax in Children from 5 to 10.* Cambridge, Mass.: MIT Press, 1969).

31
K. Nelson, "Structure and Strategy in Learning to Talk," *Monographs of the Society for Research in Child Development*, 1973.

32
H. Ginsberg and S. Opper, *Piaget's Theory of Intellectual Development* (Englewood Cliffs, N.J.: Prentice Hall, 1969).

33
I. Alschuler, "The Development and Assessment of a Parent Education Program for Increasing Young Children's Sustained Attention to Verbal Stimuli," in *Research Relating to Children* (Urbana: University of Illinois Educational Resources Information Center Clearing House on Early Childhood Education, 1974).

34
I. Alschuler, personal communication, 1976.

35
D. Seymour, "Black Children, Black Speech," *Commonweal*, 19 November 1971.

36
W. Labov, "The Logic of Nonstandard English," in F. Williams, ed., *Language and Poverty* (Chicago: Markham, 1970).

37
S. H. Houston, "A Re-Examination of Some Assumptions about the Language of the Disadvantaged Child," *Child Development* 41 (1970):947–963.

38
D. Seymour, "Black Children, Black Speech."

Personal development

Although this chapter concentrates on personal development during childhood and adolescence, it is important to remember that the various areas of growth are not separate from one another. We indicated earlier that the mind is not a discrete entity, any more than is the body. Mind and body function together and are intimately interconnected. In the same way, we cannot really separate personal development (the growth of personality) from cognitive development (the growth of intellectual skills). For example, a basic part of our personality resides in our self-concept; how we perceive and think about ourself, especially in relationship to other people, will certainly affect our personal development. Therefore, as you read this chapter, be careful not to assume that personal growth takes place in a vacuum.

To present ideas of growth and development in this very difficult area, we have based this chapter largely on Erik Erikson's elaboration of Sigmund Freud's original work. It was Erikson who transformed Freud's theories of emotional growth into a major developmental scheme as a means of understanding the process of healthy personal growth.

PERSONAL GROWTH: THE PRE-FREUDIAN VIEW
OF MINDLESS CHILDREN

Before the earthshaking discoveries of Sigmund Freud at the turn of this century, it was generally assumed that, until they reached the age of six or seven, children were mindless creatures, more like animals than humans. It was important, naturally, to meet their physical needs, but beyond that they were thought to be

Children viewed as too young to know anything

181

in a kind of incubation period, too young to know or feel anything. There was little reason to take the early years seriously as a time when anything significant could occur.

Interestingly enough, this view of young children is common to many cultures throughout the world. In both modern and primitive societies, many practices are based on the notion that children are unthinking creatures, with no mind of their own, nor emotions of any consequence. These cultures sharply demarcate the beginning of the juvenile age (about seven years of age) from the age of mindlessness (birth to six). English common law and Catholic canon law, for example, both assume that children do not know anything before their seventh year. In non-Western cultures, a variety of initiation rites, performed between the ages of six and seven, are based on similar assumptions. In fact, one culture actually killed children who became seriously ill before the age of six, in the belief that they were not really children at all, but snakes masquerading as humans.[1]

Remolding children to satisfy adult needs

In this country, one of the pioneers in establishing childhood as a significant era in human development was Lawrence K. Frank. A child psychologist of particular eminence, he devoted his entire professional life to pointing out those practices within and across cultures that were designed to meet adult needs and ignore the needs of children.[2] He documented the entire array of child-rearing practices that assumed children were little more than pieces of clay to be molded into any shape by adult "master craftsmen." Molding and shaping had everything from physical to psychological manifestations. In some cultures heads are flattened, feet are bound, necks are stretched, skin is punctured or tattooed. In other cultures natural physiological functions, such as breathing, choice of food, and sleeping patterns, are altered. The array of psychological practices is even greater, especially in the realm of what we could call character building. Using extreme forms of punishment, from beatings to severe scolding, adults have tried for centuries to defeat and deflect the process of personal growth. As L. K. Frank puts it, "Civilized man has survived *despite,* not because of, these methods of child care." The methods were too often created to suit the adult, not the child, and were based on an almost absolute ignorance of the special nature of childhood. As a result, "In the area of conduct and belief there apparently are no limits to the grotesque, the cruel and brutal, the diabolical ingenuity of man in warping and twisting human nature. . . ."[3] With these prior assumptions clearly in mind, we can now have some understanding of the impact, indeed shock wave, that was created by the works of Sigmund Freud.

FREUD: THE DISCOVERY OF CHILDHOOD

In searching for the causes of adult neuroses Freud began to create a revolutionary view of childhood that in no way resembled the prevailing view of benign emptiness. Freud, using the methods of clinical research, hypnotized his clients, or asked them to free associate ("Tell me the first thing that comes to mind") or to recount their recent dreams. He found, over and over again, that major aspects of his clients' personal development originated during their first six years of life. In fact, Freud discovered that he could understand the adult personality

Early experience and adult personality

Sigmund Freud: "The child is
father of the man."

only by examining the kind of experiences and personal relationships the adult
had had in childhood (before entering school). To know an adult, Freud would
say, know the child. Hence the famous phrase, "The child is father of the man."
In early experience could be discovered the foundations of later personal development.

EMOTIONAL GROWTH DURING CHILDHOOD: FREUD AND A NEW VIEW OF CHILDHOOD

Freud, with a kind of possessed genius, had to withstand enormous vilification as
his theories became known. He was literally hated and feared, almost like the
messenger in ancient times who was executed for being the bearer of bad news.
Freud's bad news was simple: adults must stop treating children as if they were
too young to know or experience anything. There could be no justification what-
soever for child-rearing practices that mangle, distort, inhibit, and break the

Three early Freudian
stages: oral, anal, and
phallic

young spirit. Freud discovered that during their first years of life children go through a sequence of emotional stages, much as Piaget found them to go through a sequence of cognitive stages.

In charting the course of emotional growth, Freud named three major stages of development from birth through seven years: the oral stage (0 to 18 months), the anal stage (1½ to 3 years), and the phallic stage (3 to 7 years). According to Freud, this sequence of major emotional transformations leaves an indelible imprint on the adult personality. Also, as with cognitive growth, certain dimensions of personality are maximally affected at each of these stages. During the oral stage, for example, the quality of nurturing children receive, especially that related to feelings, will maximally affect their future feelings of dependence and trust in the world. During the anal stage (the name is derived from the universal requirement for bowel training), independence and control are at the forefront of development. In the phallic stage, sexual identity is the major aspect of personality formation. Freud suggested that a period of latency (7–12 years) follows,

Training children as midget adults.

Fingers firmly gripping the thin shaft of a quill pen, many a student in an early American school labored over his copy book, tracing the elaborate dips and swirls of the ABCs and struggling with the accompanying writing exercises.

Each page of the large, clothbound text contained examples of the exacting script of the teacher. On blank lines below the teacher's writing, the students meticulously sought to achieve the same effect, repeatedly tracing garnished letters of the alphabet and copying sentences of a relentlessly uplifting tone. Hour after hour they toiled, and some of the more gifted among them ultimately went on to achieve calligraphy so ornate as to be virtually unreadable.

The reward for this drudgery was the book itself, page upon page of the most elegant penmanship, often cherished for years by such scholars as Timothy Orne.

Sigmund Freud

If there is a single name in all psychology that is synonymous with personality theory, it is Sigmund Freud. Born on the Continent in 1856, he spent his early years as a member of a tight-knit family in Central Europe. Reportedly, his youth was marked by serious personality problems, including severe bouts with depression and anxiety states. These difficulties apparently started him on a journey of discovery aimed at understanding the roots of personality and gaining insight into the relationship between personality structure and actual behavior. It was to be a long and productive professional journey, beginning with his graduation from medical school at the University of Vienna in 1881. His career extended all the way to the beginning of World War II in 1939.

After completing his medical studies, he became increasingly interested in diseases of the nervous system. Instead of continuing to look for physical and physiological reasons, he shifted his attention toward a new arena, the mind. If diseases such as hysteria, high-anxiety states, and deep personal depression were not connected to a physical cause, then the usual types of medical treatment, from actual operations on nerves to prescriptions for drugs, were bound to fail. Such activities were merely treating symptoms. Often, after these treatments, patients simply developed a new set of symptoms. As a result of these ideas, Freud decided to study with Josef Breuer, a physician famous for his treatment of hysteria through hypnosis. He found that inducing hypnotic trances was somewhat limited as a treatment of choice. Some patients could not be successfully hypnotized and others simply shifted symptoms.

Freud began to experiment with unique treatment methods, primarily asking patients to free associate and to report on their dreams. In some ways this appeared an outrageous procedure for a physician to use. Imagine Freud asking a patient to stretch out on his soon-to-be-famous couch, then suggesting that he or she say whatever came to mind (the first rule of psychoanalysis was to speak out and not repress any hidden thoughts). All the while Freud himself was sitting behind the couch quietly jotting down notes, rarely speaking. Such a procedure seemed the work of a mad genius at best or of a mountebank at worst. Not only did Freud break with the traditions of his time completely, but he even went so far as to carry on psychoanalytically oriented treatment via the mail to the father of a child patient. In the famous case of "Little Hans" he successfully treated a young boy by writing to the father and explaining step-by-

step how to cure the patient of a severe case of horse phobia. Since horses provided most transportation in those days, Hans's malady can be compared to a child who today would run and hide at the sight of an automobile.

Always an innovator, Freud continued to evolve creative treatment techniques throughout his life; however, his major contribution was his insight into the causes of behavior. Through hours of quiet listening to patients' free associations and dreams, he began to construct a theory of personality. He heard the same themes re-

peated over and over again, and gradually created his theory of infant sexuality. Adult patients were helped to gradually recall early feelings, thoughts, and sexual fantasies from their childhood. To suggest to the world that innocent little children had such sexual feelings was almost too much for the Victorian age to accept. Nevertheless, despite the enormous criticism generated and the departure of some of his closest associates, Freud continued to expand on the importance of sexuality as a determinant of personality during the early years of life. His three-part

typology of the mind—the id, the ego, and the superego—combined with his three layers of conscious, preconscious, and unconscious led to his famous dictum that all human behavior was overdetermined. His clinical approaches demonstrated that our present behavior was related to a whole series of "causes." The task of the psychologist was to uncover great amounts of psychic material and then gradually help the patient understand how many of the factors from his past had been regulating his present behavior. In fact, Freud said that the psychologist is like an archaeologist—carefully and systematically digging through the past in order to gradually uncover the intrapsychic traumas of a person's early history. Here he found the structure of the past influencing present behavior, here was the repository of events, feelings, disconnected ideas, fantasies rooted in the unconscious.

The unconscious, according to Freud, was the key to human behavior. Even though individuals may try to suppress or repress inner thoughts and feelings and push them into the unconscious, the repressed material sneaks out in disguised form. Slips of the tongue, unfortunate "accidents," forgetting important events, getting names of familiar people mixed up, and similar unusual human behavior were not just incidental activities or randomly determined. He was able to show how such events were instead a direct expression of an individual's unconscious motivation. For example, a guilt-ridden criminal might "accidentally" leave a trail a mile wide from the scene of a crime in order to bring about his own punishment. Other examples abound in everyday life.

The insights of Freud changed our level of understanding in dramatic ways. It has been said that the greatest contribution was to end, once and for all, the age of innocence. Also it has been said that it would have been impossible to understand the horrors of the twentieth century without his theories of why and how people react. His theories demonstrated the importance of both sexual and aggressive human drives. The adverse interpersonal relationships so common in this age are current reminders of this insight. The desolation created by two major world wars, the total annihilation of innocent populations, the use of ultimate weapons from A-bombs to gas chambers —these products of a so-called advanced civilization can be better understood through his views. Hopefully, his insights will teach the world the importance of recognizing and gradually developing control over these destructive human drives. Ironically he spent many of his last years as a captive of the most demonic human being of this century in Nazi Germany. His final year of life was spent in England in 1939. He watched the world he knew collapse once again in a paroxysm of hatred, moot testimony to his deepest fears for humanity.

in which the oral, anal, and phallic dimensions are integrated and no new elements are added. However, during adolescence (the genital stage), the period of so-called "sturm und drang" (a German expression meaning a period of extreme stress and strain), all the previous elements—oral, anal, and especially phallic—are brought back into play. During adolescence the basic elements are reworked into an adult character. This is a time for recapitulation, going back over the issues of dependence (oral period), independence (anal period), and identity (phallic period) to prepare for a fully functioning adulthood in which, according to Freud, we can love and work productively—a simple but profound human objective.

Adolescence as a time for recapitulation

Freud established once and for all that extremely significant personal and emotional aspects of our development are determined during the first seven years of our lives. It was no longer possible to assume that the young child has no mind or any significant emotions. Instead, Freud's theory provided valid information to buttress an old adage, "Just as the twig is bent, the tree's inclined." The adult personality is affected in major ways by the emotional experiences of childhood; or, in other words, by the quality of interaction between the child and the environment.

A PRIMER ON FREUD

A Freudian view holds to a basic principle: namely, that the quality of early experience in interpersonal relationships exerts a major influence on the adult personality. The personality, according to the Freudian view, is a structure with three major components: the id, the ego, and the superego. The id is a seething cauldron of pleasure and aggressive drives, instincts that demand immediate satisfaction. The superego is just the opposite of the id: it is the voice of a stern conscience. These two structures are, by definition, always in opposition, always at total war. The id always seeks immediate pleasure, while the superego seeks to inhibit, prevent, or stall the achievement of that pleasure. If satisfying the id would make a person "feel good," then the superego would turn that good feeling into feelings of guilt and shame.

The id: pleasure and aggression

The superego: a harsh conscience

The ego: an executive function

In the midst of this constant war between the id and the superego resides the third aspect of the personality, the ego. The ego is the voice of calm, reasoned thought that referees the two unconscious giants. The ego has to rechannel the instinctive id drives into areas that are not too unacceptable to the superego. The ego operates out of the reality principle, always mediating between the inner demands (the conflict between the id and the superego) and the outer demands of reality. In Freud's view, the extent to which our ego is able to perform this extremely difficult job depends directly on the quality of our experience in the first six years of life.

If we make it through the oral, anal, and phallic stages without suffering any psychic trauma, then our ego has passed its major test. We will probably grow in psychologically healthy directions because we will be equipped with a strong and stable ego that will enable us to see reality accurately, delay gratification when essential, focus our attention on significant tasks, and so on. If, on the other hand, our particular needs were not met at each of the three stages, then our ego will be defective. If, for example, our oral needs were frustrated during this period (premature and harsh weaning, removal of all objects to suck, including perhaps taping the thumb), then later on our ego might not be able to overcome self-defeating oral desires (alcoholism is thought to be attributable to frustrations of the oral stage). Likewise, if we were toilet trained excessively harshly during the second stage, our ego might be weakened in the areas of giving (excessive adult hoarding and miserliness are thought to be ego deficits related to this period). Finally, during the phallic period, excessively punitive warning about genital activity would have negative effects on later sexual identity (in Freudian thought, sexual impotence, frigidity, exhibitionism, and homosexuality are considered ego deficits derived from the phallic period).

In other words, the interactions between the child and significant adults during the first six years determine whether or not the adult ego will be able to function efficiently. Inadequate or negative child-rearing practices will result in an ego that is flawed, usually in one of the three areas—oral, anal, or phallic. The ego might function adequately in one or two areas, but show major deficiencies in the third area.

Erik Erikson, one of Freud's students, has done more than any other theorist to modernize Freudian theory and make it into a more complete theory of child and adolescent development. In a sense, one of the major difficulties with Freud's view was that it was too deterministic. According to Freud, by the time we are six or seven years old, personal growth is essentially all over.[4] Our basic personality structures are already set. As shown in Table 8.1, Erikson expanded the ideas of stages of development into a broader framework—a life cycle—and outlined the positive and negative dimensions of each period. This helped to clarify and balance the theory as a means of understanding personal growth.

ERIKSON: THE SEQUENCE OF STAGES AND TASKS OF PERSONAL DEVELOPMENT

Erikson: personality growth throughout the life cycle

While Freud had emphasized the negative and pathological aspects of emotional growth, Erikson directed the theory into a broader context (see Table 8.1). He saw development continuing throughout one's entire life and yet gave special significance to childhood (birth to six years), the juvenile era (six to

Table 8.1 Stages of personal development: Freud and Erikson.

Years	Freud	Erikson
0–1½	Oral	Trust and mistrust
1½–3	Anal	Autonomy and shame
3–7	Phallic	Initiative and guilt
7–12	Latency	Mastery and inferiority
12–18		Identity and identity diffusion
18–30	Genital	Intimacy and isolation
30–60		Generativity and self-absorption
60–		Integrity and disgust

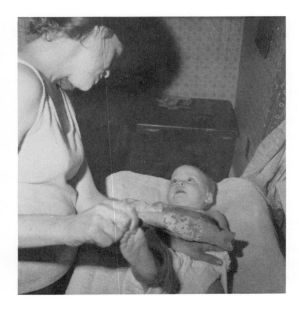

Erikson's periods of childhood almost duplicated Freud's. He labeled his first stage trust and mistrust and felt that the quality of nurturance would develop feelings of trust or distrust in the child.

twelve years), and adolescence (twelve to eighteen years). Although he has suggested stages of development well into adulthood, we will concentrate on the three categories of preschool, elementary, and secondary school years.[5]

CHILDHOOD (BIRTH TO SIX YEARS)

Trust and mistrust (0 to 18 months)

Erikson subdivided the period of childhood into three categories that almost precisely duplicate Freud's. The first of these categories, from birth to 18 months, he labeled the stage of trust and mistrust. In Freudian terms, this is the oral period, in which there is great emphasis on feeding, sucking, biting, drooling. The quality of nurture—the quality of care and affection that go into the feeding, cuddling, bathing, and clothing—will develop feelings of trust or distrust. The extent to which a baby's first experience of the world is of a dependable, warm place will create a general outlook, ranging from positive and trusting to negative and distrusting. We are not talking about the old controversy of breast feedings as opposed to bottle feeding (for a long time that seemed to be the single controversy), but rather about the need for affectionate physical contact and comfort during feeding and other child-rearing activities. A cold, tense mother breast feeding could be as lacking in good nurture as a bottleprop (a device that allows no human contact while feeding a baby).

The quality of nurture and establishing basic trust

Evidence for the importance of early experience has been provided by several researchers. Harry Harlow's continuing research has supported the concept of the importance of early mothering patterns.[6] Harlow has been raising baby monkeys under different conditions of mothering for numerous studies. Figure

Erik Erikson

Born at the turn of the century, Erik Erikson spent his early years in Europe. As a son of well-to-do parents, his education was both formal and informal. Like other upper-class children, when he finished his regular school work, he traveled the Continent. He described this period as his own "moratorium." Later in his professional career he developed a theory of human development in stages across the entire span of the life cycle. For adolescents and young adults he noted the importance of a moratorium, a temporary life space, between the completion of general academic education and the choice of a life career. He noted at the time of his own young adulthood it was fashionable to travel through Europe, gaining a perspective on civilization and one's own possible place in it. He chose the avocation of portrait painting as an activity during this time. It permitted maximum flexibility for travel and yielded some productive output as well. Obviously talented, he soon gained a reputation as a promising young artist, especially for his portraits of young children.

The turning point in his life came when he was invited to a villa in Austria to do a child's portrait. He entered the villa and was introduced to the child's father, Sigmund Freud. There began a series of informal discussions as he completed his work. A few weeks later, he received a written invitation from Freud to join the psychoanalytic institute of Vienna and study for child analysis. Erikson has commented that at this point he confronted a momentous decision, the choice between a continued moratorium, with more traveling and painting, and a commitment to a life career pattern. Fortunately for psychology and particularly for our eventual understanding of children and adolescents, Erikson ended the moratorium.

After completing his training, he migrated to this country and served from 1936 to 1939 as a research associate in psychiatry at Yale, and he worked with Henry Murray of TAT fame (Thematic Apperception Test) at Harvard. From 1939 to 1951 he served as professor at the University of California and then moved to the Austen Riggs Clinic in Pittsburgh. With each move, his reputation grew in significance. His theoretical framework was adopted in toto by the White House Conference on Children in 1950. The conference report, a national charter for child and adolescent development in this country, was almost a literal repetition of his thoughts. In 1960 he was offered a university professorship at Harvard in recognition of his national and international stature in the field of human development. The career that started so informally that day at Freud's villa culminated with almost unprecedented eminence as a professor in the country's oldest and most prestigious institution of higher education—all without the benefit of a single earned academic degree. Ironically, he was only offered associate status in the American Psychological Association as late as 1950. This oversight was partially removed in 1955 when he was elected as a Fellow of the Division of Developmental Psychology, without ever having been a member.

His work, as we have noted in the text, has been a major contribution to our understanding of healthy psychological growth during all aspects of the life cycle. In addition to the high quality of his insight, Erikson possessed a genuine flair in linguistic expression both spoken and written. In fact, one could almost compare his command of the English language with the benchmark established in this century by Winston Churchill. In many ways Erikson's scope was as broad and comprehensive as that of Churchill. Erikson's genius has been his ability to see the threefold relationship among the person, the immediate environment, and historical forces. Thus each human is partially shaped by environmental and historical events, but each human in turn shapes the environment and can change the course of history. Erikson is equally at home describing the balance of individual strengths and problems for a single "average" child or teenager as with an analysis of major historical figures such as Martin Luther and Mahatma Gandhi. He shows through personal history how events and reactions during childhood and adolescence prepare humans to be adults. Ralph Waldo Emerson said that there is no history, only biography. Erikson's work attests to this wisdom.

If there is a criticism of his overall framework it would concern his differentiation between the sexes. As might be expected, he was conditioned and shaped by the major historical and psychological forces of his own time, following in the tradition of a predominantly male-oriented theory for psychology. This reminds us of the limits set by historical circumstances which impinge on all humans. He was able to break with many of the limiting traditions of his time, particularly to move the concept of development from an exclusive pathological focus to a view that emphasized the positive and productive aspects of growth. He was, however, not successful in breaking with the cultural stereotypes regarding female growth. In sum, he personified his own theory of development in achieving a sense of personal and professional integrity. He reaches the end of life with a certain ego integrity, "an acceptance of his own responsibility for what his life is and was and of its place in the flow of history." These factors include both his limitations as well as his many successes.

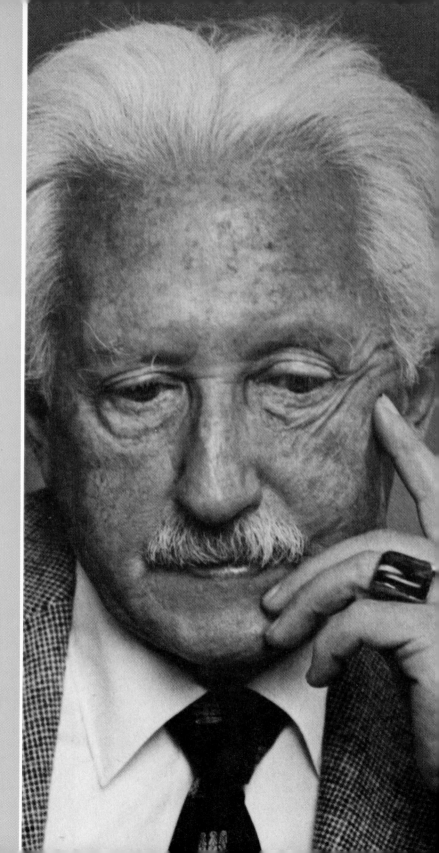

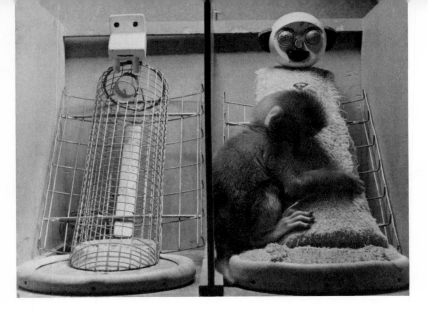

Fig. 8.1 Harlow gave baby monkeys two kinds of substitute mothers: a warm, cloth one and a cold, wire one. The wire "mother's" babies manifested bizarre behavior as adults—for example, they were unable to mate and exhibited characteristics similar to schizophrenia.

"Cloth" and "wire"
mothering patterns

8.1 depicts two types of substitute monkey mothers: a warm, soft, cloth mother and a cold, harsh, wire one. Both are capable of providing milk, but as you might expect, the wire mother's babies manifested substantial bizarre behavior as adults. They were unable to mate, to relate to strange or novel objects, and in fact, showed many behaviors reminiscent of schizophrenia. The cloth mother's babies, on the other hand, were able to explore strange and terrifying situations and demonstrated an ability to master their environment.

Equally dramatic was some clinical research conducted by Rene Spitz.[7] He studied the effects of orphanage experiences on very young children. Even though the children were given adequate physical care, washed, fed, and kept in warm, clean rooms, there was almost a complete lack of human warmth and contact. During an epidemic the orphanage children were dramatically less able to withstand disease compared to other children of nearby families. In fact, when the figures were published, they were very hard for people to accept—34 of 91 orphanage children died, compared to almost none of the other children in the area.

Sensory learning and
early experience

Erikson notes that maternal warmth and care teaches children through the senses (as Piaget might say) that they can depend on the world. The mother is practically the entire world for very young children. Through her they learn that, although she disappears at times, she also always reappears. From the regularity as well as the quality of the experience, children develop their outlook on life and prepare to move to the second stage. As with the stages of cognitive growth, the stages of personal development are sequential. This means that if their basic dependency needs are met during their first 18 months of life, they will be ready to move to the second stage of personal development. On the other hand, if these needs are not properly met, they may not be able to move on.

The dramatic studies of extreme cases of maternal deprivation cited above indicate that the failure to develop could be actual physical death (failure to thrive) or a kind of psychological death in the form of emotional withdrawal from the world (the so-called anaclitic depression). Children supposedly raised by wild animals ("feral children") have shown similar irreversible disturbances.

There is apparently no completely adequate substitute for mothering, in its best sense, during this period. Without it children are not emotionally prepared for the next developmental stage. There is also reason to question the use of professional substitute mothers during this stage. Selma Fraiberg has noted that in England in 1940 some young children were removed from their natural parents to spare them from the blitz (heavy continuous bombing of London during World War II). The children were placed in a model child-care center directed by two of the world's leading authorities, Anna Freud and Dorothy Burlingham. In spite of efforts to select the most competent staff, the children separated from their natural parents showed definite developmental lags.[8] Indeed, there may be no effective substitute for consistent regular mothering and fathering to create the growth needed to prepare the child for the second stage. Studies such as these raise serious questions about increased use of day-care centers even under ideal conditions. Current thinking about "home-care" instead of in-stitutionalized day-care for very young children is a promising new direction.

Custodial care no substitute for human care

The use of substitute mothers in World War II

Autonomy and shame (1 1/2 to 3 years)

During this second period of childhood, emotional and personal development moves into what Erikson calls the stage of autonomy and shame. This is when children emerge from their almost total dependence on mothering and begin, literally and figuratively, to stand on their own two feet. The physical maturation that allows them to crawl, walk, run, and climb provides the means for a great leap into personal autonomy. This is a time of intense exploration when they seem to be into almost everything. Physical maturation also frees them from dependence on the bottle or the breast and enables them to learn how to control their bowels and bladders. Thus the positive aspect of this period is a fundamental sense of self-direction. However, Erikson makes it clear that there can be negative emotional development, too. We noted in the first stage that children are particularly sensitive to the way in which their dependency needs are met. In this stage they need to be independent and the way that need is met will maximally affect their sense of personal autonomy. If children at this stage are punished excessively for exploring their house or neighborhood, if they receive particularly harsh and punitive bowel training, or if they are so overprotected and overmothered that they are almost "smothered," then Erikson indicates that the major emotional lesson from this period will be personal shame. The growing sense of self-control ("Mother, I can do it myself!") can be impaired as easily as it can be nurtured during this second period of childhood.

Personal autonomy and early signs of independence

It may be difficult for adults to learn not to interfere but rather to support the child's desire for freedom and autonomy. For example, if you watch a child of three trying to tie his shoes, you may see him work with extraordinary motivation even though the loops aren't matched and well over half the time as he tries for the final knot, he ends up with two separate laces, one in each hand. Then watch parents as they watch their children attempt a task like this. Too often the parent will step in and take over, tie the shoes the "right way" and

Problems of over-control and direction: defeating the child's early attempts at mastery

Children between the age of one-and-a-half and three (Erikson's period of autonomy and shame) move from almost total dependence toward greater personal autonomy.

defeat the child's growing attempt at self-mastery. The same goes for putting on boots, coats, and even how the child plays with toys. It is terribly easy to fall into the trap of almost always responding negatively to a child at this age. Commonly a mother might say "No" up to 200 times a day at this stage. Such nagging not only is negative reinforcement in the extreme, but also a constant reminder of the lack of self-control to the child.

This is also the time when language begins, and here again the child's sense of independence is clearly in the balance. Adults need to understand that their child's first attempts to speak will always be halting. All children stutter somewhat during this time just as all tumble constantly as they learn to walk and run. Attempts to speak need encouragement and modeling: adults should not baby-talk back to a child, nor should they overcorrect a child's use of language. The surest way to promote stuttering at this stage is to harp on the misuse of language. It will definitely promote a sense of personal shame if, when children first try to talk, they are criticized for not talking the "right way."

Professor Burton "Bud" White of Harvard has shown that patterns of mothering and fathering at this stage are clearly related to the child's sense of personal mastery, independence, and self-control.[9] Even at this early stage, certain patterns of interaction between parents and children can accurately predict competency and future mastery. The most successful patterns are found in homes where the mother does substantial indirect teaching. Effective mothers talk clearly and do a great deal of "labeling" ("This is a dog," and then, gradually, "This is a big dog," and so on). Children in these homes are also allowed substantial initiative in selecting activities; there is a balance between activities initiated by the mother and activities initiated by the children. Frequently, the mother asks for her children's ideas and asks questions to help them understand the activity (e.g., "Now what do you suppose will happen if I put the piece in the puzzle this way?" ". . . if you pour all the water from the big glass into this little cup?" "What will little Red Riding Hood find when she goes into the bedroom?").

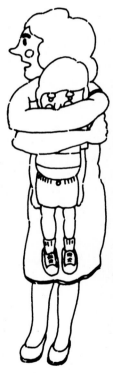

The supermother: indirect teaching

The smothering mother

Parents who provide an interesting, stimulating environment, talk frequently to their children, give them some initiative, and do a great deal of indirect teaching by asking questions and drawing out their perceptions and ideas have the most positive effect on their children's developing sense of competency. Their sense of being "doers" and of being able to control and affect the environment receives a major boost during this time.

The developing sense of personal effectiveness and mastery can also be impaired during this time. Certain patterns of mothering can directly or indirectly produce a sense of personal shame and unworthiness. While the so-called "supermother" is a great natural educator, the "smothering mother" overprotects, constantly pushes, and tells her child what to do all the time. Instead of asking, even occasionally, she literally directs every detail of her children's lives. This constant interference and nagging makes the child feel that, "Well, whatever I

do is pretty good, but it could be better." Such children can't develop the feelings of competency or self-confidence they are eventually going to need.

The overwhelmed mother

A second negative pattern is the "overwhelmed mother" who is frantic and out of control most of the time. Her disorganization creates a chaotic atmosphere that often results in genuine neglect. She may, for example, let the other children, or the neighbors, raise her own children. Almost the opposite of the smothering mother, the overwhelmed mother offers little in the way of stability. The danger is that her children will feel that the absence of maternal concern is ultimately caused by some personal defect of their own.

The zookeeper

Another pattern, perhaps more common than the overwhelmed mother, is the "zoo-keeper mother." She performs all the chores of child care, meets all the physical and even some of the emotional needs of her children. However, her responses tend to be mechanical, robotlike. She is so intent on sticking to her schedule come what may, and on going through all the proper motions, that the really essential ingredients are missing. For example, she might read a book on child psychology and learn that it is important to give her children creative, interesting, unstructured toys. She then dutifully fills the crib with such toys and leaves the child alone. One of the striking aspects of this pattern is, in fact, the extent to which these children are left alone. The routine and the schedule may never allow time for genuine interaction between mother and child. Such children resemble animals caged in the zoo—fed, watered, and washed. Naturally, this does not nurture their sense of autonomy or self-confidence; instead it tends to produce rigid, stereotyped behaviors, in response to the mother's need for routine.

If we think about these patterns for a minute, we may realize that they apply to more than just mothers. We can find parallels to the supermother, the smothering mother, the overwhelmed mother, and the zookeeper in almost any adult-child context, *including* the classroom. If you think back on your own experience, you will probably find that certain teachers loom large in your memory—*because* they fit these categories: the teacher who constantly recorrected your papers, always pointing out errors, never appearing satisfied with your work, always telling you what to do. Or the teacher (often a beginner) who appeared with a bad case of stage fright in front of your class, who seemed to swing from confusion to chaos, allowing the class to run out of control. Or perhaps there was one who always adhered to the schedule and the lesson plan as if it were a mortal sin to ever depart from the class routine. The patterns are general, then, and not limited to mother-child interactions. It is therefore most important to consider the effect such patterns have on personal development. Teachers can directly affect their pupils' sense of shame or autonomy, especially in preschool and kindergarten. The positive patterns of supermothering and, increasingly, superfathering, could also become classroom patterns of superteaching.

Similarities to the classroom

Initiative and guilt (3 to 6 years)
Personal development during the third stage of childhood takes place in the areas of initiative and guilt. This is the time when the child's identity as a boy or a girl is maximally affected. In the preceding stage the child discovers that he or she can be a person with self-direction. Now the task is to discover what

Male and female identity formation

kind of a person he or she is, especially with regard to their sense of maleness or femaleness. Children at this stage begin to identify with the appropriate adult and to model, or copy, aspects of the adult's behavior. This can be seen most readily in those families that allow children to express themselves without a lot of censoring. In such an atmosphere boys will directly express their growing maleness by becoming unusually interested in their mothers. They engage in what becomes almost a rivalry with their father for their mother's attention and affection. The same is true of girls who, in discovering their femaleness, become very attached to their fathers. Many families report the humorous comments their children make at this age. A boy may say how happy he feels when daddy leaves for work, all the while glancing rather obviously toward his mother. Similarly, a girl may wish to go off with daddy in the car and let mommy stay home and take care of the other children. There are often pointed remarks concerning marriage: "I'm not going to marry anyone," a five-year-old boy might declare, "I am going to stay home and take care of mommy when daddy gets too old!" These are not simply humorous comments, but reflect questions of sexual identity that are surfacing for the first time.

The need for positive responses to a child's sexual identity

Adults often have difficulty understanding the importance of such issues. It seems, on the face of it, rather absurd for a four- or five-year-old girl to proclaim that she would like her mother to go away. But if adults punish such statements, the child is left with strong feelings of guilt concerning her identity. To punish her for expressing her natural desire to establish herself as a female will have lasting negative effects. And ridicule or sarcasm will be just as damaging as physical punishment, for it will make her feel very small and insignificant, guilty at having expressed some of her inner feelings about what kind of a person she hopes to become. As we have seen, particular aspects of personality are unusually affected during each sensitive period. Between three and six years, it is the personal identity that is most affected. Thus it is especially important for children at this time to be reassured that they will become full-fledged adults and not made to feel guilty over these wishes. Erikson notes,

> Both the girl and the boy are now extraordinarily appreciative of any convincing promise of the fact that someday they will be as good as father or mother—perhaps better; and they are grateful for sexual enlightenment, a little at a time, and patiently repeated at intervals.[10]

PEANUTS ®   By Charles M. Schulz

© 1961 United Feature Syndicate, Inc.

Elementary-school years and sex-typing

In school itself, especially in kindergarten and the first grade, many of these same issues are plainly visible. Boys often become so enamored of their teacher that they "forget" and sometimes call their own mother by their teacher's name. "Some kids really know how to hurt a mother," one mother remarked, half humorously, when this happened to her. Recently, a first-grade teacher invited her class to her wedding. This happens every so often, but this particular wedding was featured in a television news broadcast. And there, for all the world to see, was the class—little girls in crinkly party dresses, bubbling over with excitement as they focused all their attention on the groom; and the boys, in coats and bow ties, weeping as the beaming bride swept down the aisle. This makes the point, perhaps melodramatically, that emotions and feelings at this stage are genuine, legitimate, and need to be accepted.

Children's physical size, compared to adults, can also increase any anxieties they may have at this age. In a world of adult "giants," they may fear that they will never grow big enough to be an adult. When Erikson used the phrase "perhaps better" in the previous quote, he was referring to children's need for reassurance that they will not only grow to become full-fledged adult men and women, but that they will also surpass their parents. We can imagine nothing worse than growing up to be thirty- or forty-year-old "pseudoadults" who still live in the shadow of our parents. As in child rearing, so too in teaching—the ultimate test of how effectively we assist the formation of personal identity is the extent to which we help children outgrow their need for us. By deliberately reinforcing and nurturing children's male or female identities at this stage, we will help build a firm foundation for the next stage of emotional growth. And we will help them continue their general progress from dependence to independence.

The lengthy period of childhood dependency

The human infant is born in a condition of almost complete dependence. Compared to other species, we have extremely rudimentary instincts and a drawn-out period of maturation. Erikson notes that this lengthy period carries with it the temptation for adults to exploit the period of dependency and to control and manipulate children to satisfy their own needs. For example, we could force three- to six-year-old children to comply with our wishes by manipulating their guilt feelings, since it is at this age that children are most prone to feel guilty. Make them feel guilty, and they will obey us. We can likewise exact compliance from one-and-one-half- to three-year-old children by specific use of shame. For example, we can successfully toilet train children by absolutely shaming them every time they make a mistake. This will teach them bowel control, but at a terrible price. If we adults control and manipulate children in such ways, we are victimizing them by preventing healthy personal growth. As Erikson says,

> *This long childhood exposes adults to the temptation of thoughtlessly and often cruelly exploiting the child's dependence by making him pay for the psychological debts owed to us by others, by making him victim of tensions which we will not or dare not correct in ourselves or in our surroundings. We have learned not to stunt a child's growing body with child labor; we must now learn not to break his growing spirit by making him victim of our anxieties.*[11]

THE JUVENILE PERIOD (SIX TO TWELVE YEARS)

This period has been called the time of mastery and inferiority. During the elementary-school years, Erikson indicates that personal and emotional development turns outward. Children enter a new "world"—the classroom, the neighborhood, the gang. These become the arenas for growth. The home remains an important base of operations, but the other arenas have special significance. In sheer number of hours, children now spend much more time (excluding sleeping) away from home than ever before. As juveniles they can fully participate as a member of a same-sex gang. We may recall from Piaget that not until they are six or seven years old can children genuinely listen to or talk with other children. Now that "collective monologues" have been replaced by genuine discussion, important new groups can be formed.

The polarized world of elementary-age children

During this time, neighborhood and classroom gangs become major socializing agents. As opposed to adolescent cliques, the juvenile gangs are almost always made up of all boys or all girls. Occasionally a boys' gang will "allow" a particularly talented tomboy to join, but in general the juvenile world is stable and neatly stereotyped. Their world is divided into two camps on everything: boys versus girls, good guys in white hats versus bad guys in black hats, all infants are "babies," all adults are always right (including all teachers). There is no room for relativity in anything. Again recalling Piaget, this is the stage of concrete thought. From the personal point of view, this factor provides for a period of considerable emotional stability. The juvenile usually stands in an unambiguous relationship at home. He or she may have considerable freedom to roam the neighborhood. Adults are not overly concerned about academic performance in school, while the children at this age are, in fact, interested in learning

Active learning

many of the skills that are taught. At a concrete and functional level it is "fun" to decipher words, learn to write, add, and substract, since each of these skills makes a whole new realm of experience available to them—reading for comic books, writing for notes to pass around, adding for figuring out how much a new bike will cost, and so on. There is no need to lecture children at this age about the importance of learning these skills.

The period between ages seven and twelve (Erikson's stage of mastery and inferiority) presents a special challenge to both teachers and parents. During this period, children have a natural desire to master new goals and control their environment. Robert White uses the term "competence motivation" to describe this attribute.

In addition to the many school-oriented skills, children during this period also develop a general sense of personal mastery. The sheer number of new activities and games they learn at this age is enormous—swimming, riding, sailing, skiing, roller skating, camping, boating, baseball, basketball, football, hockey, kick-the-can, sewing, cooking, collecting things (look in any child's pockets at this age!)—the list is almost endless and is testimony to the raw amount of energy and motivation for competence that exists at this age. The old saying that a child has ten thousand muscles that want to move and only one set to sit still is most appropriate. At the same time, we should understand Erikson's major point: this tremendous amount of energy can be put in the service of personal competence motivation. If children are not encouraged to actively engage with the surrounding world, their sense of personal industry will give way to personal inferiority. In other words, this is the time when the child's need to function and to actively acquire multiple skills will *maximally affect* his or her sense of personal industry.

Another theorist of personal development, Robert White, coined the phrase "competence motivation" to describe what he considered a universal attribute of humans and other species. White reviewed all the major theories and research evidence for personal development and concluded that there is an inborn

Personal mastery and competence

Also characteristic of the stage of mastery and inferiority are neighborhood and classroom gangs, which serve as major socializing agents.

The need to master the environment

"drive" to master the environment. This drive is in our very bones, so to speak. We humans—and other animal species as well—are not the "empty" organisms, or so-called black boxes, that classic stimulus-response theory would suggest, nor are we passive agents who merely react to but never act upon the world, as classic psychoanalytic theory would say.[12] White found, to the contrary, that humans and animals are naturally curious and seek to master and control the world around them. Just watch a child in a supermarket for a while, and you will see a perfect example of the need to explore and master the environment. The evidence for competence motivation comes from more sophisticated sources than observation. Animal studies have shown that rats will endure electric shock if they have to, in order to move from an empty cage to a maze filled with interesting and novel rat toys. We should remember that in animal research, electric shock (running an electric current through a wire cage) is almost always traumatic enough to condition an animal to back away. But these animals apparently wanted to manipulate and handle the objects in the other cage so much that the electricity was an ineffective deterrent.* Other studies have shown that monkeys

---

*

J. McV. Hunt, a major theorist and researcher in child development, noted that the study reported here was so controversial that the researcher (Nissen) had an extraordinarily difficult time publishing the results. The findings were too challenging to the views then held. See J. McV. Hunt, "Environmental Development and Scholastic Achievement" in M. Deutsch et al. (eds.), *Social Class, Race, and Psychological Development* (New York: Holt, Rinehart and Winston, 1968).

will work on puzzles almost endlessly for no other reward than the stimulation derived from the activity itself. You don't have to provide candy, or food pellets, or any of the other usual rewards. The animals want to work on the puzzles for the sheer enjoyment of the activity. Harlow reported that two monkeys worked on these activities for over ten hours straight, going without food and water. Thus we can say that curiosity, exploration, manipulation, and the desire to master activities is, in Robert White's words, "part of the natural makeup of an adaptive organism."

The reason this idea is so important for educators is perhaps obvious by now. Personal and emotional development from six to twelve years of age takes place largely in school. Children spend more time in school than anywhere else. Thus the classroom situation will be a major influence on their development at this stage. We too often overhear teachers making comments such as, "What can we do with a child who comes from a bad home environment?" The point is, we should not assume that we cannot have a positive effect on personal development and especially on the competence motivation of our pupils. In fact, elementary-school teachers are in a particularly strategic position to emphasize activities that can both nurture and, in some cases, restore a sense of mastery. Our elementary schools are gradually shifting away from rote learning, passive listening, and neatness ("Always color inside the lines!"), and are moving toward the open, active classroom. The so-called open classroom emphasizes many different activities, individual projects, and absorbs great amounts of energy. By stressing doing instead of listening, the active school will do much to promote the pupils' sense of personal mastery. Erikson says that children are maximally ready for active learning between the ages of six and twelve. Our task as educators is to respond to this natural tendency so as to facilitate rather than impair healthy personal growth. We shouldn't worry so much about creating quiet, orderly, neat, and polite pupils. That objective will work directly against the optunity to affect personal industry and mastery.

Classroom learning and the promotion of personal mastery

Intrinsic motivation: learning for learning's sake

ADOLESCENCE (TWELVE TO EIGHTEEN YEARS)

Adolescence, in which the major issues are identity and identity diffusion, is perhaps the most famous of Erikson's stages. Although it is impossible to pinpoint the end of adolescence and the beginning of adulthood, the major changes in most important developmental aspects of personal growth take place from about twelve years of age to about eighteen. This means that in most cases, our cognitive, physiological-glandular, and psychological systems reach their adult levels by the time we are eighteen years old. Some change may occur after seventeen or eighteen, but it does not usually qualify as a major developmental reorganization. In other words, after adolescence change tends to be quantitative, not qualitative. This does not mean that once we are adults we don't change. We do. We may gain new insights, experience new perceptions, grow in personal responsibility and maturity; but these are not usually completely new personal systems.

The changes that take place during adolescence bring about a major shift in personal development. We have already seen (Chapter 6) that cognitive developments in adolescence mean that the teenager has a completely new way

A far cry from the little red schoolhouse of the turn of the century, the Bancroft Elementary school in Andover, Massachusetts differs both structurally and philosophically from its predecessor and, indeed, from most other schools in the United States. Architecturally, the building resembles a castle (complete with towers and tunnels). On the inside, the "open classroom" look is complete, including areas for many different activities and special student projects. Such a school, with energetic and dedicated teachers, can do much to promote pupils' sense of personal mastery and growth.

to understand and think. We also have noted (Chapter 4) how the very substantial glandular changes at this time represent a major new system. Puberty obviously marks a major qualitative departure from the past. Changes of this magnitude in cognitive and physiological areas will by themselves create major psychological change. "How do I understand what is happening to me when so much is different?" a teenager might say. It is no understatement to say that of all the stages of personal development, none is more radical than adolescence. Change is the name of the game during this period.

Early adolescence and self-concept

The changes in physiology, glands, and psychological systems experienced during early adolescence constitute the most substantial shift a human being undergoes. The adolescent can now experience the world in a major new way. He or she begins to think in relativistic terms and can appreciate the difference between objective reality and subjective perception. In addition, the adolescent develops the important ability to perceive feelings and emotions both in self and others, as well as the ability to take the perspective of another person (figuratively to place yourself in another person's shoes). And finally, he or she is now able to understand as-if situations and distinguish between symbolic and literal meaning. In short, the thinking system that begins to develop during adolescence provides the teenager with a new and sophisticated mechanism for making meaning from his or her own experience, particularly in reference to understanding one's own identity as a person. To summarize, as a teenager begins to think about self and identity, he or she can perform the following operations:

1
Differentiate feelings and emotions in self and others.
2
Distinguish between objective and subjective reality.
3
Adopt the perspective of another person.
4
Understand symbolic meaning and role play "as if" situations.

In one sense, then, it seems that personal development during adolescence represents a great leap forward, since one can now be more complex, comprehensive, empathic, and abstract and maintain a broad perspective on self and others. However, as one distinguished psychologist, David Elkind, points out, such is not the case. In fact, just the reverse. The more complex thought system raises the teenager to new heights of mental operations, yet lowers him or her to new depths. Upon first entering this new stage, the thinking process of the adolescent tends to become excessively egocentric. The external world is no longer viewed as permanent and unchanging, but rather as relative, subjective, and phenomenological—accordingly, the teenager may begin to perceive himself or herself as the center of the universe.

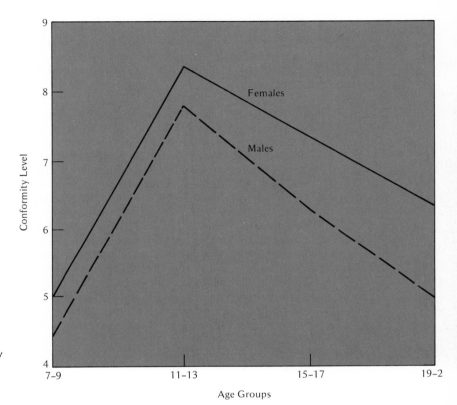

Fig. 8.2 Level of conformity at various ages.

This egocentrism, unfortunately, is accompanied by excessive self-consciousness. The teenager is unusually vulnerable to going along with the crowd. As Fig. 8.2 indicates, conformist thinking peaks during the junior-high-school years.

In another, less-formal study, researchers interviewed junior-high-aged students on their personal perceptions of self and others. The results can be summed up in the words of one of the subjects: When asked, "What is the most real thing to you?", her unhesitating reply was, "Myself."[14]

Elkind on adolescence

David Elkind, an eminent researcher and theorist, has noted that how an adolescent views his or her "self"—i.e., the self-concept—can be described along two basic dimensions of egocentric thinking: (1) the personal fable, and (2) the imaginary audience.

The personal fable.   This view comprises a deep-rooted belief in one's own personal uniqueness—the notion that no one else in the world can possibly understand how "I" really feel. Holden Caulfield in Salinger's classic novel of adolescence, *Catcher in the Rye,* stands as the extreme case. As Elkind notes, the complex beliefs create an aura—"only he can suffer with such agonized intensity or experience such exquisite rapture." To retain this image an adolescent may create a personal fable, "a story which he tells himself (and others) and which is not true."

The imaginary audience.   Essentially, this is the belief that everyone else in the world is preoccupied with the personal appearance and behavior of the adolescent, as if the entire world pauses each morning to see how a teenager is dressed for school, or waits with hushed anticipation for the adolescent to speak his or her lines. In front of such imaginary audiences teenagers can swing from excessive self-criticism (admiring one's own martyrdom) to the other extreme—self-admiration to the point of boorishness. Elkind cites the famous passage from *Tom Sawyer* of Tom witnessing his own funeral as a universal fantasy of adolescents: "They will really miss me when I'm gone and be sorry too for all the mean things they said."

On an optimistic note, Elkind finds that teenagers can be helped to gradually distinguish between real and imaginary audiences, as well as to differentiate between themselves and others in both thoughts and feelings. Given the support of adult understanding, both the personal fable and the imagined audience are progressively modified and diminished. Hopefully, as adults, we can retain some of the positive aspects of this stage, namely a healthy respect for our own individuality.[15]

Adolescents often hold the belief that everyone else in the world is preoccupied with their personal appearance and behavior. In front of this "imaginary audience," teens may be excessively self-critical or self-admiring.

The crisis of personal identity

Because adolescence represents such a major discontinuity in growth, Erikson has singled out one critical issue as the major task of this stage—resolving the crisis of personal identity. Our definition of self—how we see ourselves *and* how others see us—forms the foundation of our adult personality. If that foundation is firm and strong, an adequate resolution, a solid personal identity results; if it is not, the result is what Erikson calls a diffuse identity. Identity diffusion is something like suffering from amnesia, or like perpetually wandering over a landscape trying to "find" a self-hood. With no sense of past or future, the diffuse personality is like a stranger in his own land with no roots, no history. The sense of personal alienation prevents the establishment of a stable core for the personality.

Western societies have made it extremely difficult for adolescents to come through this stage with a firm sense of personal identity. Industrialized societies have exaggerated the marginal status of adolescents by grossly overextending the period of dependency. This is justified by the amount of special learning and training that is needed to survive in our complex world. However, it is easy to forget the negative personal effects of keeping a twenty-one-year-old, or even an eighteen-year-old, in a position of dependency. To make matters worse, adults seem to be unable to decide just when it is that a teenager becomes an adult. The age of legal adult responsibility is extremely inconsistent in this country: the legal age for marriage differs not only by sex (girls are permitted to marry without parental consent earlier than boys), but also according to state residency, with some states permitting legal marriage as early as fourteen years of age. And, there are similar discrepancies in the legal age for going to work, driving a car, entering into a legal contract, voting in elections (for most of this nation's history adolescents were old enough to die for their country in war before they were old enough to vote in elections), drinking alcoholic beverages, and enlisting in the military services.

These few examples serve to highlight the problem of identity formation. Erikson notes that the teenager is caught between two major systems, both of which are in flux. Adolescents have to cope with internal, cognitive, and glandular changes at the same time that they are confronting a series of inconsistent and changing external regulations. And they go through all this while simultaneously discarding their identity from the previous stage, the age of mastery. Kick-the-can, bike riding (the "real teenager" would rather walk than admit he or she isn't old enough to drive a car), Boy and Girl Scouts, the "Three Stooges" on TV, tomboys, and most important, the view that adults are almost always correct because they are older and bigger—these dimensions of personal development during the elementary age all have to be discarded. Adolescence is almost like entering a foreign country without knowing the language, the customs, or the culture, only it's worse because the teenager doesn't even have a guidebook. It is truly a major shock during adolescence to find that adults are not always right and, in fact, are often working very hard to cover up their mistakes. The discovery of relativism, especially in the moral behavior of adults, further exaggerates the difficulties of personal development. On the one hand, teenagers learn that some policemen take bribes, some professors plagiarize,

Adolescence and the growing sense of identity

Western society and an overly long cultural adolescence

Inconsistent legal definitions

Changes inside the person and outside: a dual discontinuity

Adults are no longer perceived as always right

Of all the stages of personal development, none is more radical than adolescence. Erikson singles out one critical issue as the major task of this stage—resolving the crisis of personal identity. The educator's objective is to provide real experience, genuine responsibility, and increasing amounts of independence during this time of stress and strain.

The overreaction: "You can't trust anyone over thirty"

some teachers copy lesson plans, some major corporations "fix" prices, some elected officials solicit bribes, some professional athletes play under the influence of drugs, and so on. On the other hand, these same adults have a tendency to lecture teenagers on the subject of responsibility, the importance of obeying rules, and above all, of showing respect to adults. The resulting teenage overreaction is well known. If you can't rely on some adults, don't trust anyone over thirty! If some businesspersons are overly materialistic, all businesspersons are Babbits! If some adults are unfaithful, all marriages are institutionalized hypocrisy! The list is endless, and serves as a poignant reminder of how difficult it is to understand the highly complicated problems of living and personal development in a modern society.

Psychological defenses during adolescence

Anna Freud has outlined the most common psychological defenses that adolescents employ.[16] She feels that much of the so-called pathology during this stage is in reality the normal upset that can be expected to accompany massive internal changes. In fact, she suggests that the only abnormality would be for teenagers to show no signs of psychological unrest. She points out that if we accept adolescent turmoil as normal, we can avoid extreme overreactions. One parent typified these feelings when she said of adolescents, "We should bury them at twelve and dig them up again at eighteen." Mark Twain allegedly commented on his own adolescence, "I thought my father was the dumbest person in the world, yet by the time I reached my twenties, he sure had learned a lot!"

Anna Freud lists the psychological systems in the following order:

Displacement: to transfer feelings and needs from one situation or person to another object. Commonly, teenagers may begin to feel attached to their parents, especially the parent of the opposite sex, and defend against this by becoming overly attached to other adults. Teenage crushes on movie stars, rock singers, and attractive school teachers are well-known examples. Displacement also is often accompanied by substantial acting-up and heightened emotional expressiveness.

Reversal of affect: to turn needs and feelings inside out. This occurs when teenagers suddenly change the manifestation of feelings from one extreme to the other. Thus, instead of showing anger, the teenager may display an exaggerated coolness. The desire for closeness may be demonstrated by withdrawal, alienation, and hiding out in one's room. Feelings and needs for excitement and curiosity may become inverted and appear as, "But, father, life is boring."

Withdrawal: to psychologically hide out. This is a more extreme defense in the sense that the teenager begins to more actively separate himself or herself from both adults and peers. There is a greater use of fantasies and a decline in reality testing. Adolescents who see themselves as the new Messiah, capable of superhuman feats or reading others' minds, are examples.

Regression: to return to an earlier stage. This is quite simply the attempt to remain a child, to avoid "growing up." Boys and girls, especially at the onset of obvious signs of puberty, may attempt to deny the changes, and dress and play as if they are still in elementary school.

Asceticism: to deny pleasure. Some adolescents may attempt to deny the development of pleasurable feelings by becoming ascetic. The increase in the depth and range of emotions is checked by (metaphorically at least) putting on a hair shirt and rejecting food, sleep, and normal comforts. Shaving heads and putting on monks' robes are other manifestations.

Uncompromising: to rigidly adhere to a narrow prescriptive ideology. This is by definition an attempt to avoid accepting the complexities of life, the shades of grey, including compromise and cooperation. All issues become dychotomized into right and wrong. Dogmatic positions abound.

> Anna Freud: if we accept adolescent turmoil as normal, we can avoid overreactions

Anna Freud also wisely points out these syndromes are common yet difficult for a teenager to understand. We all are blind to certain aspects of our own behavior and dynamics, and know that such psychological blind spots don't suddenly disappear when we are told about them. Thus, although it is important for teachers to recognize these systems, it is not necessarily wise to then confront the teenager with an interpretation. Such confrontations often make adults more defensive—and what is true for us is doubly true for teenagers. Anna Freud suggests that educators understand these common defenses, realize when a teenager is employing one, yet respond to the *person* not the *defense*. Otherwise we may find ourselves in long and unproductive arguments about whose interpretation is most accurate.

Respond to the *person* not the *defense*

One final point to remember: all of the psychological defenses are methods (some better than others) of coping with the environment as the adolescent struggles to become an adult. Adolescence is a time of double upset, "inside" the person and outside, in the surrounding environment. It really is difficult for a teenager to "get it all together," or, in Erikson's words, to achieve ego integration. Yet it is essential to develop a healthy personal identity. In ringing phrases Erikson says,

> Indeed in the social jungle of human existence there is no feeling of being alive without a sense of ego identiity. . . . The danger of this stage is identity diffusion; as Biff puts it in Arthur Miller's Death of a Salesman, 'I just can't take hold of some kind of life' . . . . Youth after youth, bewildered by some assumed role, a role forced on him by the inexorable standardization of American adolescence, runs away in one form or another; leaving schools and jobs, staying out all night, or withdrawing into bizarre and inaccessible moods. . . .[17]

As educators we need to take special note of the challenge posed by the immensely complicated problem of adolescence. There are no easy solutions. But this does not mean that nothing can be done. For years it was fashionable to say that adolescence is a tough period, but everyone outgrows it eventually, so all you can do is grin and bear it. We now realize that such advice is mere rationalization and in no way excuses us from responsibility. The number of psychological casualties during adolescence is now too obvious to permit such an attitude. For example, we now realize that teenage drug abuse is a symptom of the problem of personal identity formation, or in Erikson's terms, an attempt to solve the problem of identity diffusion. It is only an attempt because it is a nonsolution. The moment the drug wears off the same problems are still there, waiting to be attended to.

Personal identity central to a healthy personality

As we noted, educators are by definition in a strategic position to help guide personal growth. Teenagers feel a need to pull away from their own parents, so other adults can be of special significance. It is therefore our responsibility to develop effective ways to make this influence work. Erikson makes it obvious that to help teenagers grow we need to provide them with increasing amounts of independence and responsibility. In the previous stage, mastery, we said that activity was the key. In this stage our objectives as educators should be to provide real experience and genuine responsibility.

A special challenge to educators

Some adolescents may attempt to deny the development of pleasurable feelings by becoming ascetic.

A most recent report on adolescents, *Youth: Transition to Adulthood* (1974), makes the point that our society generally prevents teenagers from developing a sense of genuine responsibility. "In earlier days, responsible positions in many areas of life were common to youth, as ship captains, generals, captains of industry, statesmen, union organizers."[18] The classic novel *Captains Courageous* may be an extreme case, yet it does make the point that teenagers have responsible roles to perform and tasks to accomplish. It is our view that personal growth and the formation of an adult identity will be maximally affected by the amount of experience and responsibility we provide for teenagers. It's a simple idea in theory and almost as obvious as E. L. Thorndike's principles (see Chapter 2). If you want people to become responsible and mature adults, you must give them the experience of responsibility. Responsibility and maturity cannot be learned second-hand. Teenagers in schools and in other adult-run institutions are not given enough genuine experience and responsibility; they are forced to remain passive. We will come back to these issues and discuss them more fully in Chapter 21.

ERIKSON'S CONTRIBUTION

Each stage in personal development is characterized by certain aspects that can be maximally affected either positively or negatively. For too long, personal and emotional development was considered out of bounds for educators, as the exclusive province of child guidance clinics and of those specially trained to deal with pathological problems. Erikson's great contribution has been to bring the problems of personal growth out of the shadows of pathology and to integrate them into the overall process of healthy personality development. Erikson spells out the major personal issues for us so that we can understand much more about our pupils at each of the various stages. Such insight will hopefully guide us to more effective ways of helping children and teenagers during important, indeed critical, times.

Erikson sums it up:

> *Each successive step, then, is a potential crisis because of a radical* change in perspective. *There is, at the beginning of life, the most radical change of all: from intrauterine to extrauterine life. But in postnatal existence, too, such radical adjustments of perspective as lying relaxed, sitting firmly, and running fast must all be accomplished in their own good time. With them, the interpersonal perspective, too, changes rapidly and often radically, as is testified by the proximity in time of such opposites as "not letting mother out of sight" and "wanting to be independent." Thus,* different capacities use different opportunities *to become full-grown components of the ever-new configuration that is the growing personality.*[19]

Summary

Personal development should not be regarded as a process separate from other aspects of development. There is a common tendency to pay lip service to the idea that aspects of development are not really separate, but then to talk about these domains as if they were compartmentalized.

Prior to Freud, the common assumption about children younger than six was that they were empty, literally mindless creatures. Accordingly, little was expected of them. Freud was a pioneer in emphasizing the importance of sensitive growth periods for personal development during childhood.

The main emphasis in this chapter is on Erik Erikson's theory of a series of stages extending over the period of the life cycle. Each stage is defined by positive and negative psycho-social tasks. How adequately a person resolves each task stage helps to determine and promote strength for succeedings stages. The stages are linked together in an interdependent manner.

Trust-mistrust
Autonomy-shame
Initiative-guilt
Mastery-inferiority
Identity-diffusion

Evidence is presented to support the importance of the specified major issue at each stage. For example, Harlow's work, Spitz's research, and Anna Freud's studies all suggest the critical importance of careful, warm, and consistent parenting in the first eighteen months to establish basic trust in the infant.

Professor "Bud" White's studies detail the significance of indirect teaching, and so-called "supermothering" during preschool years as a means of building competence, autonomy, and initiative in young children.

During the child's juvenile years it is important to note the dangers of adult manipulation—namely, that children may appear to like and enjoy being told what to do. It is tempting to victimize the child, as derived from Robert White's concept of competence motivation. By reviewing the evidence in this area, educators may begin to see that their role can include the need to encourage and facilitate personal competence at each stage.

Specific difficulties and challenges of adolescent development are outlined. The stage is determined by a combination of "inside" changes (glands, physiological make-up) as well as "outside" changes (society's expectations and rites of passage). Common adolescent defense mechanisms as well as egocentric thinking patterns form a basis for understanding the interactions between the teenager and the environment.

To promote healthy personal development during adolescence has always been difficult, and these difficulties are increasing due to the passive nature of most secondary-school learning programs. This problem is underscored in this chapter, while more detailed suggestions for educational change can be found in Chapter 21.

REFERENCES

1
S. White, "Changes in Learning Processes in the Late Pre-School Years," paper presented at AERA Convention, Chicago, 1968.

2
L. K. Frank, *On the Important of Infancy* (New York: Random House, 1966).

3
L. K. Frank, "The Fundamental Needs of the Child," *Mental Hygiene* 22 (1938):353–379. Also in R. C. Sprinthall and N. A. Sprinthall, eds., *Educational Psychology: Selected Readings* (New York: Van Nostrand Reinhold, 1969), p. 71.

4
S. Freud, *A General Introduction to Psychoanalysis* (New York: Washington Square Press, 1960).

5
E. H. Erikson, "Identity and the Life Cycle," *Psychological Issues* 1 (1959), Monograph 1.

6
H. F. Harlow and M. K. Harlow, "Social Deprivation in Monkeys," *Scientific American* 207 (1962):136–146.

7
R. A. Spitz, "Hospitalism: A Follow-up Report," *Psychoanalytic Study of the Child,* vol. 2 (New York: International University Press, 1946).

8
S. Fraiberg, *The Magic Years* (New York: Scribner, 1959).

9
B. L. White, *The First Three Years of Life* (Englewood, N.J.: Prentice-Hall, 1976).

10
E. Erikson, "Identity and the Life Cycle," *Psychological Issues*, Vol. 1, no. 1, p. 78. Reprinted by permission of W. W. Norton & Co., Inc. Copyright © 1959 by International Universities Press, Inc.

11
E. Erikson, "Identity and the Life Cycle." *Psychological Issues*, Vol. 1, no. 1, p. 100. Reprinted by permission of W. W. Norton & Co., Inc. Copyright © 1959 by International Universities Press, Inc.

12
R. W. White, "Motivation Reconsidered: The Concept of Competence," *Psychological Review* 66 (1959):297–333.

13
P. R. Costanzo and M. E. Shaw, "Conformity as a Function of Age Level," *Child Development* 37 (1966):967–975.

14
L. Kohlberg and C. Gilligan, "The Adolescent as a Philosopher," *Daedalus* 100, no. 4 (1971):1051–1086.

15
D. Elkind, *Children and Adolescents* (New York: Oxford, 1970).

16
A. Freud, "Adolescence," *Psychoanalytic Study of the Child* 13 (1958):255–276.

17
E. Erikson, "Identity and the Life Cycle," *Psychological Issues*, Vol. 1, no. 1, pp. 90–91. Reprinted by permission of W. W. Norton & Co., Inc. Copyright © 1959 by International Universities Press, Inc.

18
J. S. Coleman et al., *Youth: Transition to Adulthood* (Chicago: University of Chicago Press, 1974).

19
E. Erikson, "Identity and the Life Cycle," *Psychological Issues*, Vol. 1, no. 1, p. 55. Reprinted by permission of W. W. Norton & Co., Inc. Copyright © 1959 by International Universities Press, Inc.

9

Education and student discipline

Since the beginning of time, almost any teacher asked to identify his or her most difficult problem has complained of student discipline. An archaeologist reportedly found evidence of the antiquity of this problem in the ruins of ancient Sumeria. He is supposed to have dug up some clay tablets recording a conversation between an adult and a teenager. According to the archaeologist's translation, the adult harangued the teenager as follows, "Grow up. Stop hanging around the public square and wandering up and down the street. Go to school. Night and day you torture me. Night and day you waste your time having fun."[1] These words were spoken some 4000 years ago; the problem—lack of discipline, unruliness, wasting time. The more recently discovered memoirs of President Everett of Harvard suggest that he spent the most miserable three years of his life (1846-1849) dealing with problems of student discipline. As a scholar, Everett was regarded as equal to "Pericles in Athens," yet he complained bitterly about his students:

> Hateful duties in the morning to question three students about beckoning to loose women in the College Yard on Sunday afternoon; to two others about whistling in the passage; to another about smoking in the College Yard. Is this all I am fit for? . . . The life I am now leading must end, or it will end me.
>
> . . . My time taken up all day with the most disgusting details of discipline, such as make the heart perfectly sick—fraud, deception, falsehood, unhandsome conduct, parents and friends harassing me all the time and foolishly believing the lies their children tell them.[2]

If we turn to fiction we find similar sentiments. The tragic figure of the father in John Updike's novel, *The Centaur*, is likewise upset and in despair concerning student behavior and discipline. Mr. Caldwell, perhaps overstating the problem for effect, turned to a particularly "slow-witted" pupil, Deifendorf:

> *"The Founding Fathers," he explained, "in their wisdom decided that children were all an unnatural strain on parents. So they provided jails called schools, equipped with tortures called an education. . . . I am a paid keeper of society's unusables—the lame, the halt, the insane and the ignorant. The only incentive I can give you, kid, to behave yourself is this: if you don't buckle down and learn something, you'll be as dumb as I am, and you'll have to teach school to earn a living."*[3]

It seems safe to conclude that problems of student behavior and discipline have been with us for a long time and will probably be with us for a long time to come. Recent studies of teachers' attitudes toward children's behavior have revealed concerns exactly like those revealed by the ruins of ancient Sumeria, by President Everett of Harvard, and by Updike's Mr. Caldwell. In 1928, for example, a study found that the greatest concern of most teachers was acting-out, loud, disruptive children.[4] Some forty years later, in a replication, another researcher came to very much the same conclusion.[5] A particularly tragic effect of this preoccupation is that teachers may fail to recognize one of the most common mental-health problems—excessive inhibition—because their attention is diverted by the noisy, aggressive pupils. Even though educational psychologists have been trying to convince teachers to look beyond the obvious and recognize that withdrawn children may be a more serious problem than loud, active children, there is still a very strong tendency to equate activity and noise with a discipline problem and to ignore passivity.

STUDENT DISCIPLINE AND THE FALLACY OF CHARACTER EDUCATION

A general assumption we all tend to make about discipline is that pupils learn best when they are quiet. When we say, "Learn with your eyes and ears but not with your mouth," we are assuming that we can't learn anything if we are talking, making noise, or moving around. When all the students are sitting quietly, listening in rapt attention to the teacher, it does look as though they are learning. However, as we have already noted in Chapters 5 and 6, appearances are deceiving.

Quiet learning: "sit up straight in your chairs and listen"

If we accept the idea that a quiet atmosphere promotes learning, it follows that any breach of that atmosphere is not to be tolerated. In fact, to carry this logic a step further, it becomes the teacher's moral duty to keep peace in the classroom, because it is by this means that pupils develop the proper moral character. Thus, the teacher's role is seen in terms of simple-minded character training or moral education.

Teaching and keeping the peace

Because of the seriousness with which moral education is viewed, no latitude or flexibility can be allowed. Student behavior is an indication of character, so teachers may react strongly to noncompliant behavior: there is no room for give and take when we are dealing with issues of character.

Teachers often assume that silent attention is a sign of learning
and that orderly obedience is a sign of character building.
The teacher must face the conflict between the need for
classroom control and the encouragement of self-reliance and
responsibility.

Finally, to make matters even worse, this view assumes that by forcing
obedience and conformity on children in school, self-directing and self-con-
trolled adults will result. To many of us, however, it seems strangely paradoxical
to teach self-control, personal independence, and responsibility by forcing students to be dependent and controlled. The discontinuity between demanding
one set of behaviors when people are young and expecting a completely opposite set when they are older strikes us as counterproductive. Education will
simply not promote personal independence if we insist on dependence and
conformity during the formative years. We noted earlier in this volume the almost indelible effect of early experience on later behavior. Teaching dependence
and conformity will tend to enhance those behaviors rather than promote independence, inquiry, and self-direction.

*The paradox: teaching
for conformity and
self-direction*

The teacher as a Western marshall with a white hat.

MODELS FOR CLASSROOM CONTROL

Before turning to the general issue of education for personal independence, we will present some of the common models of classroom control to illustrate the direct relationship between method of control (teacher sanctions) used and resulting student behaviors. Given this relationship, we can no longer say that students are discipline problems, or even that students misbehave, or that they are bad; that would ignore the other half of the problem, the teacher. Neither can we say, as some critics do, that discipline problems are created by teachers so they can apply the sanctions, since this would again ignore half of the problem. We can say that discipline is a function of the interaction between teacher and student, not the single property of either. We noted in Chapter 1 that the concept of ecology was important for educators. The discipline question is a good example. Children and teachers together form the ecology of the classroom environment—their interaction produces either a positive or negative learning atmosphere. The following illustrations have been drawn from over a decade of observation of initial and inservice teaching in a variety of settings. We have selected them as the most obvious samples of classroom difficulties.

Western drama in the classroom

In this situation the teacher is a genuine stickler for obedience, an advocate of "law and order." The most minor breach of peace brings out all the forces for control. Like the marshal in a Western drama, the teacher strides through the class, the "white hat" defending his or her honor and the reputation of the classroom. The confrontation, when it comes, almost inevitably arises over a minor issue, permitting the teacher to set a genuine example before all other pupils of what happens to wrongdoers, even for minor transgressions.

Unfortunately, once this process is set in motion, both teacher and pupil begin to function according to the "script." Neither can afford to lose face or back down. The teacher strides menacingly toward the pupil who stands his ground; the class watches silently, rooting for the underdog but knowing the outcome. Of course, the "marshal" wins the shoot-out. The duel over, the pupil vanquished once again silently waits to get even next time.

The interaction pattern is set. Another day will bring another contender to challenge the teacher. The scene will be repeated. Neither teacher nor pupil interact as human beings. Each represents a position or posture, and the outcome is as predictable as the classic Western plot. Once the challenge is issued, it all follows automatically. The participants don't really talk to each other, nor do they understand each other.

Head-in-the-sand: the permissive/explosive syndrome

A second interaction, quite the opposite of the Western drama, is the head-in-the-sand approach. The teacher is studiously indifferent to student misbehavior and ignores all the usual class rules: he or she doesn't seem to mind when pupils leave their seats, talk, or come to class unprepared. In a sense, all the surefire techniques for getting a teacher to explode and lose control in the classroom don't seem to work here. If character is to be built, it will not be by enforcing discipline but by ignoring misbehavior. The teacher seems a model of forbearance, though in reality he or she is more like the ostrich who buries its head in the sand. Eventually, of course, the teacher does have to look up and witness the classroom anarchy. What he or she usually doesn't see, however, is the subtle sets of teacher-student interactions. It is the teacher's gradual withdrawal and indifference that prompt the students to react: their boldness grows as his or her withdrawal increases. This type of interaction is more subtle than the Western drama but equally programmed. Noncontrol is no more a solution to the problem of discipline than the law-and-order approach. Also, the permissive teacher often finally breaks down and explodes or permanently retreats and runs for cover. The experiences of certain well-meaning but permissive, or what we could term laissez-faire, teachers who have gone into urban classrooms illustrate this point. Unfortunately, their behavior has too often tended to encourage student acting-out. Such teachers may be literally driven out of the classroom, their good intentions dashed and their hopes shattered. Few apparently ever realize how their interactions with pupils created a devastating environment. To replace an autocrat or a tough Marine sergeant with an ostrich simply creates a new set of educational problems.[6]

The head-in-the-sand approach.

Mary Poppins in the classroom. Entertainment replaces classroom learning.

Keep the little devils busy: Mary Poppins in the classroom

In this case the teacher usually agrees with the old adage about the devil and idle hands and solves the problem of classroom control by keeping the students busy all the time. By carefully sequencing activities, the teacher moves the pupils through each class with rapid-fire speed. Discussions are brief. The class moves along, almost breathlessly trying to keep up with the teacher. Of course, what usually happens is that the class senses the game and rises to the occasion. By figuring out how to dispense with the busy work in short order, students leave themselves free time, and so defeat the system. Or, more likely, they join the game and play it into absurdity. Sooner or later the teacher realizes that it is impossible to plan enough activities to occupy the "little devils," and may then play for a stalemate in which both sides acknowledge the game and allow some accommodation. This may result in a semblance of teacher control, but probably little in the way of learning. "Fun in the classroom" activities to entertain and control the pupils lose their uniqueness after awhile. How many times could you play spelling-baseball or math-jeopardy or Botticelli before you grew bored? A Mary Poppins may have the ingenuity and energy to keep it up day after day, but even then the pupils may simply sit back and wait to be entertained.

The collective: how to use group coercion to control the classroom

Some teachers discover how to use students to control the classroom. This goes well beyond the old-fashioned system of using students as hall monitors, door-keepers, and classroom guards. In the collective, the teacher finds that effective sanctions can be invoked to coerce and control individual students. In fact, the group may be quite eager to punish individual members: the teacher convinces the class to accept certain rules, such as prompt arrival, good posture, assignments handed in on time, etc. If an individual does not perform, then the group as a whole may be punished. The phrases are all too familiar:

THERE WILL BE NO RECESS TODAY...

> "All right, class, we will sit here until the person who threw the spitball gives himself up." Or, "you will all redo the assignment because some were handed in late." "There will be no recess today." "All athletic games have been canceled because . . . ." "Unless the person who stole the class-picture money confesses, the picnic will be canceled."

The main point, of course, is the degree to which pupil compliance can be forced through the application of group pressure. Pupils will soon turn against one of their peers if the teacher keeps after them, for it is much easier to take it out on the individual pupil than to buck the teacher. The group agrees with the leader because it has no choice. The individual quickly learns to conform to the group at the risk of being ostracized. This is an exceedingly high price to pay for individuality. Some of the recent anthropological studies (where researchers actually sit in classrooms and observe over long periods of time) show that many teachers do manipulate group sanctions, so that classroom democracy becomes a guise for almost total control. Apparently teachers tend to fall into this system more by default than through deliberate planning.[7]

The Wizard of Oz: the master/puppet system (or 1984?)

Probably the most difficult system of teacher control to describe is the Wizard of Oz approach. The teacher may be so skilled at carefully sequencing rewards and punishments that the pupils never realize they are being manipulated. Through subtle psychological manipulation, the teacher remains the actual hub of the entire classroom. This approach is most common at the elementary level. Very young children can be quite easily exploited. The patronage system becomes highly "efficient":

> "Let's see which big, strong young man will open the windows for us." "Since Mary's paper is so neat, she can collect the milk money for us today."

Public recognition and humiliation through the use of shame can be exploited to orchestrate a class with all the skill of a fine conductor. Control is virtually total. Behavior is manipulated to suit the teacher's needs. From an educational point of view, what is probably most harmful is that pupils often indicate they enjoy and are happy with such teachers. The manipulation can be so expert and subtle that the pupils themselves do not recognize it. However, if an

The master/puppet system. Skillful manipulation takes the place of teaching.

observer watches such a class carefully, it will soon be apparent that every activity, every movement, almost every expressed thought is being controlled by the teacher. Spontaneity is nonexistent—the children are little more than puppets.

In Chapter 7 we discussed the lengthy period of human dependency, from birth to adulthood, that led Erik Erikson to warn adults against giving in to the temptation to exploit children and teenagers. Educators especially should heed this warning, since so much time is spent and so much interaction during this period occurs in classrooms. We need to avoid developing our own powers at the expense of children and teenagers.[8]

DISCIPLINE AND MORAL DEVELOPMENT

The various methods of control teachers commonly use are, at best, temporary means of coping. Discipline problems are all too often blamed on defects in the pupil's character or home environment. We noted in Chapter 1 that teachers have a tendency to relegate pupils to fixed categories by such statements as, "That boy is a poor student because he is a discipline problem." Philosophers have a name for such statements: nominal fallacies. A nominal fallacy mistakes a description for an explanation. It is meaningless to say that someone is a discipline problem. Both parts of the statement are descriptions; they cannot be related as cause and effect.

Nominal fallacy: confusing description with causation

In addition to the misguided assumption that you can explain upsetting behavior by merely labeling it a behavior problem, teachers sometimes mistakenly assume that children are undersized adults—a notion we call the Lord of the Flies syndrome. In Chapters 3 and 8 we noted this tendency. Also recall the array of procedures adults have developed to mold children's minds and bodies to fit that view. Probably in no area is this as apparent as in moral development and pupil discipline. For thousands of years adults have universally put great effort and energy into shaping the moral growth of the young: character education seems to have been a major emphasis throughout the history of civilization. The approach to moral development and character education, however, usually assumes that we begin life as formless organisms that, if given half a chance, will grow up into vicious and uncontrollable savages. According to this view, children require constant adult surveillance so that they will not be consumed by primitive/destructive impulses. The role of character education was to tame the wild and ferocious child into a model of adult decorum, to make the little beasts over into civilized ladies and gentlemen.

William Golding's 1954 novel *Lord of the Flies* describes what happens to a group of English schoolboys who are stranded alone on an island. At the outset the children are proper English gentlemen who sing the school songs and work cooperatively in the finest tradition of English character. Gradually, however, their civilized behavior, their manners, dress, and deportment, are grotesquely transformed. The polite schoolboys become little savages who lose all self-control and desire to cooperate: dressed in war paint and loincloths and carrying spears, they begin a blood lust that ends in murder. And, just as a second murder is about to take place, a British naval force lands on the island and discovers the children. The commander, viewing the children for the first time, says slowly, "I would have expected more from English children."

We have been stressing an alternative to the view of children presented in *Lord of the Flies*. Yet it is probably true that most adults consider children to be on the verge of self-destruction. It is certainly true that many teachers treat their pupils as if they were about to erupt into some primitive orgy of wanton destruction. Our point here is simply that a view such as that expressed in *Lord of the Flies* will lead a teacher to invoke strict and continuous sanctions against the children. We are not opposed to sanctions—we have already seen what happens when a teacher pretends not to notice loud and noisy behavior. However, we must question what the teacher's punishment accomplishes. What basic objective do teachers achieve by invoking these sanctions? If their objective is to prevent the children from becoming savages, because the teachers believe that children, unlike adults, possess only a thin veneer of "civilization," then the teachers are trapped by their own assumptions. Children are no more or less

Character education
to tame the beast
within the breast

inherently aggressive than adults. Nor is there any evidence that teachers, or for that matter any other adult, can deliberately develop character in children by employing the usual teaching techniques. There are exceptions, of course, but in general the evidence indicates that the usual approaches to character education have no positive effects.

HARTSHORNE AND MAY: THE FAILURE OF THE BAG-OF-VIRTUES APPROACH

In the literature of almost any school, "character building" can be found as a stated objective. The Boston Public Schools' "Curriculum Guide in Character Education" proclaims that

> We are unfit for any trust til we can and do obey.
> Honor thy father and mother.
> True obedience is true liberty.
> The first law ever God gave to man was a law of obedience.

Each agency has its own list of virtues to be taught to pupils. Some endorse honesty, service to others, self-control; others promote courage, responsibility, friendliness. Practically every man remembers the Boy Scout Oath or at least the last line, "Brave, Clean, and Reverent." Similarly, most women probably remember memorizing the Girl Scout Oath or the Camp Fire Creed. The idea behind these rituals is quite simple: to instill in the young particular traits and virtues. Character building was thought to be the means of achieving discipline in the classroom as well as in life. In fact, it is truly amazing that this notion was accepted for centuries before someone finally examined how effective the process actually was.

In the 1920s two researchers, Hartshorne and May at the University of Chicago, conducted a long series of studies, which they replicated again and again.[9] Their results were a bombshell. In every study they arrived at the same conclusion: formal character instruction had no positive effect. They studied regular school classes in character education, special Sunday-school classes, Boy Scout classes, and others. In every case they concluded that there was no correlation at all (essentially an r of 0) between character-education/virtue training and actual behavior (such as cheating). They also found essentially no consistent moral behavior in the same person from one situation to another based on character education. This seemed to imply that people who cheat in one situation may or may not cheat in the next situation. (The sample honesty tests accompanying this discussion may help demonstrate such an assertion.) In general, moral behavior seemed unpredictable and moral character traits mythical. If ingrained character traits such as honesty or dishonesty did exist, then it would be possible to predict behavior accurately.

To make matters worse (Hartshorne and May were as dismayed as everyone else), the researchers also found no relationship between what people said about morality and the way these same people acted. People who express great disapproval of cheating or stealing actually steal and cheat as much as anyone else. Hartshorne and May concluded that it was meaningless to divide people into simple categories and label them as either honest or dishonest. Almost

No correlation between character education and moral behavior

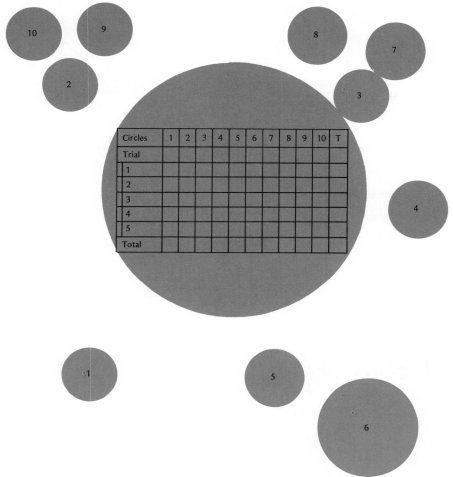

Circles	1	2	3	4	5	6	7	8	9	10	T
Trial											
1											
2											
3											
4											
5											
Total											

Sample honesty tests. The Eye-Hand Coordination and Memory Test

At the signal for each trial place your pencil at point X. Study the circles, then *close your eyes* and write the number 1 in the first circle, the second circle, the third circle, etc. For the second trial open your eyes, place your pencil at point X, *close your eyes* and write the number 2 in the first circle, the second circle, and so on. For the third trial, follow the same procedure and write the number 3, etc. Proceed for five trials.

After each trial, put a check mark in the score box for each time you hit the correct circle. Count the checks and enter the total in column T. After the last trial, add up column T. This is your total score. The maximum is 50.

everyone is dishonest some of the time. And like so many other aspects of human nature, cheating is normally distributed around a level of moderate cheating. A normal distribution means we can fit the results of tests that detect cheating on a bell-shaped curve. The distribution will look the same as that for measured intelligence, height, weight, or coin flipping for heads or tails. (See Chapter 16 for further discussion on the meaning of normal distribution.) Hartshorne and May found that what was true for supposed traits such as honesty/dishonesty was also true for traits such as altruism/selfishness and self-control/impulsiveness. What this does, of course, is call into question the entire con-

Maze no.	Score value
1	1
2	1
3	1
4	1
5	1
6	2
7	2
8	2
9	2
10	2
11	5
12	10
13	15
14	20
15	35
Total	100

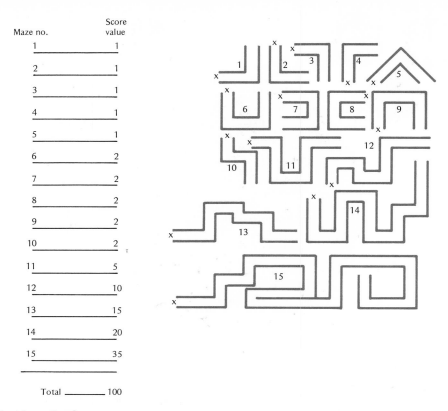

Sample honesty test. The Mazes Puzzle

Wait for signal before beginning each maze. Each time, put the point of your pencil on the cross. Then, when the signal is given, shut your eyes and move the pencil through the maze without touching the sides. After each successful effort enter the score value on the line at the left after the maze number. The score value of the maze is given in the right-hand column. When through, add your scores. The maximum score is 100.

Character traits as a bag of virtues

cept of character traits. What is true for Hartshorne and May's seemingly old-fashioned virtues is equally true for the virtues we may cherish today. This means that if we ridicule the idea of teaching children to be "thrifty, brave, clean, and reverent," an antiquated bag of virtues, it is also meaningless to try to teach children to be "spontaneous, open, authentic, or genuine." A bag of virtues is a bag of virtues. None is particularly amenable to being taught. Merely changing the content of the virtues to be taught will not change the outcome. We may prefer the more modern traits, but this does not advance the educational problems of student growth and discipline. In Chapter 2 we said that "telling" was not teaching, and the same holds true for character development. Telling children and teenagers to adopt particular virtues or manipulating them until they say the right words will not produce significant personal or cognitive development.

Problems of student discipline are actually interaction problems. It is the teacher *and* pupil interacting that create behavior or deportment difficulties. A view that excludes either one is incomplete.

DISCIPLINE AND THE CLASSROOM: SOME SUGGESTIONS

By now it probably seems almost hopeless to consider suggestions about pupil discipline. Our major point, of course, is that problems of student discipline are in large part interaction problems arising from assumptions adults hold concerning the nature of child and adolescent development. Teacher-pupil interaction can create either a positive or negative environment for learning. The old biblical view that pupils were to sit, listen, mark, and "inwardly digest" as passive receptacles is a gross distortion of the teaching-learning process. Thus, how we develop classroom atmospheres is dependent on our understanding of this process. In the next chapter, we discuss a comprehensive framework for viewing the general process of moral development. At this time, therefore, we will make only a few process recommendations concerning classroom interactions.

1

Carefully review, either by systematic counting or even by tape recording some typical classroom discussions, the ratio of positive to negative comments made by you. Recent studies have suggested that teachers average somewhere in the vicinity of 8:1, negative to positive comments. If you find you are more negative than positive, deliberately attempt to increase your number of supportive, accepting comments to achieve a more balanced atmosphere.

2

Practice employing "I-messages," a technique developed by Thomas Gordon.[10] This is a system of responding to pupils without shaming or cutting them off at the ankles. In an I-message, you describe the child's behavior, your own feeling, and the general effect or consequence. More precisely the three components of an "I" message are:

a. a nonjudgmental, precise, objective statement of the pupil's behavior—"When you interrupt . . ." (not, "When you impulsively, inconsiderately, and snearingly blurt, shout, and scream out your answers. . . .")

b. a statement explaining why the behavior is troublesome—"I can't hear what Nancy was trying to say . . ." (not, "I cannot let you run over, steamroller, cut people off, have your own way, be so self-centered. . . .")

c. a statement of how you feel—"I feel frustrated trying to listen to two people at once . . ." (not, "I feel ashamed to have such a poor citizen in my class who casts such a terrible reflection on the rest of us. How do you ever expect to grow up and not end up on welfare?").

3

Review the physical environment and make adjustments to reduce the possibilities of unnecessary conflict. Naturally expecting all pupils to sit in neat rows, faces forward, erect and attentive for long periods of time is bound to create discipline problems. Increase the variety of teaching-learning strategies—"learning centers" within a classroom, small-group tasks, and cooperative teaching. We would particularly recommend a new paperback, *Learning Together and Alone,* for examples of small-group, cooperative learning atmospheres and how to rearrange the physical environment.[11]

4

Initiate classroom discussions on the problem of discipline. The class-meeting procedure developed by William Glasser is particularly useful in building class cohesion and joint responsibility between the teacher and pupils. Obviously, it is important to gradually share the responsibility for reasonable control with the pupils—interaction means that everybody is in the same boat. No one really enjoys or learns in an atmosphere of chaos or excessive punitiveness. It will require time and patience to develop this atmosphere of joint responsibility, but when you reach your goal, the rewards are substantial. No longer will you be burdened with the responsibility of single-handedly maintaining the peace.[12]

5

Finally, remember that creating positive atmospheres requires time. Studies have shown that the transition periods are the worst. When you alter the classroom atmosphere from an authoritarian to a more-democratic climate, the children need time to adjust to new expectations and test out the new and broader limits. This is difficult, also, because you are essentially trying to shift the balance of control from external to internal sources. Authoritarian control does work to a point, yet it requires constant external vigilance. When you seek to help pupils develop internal self-control, you are attempting to lay the foundations of personal self-management—no easy task for children, teenagers, or adults, for that matter.

Summary

Student discipline problems seem endemic to teaching. Examples from ancient Sumeria, the Harvard College riots in the 1800s, down to the present, all suggest a long-standing pattern of difficulty in finding solutions.

Part of the pattern derives from the fallacy of so-called character education—the attempt to enforce pupil silence, instill discipline from the outside, and force pupils to listen, attend, and inwardly mark.

A second aspect of the difficulty derives from the singular view that discipline problems are almost always the fault of the pupils. This isomorphic view suggests that all problems are safely and neatly "inside" each pupil. He or she is to be trained, socialized, and conditioned like a robot to obey adult commands.

Teacher behavior patterns are outlined to illustrate common teacher responses. In our view, discipline problems are in reality interaction problems—a combination of teacher-pupil relationships. Children and teachers together form the ecology of the classroom.

Hartshorne and May's work demonstrated the total ineffectiveness of old-fashioned character education. Boy Scouts, Sunday school, Girl Scouts, and other means of "building character" usually fail due to their narrow base—telling, lecturing, extolling on one hand and a narrow goal on the other. Traits like honesty versus dishonesty, truth versus falsehood, right versus wrong, etc. are too stereotyped, fixed, and static as learning outcomes. There is need for a comprehensive moral theory to explain the complex process of value, ethical, and moral development.

Examples are presented of some of the newer techniques to promote positive classroom atmospheres as a means of avoiding disciplinary confrontation. Process recommendations include: review the ratio of negative to positive teacher comments; practice the use of "I messages"; adjust the learning atmosphere and make use of cooperative teaching; utilize classroom meetings to discuss discipline issues; and, finally, be particularly sensitive to "transition" periods in switching classes from authoritarian to more democratic classroom climates.

REFERENCES

1
Quoted from *Everyday Life in Bible Times,* National Geographic Society, 1968.

2
Quoted in *Harvard Alumni Bulletin,* May 1, 1965, p. 583.

3
J. Updike, *The Centaur* (New York: Alfred A. Knopf, 1963), pp. 80–81. Reprinted by permission.

4
E. K. Wickman, *Children's Behavior and Teacher's Attitudes* (New York: Commonwealth Fund, 1928).

5
H. Beilin, "Teachers' and Clinicians' Attitudes toward the Behavior Problems of Children: A Reappraisal," *Child Development* 30 (1959):9–25.

6
E. Fuchs, *Teachers Talk* (New York: Doubleday, 1969).

7
P. Jackson, *Life in Classrooms* (New York: Holt, Rinehart and Winston, 1968).

8
See particularly:

J. Henry, "American Schoolrooms: Learning the Nightmare," in R. C. Sprinthall and N. A. Sprinthall, eds., *Educational Psychology: Selected Readings* (New York: Van Nostrand Reinhold, 1969).

E. Z. Friedenberg, *The Vanishing Adolescent* (Boston: Beacon Press, 1959).

H. Becker, "Social Class Variations in the Teacher-Pupil Relationships," in Sprinthall and Sprinthall, *Educational Psychology.*

9
H. Hartshorne and M. May, *Studies in the Nature of Character,* vols. 1, 2, 3, (New York: Macmillan, 1928–1930).

10
T. Gordon, *Teacher Effectiveness Training* (New York: Wyden, 1974).

11
D. W. Johnson and R. T. Johnson, *Learning Together and Alone* (New Jersey: Prentice-Hall, 1975).

12
W. Glasser, *Schools without Failure* (New York: Harper & Row, 1961).

10

Moral education

In the preceding chapter we described some of the common problems of student discipline. The major difficulty, we concluded, is that teachers have assumed they must force children to "mark, learn, and inwardly digest" what we have to tell them. Transgressions are usually dealt with severely, lest the pupils gain unbridled ascendancy. This unfortunately traps teachers into viewing discipline problems as basically out of their control, since the problem is thought to be isolated within the child.

An alternative view—our view—assumes that discipline problems are more likely the result of interactions between teachers and pupils. Therefore, a teacher, or for that matter any adult, really has to understand the process of personal and moral development in children. If this development is understood, discipline problems can be used for creative interaction between adults and students. In this chapter, we discuss what has been discovered about the process of moral development in children and adolescents.

MORAL GROWTH AS A DEVELOPMENTAL PROCESS:
KOHLBERG'S THEORY

After the work of Hartshorne and May in the 1920s and early 1930s, very little attention, theoretical or practical, was paid to the area of moral development as an educational problem. In some ways it was simply not fashionable to examine that goal as an educational concern. Instead, teachers were taught a series of classroom-management techniques. It was considered unnecessary to worry about the children's development. Either they would unfold magically, as a

Lawrence Kohlberg

Gesell might say (see Chapter 6), or, if they were incorrigible, teachers should limit their efforts to keeping the lid on while they were in class. A new theory was needed to provide insight into the problem.

Professor Lawrence Kohlberg, working first at Chicago and more recently at Harvard, has revolutionized our understanding of moral development. He found that people cannot be grouped into neat compartments with simplistic labels, "This group is honest," or "This group cheats," or "This group is reverent." Instead, he found that moral character develops. And this idea, that moral growth occurs in a developmental sequence, has completely revised our basic assumptions.

After conducting a long series of studies with children and adults, Kohlberg found that moral growth occurs in a specific sequence of developmental stages regardless of culture or subculture, continent or country. This means that we can no longer think of moral character in either/or terms, or assume that character is something we do or do not have. Instead of existing as fixed traits, moral character occurs in a series of developmental stages. In other words, what Piaget identified as stages of cognitive development, and what Erikson suggested to be stages of personal development, Kohlberg described as stages of moral development.[1] You may recall from the chapter on cognitive growth (Chapter 6) that a developmental stage, by definition, has four components. Each stage has the following features:

Kohlberg's view: stages of moral growth

Definition of stage sequences

1
It is qualitatively different from the preceding stage.

2
It represents a new and more comprehensive system of "mental" organization.

3
It occurs in an invariant sequence.

4
It is age-related within general groupings.

With this definition in mind, we can now examine some of the specific aspects of this view.

KOHLBERG'S SIX STAGES OF MORAL GROWTH

Kohlberg identified six stages of moral growth, each distinctly different. He derived the stages by studying the system of thinking people actually employ in dealing with moral questions. By asking people from different backgrounds and of different ages to respond to problems involving moral dilemmas, he found that their responses fell into six judgmental systems, on which he based his six categories. The following two examples illustrate the type of problem he used.

Examples of moral dilemmas

1

Joe's father promised he could go to camp if he earned the $50.00 for it, and then changed his mind and asked Joe to give him the money he had earned. Joe lied and said he had only earned $10.00 and went to camp using the other $40.00 he had made. Before he went, he told his younger brother Alex about the money and about lying to their father. Should Alex tell their father?

2

In Europe, a woman was near death from a special kind of cancer. There was one drug that the doctors thought might save her. It was a form of radium that a druggist in the same town had recently discovered. The drug was expensive to make, but the druggist was charging ten times what the drug cost him to make. He paid $200.00 for the radium and charged $2000.00 for a small dose of the drug. The sick woman's husband, Heinz, went to everyone he knew to borrow the money, but he could only get together about $1000.00, which is half of what it cost. He told the druggist that his wife was dying and asked him to sell it cheaper or let him pay later. But the druggist said: "No, I discovered the drug and I'm going to make money from it." So Heinz got desperate and broke into the man's store to steal the drug for his wife. Should the husband have done that?

Moral development—like both cognitive and personal development—appears to proceed in an invariant sequence of development stages. Children cannot skip stages in moral development but, interestingly, a child will prefer moral judgments one level beyond his or her own. This fact has significant implications for the classroom teacher.

As you can see, the problems are complex; they have no single, correct answer. In fact, the least-significant part of the response is the direct answer "Yes" or "No." Most significant are the reasons given for why the person should or should not behave in certain ways. In other words, the way in which suggested behavior is justified defines the respondent's level of moral development. Table 10.1 outlines the six stages of moral growth.

Table 10.1 Kohlberg's stages of moral growth.

Basis of Judgment	Stages of Development
Preconventional moral values reside in external, quasi-physical happenings, in bad acts, or in quasi-physical needs rather than in persons and standards.	*Stage I:* Concern about self. Obedience to a powerful authority. Fear of punishment dominates motives. One sees oneself as being dominated by other forces. Actions are judged in terms of their *physical consequences.* 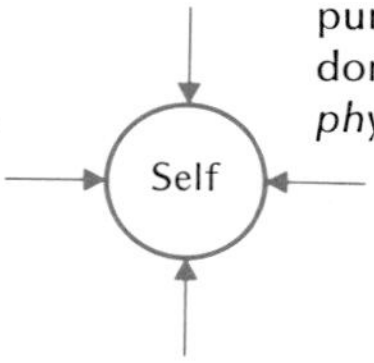
	Stage II: One-way concern about another person (what he/she can do for me, how we can agree to act so *I* will benefit.) The basic motive is to *satisfy my own needs.* I do not consider the needs of the other person, unless I think it will benefit me to do so. 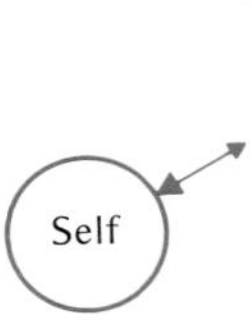
Conventional moral values reside in performing good or right roles, in maintaining the conventional order, and in meeting others' expectations	*Stage III:* Concern about groups of people, and conformity to group norms. There is a two-way relationship (we are good to each other). Motive is to be a "nice guy/gal," to be accepted. Affection plays a strong role. 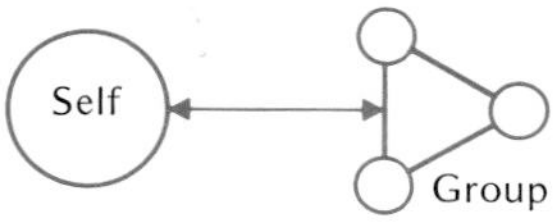
	Stage IV: Concern for order in *society.* Honor and duty come from keeping the rules of the society. The focus is on *preserving the society* (not just obeying, as in Stage I). 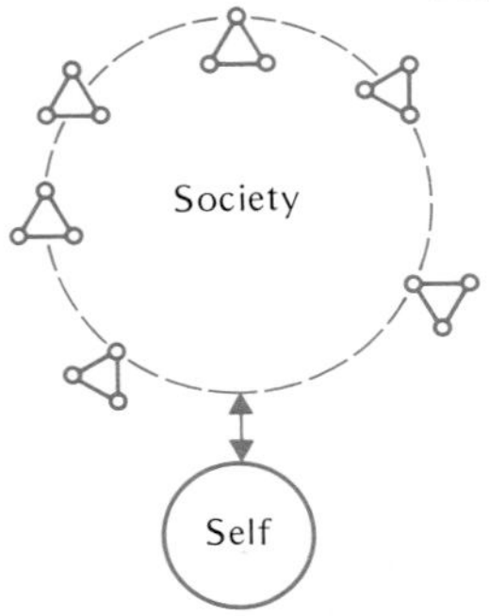

Diagram labels: Self; Other, Self; Self, Group; Society, Self

Basis of Judgment	Stages of Development

Postconventional moral values are derived from principles which can be applied universally

Stage V: Social contract, legalistic orientation. What is right is what the whole society decides. There are no legal absolutes. The society can *change standards* by everyone agreeing to the change. Changes in the law are usually made for reasons of the greatest good for the greatest number of people. Where law is not affected, what is right is a matter of personal opinion and agreement between persons. The U.S. Constitution is written in Stage 5 terms.

Stage VI: Universal ethical principles. What is right is a decision of one's conscience, based on ideas about rightness that apply to *everyone* (all nations, people, etc.). These are called *ethical principles*. An ethical principle is different from a rule. A rule is specific (Thou shalt not kill). An ethical principle is *general* (All persons are created equal). The most important ethical principles deal with justice, equality, and the dignity of all people. These principles are *higher* than any given law.

Free agreement and contract

Self

Democratic agreement on rights, standards, change

Universal principles of justice for all

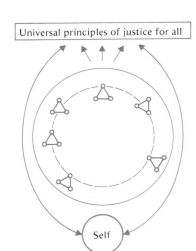

Self

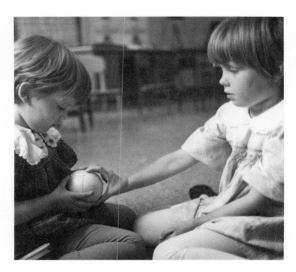

Kohlberg's Stage II actions are based largely on satisfying one's own personal needs.

PRECONVENTIONAL MORALITY: STAGES I AND II

Stage I: punishment and obedience

Stage I obedience and moral decisions are based on very simple physical and material power—"Big fish eat little fish." "Might makes right." "The survival of the fittest." Stage I behavior is based on the desire to avoid severe physical punishment by a superior power.

Stage II: "watch out for number one"

Stage II actions are based largely on satisfying one's own personal needs, or "Looking out for number one." Figure out ways to make trades and exchange favors, "You scratch my back and I'll scratch yours"—but see if you can come out a little bit ahead on each trade. The orientation is materialistic in that moral discussions are expressed in instrumental and physical terms. If, for example, a person is caught stealing a car, punishment is determined by how much the car cost. This also means that it is perfectly permissible to use influence to fix up any so-called wrongdoings. Fixing traffic tickets, bribing people, stealing from the boss, and similar misdemeanors are OK as long as you get away with it. If students alter their report cards, it's a Stage II response, providing they are successful. The clever con man or flim-flam artist are further examples. In philosophical terms this category of moral thinking is referred to as instrumental hedonism, characterized by little human regard for the other person. "Nice guys finish last," genuine empathy is lacking.

In spite of the obvious shortcomings as a system of moral thinking, Stage II, "let's make a deal," does represent an advance over Stage I. Gypping people financially, ignoring others' feelings, cheating at elections and similar behaviors are not as bad as physical torture or death. Thus Stage II thinking represents a more adequate method of problem solving, but only when compared to Stage I, where right and wrong are determined by the fastest gun, the quickest fist, or the biggest bomb.

These first two stages are sometimes classified together as the preconventional stage of moral development. The reason for the term preconventional will be obvious when we look at the next level, Stages III and IV.

CONVENTIONAL MORALITY: STAGES III AND IV

Stage III is the "good-boy" and "good-girl" orientation. At this stage a person makes moral judgments in order to do what is nice and pleases others. At the same time, Stage III thinking is more comprehensive and more complex than Stage II. At this level a person does begin to take into account how others genuinely view the dilemma situation. The egocentrism of Stage II is replaced by the ability to empathize, to feel what others may be feeling, or, as it's called, an increase in social-role-taking perspective.

Stage III: conformity and being nice

The problem with this stage, however, is that individuals may have great difficulty in resolving the conflicting feelings of all those involved in a dilemma situation. Thus in the Heinz case mentioned above, a Stage III response would probably conclude that it was wrong to steal because almost all the people in the community say that stealing is wrong. "I will go along with the majority consensus, or social convention. I understand that most people hold that view and I would feel very uncomfortable going against the wishes of the majority." Thus moral judgment is equated with following the leading crowd.

Stage III moral thinking depends on distinct stereotypes and sharp differences. Relativism and complexity are absent. In this sense, moral behavior is other-directed. Stage III behavior conforms strictly to the fixed conventions of the society in which we live. We don't look inward to our own "self" and attempt to work through a decision independently. Kohlberg often illustrates Stage III behavior by referring to the comic-strip character, Charlie Brown. Charlie is usually caught in a hopeless predicament from trying to please everyone. His pleading with the iron-willed Lucy is both a comic and a poignant illustration of what it is like to try to live life always looking to other people for direction.

At *Stage IV,* the individual looks to rules, laws, or codes for guidance in dilemma situations. In one sense, civil- and criminal-law codes in our society represent a more stable and comprehensive system of resolving moral dilemmas than attempting to solve such questions on the basis of social conventions, community popularity, and what the leading crowd decides is the "nice" thing to do. Laws and rules as codified wisdom can be viewed as a positive glue, providing a society with stability and cohesion by guarding against rampant fads, quickly changing social customs, and societal anarchy or mob rule. The laws or rules represent society's attempt to set the same standards of conduct for all its citizens. Moral judgments are made by individuals in accordance with those rules. A person thinking at this level, then, does not simply look out for number one (Stage II) or follow the leading crowd (Stage III), but rather makes decisions that square with the existing legal codes.

Stage IV: follow the rules

Difficulties arise, however, with this rigid, law-and-order orientation. What do we do when the laws conflict, or are unclear? Lawyers have a saying that difficult and complex social problems make for "bad" laws. In the Heinz case, for example, the law protects the druggist against stealing, but what about an equal-rights law that gives the wife a right to life? It is always possible to come up with exceptional cases to any comprehensive fixed law. For example, there are a few cases each winter where an electric or gas company has turned off the heat on a customer for nonpayment. Contract law is clear: if a person doesn't pay the bill, then the provider of the service is not obligated to continue service. But what happens when the nonpayee dies from the cold? This may be an overly dramatic example, but such exceptional cases do occur. To handle such questions more comprehensively we need recourse to a higher stage of reasoning.

POSTCONVENTIONAL STAGES: V AND VI

Stage V: a system of laws

In the Kohlberg scheme, an individual at the highest stage of moral development behaves according to a social contract (Stage V) or to a universal principle such as justice (Stage VI). Moral thinking and judgments are complex and comprehensive. Diverse points of view are considered. Each situation is examined carefully in order to derive general principles to guide behavior appropriate for all. There are never any easy solutions to complex human problems and moral dilemmas. Judgments and decisions are neither simply situational and conveniently relative, nor are they an easy and fixed application of a rule. At this level, we have to account simultaneously for all the situational aspects, motivations, and general principles involved.

The system of thinking at this level, then, represents a more adequate method of problem solving. Laws are viewed as a system of governance—each law can be judged in terms of the extent to which it squares with the principles of the system.

At Stage V the principles are usually written as a document of assumptions or declaration of ideals. For example, the United States Constitution sets forth a series of principled rights as the basis for judging the adequacy of each law. As you can readily see, the key question becomes resolving dilemmas and conflicting laws by interpreting the intent of these written principles—justice, freedom, liberty, and equality of opportunity, to name a few.

PEANUTS •   By Charles M. Schulz

It is also important to realize that problem solving on moral questions, social justice, or squaring my freedom with your freedom is not necessarily simpler at Stage V. Commonly, there is confusion on this issue: people believe that higher-stage reasoning is better because it's easier. Such is not the case. Reasoning at this level requires the ability to think abstractly (to view laws as a system of governance), to weigh competing claims, to take into account both the logical and emotional domains, to take a stand and yet remain open to future, more adequate interpretations of social justice.*

At Stage VI the principles of social justice are universal, yet not necessarily in written form. It is always difficult to explain the exact difference between Stage V and VI, because in some ways both systems are based on similar concepts. Also, analytical philosophers themselves are unclear as to the distinctions. The "official" definition of Stage VI is that the principles are abstract, ethical, universal, and consistent. As Kohlberg notes, "At heart, these are universal principles of justice, of the reciprocity and equality of human rights, and of the respect for the dignity of human beings as individual persons."[2]

Stage VI: universal principles

One way to see the different levels of complexity involved in judgments at each stage is to examine and compare the different response patterns associated with the preconventional (Stages I and II), conventional (Stages III and IV), and postconventional (Stages V and VI) levels. Let's look at some typical responses, at different levels, to the Heinz case.

A Stage I or II response (preconventional) would say that it was OK for Heinz to steal the drug because the druggist was himself a robber, or simply because Heinz needed it. However, he should be smart enough not to get caught. A Stage III or IV response (conventional) would say that Heinz was wrong in breaking into the store. Either it isn't nice to steal ("What if everyone went around just taking things?"), or the law must always be obeyed regardless of circumstance ("What happens to a society if we all break laws according to our own whim?"). In either case, the social convention or the rule says unequivocally, "Thou shalt not steal." Heinz should be judged the same way an escaped convict would be judged. There is no difference between Heinz and Clyde Barrow of "Bonnie and Clyde" fame. A Stage V or VI response (postconventional) would weigh Heinz's behavior against universal principles. How does the value of life compare to the value of property? What general rights do all people have? What constitutional provisions are there for such behavior? Also, what are the provisions for changing laws? Since there may be bad laws, what avenues are available for seeking redress? Is the law that allows the druggist to make whatever profit he can such a bad law? If so, does this justify, or does it simply rationalize, Heinz's theft? These are essentially Stage V considerations. Moral decisions are based on a system of laws themselves judged on the basis of the common good and social utility. This means that at Stage V we don't view the problem in terms of a single law, but in terms of the entire system.

Examples of answers to the Heinz dilemma

---

*
In a sense the legal interpretations of the Supreme Court in this country exemplify this process. It is possible to judge the moral-justice adequacy of the Court's interpretations over time. The difference between *Dred Scott* and *Brown v. the Board of Education* is an obvious case in point. The voting-rights extension of the Fourteenth Amendment is another obvious example.

At Stage VI the consideration would be based not so much on a system of laws (such as a written constitution), but on unwritten, moral, and universal principles. A moral principle would be something like the Golden Rule ("Do unto others as you would have them do unto you," which is different from the Stage IV Ten Commandments), or it would be an ethical principle like Immanuel Kant's categorical imperative ("Act only as you would be willing that everyone should act in the same situation"). Stage VI principles apply across all social classes and cultures and, in fact, can be considered genuine principles only if they can be applied universally. Thus at this stage decisions are made on the basis of a universal law, or a "higher" law that may not be written or even codified. However, the principles are implicit: value for human life, equality, and dignity. These are distinguished from static virtues and character traits, because the values and principles are universal and dynamic. This also distinguishes such principles as "justice" from narrow and prescribed rules, such as "Thou shalt not steal." Stage VI requires that we consider the circumstances and the situation, as well as the general principles and the reasons behind the rules.

Thus in the Heinz case, a Stage VI response might consider Heinz to be justified in stealing the drug since the value of human life is greater than the value of property—a universal principle. At the same time, Heinz should also be willing to accept legal punishment for stealing. The key here is the reasoning that makes it clear that Heinz deliberately challenged the law that allowed the druggist to make large profits, that he committed an act of civil disobedience and was willing to accept society's punishment for stealing. Socrates' refusal to alter his principles even to save his own life is an example of a Stage VI response. This is an important distinction. A certain behavior in and of itself is not necessarily an indicator of high-moral-stage thinking. For example, in the 1960s, a series of college-campus protests concerning our participation in the Viet Nam war were held: the Berkeley "Free Speech Movement," the Harvard Strike, the Kent State and Jackson State demonstrations, as well as others. From a moral-development perspective it would be important to know each individual's reasons for sitting-in and/or not sitting-in. Obviously there is a difference between a person sitting-in for "kicks"—"man, what a high!"—or because "all my friends are here" and someone who wishes to contest injustice by deliberately being arrested.* These are not simply trivial distinctions; they force us to look at both the action as well as the reasons behind the action.

The accompanying excerpt from Martin Luther King, Jr.'s "Letter from the Birmingham City Jail" (1963) is an example of Stage VI judgment:

> You express a great deal of anxiety over our willingness to break laws. This is certainly a legitimate concern. Since we so diligently urge people to obey the Supreme Court's decision of 1954 outlawing segregation in the public

---

* It is interesting to note that student participants in the famous Berkeley and Columbia campus disorders in the late 1960s were split into two distinct groups. Research on the student activists revealed moral development at either Stage VI or Stage II. L. Kohlberg and R. Kramer, "Continuities and Discontinuities in Childhood and Adult Moral Development," *Human Development* 12 (1969):93–120.

schools, at first glance it may seem rather paradoxical for us consciously to break laws. One may well ask: "How can you advocate breaking some laws and obeying others?" The answer lies in the fact that there are two types of laws: just and unjust. One has not only a legal but a moral responsibility to obey just laws. Conversely, one has a moral responsibility to disobey unjust laws. I would agree with Saint Augustine that "an unjust law is no law at all."

Now what is the difference between the two? How does one determine when a law is just or unjust? A just law is a man-made code that squares with the moral law or the law of God. An unjust law is a code that is out of harmony with the moral law. To put it in the terms of St. Thomas Aquinas: An unjust law is a human law that is not rooted in eternal law and natural law. Any law that uplifts human personality is just. Any law that degrades human personality is unjust.[3]

THE RESEARCH EVIDENCE

Figure 10.1 (page 248) indicates the results of a series of cross-cultural studies. There are a number of important points to note. First, the trends are constant. Stage I and II behavior becomes less frequent as age increases, and Stage IV, V, and VI behavior increases during the same span. From this point of view we can say the sequence is developmental and invariant. The stages occur in order; that is, moral behavior develops from lower to higher stages, and no stages are skipped over. In this way, moral growth is similar to cognitive growth as detailed by Piaget (see Chapter 6). In fact, there is a clear, logical connection between the stages of cognitive growth and the stages of moral development. For example, people cannot possibly operate at Stage V or VI if their own cognitive structures could not accommodate abstract thinking and "formal" operations. Similarly, there is clearly a relationship between concrete thinking (ages seven to eleven, according to Piaget) and the second and third stages of moral development, where children would clearly understand physical punishment (Stage II), or severe disapproval from peers or family (Stage III). At the same time, children at this stage cannot skip ahead and genuinely understand that they should act as if their behavior were a guide for all mankind to follow (Stage VI)!

An invariant sequence: always from lower stages to higher

A second aspect of the sequence of development is particularly critical for teaching. While people cannot skip stages, they do prefer moral judgment that is one stage beyond their own present level. Thus someone operating at Stage II can begin to understand and will prefer a Stage III moral position, while someone operating at Stage V can understand and will prefer Stage VI. The explanation for this probably lies in our ability to understand ideas just beyond our coherent level. Remember William James's comment in Chapter 2 about the good teacher being one who presents an idea just slightly ahead of the students' present understanding? What this means is that, in general, we can appreciate and understand the next stage because it represents a more adequate, comprehensive, integrated, or even a more aesthetic system than our own. The higher stage is a better cognitive organization than the preceding. The implication for teaching is enormous. Students can understand all levels up to their own, but

A preference for one stage "up"

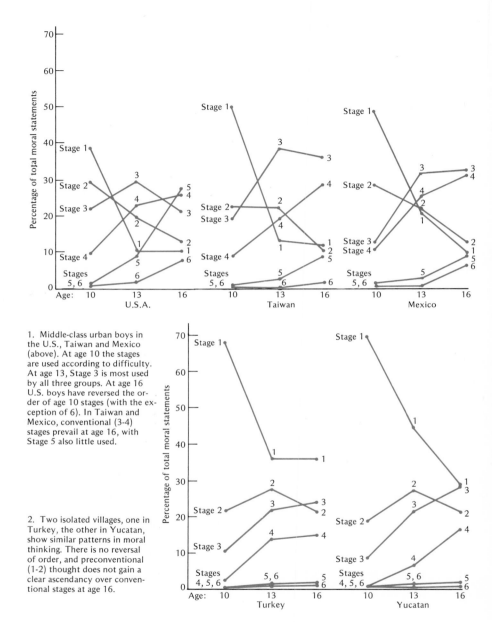

1. Middle-class urban boys in the U.S., Taiwan and Mexico (above). At age 10 the stages are used according to difficulty. At age 13, Stage 3 is most used by all three groups. At age 16 U.S. boys have reversed the order of age 10 stages (with the exception of 6). In Taiwan and Mexico, conventional (3-4) stages prevail at age 16, with Stage 5 also little used.

2. Two isolated villages, one in Turkey, the other in Yucatan, show similar patterns in moral thinking. There is no reversal of order, and preconventional (1-2) thought does not gain a clear ascendancy over conventional stages at age 16.

Fig. 10.1 Cross-cultural studies.

Table 10.2 Comparison of Piaget and Kohlberg.

Piaget (Cognitive Stage)		Kohlberg (Moral Stage)	
Age	Stage	Age	Stage
0–2	Sensori-motor	0–9	Preconventional (Stages I and II)
2–7	Intuitive/preoperational		
7–11	Operational/concrete	9–15	Conventional (Stages III and IV)
11 and up	Formal/abstract thinking	16 and up	Postconventional (Stages V and VI)

Comparing Kohlberg to Piaget

they prefer the next stage above. This means that pupils can become aware of a higher level of moral development if only someone presents it to them. In fact, a series of recent studies have shown that classroom discussions of moral dilemmas (like the Heinz case) can actually contribute to changing, within limits, students' level of moral judgment. The limits, of course, are set by the boundaries of the developmental stages and ages.[4] Table 10.2 compares Piaget's cognitive stages and Kohlberg's moral stages.

COGNITIVE DEVELOPMENT AND MORAL DEVELOPMENT

The relationship between the Piaget and Kohlberg systems is not exactly one to one, but it is significant. In general, the stages of moral development tend to lag slightly behind the stages of cognitive growth. This is certainly understandable when we consider that moral judgments at each stage are considerably more complicated than overall cognitive capacity at each stage.* For example, it is one thing to be able to recognize and understand abstract thought (during adolescence, formal operations allow us to realize that metaphors and similes are symbols), but it is more difficult to take an abstract concept like the Golden Rule and apply it to a difficult human dilemma, such as that represented in the Heinz problem, and come out with a response equivalent to Stage V or VI.

CAN WE SPEED UP MORAL GROWTH?

There are broad limits to the development of moral judgment. For example, we cannot expect elementary-aged children to understand moral thinking at the postconventional levels, nor is it possible to speed up their rate of moral devel-

---

*

We also must realize that there is considerable variability during adolescence in the development of formal operations and abstract thought itself. All children by eleven years attain a clear capacity for logical reasoning at a concrete level. This is not true for formal operations. At ages sixteen to twenty, only 53 percent of those late adolescents had clearly demonstrated a comprehensive capacity for formal operations. L. Kohlberg and C. Gilligan, "The Adolescent as a Philosopher," *Daedalus* 100, no. 4 (Fall 1971):1051–1086.

Acceleration vs. maximum development within each stage

opment. Even if we set up a special intensive program in moral education we would not be able to turn a nine- or ten-year-old into a Stage VI moral thinker and doer. Again, recall Piaget's comments on the so-called American question, "Can we speed up cognitive growth?" (see Chapter 6). We cannot accelerate growth beyond the limits set by the psychological framework. Does this mean, however, that we can do nothing but sit back and hope for an unfolding of a developmental sequence completely internally determined? Obviously not. While almost all adults have successfully passed through the four major stages of cognitive growth and since late adolescents have been able to use at least some formal operations (abstract thinking), very few of them actually ever reach the fifth or sixth stage of moral development; and many do not even reach the third or fourth stage! This means the American question should be rephrased to: "Can we educate pupils during the elementary and secondary school years so they can reach higher levels of moral maturity than is now the case?" If we don't ask ourselves this question, we will fail to educate—by default.

STAGES OF MORAL DEVELOPMENT AND AGE TRENDS

Figure 10.2 shows the ages and predominant, or modal (most common), stages of moral maturity.[5] Between ten and sixteen years of age a major shift occurs: Stage I and II thinking accounts for 66 percent of moral judgments at ten years of age, but for only 20 percent by sixteen years of age. By sixteen there is a double shift: Stage II thinking declines sharply and there is a simultaneous and substantial increase in Stage III and IV thinking (from 32 to 44 percent). By sixteen, then, the modal stage is clearly the conventional stage. There is also a dramatic increase in Stage V and VI thinking, from almost none at all to ten years, to 35 percent by sixteen. Thus, at sixteen the greatest proportional increase is in Stage V and VI thinking from 1 to 35 percent, while the most common stages are III and V.

Also noteworthy in Fig. 10.2 is the relatively slight change in moral growth from sixteen to twenty-five years of age. This indicates that, at least under present conditions, the level of moral maturity stabilizes by late adolescence and early adulthood, approximately between the ages of sixteen and twenty-five. There may be shifts within the broad stages by both age and sex. For example, between the ages of sixteen and twenty-five, women usually remain at Stage III, while men tend to move to Stage IV. Both groups remain at the level of conventional morality, but emphasize different aspects. Women tend to think and act on moral questions in order to please others (Stage III), while men tend to think and act in compliance with fixed and arbitrary "law and order" (Stage IV).*

Stabilization of moral maturity at Stages III and IV by adolescence

---

*
This difference between men and women probably derives from the differing patterns of social and work interaction. The official "morality" of the still predominantly male business world, in trade unions as well as among business executives, tends to be a legal-contractual Stage IV. Housewives, however, tend to interact more within the conventional morality of the neighborhood. We will examine the question of general sex differences in greater detail in the last chapter.

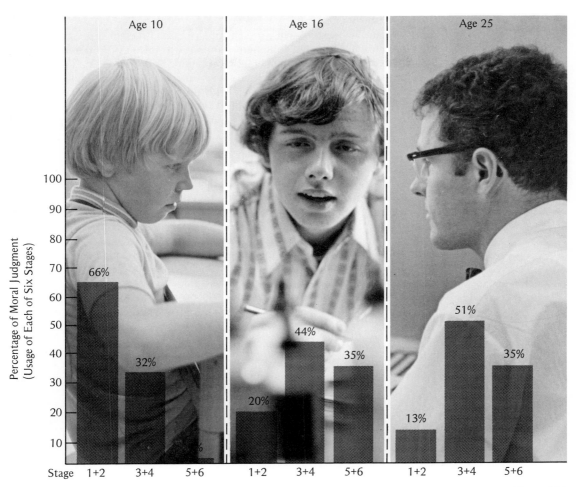

Figure 10.2

Between sixteen and twenty-five years of age, there are also shifts within the postconventional categories (Stages V and VI). The total amount of postconventional activity remains stable at approximately 35 percent. However, the amount of Stage VI thinking doubles from 5 to 10 percent. During this period, then, postconventional activity tends to shift slightly from Stage V to Stage VI.

At present we do not know whether this stabilization of moral-judgment thinking is, in fact, permanent. The first Kohlberg sample of fifty subjects represents an original longitudinal study. Their responses to dilemma situations are scored at three-year intervals to provide a longitudinal basis for understanding the process of development during adulthood. The original testing was done in 1957, so that in 1977 the subjects who were between ten and sixteen years of age are now thirty-one to thirty-seven years of age. Needless to say, the results of such longitudinal testing will provide much needed insight into whether and under what conditions moral judgment continues to develop. Preliminary analysis seems to indicate that under specific conditions moral judgment may, in fact, continue to move toward higher stages for particular individuals.[6]

For the educator who is concerned with both theory and practice, the possible implication of these outcomes could be very significant. We may have to reexamine all of our assumptions concerning stages of adult development.

MORAL GROWTH: AN INVARIANT SEQUENCE

The series of research studies that provided the data in Fig. 10.2 also examined a further question particularly important to the concept of development. To qualify as a developmental change, as we may recall from Chapter 6, a change can only take one direction: up. A developmental change can only occur from a lower to a higher stage. As we can see from Fig. 10.2, not all people end up at Stage VI with Gandhi, Martin Luther King, Abraham Lincoln, Thoreau, or Socrates. However, there can be no reversals! With a few extreme exceptions (e.g., schizophrenics and other institutionalized patients), the researchers have found that major regressions in moral growth do not occur.

MORAL JUDGMENTS AND MORAL ACTION

Moral thinking and moral behavior

A key element so far missing from this discussion is the connection between stages of moral growth and actual behavior in the "heat of battle," so to speak. This is an important issue, especially in this book where we have stressed that thinking about issues is no substitute for acting in real situations. The evidence for moral maturity and moral behavior comes from a series of studies. Naturally, if the theory of moral development has any meaning, we would predict significantly different behavior according to significantly different levels of moral judgment. For example, we would expect that almost everyone who responded to the Heinz dilemma at Stage I or II ("It's all right to steal, especially if you get away with it") themselves would cheat or steal if given any chance at all. And, at the opposite extreme, we would expect that almost no one who responded at Stage V or VI would themselves cheat or steal.

To put this expectation to the test, a series of studies have been conducted using "cheating" tests. In one group of thirteen-year-olds, 75 percent of the preconventional and conventional pupils (Stages I to IV) actually cheated. At the same time, only 20 percent of the postconventional pupils (Stages V and VI) cheated in the same situation.

Cheating test results

In an older population (eighteen-year-olds) the same trends occurred, but, as we would predict, in different proportions: 42 percent of the preconventional and conventional students (Stages I to V) cheated and 11 percent of the postconventional students (Stages V and VI) cheated. Thus there is obviously a direct relationship between the rated level of moral judgment and behavior on the tests of cheating.

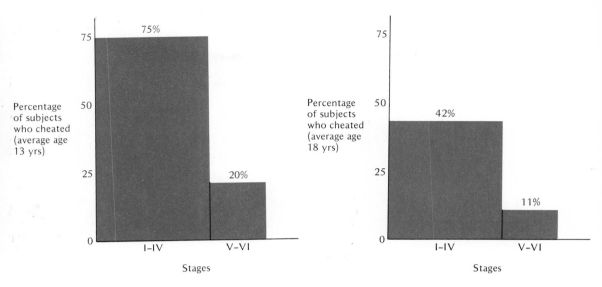

"Cheating" test results.

In another, more dramatic study, the moral-judgment tests were administered to subjects who had participated in the famous Milgram experiments, in
order to rate their level of moral maturity. Briefly, in the Milgram experiments
research subjects were told to "follow orders" exactly as specified by a scientific
investigator. The subjects were told that they were going to administer a series
of strong electric shocks to an innocent "victim" in the next room. The subjects
could hear the "victim" pounding on the door, wincing, and screaming every
time they pushed a button marked "high voltage." The experiment was set up
to test how long subjects would follow orders and continue to administer increasing amounts of electricity to another human being (in fact, of course, the
supposed victim was part of the experiment and was not actually hooked up to
the electric current). The study itself caused a tremendous stir, because the results revealed that, in general, fully 65 percent of all subjects, regardless of age,
background, or educational level, were willing to obey orders, no matter what!
In other words, in spite of the screaming, pounding, and pleading from the
"victim" in the next room, almost two-thirds of the subjects were willing to
follow the scientist's directions. Figure 10.3 shows various phases of this classic
experiment.

The results of the moral judgment testing showed that only 13 percent of
the subjects rated at Stages I to IV actually refused to obey the orders while 75
percent of the subjects rated at Stages V and VI refused to obey. This, of course,
fits very closely the concept of moral maturity at the postconventional level.
Only at that level would we expect a person to refuse to follow the rules and

**The Milgram study of
obedience**

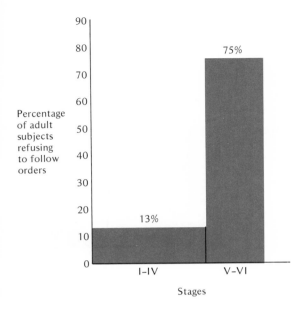

Fig. 10.3 Various phases of Milgram's classic experiment. At top right, a shock generator; at right, a subject being strapped into place. At lower left, a subject refusing to obey orders; at lower right, an obedient subject being introduced to his unharmed "victim." © 1965 by Stanley Milgram. From the film *Obedience*, distributed by the New York University Film Library.

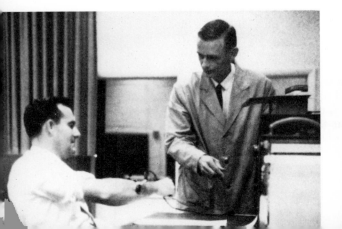

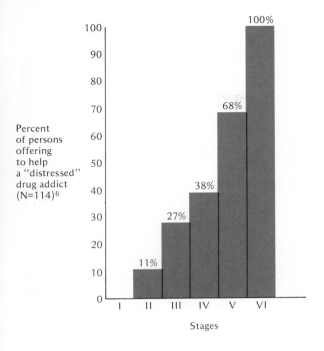

100%

Percent
of persons
offering
to help
a "distressed"
drug addict
(N=114)[6]

68%

38%

27%

11%

Stages

Kohlberg's stages of moral growth applied to persons offering to help a drug addict.

say, in effect, "I really don't care what the experiment is all about or whether a scientist tells me I must do what he says, I will not deliberately inflict harm on that guy in the next room. He is more important than any experiment." In other words, only at that level could a person disinguish between obeying the "law" and valuing human life. We might recall at this point the number of times in history that humans have been willing to exterminate helpless victims on the grounds that they were "just following orders."*

IMPLICATIONS: MORAL DEVELOPMENT, CLASSROOM BEHAVIOR, AND EDUCATION

Student discipline has been a major educational concern for centuries. In general, teachers have seen it in a most singular way. They viewed discipline problems as being conveniently (we would say) out of their reach, inside the pupils. Added to this idea was the notion that some children and adolescents are inherently "bad," perpetually on the verge of revolt. If this is your view of children, it is perhaps logical to limt your role to keeping them in their place by means of the various rewards and punishments we described in Chapter 9. Also, recall that these sanctions are generally employed to produce a quiet, obedient,

---

*

It is interesting to note that the single American GI who refused to follow the orders indicating that a small hamlet in Viet Nam was a "free fire zone" was rated at Stage VI in regard to moral dilemmas. Such behavior in an extraordinarily stressful situation may be the best real evidence for the relation between judgment and behavior, even though the sample consisted of only one person! (Kohlberg, personal communication, 1973)

Lawrence Kohlberg

Born in 1927, Lawrence Kohlberg spent three years as a junior engineer in the merchant marine before entering college. After those years at sea, he was ready to buckle down and push through the rigorous program at Chicago in record time. He completed the four-year B.A. degree in 1949 after only two years' work. He clearly demonstrated a great capacity for academic scholarship, and it was natural for him to enroll as a Ph.D. candidate at the same university. He completed his doctorate in 1958; after two years for his undergraduate studies, it took him nine years for the Ph.D. He remarked wryly that it only proved you couldn't accurately predict human behavior in all cases.

One of the major reasons for delay was his eventual topic, moral development in children and adolescents. A major portion of his doctoral work was in traditional areas of clinical psychology and child development, including a traineeship at the famous Children's Hospital in Boston. A substantial part of his difficulty was that all the time he was learning the traditional theories, including psychoanalytic views, he found in himself a growing skepticism. He began to evolve an alternative set of ideas to explain how children develop moral reasoning. What started as a traditional thesis on the relation between the superego (Freudian term for conscience) and moral behavior was transformed into a remarkably original framework for moral development in stages. It is rare for a young Ph.D. candidate to produce truly new insights in human behavior theory. It was uniquely creative for his thesis to force almost a complete revision of moral development theory as well.

With the completion of the thesis, finally, after nine years of work, he accepted an assistant professorship at the University of Chicago in 1962. Just six years later he was offered and accepted a full professorship at Harvard University and joined that faculty to form an innovative graduate program in human development. He was also awarded a special five-year Research Career Award by the National Institute of Mental Health to promote his longitudinal study on stages of moral development in adults as well as in children and adolescents. His major significance derives from the possible applications of the theory to promote psychologically healthy human beings. He is presently developing a series of intervention and teaching procedures which show promise of deliberately improving our level of moral judgment and moral maturity. Although so modest by nature that he suggests that his work is simply warmed-over Dewey, Kohlberg's work is much more than that. If we are concerned about improving the quality of interpersonal human relationships, his work at present represents the most helpful insights and processes to help us attain that objective.

and conforming pupil. Such an approach, we concluded, is an attempt to brainwash pupils in the name of building character. By molding and shaping pupils' behavior, teachers supposedly turn wild and unruly children into quiet, "good" pupils.

In our opinion, this old approach to student discipline is virtually useless. Studies have shown that direct exhortation combined with positive and negative sanctions has absolutely no long-lasting positive effects. Neither the old-fashioned values, such as honesty, self-control, and obedience, nor the newer "mod" values, such as spontaneity, openness, or "doing your own thing," develop as a result of forcing pupils to comply. Certainly any teacher, like any parent, can make a pupil "behave," at least up to a point. However, to say that such forced compliance will result in any long-term positive effect on the pupils' character or moral development is not only inaccurate but results in a gross misuse of educational time and effort.

To rescue the problems of student discipline and moral development from the simple-minded approach of lecturing and yelling at pupils, we presented an extensive discussion of Lawrence Kohlberg's developmental view. We now turn to the educational implications of Professor Kohlberg's theory.

Moral development: an interaction

Moral development determined by interaction

In contrast to the old view, the first implication of Kohlberg's theory is that moral development is determined by interaction, interaction between children and adults as well as between children themselves. We cannot approach discipline problems without recognizing the importance of the relationship between the students and their teacher, a relationship as critical as that between the child and his or her parents. Thus, we have another way in which the process of moral development is parallel to the processes of cognitive and intellectual development. Recall that intelligence develops as a result of the interaction between heredity and environment, and that this interaction determines the growth of intelligence. In the moral sphere, too, growth depends on interaction. It is one of our great misfortunes that our educational institutions underestimate the importance of this idea.

Moral development: stages universal across cultures

Similarity across social classes in level of moral judgments

The second implication of Kohlberg's theory is that moral development proceeds according to a series of psychological stages. Kohlberg has clearly demonstrated, both across cultures (from Malaysian aborigines to white middle-class Americans) and within cultures (lower- to upper-class Americans), that the sequence is the same not only within country, class, and caste, but also within major religious categories. Kohlberg's stages, like Piaget's and Erikson's, represent a systematic, one-way sequence from preconventional levels (Stages I and II), to conventional levels (Stages III and IV), and culminating in postconventional levels (Stages V and VI). See Table 10.3.

This means that the formal sequence of understanding and developing moral judgment is limited by developmental age and stage. The content may

Table 10.3 Stages of moral development: predominant judgments.

Age	Stage
Birth to nine years	Stages I and II (preconventional)
Nine to fifteen years	Stages III and IV (conventional)
Sixteen to adulthood	Stages V and VI (postconventional)

vary but the structure of judgment may not. Thus, a ten-year-old Taiwanese village boy would say it was OK for Heinz to steal the drug, "Otherwise the wife would die and he'd have to pay for the funeral and they cost a lot"; and a ten-year-old Malaysian boy would say it was OK to steal the drug, "Otherwise the wife dies and he needs her to cook for him"; and an American middle-class boy the same age would say he should steal the drug, "Especially if the wife could turn out to be an important person—or if she died then he would have to go to the trouble of finding a new wife." The logical structure in all three cases is the same. The wife is viewed exclusively as an instrument of the husband in concrete and operational terms.

Thus far research has shown that the stages of moral development themselves are far more significant in determining the structure of moral judgment than differences across cultures, within cultures, across social and economic classes, or by sex. Differences do exist because of these factors, but not major differences. For example, lower-class children lag slightly behind middle-class children on attained levels of moral maturity at each age, but the sequence of growth is still the same.

Not all adolescents, or adults, reach stages V and VI, since development is not automatic. Without certain types of necessary experiences, people will remain at lower levels of the sequence. Evidence on this point indicates that moral maturity is heavily influenced by the amount of significant responsibility an individual experiences. This means that actual participation/activity in social roles and interpersonal relationships helps educate for moral maturity. We will say more on this question in the next two sections, but want to underscore here the developmental nature of the process. Recall that Piaget almost equates cognitive growth with the extent to which an individual interacts with his or her environment. In a similar way, Kohlberg finds that moral growth within each stage depends on active participation in a variety of social roles.

Social role participation: experience as a teacher

Moral growth: understanding at your own stage and one stage "up"
We have seen that children and adolescents generally understand moral judgments at their own stage and one stage above. Generally, people operate out of one major stage (such as Stage III, the "good-boy" orientation), but they also incorporate a few elements from the next higher stage (in this case, Stage IV, the "law-and-order" orientation). This enables them to understand judgments one stage "up" and also, because of the nature of development, to prefer it to

Presenting views one stage "up" to encourage growth

their own mode. Each higher stage is more universal and less self-centered and so requires fewer rationalizations. At the same time, it is useless to present people with moral systems more than one stage beyond their own. Students, or adults for that matter, simply cannot comprehend that far in advance of their present level of understanding.

From an educational point of view, it is well to remember that we can get pupils or adults to make rote statements that sound like the very highest level of moral development. However, if they themselves are more than one stage "down" from the moral system embodied in such memorized statements, they will not internalize that system. Instead, we will succeed only in producing more lip service. Say, for example, that we wanted to coach the high-school debating team to present their arguments at Stage VI. We could teach them to mouth the concepts of universal principles of justice to support their position. However, unless they were already close to that level themselves, we would find, much to our chagrin, that when it came time for the rebuttal, our game plan would fail miserably. Once on their own, our debaters would immediately lapse back into their own level (probably Stage II, III, or IV), undoing all our work. Instead of arguments based on principles such as justice, we would hear arguments in accord with their own natural levels. In the classroom, too, there is a need to match the level of discussion to the pupils' developmental stage. The research evidence on this point is supportive. All children were able to understand and represent correctly all stages below their own as well as those at their own level. Some children could spontaneously understand and represent thinking one stage "up" from their own level. Almost none were able to comprehend and translate thinking two or more stages above their level.

Moral education in the classroom

Recent evidence indicates that special classroom teaching techniques can affect the level of the pupils' moral maturity. It is also important to note the factors that make a difference. Because of the limits imposed by developmental stages, it makes little sense to start discussing moral dilemmas before students reach elementary-school age. There is the possibility, however, of starting discussions then to promote the idea of choosing from alternatives in everyday situations. Also, it is possible for pupils in elementary school to gain a sense of seeking reasons behind actions. Such discussions would help students become aware of a series of reasons for rules and would help them compare these ideas.

Moral education during the later elementary years

Between ages nine and twelve, however, just prior to the onset of Piaget's stage of formal operations, such discussions are highly recommended, since at that point children are ready to move from Stages II and III to IV and possibly to Stage V.

Discipline and moral development can become a direct part of a positive educational program. Discussions of moral dilemmas can be introduced to classes. Headline stories from newspapers, everyday incidents, popular moral issues (e.g., capital punishment, civil disobedience, an "attractive" nuisance), incidents from movies or readings can be used. The teacher's job is to present the case material in a systematic and provocative way by asking questions. The idea is to promote a flow of ideas about what actions might be proposed. If, for example, children say capital punishment should be abolished, their reasons should be explored. Reasons for and against capital punishment can be outlined by moral stage:

	Pro	Con
Stage II	An eye for an eye— to put a murderer to death is a fair trade.	It takes too much time, energy, and money to convict a person of a capital offense. It's too expensive.
Stage III	Society shouldn't keep "bad apples" around— they infect others.	Civilized societies shouldn't themselves murder humans. It isn't a "nice" thing to do.
Stage IV	A law declares that if a murderer is tried and convicted, then electrocution is simply carrying out the law.	A law declares that cruel and unusual punishment is not justified. It's the law.

Of course, the teacher needs practice identifying the levels of response. But, In most cases, the differences in stages become quite apparent as long as the teacher resists the temptation to take over and do all the talking. By rephrasing and clarifying certain reasons produced by pupils in the class, the teacher can help them begin to hear and understand one stage "up."

A further point: Don't wait until a student in your class does something wrong before starting discussions of moral values. That is the worst possible time educationally; from the child's point of view, it's like being caught with one hand in the cookie jar. Shaming does not teach.

Shaming does not teach

Another teaching point to remember: stifle your own tendency to overreact. You may be more than surprised, and somewhat dismayed, if you succeed in getting the children to say what they really think about certain issues. For example, children at this age frequently express highly racist and narrow-minded views. It may be quite natural to want to challenge and ridicule such ideas, and insist that they stop talking "that way." For example, in a recent sixth-grade class in social studies, the children were discussing welfare. They unanimously agreed that some people were not able to work through no fault of their own. The students' middle-class backgrounds made it proper to say things like, "We should help those less fortunate than we." They had also done extensive reading, watched films, and even interviewed economically "poor" people. They all agreed that in most cases, through a series of often dramatic and poignant events, the grinding cycle of poverty acted as an overwhelming social force. Individuals have been destroyed, their will to act energetically has been broken, and so on.

At this point, the teacher presented a hypothetical case of a welfare family, a mother with six children, ages fourteen to two, and an institutionalized husband. The class was asked to develop a budget of needed financial assistance. At this point all empathy vanished from the classroom. The pupils decided that the family didn't need a dining room table or chairs ("They could eat sitting on the floor"); that they needed only a few beds ("They could take turns sleeping"); that all children above the age of eight could go to work, even though this meant dropping out of school; and that the mother could work at night when the older children returned from their jobs ("It's good for people to make their own money and not beg")! Obviously the entire objective had been missed; there was a total lack of comprehension. As you might guess, the teacher then got angry at the class. She sermonized at them for the balance of the period. The next day the pupils were back in class talking about the need for welfare programs to help unfortunate poor people.

Clarify the students' reasons—avoid moralizing

The teacher, of course, had really missed the key opportunity in the lesson, i.e., that of discussing the discrepancy between the students' "budget" and their high-sounding ethics, and then of gradually moving them to a higher stage of moral awareness. Had she discussed the legal framework (Stage IV), for example, she could have led them to step beyond the Stage II and III arguments they had presented. Child-labor laws, compulsory-school-attendance laws, limitations on working mothers' hours, and so on, could have become a means of examining the reasons for such laws and the need to protect individual rights. In this way a slightly "higher" explanation could have been introduced and thought about.

A classroom discussion that backfired

Kohlberg's developmental framework, then, suggests that children between nine and twelve years of age are maximally ready to discuss and examine questions of moral judgment, decisions concerning the value of life versus property, and others. This is the time, both cognitively and personally, for them to move into Stages III and IV of moral judgment. This is when it makes most sense educationally to provide experiences and classroom discussion to ensure growth beyond Stages I and II, that is, past the level where moral judgments are exclusively self-serving or egocentric.

For adolescents, the problem of moral education is similar, but, of course, at a higher level. By the time teenagers reach high school, the greatest proportion have stabilized at Stages III and IV. We noted earlier that at sixteen years of age almost one-half were "conventional" moral thinkers, and only 35 percent were post-conventional. At this time, then, it would be most appropriate, developmentally, to educate for the postconventional levels. Late adolescence is maximally sensitive for growth and development to Stages V and VI, where moral judgments are based on abstract principles. Programs instituted earlier or later might be less effective. It is important to remember that the shift from conventional to postconventional levels does not occur automatically. As Kohlberg notes, "You have to be cognitively mature to reason at the level of principled morality, but you can be smart and never reason morally."[8]

Moral education in high school

The educational problem, then, is to create systematic experiences and discussions on moral issues in order to aid the growth from Stages III and IV to Stages V and VI. Research has shown that, especially during adolescence, moral development is most likely to occur where there is sufficient opportunity for role-

playing (seeing events from a different perspective, putting oneself in someone else's shoes). Effective role-playing requires that we set aside some of our own preconceived views. To genuinely perceive or experience different points of view broaden's one's own experience. However, it is well to remember that "raw" experience by itself is not enough. It is the examination of the experience that allows the process to "take." Only by reflecting on questions of moral judgment and by seeing moral situations from a variety of points of view can we hope to internalize the learning.

Experience and reflection

To stimulate growth, the teacher has to be provocative and challenging. Otherwise students will tend to remain at their present levels. By providing significant role-playing experiences at maximally responsive stages, we can promote growth and prevent the stabilization of moral judgments at less-mature levels.

One of Kohlberg's associates, Dr. Mosher Blatt, has conducted an original set of studies demonstrating the usefulness of classroom discussions of moral dilemmas. An actual transcript of the classroom interactions follows. Note how Blatt does not put-down, criticize, or judge each pupil's comments. Also note how he clarifies responses, asks for elaboration, gently probes, and suggests alternative views. The power of this process really depends on the teacher's ability to lead discussions using such an indirect format (see Chapter 14 for further information on "indirect" teaching).

Dilemma

There was a case in court the other day about a man, Mr. Jones, who had an accident in his house. His child, Mike, was wounded in the chest. He was bleeding heavily, his shoes and pants were soaked with blood. Mike was scared. He began screaming until he finally lost consciousness.

His parents were scared, too. His mother began screaming, crying. She thought her child was dying. The father no longer hesitated; he lifted Mike up, ran down the stairs and went outside in hopes of getting a cab and going to the hospital. He thought that getting a cab would be quicker than calling an ambulance. But, there were no cabs on the street and Mike's bleeding seemed worse.

Suddenly, Mike's father noticed a man parking his car. He ran up and asked the man to take him to the hospital. The man replied, "Look, I have an appointment with a man about an important job. I really must be on time. I'd like to help you but I can't." So Mr. Jones said, "Just give me the car." The man said, "Look, I don't know you. I don't trust you." Mr. Jones told Mrs. Jones to hold Mike. She did. Then Mr. Jones punched the man, beat him up, took his keys and drove away toward the hospital. The man got up from the street, called the police, and took them to the hospital. The police arrested Mr. Jones for car theft and aggravated battery.

Mr. Blatt: What is the problem? Was the man legally wrong for refusing to drive Mr. Jones and Mike to the hospital?

Student A: It's his car, he doesn't have to drive.

Mr. B: Well, Mike was hurt. You said no, he's not legally responsible, because, why not?

Student A: Because it's his car.

Mr. B: It's his car. It's his property, and he has the right of property and he can legally—

Student B: But a life is at stake.

Mr. B: Okay. It's not so easy. Like here is property, but here is life, so the conflict here is between life, Mike's life, or that man's car.

Student B: But if Mike died, then that guy could be charged with murder, because, you know. . . .

Student C: No, he couldn't. . . .

Mr. B: But do you people think this man has a right, a legal right, to refuse to give Mr. Jones the car?

Student D: Does that man have children; he probably has to support a family, he's got a family, he can't just—

Student E: So? He can always find a job—

Mr. B: The question is, do you think that the man who had the job, wouldn't he understand if you came up to him and said, "Look, I was here, I wanted to be on time, but I saw this boy bleeding, and I wanted to help him out." Don't you think he would understand? (Chorus of "yes" and "no.")

Student F: No, because if you're supposed to go on the job—

Student G: You could make him show some proof.

Student F: Bring the kid there when he's well.

Mr. B: All right. This man who refused to give the car was not legally wrong. You couldn't take him to court. But do you think he was wrong in any way? (Chorus of "yes.")

Student B: He was just all wrong because if that kid died, I don't know what he'd be charged with, but he'd be charged with something. There's something, I don't know what it is, but there's something they could charge him with.

Mr. B: I don't know if they could charge him legally, but you're right; there's something very wrong with that, because what is this man doing? Which is more important: property or life? (Chorus of "life.") Why? (Confused answers, on the principle that life is irreplaceable.) Life is something you can't replace, right? Everybody wants to live. Now this guy, what was he putting first, life or a job? What do you think is more important, losing a job and maybe getting another one, or saving a life? (Answers: "Saving a life.") Helping to save a life. But this guy refuses to help Mr. Jones and Mike out, to take them to the hospital. What was he doing? He was putting his property before somebody else's life. He said, "This is my car." Mr. Jones asked him, "Look, I'd like you to lend me your car; I'll bring it back." The guy said, "No, I don't trust you."

Student A: Well, he didn't know Mr. Jones, maybe he didn't trust him.

Student D: What did he look like?

Student A: Yeah, I wouldn't trust nobody with my car.

Student H: Well, I would trust him if I knew him. (Confused comments about whether they would or would not trust somebody with their car.)

Student B: Would you care if you trust him or not?

Student E: Well, I wouldn't go so far as to beat him up and to take his car. He might still need it. (Conversation on beating up somebody.)

Mr. B: So what you're saying is, this man's value, what he thought was most important was his property. His property was more important to him than somebody else's life. You said legally he was right. Right? (Agreements.) Can you say morally he was right? (Undistinguishable answers.) What do you mean by morally? Can somebody tell us what is meant by morally?

Student C: It's—there's not a law but—

Mr. B: What kind of a law may be involved? It's not a legal law, although it may be, it doesn't have to be. What kind of law is it? What were you saying before, about your mother? What did she say?

Student B: God's law.

Mr. B: God's law, what does it say about killing?

Student B: Thou shalt not kill.

Students B and F: God's law is moral law.

Mr. B: What do you mean?

Student B: Cause this is the laws of his country and God has moral laws for everybody.

Mr. B: Oh, so what you're saying is—did you listen to what he's saying? Would you repeat what you said? It's very important.

Student B: God's law is for everyone and there's different laws in different countries, so God's law, his moral laws are for everyone.

Student D: God's laws include more people than laws down here, yes.

Mr. B: Now what you're saying is that God's laws are for all people regardless of where you live. And so, they're universal laws, right? They're for the whole universe, is what you're saying. All right. Now you said, from the legal point of view he was right, from a moral point of view he was wrong. He had a legal right to refuse his property but no moral right to do so. Now what about Mr. Jones? Was Mr. Jones justified, from a legal point of view, in beating up the man and taking his car? (Chorus of "no.") Why not?

Student B: Because there's a law that like, that guy's car, you know, he can say whatever he likes about it, he has a right to do what he wants with it, but with the moral law [Mr. Jones] was doing pretty good.

Mr. B: He was doing right? Do you agree with him? He says that Mr. Jones was doing right from a moral point of view.

Student B: But it still went outside God's law, going against the law. Thou shalt not steal.

Mr. B: So what you're saying is—

Student D: There's a problem. It's still stealing.

Student F: Yes, he should have asked him. If the man said no, that should have been the answer.

Mr. B: Did he have a moral right to beat up the man and take his car? (Chorus of "no.") Why not?

Student F: He didn't have no right to do it.

Student B: There's another moral law....[9]

Blatt's studies have shown that pupils improve in their ability to think at more comprehensive and empathic levels as a result of moral-dilemma discussions through indirect teaching. Whether this process actually works is dependent on the teacher's skill in facilitating participation, creating a supportive atmosphere so all can talk, and helping pupils actually listen to each other's points of view. The process is complex, as the transcript demonstrates.

In conclusion, we reiterate the importance of understanding the processes of child and adolescent development, especially in the area of moral growth. In no single aspect of educational psychology has there been more confusion. Kohlberg's developmental framework moves discipline problems into a new arena. Moral judgment and growth become educational problems, not discipline problems. Rather than attempting to build character by superficial exhortations on static traits like honesty, neatness, and obedience, a teacher can provide experiences and discussions tailored to the pupils' developmental stages. We cannot simply talk about stages of moral maturity in the abstract. Classroom interactions between pupils and teacher represent an opportunity for significant growth experiences designed to facilitate genuine moral maturation.

Summary

The theoretical breakthrough provided by Professor Kohlberg revolutionized our understanding of moral development. His work parallels Piaget and Erikson in that it includes specific, age-related stages of growth. Each stage represents a system of thinking defined by how we process moral/ethical and value questions. Each stage is also part of an invariant sequence and represents a qualitatively more comprehensive system of understanding than the previous one.

The Kohlberg framework "emerged" from interviews with his research subjects. By presenting moral dilemmas to people from different backgrounds, he was able to sample the system of reasoning, thinking, and judging—the reasons behind their decision. In analyzing these reasons, Kohlberg formed the six-stage category system. Then he set out to cross-validate the system both cross-sectionally and now longitudinally.

The stages are defined by the major set of assumptions a person uses to think through, reason, rationalize/justify an important ethical decision. Each stage is "better" than its preceding one; higher stages take into account an increasingly broader perspective, represent more complex and abstract thought, contain more personal empathy, and "solve" social problems more on the basis of principles. Thus the direction of the system is highly congruent with the principles of a democratic society—values and ethics based on principles of justice.

There is not an exact one-to-one relation between moral stage and actual behavior. However, the trends in practically all studies are almost always consistent with the theory—whether it be performance on "cheating" tests, riots on college campuses, or the Milgram study.

In relating the Kohlberg system to the classroom, the teacher's job is to present or to encourage statements and reasons that are slightly ahead of those of the majority of the class. This means that the teacher must do a great deal of probing, asking clarifying questions, and seeking elaboration of the pupils' thought processes. It also means the teacher has to withhold his or her own judgments, not get overly angry or lecture at the pupils. Exhortation, though tempting, is not teaching for moral development.

The teaching for moral development needs to be understood as a slow and complex process. We cannot really accelerate moral development beyond the limits set by the stage concepts. On the other hand, especially after the long recent educational history of relativism, we cannot just sit by and beg the value question.

Undoubtedly the most important aspect of the entire chapter is that it confronts educational psychology with questions of character education in the form of stages of moral maturity. For almost half a century such questions of moral education and general education have been avoided or not considered a legitimate area for inquiry. Kohlberg has changed all that. We now must think through the value questions as part of a developmental sequence.

REFERENCES

1
L. Kohlberg, "Stage and Sequence: The Cognitive-Developmental Approach to Socialization," in D. Goslin, ed., *Handbook of Socialization Theory and Research* (New York: Rand McNally, 1969).

2
L. Kohlberg, "The Cognitive-Developmental Approach to Moral Development," *Phi Delta Kappan* 56, no. 10 (1975):671.

3
M. L. King, "Letter from Birmingham Jail," *Why We Can't Wait* (New York: Harper & Row, 1963), pp. 84–85. Reprinted by permission of Joan Daves. Copyright © 1963, 1964 by Martin Luther King, Jr.

4
L. Kohlberg and E. Turiel, "Moral Development and Moral Education," in G. Lesser, ed., *Psychology and Educational Practice* (Glenview, Ill.: Scott Foresman, 1971).

5
L. Kohlberg and R. Kramer, "Continuities and Discontinuities in Childhood and Adult Moral Development," *Human Development* 12 (1969):93–120.

6
L. Kohlberg, personal communication, January 23, 1976.

7
L. Kohlberg, *Collected Papers* (Cambridge, Mass.: Harvard Graduate School of Education, 1974).

8
L. Kohlberg, "From Is to Ought," in T. Mischel, ed., *Cognitive Development and Epistemology* (New York: Academic Press, 1971), p. 54.

9
L. Kohlberg, *Collected Papers.*

UNIT III

The nature of learning

11

Learning backgrounds

The study of learning has been at the very heart of psychology, especially American psychology, since its origin about 100 years ago. During the 1870s the great Harvard psychologist William James discussed the importance of learning, and later he called habit that "enormous fly-wheel of society, its most precious conservative agent. . . . It keeps the fisherman and deckhand at sea through winter; it holds the miner in his darkness. . . . It keeps different social strata from mixing."[1] James felt that learning, especially during childhood, shapes and directs our later lives: "Could the young but realize how soon they will become mere walking bundles of habits, they would give more heed to their conduct while in the plastic state."[2] We might paraphrase James by saying that if society realized how soon its children would become walking bundles of habits, that society would give more heed to the importance of its early childhood education programs.

James stresses the importance of habit

Though the study of learning has been the core area of American psychology, the pursuit of this study has been anything but serene. Great debates, full of sound and fury, over the nature and process of learning all but shattered the foundation of the fledgling discipline. Some psychologists, rigid behaviorists like John B. Watson, felt that learning involved the patterning of overt responses. Knowledge, to these psychologists, resides in muscular reactions, not in cerebral exercise. In driving to your favorite ice-cream store, it would be your arms and legs that would "know" the route, not your head. These psychologists were correct—to some extent. Certain kinds of learning do occur as a result of response patterning. For example, try explaining to a youngster how to tie a necktie. It is almost impossible to transmit this knowledge through words alone, for it

The study of learning has been at the heart of American psychology

271

doesn't exist completely at the conceptual level. You will probably find that you have to demonstrate and, even then, you will stand behind the child, since your responses are so restricted and rigid that you can't tie a necktie while facing it. In playing the piano, knowledge of certain intricate passages seems to reside in your fingers. You may have forgotten a certain tune, but after fiddling around on the keys for a few minutes, your fingers suddenly "remember." Or in sports like skiing and golf, despite hours of verbal instruction, you ultimately have to learn a certain "feel," a certain muscular patterning.

Behaviorists and cognitive theorists disagree on how and where learning takes place

Other psychologists, cognitive theorists like Wertheimer, Kohler, and Lewin, felt that learning required thinking and insight. In driving to your favorite ice-cream store, to return to a previous example, your arms and legs wouldn't be any help without a more general, cognitive map, probably located in your brain. To the cognitive theorists, teaching children by drill or rote is like training a bunch of parrots. Children really learn only when they discover solutions for themselves, only when they "understand."

THE TWO BASIC POSITIONS

Now that the dust has settled on some of the great theoretical debates of the past, two main schools of thought on learning have emerged, though many variations still exist. These two main schools of thought are association learning and cognitive learning.

The behaviorists view learning as a result of an association between stimuli and responses

Association theorists see learning as the result of connections (associations) between stimuli (sense impressions) and responses. Dogs salivating when they hear the can opener opening their food, or babies waving "bye-bye" on cue from their mothers, or fifth graders saying "72" to the stimulus "9 times 8" are all examples of association learning. A bond has been formed between two elements, a stimulus and a response.

The cognitive theorists view learning as a result of a reorganization of perceptions

Cognitive theorists, on the other hand, view learning as a reorganization of a number of perceptions. This reorganization allows the learner to perceive new relationships, solve new problems, and gain a basic understanding of a subject area. A fifth grader suddenly realizing that multiplication is successive addition; or an ape suddenly understanding that by putting two short sticks together, a banana that was out of reach is now obtainable; or an eighth grader discovering a way to calculate the area of a parallelogram—these are all examples of cognitive learning.

These two views of learning parallel the two sides of another controversy that has historically split the field of psychology: behaviorism versus gestalt psychology. The behaviorists have typically been associationists, whereas the gestaltists have traditionally been cognitive theorists.

THE ORIGINS: JAMES AND WUNDT

It must be remembered that psychology as a separate discipline was a product of the late nineteenth century. Its origins are philosophy and physiology. For example, many philosophical overtones are apparent in the work of the first major American psychologist, William James. In fact, James had great difficulty deciding whether to cast his lot with philosophy or with psychology, being first in one department and then in the other at Harvard. This in spite of the fact that he created Harvard's psychology department.

Wilhelm Wundt, who set up the first experimental-psychology laboratory in Europe (around 1879), was also strongly influenced by philosophy. However, he was also influenced by physiology, having begun his career as a physician and having later become a physiologist. Like the philosophers who preceded him, Wundt was interested in studying man's conscious experience, and he sought to do this by analyzing consciousness into its smallest components. He was looking for the basic elements of psychology, the smallest parts of analyzable consciousness. This was analogous to the physicists having, at roughly the same time in history, constructed the atomic table. As physics had its elements, so, too, thought Wundt, would psychology. Wundt felt that by analyzing consciousness into these tiny elements, or "atoms," he could make psychology as respectable a science as physics.

The main thesis of Wundt's work was that these basic elements of the mind are connected through association; that is, the mind is composed of individual elements, or items of experience, linked by associations. The problem was to ferret these elements out for study. To accomplish this, Wundt used the technique of introspection. He trained subjects to look within themselves and report all their most fleeting and minute feelings and sensations.[3] Both behaviorism and gestalt psychology began in reaction to Wundt; he set the stage for the great controversy to come.

THE GESTALTISTS ATTACK WUNDT

A group of psychologists, led by Max Wertheimer, got together around 1910 at the University of Frankfurt and began the school of psychology known as Gestalt psychology.* The gestaltists felt that Wundt had led psychology down the primrose path, that in order to produce his neat atomic chart of psychology, Wundt had lost sight of the reality of human experience. They felt that by analyzing experience into its smallest parts, Wundt had, in effect, destroyed the total experience. He was like a musician analyzing each note separately and never hearing the melody. "The whole is more than the sum of its parts," thundered Wertheimer. You must study the whole, the totality, the entire configuration, or, to use the German word, the *Gestalt*. The gestaltists felt that the study of the associations formed between tiny elements, whether they are elements of consciousness or stimuli-response connections, is misleading. It is misleading because elements often act and look differently when they are taken out of context. For example, Wertheimer would say that if you were to study each frame in a motion picture, you would never see movement, which is what a motion-picture film is all about.

James creates first experimental-psychology department in America

Wundt attempts to make psychology a science

Wertheimer introduces Gestalt psychology

---

*
Schools of psychology refer to schools of thought, not specific colleges and universities.

THE BEHAVIORISTS ATTACK WUNDT

The school of behaviorism was born under the impetus of John B. Watson at Johns Hopkins University. The behaviorists attacked Wundt because of his use of introspection as a scientific tool. The behaviorists believed in elements, all right, but they didn't like the way Wundt went about finding them. In the now classic paper, "Psychology as the Behaviorist Views It," Watson proclaimed that behavior is the real data of psychology.[4] According to Watson, introspection is as useless to psychology as it would be to chemistry or physics. The only thing that is really observable and therefore the only thing that really allows for the use of the scientific method is the subject's overt behavior. Watson also announced to the world what would and what would not be proper areas for psychologists to study. If consciousness can be studied only through introspection, and if it has no behavioral correlates, then throw it out of psychology. As we have seen, John B. Watson was not one to equivocate.

Watson: the only proper data for psychology is behavior

BEHAVIORISTS AND GESTALTISTS ATTACK EACH OTHER

Although these two powerful schools of psychology began by fighting independent battles with Wundt, the scene of battle soon shifted and they began fighting each other. Watson fell in with a powerful ally, Ivan Pavlov, the Russian

The Russian Ivan Pavlov's work on the conditioned reflex provided Watson with evidence to support his contention that learning was the result of associations between stimuli and responses. Pavlov discovered the phenomenon of the conditioned reflex in the course of his research on his major interest, the digestive ability of dogs. He won a Nobel Prize in 1904.

whose work on the conditioned reflex was being recognized at about the same time Watson was preparing for combat. Watson found just what he needed when he needed it—the conditioned reflex, something observable to replace Wundt's nonobservable elements. Watson soon felt that all learning could be explained on the basis of conditioning, that is, the association of stimuli with responses. A new unit of analysis had been found that was both observable and consistent with the principle of association. Watson was ready to take over American psychology, and through his direct influence and through the indirect influence of those who followed—Guthrie, Hull, Thorndike,* and B. F. Skinner —Watson certainly did manage to shape and direct the course American psychology was to take. Learning was a matter of accumulating a series of stimulus-response associations. There is no need to study insight or even thinking in the traditional sense, for conditioning pretty much explains it all.

Watson borrows Pavlov's concept of conditioning

The gestaltists did not agree. Wertheimer, and later Kohler and Lewin, felt that learning could not be dissected into little S-R associations and still be consistent with what they saw as reality. Children could be conditioned ad nauseam, trained to recite the multiplication tables, the state capitals, the major agricultural products of each country—and yet without insight or real understanding, the information would be virtually useless. According to the gestaltists, if you want children to learn nonsense, go ahead and condition them; but if you want them to learn meaningful relationships, then a different approach is needed —a cognitive approach.

The gestaltists disagree with Watson

EBBINGHAUS: THE PIONEER

The experimental study of learning had quiet beginnings. In Germany during the 1880s, Hermann Ebbinghaus carried out the first of these studies, pioneering work that eventually earned him the title "father of learning psychology." Because he wanted to study learning in its pure form, he had to control for the influence of meaningfulness. In order to to do this Ebbinghaus used long lists of nonsense syllables (cav, lek, pum, etc.) which, he felt, allowed him to control for difficulty. Since many words have past associations or inherent interest, they might be easier to learn than others, whereas all lists of nonsense syllables would be of comparable difficulty and would have to be learned from scratch. Ebbinghaus was his own subject and he spent many hours learning these meaningless words. His work led him to draw two major conclusions:

Ebbinghaus carries out the first experimental studies of learning

1

Once something is learned it is not forgotten at an even rate. Most of what is forgotten is lost very quickly, and the rest is lost at a slow and fairly stable rate.

2

In order to learn new material, it is more efficient to space practice than to mass it. For example, if you had one hour to learn something, you would re-

---

*

Even though some of Thorndike's writings predate Watson's, Watson's influence on Thorndike became very powerful.

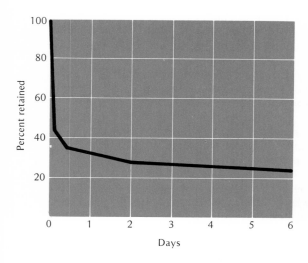

Ebbinghaus' retention curve. Most of the learned material is lost very rapidly and the rest more and more slowly.

Hermann Ebbinghaus hoped to lay the basis for a scientific study of learning by memorizing long lists of "nonsense syllables" and then measuring his retention capacity. His pioneering research on learning earned him the title "father of learning psychology."

tain more by taking four 15-minute practice sessions spread over a few days, than by spending one full hour working without a break.[5]

The results of these studies, while interesting to the learning theorist, have limited practical use in the classroom. Laws governing the learning of meaningless information may not be generalized to the learning of meaningful material. Material learned in the classroom should be meaningful, though unfortunately students are still being made to memorize vocabulary, passages from poems, and grammatical rules—material that may be no more meaningful to them than the nonsense syllables were to Ebbinghaus.

THE ASSOCIATIONISTS VERSUS THE GESTALTISTS

We now turn to a discussion of how the association-learning and cognitive-learning positions were formed and eventually translated into action. We begin with those theories that dominated the first half of the twentieth century, spotlighting the early associationists Thorndike, Pavlov, and Guthrie, in that order. J. B. Watson, though not singled out for independent coverage in this section, is intermittently mentioned in the discussions of the other three. Watson's influence on the early behaviorist-associationist movement was very significant.

The discussion of the early cognitive theorists focuses on Wertheimer and Kohler, two gestaltists who made important contributions to our current knowledge of cognitive learning. In Chapter 12 we examine in some detail the two current spokesmen for each position: B. F. Skinner and Jerome Bruner. The present chapter provides a background for appreciating the significance of Skinner and Bruner in education today.

THE EARLY ASSOCIATION THEORISTS

Thorndike

In 1899 Edward Lee Thorndike published a paper entitled "Animal Intelligence," and thereby catapulted to the forefront of the emerging field of learning psychology. From his headquarters at Columbia Teachers College, Thorndike issued his concepts and laws of learning for many years thereafter. For most of the first half of the twentieth century he was truly Mr. Educational Psychology in the United States. His studies of cats learning to escape from puzzle boxes are now legendary.

Thorndike becomes the leading figure in American educational psychology

Thorndike viewed learning as a series of stimulus-response connections, or bonds. His theory of learning described the ways in which these S-R connections could be strengthened or weakened. He felt that learning was basically a trial-and-error enterprise, and he paid little attention to the possibility of concept formation or thinking.[6]

The three major laws. Thorndike postulated three major laws of learning: readiness, exercise, and effect.

1

The law of readiness. When an organism is in a state where the conduction units (S–R connections) are ready to conduct, then the conduction is satisfying. If the conduction unit is not ready to conduct, then conduction is annoying. Thorndike was speaking here of a brief, neurological readiness, not the kind of maturational readiness which, as we saw in Chapter 5, was of concern to Myrtle McGraw. Thorndike was referring to a more momentary phenomenon, a kind of neurologically teachable moment.

The neurologically teachable moment

2

The law of exercise. This law, also called the law of use and disuse, states that the more an S–R connection is used the stronger it will become, and the less it is used the weaker it will become. This law is obviously based on the old maxim about practice making perfect. Thorndike, especially in his later writings, made it clear that practice led to improvement only when it was followed by positive feedback or reward. Blind practice, with no knowledge of the consequences of the act, had no effect on learning.

Practice makes perfect

3

The law of effect. This was by far Thorndike's most important law. It states that when an S–R connection is followed by satisfaction (reward), the connection is strengthened. Also, if the connection is followed by annoyance (punishment), it is weakened. In later years Thorndike played down the importance of the second part of the law. In fact, he changed his mind about the significance of punishment as a means of weakening learned associations. He came to feel that reward strengthened learning far more than punishment weakened it. His evidence for changing his position on this issue was, to say the least, rather flimsy. It was based on a study of symbolic re-

Reward and punish-
ment shape learning

ward and punishment, where the reward consisted of saying "Right" to the
student and the punishment consisted of saying "Wrong." The results might
have been quite different if the reward had been a candy bar and the punishment a mild electric shock.

There is no doubt that Thorndike had a dehumanizing effect on American
education. His first work involved the study of how cats solve problems. He saw
little basic difference between animal and human learning—never mind the
qualitative differences in learning which Piaget insists occur at different periods
during human development. Thorndike spread a kind of mechanical-man gospel
that viewed animals and children as akin to robots.

His contribution to education, however, cannot be minimized. He was,
through his law of effect, the first psychologist to stress the importance of motivation in learning. When an individual is rewarded for learning, then learning
is far more apt to occur. This aspect of learning seems to have been overlooked
by Ebbinghaus. Since he was so close to his experiments (he was, after all, his
own subject), Ebbinghaus could hardly take note of his own fantastically high
motivation. If you have any doubts about the strength of Ebbinghaus's motiva-

Thorndike first stressed the importance of motivation in learning,
an aspect overlooked by Ebbinghaus.

tion, try spending a few months doing virtually nothing but learning lists of nonsense syllables.

In addition to stressing the importance of motivation in learning, Thorndike also made much of another crucial concept, that of transfer. His law of identical elements specified that the learner is better able to confront new problems if these new problems contain elements similar to those the learner has already mastered. This, after all, is largely what schooling is all about. If we learned how to use an encyclopedia while we were in school, we are more likely now to be able to diagnose what is wrong with our car by looking it up in our owner's manual, or to prepare a gourmet meal from the directions in a cookbook, or to plan an advertising campaign by making use of appropriate library resources. Transfer will be discussed in greater depth in the next chapter.

Thorndike emphasizes transfer of learning

Pavlov

The laboratory work of the Russian physiologist Ivan P. Pavlov was of great importance to the study of learning. Though most modern physiological psychologists consider his theory of the neurological process of learning a historical curio, his laboratory techniques and findings are still of great significance. In 1904 Pavlov won the Nobel Prize in medicine for his work on the digestive activity of dogs. His lasting fame, however, resulted from what at the time were incidental and chance observations regarding digestion in his dogs. Pavlov noted that the dogs salivated not only when meat powder was placed directly in their mouths, but also well before that (for example, when they heard the trainer's footsteps coming down the stairs). Pavlov later coined the term: "conditioned reflex" to describe this phenomenon.[7]

Pavlov and his chance discovery

A reflex must have an identifiable stimulus that automatically elicits the response, even though no learning has occurred. For example, when a bright light shines directly into a person's eyes, the pupils automatically contract. No learning or training is required for this to occur. Similarly, when food is placed in a dog's mouth, salivation automatically occurs. Reflexes are therefore directly caused by an unconditioned stimulus (UCS), much as pulling the trigger of a loaded gun automatically causes the gun to fire.

Pavlov also noted that if a neutral stimulus—one that does not elicit a certain response—is repeatedly paired with an unconditioned stimulus—one that does automatically elicit a certain response—the neutral stimulus will eventually take on the power to elicit the response. This is now called classical conditioning, and an example will illustrate. When meat powder is placed directly in a dog's mouth, the dog automatically salivates. This is a reflex action and does not have to be learned. However, if a 500-cycle tone is presented immediately before the meat powder, the tone soon comes to evoke the salivation. Through association with the meat powder, the tone begins to act as a signal that meat powder will follow, and the dog eventually learns to respond to the signal the same way it used to respond only to the meat powder. Technically, the meat powder is called the unconditioned stimulus (UCS), since responding to it does not depend on prior experience or learning. The tone or signal is called the conditioned stimulus (CS), since the response to it must be learned. For the same reasons, salivating to the meat powder is called the unconditioned response (UCR), and salivating to the tone is called a conditioned response (CR).

The conditioned reflex

Conditioned stimuli act as signals

When John B. Watson studied the acquisition of fear in the baby Albert, this was the technique he used (see Chapter 3). When Watson first presented Albert with a white rat, Albert showed no sign of fear. Then Watson struck a steel bar right beside Albert's head, and this loud sound (unconditioned stimulus) automatically made Albert cry (unconditioned response). After repeated pairings of the white rat and the loud sound, Albert began crying as soon as the rat came in view, even when he heard no loud sound. The rat (conditioned stimulus) took on the power to elicit the crying (conditioned response). Note that the conditioned and unconditioned responses are the same, salivation in the case of Pavlov's dogs and crying in the case of Watson's baby. The difference is what brings them about. The conditioned response is one that is elicited by a stimulus which had to be learned through association.

Watson used Pavlovian techniques in conditioning Albert

One reason educators must know about conditioning is that a great number of autonomic reflexes can be conditioned while the child is still in school. Just as Albert was conditioned to fear a rat, so the schoolchild may be conditioned to fear math, science, spelling, or any other school subject. Autonomic responses, such as sweating, rapid heartbeat, or general feelings of anxiety, may be conditioned by certain cues that come to be associated with various aspects of the school setting. Children who have been conditioned to such an extent that they are literally paralyzed by fear at the mere sight of a math problem are unlikely to be able to learn much math. They might sincerely try to learn the subject, but because of a great and crippling discomfort, they are just not able to.

This is not to say that teachers deliberately create these fears, but they can unwittingly set the stage for such conditioning. For example, a math problem is presented, followed by some other action of the teacher which may already be associated in the child's past experience with feelings of tension, and now the math problem itself triggers autonomic reactions of anxiety on the part of the child. After a few associations of this kind, the mere presentation of the math problem (CS) begins to elicit anxiety (CR). Sometimes this process occurs because teachers themselves have a conditioned fear of math and unwittingly transmit it to their students in the form of scolding, bullying, or a generally "up-tight" approach to learning the subject.

Children may be unwittingly conditioned to fail in school

Stimulus generalization. Pavlov found that reflex conditioning had some extremely important by-products. For example, once a dog was conditioned to salivate to a 500-cycle tone, it would also salivate to a 200- or 700-cycle tone, even though these new stimuli were never used in training. In other words, once a given conditioned stimulus is associated with a reflex, other similar stimuli also take on the power to elicit the response. This is called stimulus generalization. The original conditioned stimulus becomes generalized, and the organism begins responding to other stimuli which are in some way similar to the original one. In the case of Watson's young subject, Albert, once he was conditioned to fear the rat, it was found that he was also afraid of a Santa Claus mask, a sealskin coat, human hair, a dog, a rabbit, and cotton wool. The point is, reflex conditioning has wide-ranging effects. A child who is conditioned to fear math problems may generalize this fear to many other school subjects, perhaps even the

Stimulus generalization

entire school situation. Phobic reactions can be understood in this way. Suppose an unruly child is punished by being locked in a closet. The conditioned stimulus might be generalized so that the child became fearful of any enclosed area. The result, claustrophobia, could carry over into adulthood, and the person so afflicted might live a severely restricted life.

Pavlov found that the only way to break the association between a conditioned stimulus and a conditioned response was through a process called extinction. Extinction is achieved when the CS loses its power to evoke the CR; it is accomplished by repeatedly presenting the CS without following it up with the UCS. Thus if the 500-cycle tone is consistently presented without the meat powder, the dog eventually stops salivating when he hears it. It is important to note that for extinction to occur, the conditioned stimuius must be repeatedly presented by itself. Unfortunately, when the conditioned reflex is fear, the afflicted individual naturally avoids the conditioned stimulus and extinction is never allowed to occur. Joseph Wolpe, a famous psychotherapist, uses techniques of classical conditioning and extinction in treating his phobic patients.

Extinction

Classical conditioning and psychotherapy

Guthrie

The last of the early associationists we will cover here is Edwin Guthrie. Guthrie was the behaviorist-associationist par excellence. Following directly in Watson's footsteps, he rejected any psychological concepts that might have "mentalistic" overtones. He postulated one law of learning: learning by association or, as he called it, "contiguity." According to Guthrie, if a certain stimulus (or pattern of stimuli) is followed by a response, then the next time that stimulus appears the same response will follow. That's all there is to it—stimuli and responses in sequence. There is no need to call upon reward, reinforcement, or "effect" in order to explain how learning occurs. He also believed that learning occurs the first time the stimulus and response become associated.[8]

Guthrie's one law of learning

To create conditions that will promote learning, Guthrie believed that the teacher should provide the stimulus and the student should respond. For example, the teacher might point to a map and the students would then reply with the name of the city. The important thing is for the appropriate stimulus to be presented before the desired response occurs.

A frenzied mother once brought her child to Guthrie. The child had been in the habit, on coming home from school, of opening the door of his home, taking off his coat, and throwing it on the floor. The mother told Guthrie that no matter how many times she told her child to pick up the coat and hang it in the closet, the child continued this behavior. Guthrie did not reach for any deep psychological explanation, like finding out what throwing the coat on the floor symbolized, what it "meant" to the child. He simply told the mother to rearrange the stimulus-response sequence. When the child throws his coat on the floor, he should not be told to hang it up. He should instead be told to put the coat on, go back outside, come through the door and, only then, hang up the coat. Thus hanging up the coat could become a response to the stimulus of entering the house, rather than to the stimulus of the mother's command, "Take your coat off the floor and hang it up."

Max Wertheimer

Max Wertheimer was born in Prague in 1880, the son of a school teacher. As a student, young Wertheimer's interests were far ranging. He studied law for awhile, then switched to philosophy, and finally began to study psychology. After attending a number of schools and universities, Wertheimer received his Ph.D. degree at Wurtzburg in 1904. For the next six years he continued his work in psychology at Prague, Vienna, and Berlin.

Wertheimer had been schooled in the stucturalist psychological tradition, a point of view which held that all psychological phenomena could be broken down and analyzed into their smallest parts or elements. In 1910, while traveling by train from Vienna to a Rhineland vacation resort, Wertheimer was suddenly struck by an idea. He began to ponder this structuralistic viewpoint, and the more he pondered, the more he doubted. Suddenly he decided to forget his planned vacation and left the train at Frankfurt. He rushed to the nearest toy store and purchased a child's stroboscope. This was in the days before motion pictures, and a stroboscope was a device which, when turned at a constant speed, exposed a series of still pictures that appeared to move. In his hotel room Wertheimer examined his new purchase. He spun the stroboscope, fascinated by the apparent movement which the device produced, and in one of the history of psychology's great examples of insight, thought, "Aha, Wundt and the structuralists must be wrong." Here was a psychological perception, apparent movement, which simply could not be explained or understood by analyzing the individual still pictures. When the elements of this perception were studied individually, the total phenomenon of perceived movement was lost. The whole must be more than just the sum of its parts. In order to understand this perception of movement, one had to study all the parts together in their particular "Gestalt," a German word which means whole, or totality, or configuration.

Wertheimer went to the University of Frankfurt and began a series of controlled experiments. His first subject was Wolfgang Kohler, who was later joined by Kurt Koffka. Early in 1912 Wertheimer explained to Kohler and Koffka the results and meaning of his studies. Gestalt psychology had been born. Both Kohler and Koffka became zealous advocates of this new school of thought, and both went on to produce many experiments, articles, and books in support of it. Both became famous Gestalt psychologists in their own right.

In 1912 Wertheimer published his now famous article, "Experimental Studies of the Perception of Movement." As a result of this single, revolutionary article, a tremendous new movement in psychology was under way, and, as a result, thousands of articles and

books were written and are still being written on this important subject.

In 1916 Wertheimer joined the faculty at the University of Berlin, where he worked with another soon-to-be-famous Gestalt psychologist, Kurt Lewin. In 1933 Wertheimer came to the United States, where he taught at the New School for Social Research in New York City. He remained at the New School until his death in 1943.

Wertheimer was a man with a cause, but he was not arrogant or authoritarian. He was a gentle, warm, deep-thinking man. He had a close personal relationship with Albert Einstein, and he was deeply concerned with the social and ethical issues of his times.

Wertheimer was also interested in education and the techniques of good teaching. He pointed out the importance of Gestalt principles as they apply to learning in the classroom. He criticized the use of repetition and rote memorization, explaining that such procedures lead only to blind, nonproductive learning on the part of students. He insisted that educators should teach for understanding, and this is made possible when the teacher arranges the material so that the student can see the "whole" or the Gestalt, and not just a series of seemingly unrelated parts. In his book *Productive Thinking*, Wertheimer stressed the importance of Gestalt theory in the practical problem of educating children.

Whereas Watson and Guthrie were concerned with overt responses, stressing always what the student *did*, Wertheimer placed his emphasis on the child's process of mental organization, stressing instead what the student *understood*.

The advice apparently worked, for from then on the child hung up his coat correctly. Fortunately for Guthrie, and especially for the child, a longer sequence of S-R associations did not form. That is, according to Guthrie's system, the child might have forever learned to come home, open the door, throw the coat on the floor, pick it up, put it on, go back outside, come back in, then hang up the coat!

THE EARLY COGNITIVE THEORISTS

Wertheimer

Max Wertheimer, as noted before, founded the school of psychology called gestaltism or configurationism. Wertheimer insisted that it was useless to study small parts of psychological concepts, like perception or learning. Studying parts in isolation was unjustified, because changing any single part necessarily changes

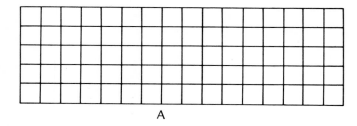

A

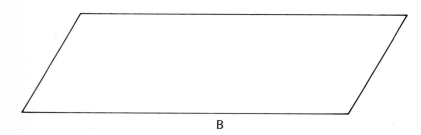

B

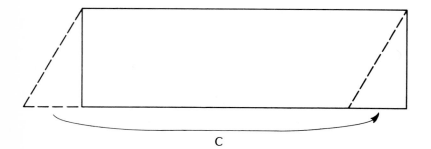

C

Fig. 11.1 Wertheimer's parallelogram problem. Part A shows Wertheimer's way of explaining why the area of a rectangle equals the product of length times width, in this case sixteen by five. Part B shows the parallelogram for which he asked subjects to find the area. Part C shows one person's solution to the problem, cutting off one end, moving it to the other end, and thus converting the parallelogram into a rectangle.

the whole, or the gestalt. Similarly, the whole may remain, even when all the parts have changed. For example, if we play a tune in two different keys, even though the individual notes are different each time, the tune retains the integrity of its gestalt.

Wertheimer was concerned with the way children learn, particularly in school. He was against the use of rote memorization, especially when it so often seemed to be an end in itself. Above all else, he wanted children to achieve understanding, to have insight into the nature of the problem.

Wertheimer explained that there are two kinds of solutions to problems, type A and type B. Type A solutions are those that use originality and insight, whereas type B solutions are those that make use of past associations in a rigid, inappropriate way. Wertheimer used the example of teaching a child how to find the area of a parallelogram (see Fig. 11.1).

The child is first taught how to find the area of a rectangle, not by memorizing the formula but by understanding why the formula works. The rectangle is divided into smaller squares, and the child sees that the total area is composed of the number of squares in a row times the number of rows. Wertheimer then cut a parallelogram out of paper and asked the child to determine its area. Some children persisted in multiplying the length times the height, a type B solution. Others used type A solutions, like cutting off one of the triangular ends and fitting it against the other end. At this point, the child had created a rectangle and could correctly utilize the previously learned formula. Another type A solution involved bending the parallelogram into a loop with the two angular ends abutting each other, then making one vertical cut which would also create a rectangle. The children using type A solutions had obviously discovered a real geometric relationship.[9]

Kohler

Wolfgang Kohler, who had worked with Wertheimer at the University of Frankfurt, spent a few years during World War I on the island of Tenerife off the coast of Africa. There he performed gestalt psychology's most famous animal studies. Kohler arranged an ape's cage so that there were bananas hanging from the top and a couple of boxes on the floor. In order to reach the bananas the ape had to stack one box on top of another and then climb to the top. The ape's solution to the problem appeared to Kohler not to be one of blind trial and error. Instead, the ape seemed to size up the situation and then, almost in a flash, he understood the problem and "saw" the solution. The ape displayed what Kohler called insight, and Kohler felt that this was more typical of learning, especially human learning, than Thorndike's concept of blind trial and error.

In another experiment, Kohler put food outside the cage, beyond even an ape's long reach. Inside the cage, however, there were some sticks. At first the apes would throw the sticks at the banana. Then they "realized" that by using the stick as a kind of tool they could reach out and rake the banana in. One especially intelligent ape, named Sultan, was even able to join two short sticks together to rake the food in.

Kohler's explanation was that the apes were able to see the problem as a unified whole. In the box-stacking problem, the ape did not see the boxes and

Wertheimer stresses insight and understanding in learning

Type A and B solutions

Kohler challenges the notion of learning by trial and error

Kohler's ape demonstrates "insight"

bananas as separate elements but came to realize that they belonged together as part of a total gestalt. Similarly, the sticks and bananas were perceived as belonging together, and it was only after this reorganization of perceptions that insight into the solution to the problem occurred.

Insight has been called the "a-ha" phenomenon. Kohler made much of the concept of insight, perhaps too much. He felt that insight learning did not depend on past experience, that it was not just a special case of transfer. As we shall see in a later chapter, Harry Harlow's studies on learning sets have since cast some doubt on the validity of Kohler's interpretation.

NEW DIRECTIONS IN PSYCHOLOGY AND EDUCATION

You may now be wondering why nobody tried to bridge the gap between the two learning-theory traditions, for both positions evidently have some merit. The behaviorists did have a strong case for insisting that overt responses are the appropriate data for psychology. If you were trying to judge your friends' attitudes toward some issue, you would, in all probability, be more influenced by what they did than by what they said. For example, if your boss constantly bragged of being an equal opportunity employer and yet never hired black applicants, you might rightly feel that "actions speak louder than words."

Yet you probably feel equally sure that the gestaltists also had a good case; learning, understanding, discovering new relationships must be more than just the mere conditioning of certain responses. Some reorganization of perceptions, something going on within the organism must account for understanding and discovery.

In fact, some psychologists did attempt to bridge the gap. E. C. Tolman, for example, produced a theory called purposive behaviorism. It was called purposive because Tolman insisted that, far from being random and chaotic, learning was goal-directed. The learning organism is a striving organism, striving to give meaning to behavor. Yet Tolman's theory was also behavioristic, because he believed that scientific validity could be achieved only by observing objective behavior.

Tolman stated that both rats and humans learn by forming "cognitive maps" of their environment.[10] This explains how organisms get from place to place. They form hypotheses, see relationships, and then select out appropriate responses on the basis of their cognitive maps. Although Tolman did not emphasize stimuius-response connections as the basic unit of analysis, he was still an associationist because he saw learning as a result of bonds formed among a number of stimuli. The learner forms an association between some new stimulus, or sign, and a previously encountered and therefore meaningful stimulus or significate. Tolman's behaviorism is therefore an S-S (sign-significate) psychology, rather than a Watsonian S-R psychology.

Tolman was more responsive to the work of the developmental psychologists than were most of the other behaviorists. He postulated his famous H-A-T-E variables (Heredity, Age, Training, Endocrine) as of crucial importance in understanding and predicting behavior. Heredity sets certain limits on what environmental manipulation can accomplish. Age determines how much impact training can have. Training is, of course, vital, since learning cannot occur in

Tolman and purposive behaviorism *(margin note)*

The H-A-T-E variables *(margin note)*

a static environment. Endocrine, or internal physiological, factors also play an important role in learning. Thus Tolman, perhaps more than any other learning theorist, understood the importance of individual differences. Recent studies, such as those by Krech, have shown how strong the relationships between training variables and the internal physiology of the organism are.[11]

With all its sophistication and thoroughness, Tolman's system never really caught on in education. Tolman never exerted the influence on teachers that Thorndike or Watson did. Though he may be rediscovered in the next decade, and in the long run may have more influence than Thorndike, this is not yet the case.

Why was Tolman so ignored by the field of education during his lifetime? There are a number of reasons, but it is primarily because he never translated theory into practice. The teacher might learn from Tolman that a rat at a choice-point in a maze hypothesizes a solution before acting, but this hardly helps the teacher in the classroom. The teacher wants answers to specific questions regarding learning and discipline in the classroom, not sophisticated and elegant theorizing. Further, Tolman failed to develop his theory to its fullest potential. He didn't do enough experiments to make his cognitive position firm enough to generate precise predictions. As Winfred Hill, a modern expert in the field of learning, has said of Tolman, "His system is more a road sign or a pious hope than it is an accomplished fact."[12]

And so educational psychology turned away from the old-line theorists and turned toward psychology's "new breed" theorists, psychologists who talked to teachers, who told teachers what to do in given situations, who told teachers how to produce desired behavior changes or set up conditions that aid discovery. Educational psychology turned to Skinner and Bruner.

Summary

The study of learning has been of utmost importance in psychology for over a century. Though psychologists agreed on the importance of learning as an object of study, they disagreed on the mechanics of how the learning process occurred.

The major schools of thought were:

1
Behaviorist-associationists: those who viewed learning as resulting from the forming of connections between stimuli and observable responses.

2
Cognitive-gestaltists: those who believed that learning resulted from the reorganization of perceptions and the forming of new relationships.

Both the behaviorists and the gestaltists began their schools of thought as reactions to Wundt's associationist-introspectionist brand of psychology. The gestaltists, led by Wertheimer, challenged Wundt's associationist position, while the behaviorists, led by Watson, attacked Wundt's use of introspection.

Wertheimer and the gestaltists argued that psychological phenomena could not be understood by studying simple associations among tiny elements, but must be viewed as a total configuration, or to use the German word, as a *Gestalt.* Wertheimer argued that the whole (the Gestalt) is more than just the sum of a group of separate parts. Learning was seen as the understanding of a total, meaningful relationship, and the only acceptable approach to the study of learning was a cognitive one. Watson and the behaviorists, while not objecting to the study of separate parts, did denounce Wundt's use of introspection. Watson argued that the only true scientific data in the field of psychology were *observable responses*. Thus, if a concept such as "consciousness" could not be seen, touched, or observed in any way, it should be thrown out of psychology. Watson believed that learning could be thoroughly understood on the basis of Pavlov's principles of classical conditioning.

The first experimental studies of learning were conducted by Hermann Ebbinghaus during the late nineteenth century. In order to control for past associations, Ebbinghaus studied the learning of nonsense syllables. He discovered that the forgetting of learned material does not occur at an even rate, that most of what is forgotten occurs very quickly, and that the rate of forgetting eventually slows down to a fairly even rate.

E. L. Thorndike, an early associationist, posited three major laws of learning: (1) the law of readiness—showing the importance of neurological anticipation; (2) the law of excercise—showing the importance of practice; and (3) the law of effect—indicating the importance of motivation.

I. P. Pavlov, a Russian physiologist, discovered some lawful relationships between stimuli and responses. He showed how learning could take place through *conditioning,* a trained association among stimuli and a certain response. Pavlov's system is now called classical conditioning, and applies only to reflex activity. Pavlov also introduced such concepts as extinction, stimulus generalization, and discrimination learning.

Guthrie, a psychologist in the behaviorist-associationist tradition, felt that all learning was a result of stimuli and responses in sequence. Guthrie saw no need to use concepts such as motivation or reinforcement to explain learning.

Wertheimer, the first of the cognitive-gestalt psychologists, was concerned with how the learner achieved understanding and insight when confronted with a problem. He felt that rote memorization did not lead to real understanding.

Kohler, also of the cognitive-gestalt school, performed several important animal studies. Kohler's studies on apes led him to conclude that learning was a result of a series of insightful solutions, not blind trial-and-error.

E. C. Tolman attempted to bridge the gap between behaviorists and gestaltists, and created a type of psychology called purposive behaviorism. Tolman thought that striving toward a goal gave meaning to the resulting behavior. Learning occurs when a new stimulus (or sign) is associated with a previously encountered and therefore meaningful stimulus (significate).

The two basic positions, behaviorist-associationist and cognitive-gestaltist, have their contemporary proponents in B. F. Skinner and Jerome Bruner. Skinner (the behaviorist) and Bruner (the cognitive theorist) are especially important in educational psychology today, for each devotes a great deal of time talking directly to the classroom teacher.

REFERENCES

1
W. James, *The Principles of Psychology* (New York: Henry Holt, 1890).

2
Ibid.

3
W. Wundt, *Physiological Psychology*, 5th ed. (New York: Macmillan, 1910).

4
J. B. Watson, "Psychology as the Behaviorist Sees It," *Psychological Review* 20 (1913): 158–177.

5
H. Ebbinghaus, *Memory: A Contribution to Experimental Psychology*, trans. by H. A. Ruger and C. E. Bussenius (New York: Teachers College, Columbia University Press, 1913).

6
E. D. Thorndike, "Animal Intelligence," *Psychological Review, Monograph Supplement* 2, no. 8 (1898).

7
I. P. Pavlov, *Conditioned Reflexes* (London: Oxford University Press, 1927).

8
E. R. Guthrie, *The Psychology of Learning* (New York: Harper, 1935).

9
M. Wertheimer, *Productive Thinking* (New York: Harper, 1945).

10
E. C. Tolman, "Cognitive Maps in Rats and Men," *Psychological Review* 55 (1948):1–4.

11
D. Krech, "The Chemistry of Learning," in R. C. Sprinthall and N. A. Sprinthall, *Educational Psychology: Selected Readings* (New York: Van Nostrand-Reinhold, 1969), pp. 152–156.

12
W. F. Hill, *Learning: A Survey of Psychological Interpretations* (Scranton, Pa.: Chandler, 1971), p. 129.

SUGGESTIONS FOR FURTHER READING

Bugelski, B. R. *The Psychology of Learning Applied to Teaching.* 2d ed. New York: Bobbs-Merrill, 1971.

Hilgard, E. R., and G. H. Bower. *Theories of Learning.* 3d ed. New York: Appleton-Century-Crofts, 1966.

Hill, W. F. *Learning: A Survey of Psychological Interpretations.* Scranton, Pa.: Chandler, 1971.

12

Learning theory today

Now that we have had a look at some of the positions learning theorists have taken over the years, you may be questioning whether there is anything in all these theories for you, the future classroom teacher. If the study of learning is so complicated as to have generated so many different and often conflicting explanations, how can the prospective teacher begin to understand the learning process, let alone stand up in front of a roomful of children and help them learn? Is the study of learning really as complicated as the controversies we have outlined seem to indicate?

Part of the reason there are so many theoretical positions is that learning means so many different things—from a child memorizing a poem, to a rat finding its way through a maze, to a baby trying to imitate an adult saying "bye-bye," a smoker choosing one brand of cigarettes over another, a teenage boy fearing and thus avoiding all contact sports, a young geometry student suddenly seeing the solution to a difficult problem, and on and on. Almost all our thoughts and behavior have been learned. Learning may be adaptive or non-adaptive, conscious or unconscious, overt or covert. Feelings and attitudes are learned just as certainly as facts and skills. Learning means so many different things that controversies sometimes result merely because different theorists are studying different aspects of learning. Like the blind men feeling the elephant, each one describes only that part with which he happens to come in contact. And yet, our present knowledge of learning is neither so incomplete nor so complicated that the classroom teacher can't profit from it. There are scientific principles of learning that can be translated into classroom use in order to make learning more efficient and productive.

Different theorists often studied different aspects of learning

291

In this chapter the spotlight falls on two contemporary theorists, B. F. Skinner and Jerome Bruner. Each has a different philosophical lineage: B. F. Skinner is today's most eloquent behaviorist-associationist; Bruner is the most influential cognitive-gestaltist. Each also has a great deal to say to the practicing classroom teacher. Part of the problem in the past was that some learning theorists were of virtually no help to the educator. It may have been glorious to contemplate the elegance of Hull's "oscillation of reaction potential" or Spence's paper on the transposition controversy, but neither gave much comfort to the teacher trying to find out why Johnny couldn't read.

Some learning theorists were of little help to the working teacher

B. F. SKINNER AND RESPONSE ANALYSIS

No psychologist ever dominated American behaviorism to the extent that B. F. Skinner does today. John B. Watson commented that behavior is the data of psychology, and felt that responses, not conscious experience, should be studied and analyzed. B. F. Skinner wholeheartedly agrees, and since the 1938 publication of his *Behavior of Organisms,* has outlined a system of response analysis that is far more thorough and detailed than anything seen before. While behaviorists were preoccupied with response analysis up through the mid-1930s, Skinner's arrival changed this preoccupation to a near obsession. To the Skinnerians every little squiggle on the cumulative recorder* is fraught with profound significance.

Skinner not concerned with what goes on inside the child

Skinner's work is not concerned with what goes on inside the organism, the organism's motivational or emotional state, or even its neurology. Skinner's psychology is an "empty organism" psychology, a psychology of environmental conditions (stimuli) associating with and affecting the organism's response repertoire.

Skinner's line of descent, back through Watson, Thorndike, and the other early associationists, is clear and direct. He views learning as an association be-

---

*

A device that records the responses made by an animal in the experimental chamber.

tween stimuli and responses, although not always in that order, and emphasizes R-S associations as much as S-R associations; that is, he has found that conditioning takes place when a response is followed by a reinforcing stimulus.

Skinnerian psychology is based on a totally environmental view of behavior. Since the consequences of a response influence further action, and since these consequences occur in the outer environment, it is the environment that causes changes in behavior. This is essentially Skinner's "theme song."

Throughout our discussion of Skinner's system, we focus on the conditioning of rats and pigeons. Although his data were derived primarily from work with these animals, Skinner's findings are, nonetheless, relevant to education. A fairly thorough knowledge of Skinner is essential to the classroom teacher, for as we shall see later, Skinner's techniques do work in the classroom just as surely as in the aseptic confines of the Skinner box.

Skinner's data result from experiments on rats and pigeons

REINFORCEMENT

Skinner picks up the behaviorist-associationist tradition about where Thorndike left off. You may recall that one of Thorndike's three major laws of learning was the law of effect, which stated that learning is an association between a stimulus and a response as a result of the consequences of an act. If the S-R sequence is followed by a satisfying state of affairs, the association is strengthened; that is, learning takes place.

B. F. Skinner and a pigeon used in his research. Skinner's data came primarily from working with rats and pigeons.

Burrhus Frederic Skinner

B. F. Skinner was born in Susquehanna, Pennsylvania, in 1904. His father was a lawyer in Susquehanna, and young Skinner attended the local schools, graduating from high school in 1922. He then went to Hamilton College in New York, where he majored in English and also took several courses in Greek. In 1926 he graduated from Hamilton and was awarded the coveted Hawley Greek Prize.

During his senior year in college, Skinner had written some poetry which he sent to Robert Frost for comment and evaluation. Frost's response was so flattering that following college graduation, Skinner took time out to do some serious writing. He was not pleased with the result. Says Skinner of this experience, "I discovered the unhappy fact that I had nothing to say, and went on to graduate study in psychology, hoping to remedy that shortcoming." And remedy it he apparently did, for Skinner has not been at a loss for something to say ever since.

In 1928 Skinner entered Harvard, where he found himself attracted to the ideas of John B. Watson. Watson, though not at Harvard himself, was very influential in American psychology, especially in the twenties and thirties. Skinner pursued a degree in experimental psychology and received his Ph.D. in 1931. He remained at Harvard under various research fellowships until the fall of 1936. At this time he went to the University of Minnesota as an instructor. In 1937 he was made an assistant professor and, in 1939, an associate professor. In 1944 he won a Guggenheim Fellowship. During World War II, Skinner participated in a government research project, the results of which were not made public until 1959. He had been conditioning pigeons to pilot missiles and torpedoes. The pigeons were so highly trained that they could guide a missile right down into the smokestack of a naval destroyer.

In 1945 Skinner went to the University of Indiana as chairman of the psychology department, a job he held until 1948. During this time he developed the now-famous air crib, a soundproof, air-conditioned, germfree, glass-enclosed box for raising children in a scientifically controlled environment. One of his daughters, Deborah, spent much of her first two years of life in an air crib. The device, however, was not widely acclaimed by the mothers of America.

In 1948 Skinner was appointed to the faculty at Harvard, and from his command post in Cambridge he has influ-

enced a whole generation of students in experimental psychology. While at Harvard he developed the experimental chamber, or Skinner box, for the study of learning in rats and pigeons. This device has enabled American psychologists to study animal responses with a precision and ease never before possible. While the animal is in the Skinner box its every movement can be recorded and made ready for analysis by automated equipment.

Skinner later became very interested in educational psychology, after visiting his daughter's arithmetic class in elementary school. He says of that visit that he had been a witness to "minds being destroyed." He felt that human beings could be trained in much the same fashion as the rats and pigeons that he had conditioned in the Skinner box. Children, too, could be conditioned, step by step, each correct response followed by reinforcement, until they acquired complex forms of behavior. He developed and tested his first "teaching machine" in the '50s, and as a result has been credited with creating a revolution in the technology of education. The teaching machine, or programed instruction, was seen as a threat to their jobs by many teachers. Skinner has assured the teachers that programed instruction is a learning aid, not a substitute teacher. He has also assured educators that the children trained with this device will not become mechanized little ro-

bots, but instead will be more likely to reach their intellectual potential.

Skinner's analysis of the learning situation into operant responses and reinforcing stimuli also led to the development of behavior-modification techniques in the classroom. Under this system, teachers are trained to wait for their students to emit appropriate responses and then reinforce these responses speedily and consistently. Behavior modification is the second revolution in teaching technology attributed to Skinner.

Skinner has been a most prolific researcher and writer. His books and papers are far too numerous to summarize here, but his best-known works are: *The Behavior of Organisms* (1938), *Walden Two*, a novel about a utopian society

where everyone's behavior has been shaped according to conditioning principles (1948), *Science and Human Behavior* (1953), *Verbal Behavior* (1957), *Schedules of Reinforcement* (1957), *Cumulative Record* (1959), *The Technology of Teaching* (1968), and *Beyond Freedom and Dignity* (1971). Skinner has recently published a lively autobiography, *Particulars of My Life* (1976), in which he discusses many intimate details of his life history.

In 1958 Skinner received the American Psychological Association's Distinguished Scientific Contribution Award. Skinner is an avowed behaviorist in the tradition of J. B. Watson. Though now retired from active teaching, Skinner is today America's most important and honored behaviorist psychologist.

Skinner streamlined
Thorndike's law
of effect

Skinner borrowed the law of effect, streamlined it somewhat, and called it reinforcement. Thorndike had spent considerable time defending his law of effect against the charge that it was subjective and mentalistic (a charge leveled by behaviorists who were even more tough-minded than Thorndike). Skinner's concept of reinforcement needs no such defense. Skinner totally stripped his concept of any subjective or mentalistic overtones. Reinforcement neither offers a reward nor does it create a feeling of satisfaction in the learner. Reinforcement, like all of Skinner's concepts, is defined strictly in operational terms, that

Positive and negative
reinforcement

is, in terms of the way it is observed or measured. Thus a positive reinforcement is any stimulus which, when added to the situation, increases the likelihood of the response occurring. Similarly, a negative reinforcement is any stimulus which, when removed from the situation, increases the probability of the response occurring. That is all there is to it. There is no mention of subjective feelings, only a description of the observed events. If a pellet of food is a positive reinforcer to a hungry rat, it is only because the rat pressed a lever to get another pellet. Reinforcement is defined as something that is observed to increase the likelihood of a response recurring. Skinner is no hedonist, basing his concepts on the search for pleasure, but an objectivist defining his concepts in operational terms.

RESPONSES ARE OF TWO TYPES

Skinner, like the earlier behaviorists, bases his system on the observation of overt responses. He divides all responses into two categories: respondents and operants.[1]

Respondents

Respondents are
reflexes

Respondents are those responses that can be automatically triggered by a specific unlearned or unconditioned stimulus; Pavlov called them reflexes. Pavlov, and later Watson, based a whole system of learning on the fact that reflexes can be conditioned. Skinner accepts the fact that respondents can be conditioned in precisely the manner Pavlov described, but he doesn't consider respondent conditioning nearly so important as Pavlov and Watson did. The reason for this is that so many living organisms have so few respondents. To generalize the laws of classical conditioning to the whole range of human behavior is to carelessly overwork a fairly restricted formula. As Skinner pointed out (1953), a human

Humans have rela-
tively few respondents

being is far more than a mere jack-in-the-box with a list of tricks to be elicited by pressing the correct button. The bulk of an individual's response repertoire takes another form.

Operants

Operants are all those responses that cannot be classified as respondents. An operant is a response that occurs spontaneously, without having to be triggered by an unconditioned stimulus. For example, when you stretch your legs, or raise your hand, or shift in your seat, there are no known unconditioned stimuli which automatically force those responses.

An operant is therefore a response for which the original stimulus is either unidentified or nonexistent; it may be loosely thought of as voluntary behavior. The consequences of operant behavior can be observed, even though the stimulus is not known. In operant conditioning, reinforcement is contingent on the operant first being emitted. Thus, the organism must "operate" on the environment in order that the reinforcement will follow. Earlier psychologists called operant responding *instrumental* responding. Skinner believes that most human behavior is of the operant type.

Some responses we first think are respondents turn out not to be when they are subjected to further analysis. For example, putting your foot on the brake pedal to the stimulus of a red traffic light is not a reflex. You had to learn the significance of a red traffic light. You didn't come into the world already equipped to press your foot down automatically at the sight of a red light. This response is an example of a conditioned operant.

OPERANT CONDITIONING

The best way to understand operant conditioning is to examine the experimental situation Skinner has used over the years. Figure 12.1 is an illustration of the experimental chamber, or as it is so often called, the Skinner box. It is a small box, the side and top of which are made of clear plastic. A lever protrudes from one side and there is a tube which empties into the food cup next to the lever. The experimenter decides which operant to condition; in this case it will be pressing the lever. The experimenter then simply waits while the rat explores the cage. Since there aren't that many things to do in a Skinner box, the rat eventually presses the lever. A pellet of food (a reinforcing stimulus) immediately drops down the tube into the food cup. The rat pounces on the food, and conditioning has begun. It is important to note that when the rat, after wandering

The experimental chamber, or Skinner box

Fig. 12.1 The experimental chamber, often called the Skinner box.

around the cage for a while, chances to press the food-producing lever, the response is not a reflex action triggered by a particular unconditioned stimulus. Skinner says that operants are emitted by the organism, whereas reflexes or respondents are elicited by unconditioned stimuli.

Thus the sequence of events for operant conditioning is:

1

the emitting of the free operant (the rat chancing to press the lever); followed by

2

the presentation of a reinforcing stimulus (the rat is given a pellet of food); followed by

3

an increase in the probability of the response occurring again.

**In operant condition-
ing the reinforcing
stimulus must follow
the response**

The response is now becoming controlled, or predictable. Note that the events must follow in the order specified above. The food must come after the response is emitted. How long after? The sooner the better. For optimum conditioning, the reinforcement should immediately follow the response. This is an important Skinnerian principle. Skinner believes that in the classroom the student should be reinforced as soon as the appropriate response is emitted.

> *A student in a class contributes very little to classroom discussions. The teacher is concerned and wants to increase the student's active participation. Finally, the student asks a question. The teacher, using Skinnerian psychology, looks at the student, pauses a while, and then proceeds to comment on the good quality of the question and adds that if more questions of such quality were introduced the sessions would be more profitable to the whole class. The episode is followed by a dramatic increase in the asking of questions on the part of this student. The teacher's commendation is hence deemed reinforcing (rewarding). But for some students, approval from the teacher may act as a negative stimulus. Consequently, the art of teaching, according to Skinner, must include the identification of events that reinforce each student and the setting up of conditions that provide the opportunity for each to experience reinforcement upon making desired responses and showing progress.[2]*

Note that, unlike reflex or respondent conditioning, the experimenter cannot force the response to occur. The experimenter may have to wait awhile until the rat chances upon the lever and emits the appropriate operant. Pavlov had no such wait, for he could automatically trigger the desired response (salivation) by simply presenting the unconditioned stimulus (meat powder).

In operant conditioning, although the experimenter might have to wait as long as fifteen or twenty minutes before the rat presses the lever for the first time, after a few reinforced responses the rat begins pressing ever more frequently. It is not unusual to see a conditioned animal pressing the lever 300 to 400 times in the space of one hour. With a highly conditioned rat, the sound of lever-pressing emanating from the Skinner box is reminiscent of the sound of a high-speed typist.

THE LAW OF OPERANT CONDITIONING

We may now state Skinner's general principle: If the occurrence of the operant is followed by a reinforcing stimulus, the rate of responding, for that particular operant, will increase.

Remember that the free operant originally had no connection with a stimulus. In operant conditioning, the response produces the reinforcing stimulus, or in Skinner's terms, the reinforcement is contingent upon the occurrence of the response. In this case, then, a response-stimulus connection is formed, not a stimulus-response connection.

Operant Level

We have said a number of times that as conditioning proceeds, the rate of responding increases. Increases over what? The rate increases over what is known as the operant level, or the frequency with which the response typically occurs in the untrained animal. For conditioning to take place, a response must occur before it can be reinforced. The experimenter must therefore select a response that the animal is apt to make on its own, such as rising on its hind legs, stretching its neck, or more commonly, pressing a lever. When first placed in the experimental chamber, the naive rat may happen to press the lever three or four times during the course of an hour, even though the lever is not producing any food. That is, the animal will occasionally press the lever even without positive reinforcement. The operant level is, therefore, the rate with which the free operant is typically emitted prior to conditioning.

> The operant level: the response rate before conditioning

EXTINCTION

Extinction may be loosely thought of as a kind of forgetting process. For example, as has been seen, an animal may be conditioned to the point where it is pressing the lever 400 times per hour. Similarly, the animal may be extinguished or "deconditioned" back to the point where it will press the lever only three or four times per hour. The technique is simple. Allow the conditioned response to occur, but do not reinforce it. With the Skinner box, this means that pressing the bar no longer produces a food pellet. After enough nonreinforced lever presses, the animal "gives up," and the rate of response returns to its pre-conditioned, or operant, level. Note that extinction does not cause the animal to stop pressing the lever completely, but it does cause the response frequency to return to the operant level.

> Nonreinforced responses become extinguished

It is important to remember that extinction requires that the animal emit the response, and that the response not be reinforced. If the animal were somehow prevented from making the response, extinction would not occur. For example, if a conditioned animal were removed from the Skinner box and returned to its home cage, where there was no lever to press, the animal would retain the conditioning. If the animal were returned to the Skinner box, even a year later, lever-pressing would be resumed.

Spontaneous recovery

The first time a conditioned animal is extinguished, spontaneous recovery of the response will occur. This requires time, though sometimes as little as an hour. If

> Spontaneous recovery follows extinction

the extinguished animal is taken out of the Skinner box for an hour or so and then returned to it, lever-pressing will resume even though no new training has taken place. These spontaneously recovered responses will extinguish more quickly, however, than did the original extinction. Several extinction-spontaneous recovery sequences may be necessary before extinction is complete to the point where the animal remains at the operant level with no further evidence of spontaneous recovery.

DISCRIMINATION

Discriminated operants

Although in its original state the free operant is not attached to a stimulus, it may become so through training. This technique is called discrimination training, and the operant that has become associated with the stimulus is called a discriminated operant. Discrimination training is accomplished in the following manner: we introduce a new stimulus to an animal that has been conditioned to press the lever, such as a light that we turn off and on in a random time sequence. We now reinforce the animal only for pressing the lever when the light is on. Since any lever-pressing that takes place when the light is off is not reinforced, the response is extinguished as far as periods of no light are concerned. The animal emits the response only when the light is on; that is, the operant has become attached to the stimulus "light on." At this point the operant is no longer free, but is firmly controlled by the stimulus.

Technically, the stimulus for which responding is reinforced is called the discriminated stimulus, or the S^D—in this case "light on." The stimulus for which responding is extinguished is called the stimulus delta, or S^Δ—in this case "light off." Responding to the discriminated stimulus (pressing the lever) is followed by reinforcement (food pellets). This sequence of events is crucial to the development of discrimination: (1) stimulus, (2) response, and (3) reinforcement.

STIMULUS GENERALIZATION

Once discrimination training has been completed—that is, once the animal has attached an operant to a certain stimulus—the stimulus may become generalized. Stimulus generalization means that other stimuli, similar to the one used in training, may take on the power to produce the response. If the animal has been trained to respond to a bright light, through generalization it may also respond to a dim light, even though the dim light was never used in training. Or perhaps a buzzer was used as the stimulus; through generalization, the animal may also be found to respond to a clicking sound or even a bell.

When generalization is noted, further discrimination training may be used to train the animal to respond only to a fairly specific stimulus magnitude. For example, if the original discrimination training used "light on" as the S^D and "light off" as the S^Δ, the animal will eventually respond only when the light is on. However, because of generalization, responses will occur at many different light intensities. Perhaps the original S^D was a fairly bright light, but because of generalization the animal also responds to a dim light. We may now "correct" for this generalization by a new discrimination series in which the bright light is the S^D and the dim light is the S^Δ. That is, we continue reinforcing responses to the bright light, while extinguishing responses to the dim light. This procedure allows the experimenter to determine the animal's capacity for distinguishing between rather subtle stimulus differences. For example, we can probe such questions as how small a difference in light intensity the animal is capable of identifying. Experiments have even been carried out in which the S^Δ was a card printed with the words "Don't Press," and the S^D a card with the word "Press." The experimental animal then displays the seemingly uncanny ability to "read," rushing over to the lever and pressing whenever the "Press" card is shown. The rat reacts on cue, much the way that a studio audience on a TV show frantically claps when the "applause" sign is presented.

Animals exhibit ability to "read"

CONDITIONED REINFORCEMENT
A stimulus that is not originally reinforcing may become so through repeated presentation with one that is. For example, if lever-pressing produces both a light and a food pellet, the light, by association with the food, will take on the power to reinforce. The sequence of events for establishing conditioned reinforcement is (1) response; (2) neutral stimulus, such as a light or buzzer; followed by (3) the primary reinforcement. It is important that this order of events be followed, for if the neutral stimulus is presented before, rather than after, the response, discrimination, and not conditioned reinforcement, will result. If a light is presented before the response has been emitted, the light will become an S^D, whereas if it follows the response, it becomes a conditioned reinforcer. In a sense, discrimination training teaches the rat to respond *to* the light, whereas conditioned reinforcement teaches the rat to respond *for*, or in order to get, the light.

The conditioned reinforcer follows the response, but precedes the primary reinforcer

Although the teacher may sometimes use primary reinforcers such as candy, conditioned reinforcers such as good grades, promotions, prizes, and teacher approval are usually more appropriate.

SCHEDULES OF REINFORCEMENT

Five major schedules
of reinforcement

The way in which the reinforcers are arranged determines in large measure the strength of the resulting conditioning. Responses that are reinforced periodically, rather than each time they are emitted, tend to be conditioned more strongly and are thus more difficult to extinguish. Though there are many variations on the major themes, Skinner has identified five major schedules of reinforcement.

1
Continuous Reinforcement (Crf).   As the name implies, the Crf schedule provides for reinforcement each time the operant is emitted. For example, a rat in a Skinner box will receive a pellet of food every time the lever is pressed.

2
Fixed Ratio (F.R.).   Under the F.R. schedule the reinforcement occurs only after a fixed number of operants have been emitted. For example, on an F.R. schedule of 3:1, the rat in a Skinner box must press the lever three times in order to get one pellet of food. Skinner has demonstrated that the ratio can go as high as 196:1 and still maintain the conditioning.

3
Fixed Interval (F.I.).   Rather than being based on the number of responses being emitted, the F.I. schedule is keyed to a fixed *time* interval. That is, a given period of time must elapse, regardless of what the organism is doing, before the reinforcement is presented. On an F.I. schedule of say thirty seconds, this thirty-second time period must be allowed to elapse before the organism's next response will be reinforced.

4
Variable Ratio (V.R.).   Like the F.R., the V.R. schedule is also based on the number of responses being emitted. Under the V.R. schedule, however, the ratio is constantly being varied so that the organism never knows which response will be reinforced. The rat might be reinforced after five responses, then after fifteen responses, then after the very next response and so on.

5
Variable Interval (V.I.).   On this schedule the time periods, rather than numbers of responses, are varied. The rat may have to wait thirty seconds, then five seconds, then fifty seconds and so on before pressing the lever will deliver the reinforcement.

ANALYSIS OF THE REINFORCEMENT SCHEDULES

Each of the reinforcement schedules creates differences in the way the resulting conditioning is exhibited. The Crf schedule, though extremely useful for the acquiring of new behavior, does not result in a great deal of perseverance. Extinction can occur rather rapidly when a response has been conditioned on the continuous schedule. Parents in the United States may be guilty of using too much reinforcement in bringing up their children, and consequently nurture such qualities as a lack of perseverance, low frustration tolerance, impulsiveness, impatience, and a generally low level of ego strength.

Children at home, or rats in the Skinner box, tend to give up easily (have a low resistance to extinction) when the reinforcers are continuous. This is especially true in a highly industrialized nation in which continuous reinforcement is built into the society.

> *The conveniences provided by technological gadgets work in concert with parental indulgence by providing immediate gratification with great consistency while requiring little effort. Coke machines, television sets, automobiles, and many other devices yield rewards quickly and consistently with a minimum of sweat. Indulgent parents, who readily provide their children the means for making life easy and convenient, should not be surprised to find that their children lack some of the old-fashioned traits that the parents were taught to admire in their early lives.*[3]

The other schedules, F.R., F.I., V.R., and V.I. are all of the *intermittent* type: they require that the organism learn to wait out the hard times. Responses conditioned in this way become highly resistant to extinction. Intermittent reinforcement does condition perseverance and perhaps "hope."

Responses conditioned by intermittent schedules are highly resistant to extinction

Life outside the Skinner box creates many conditions that are analogous to the various intermittent schedules. For example, factory workers or farm laborers who are paid on a piece-work basis are being conditioned on an F.R schedule. In piece work one's pay is based on a set number of items produced or apples picked. Workers who are paid by the hour or by the week illustrate the F.I. schedule. An example of the V.R. schedule might be a door-to-door encyclopedia salesman who is paid on a commission basis. The salesman knows he must emit a number of responses, but he never knows which response is going to lead to a pay-off. Slot machines and other forms of gambling are set up on a V.R. basis. Because the V.R. schedule creates responses that are highly resistant to extinction, people can often become addicted to gambling. This helps explain why the gambler can persevere through long dry spells and still go back to the game. The V.I. schedule also creates strongly conditioned responses that are maintained at a rapid rate and are highly resistant to extinction.

The variable schedules are typical of most social situations. Human interaction is characterized by inconsistent reinforcement, and the result is a repertoire of responses that may become almost extinction-proof. Habit, as William James has told us, that great fly-wheel of society, keeps people doing the same things over and over again, even when the habits are self-destructive.

Human interaction is characterized by inconsistent reinforcement

THE ENGINEERING OF SOCIETY

Skinner suggests that through the judicious use of reinforcement schedules, a society free of war, crime, poverty, and pollution can be behaviorally engineered. The individuals in the society could be shaped to reflect the best of human traits: honesty, altruism, ambition, and so on. It is Skinner's conviction that this not only could be done, but should be done. A culture should be designed in which the behavior of the individuals is systematically controlled—and Skinner is not overly concerned about who will decide which behaviors are to be reinforced and which are to be extinguished.

The relation between the controller and the controlled is reciprocal. The scientist in the laboratory, studying the behavior of a pigeon, designs contingencies and observes their effects. His apparatus exerts a conspicuous control on the pigeon, but we must not overlook the control exerted by the pigeon. The behavior of the pigeon has determined the design of the apparatus and the procedures in which it is used.[4]

Thus, just as the scientist in the laboratory is to some extent under the control of the pigeon, so too will the controller of a society be influenced by the members of that society. Despite Skinner's view on the apparent equality between the controller and controllee, some of you may feel you'd prefer the role of experimenter to that of pigeon.

VERBAL BEHAVIOR

Skinner: learning to talk is a result of operant conditioning

Skinner uses his system to explain all animal and human learning. For example, Skinner believes that learning to talk follows the principles of operant conditioning. Picture for a moment a one-and-a-half-year-old baby contentedly lying in a crib. The baby is cooing, gurgling, uttering a whole series of disconnected sounds. Suddenly, from out of the babble, and surely by accident, the baby chances on the sound "da-da." The parents, who have been listening intently, are beside themselves with joy. They heap praise on the baby and, sure enough, the baby soon says "da-da" again.

In technical Skinnerian terms, from the entire repertoire of possible verbal operants, the baby has emitted the operant "da-da." This is immediately followed by positive reinforcement, increasing the probability that the operant will be repeated. After more "da-da" responses are followed by more reinforcements, the baby will emit the operant at a fairly frequent rate. Conditioning of the operant has occurred. Now, however, the parents' expectations are raised so that reinforcement no longer follows each and every utterance of the magic "word." The parents begin teaching the baby to discriminate, so that only when the father himself is presented as the stimulus does baby get reinforced. When the baby says "da-da" to the mother's presence, no reinforcement follows, and the response to that stimulus is extinguished. In this case the father is the S^D, the stimulus for which responding will be reinforced, and the mother is the S^Δ, the stimulus for which responding will be extinguished.

This discrimination will occur quickly, but because of stimulus generalization, the family may be in for an embarrassing moment. A few days later the milkman stops in with his delivery. The baby, seeing the male figure, proudly calls out "da-da." Obviously, further discrimination training is in order. When the baby says "da-da" to other male figures, reinforcement is withheld. Finally, the father is perceived as the only appropriate S^D for that operant, and the family perhaps breathes a sigh of relief.

Skinner believes that language is learned in precisely this manner: an operant is conditioned so that it occurs regularly, and then, through discrimination training, it is attached to its appropriate stimulus. Perhaps the child later generalizes the word "car" to include all wheeled vehicles. Through discrimination training, the child then learns the appropriate responses that will correct for this stimulus generalization.

Skinner's contention that verbal behavior is learned strictly through operant conditioning has not gone unchallenged. Specialists in the field of psycholinguistics believe that language acquisition is not a mere matter of conditioning. Noam Chomsky, for example, sees the child as genetically prewired, born with biological givens that direct the course of language development. In this way, Chomsky can explain how children learn sentence structure and the complex grammatical sequencing of words—both of which he feels children learn far more easily than the principles of operant conditioning would predict.[5,6]

Chomsky challenges Skinner's position on language development

OPERANT CONDITIONING IN THE CLASSROOM

Only Skinner's general apporach to the problem of classroom teaching will be treated in this section. Specific techniques, such as teaching machines and the arrangement of reinforcements to promote student control, will be covered in the next chapter.

Education is the learning of certain responses that will be useful later in life. How can this best be accomplished? The teacher, says Skinner, should use the techniques that produce meaningful behavioral changes. Though the teacher may sometimes use primary reinforcers such as M & M candy, conditioned reinforcers such as good grades, promotions, prizes, and the generalized social reinforcement of approval are usually more appropriate. One of the real problems with the use of conditioned reinforcers, however, is that they are often too distant. As we have seen, operant conditioning is most effective when reinforcement is immediate. This is one of the reasons why Skinner strongly favors the use of the teaching machine. It can provide immediate reinforcement and help bridge the gap between student behavior and the more distant conditioned reinforcers such as promotion or grades. Skinner is against the use of punishment in the classroom, not because it won't control behavior—it will—but because it may produce a host of negative emotional reactions. Negative emotional reactions, conditioned through the use of punishment, may prevent further learning and even further school attendance. Punishment always leads to attempts to escape, and when children do escape from the classroom situation, formal learning in the classroom is obviously impossible.

Conditioned reinforcement in the classroom

Just what is the goal of education according to Skinner? Skinner believes that education should maximize "knowledge." This is done through operant conditioning, through building up a student's repertoire of responses. Understanding a subject, such as history, is simply the result of having learned a verbal repertoire. Skinner insists that when students can answer questions in a given area, and speak and write fluently about the area, then, by definition, they understand that area. A verbal repertoire is not a sign of knowledge, it is the knowledge. In order to teach a knowledge of biology, one must teach the specific behavior from which the "knowledge" is inferred. That is, in order to say that students "know" something, we must observe certain responses: how they speak, the diagrams they draw, the equations they can solve, and so on. These, then, are the very responses that should be trained into the students who don't display this knowledge.

Skinner sees "knowledge" as a repertoire of responses

Observe what students "do" to see what they "know"

Good teaching is thus the ability to arrange the proper sequence of reinforcements and to make sure that these reinforcements are contingent upon students emitting the appropriate responses.

MEDIATION THEORY AND VERBAL LEARNING

Before turning to Bruner, it should be pointed out that some of today's association theorists do try to bridge the gap between response learning and cognitive learning. These theorists, for example Kendler, explain a large part of learning by the use of what they call mediation theory. Mediation theory suggests that much of our learned behavior can be explained on the basis of internal, nonobservable S-R systems that are chained to overt stimuli and responses. The internal mediators can be such things as words, concepts, sets, and images. This can be most easily seen in the case of words. As children begin to develop the use of language, they can use verbal labels to expedite the learning of everything from visual discriminations and generalizations to motor responses; that is, children (or adults) will make learning easier by inserting a word (a mediator) between the stimulus and the response. For example, if three-year-old children are trying to learn the differences between a circle, a triangle, and a square, they will learn far more quickly if they are given verbal labels for each form. The verbal labels help make the stimuli more distinctive and, therefore, easier to learn and remember. Also, there are certain kinds of learning that can be explained far more simply by mediation theory than by any other current theory. This is true, for example, in the case of paired-associate learning. In this situation, pairs of words, typically up to a dozen pairs, are presented to the subject for memorization. Subjects learn the associations far more quickly when the pairs of words are mediated by some meaningful connection than when random pairs are presented. For example, a subject will learn to associate "cat-dog" more easily than "cat-inch."

In summary, the more that verbal labels make stimuli more distinctive, the easier it is to learn a discrimination. Conversely, the more that verbal labels make stimuli equivalent, the easier it is to learn a generalization.

Finally, some theorists believe that the association of the verbal label and the stimulus forms a linkage within the central nervous system.[7]

MNEMONIC DEVICES

Verbal mediators may be used in the form of mnemonic devices to aid memory. The fifth grader, for example, may learn the word "homes" in order to remember the Great Lakes: Huron, Ontario, Michigan, Erie, and Superior. Using the word "homes" is called a first-letter mnemonic, since homes, called the peg word, includes the first letters of all the items that must be recalled. Research in this area has shown rather conclusively that if the peg word itself is not too complicated, the use of the first-letter mnemonic definitely aids recall.[8]

Another type of mnemonic device is used to indicate directions. The novice boatsman might learn the phrase "red, right, returning" in order to recall that the red buoys should be on the right when returning to the harbor. Many of the

Kendler's mediation theory

Verbal labels make stimuli easier to remember

Memory experts use mnemonic devices

so-called memory experts utilize long and intricate mnemonic devices when performing their amazing feats of recall.

The mnemonic device, however, may be so complex that recalling the original stimuli is even more difficult than it would have been without it. One college student had learned a long poem which was designed to ensure the memorization of all the U.S. presidents in order. The first letter in each word of the poem corresponded to the first letter in the last name of the president. Sometimes, however, the student would forget a word or line from the poem, and at other times he would forget the name the letter had designated. For example, once when asked who the thirteenth president was, he paused, repeated the poem to himself, and then proudly answered, "Franklin." (This is not to suggest, of course, that he also believed that Filmore was the name of a stove.)

BRUNER AND THE PROCESS OF THOUGHT

Whereas Skinner has presented a behaviorist-associationist account of learning, borrowing heavily from Watson and Thorndike, Bruner's position is more consistent with the cognitive-gestaltist position. For example, Bruner insists that the final goal of teaching is to promote the "general understanding of the structure of a subject matter."[9] When the student understands the structure of a subject, he or she sees it as a related whole. "Grasping the structure of a subject is understanding it in a way that permits many other things to be related to it meaningfully."[10] These are hardly the words of a behaviorist-associationist. Bruner

Bruner's theory of instruction

Bruner tells the teacher—and he constantly aims his message at the working classroom teacher—to help promote conditions in which the student can perceive the structure of a given subject: "Any idea or problem or body of knowledge can be presented in a form simple enough so that any particular learner can understand it in a recognizable form."

Jerome Bruner

Jerome Bruner was born in 1915 in New York. His family was successful upper-middle class, and they fully expected young Bruner to become a lawyer. Bruner, however, had other ideas. He graduated from Duke University in 1937 and immediately entered Duke's graduate school in psychology. The following year he transferred to Harvard, where he received his Ph.D. degree in psychology in 1941.

When Bruner first arrived at Harvard his interest focused on the investigation of perception in animals. Harvard had only recently (1933) created an independent department of psychology, and under its chairman, E. G. Boring, the research emphasis was aimed at experimentation in animal learning and perception. Bruner studied under the great Harvard researcher and physiological psychologist Karl S. Lashley. With the outbreak of World War II, Bruner's interests shifted to social psychology, and he wrote his doctoral thesis on the techniques of Nazi propagandists. During the war, Bruner entered the army and worked on psychological warfare in General Eisenhower's headquarters in SHAEF (Supreme Headquarters Allied Expeditionary Force). He returned to Harvard in 1945, and in 1947 he published an important paper on the importance of needs as they influence perception. In this study he showed that poor children tend to overestimate the size of coins more than do well-to-do children. From this study he concluded that values and needs strongly affect human perception and also that people make meaning out of their perceptions by making them consistent with their past experiences. Humans are thus able to reduce the possibility of mental strain by viewing the world in such a way as to reduce environmental surprises. These findings led to what became known as the "new look" in perception theory and also laid the groundwork for an American school of cognitive psychology. Cognitive psychology deals with the human being's ability to obtain knowledge and develop intellectually. Although the field of cognitive psychology has been important in Europe, America under the heavy influence of the behavioristic tradition had turned a deaf ear to anything as subjective and "unscientific" as the study of thinking. Bruner changed all that. By 1960 he had helped found Harvard University's Center for Cognitive Studies, and although he didn't invent cognitive psychology, he certainly went a long way toward making it systematic and consistent with the rules of science.

Always the empiricist, Bruner kept science's basic rule clearly in mind: begin by observing the data from which the conclusions are to be drawn. Once when a group of academic psychologists was debating the possible impact a certain film might have on children, Bruner was brought in as a consultant. After listening to this group of armchair speculators for awhile, Bruner suddenly interrupted them and said, "I've got it! We'll get a child, show him the film, and then we'll ask him what he thought of it."

This is also Bruner's approach to the problems of educational psychology. If you want to know how children go about the business of learning in the school situation, then study children in the classroom, not rats and pigeons in cages.

In 1960 Bruner published the important work *The Process of Education*. As *Harper's Magazine* said, "To people starved for reasonable comments on education in intelligible English, Bruner's writings are above reproach." In this book Bruner developed three important points. First, schools should strive to teach the general nature, or the "structure," of a subject rather than all the details and facts of a subject. Second, any subject can be taught effectively in some intellectually honest form to any child at any stage of development. And finally, Bruner stressed the importance of intuition in learning. Intuition is a problem-solving technique whereby a child relies on insight or immediate apprehensions rather than planned steps of analysis.

Bruner's work has not gone unnoticed by his colleagues. In 1963 the American Psychological Association awarded him the Distinguished Scientific Award. In 1965 Bruner was elected president of the American Psychological Association.

When the spring semester at Harvard came to a close, Bruner would leave the summer heat of Cambridge for the fresh winds of the sea. On his sailboat, Bruner and his wife and children confronted the natural forces of wind and tide. He is as skilled a navigator as he is psychologist and researcher.

In 1972, more than thirty years after his arrival at Harvard as a graduate student, Bruner left to begin the newly created duties of Watts Professor of Psychology at Oxford University in England.

Jerome Bruner has made things happen in educational psychology. Says *Harper's,* "He is the first person to come along in years—perhaps the first since John Dewey—who can speak intelligently about education to his fellow scholars as well as to educators."

stresses the importance in learning of forming global concepts, of building coherent generalizations, of creating cognitive gestalts. Bruner tells the teacher—and he constantly aims his message at the working classroom teacher—to help promote conditions in which the student can perceive the structure of a given subject. When learning is based on a structure, it is more long-lasting and less easily forgotten. The student who once studied biology, for example, may forget many of the details over the years, but these details can be more easily and quickly reconstructed if the general structure is still there.

Bruner calls his position a theory of instruction, not a learning theory. He feels that a learning theory is *descriptive;* that is, it describes what happens after the fact. A theory of instruction, on the other hand, is *prescriptive;* it prescribes in advance how a given subject can best be taught. If a learning theory tells us that children at age six are not yet ready to understand the concept of reversibility, a theory of instruction would prescribe how best to lead the child toward this concept when he or she is old enough to understand it.

Bruner's theory has four major principles: motivation, structure, sequence, and reinforcement.

BRUNER'S FIRST PRINCIPLE: MOTIVATION

Bruner's first principle specifies the conditions that predispose an individual toward learning. What are the critical variables, especially during the preschool years, that help motivate and enable the child to learn? Implicit in Bruner's principles is the belief that almost all children have a built-in "will to learn." However, Bruner has not discarded the notion of reinforcement. He believes that reinforcement, or external reward, may be important for initiating certain actions or for making sure they are repeated. He insists, however, that it is only

Curiosity is perhaps the best example of intrinsic motivation. Bruner's principles stress that almost all children have a built-in "will to learn."

Teenagers playing in a high-school orchestra exemplify two
other motivating factors: a drive to achieve competence and
reciprocity, and a need to work with others cooperatively.

through intrinsic motivation that the will to learn is sustained. Bruner is far
more concerned with intrinsic motivation than with what he believes to be the
more transitory effects of external motivation.

Perhaps the best example of intrinsic motivation is curiosity. Bruner believes
that we come into the world equipped with a curiosity drive. He feels this drive
is biologically relevant, that curiosity is necessary to the survival of the species.
Bruner suggests that young children are often too curious; they are unable to
"stick with" any one activity. Their curiosity leads them to turn from one activity to another in rapid succession, and it must therefore be channeled into a
more powerful intellectual pursuit. Games like Twenty Questions help develop
a sense of curiosity discipline in the child.

The curiosity drive

Another motivation we bring into the world with us is the drive to achieve
competence. Children become interested in what they are good at, and it is
virtually impossible to motivate them to engage in activities in which they have
no degree of competence.

**The drive for compe-
tence**

Finally, Bruner lists reciprocity as a motivation that is built into the species.
Reciprocity involves a need to work with others cooperatively, and Bruner feels
that society itself developed as a result of this most basic motivation.

According to Bruner, the intrinsic motivations are rewarding in themselves and are therefore self-sustaining. How can the teacher take advantage of this in the classroom situation? Bruner's answer is that teachers must facilitate and regulate their students' exploration of alternatives. Since learning and problem-solving demand the exploration of alternatives, this is at the very core of the issue and is critical in creating a predisposition to the long-term pursuit of learning.

Exploration of alternatives

The exploration of alternatives has three phases: activation, maintenance, and direction.

Activation

In order to activate exploration, in order to get it started, children must experience a certain level of uncertainty. If the task is too easy, they will be too bored to explore alternatives, and yet if it is too difficult, they will be too confused to explore alternatives. This is similar to J. McV. Hunt's problem of the match, already discussed in Chapter 5. The teacher must provide students with problems that are just difficult enough for the children's intrinsic curiosity motivation to itself activate exploration.

Problems must be difficult enough to arouse a level of student uncertainty

This brings up a further question: Is there a curiosity drive, a drive which is satisfied not by food, drink, or praise, but simply by getting the answer? There is growing evidence that this might indeed be the case. For example, monkeys have been observed taking apart and reassembling a metal lock arrangement. Just like the child who takes a watch apart to see what makes it tick, monkeys will manipulate mechanical puzzles for no reinforcement other than the sheer joy of manipulation. One monkey continued taking a complicated metal lock apart for ten straight hours. "At this point the experiment was terminated because of experimenter fatigue; the monkey was still going strong."[11]

Lower primates demonstrate an inherent curiosity, too

In another study, a monkey was trained to push a certain panel inside the cage, with food as the positive reinforcer. In order to observe the monkey during the learning trials, the experimenter made a small peephole in the screen which separated him from the monkey. The peephole, however, immediately became an object of great fascination for the monkey, and when the experimenter tried to peer through the hole, all he could see was the eye of the monkey peering back. Monkeys have actually been conditioned to discriminate between stimuli (a blue card and a yellow card) with the only reinforcer being the opportunity to open a small door in the training box and look out. Thus the drive to manipulate objects and explore the world visually "is fundamental and primary in monkeys and man."[12]

Berlyne's theory of brain excitation

Berlyne has suggested that when a person (or an animal) is in a situation where conflicting responses are possible, a curiosity drive is generated and the person (or animal) is motivated to seek further information just to satisfy this drive. This could mean that discovery learning, as Bruner has suggested, is indeed self-reinforcing. Berlyne believes that there is an optimum level of arousal which is physiologically based. Berlyne sees arousal level as a function of brain excitation: if the arousal level is too low, the child might attempt to increase it by taking in new stimuli; if the arousal level is too high, however, the child will attempt to lower it by reducing the stimulus inputs.[13]

Harlow's evidence supports the theory of an innate curiosity drive. One monkey continued taking a complicated metal lock apart for ten straight hours.

Now we return to the various ways Bruner suggests for guiding students' exploration of educational alternatives. Activating that exploration, especially by arousing curiosity, was the first phase. The second and third phases are the maintenance and direction of the exploration.

Maintenance

Once activated, exploration must be maintained. This involves assuring children that exploration is not going to be a dangerous or painful experience. Children must view exploration under the guiding hand of the teacher as less risky, less dangerous than exploration on their own. The advantages of exploration must be made greater than the risks.

The student must view exploration as being safe

Direction

Meaningful exploration must have direction. The direction of exploration is a function of two factors: knowledge of the goal, and knowledge that the exploration of alternatives is relevant to the achievement of that goal. Children must know what the goal is and how close they are to achieving it.

Thus Bruner's first principle indicates that children have a built-in will to learn. Teachers must manage and enhance this motivation so that children will see that guided exploration is more meaningful and satisfying than the spontaneous learning they can achieve on their own. In short, Bruner's first principle is a justification for formal schooling.

BRUNER'S SECOND PRINCIPLE: STRUCTURE

Bruner's second principle states that any given subject area, any body of knowledge, can be organized in some optimal fashion so that it can be transmitted to and understood by almost any student. If appropriately structured, "any idea or problem or body of knowledge can be presented in a form simple enough so that any particular learner can understand it in a recognizable form."[14] This is not to say that all of the nuances of Einstein's theory of relativity can be fully mastered by a six-year-old child. It does mean, however, that if properly structured, Einstein's general position could be understood by the child, and that under questioning the child could convey to a physicist a recognizable account of the theory.

Bruner's three means of achieving understanding

According to Bruner, the structure of any body of knowledge can be characterized in three ways: mode of presentation, economy, and power.

Mode of presentation

Mode of presentation refers to the technique, the method, whereby information is communicated. One of the reasons teachers despair of trying to explain some fundamental point to a seemingly uncomprehending child is that the teacher's mode of presentation simply does not fit with the child's level of experience. The child will remain uncomprehending as long as the message is incomprehensible. Bruner believes that a person has three means of achieving understanding: enactive, iconic, and symbolic representation.

The wordless messages of enactive communication

Enactive representation. Very young children can understand things best in terms of actions. For example, children can demonstrate their understanding of the principles of a balance beam by referring to their experiences on a seesaw. If the child on the other end is heavier, you compensate by sliding further back on your own end; if the other child is lighter, you push yourself farther forward. Young children also define words in terms of the actions which are associated with them: a chair is to sit on, a spoon is to eat with, and so on. When children are in the enactive stage of thinking, it is important that the teacher's messages somehow make contact with their muscles. Even adults may revert to enactive representation when learning something new, especially a new motor skill. Teaching an adult to ski is best accomplished wordlessly. A skilled ski instructor doesn't just tell students to "edge into the hill," but will instead ask them to imitate her own stance.

In short, when young children are in the enactive stage of thinking, the best, the most comprehensible, messages are wordless ones.

A picture often tells a thousand words: the iconic level

Iconic representation. Somewhat older children learn to think at a different level, the iconic level. Objects become conceivable without action. Children can now draw a picture of a spoon, without acting out the eating process. They may even be able, at this stage, to draw a diagram of a balance beam, for they now possess an image of it which no longer depends on action. This is a significant breakthrough in the development of intellect, for the use of pictures or diagrams allows children at this stage to be tutored in simpler ways.

At the iconic level, subjects become conceivable without having to be acted out.

Symbolic representation. At this stage children can translate experience into language. The balance beam can be explained through the use of words rather than pictures. Symbolic representation allows children to begin making logical derivations and to think more compactly. Bruner says that through symbolic representation "powerful representations of the world of possible experiences are constructed and used as search models in problem solving."[15]

Language—the symbolic level

Which of these modes should the teacher choose in order to facilitate the learning process? It depends on the learner's age and background, and on the subject matter itself. For example, Bruner believes that teaching a problem in law demands symbolic representation, whereas geography is well suited to the iconic. New motor skills are often best communicated by enactive representation, especially at first. Mathematics can be represented, and often should be, by all three modes.

Economy of Presentation

Economy in communicating a body of knowledge depends on the amount of information the learner must keep in mind in order to continue learning. The fewer bits of information, the fewer facts the learner must bear in mind, the greater the economy. The best way to provide economy in teaching is to give the learner concise summaries. For example, Bruner feels that it is more economical to "summarize the American Civil War as a battle over slavery than as a struggle between an expanding industrial region and one built upon a class society for control of federal economic power."[16]

Concise summaries lead to economy

Power of Presentation

Bruner believes that nature is simple; hence, to be powerful, a presentation of some aspect of nature should reflect nature's simplicity. Teachers often make difficult what is inherently easy. A powerful presentation is a simple presentation, one that is easily understood. It allows the learner to see new relationships, to find connections between facts that may at first seem quite separate. Bruner feels that a powerful presentation is especially important in the field of mathematics.

BRUNER'S THIRD PRINCIPLE: SEQUENCE

The extent to which a student finds it difficult to master a given subject depends largely on the sequence in which the material is presented. Teaching involves leading the learner through a certain sequence of the various aspects of the subject. Since Bruner believes that intellectual development is innately sequential, moving from enactive, through iconic, to symbolic representation, he feels it is highly probable that this is also the best sequence for any subject to take. Thus the teacher should begin teaching any new subject with wordless messages, speaking mainly to the learner's muscular responses. Then the student should be encouraged to explore the use of diagrams and various pictorial representations. Finally, the message should be communicated symbolically, through the use of words. This is obviously a very conservative approach. Some children, because of their age and background, may seem to be able to begin a new area at the symbolic level. But, though conservative, this sequence is safe. Children who seem ready to handle new material at the symbolic level may suddenly become lost and confused if they haven't been given the basic imagery to fall back on.

The sequence in which new material is presented is also important during exploration. Sometimes the child should be encouraged to explore a wide vari-

Mathematics is a subject often best taught by using all three modes of presentation Bruner names: enactive representation, iconic representation, and symbolic representation.

ety of alternatives, whereas at other times the thorough analysis of a single alternative should be stressed.

Finally, sequencing is a significant aspect of motivation. Bruner feels that it is necessary to specify in any sequence the amount of tension children must feel so that problem solving will be both activated and maintained. Bruner is not overly specific on this point; he simply says that the tension should be such that children are somewhere between boredom and wild excitement.

BRUNER'S FOURTH PRINCIPLE: REINFORCEMENT

Learning requires reinforcement. In order to achieve mastery of a problem, we must receive feedback as to how we are doing. The timing of the reinforcement is crucial to success in learning. The results must be learned at the very time a student is evaluating his or her own performance. If the results are known too soon, the learner will become confused and his or her explorations are stifled. If it comes too late, the learner may have gone two or three choice-points beyond the point where it would have been helpful, and may by this time have incorporated false information. The teacher's role is, thus, indeed sensitive. If the learner has gone on to incorporate false information, this must now be unlearned in order for the learner to get back on the right track.

Bruner agrees with Skinner on the importance of reinforcement

Not only is the timing of the reinforcement important, but the reinforcement must also be in a form that the learner will understand. If the learner is operating at the enactive level, reinforcement at the iconic or symbolic level may be useless. To be helpful, feedback must be made understandable to the learner.

Reinforcement must be understandable to the learner

Finally, Bruner emphasizes that "instruction is a provisional state that has as its object to make the learner or problem-solver self-sufficient."[17] Thus, the learner cannot become so dependent on the teacher's reinforcement that the teacher must be perpetually present. Ultimately, the learner must take on a self-corrective function.

Teacher's goal is to make the problem solver self-sufficient

Understanding reached through exploration and discovery is more meaningful to the student, and facts and relationships thus acquired are better retained than when the material has simply been memorized.

DISCOVERY

Though it is possible to memorize a poem, or the multiplication tables, or the state capitals, meaningful learning often requires actual discovery. The facts and relationships children discover through their own explorations are more usable and tend to be better retained than material they have merely committed to memory. Teachers can provide the conditions in which discovery is nourished and will grow. One way they can do this is to guess at answers and let the class know they are guessing. The students can then analyze the teacher's answer. This helps prove to them that exploration can be both rewarding and safe, and it is thus a valuable technique for building lifelong discovery habits in the students.

Bruner is not saying that discovery is the only form of learning. Nor is he saying that students must discover for themselves the solutions to every problem in a given field. This would be extremely wasteful, if it were even possible, for it would mean that each generation would have to rediscover the ideas and technology of their culture. Beginning physics students, for example, shouldn't have to discover the technology of radio transmission, as Marconi once did. Students can, however, through insightful questioning and prompting by the teacher, discover for themselves some of the basic principles that account for radio transmission. Learning in this way allows the student to reach a level of understanding that far surpasses the rote memorization of a radio chapter in an electronics book.

Teaching for discovery is obviously not easy. The teacher must be bright, flexible, and really know the subject matter. In order to communicate knowledge, the teacher must have mastery of that knowledge. Finally, the good teacher is a patient teacher, for discovery teaching cannot be hurried. It is often frustratingly slow, but the goal of real student understanding is well worth the wait.

A FINAL COMPARISON

At times it may seem that Skinner and Bruner are from two different worlds, that they discuss entirely different concepts. In part this is true. Skinner's data came primarily from his work with rats and pigeons; Bruner's from his observations of children in learning situations. Skinner is an associationist; Bruner a cognitive theorist. Skinner is an avowed behaviorist; Bruner speculates on events occurring within the child's mind. Yet both are discussing learning, and both are talking to working teachers. Skinner speaks of the laws of conditioning, and Bruner, acknowledging that the teacher is a potent reinforcer, insists that the teacher should know these laws.

Piaget's P learning and LM learning

Piaget has stated that there are really two kinds of learning, P learning and LM learning. P learning is physical learning, learning that takes place when physical things act on us. LM learning is logico-mathematical learning, learning that results from our actions on things.

P learning results from the environment acting on the learner

This distinction of Piaget's is similar to the distinction between associative and cognitive learning. P learning is, in effect, conditioning, and it's the kind of learning that has been so thoroughly analyzed by Watson, Thorndike, Guthrie, and Skinner. P learning is externally motivated; it is the properties of the physical objects that act upon us (the sweetness of candy or the aversive properties of punishment) which have a potential reinforcing effect. This, of course, is precisely the way the behaviorists have described motivation in learning; and indeed this is exactly the way they should have described it, since they have been describing P learning almost exclusively. When Skinner tells us that learning is the result of a given response followed by a reinforcing stimulus, he is in effect defining P learning—a physical event acting upon the learner. LM learning, on the other hand, has been more the province of the cognitive-gestaltist theorists. LM learning is the result of our continuous experience of organizing and reorganizing our actions as we proceed toward the goal of understanding. Piaget says that LM learning is intrinsically motivated; that is, the discovery of a new relationship is self-rewarding. When children experience new LM relationships that they have discovered through their own actions, they feel pleased, a joy that swells up from within.

LM learning results from the learner acting on the environment

After examining the positions of Skinner and Bruner, can we now say which one is right—which theory says it all? The answer, of course, is that both are right, though neither one is likely to have the supertheory. Skinner's laws of conditioning are certainly valid. The evidence with regard to operant conditioning overwhelmingly supports his position. Skinner has much to teach us about how to teach. He has simplified and made more efficient the learning of the informational background children need in order to think creatively. It must be remembered that P learning, though perhaps not as glamorous as LM, is crucial to intellectual growth. Skinner has given us invaluable aids for transmitting this P-learning base.

Bruner, too, has made an extremely important contribution, but at a different level. In his theory of instruction he has pointed out ways of carrying children beyond mere simple conditioning, or P learning. Bruner's interest is more in the area of the cognitive organization, understanding, LM learning. To some extent, Bruner's theory may be more speculative than Skinner's, but exciting advances in science have often in the past been foreshadowd by sophisticated speculation. This isn't to imply that Bruner's position is not perched on an empirical base. After all, Bruner has spent long hours watching children going about the business of learning.

It is certainly true that all the answers are not yet in on this complex phenomenon called learning, but it is also true that Skinner and Bruner have pointed us in the direction of knowing more about what the questions are.

Summary

Two major theorists in educational psychology are spotlighted in this chapter: Skinner, representing the behaviorist-associationist tradition, and Bruner, representing the cognitive-gestalt tradition. Both Skinner and Bruner discuss issues in learning which are of practical importance to the classroom teacher.

Skinner bases his concept of learning on the experimental facts of operant conditioning. Operant conditioning occurs when a response is followed by a reinforcing stimulus. The rate of responding then increases. Skinner distinguishes between operants, responses that need no stimuli to set them off, and respondents, which do need unconditioned stimuli to be activated. Skinner uses the term "respondent" to describe the same kind of behavior that Pavlov had previously described during his conditioning studies on dogs—that is, Skinner's "respondent" is synonymous with Pavlov's "reflex."

The operant conditioning system also includes such other concepts and techniques as extinction, spontaneous recovery, discrimination, stimulus generalization, and conditioned reinforcement.

Skinner has also conducted research into the schedules of reinforcement—that is, the methods by which reinforcers are arranged. Responses that are reinforced periodically, either on the basis of time or the number of responses emitted, are conditioned more strongly and are thus more difficult to extinguish.

Skinner indicates that language is learned via the principles of operant conditioning. Also, such cognitive-sounding concepts as an "understanding" of history, or mathematics, or even knowledge itself, are really examples of operant conditioning. In order to gain knowledge one must be equipped with the specific set of responses from which that knowledge may be inferred.

Good teaching, according to Skinner, is the ability to arrange the proper sequences of reinforcements for the student, and then to be certain that the presentation of these reinforcers is contingent on the student emitting the correct response.

Somewhere between the behaviorist-associationist position and the cognitive-gestalt position lies a theory of learning called mediation theory. Mediation theory tells us that much of one's learning can be explained on the basis of internal, nonobservable S-R systems, such as words and images, which are chained to the overt stimuli and responses. Learning is aided immeasurably by the use of internal mediators.

Bruner's position regarding learning is the cognitive-gestalt tradition. His goal is to create a theory of instruction which will allow a teacher to prescribe how a given subject can best be taught.

Bruner's theory has four major principles: (a) motivation, (b) structure, (3) sequence, and (d) reinforcement. These four principles are aimed at producing a learning based on understanding and meaning, rather than on the conditioning of facts and details.

Bruner insists that meaningful learning requires the child to actively search for solutions. Such "discovery learning" is far more long-lasting and useful than learning based on memorization and conditioning. Good teaching demands that the student be encouraged to explore alternatives and discover new relationships. Bruner also insists that when presented appropriately, any subject matter can be understood by almost any child.

The theories of Skinner and Bruner, though seemingly diametrically opposed, share a common framework when viewed from the position of Jean Piaget. Piaget distinguishes between P learning, learning that takes place when physical things act on us, and LM learning, which results from our actions on things. Skinner's position seems consistent with Piaget's P learning, while Bruner may be discussing Piaget's LM learning.

REFERENCES

1
B. F. Skinner, *The Behavior of Organisms: An Experimental Analysis* (New York: Appleton-Century-Crofts, 1938).

2
F. Carpenter, *The Skinner Primer* (New York: The Free Press, 1974), pp. 8–9.

3
F. Carpenter, *The Skinner Primer* (New York: The Free Press, 1974), p. 28. Reprinted by permission.

4
B. F. Skinner, *Beyond Freedom and Dignity* (New York: Knopf, 1971), p. 169.

5
N. Chomsky, *Syntactic Structures* (The Hague: Mouton, 1957).

6
N. Chomsky, *Aspects of the Theory of Syntax* (Cambridge, Mass.: MIT Press, 1965).

7
H. H. Kendler and T. S. Kendler, "Vertical and Horizontal Processes in Problem Solving," *Psychological Review* 69 (1962):1–16.

8
D. L. Nelson and C. S. Archer, "The First Letter Mnemonic," *Journal of Educational Psychology* 63, no. 5 (1972):482–486. ,

9
J. S. Bruner, *The Process of Education* (Cambridge, Mass.: Harvard University Press, 1962), p. 6.

10
Ibid.

11
H. F. Harlow, J. L. McGaugh, and R. F. Thompson, *Psychology* (San Francisco: Albion, 1971), p. 271.

12
Ibid., p. 272.

13
D. E. Berlyne, *Conflict, Arousal and Curiosity* (New York: McGraw-Hill, 1960).

14
J. S. Bruner, *Toward a Theory of Instruction* (Cambridge, Mass.: Harvard University Press, 1966), p. 44.

15
Ibid., p. 14.

16
Ibid., p. 46.

17
Ibid., p. 53.

SUGGESTIONS FOR FURTHER READING

Bruner, J. S. *Toward a Theory of Instruction.* Cambridge, Mass.: Harvard University Press, 1966.

Carpenter, F. *The Skinner Primer.* New York: The Free Press, 1974.

Skinner, B. F. *The Technology of Teaching.* New York: Appleton-Century-Crofts, 1968.

13

Learning in the classroom

"In an American school, if you ask for the salt in good French, you get an A. In France you get the salt." This statement by B. F. Skinner (1953) illustrates perhaps the major feature of the educational process.[1] The concepts, skills, and techniques we teach are not only useful in the present, but more important, will be useful at some later time. One of the major goals of education is to equip us to transfer what we learn in the classroom to future situations. Learning to add, subtract, and spell has the immediate advantage of good grades, a gold star, a promotion to the next grade, or perhaps a teacher's or parent's general approval. Eventually, however, the advantages become more compelling. In later life we learn that our ability to spell, or multiply, or derive square roots has enormous practical consequences, for example in helping us earn a living. Some of us learn this too late. "If only I had paid more attention in school," we moan. And, we might add, we might have paid more attention if our classroom experience had been structured differently.

TRANSFER

Transfer is the key to classroom learning. Transfer takes place when learning task A influences learning task B. Transfer may be positive or negative. When learning A facilitates learning B, positive transfer is said to have taken place; conversely, when learning A inhibits learning B, negative transfer has occurred. Here are a few examples of positive transfer: learning to ride a motorcycle is easier if you already know how to ride a bike, learning Italian is easier if you already know Latin, writing a letter to Santa Claus is easy if you have learned

Positive transfer

Negative transfer

323

A suggestion before a final exam—take a nap. Or do something as remotely connected as possible to the subject matter you are studying. Such "breathers" prevent retroactive inhibition.

your second-grade spelling. Here are some examples of negative transfer: learning to lean forward while snow skiing may cause you to fall on your face when you learn to waterski, learning to keep your elbows away from your body to hit a baseball may cause a disastrous slice when you learn to hit a golf ball, studying a French assignment until the wee hours may wreak havoc with the Spanish exam you take the next morning.

Retroactive inhibition

There is also a special case of negative transfer in which the influence works in reverse. You successfully learn A and then learn B; when you try to recall A, you draw a complete blank. This is called retroactive inhibition, and it happens when the second task works retroactively to inhibit recall of the first task. If you spend four hours studying for a French exam and then spend four hours on a Spanish assignment, when you later take the French exam you may very likely confuse the "estar" with the "êtres." Your knowledge of French might have remained intact had you not spent the intervening time working on the Spanish. Some students cram for a final until they drop off to sleep in the early morning hours in a state of exhausted confusion. On awakening, just before the exam, the material suddenly seems less confusing and more understandable. Some students attribute this to the fact that they have continued learning in some mysterious way while sleeping. Though this theory is admittedly seductive, a simpler explanation is that sleeping prevented retroactive inhibition. Going to sleep, rather than adding to the store of knowledge, simply prevents interference. One general rule to follow is that the best way to take a break while studying for an exam is to do something as different as possible from the exam material. For example, if you are studying for an educational psychology exam, it's better to take a fifteen-minute Ping-Pong break than to read your sociology notes.

FORMAL DISCIPLINE

Current theories of transfer can be traced back to the early Greek notion of formal discipline. According to this view, the role of the school is to discipline the students' minds. It was thought that the mind, like an athlete's muscles, must be systematically exercised until it becomes so strong it can learn and understand virtually any new material. The theory of formal discipline remained in vogue until the early twentieth century. Subjects such as logic, Latin, and Greek were taught, not for their practical value, but because they were thought to strengthen the student's mind to the point where all later problem solving would be easy.

THE CHALLENGES TO FORMAL DISCIPLINE

The theory of formal discipline was challenged around the turn of the century by three important psychologists. The first, William James, put the theory to the test.[2] He spent 132 minutes, over an eight-day period, memorizing a long segment of poetry (Victor Hugo's *Satyr*). He reasoned that if the theory of formal discipline was correct, exercising the mind by memorizing another poem would make further memorization easier. He therefore spent the next thirty-eight days memorizing Book I of Milton's *Paradise Lost*. Finally, he tried to memorize another segment of the *Satyr,* equal in length to the first segment he had memorized, only to find that it took him even longer than it had previously. The results of this rather informal test led James to suspect the validity of the theory of formal discipline.

James tests the theory of formal discipline

The second challenger, E. L. Thorndike, had subjects practice estimating the length of lines one-half to one-and-one-half inches long.[3] When these subjects achieved a certain degree of accuracy in this task, Thorndike introduced a different, though similar task: estimating the length of lines six to twelve inches long. Thorndike found that there was little, if any, improvement on the second task as a result of the practice gained from the first task. Although he believed that he had thoroughly refuted the theory of formal discipline, Thorndike still maintained that transfer could occur. Thorndike based his explanation of transfer on the existence of certain elements in the second task that were identical to those in the first task.

Thorndike challenges formal discipline

The third challenger, Charles Judd, took on both the theory of formal discipline and Thorndike's "identical elements." In a classic experiment, Judd trained two groups of boys to hit a target submerged twelve inches in water.[4] One group of boys, the experimental group, was instructed in the general principles of refraction, while the control group was not. Although both groups did equally well while the target was at the twelve-inch depth, when it was later raised to a depth of four inches, the boys in the experimental group performed significantly better. The boys in the control group, who had not been given any of the principles of refraction, responded to the new task as though it were a completely new problem. On the basis of this experiment, Judd postulated the theory of transfer by generalization, which stated that transfer is far more efficient when the theory or the generalization behind the task is learned. The boys who had simply learned to hit a target submerged in twelve inches of water transferred this skill only to other targets also submerged twelve inches deep. When the target depth was changed, no transfer took place.

Judd thus insisted that classroom students should be taught abstractions and generalizations as well as the details of a subject. Students should still learn certain facts and possess certain information, but their ability to transfer depended equally on a basic understanding of the theoretical generalizations which allow those facts to be interpreted. Travers says:

> the student of geography must have certain essential information about a nation, such as location, population, resources and economy. . . . Yet, mastery of this knowledge for the sake of mastery is insufficient. The instructor should guide his students to realize that economic diversity, for instance, in modern society is a necessity for any nation. Dependence on one crop is disastrous if the world market would shift its need for this single item.[5]

THE LEARNING CURVE

Many studies of the learning process have shown that the acquisition of new information or of a new skill proceeds in a predictable fashion. When first confronting a new subject we begin learning slowly and then pick up speed rather dramatically. Finally, our pace slows down and begins to level off.

Figure 13.1 shows a typical learning curve. It is said to be negatively accelerated because as the number of trials increases, there is less and less increase in the amount learned. After the first few trials, in which the learner is "catching on" to the basic procedures, rather huge gulps of new learning are quickly assimilated. As time goes on, however, improvement becomes less and less pronounced and finally levels off. This leveling off is called a *plateau*. Novice golfers may score 150 their first few times around the course, but after their fourth or fifth round they may be down to around 120. At this point they may feel that it's easy to excel at golf and that, if they can continue lopping 30 strokes off their score, they will soon be ready for "the tour." They soon learn, however, that lowering their score from 100 to 90 is far more difficult than lowering it from 120 to 110.

Students learning a new skill may reach a whole series of plateaus. Typing students, for example, may proceed fairly rapidly at first and then level off. Perhaps they were learning the keyboard letter by letter. Suddenly, they notice another increase in performance, for now they have learned certain letter

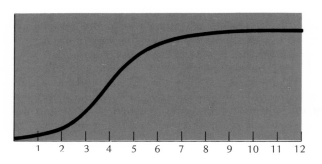

Fig. 13.1 A typical learning curve.

sequences like ING, or TION, or THE, which can be rattled off as though they were single letters. This is actually an example of positive transfer, where the previous learning finally builds up to the point where a sharp increase in new learning has become possible.

LEARNING SETS

Harry Harlow has done some important research in learning, using monkeys as subjects. Harlow coined the phrase "learning set" to describe the phenomenon of learning how to learn. He found that with practice his monkeys became increasingly skilled at solving discrimination problems. They improved, not only on the previously learned problems, but on novel problems as well. The fact that the monkeys developed these learning sets freed "them from the restrictions of the slow, trial-and-error process of the original attempts."[6] Harlow feels that his concept of learning sets has explained what the gestalt psychologists had labeled "insight." He sees the sudden spurt in learning, the so-called "a-ha" phenomenon, as just another extension of the theoretical concept of transfer.

Harlow's learning sets: an explanation for "insight"

MASSED VERSUS DISTRIBUTED LEARNING

If you had four hours to parcel out any way you wished, how could you make the most of this time to learn a new skill? In learning new motor skills, the evidence is fairly clear—distributed practice of, say, sixteen fifteen-minute segments is more efficient than a massive dose of four straight hours. When learning to skate, ride a bike, or perform a new skill in a physical-education class, this distributed practice prescription is indeed sound advice. Not only are the shorter sessions less fatiguing, but by their very nature, motor skills are best learned a step at a time. When it comes to more-intellectual tasks, however, the situation is somewhat different. To learn a simple problem or a passage of poetry, it is probably best to use a single sitting of massed practice, since breaking this kind of material down into smaller units makes it less meaningful. Bruner has stressed the importance of keeping a subject internally coherent and meaningful when setting up efficient learning conditions. When longer material must be learned, a compromise can be worked out; the material can be divided into meaningful units and learned in several massed-practice sessions.

Spaced practice better on motor tasks

WHOLE VERSUS PART LEARNING

The question of whether the material to be learned should be carved up and doled out in small units, or whether it should be presented as an integrated whole, if only sketchily, is of great concern to educators. Is it more efficient for you, the reader, to try to master the material in this chapter by reading three pages a day, or by reading through the whole chapter first and then going back and attempting to iron out the details? The message from Jerome Bruner is clear—the more meaningful the material, the easier it is to learn. Therefore, breaking it down into parts is a risky venture, unless the material to be learned is something like Ebbinghaus's nonsense syllables. The trouble with learning

The more meaningful the material, the easier it is to learn.
When introducing new material to students, give a general
overview of the subject matter before introducing the details.

material in parts is that the parts eventually have to be pieced back together, and this can be extremely time consuming. In many learning situations the best approach is to work first on the whole and then to go back to the various parts. When presenting a new unit in, say, social studies, the teacher should spend some time discussing the general point of view of the whole unit before introducing the details. Giving the student an overview of the whole unit makes even the use of a teaching machine more effective (see p. 346).

SOCIAL LEARNING OR MODELING

Albert Bandura, an important contemporary psychologist, has suggested that a significant part of what a person learns occurs through imitation or modeling. Bandura has been called a *social learning theorist,* in that he is concerned with the learning that takes place in the context of the social situation. During social interactions an individual may learn to modify his or her behavior as a result of how others in the group are responding.

Bandura studies learning that takes place in a social context

Modeling versus operant conditioning

Though recognizing the importance of Skinner's operant conditioning, Bandura insists that not all learning takes place as a result of the direct reinforcement of responses. People also learn by imitating the behavior of other people, or models, and this learning takes place even though these imitative responses are not themselves being directly reinforced. For example, a young child may stand up when the "Star Spangled Banner" is played because he sees his parents stand. The child's response in this instance was not immediately followed by an M&M candy or any other primary reinforcer. The child simply imitated the response made by his parents.

Learning new responses

In the previous example, the child's ability to stand up was, of course, already a part of his behavioral repertoire. Bandura further says that people can also learn *new* responses simply by observing the behavior of others. A child learns to ski, or an adult learns to stroke a tennis ball, simply by imitating the behavior of the instructor. The "language-lab" method of teaching a foreign language is based on the premise that people can efficiently learn to imitate the sentences and phrases that are electronically reproduced for them to hear. The list of new forms of behavior that can be learned through modeling is virtually endless, and though the previous examples stress positive forms of learning, modeling may also create undesirable responses. A child may learn to become overly aggressive, or deceitful and dishonest through the modeling mechanism.

People also learn by imitating the behavior of other people, or models.

In a now-classic study, Bandura subjected a group of young
children to the improbable spectacle of adults punching,
kicking, and yelling at a large, inflated "Bobo" doll. When
allowed to play with Bobo later, these children displayed
twice as many aggressive responses as a control group
of children which had not witnessed this performance.

The learning of aggressive behavior

In a now-classic study, Bandura subjected a group of young children (ages three
to six) to the improbable spectacle of watching adult models punch, kick, and
yell at a large, inflated "Bobo" doll.[7] When later allowed to play with "Bobo"
themselves, these children displayed twice as many aggressive responses as a
control group of children which had not witnessed this performance. The form
of imitation in this study was indeed direct. The children even yelled the same
phrases the adults had used: "Kick him," "Sock him in the nose," etc. One might
speculate that had the adults danced with "Bobo" rather than punching him, the
children, too, would have behaved in this gentler fashion.

Children imitate adult models punching "Bobo" doll

Reinforcement and modeling

Though, as has been shown, learning through modeling does not require direct
and immediate reinforcement, Bandura has suggested that reinforcement may
still be involved. In the first place, many of the significant models in the child's
world, parents and teachers, are also in charge of the child's reinforcement
schedule. The parent may not only provide the modeling stimulus, but may also
reinforce the child when the behavior is imitated. Secondly, Bandura has demonstrated that a child is more apt to imitate an adult model's response when the
adult is himself being reinforced for that response.[8] In other words, the child
who observes an adult being praised for a certain action is more likely to
respond in the same way than is a child who views the action but not the subsequent reinforcement. Bandura calls this *vicarious* learning, since the learner
in this instance is not the one being reinforced, but is merely witnessing the
reinforcement.

   Thus, reinforcement and modeling can together create very potent conditions for behavior change. Many of our most persistent habits and attitudes are
a result of this combination of powerful forces.

Modeling as a therapy technique

Bandura has also shown that the modeling process can be used as a technique in
psychotherapy. Just as persons can learn certain fears through modeling, so, too,
can these fears become unlearned. A child, for example, may learn to fear
snakes by observing his father recoil in horror at the sight of a snake. In one
study, Bandura attempted to cure a group of individuals, all of whom had severe
snake phobias.[9] The subjects in one group watched, in various stages of agitation,
while the experimenter or model handled and played with a king snake. The
experimenter then urged the subjects to imitate his behavior, asking them
first to touch the snake while wearing gloves, and later with their bare hands.

Modeling can be a helpful technique in psychotherapy

After ten sessions, the cure rate was a phenomenal 100 percent. All of the subjects in the "Live Modeling" group were able to pass the criterion test, that is, sit quietly for thirty seconds while a large snake was allowed to crawl all over them.

Significance in the classroom

Other than the parents, the classroom teacher may be the most important model in the child's environment. Many children have been known to model their teacher's behavior so closely that they in a sense "become" the teacher when interacting with younger brothers and sisters at home. In some cases, these children demand that the younger siblings call them by their teacher's name— "I'm not Debbie, I'm Mrs. D." The teacher's likes and dislikes regarding subject matter may become obvious to the students and result in imitative attitudes. The teacher who loves music but hates math may, through vicarious learning, transmit these feelings to the class. So called "math blocks" may be created in this way, and the student could be permanently affected.

Other types of negative teacher behavior may also be imitated by the students. A first-grade teacher was having a very difficult time maintaining what she considered to be proper discipline in her classroom. She began spending more and more time screaming at the children. The parents of one of the children found that each day, after school, she would shut herself up in her room and scream at her dolls (even using the same words the teacher had used). A teacher's attitude toward minority-group students can also have a significant effect, both on how the minority student learns to perceive himself or herself, and on how the student is perceived by the other members of the class. In short, teachers provide conditions for learning in the classroom, not only by what they say but also by what they do.

OPERANT CONDITIONING IN THE CLASSROOM

Translating theory into practice

As we saw in the previous chapter, Skinner's principles of operant conditioning can be translated into specific classroom techniques. The Skinnerians feel that colleges have failed to equip prospective teachers for the actual day-to-day job of educating children. The new teacher, no matter how knowledgeable in educational theory, is usually at a complete loss when it comes to putting theory into practice. The teacher may understand the importance of recognizing individual differences, and may know full well that learning requires motivation and that the students' interest must be captured, but then what? What happens when, in order to motivate students, the new teacher proudly displays the best student's written work on the bulletin board, only to find the next day that the essay is on the floor and the thumbtacks have been stolen? What happens when the new teacher, steeped in the philosophy of "fairness," leaves the room and asks the students to cover their eyes so that the one guilty child can come discreetly forward and return a dime that has been stolen from another child? Not only is the dime not returned, but one young philanthropist, missing the teacher's point entirely, loudly offers to contribute a dime to the aggrieved child so that the class can go on to important matters. What happens when the new teacher demands that an unruly child sit down and be quiet, only to have the child stare back coolly and say, "Make me!"? What happens when . . . and on, and on.

The current popularity of operant conditioning techniques is due in large measure to the fact that operant conditioning offers the teacher a precise prescription for handling specific classroom situations. The Skinnerians do not resort to such cliches as "seizing the teachable moment" or being an "educational provocateur." The Skinnerians are specific, and they urge the teacher to be just as specific.

Operant conditioning offers teacher precise prescriptions for specific situations

THE CASE FOR BEHAVIOR MODIFICATION

Some of the essentials of this thing we now call behavior modification have probably been with us since time immemorial. As soon as humans "discovered" that their behavior could be affected by environmental conditions, some aspects of behavior modification came into being. Many of today's college students, on hearing their first lecture on behavior modification, respond with a smug yawn and ask, "So what else is new?".

The fact is, however, that despite its apparently long history, and despite its obvious overtones of "mere common sense," behavior modification as it is technically understood and used today is of fairly recent origin. A recent issue of the *American Psychologist* distinguishes between *behavior influence* and *behavior modification*.[10]

1
Behavior influence: a very general phenomenon that occurs anytime one person is able to exert some degree of control over the behavior of another person. "This occurs constantly in such diverse situations as formal school education, advertising, child-rearing, political campaigning, and other normal interpersonal interactions."[11]

2
Behavior modification: a specific type of behavior influence that translates the theories and principles of learning derived from experimental psychology into an applied technique for behavior change. The technique should always be used in the pursuit of positive goals, that is, to reduce human suffering and increase human functioning. "Behavior modification emphasizes systematic monitoring and evaluation of the effectiveness of these applications . . . and is intended to facilitate improved self-control by expanding individuals' skills, abilities, and independence."[13]

Thus, behavior influence occurs normally whenever people interact and may result in either positive or negative consequences for the people involved. Behavior modification is a precise form of influence, based on research findings and used to promote positive behavior changes.

Finally, it should be pointed out that behavior modification, unlike Freud's theory of psychoanalysis, assumes that the most important forces affecting any individual are the current life experiences, not the memories of childhood events and traumas.

Behavior modification assumes current, not past, life experiences affect individual the most

Defining objectives

Objectives must be specified in behavioral terms

Every teacher has a general idea of educational goals for the class as a whole or for individual students. It is crucial that these goals be specifically stated in objective, behavioral terms, so that both the teacher and the students know what the goals are and when they have been reached. Furthermore, goals should be specified not just for the term, but for each day of the term.

Behavioral terminology avoids words such as "understanding"—that is, words that do not describe a demonstrable behavior. A behaviorally formulated objective is one that describes the *behavior* that will result when the objective is attained. For example, students can be said to have learned multiplication when they can recite the multiplication table with no errors. In terms of daily goals they may be expected to make no more than five errors the first day, no more than two the second day, and none at all the third day. Each time a goal, or "terminal behavior," is reached, a new goal is set so that the first goal is just a step in a continuing process toward an overall goal.

Terminal behavior—a specific goal

Say the goal, or the terminal behavior, for a certain child is to develop better study habits in the classroom. This must then be defined in behavioral terms. Perhaps the teacher wants the child to not gaze into space, to talk and fidget less, and to read and write more. When objectified in this way, it can be accurately judged whether or not the terminal behavior is achieved, and if it is, exactly when.

Anything that can be taught can be objectified

Reading skills can be objectified as the ability to recognize correct definitions for 100 selected words. Music appreciation can be objectified as the ability to identify the composers of 20 musical compositions. The proponents of behavior modification argue that anything that can be taught can be objectified, and that all educational goals can be stated in behavioral terms. Critics may argue that being able to recognize 20 composers "isn't what we mean by musical appreciation," or that recognizing definitions of 100 selected words "isn't what we mean by reading skills." If so, the Skinnerians would say it is up to the critics to state clearly what they do mean in order that these goals can be knowingly reached:

> *Mathematical behavior is usually regarded, not as a repertoire of responses involving numbers and numerical operations, but as evidences of mathematical ability or the exercise of the power of reason. It is true that the techniques which are emerging from the experimental study of learning are not designed to "develop the mind" or to further some vague "understanding" of mathematical relationships. They are designed, on the contrary, to establish the very behaviors which are taken to be evidences of such mental states or processes.*[13]

Establishing the operant level

Once the goal has been defined (and nobody says this is easy, but then, good teaching is not easy), the teacher must observe the student and establish the operant level, or the rate at which the behavior occurs naturally in the classroom. Since student responses are so often specific to the stimulus situation, it is important that the operant level be established by observing the classroom.

Many children who are disruptive in class are as good as gold in the counselor's or principal's office. If unruly students are sent to the psychologist's office, they are not as likely to display their disruptive behavior, since the releasers for this behavior remain back in the classroom.

Let's visit a fifth-grade classroom and observe the behavior of an eleven-year-old boy, Walter S. An art lesson is in progress. As the teacher begins giving the directions for today's project, Walter stands on top of his desk and calls out his own name, "Wally, Wally, Wally," and makes strange, grunting sounds for two minutes. After the teacher's tenth request, Walter sits down and remains silent for just over one minute. The students then file toward the front of the room to pick up their supplies. Walter spends the next two minutes running back and forth, occasionally sliding, as though going into home plate. The teacher brings Walter's supplies to his desk, where Walter remains seated quietly for almost three minutes. Among the art supplies are some elastic bands which he suddenly discovers can be put to use in an aggressive way. He flicks them at the other students for the next thirty seconds, or until he runs out. One girl receives a direct hit and calls loudly to the teacher who is three rows away helping another student. Walter laughs at the girl's discomfort, but immediately takes his seat when the teacher comes over to investigate the uproar. Walter finally gets down to work and remains quietly at his seat for almost ten minutes. Suddenly, he discovers that a certain piece of cardboard, which he had previously cut, doesn't quite fit where he had planned to glue it. He leaps back up on top of his desk, makes loud noises, and contorts his face. The class seems to enjoy his performance, and despite the teacher's pleas, he remains on top of his desk for almost three minutes.

Out of twenty-two total minutes of class time, Walter has now spent just over seven minutes engaging in disruptive behavior. His operant level for disruptive behavior is, thus, a little over 34 percent.

What should be done with Walter? Behavior-modification experts, like Charles and Clifford Madsen, say that the teacher has the responsibility to help Walter. He is obviously a problem child. In testing Walter, the school psychologist discovered that Walter's home life was extremely bad: he has no father, his older siblings engage in delinquent behavior, there is no supervision in the home at all, and so on. Walter's test scores show him to be "precariously adjusted" and, of course, his home life is terrible. Perhaps the teacher now feels a sense of compassion toward Walter, and even some guilt for having disliked him so. Walter is probably headed for real trouble and may someday spend a great deal of time in a more structured institution than a school. Should the teacher throw up her arms in dismay and give up trying to interact meaningfully with Walter? The proponents of behavior modification say, "No."

In discussing the problem child, in this case the proverbial "Johnny," Madsen and Madsen say:

> The truly pathetic situation is that no one will teach Johnny. The one place where there is some hope for Johnny is the school. Yet, many teachers quickly abdicate responsibility once his history is known. Johnny can discriminate. He can be taught new responses to deal with that world outside the home. He can learn to read, write, spell; he can learn new rules of

social interaction and thereby break the cycle of the past. If cooperation (with the home) is impossible, he can even learn these responses in spite of a bad home. It is not easy to deal with the Johnnies (or the Walters). They take time, energy and a disciplined teacher. All the Johnnies do not survive; yet for these children the school is their only hope. Who has the responsibility of discipline?—The teacher.[14]

The modification of behavior

Once the educational goals have been defined behaviorally, and the operant level assessed, one can begin the job of modifying behavior. The techniques used are those outlined in Chapter 12. In order to change responses, in order to modify behavior, we must allow the operant to occur and then provide an appropriate stimulus situation. For example, if we wish to strengthen a certain response, i.e., increase the rate of a given operant, the response must be allowed to occur and then be followed by positive or negative reinforcement. Recall that a positive reinforcement is a stimulus that, following a given response, increases the rate of that response. A negative reinforcement is a stimulus that, when removed, increases the response rate. Both positive and negative reinforcement increase rather than decrease the strength of a given response. Punishment, on the other hand, is an aversive stimulus that reduces the rate of the response. We will discuss punishment in detail later in the chapter, but it is important to note now that punishment and negative reinforcement are very different kinds of stimulus situations which have exactly opposite effects on response rates.

Punishment is an aversive stimulus that reduces the rate of response

POSITIVE REINFORCEMENT

In the classroom, positive reinforcement may be provided by a primary reinforcer, such as milk, cereal, or candy, or it may be a conditioned reinforcer, such as gold stars, high grades, social approval, or, in the case of younger pupils, physical contact.

A certain student, John D., would not remain attentive or even attempt to do his numerical reason problems. The teacher set the behavioral goal of nineteen correct solutions out of twenty problems. Observation of the student indicated that his operant level was zero; he simply would not do the work. After a conference with his parents, the boy was sent to school each morning without any breakfast. The teacher used milk and cereal as the positive reinforcers for correct math solutions. The student reached the desired goal on the fourth day.

Tommy L., a third-grade student, was boisterous and noisy in class and prevented other students from concentrating on their own work. The first behavioral goal was set at thirty minutes of complete silence. Tommy was presented with an M & M candy each time he remained quiet for forty-five seconds. On the eighth day the goal was reached. At this point a new goal was set for sixty minutes of silence. Also the reinforcement schedule was altered so that Tommy had to remain silent for two minutes in order to receive the M & M reinforcement. This new goal was reached in only three days.

Such primary reinforcers as food for the child who has had no breakfast or candy for the child who loves sweets are obviously of a positive valence. When it comes to conditioned reinforcers, however, the teacher must observe the situation closely, for, as the proverb states, "One man's meat may be another man's poison." What the teacher may consider a positive reinforcer will not necessarily be such for each and every student. Usually, however, the teacher can select from such conditioned reinforcers as the following, suggested by Madsen and Madsen:[15]

1
Words—spoken and written

2
Expressions—facial and bodily

3
Closeness—nearness and touching

4
Activities and privileges

5
Things—materials, awards, toys

NEGATIVE REINFORCEMENT

Negative reinforcement—the removal of an aversive stimulus in order to increase response rate—has been used in a variety of school settings. One fairly common use of this is the so-called *time-out* procedure, a technique, incidentally, that is commonly used by parents in the home.[16] In a study now being conducted at the University of Kansas on preschool children with poor cognitive, language, and social skills, this time-out procedure has produced some dramatic results. A child who exhibits low self-control is placed for brief periods of time in a small room next to the classroom. When the child's behavior becomes more positive and less hyperactive, he or she is allowed to return (aversive stimulus is removed) to the regular classroom. This technique is combined with the use of various positive reinforcers to enhance the build-up of desirable responses.[17]

Negative reinforcement has proved successful in shaping a variety of desired responses. In one instance a student who had not done his homework assignment was placed in a time-out room and told to complete the work. Only when the assignment was finally completed was the student allowed back in the classroom. In this case, the removal of the aversive stimulus (escape from the isolation room) acted to strengthen the behavior (doing the assignment).

Another example of negative reinforcement, cited by Madsen and Madsen, involved a second-grade boy whose teacher made him wear a girl's ribbon in his hair until he began acting in a more controlled fashion. Whenever his behavior improved, the hair ribbon was removed. Madsen and Madsen question the advisability of this particular technique on the grounds that it might affect the child's perception of his sex identification.

Negative reinforcement should only be used with great caution. A teacher should examine carefully the possible disturbing consequences whenever considering the use of negative reinforcement. There is a real difference between

Punishment and negative reinforcement affect response rates in opposite ways

Negative reinforcement should only be used with great caution placing children in a time-out room, where they have the opportunity to finish their work, and shoving them into an unlighted closet with the door closed. It is obviously very easy for the teacher's intended negative reinforcement to become simple punishment. When that occurs, as Skinner has pointed out, the whole purpose of reinforcement is defeated.[18] Control by aversive means may provoke a counterattack; day dreaming, dropping out, vandalism, refusal to learn assignments are all common indications of an attempt to avoid aversive control.

CONSISTENCY

Consistency—the key ingredient in any behavior-modification program

Perhaps the major premise underlying the technique of behavior modification is that consistency should be observed at all times. Once a child is placed on a reinforcement program, the teacher must not waver. As Skinner's research on animals has shown, behavior that is intermittently reinforced is the most difficult to extinguish. If children are told that every time they act in a certain way they will be sent to the principal's office, they must be sent to the office every time they act that way. There can be no exceptions. Inconsistency teaches just that—inconsistency. As Madsen and Madsen point out:

> The child does not remember the 1,321 times he went to bed at 8 P.M., he remembers the two times he got to stay up. The third grader does not really believe that the teacher will send him to the time-out room (isolation) for ten minutes. This is already the sixth time the teacher has threatened and nothing has happened yet. The ninth grader cheated before and didn't get caught; why should he get caught this time? The college student has turned in late papers before; why should this professor be such a hard nose?[19]

Consistency is a key ingredient in the success of any behavior-modification program. The cute little student who pleads, "Can't you make an exception just this once," may be hard for the teacher to resist, but resist the teacher must. Once the teacher breaks the rules, the children learn only too well that the rules are there for the breaking.

> A ninth-grade creative writing class was slowly but surely getting out of control; assignments were not being turned in, the students were becoming increasingly boisterous and rude both to the teacher and to each other. The teacher, Miss W., pleaded with the students to be fair and meet her half way, but this had no effect. It was suggested to Miss W. that reinforcement principles might be applied. She thereupon informed the class that if they behaved well for two successive days, they would go on a trip downtown to see the movie, "Hamlet." The next two days found the class no different, just as rowdy, just as out of control. Virtually every five minutes Miss W. shouted (to those who could hear her) that if they didn't behave, the trip would be cancelled. In fact, she actually cancelled the trip three times, but on the third day, the class pleaded with her and she relented. They saw the movie, and the next day the classroom situation became even more de-

teriorated. Miss W. was beside herself. "I've tried everything, even behavior modification, and nothing works." She went back to class and pleaded with the students to be fair.

THE TIMING OF REINFORCEMENT

To modify behavior effectively, the reinforcement must be timed to occur after the desired response has occurred. The teacher should never, never deliver the reinforcement on the promise that the behavior will occur later. For example, a teacher asks the students in her class to turn in their assignments at the beginning of each class period. At the start of the next class period no assignments are handed in. The teacher then tells them that if they promise to begin turning in their assignments the following Monday, they can have a record party for the last half hour of today's class period. The class quickly promises, has the record party, and the teacher is still waiting for the homework.

A seven-year-old boy enters his house muttering an innocuous swear word. His mother becomes upset and urges the boy never to say that word again. In exchange for his promise to obey her, the mother gives him a quarter. An hour later he returns demanding a dollar, saying, "If you think that word was bad, wait 'til you hear this!"

Reinforcement must follow actual behavior. We learn by doing, not by talking about doing or by promising to do. As the behavior modifiers argue, the reinforcement must be made contingent on the appropriate response.

Reinforcement is contingent upon the desired response

PUNISHMENT

The use of punishment to control behavior has been a controversial issue among both learning theorists and educators. Thorndike, for example, changed his position on the question of punishment. His original law of effect stated that reward and punishment had equal but opposite effects, reward strengthening and punishment weakening a learned stimulus-response connection. Later in his career, Thorndike revised this law drastically, saying that reward was far more effective in reinforcing learning than punishment was in weakening it. Later still, the Skinnerians demonstrated that if a rat was reinforced, say, 100 times for pressing a lever and thus had a rather large build-up of responses waiting to be emitted, punishment would temporarily slow down the response rate, but would not reduce the number of responses that would be emitted once the punishment was removed.

Punishment temporarily slows response rate

The typical experiment used a rat in an experimental chamber. The rat was reinforced with a food pellet for each lever press, until lever-pressing became highly resistant to extinction (the rat's lever-pressing response was strengthened until he would emit, say, 200 responses without being further reinforced). The lever was then electrified so that the rat now received a punishing shock every time he pressed the lever. The rat learned very quickly to stay away from the lever. However, once the shock was removed, he went determinedly back to the lever and all 200 responses were finally emitted. Punishment had merely held the responses in abeyance, suppressing them temporarily until the aversive stimulus was removed.

Because of Thorndike's changed position, the rat data from the Skinnerians, and other studies and theoretical positions, many psychologists and educators assumed that punishment had no real effect on learning. This scientific news was greeted with some skepticism, especially by older teachers who recalled the effect of the hickory stick on class control. Many parents and grandparents also found it difficult to mesh this "scientific breakthrough" with their own experiences raising children.

More recent psychological studies, especially those carried out in the past ten years, have shown that punishment is indeed an effective technique for controlling behavior. The problem with the previously mentioned rat study was that it was an extremely artificial situation. In the first place, the rats were exceptionally highly motivated to press the lever—the lever was the route to life-sustaining food for these poor starving creatures. In the second place, no alternative response would produce the reinforcement. If a rat is given another response option during the time the punishment is in force, the original lever-pressing response does indeed weaken very rapidly. Punishment may not be a humane conditioning technique, and it may create some serious side effects, but it does control behavior. Even the most humanitarian parent seems to know this in moments of crisis. A child who is playing on a busy highway is quickly punished and then shown another area where he can play safely. A baby is not "reasoned with" when she is found poking her fingers into a light socket.

Punishment may not be humane, but it does control behavior

Punishment in the classroom usually takes the form of disapproval or of withholding a positive reinforcer. Severe disapproval by the teacher may often be an effective form of controlling behavior, but it does not instill a love of learning. Withholding a positive reinforcer, if the rule of consistency is religiously followed, is also an extremely effective behavior modifier. This method of aversive control takes such forms as the loss of privileges, objects, or pastimes the students value. The purist should note that withholding a positive reinforcer when used as punishment is not the same as extinction.

> *In extinction, consequences that ordinarily follow the behavior are simply discontinued; in punishment, behavior results in the application of aversive consequences through forfeiture of positive reinforcers. Thus in extinguishing aggression sustained by peer attention, the behavior is consistently ignored; under the punishment contingency, however, the rewards of peer attention are pitted against the negative effects of confinement to one's room, loss of television privileges, or some other type of negative outcome.[20]*

Proponents of behavior modification have made extensive use of punishment in psychotherapy. For example, male homosexuals have been treated by showing them slides of nude men and women. While viewing the slides of male nudes the patient receives an unpleasant shock through electrodes attached to his leg. While viewing the female nudes, no such punishment is administered. This technique has apparently been successful in changing the sexual orientation of a number of subjects.

Children who suffer from stuttering have also been treated by the administration of electric shock whenever they begin stammering. Fairly dramatic recovery rates, of two weeks or less, have been attributed to the use of this technique.

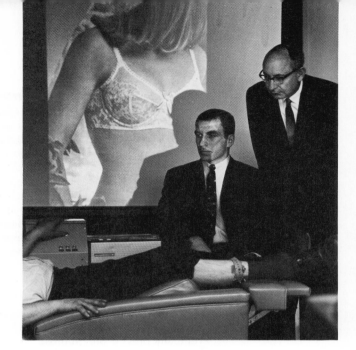

Receiving an unpleasant shock when viewing slides of nude males has apparently been successful in changing the sexual orientation of a number of homosexuals. The shock is not delivered when slides of females are shown.

Punishment has even proved effective with severely disturbed children, children who unless restrained bang their heads against hard objects, tear and bite off pieces of their own flesh, pummel their own faces, and so on. Despite the fact that these children might be assumed to enjoy being hurt, they apparently don't enjoy being hurt by others. Research in this area indicates that the use of shock, administered whenever self-injurious behavior is observed, can drastically reduce and even eliminate self-destruction responses.

There is, however, growing concern that the use of electric shock on humans may be ethically wrong and an infringement on the individual's civil liberties.[21] No doubt, there are moral issues and even problems of possible physical harm to be considered. In one report, a psychotic child was given painful electric shocks with a cattle-prod device for self-injurious behavior. This technique resulted in the total elimination of such behavior after *167 days of treatment*.[22] American companies are even advertising radio-controlled "Remote Shockers" that can "deliver a painful shock from up to 300 feet away." These devices have been displayed at psychology conventions. Recently a plea has been advanced that if a person, who may not have the capacity to give full and informed consent, is to be subjected to such aversive conditioning procedures, then an outside, objective advocate should be called in to determine the person's best interests.[23] Thus, retarded or psychotic children and adults will be protected from the possible abuses arising from the indiscriminate use of a painful shock as an aversive stimulus.

AVERSIVE STIMULI IN THE CLASSROOM

The use of aversive stimuli in the classroom, whether as negative reinforcement or as punishment, should be viewed with extreme caution. While certainly an effective means of controlling behavior, it rarely instills in the student a joyful love of learning. Aversive stimuli can also act to classically condition emotional responses that can cause "blocks" to future learning (see Chapter 11). If punishment is to be used, it should be used sparingly and only in conjunction with a positive reinforcement of some alternative response. That is, while the punishment is suppressing an undesirable response, positive reinforcement should be used to strengthen a socially approved alternative response. Punishment has only a short-lived effect on people who have few response options. This is why it is so often ineffective in the case of criminals—they have few, if any, socially approved means of achieving the material things our society values. In short, behavior modification brought about through positive reinforcement is more likely to be lasting and, eventually, self-perpetuating, than that brought about through the use of aversive controls.

EXTINCTION

A basic principle in learning is that behavior which is not reinforced will slowly be extinguished. A rat that has learned to press a lever 400 times per hour will eventually press it only four or five times per hour if his lever-pressing response ceases to be reinforced. Learned responses are abandoned when they no longer result in a payoff.

During extinction, response rates often increase before decreasing

Studies of extinction in rats and humans have uncovered an interesting phenomenon. During extinction the rate of responding initially increases before it begins to peter out. The teacher who discovers that her display of anger toward a certain student somehow positively reinforces his undesirable behavior decides that she will simply ignore the student in order to extinguish his behavior. To her dismay, the teacher notes that the student's behavior increases rather than decreases. At this point consistency may be difficult, but it must be maintained if the extinction technique is to be successful. The student, who is suddenly denied reinforcement for his undesired behavior, tries even harder before finally realizing that the situation has really changed.

Extinction techniques will work only if the teacher can:

1
Identify what is reinforcing the student's behavior

2
Eliminate that reinforcer

3
Remain faithful to the program.

SHAPING

Shaping is the technique of reinforcement by successive approximation until the desired response is emitted. For example, a rat newly introduced into an experimental chamber doesn't immediately rush over to the lever and start pressing it in order to receive the reinforcer. If left completely on its own, the rat may take an hour or even longer to stumble upon the lever. In order to speed up the conditioning process, the experimenter will shape the rat's behavior by reinforcing it first for simply facing the lever; then, each time the rat makes a new response that results in a further approach to the lever, the behavior is immediately reinforced. The point is to get the animal winning as quickly as possible, even if the ultimate behavioral goal has not been exhibited.

In the classroom this shaping technique is an important aspect of behavior modification. It is important, especially in the younger grades, that children attain success *quickly and often*. Later, the number of reinforcements may be stretched over longer periods of time and thereby reduced. With young children, the use of food is extremely effective. Again, as time goes by, the food may be paired with social stimuli such as smiling, nodding, praising, so that later on conditioned reinforcers may replace the primary reinforcers.

Shaping allows children to attain success quickly

Madsen and Madsen provide an excellent example of shaping in which M & M candy is used to reinforce the responses of young children on the first day of school.

> The teacher may start the very first class with an M & M party. While the children are eating, the teacher says, "We will have another M & M party if everyone is quiet while I count to ten." The teacher counts aloud quickly, making sure they win. After giving the candy the teacher says, "If everyone is quiet for five minutes we will have another party, but if someone talks we will not get to have one." Now the teacher sits back and waits; in all probability someone will talk, whereupon the teacher says, "Oh, I'm very sorry. Mary talked before our time was up; now we will not get to have a party. Maybe tomorrow we may have one if everyone is quiet." Some children will think this is not fair. Because the teacher does not get angry at Mary, Mary cannot give her problem to the teacher.[24]

THE TOKEN SYSTEM

Another behavior modification technique that is being used more and more is the token system or the token economy.[25] In this system individuals receive various tokens for emitting desired responses, and these tokens are later exchanged for prizes or privileges (just like the use of money). The token system is simply another method for employing a work-payment incentive program. Rather than keeping a large refrigerator stocked with tasty food and drink beside the desk, the classroom teacher can set up a token economy.

Tokens, or conditioned reinforcers, can be virtually anything the teacher has available: pieces of colored cardboard, colored wool, gold stars, or poker chips, for example. The tokens are assigned point values and may eventually be turned in for some treasured prize, privilege, or desired activity. Tokens are awarded for desirable student behavior: accurate spelling, a certain number of correctly solved math problems, learning a specified number of lines of poetry, participating in class discussions, whatever. The colored pieces of cardboard may be set so that a red piece is worth, say, five points, a blue piece three points, and a white piece one point. Point values are assigned to the prizes so that a child can accumulate enough points in one day to earn a moderately valued prize, but may have to spend an entire week working toward a particularly desirable prize. This system has two advantages: it maintains a high daily rate of desirable responses and it teaches delayed gratification, or an ability to think in long-range terms.

Tokens as conditioned reinforcers

Token system used
with retarded chil-
dren

One example of the use of the token system involved a group of retarded children. One of the girls, who had been labeled "trainable retardate," especially enjoyed listening to records. Every time she earned twenty points for various academic accomplishments she was allowed ten minutes at the record player. "Under this reinforcement system she was learning to read, write, and do arithmetic, skills that were thought impossible for her. Needless to say, she now had a teacher who didn't believe in limiting children by categories, but who started with what the student could do and tried to take her further. This teacher's only complaint was that he had to spend so much time developing new materials as his 'trainables' learned the old."[26]

Some psychologists have questioned the use of the token system for two reasons. First, since the token system relies for its effect on extrinsic reinforcement, it may in the long run decrease a student's intrinsic motivation to learn. Second, it may be that once the tokens are withdrawn (and a student cannot be kept on a token system forever), the resulting behavior changes may be extinguished.[27]

THE PREMACK PRINCIPLE

High-frequency re-
sponses may be used
to reinforce low-fre-
quency responses

The Premack principle states that behavior that occurs at a naturally high rate of frequency may be used to reinforce behavior that occurs at a naturally low rate of frequency.[28] For example, if left to their own devices, many children will spend far more time watching TV than reading. According to Premack, when such children have finished a given amount of reading, allow them to go watch TV for a while. The teacher should carefully observe the children during free-choice periods and note the behaviors that naturally occur most frequently. These behaviors can then be used as positive reinforcers for low-probability responses. Teachers usually find that academic behavior has a low natural frequency, meaning that, when given a choice, most children prefer not to do school work.

PROGRAMED INSTRUCTION

The general concept of programed instruction is probably as old as formal schooling itself. Each grade level has a certain small portion of our accumulated knowledge allotted to it, and each child is expected to master that segment before being allowed to proceed to the next grade. Children who don't keep up with the rest of the class are held back and repeat the year. Children who are not challenged by the content in their grade are skipped ahead to a level more consistent with their ability. The proponents of behavior modification agree with this practice in general (except in cases where the pressure of the social promotion pushes all the children ahead, regardless of achievement), but they argue that the practice is too general and not tailored to the needs of the individual child. The individual child, they urge, needs a system of precision teaching, an educational prescription written just for him or her.

Programing is the arrangement of the material to be learned in a sequence of steps designed to lead the students to the final goal. The steps are usually quite close together, ensuring a gradual increase in difficulty. The material being presented is broken down into small units called frames. The entire program may have hundreds of frames, and the frames are written in such a way as to maximize the possibility of success. They may sometimes seem repetitious, but this is the result of a deliberate attempt to prevent any misconceptions from forming in the student's mind. A good program is one in which the students make very few errors, no more than five percent. This means, of course, that they are constantly experiencing success, or that they are on what is close to a continuous reinforcement schedule. Teachers can add their own reinforcers (such as prizes or desired activities) for the completion of, say, every twenty-five items. This puts the students on an intermittent schedule of reinforcement (fixed ratio) for the external reinforcers, while they remain on a continuous reinforcement schedule for the intrinsic, success reinforcer.

A good academic program may employ various techniques in the construction of frames. Certain frames may consist basically of words which serve as prompts through familiarity and experience. Other frames may merely introduce new material and ask easy questions about it. Logical order is another criterion used to determine the next frame to be presented, and degree of difficulty is still another consideration. At various times in the program a word might be requested which requires a synthesis of earlier concepts. From time to time frames may review previous material or require that it be used in new contexts. Programming, then, is not a sterile, mechanized technique, but offers a wide range of possible responses.[29]

Almost anyone with some degree of literacy can go through a program. Students will not all proceed at the same rate, but that, after all, is the story of individual differences. The first frame is always very easy, and the students are led by small steps into more complicated frames until the unit is completed, or the students have achieved the desired "terminal behavior."

Programs can be written in book form, with the questions on one page and the answers on the facing page. The students cover the answers, respond, and then uncover the answer as a self-check. Programs may also be placed in machines which are set so as not to move from one frame to the next until each one in turn has been successfully completed. Some machines are even equipped with a buzzer or a bell which sounds when a correct response has been given. The buzzers and bells act as further conditioned reinforcers for correct responses.

Programed instruction has several key advantages:

1

The student must pay attention, for if the program is to continue, responses must be given. The student is, therefore, an active participant in the learning process, not a mere passive observer.

2

Each student proceeds at his or her own rate. One student may finish in one hour a program that takes another student five hours to complete.

3

Reinforcement, to use Skinner's term, or feedback, to use Bruner's, is immediate. There are no delays between the response and knowledge of results.

4

Learning that takes place in a programed setting is always by positive reinforcement. Aversive techniques are never used. Machines don't shout, or
hit, or "tell parents."

5

Machines can be set automatically to keep track of errors. These can be
discussed later with the student, and in this important student-teacher dialogue, misconceptions about the subject matter can be allayed.

Probably the main disadvantage to programed instruction is that many students report finding it boring. "If that same question is asked one more time
I'll scream," said one student facing the seventeenth successive frame making
the same point. In their zeal to increase frame difficulty ever so slowly, certain
programers have simply not increased the frame difficulty at all for long periods
in the program. This is often resented by the alert student.

CAN THE MACHINE REPLACE THE TEACHER?

This question was debated seriously in the early 1960s when teaching machines
first began attracting a great deal of attention. Many teachers acknowledged the
benefits to be derived from the scientific programing of a teaching machine, but
then asked plaintively, "Is there still room for me?" The good teacher should
never be concerned over the possibility of being replaced by the machine. The
teaching machine is another audiovisual device, like motion pictures, TV, and
records, which when used appropriately can enhance the learning process.
Rather than taking the place of the warm, encouraging, dedicated teacher, the
teaching machine, like books and chalk, assists the teacher in the job of communicating with students. Part of the apparent early success of the teaching
machine, it now appears, was due to the novelty effect, the capturing of student interest merely because it was something new. Even the teaching machine
may be phased out and replaced by what is called "C.A.I.," or Computer As-

The C.A.I. system

sisted Instruction. The C.A.I. system involves the putting together of computers,
TV screens, and automatic typewriters to instruct students, not just in specific
facts, but in complex skills as well. C.A.I. systems can be designed so that hundreds of students can be involved at one time.

*Teaching machines
most effective for
transmitting specific
facts*

Teaching machines are probably very effective in the transmission of specific facts, but the teacher is needed to tie these facts into global concepts. The
teacher can use current examples of certain principles, thus helping to make
the machine seem more alive and, thus, effective. Bruner has said that the student must have a background of facts, the "stuff of learning," before discovery
learning can take place. A teaching machine can provide that "stuff." Knowing
a few "names and dates" allows for a certain level of understanding which will
aid a student in further exploration and discovery. A student who thinks that
John Dewey and Aristotle were classmates at Columbia, for example, may find
it difficult to appreciate the significance of the historical succession of philosophical ideas. There are, however, many areas that just can't be adequately
taught by machine. History and literature would be reduced to a pile of bits and
pieces, names and dates, were not the teacher there to integrate the material
into a living picture.

Rather than taking the place of the dedicated teacher, the teaching machine assists the teacher in the job of communicating with students.

As we saw in the beginning of this chapter during the discussion of whole-part learning, when material is learned in discrete units, these parts must be put back together. No programer can ever anticipate all the ways in which children may misinterpret the way the separate parts should be glued back together into a meaningful whole. The teacher is there, on the spot, guiding, motivating, doing the real job of teaching in its true sense.

Summary

Learning in the classroom revolves around the concept of transfer. What is learned in class is thought to transfer into later-life situations, so as to enable the learner to earn a living and enjoy a fuller life.

Modern theories of transfer date back to the early Greek notion of formal discipline, in which the mind, considered comparable to an athlete's muscles, was thought to require systematic exercise if it were to grow. Even as late as the early twentieth century, proponents of this position created academic curricula that stressed such subjects as logic, Greek, and Latin, not because these subjects had any practical value, but because they "strengthened" the mind.

Formal-discipline theory was seriously challenged by a number of psychologists, including William James, E. L. Thorndike, and Charles Judd. All of their studies pointed to the fact that "training the mind" had little if any lasting benefits, that learning Latin in order to understand English, for example, was a circuitous and wasteful route.

Educators today are no longer concerned with the theory of mental discipline, but they are concerned with promoting positive transfer between learning in the classroom and living effectively in later life.

The learning curve, a plotting out of one's learning speed, is typically negatively accelerated, which means that when confronted with a new subject, students learn a great deal of the material in a relatively short time, and then, with increased practice, add less and less new learning.

The term "learning sets" was coined by Harlow to explain what gestalt psychologists had previously labeled as "insight."

The issue of massed versus distributed practice results from the question of how the learner should allocate his or her time for maximum efficiency. When learning a new physical skill, distributed practice (an hour a day for a week) is more efficient than massed practice (seven straight hours in one day). On intellectual tasks, however, distributed practice may destroy the meaning of the material. In this case it is best to divide the material into meaningful units and then work on each unit in a massed-learning session.

The issue of whole versus part learning is based on the question of whether learning is most efficient when the material is broken down into small, discrete units or left in a total, organized whole. The best method seems to be to work first on the whole to gain a general overview of the material, and then go back and work on the various parts.

Albert Bandura has suggested that a large part of what a person learns occurs through imitation or modeling. This is called social-learning theory, since it is concerned with learning that takes place within a social situation. Bandura has shown that learning that occurs through modeling need not be based on direct reinforcement of the response. Other than the parents, the teacher may be the most important model in the child's environment. Conditions for learning are thus established not only by what the teacher says, but by what he or she does.

The current popularity of operant-conditioning techniques in the classroom is due in large part to the fact that the teacher is presented with a very precise prescription for handling specific classroom problems. Changing a student's behavior through the use of conditioning techniques is called behavior modification.

In order to use the behavior-modification techniques, the teacher must first define the educational objectives in behavioral terms, that is, determine exactly *what* the student should learn and *how* the student is to show that the learning has taken place. The teacher can only infer that learning or understanding has taken place by observing the *behavior* of the student.

Once the objectives have been defined, the teacher observes the student's initial rate of response, or operant level, for the activity in question. The operant level, or base rate, for the given activity should be observed in the classroom situation, not the principal's or guidance counselor's office.

After the behavioral goal is set and the student's operant level is established, the teacher can use reinforcement to strengthen (condition) some student behavior and withhold reinforcement (extinguish) other student behavior. Reinforcement always increases response rate. Positive reinforcement is when the response rate increases by adding the reinforcer (giving the student M&M candies, or gold stars, or high grades), and negative reinforcement is when the response rate increases by taking away the reinforcer (removing an aversive stimulus when the desired behavior is emitted). Aversive stimuli should be used as negative reinforcement or punishment *only* with great caution, since it can result in the student acquiring not only the goal behavior the teacher intended, but also other potentially damaging responses. For example, aversive stimuli may condition the student not only to be able to recite the multiplication tables, but also to fear the whole area of math, thus blocking any future learning.

The key to the successful use of behavior-modification techniques is *consistency*. The teacher must follow through on the established reinforcement schedule without wavering. Exceptions cannot be made, not even once.

Reinforcement must *follow*, not precede, the student's response. That is, reinforcement must always be made contingent on the student displaying the appropriate behavior. Usually the sooner the reinforcement follows the response, the more impact it will have in changing behavior.

Behavior-modification proponents also make use of the token system, a system based on the use of conditioned reinforcers. The teacher assigns point values to various stimuli, such as different colored pieces of cardboard. When the student emits the desired response, the tokens are awarded, and when enough points have been accumulated, the student may select a prize. The token system has two main advantages: (1) it maintains a high daily rate of desirable responses, and (2) it teaches delayed gratification.

The Premack principle states that behavior that naturally occurs at a high rate can be used to reinforce behavior that occurs at a naturally low rate. Thus, one set of responses may be used to reinforce another set of responses. If a student has a higher rate of TV-viewing responses than reading responses, then viewing TV can be used as reinforcement for a certain amount of reading.

Programed instruction is based on the arrangement of the material to be learned in an orderly sequence of steps designed to reach a certain goal. The steps are arranged so as to be very close together, ensuring only a very gradual increase in difficulty. A good program is one in which the student actually makes very few errors (less than 5 percent). The material to be learned is broken down into small units, called frames, and is usually presented to the students by mechanical means (the teaching machine). The basic advantage of programed instruction is that each student can proceed at his or her own rate. On the other hand, some students, especially brighter students, become bored with the long succession of similar items. Also, when material is learned in bits and pieces, it is often hard for the student to integrate it back into a meaningful whole.

REFERENCES

1
B. F. Skinner, *Science and Human Behavior* (New York: Macmillan, 1953), p. 402.

2
W. James, *The Principles of Psychology* (New York: Henry Holt, 1890).

3
E. L. Thorndike and R. S. Woodworth, "The Influence of Improvement in One Mental Function upon the Efficiency of Other Functions," *Psychological Review* 8 (1901):247–261, 384–395, 553–564.

4
C. H. Judd, "The Relation of Special Training to General Intelligence," *Educational Review* 36 (1908):28–42.

5
J. F. Travers, *Learning: Analysis and Application* (New York: McKay, 1972), p. 166. Copyright © 1965, 1972 by John F. Travers. From the book *Learning: Analysis and Application,* by John F. Travers. Published by the David McKay Company, Inc. Reprinted by permission of the publishers.

6
H. F. Harlow, J. L. McGaugh, and R. F. Thompson, *Psychology* (San Francisco: Albion, 1971), p. 301.

7
A. Bandura, D. Ross, and S. A. Ross, "Imitation of Film-Mediated Aggressive Models," *Journal of Abnormal and Social Psychology* 66 (1963):3–11.

8
A. Bandura and F. J. McDonald, "Influence of Social Reinforcement and the Behavior of Models in Shaping Children's Moral Judgments," *Journal of Abnormal and Social Psychology* 67 (1963):274–281.

9
A. Bandura, E. B. Blanchard, and B. Ritter, "Relative Efficacy of Desensitization and Modeling Approaches for Inducing Behavioral Affective and Attitudinal Changes," *Journal of Personality and Social Psychology* 13 (1969):173–199.

10
S. B. Stolz, L. A. Wienckowski, and B. S. Brown, "Behavior Modification: A Perspective on Critical Issues," *American Psychologist* 30, no. 11 (1975):1027–1048.

11
Ibid., p. 1027.

12
Ibid., p. 1028.

13
B. F. Skinner, "The Science of Learning and the Art of Teaching," *Harvard Educational Review* 24 (1954):86–87.

14
C. H. Madsen and C. K. Madsen, *Teaching-Discipline* (Boston: Allyn and Bacon, 1970), p. 14. Reprinted by permission.

15
Ibid., p. 116.

16
R. R. Sears, E. Maccoby, and H. Levin, *Patterns of Child Rearing* (Evanston, Ill.: Row, Peterson, 1957).

17
D. M. Baer, "The Control of Developmental Process: Why Wait?" in J. R. Nessebroade and H. W. Reese, *Life-Span Developmental Psychology: Methodological Issues* (New York: Academic Press, 1973).

18
B. F. Skinner, "Why Teachers Fail" (1965), in R. C. Sprinthall and N. A. Sprinthall, eds., *Educational Psychology: Selected Readings* (New York: Van Nostrand-Reinhold, 1969), pp. 164–172.

19
Madsen and Madsen, *Teaching-Discipline,* p. 34. Reprinted by permission.

20
A. Bandura, *Principles of Behavior Modification* (New York: Holt, Reinhart and Winston, 1969), p. 338. Reprinted by permission.

21
G. C. Davison and R. B. Stuart, "Behavior Therapy and Civil Liberties," *American Psychologist* 30 (1975):755–763.

22
B. G. Tate and A. S. Baroff, "Aversive Control of Self-Injurious Behavior in a Psychotic Boy," *Behavior Research and Therapy* 4 (1966):281–287.

23
G. P. Koocher, "Civil Liberties and Aversive Conditioning for Children," *American Psychologist* 31 (1976): 94–95.

24
Madsen and Madsen, *Teaching-Discipline*, p. 26. Reprinted by permission.

25
T. Ayllon and N. H. Azrin, *The Token Economy* (New York: Appleton-Century-Crofts, 1968).

26
M. F. Meacham and A. E. Wiesen, *Changing Classroom Behavior* (Scranton, Pa.: International Textbook, 1969), p. 50. Copyright 1969, by International Textbook Company. Reprinted from *Changing Classroom Behavior: A Manual for Precision Teaching* by Merle L. Meacham and Allen E. Wiesen by permission of Intext Educational Publishers.

27
F. M. Levine and G. Fasnacht, "Token Rewards May Lead to Token Learning," *American Psychologist* 29 (1974):816–820.

28
D. Premack, "Reinforcement Theory," in D. Levine, *Nebraska Symposium on Motivation* (Lincoln: University of Nebraska Press, 1965), pp. 123–180.

29
Meacham and Wiesen, *Changing Classroom Behavior*, p. 100. Copyright 1969, by International Textbook Company. Reprinted from *Changing Classroom Behavior: A Manual for Precision Teaching* by Merle L. Meacham and Allen E. Wiesen by permission of Intext Educational Publishers.

SUGGESTIONS FOR FURTHER READING

Bandura, A. *Principles of Behavior Modification.* New York: Holt, Rinehart and Winston, 1969.

Madsen, C. H., and C. K. Madsen. *Teaching-Discipline.* Boston: Allyn and Bacon, 1970.

Meacham, M. F., and A. E. Wiesen. *Changing Classroom Behavior.* Scranton, Pa.: International Textbook, 1969.

Travers, J. F. *Learning: Analysis and Application.* New York: McKay, 1972.

Teaching relationships

14

Teaching and education

Throughout this volume we have stressed the view that teaching is the management of instruction. Teaching may look deceptively simple (remember some of the attitudes we discussed in the first two chapters). One of the reasons for this apparent simplicity is that there is a fundamenal confusion between teaching and telling. Too often people say they are teachers and yet, if we were to observe their performance in the classroom, we would see that they don't really teach at all, but simply tell pupils what to do—as if pupils were little mechanical robots or walking computers. If you've had any experience running a computer, or using an adding machine, or even driving a car, you know you can tell those things what to do. However, you can hardly say your relationship to such machines bears any resemblance to a teaching relationship, for no interaction is involved. The teacher tries to create conditions under which the pupils will come to learn, to know, and to act upon their knowledge. Telling them or getting them to say or to repeat is not teaching, since these techniques merely call for parrotlike responses.

As soon as we realize that our job as teachers is to manage and direct the instructional process, not the telling process, we have begun to understand the complexity of the teacher's job. And since our approach to teaching will depend to an important extent on our own conception of our role, and since a number of different teaching models exist that may influence our conception, we discuss below some of the common teaching models. Three distinctly different views of the teacher's role can be identified.

Teaching is interactive, and the teacher's job is to manage
and direct the instructional process, not the telling process.

MODEL ONE: THE TRANSMITTER OF KNOWLEDGE

Teaching as the trans-
mission of knowledge

Probably the most common teaching model, and certainly the one with the
longest tradition, is that which views teaching as the transmission of knowledge.
This view assumes that there exists a well-known and finite body of knowledge
from which the teacher selects certain facts to pass on to pupils. In a metaphori-
cal sense, the teacher looks over all the knowledge "stored" in the Library of
Congress, pours through books and pamphlets, reads and digests everything, and
takes some of it to school where it will be disseminated.

This model emphasizes giving pupils basic facts and information before they
can be expected to think for themselves. They need to learn what is already
known before they can come up with any new ideas that might fit in with the
existing knowledge. At least part of the difficulty with this model is that it assigns
most of the activity, most of the work, and most of the decisions to the teacher
who, ironically, ends up learning more than the pupil. Recall Piaget's emphasis
on pupil initiative and pupil activity as a key element in the growth of cognitive
structures. The transmission-of-information view of teaching runs exactly contrary to Piaget's advice, emphasizing, as it does, passivity and rote learning. In
a sense, then, the transmission-of-knowledge model provides only a partial explanation of teaching and learning. We can learn some information and some
facts through this mode, but the model has major shortcomings, as we have
noted (see especially Chapter 2).

MODEL TWO: REVEALING THE STRUCTURE OF THE DISCIPLINE

Another common teaching model that has come into vogue in the last decade suggests that the teacher's role is to reveal or unveil the fundamental structure of a discipline. The idea here is to teach concepts or the process of inquiry, not facts. In some ways this is like teaching for problem solving, whereby we learn to solve problems by understanding the framework or the structure of the concepts. For example, pupils used to learn to cross-multiply fractions to solve a division problem. In model two, the teacher focuses on the concepts of fractions and division so that the pupils understand that cross-multiplying is really dividing both sides of an equation by a common number. Similarly, in a class in social studies, or what used to be called geography, pupils are no longer asked to memorize the principal cities and products of a state. Rather, they might be given a blank map showing topographical features such as hills, mountains, valleys, rivers, and lakes and then be asked to figure out where cities might be located. In other words, they go through an inquiry process that helps them understand why big cities grow in certain locations. The model-two teacher produces minischolars in the various disciplines.

Teaching knowledge as a "structure"

According to this model, the sheer intellectual excitement of discovering the reasons behind events, the logic a historian or a mathematician actually use, motivates the pupils to further activity and exploration. Teaching and learning resemble an archaeologist's uncovering of one fragment after another of some mysterious object. The archaeologist's curiosity about the fragments naturally makes her want to make sense of the puzzle; this curiosity produces both activity and excitement. The so-called discovery method of teaching is based on this model. The teacher, by analyzing material and asking questions, but not giving answers, spurs the pupils to learn by helping them discover the answer. The experience and the insight resulting from having put the puzzle together nurtures the entire educational process.

It is, of course, possible to overemphasize learning by discovery. It can be exasperating to never have any of your questions answered. It isn't necessary to discover everything for yourself in order to learn. Most important, however, it is difficult to know, especially at the elementary level and in junior high, exactly how much the pupils genuinely understand about the structure of a discipline taught this way. The idea of a structure is itself abstract and therefore beyond the comprehension of the concrete stage of thinking which most of these children are in. To understand such concepts and such processes, substantial cognitive sophistication is necessary. For example, to learn how a historian "thinks," we must understand concepts such as a fact, an opinion, a value, cultural relativism, subjectivity, and objectivity—to name a few.

A major debate is now going on between those who advocate this approach and those who hold other views. Jerome Bruner, formerly a professor at the Harvard Center for Cognitive Studies, is a leading advocate of teaching for the structure of knowledge.[1] One of his most provocative statements promotes this view: "Any subject can be taught effectively in some intellectually honest form to any child at any stage of development." Thus, according to Bruner, the six-year-old minischolar can learn to think like a historian or a mathematician.

We have already mentioned (Chapter 6) some of the problems inherent in the so-called spiral curriculum, a system that teaches children the same con-

The spiral curriculum: some problems

The difficulty in
teaching abstractions

cepts, with increasing sophistication, throughout their entire schooling. The difficulties, especially at the elementary level, are enormous. The cognitive structure of elementary-age children makes it difficult for them to understand abstract concepts, and therefore they tend to translate the abstractions into concrete terms and miss the connections altogether. Piaget has said that Bruner's statement "has always filled me with the deepest wonderment." Imagine, for a moment, trying to teach a three- or four-year-old the structure of algebra or the idea that historical knowledge is relative and biased.

Nor is the educational problem strictly limited to the elementary ages. Much secondary-school material is based on the assumption that all teenagers can make use of formal operations. We have already noted (Chapter 10) that over 50 percent of secondary-age pupils never fully achieve cognitive maturity (Kohlberg's fifth and sixth stages). This means that they are unable to translate and understand the abstractions of the spiral curriculum. Model-two teaching, though it has a laudable objective, rests on a doubtful assumption. There is a difference between assuming the ability to think abstractly and carefully creating a series of experiences that will nurture and promote the development of this ability. Teaching to reveal the abstract structure of the disciplines too often results in a mismatch between the curriculum on the one hand and the pupils on the other.

Thus, as was the case with Model One, Model Two suffers from certain deficiencies. In evaluating Model Two, it is important to recognize that the difficulty is not really with the instructional method—so called discovery teaching or inductive learning is a useful technique. The problem is with the assumption that children can grasp the idea that each subject-matter discipline has a unique structure. This assumes that pupils can develop a meta-structure (or super framework) to understand both the frame of reference and the process of inquiry across a variety of disciplines.

MODEL THREE: INTERPERSONAL LEARNING

While the first and most common teaching model emphasizes learning the facts and the second stresses the discovery of concepts, the third and most recent model stresses the development of warm human relationships between teacher and pupil. If the teacher can convey a genuine affection and empathy, a warm, facilitative classroom climate will be created, and the pupils will take it from there. The quality of the human interaction, especially the degree to which the teacher treats the pupils with sincerity and honesty, is the key to creating the best environment for learning.

Teaching as a process
of interpersonal
relationships

A leading exponent of this third model is Carl Rogers. Rogers has said that teaching as deliberate instruction is a vastly overrated function. The educator should instead concentrate much more attention on creating the conditions that will promote experiential learning. Rogers emphasizes experience and feeling, rather than thinking or reading as the proper pathway to knowledge—an odd thought, no doubt, as you sit reading a textbook! Rogers is convinced that traditional learning is so impersonal, cold, and aloof that it really goes in one ear and out the other. According to him, we learn only what is really important and relevant to us as people. In his classic work *Freedom to Learn*, Rogers presents three necessary and sufficient conditions for the promotion of learning: empa-

Carl Rogers, a leading exponent of interpersonal learning.

thy; unconditional positive regard; and congruence, or genuineness. Empathy allows us to communicate to our pupils that we really understand the emotions they are experiencing, to accurately "read" their feelings. Unconditional positive regard allows us to accept our students for what they are without passing judgment. This acceptance is unconditional and involves none of the usual bargaining ("If you do this for me, then I will like you!"). Rogers repeatedly says that teachers must place no conditions on these relationships and must accept students without reservation. Congruence, or genuineness, means being "real," honest. Going through the motions and pretending we like children, or listening to their feelings and emotions half-heartedly is not enough.

If teachers provide these conditions, then, according to Rogers, the children will be free to learn. The natural makeup of children and teenagers is such that if we remove the inhibitions imposed by outside direction, then self-directed learning will follow.[2]

Model-three teaching is not as concerned as model one is with disseminating appropriate information, nor does it worry too much about understanding concepts or discovering the structures of a discipline. Model-three teaching is primarily concerned with human interaction. This may also be its major drawback.

We realize that classroom atmospheres are important; clearly, pupils have difficulty learning anything if the anxiety levels are high. Under such conditions our perception, how much we can "see," becomes narrow. Studies have shown that nonsupportive, critical, and negative classroom "climates" have adverse psychological and physiological effects on the pupils: heart beats increase, the Galvanic Skin Response (GSR is a scientific term for sweaty palms, etc.) goes up, the Resistance Level (measured in ohms) increases. In the psychological domain, the pupil's self-concept as a learner decreases and self-direction in learning

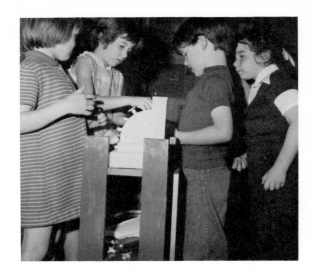

declines. Also, as one might expect, negative attitudes toward the teacher increase. Finally, and perhaps most importantly, the academic achievement of the pupils declines under the stressful directive-critical teaching atmospheres. Even their voice tones—both the content of what pupils say as well as how they say it—reveal differences clearly in favor of supportive classroom atmospheres. Thus the quality of the interpersonal relationship between the teacher and pupils does impact many facets of classroom interaction, and how much the pupil actually learns is related.[3]

On the other hand, we cannot necessarily conclude that teaching and learning can be explained exclusively by the three Rogerian conditions. We can all think of examples from our own experience where ideas, directions, and other types of academic content were important, and a skeptic might be quick to conclude that love alone is not enough. We are not suggesting either extreme. Obviously unconditional positive regard is not sufficient; but just as obviously, such facilitating conditions are important and necessary.

All three models—the transmittal of knowledge, revealing the structure of the discipline, and interpersonal learning—are important to the classroom teacher, and effective teaching demands a combination of the three. Certainly it would be a mistake to depend exclusively on any one.

SUMMARY OF THE THREE MODELS

There is obviously something to be said in favor of all three of these models. But we would be making a great mistake if we decided that teaching was exclusively any one of these models. The most important thing to remember is that teaching—the management of learning, of helping others grow and develop both cognitively and emotionally—is an extraordinarily difficult and complex task. It is not to be taken lightly or entered into on a lark. Since we are dealing with other people's lives, we must realize that we are facing both a great responsibility and a great challenge. To place these problems in some perspective, we now turn to the question of teaching objectives and the problem of what to teach.

EDUCATIONAL OBJECTIVES: THE PROBLEM OF WHAT TO TEACH

Even though we may realize that effective teaching probably requires inputs from each of three models, the question of objectives remains. What objectives do we want to achieve in teaching anybody anything?

A few years ago, this very question was given perhaps its best portrayal in _The Saber-Tooth Curriculum_, a book written under the pen name of J. Abner Peddiwell. It was a spoof, but it made its point most dramatically and effectively. In Paleolithic times a tribe developed an educational curriculum based on survival needs. The young were taught how to scare away saber-toothed tigers with firebrands, how to club woolly horses for clothing, and how to fish with their hands. However, as time passed and the Ice Age began, the survival needs changed: the tigers caught cold and died, the woolly horses ran away, and the fish disappeared in muddy water. In their places came big, ferocious bears that weren't scared by firebrands, a herd of antelope that could run like the wind (the woolly horses had been slow-footed and clumsy), and new fish that hid in the muddy water. It soon occurred to the tribe that their educational curriculum was, in today's parlance, not relevant. Scaring tigers, clubbing horses, and catching fish by hand were relics of the old days. The tribe now needed to

Carl R. Rogers

Born at the turn of the century in a Chicago suburb, Carl Rogers spent his early years deciding how to focus his career. In 1919 his first interest at the University of Wisconsin was in scientific farming. Simultaneously he was extremely active in church work, including attendance at a Christian youth conference in Peking, China. Upon his return to this country he shifted his undergraduate major to history. He felt that such a change was more in line with his emerging desire to go into evangelical work. He received an A.B. in history in 1924 from Wisconsin. Ironically, in view of his subsequent eminence in the field, he had but a single academic course in psychology as an undergraduate, and that by correspondence.

To prepare for the ministry, Rogers attended Union Theological Seminary in New York. There he began to change his emphasis once again, in this case from the dogma of religion to more general questions concerning the nature of the helping relationship. His interest in the healthy personal and psychological development of each person as an individual became more important than the formal, organized practice of religion. It was here that one of his key concepts took shape, the unique and special nature of "person-hood." Much later this idea was actualized with the establishment of his famous Center for Studies of the Person. With this shift in focus, it was not surprising for Rogers to transfer from Union to Columbia Teachers College. He received his Ph.D. in 1931, having spent much of his time doing field work in Rochester, New York, with the city's child study department for the prevention of cruelty to children.

His interest in preventive treatment for mental-health problems, another lifelong theme of his professional career, had its roots in this early work. One of the major difficulties that psychological treatment as a concept has grappled with almost from its inception has been this matter of preventive treatment. To provide help after a person becomes emotionally upset, or treatment after the fact, had been a major model of psychotherapy. It was really borrowed from the practice of medicine. Psychological help, then, in this view, takes the form of diagnosis, prognosis, treatment, and the cure process. People with problems would be classed into categories of mental illness, become patients, and, if the psychotherapy was successful, would be cured. Rogers felt almost from the beginning that this approach

had severe limitations. Diagnostic categories easily became negative labels. Focusing on mental disturbance could cause therapists to overlook the positive forces for growth inside each person. Treatments designed to help people often encouraged dependency or became a purchase of friendship. Rogers waged a long battle with the traditional psychological and psychiatric establishment on these issues. From his view, it was most important to prevent personal problems from being treated as long-term mental illness. An ounce of prevention is always worth more than a pound of cure. In this vein, he tried to develop counseling techniques that would encourage the positive growth forces within each human. To grow psychologically strong people was his answer to the treatment question.

Essentially the entire career of Carl Rogers has been a pilgrim's progress toward the goal of personhood for all. After spending almost a decade at the Rochester Clinic, he moved into the university setting, first at Ohio State from 1940 to 1945 and then at the University of Chicago. At Chicago he created a now-famous client-centered counseling agency for the university. With this as a laboratory, he began to

provide not only a significant new approach to college counseling, but also established a research base to document his work. He was the first counselor therapist to tape-record his sessions. By analyzing the actual transcripts of the counseling interactions he was able to dispel many of the myths surrounding psychological treatment. He was not well received by the more orthodox establishment. His openness in providing a public record of counseling challenged therapists to examine their own work and attest to its effectiveness. Up to that time, treatment failures were almost always blamed on the patient. If the patient didn't get well, there were three possible explanations: he might be too disturbed, he might be untreatable, or he might have a chronically weak ego. Rogers was able to show that many treatment problems were actually derived from the therapists. Research on the counseling process began to show that particular conditions were absolutely essential if the person was to be helped. In a series of significant research studies started first at Chicago and then moved to Madison, Wisconsin, Rogers concluded that three conditions represented the core of the therapeutic relationship: unconditional positive regard,

empathy, and congruence (these are explained in the text). The famous Rogerian triad became the central ingredient in the helping process. What was true for psychotherapy, he felt, applied equally to counseling and teaching.

Throughout his career, he has stressed the importance of the quality of interpersonal relationships, that how we relate to each other as human beings is central to the development of the person. Too often, he would say, we neglect this fundamental truism. Just as John Dewey can be thought of as the major

proponent of education as a democratic ideal, so Carl Rogers can be viewed as a lifelong fighter to democratize counseling and psychotherapy. He saw and still sees today the need to develop equal and genuine relationships between people. The ability to help and care, according to Rogers, is an important resource within each human being, and we all have a responsibility to use it, as part of our mutual human interdependence. His work has always focused on that goal. In his invited address to the American Psychological Association

in 1972 he once again challenged psychologists to move out of a narrow scientific and even narrower professional stance and teach the principles of healthy growth to all people. "If we did away with 'the expert,' the 'certified professional,' the 'licensed psychologist,' we might open our profession to a breeze of fresh air, to a surge of creativity, such as it has not known for years." Now in his seventh decade, Carl Rogers still stands for the same principles of helping and caring in interpersonal relations.

learn how to trap bears, snare antelopes, and build fish nets. However, the "educational establishment" of the tribe declared in august tones:

> Don't be foolish . . . . We don't teach fish-grabbing to grab fish; we teach it to develop a generalized agility which can never be developed by mere training (in net-making). We don't teach horse-clubbing to club horses; we teach it to develop a generalized strength in the learner which he can never get from so prosaic and specialized a thing as antelope-snare setting. We don't teach tiger-scaring to scare tigers; we teach it for the purpose of giving that noble courage. . . .[4]

The debate of educational objectives has a long history. The controversy usually covers the same terrain; namely, advocates of teaching skills for survival are in opposition to those who would teach for intrinsic and general education. Each side has some merit. We certainly do need to learn survival skills, but if that is all we learn, it is obvious our skills are destined to become obsolete. Critics compare this approach to training a generation of dinosaurs, animals which, because of their inability to adapt to changing times, were unable to survive.

Teaching for survival skills or for general education

On the other hand, proponents of learning for its own sake claim that a "classical education" will train the mind for disciplined thought. Mind training could never become obsolete, because skills we have developed can be brought to bear on any problem we meet in life. However, as you may recall from Chapter 2, E. L. Thorndike conducted a series of studies showing that the theory of mind training through the study of Greek and Latin was false. Such learning did not generalize.

Learning for its own sake

EDUCATIONAL GOALS: BLOOM'S TAXONOMY

Thus education has always been unable to decide between those who advocate a curriculum of relevance and those who desire a program of general education. In the mid-1950s a team led by Professor Benjamin Bloom of the University of Chicago bravely decided to settle the matter once and for all, and developed the now famous taxonomy, or classification, of educational objectives.[5]

Categories of teaching objectives

Bloom felt that one of the major difficulties confronting anyone interested in education had to do with the definition of goals; that is, what we want to strive for as teachers, counselors, or educational administrators. If you ask any of your friends to define their goals as teachers, you are likely to receive either an impossibly abstract statement ("I want to help students realize their full potential as individuals—to become self-actualizing"), or some very explicit and narrow statement ("My job is to teach the multiplication tables").

Bloom examined this problem of considering educational objectives from either an impossibly cosmic or hopelessly trivial point of view. He came up with a scheme that classifies educational objectives and relates each objective to specific classroom procedures. Bloom's approach has a very healthy effect in that it forces teachers to specify their goals and the means of getting there; it fits procedures and materials to instructional strategies. Bloom's system also specifies a sequence of stages or levels of objectives that are matched to a sequence

The problem: cosmic objectives or trivial goals

of assessment strategies. We will describe each of the six levels of his system by defining their content and briefly discussing their associated assessment procedures.

Level one: basic knowledge

Level one: teaching facts

Definition.   Students are responsible for information, ideas, material, or phenomena. They have to know specific facts, terms, and methods.

Assessment.   Direct questions and multiple-choice tests. The object is to test the students' ability to recall the facts, to identify and repeat the information provided. The teacher doesn't ask the students to form new judgments or to analyze ideas; he or she simply tries to find out how much material they can recall. When Piaget said that "to know by heart is not really to know," he was referring to this level of knowing.

Level two: comprehension

Level two: facts plus some comprehension

Definition.   Students must show they understand the material, ideas, facts, and theories.

Assessment.   A variety of procedures are applicable. Students can restate the material in their own words, reorder or extrapolate ideas, predict or estimate. In other words, at this level students are assessed on the basis of their capacity to act upon, or process, information. Assessment at this level requires more activity from the pupil than assessment at level one. Objective or multiple-choice questions can still be used, but they would be of a different order, since they must provide evidence that the pupils have some understanding or comprehension of what they are saying.

Level three: application

Level three: applying ideas and facts

Definition.   Students must be able to apply their knowledge to real situations. At level two we are satisfied if they understand their ideas. At level three we want them to demonstrate that they can actually apply their ideas correctly.

This particular level has been one of the stumbling blocks of educational psychology itself. In Chapter 2 we raised the question of why, after fifty years, the mode of classroom teaching has changed so little. We also cited the research showing the predominance of what we called trivia in the classroom. Educational psychology, as a field, contains much basic knowledge (level one) and understands much of it (level two), but has been unable to apply the ideas to real situations (level three). The application of knowledge is critical because it means putting knowledge into action, rather than merely talking about what might be done.

Assessment.   We have to go well beyond the usual procedures in order to assess how well students apply what they learn. If, for example, we are teaching them to play volleyball, the test would be obvious: put them on either side of a net and evaluate their performance. It is easy to see whether children can apply their knowledge of addition or subtraction: just give them some money, have them "buy" things in a mock store, and see if they end up with the correct change. Or, in geometry, have them construct a right-angled triangle out of wood and then measure the length of each side. In physics children can wire a bell and see whether or not it will ring. The one drawback, however, to tests of this sort is the possibility that pupils may learn by rote how to apply the information. The teacher needs to be aware of this possibility and to vary application tests to ensure that pupils can genuinely put their knowledge into practice.

Unfortunately, testing for application at advanced levels of courses in the humanities is more complicated. In fact, it is interesting to note that Bloom and his associates could find no examples from the humanities. Perhaps as we develop more active methods of teaching in the humanities, we will find it possible to test applications.

Examples of assessment

Level four: analysis

Definition.   Analysis is essentially a more advanced aspect of level two (comprehension). Analysis requires that pupils classify or break material down into its components, understand the relationship between the components, and recognize the principle that organizes the structure or the system. (As you can see, it becomes increasingly difficult to describe the levels, as we move from the simple and the concrete to the complex and abstract.)

Level four: classification and organizing principles

Assessment.   The ability to analyze material can be assessed in a number of ways. For example, we might see whether students can identify the assumptions behind an argument or a debate. For example, an advocate of the use of preventive nuclear war might argue that "in times of extreme danger, with national survival at stake, a country has to defend itself by striking and destroying the enemy, before the enemy attacks it." Students would be asked to identify the assumption from which his argument is constructed. In order to analyze the statement, students would have to ask some of the following questions: How extreme is the danger? Does the end (survival) justify the means (a nuclear war)? In everyday language, this kind of analysis is called critical thinking. Critical thinking allows us to separate fact from opinion and to compare theories so that we can take a position based on logic. Piaget's stage of formal operations involves just this kind of logical thinking.

Learning to separate facts from opinions and theories

Level five: objective synthesis

Definition.   The educational objective at level five is to learn to synthesize material. This means making something new, bringing ideas together to form a new theory, going beyond what is now known, providing new insights. This is a "tall order," since it means guiding pupils beyond our own level of understanding— to help them create new ideas and outgrow ours!

Level five: building new knowledge

Assessment.   Assessment should be designed to produce new ideas, methods, or procedures. Some obvious examples might be writing an original short story, play, or poem; painting a picture; composing music. In other areas, term papers or essays might be vehicles for synthesis. Unfortunately, it is often difficult to judge whether an essay or term paper is a genuine synthesis, one that is indeed a novel or creative approach to a topic. We will devote more space to the question of creativity in Chapter 18; for now, it is enough to remember that creativity itself is a highly subjective matter and very difficult to measure. You might just see whether or not you find yourself saying, "Now, why didn't I think of that?" One of the major rewards of teaching comes when we realize that one of our pupils is breaking new ground, advancing our knowledge.

Level six: objective evaluation

Level six: value judgments

Definition.   Level six, the learning of value judgments, involves all the previous levels to some degree. Pupils are developing the ability to create standards of judgment, to weigh, to examine, to analyze, and most of all, to avoid hasty judgment. Evaluation requires a lengthy process of scholarly care, of minute examination.

Assessment.   Although it may sound circular, it is possible to evaluate evaluation—there are standards for judging the way others pass judgments. For example, we can judge the performance of an umpire at a baseball game (the fans, managers, and players do so all the time). In the same way, we can judge the performance of a trial judge, or a labor arbitrator, or a newspaper editor. It is possible, but it is also difficult. Chapter 16 presents some of the means we have for judging the adequacy of assessment procedures and, since the procedures are special, we will postpone our discussion of level-six assessment to that chapter.

RELATION BETWEEN BLOOM'S TAXONOMY AND DEVELOPMENTAL STAGES

Although Bloom and his associates did not directly connect their objectives to developmental and Piagetian cognitive stages, there is an implicit relationship. Bloom's levels one, two, and three—basic knowledge and facts, comprehension, and application—are all clearly within the grasp of elementary-age concrete thinkers. When we reach levels four, five, and six, we are moving toward the need for symbolic and logical thinking in Piaget's formal-operations sense. As you read the descriptions of the style of thinking required at these levels, you realize the importance of a careful instructional sequence to promote the growth of abstract thinking. We cannot assume that adolescents are automatically able to use formal operations at Bloom's levels four to six without deliberate teaching toward these objectives.

DAVID HUNT AND DEVELOPMENTAL EDUCATIONAL OBJECTIVES

The recent work of David Hunt represents a more direct connection between educational objectives and developmental stages. Hunt, along with a colleague, Edward Sullivan, has been able to specify the interaction between the conceptual level of the pupils and the expectations, learning atmospheres, and conceptual

Benjamin Bloom

This eminent psychologist and scholar was born in 1913. After completing his undergraduate work and master's degree at Penn State, Professor Bloom moved to the University of Chicago. He was named instructor of educational psychology in 1940, completed his Ph.D. in 1942, and has remained there for over thirty years. He rose through the ranks to a full professorship, all the while building a reputation for careful and significant scholarship. His insistence on precision in educational thought soon led to the now-famous taxonomy for educational objectives in both the cognitive and affective domains, scholarship that literally revolutionized the process of lesson planning for classroom teaching. His category system soon became the standard for describing objectives and the process of achieving those specified goals. Not content to rest on these laurels, Professor Bloom next stepped into the raging controversy concerning the nature of intelligence. His scholarship and care were once more tested. He published the classic *Stability and Change in Human Characteristics*, in which he attempted to resolve the nature versus nurture controversy. His work clearly indicated the significance of early experience and the critical nature of early learning as factors that promote intellectual growth. A lifetime of significant scholarship for educational psychology perhaps best sums up his valuable contributions to the field.

Hunt and Sullivan's
three-stage frame-
work

level of the teachers. We have stressed throughout this text that a developmental approach to education means we have to look both ways, so to speak: at the pupils and their levels of development, and at the teachers. Hunt and Sullivan suggest that if it is important to assess the levels of the pupils, it is equally important to assess the levels of the teachers (and as we will note later, the level of the curriculum material itself). Thus Hunt and Sullivan present a three-stage framework for educational objectives and instructional strategies.[6]

Conceptual level proceeds through three general stages, characterized as follows:

> *Stage A—Concrete thought.*   Need for high structure. Careful directions, explicit instructions. Dependent on external direction. Easily confused passive acceptance of fate control.

> *Stage B—Complex and abstract thought emerges.*   Convergent thinking. Conformist. Recall and comprehension important. Empirical orientation. Follow the rules. Orderly, quiet, and attentive.

> *Stage C—Multiple frames of reference at symbolic/abstract level.*   Compare and contrast two or more concepts. Employ a variety of points of view. Low structure. Creative and interdependent.

Young children tend to think very concretely (Stage A) and need careful and explicit directions. Pupil "growth" proceeds in a developmental sequence from concrete to abstract, from simple to complex, and from being dependent on others toward self-direction. Most importantly, Hunt and Sullivan show that such developmental growth *does* depend on how the teacher structures the learning experiences. To facilitate the pupils' achieving increased levels of intellectual complexity, teachers need to match the learning tasks with the actual developmental functioning of the pupils. Thus for Stage A pupils, teachers need to provide high structure, explicit assignments, frequent feedback, and consistent

and concrete rewards. For Stage C pupils, of course, a significantly different environment, characterized by low structure, substantial freedom for pupils to develop their own assignments, less-frequent feedback, and more abstract and intrinsic rewards, would be required.

Perhaps most significantly, Hunt and Sullivan have found that if the teachers themselves are at the more complex levels (Stage C), they can more effectively adapt the learning tasks to match the pupils' needs. Teachers at these higher stages were able to respond to the individual differences of pupils, use a greater variety of learning tasks, adapt their teaching to changing conditions, and were less distractable and more empathic. This last point needs special emphasis: the more-effective teachers were not only more intellectually flexible, but also more responsive interpersonally.

More-effective teachers were more responsive interpersonally

The Hunt-Sullivan framework is unusually important because it demonstrates (1) a sequence of educational objectives, and (2) the relationship between what and how the teacher teaches and pupil learning.

WILLIAM PERRY AND DEVELOPMENTAL EDUCATIONAL OBJECTIVES

Working independently of Hunt and Sullivan and with a different population of students, William Perry has also provided significant new insights into the identification of stage-related educational objectives and instructional strategies. Although Perry's original work was based on a college-age population, the overall framework has implications for the full range of pupils (K–college).[7]

Perry's system employs four general levels of intellectual complexity.

1

Single frame of reference—concrete. Material, essay questions, readings, etc., at this level are highly specific and literal, calling for few abstractions or inferences. Answers are either totally correct or totally wrong. "Name the state capitals." "How many ships did Columbus and crew sail in?"

2

Multiple frame of reference—concrete. Material at this level is the same as at level one except that two or more frames of reference are employed. The questions still call for concrete facts and descriptions but do not call for interpretations, theorizing, critical analysis, or comparisons. "Compare Achilles and Superman." "Name the state capitals, dates of admission, and chief products." "Describe the five causes of World War One." "Name Kohlberg's stages of moral development and Piaget's stages of cognitive development."

3

Single frame of reference—abstract. Material at this level employs abstractions and inferences, and distinguishes between facts and theories, from one frame of reference. Answers are graded by degree of comprehensiveness. How adequate, logical, and consistent are the explanations and assumptions? "Show that westward expansion in the nineteenth century was manifest destiny only in a Machiavellian sense." "Describe the major theoretical assumption of Piaget's conception of intellectual growth." "Critically analyze Rousseau's conception of the general will." "Describe Shakespeare's conception of a tragic hero."

4

Multiple frame of reference—abstract.   Material at this level is similar to level three except that multiple frames of reference are employed. These questions call for the ability to analyze the comparative explanatory power of multiple theoretical frames of reference. "Compare the conceptions of national leadership exemplified by Catherine the Great, Queen Elizabeth the Second, and Cleopatra." "Present a case study of a child according to Freudian theory, Skinnerian constructs, and common sense." "Describe and compare the author's conception of a tragic hero in *Death of a Salesman, Go Ask Alice,* and *Julius Caesar.*" "Compare and contrast the wave theory to the particle theory in the transmission of light."

As was the case with Hunt and Sullivan, Perry also included assessments of the learning environment. Instead of actually "testing the teachers," however, Perry assessed the conceptual complexity of the learning tasks by rating the examination questions. This is an important point, for it reminds us of the necessity of examining the pupil (where he or she is coming from) as well as the conceptual level of the tasks we are asking the pupil to learn. Perry reviewed the final-examination questions and rated them by subject matter. Since all the questions were from the Harvard College files, it was not surprising that most called for abstract answers. However, it was surprising to note the significant shift over the sixty-year span examined to a greater percentage of questions requiring abstract thinking from multiple frames of reference—from less than 10 percent in 1900 to 50 percent in 1960. Also noteworthy are the differences according to specific subject-matter disciplines. Government (or political science) demonstrated the most significant increase in questions calling for the most-complex level of thinking, while English literature and foreign languages showed the smallest shift.

Perry's levels of intellectual complexity

To familiarize yourself with the levels of intellectual complexity, you may wish to try categorizing the following essay questions as representing:

A. Single frame of reference and concrete
B. Multiple frame of reference and concrete
C. Single frame of reference and abstract
D. Multiple frame of reference and abstract

1. Name the state capitals, dates of admission, and chief products.

2. Compare Marilyn Monroe, Ethel Kennedy, and Golda Meir.

3. How are pity and sorrow the same; how are they different?

4. Outline the critical dates leading to the Revolutionary War.

5. Write a letter to Sam Adams explaining the Tory point of view.

6. Compare the conception of tragic hero in Achilles and Willie Loman.

7. Compare Holden Caulfield and Alice (in *Go Ask Alice*).

8. Compare the shifting social roles of women in *Florence Nightingale, The Autobiography of Jane Pittman,* and Xaviera Hollander.

9. Describe the wave theory in reference to the transmission of light.

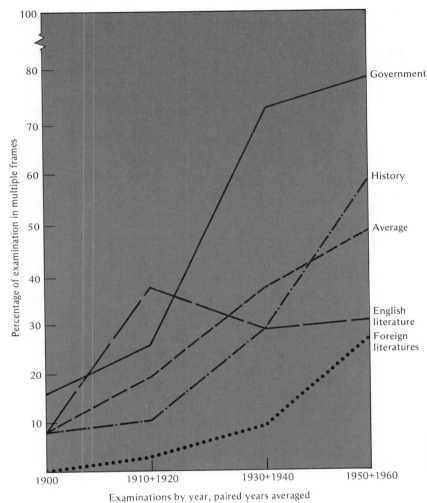

Harvard College examination questions, charted over a sixty-year span.

10. Show westward expansion was manifest destiny.

11. Describe the impact of westward expansion from the points of view of Native Americans, Hungarian railroad workers, and the Harriman family. Include social, ethical, and economic considerations.

12. Compare the dilemmas confronted by J. Robert Oppenheimer, Rose Mary Wood, Adolf Eichmann, and Antigone. Compare their responses.

13. Compare *The Exorcist, The Crucible,* and *The Diary of Anne Frank* in terms of the concept of free will and feminine development.

Answers: 1(A), 2(B), 3(D), 4(A), 5(C), 6(D), 7(B), 8(D), 9(C), 10(C), 11(D), 12(D), 13(D).

Table 14.1 Summary: stages of intellectual development.

Approximate chronological age	Bloom	Piaget (Bruner)	Perry	Hunt and Sullivan
Elementary-school ages, grades K–5	Rote memory Concrete under-standing	Concrete operations (iconic)	Concrete single frame	Stage A
	Application		Concrete multiple frame	
Early adolescence, grades 6–9	Analysis	Formal operations (symbolic)	Abstract single frame	Stage B
Late adolescence, early adult, "grades" 10–Adult	Synthesis Evaluation		Abstract multiple frame	Stage C

As you can readily see, questions differ qualitatively across these conceptual levels as to what the pupil is expected to "know." Yet the developmental frameworks do share logical similarities. Table 14.1 attempts to connect these various frames of reference as systems of understanding levels of intellectual development. (The table itself, then, is hopefully an example of Bloom's synthesis, Perry's multiple frames, and Hunt and Sullivan's Stage C.) Also, for purposes of recall, we have included reference to Piaget's stages of concrete and formal operations as well as Bruner's iconic and symbolic phases.

ASSESSING THE PUPIL'S CONCEPTUAL LEVEL

From a logical standpoint, the various theoretical perspectives are obviously related, even though, as we have pointed out repeatedly, all the theorists mentioned have worked independently, in widely different parts of the globe, with different assessment procedures, and employing dissimilar research populations. To summarize all these systems does some violence to each, yet from a broad perspective it may be useful to combine the strands into a general framework representing stages of intellectual growth as well as educational objectives. This framework then becomes a useful means of locating children in terms of the system of thinking they currently employ in processing information. A critical step for you as the teacher is to identify the system of thinking each pupil uses in problem-solving situations. Open-ended inquiry, probing questions, listening for assumptions, asking for clarification—all are helpful in pinpointing the pupil's thinking process. Also remember that conceptual development does not necessarily proceed completely in all domains simultaneously. A junior- or senior-high pupil may be adept at high levels of abstraction in mathematics, or history, but have difficulty in understanding poetic symbolism. Similarly, in a course such as

Conceptual development does not proceed in all domains simultaneously educational psychology, some college and graduate students can think abstractly about the nature of child development, yet revert to concrete thinking when statistics are involved. Thus you can expect some unevenness in conceptual development by subject areas from your pupils.

ASSESSING THE CONCEPTUAL LEVEL OF THE CURRICULUM

Since Piaget has stressed the interactive nature of development, the teacher needs to examine the assumptions and level of abstraction of the curriculum materials, in addition to assessing the conceptual level of the pupils. A developmental approach forces us, as educators, to consider the pupils and the learning tasks simultaneously. Remember that Perry examined the conceptual level of the final-examination questions at Harvard as an indicator of the actual conceptual level of that learning task.

In other words, one can take a "piece" of curriculum material, examine the content, and place it on the conceptual-level scheme according to assumptions and level of intellectual complexity. In the next section, we provide examples of such ratings to help you understand how to logically analyze the conceptual structure of learning tasks.

ETHICAL DEVELOPMENT AND EDUCATIONAL OBJECTIVES

As noted previously, education by definition is not value free or neutral. Curriculum materials, teaching procedures, readings, and films all to a greater or lesser degree teach values. Certainly, a free democratic society clearly rests on a very explicit value structure; to be an informed and intelligent democratic citizen means that we value principles of social justice, the consent of the governed, a free press, and equal rights and opportunities—the basic construct of a democratic constitution. A free public-school system, supported by public funds, is, at least ostensibly, designed as an instrument to teach pupils how to function effectively in a democratic society. This process includes both rational and ethical domains or, as philosophers would say, the epistomology and the axiology—how we know something and how we value. Thus, in addition to the so-called intellectual domain, or levels of conceptual development, we need to consider the ethical domain.

Education by definition is not value free or neutral

The recent work of Kohlberg (see Chapter 10) and the earlier theory of Dewey suggest a framework for categorizing levels of ethical development. A brief review follows with reference to ethical level and general conceptions of human development.

A framework for categorizing levels of ethical development

Level one: "Might makes right," humans and subhumans. At this level, the conception of social justice is stark and direct: an eye for an eye, big fish eat little fish, justice equals the fastest gun.

Level two: Humans as objects of exploitation. At this level, people are deliberately exploited for profit. The concept of social justice is based on a trading mentality. Humans are to serve as instruments of pleasure and/or profit for society's ruling class.

Level three: Social conventions, stereotyped thinking as justice. Ethical development at this level is largely reflected by the predominant social conventions of the middle-class majority. Middle-class culture is seen as "right," because it's what everyone really wants. Some concern with empathy and a developing recognition of the importance of feelings can be detected.

Level four: Laws and fixed standards and codes. Ethical thinking at this level is based on societal standards and laws rather than just social conventions. The standards are usually legislated, abstract guidelines intended to regulate human behavior. Positive aspects of law and tradition are stressed; justice is seen as following the law. Ultimately, the individual is expected to respect and follow the law.

Level five: Laws and rules as a system for social justice. At this level, individual laws are not seen as unchanging, but rather as part of a flexible, evolving system. A given law may be unjust, and ethical thinking involves changing and challenging "unjust" laws.

Level six: Ethical standards are based on universal principles of justice. Ethics at this level involve conceptions of universal principles, such as the "Golden Rule," respect for human personality, or belief in the essential dignity of human beings.

Decisions are made in accord with such principled standards.

ASSESSING ETHICAL LEVELS

In a manner similar to conceptual-level assessment, you can evaluate the system of ethical thinking a person employs by learning to listen to the assumptions he or she uses to justify and/or defend a particular view. By careful inquiry, probing, posing open-ended questions, and asking for clarification, you will be able to "hear" the system or frame of reference as an indication of "where the person is coming from."

For example, a person's ethical level and their belief in democratic principles could be easily pinpointed by their reaction to the statements on page 377.

You could similarly detect a person's general attitude toward other groups by retaining this format and simply replacing the phrase "retarded/handicapped" with blacks, Native Americans, women, Chicanos, or others. At a more complex level, you could ask the person to explain why he or she takes such a position and how they think and feel about particular issues.

The same framework is also applicable to general curriculum materials. For example, specific ethical principles are clearly embedded in many works of literature and films. Also, clear differences in the levels of principles can be noted. For example, the ethical assumptions in a novel like *The Exorcist* reinforce the idea that twelve-year-old girls are susceptible to the devil, that ghosts and demons are real, that intuitive and preoperational thinking is higher and more comprehensive than abstract symbolic and rational thought. Compare those ethical and intellectual assumptions with the thinking and behavior of the heroine in *The Diary of Anne Frank*. *The Diary* portrays a major ethical struggle

Specific ethical principles may be embedded in curriculum materials

Ethical Attitudes	Agree	Disagree
Retarded children don't value life the way normal pupils do.	———	———
Physically handicapped children shouldn't expect to be involved in sports programs in schools.	———	———
Schools should devote more resources to exceptionally bright and gifted children, since they will be future leaders.	———	———
It's only right that normal children do not have to mingle with grossly physically handicapped and slow learners.	———	———
Placing special-education pupils with regular pupils is a fine idea as long as it's not my child.	———	———
Handicapped and retarded pupils are happier in their own classes rather than trying to compete with regular children.	———	———

between a regime that believed in "demons," in the right of nations to punish and "waste" evil girls versus a conception of loyalty to a cause more just than blind obedience to fanaticism. If we examine curriculum materials, films, attitudes, perhaps even teaching styles themselves with the goal of identifying inherent assumptions, we shall have a clearer picture not only of the material's surface content, but of its subtler ethical content as well.

INTELLECTUAL AND ETHICAL DEVELOPMENT: A COMBINATION

By combining or synthesizing the intellectual and the ethical domains, we hope to provide you with a reference point for assessing the level of a pupil's current thinking, the level of the material you are using, and some of your own assumptions. This double framework hopefully will help you to more explicitly identify where you are in the teaching-learning process, as well as where you may want to go—i.e., your educational objectives.

The following examples from well-known works of literature should help to clarify this intellectual/ethical double vision. Remember that these ratings are to serve as illustrations of differences in both conceptual and ethical complexity. Also, they are only approximations and should by no means be considered absolute, fixed, or permanent. As indicated at the outset, this combination of developmental theories is itself only a first step toward a synthesis of ideas. We see it, obviously, as a promising trend, as useful for educational exploration, and as an open system that appears to have significant heuristic value in promoting exploration and examination of developmental concepts to guide teaching practice.

Summary: A Two-Way Analysis
Conceptual and Ethical Levels

Since neither domain by itself is really sufficiently comprehensive, we can suggest combining these to include ratings of conceptual level (1–6) on one axis *and* level of ethical development (1–6) on the other.

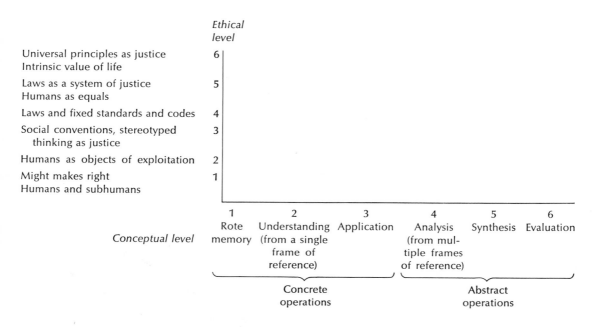

	Ethical level					
Universal principles as justice Intrinsic value of life	6					
Laws as a system of justice Humans as equals	5					
Laws and fixed standards and codes	4					
Social conventions, stereotyped thinking as justice	3					
Humans as objects of exploitation	2					
Might makes right Humans and subhumans	1					
	1 Rote memory	2 Understanding (from a single frame of reference)	3 Application	4 Analysis (from mul- tiple frames of reference)	5 Synthesis	6 Evaluation

Conceptual level

Concrete operations (under levels 1–3)   Abstract operations (under levels 4–6)

Examples from well-known works of literature to illustrate the two dimensions

Title	Conceptual level	Ethical level
1 *Kindergarten-elementary levels*		
Dr. Seuss Series	2 Highly concrete descriptions. Functional action oriented.	3 Tends to teach conventional, somewhat stereotyped roles for humans. More imaginative for animals.
Little Engine that Could	2 Single frame of reference. Concrete.	3 Success comes from simple hard work.
Lassie Series	4 Actually can be read at two or four depending on how much emphasis there is toward humane treatment of animals.	3 Humans in stereotyped roles. Women almost always "domestic."

Title	Conceptual level	Ethical level
Hardy Boy Series	2 Concrete, action oriented, mostly from a single frame of reference.	3 Stereotyped depiction of "good" versus "bad." Stereotyped roles for men and women.
Little Prince	4 or 5 Multiple levels of abstraction. Requires synthesis.	4 Abstract standards and laws.
Tom Sawyer	4 Understanding and analysis from multiple frames of reference. Imaginative depiction of "boyhood."	2 or 3 Adults in stereotyped roles. Minority persons depicted as subhuman.
Hans Brinker	2 or 3 Straightforward adventure story. Singular plot.	3 Overly simplistic view of "rags to riches."
The Exorcist	2 or 3 Magical and pseudo postrational thinking.	1 Deliberately designed to foster supernatural beliefs of ghosts and demons.
The Diary of Anne Frank	4 Presents ideas from a variety of views. Employs levels of abstraction on questions of human survival.	5 or 6 The struggle is between justice and might. Empathically portrayed.
Lord of the Flies	4 In-depth study of system of governance. Symbolic messages.	4 Without rigid enforcement of rules, anarchy awaits.
Gone With the Wind	4 Some in-depth analysis of the structure of the antebellum society in crisis.	3 or 4 Most characters (black and white) are highly stereotyped. Honor is generally more important than justice.

2
Secondary-school level:

Title	Conceptual level	Ethical level
Catcher in the Rye	4 or 5 Analysis and synthesis of a variety of concepts on adolescence.	4 Protagonist attempts to think on major issues beyond a conventional "level three."
To Kill a Mockingbird	4 or 5 Analysis and synthesis of abstract conceptions of human interdependence.	5 Father thinks and acts in accord with principles. Speaks of reasons "behind" laws.

Title	Conceptual level	Ethical level
Billy Budd	4 Analysis of abstract conceptions of military justice.	4 The captain refuses to break a law to save a life.
Mister Roberts	4 Analyzes a sailor's life during war time from multiple perspectives. Also examines the system of command.	5 Lead character consistently looks for reasons behind rules and exhibits empathy for all crew members.
The Crucible	4 or 5 Abstract levels of analysis on mixing religion and governance.	5 or 6 An object lesson in human exploitation and scapegoating.
Profiles in Courage	4 or 5 Analyzes and synthesizes questions of law and principle.	5 or 6 Main characters depict the lonely struggle of standing up for principles versus expediency.
Bridge on the River Kwai	4 or 5 Multiple frames of reference and abstract levels of analysis.	5 or 6 An object lesson on fanaticism and the destructive effects of blind obedience to a "cause."
Animal Farm	4 or 5 Heavy use of metaphors, multiple perspectives and levels of abstractions.	5 or 6 Demonstrates the corrupting effects of political power, pre-Watergate.
Streetcar Named Desire	4 Use of multiple perspectives and abstract levels in analyzing a family structure.	2 Women accept exploitation as their "lot." The female fantasy world is juxtaposed with the aggressive egocentric male world.
Sounder	4 Skillful use of multiple frames of references in analyzing a society.	5 or 6 Illustrates the injustice of Southern justice. Empathic portrayal of family relationships.

EDUCATIONAL OBJECTIVES AND THE INTELLECTUAL AND ETHICAL DOMAINS: A SUMMARY

To help you understand the pupil more fully, we have discussed some of the fundamental psychological needs of children and teenagers, growing at different rates through different stages of development, and in different domains—such as intellectual, physical, personal, and ethical. We have also stressed the importance of the teacher's role. How you view the learning-instructional process, your perception of pupils, your conception of "knowledge," your understanding of your own educational assumptions as you set objectives for pupils—all these aspects are critical determinants of whether the teaching-learning process is positive, developmental, and successful for both teachers and pupils.

At this point you may be saying to yourself, it all seems too complicated, the various theories don't seem to agree. How can I continuously monitor each child's progress, create positive learning atmospheres, stay up-to-date in my subject area, watch for development along three or four separate domains simultaneously, remain ever conscious of my own values—let alone keep up with the routine "traffic" duties of classroom management? Admittedly, it seems as if we are asking the impossible, like shooting baskets and holding your pants up at the same time or administering artificial respiration while you're still in the lake.

At a very general level, teaching and learning will always remain a paradox. Given the complexities of the teaching-learning situation we simply cannot resolve all of the apparent inconsistencies; in the language of organizational theories, the classroom will always be an "open-system" and can never be reduced to a formula or program. Thus the perspective we referred to at the outset is important: we must view the problems (and opportunities) from a series of successive approximations.

DELIBERATE INSTRUCTION AND LESSON PLANNING

As we have made clear, the question of what we teach to whom, as well as how we teach it from the educational objectives, is critically important. But we must not overlook the significance of teaching methods, the means of achieving our goals and objectives. After all, we cannot achieve our objectives by blind luck —we have to know how to get where we are going. The lesson plan is a kind of road map, containing a number of strategies or routes, any one of which may be appropriate on a given day with a particular class. In other words, it is an outline of ideas for making systematic use of classroom time. One danger associated with lesson planning is a tendency (especially for a beginning teacher) to stick too rigidly to the plan. After spending time working up a good unit, the teacher may feel duty-bound to cover every point in the exact order, no matter what. The following is a classic example of excessive rigidity.

The lesson plan as a road map—a series of routes

A beginning teacher was presenting a lesson he had just worked up. The lesson was titled "World War I Armaments: The Machine Gun." The objective was to convey level-one information (the technological development of a rapid-continuous-firing gun) and level-two comprehension (the effect of this new weapon on strategy). He wanted to show the students that the development of the machine gun helped create a stalemate. To emphasize his point, the teacher had assembled pictures showing infantry and cavalry futilely attempting to charge machine-gun nests and being cut to ribbons in the process.

However, as is almost always the case in good teaching, the presentation was making the pupils think. One boy in the third row raised his hand, "I see what you mean about the machine guns. It meant it was easier to defend than attack. But didn't that lead to the tank? Wasn't it near the end of the war that they brought tanks in?"

At this point the teacher got himself trapped in his own lesson plan. Since the subject was machine guns, he said brightly (after a few anxious moments of silence), "Yes, that's right, tanks were also introduced in World War I, and on top of each tank, they put a machine gun."*

Sticking too close to the lesson plan

But if sticking too close to the plan will make us miss a golden opportunity for learning, it is also risky to have no lesson plan at all. It has recently been fashionable to accuse the lesson plan of spoiling teaching. Anything that interferes with spontaneous interaction between teachers and pupils hinders growth. In this somewhat romantic view, the teacher must operate exclusively from intuition. Planning is equated with programing and is thus considered mechanical. It is also equated with structuring the class and is therefore seen as dehumanizing. The teacher as an authority is equated with the teacher as an authoritarian. And planning a lesson in advance, providing structure, or allowing the teacher to be an authority are all regarded as artificial barriers to learning. Instead, teachers are advised to reject structure, planning, and, indeed, their own authority and to replace all these things with what is called "flying by the seat of one's pants." "We do what the class feels like doing," a teacher might say.

The theory of spontaneous teaching is to some degree an overreaction to the rigid lesson plan. After all, if blind adherence to the lesson plan leads to rigid authoritarianism, then its total rejection can lead to classroom anarchy. Neither is appropriate. However tiresome, we still hear the same endless debates between these extremes: structure versus nonstructure, leading versus participating, planning versus spontaneity. Instead of joining either camp, we suggest the importance of avoiding both of them.

Nonplanning can lead to classroom anarchy

EFFECTIVE TEACHING

Effective teaching a synthesis

We can say by way of summary that effective teaching incorporates a series of different but related dimensions. It demands a combination of all three of the most common models: transmitting knowledge, teaching for the process of inquiry, and encouraging interpersonal relations. In terms of teaching objectives, especially for the first two models, Bloom's taxonomy can help us set our teaching goals according to the kind of understanding we want to develop, from elementary facts (level one) all the way to evaluation (level six). The way we teach and assess our teaching will depend on the level and goal we select. As for the lesson plan itself, it gives us a systematic and operational guide to follow in the classroom. It should never become the be-all and end-all of teaching. Unless teachers can translate the models and the obectives into practice in the real world of the classroom with real pupils, they will accomplish nothing.

THE LESSON PLAN IN ACTION: INDIRECT
TEACHING AND COGNITIVE FLEXIBILITY IN TEACHING

When we begin to translate our educational objectives to the classroom, we begin the teaching-learning process. The interaction of teachers, pupils, ideas, and emotions involves a complex of transactions almost as chaotic as a three-

---

*

We are indebted to Professor Ralph Mosher for relaying this classroom incident to us.

Ned Flanders: "Two major systems of teaching are actually practiced—direct teaching and indirect teaching."

ring circus. So much is going on at once that it is very difficult to observe a classroom, let alone direct the process.

In the complex world of teaching and learning at the operational level, educational psychology has started to produce some important findings. By far the most promising and comprehensive approach has been developed in the recent work of Professor Ned Flanders.

The Flanders system: indirect teaching

We noted earlier that educational research has come up with very few significant findings. We also noted the importance of studying the question of effective teaching, not in the laboratory with captive audiences (neither the white rat nor the college freshman recruited as a research subject), but in the natural setting, in the field of action. Flanders is part of a new wave of educational researchers who examine important questions in the natural classroom environment.

Flanders conducted a series of studies that led him to conclude that two major systems of teaching are actually practiced: direct teaching and indirect teaching. In direct teaching the teachers do almost all the talking—lecturing, giving directions, and justifying or explaining their own views. (Recall the studies we discussed in Chapter 2 that indicated that teachers tend to do almost all the

Direct vs. indirect teaching

talking in a class.) Flanders has found that direct teachers actually talk for about *85 percent* of each class period. Direct teaching is not only direct, it is also a monologue.

In indirect teaching, teachers ask open-ended questions that require more than rote responses. Indirect teachers also clarify student responses, praise and encourage the content, and accept/clarify feelings expressed.

Table 14.2 Categories for Flanders interaction analysis.

TEACHER TALK	**INDIRECT INFLUENCE**	**1** **Accepts feelings.** Accepts and clarifies the tone of feeling of the students in an unthreatening manner. Feelings may be positive or negative. Predicting or recalling feelings are included.
		2 **Praises or encourages.** Praises or encourages student action or behavior. Jokes that release tension, but not at the expense of another individual, nodding head and saying "um hm?" or "go on" are included.
		3 **Accepts or uses ideas of students.** Clarifies, builds, or develops ideas suggested by a student. As teacher brings more of his own ideas into play, shift to #5.
		4 **Asks questions.** Asks a question about content or procedure with the intent that the student answer.
	DIRECT INFLUENCE	**5** **Lecturing.** Gives facts or opinion about content or procedure; expresses his own ideas, asking rhetorical questions.
		6 **Giving directions.** Directs, commands, or orders that students are expected to comply with.
		7 **Criticizing or justifying authority.** Statements intended to change student behavior from unacceptable to acceptable pattern; bawling someone out; stating why the teacher is doing what he is doing; extreme self-reference.
STUDENT TALK		**8** **Student talk—response.** Talk by students in response to teacher. Teacher initiates the contact or solicits student statement.
		9 **Student talk—initiation.** Talk initiated by students. If "calling on" student is only to indicate who may talk next, observer must decide whether student wanted to talk.
		10 **Silence or confusion.** Pauses, short periods of silence, and periods of confusion in which communication cannot be understood by the observer.

From N. A. Flanders, *Analyzing Teacher Behavior* (Reading, Mass.: Addison-Wesley, 1970), p. 34. Reprinted by permission.

Flanders then compared the learning gains of students of indirect teachers with those of students of direct teachers. Where the predominant mode of teaching was indirect, he found that the pupils, when tested independently, showed greater gains in learning than did comparable groups where the direct mode was predominant. In other words, the academic achievement of pupils taught by the indirect mode was significantly greater than that of pupils taught by the direct mode, in scientific subjects (mathematics), in social-science subjects (social studies), and in the humanities (English). Also, students' attitudes toward school were more positive in the classes with indirect teaching. Flanders commented, "It appears that when classroom interaction patterns indicate that pupils have opportunities to express their ideas, and when these ideas are incorporated into learning activities, then the pupils seem to *learn more* and to develop *more positive attitudes toward the teacher and the learning activities.*"[8]

In six out of seven studies the same findings turned up. It seems that neither the academic discipline nor the quality of the pupils' intelligence makes a crucial difference (the statistical procedures adjusted all the classes to equivalence). Indirect teaching results in improved academic performance and an increase in positive student attitudes.

Evidence in favor of indirect teaching

The Flanders rating system is outlined in Table 14.2. As you can see, it is easy to understand and to use. In fact, you might try it yourself in your next class. Each time the teacher or a pupil says something, try to place the statement into one of the ten categories. After you get the hang of it, try it in some of your other classes. This will give you a picture of how your own teachers are instructing you. You might even try taping your own attempts to teach somebody and rating your own interaction. You don't have to be teaching a formal class—you could be giving an individual tutorial, helping a friend in educational psychology, or teaching someone to knit, dance, do fractions, or whatever. Your purpose would be to examine the ratio of your talk and the pupil's talk to see whether you use up all the time yourself and to see whether you use the direct or the indirect method. After you have tried it once or twice on yourself, deliberately try to change your patterns. If, for example, you find yourself using categories 5, 6, and 7—lecturing, giving directions, and criticizing—try to use categories 1, 2, 3, and 4 more frequently. If you can accomplish this, you should notice a change in the student-talk categories from 8 to 9, from response to initiation.

Applying Flanders to your own practice

Cognitive flexibility in teaching

Flanders' findings about the indirect mode are quite similar to what has been called cognitive flexibility in teaching. Flexibility in the classroom means the ability to think on your feet, to adapt and change teachng objectives to fit the classroom objectives and classroom interaction, and to respond to both the ideas and the feelings of the pupils.

Cognitive flexibility and indirect teaching

Flexibility also means not jumping to conclusions, keeping an open mind. Under conditions of stress and anxiety, cognitive flexibility allows us to keep our wits about us. Teachers who are not flexible literally do not see most of what goes on in their classroom; nor do they hear much of the interaction. Their perceptual field is so narrow that they are able to concentrate only on what they themselves are saying. Thus, the opposite of flexibility in teaching is a kind of

Born in 1918 and raised on the West Coast, Professor Flanders gradually migrated eastward. He completed an A.B. degree at the University of California in 1940 and a B.S. from Oregon State College in 1944. He then left the Coast and completely changed his field of academic interest. From his undergraduate work of chemistry and a B.S. in electrical engineering, he shifted to educational psychology, completing both a master's degree and a Ph.D. at the University of Chicago. He remained at Chicago for a brief period and then, from 1949 to 1962, he served as an assistant and then associate professor of educational psychology at the University of Minnesota.

It was during this period at Minnesota that his research focus matured. He began to successfully crack one of the most difficult problems in education—a theoretical and practical model to define teaching effectiveness. For years prior to his work, hundreds of research studies had been conducted in this area, almost always yielding insignificant results. Researchers had tried to correlate personality characteristics, temperamental traits, personal interests, cultural backgrounds, social and economic status, marital state, birth order, and similar variables to effective teaching performance. Attempts had also been made to relate measures of a teacher's "warmth" or knowledge of subject matter to effective performance in the classroom. These so-called characteristic studies produced very little valuable information; instead, the results were inconclusive and often contradictory. One study might find a small but statistically significant correlation between a trait such as "friendliness" and teaching effectiveness, and just as likely the next study would show no relationship.

When Flanders began to develop the concept of "direct" versus "indirect" teaching, he also started a series of field studies to test out the possible relationships. As we have noted in the text, his central findings remained consistent through a long series of studies. With various subject matters, different grade levels, and in different school settings, teachers employing "indirect" teaching styles were producing higher levels of academic learning in their pupils than were "direct" teachers.

As we move toward educational accountability, with the general public demanding increasing documentation of teaching effectiveness, the Flanders system gives evidence of becoming a major index of effective teaching. In 1962 Professor Flanders moved from Minnesota to the University of Michigan, where his work continued. He has published *Teaching with Groups* and *Analyzing Teacher Behavior*, as well as numerous articles reporting his research on teacher interaction analysis. In 1970 Flanders returned to California where he is currently directing the Far West Laboratory for research in teaching.

Ned A. Flanders

egocentric, or teacher-centered, performance, in which the pupils are pretty much left out of the learning process.

Studies conducted by one of the coauthors and a group of colleagues indicated that effective classroom teaching was directly related to cognitive flexibility.[9] The rating scales used to assess the degree of flexibility or rigidity of observed teacher performances are reproduced in Table 14.3. You will note that the descriptions of flexible behaviors (the left-hand column) are similar to Flanders' description of the indirect mode. In other words, it is probably fair to say that in order to operate in the indirect mode, one must be cognitively flexible. To accept the pupils' ideas and feelings, to listen to them well enough to be able to ask clarifying questions, to be open enough to follow up on "wrong" answers (help them see how they got off the track or misunderstood what you said)—to meet all these challenges in the heat of battle requires the kind of cognitive flexibility we have been describing. Teachers often report that there are days when things are popping out so fast and furiously that the classroom seems on the verge of revolution. At times like that, the teacher's ability to remain flexible meets its most severe test.

LEARNING TO TEACH

At this point you may say to yourself, "Okay, so I'll be flexible," and then march right into the classroom full of hope and eagerness only to fall flat on your face. A word of caution: it takes much practice and a great deal of support from friends and supervisors to reach the point where you can consistently maintain a focus on your pupils, tune in on their thinking, carefully analyze their comments as feedback, and modify your own objectives as you go along. It is hard enough to learn to listen to a single person, let alone twenty-five other people. It used to be said that great teachers are born, not made; yet that is surely over-simplifying matters. Certainly, it is difficult to learn new behaviors, especially when the behavior is so complex and when it is a natural human tendency to resist change. However, they can be learned, given the opportunity to practice and try out different approaches in the classroom.

Learning new teaching behaviors: a slow process

Practice must include a careful examination of your performance as soon as possible after each venture. The analysis of your own practice is the most valuable tool for improving your teaching. Without it, your teaching will remain pretty much as good or as bad as it was the first few trials. By tape-recording, or even better, videotaping your performance, you can go back over what you actually did and compare it to your objectives. The building of professional competence in teaching takes both time and effort, but most of all it takes the ability to look objectively at your own work.

Videotaping and microteaching

One promising method for learning new teaching behaviors is called microteaching.[10] We highly recommend this procedure, especially for beginning teachers. The central idea of microteaching is to select one aspect of teaching to work on at a time. These aspects include asking questions, learning to clarify student answers, recognizing nonverbal cues, and positively reinforcing student participation. Video equipment can be used for feedback and for concentrating on one aspect of instruction at a time—i.e., you can select one specific aspect of your

Table 14.3 Teacher rating scale for apprentice teachers.

I. Personal cognitive characteristics

   A. *Intellectual process*

1	2	3	4	5
	Flexible		Rigid	

Ideas and language appropriate to age and ability level of pupils and subject matter.

Teaches at an abstract level of language and ideas too advanced for pupils. A significant proportion of pupils doesn't appear to understand what intern is saying. Intern not sensitive to ambiguous meaning of own language.

   B. *Behavior under stress*

1	2	3	4	5
	Flexible		Rigid	

Stress and anxiety do not drastically narrow the perceptual field. Intern remains "open"—sees what is going on and can report the range of behavior in the class.

Under stress, the perceptual field is narrowed—intern erects a perceptual screen between self and class—little differentiation, e.g., misses pupils' inattention and contributions. Inability to focus on individual and group at the same time.

   C. *Perspective of*

1	2	3	4	5
	Flexible		Rigid	

Proper perspective of self is maintained; can use humor and other devices to look beyond the immediate situation. Perceives what self is doing in class, suggests new strategies, and makes good use of supervisor's suggestions.

Can't see self or situation in perspective. Intern makes excuses, is on defensive, e.g., may blame disinterested pupils on poor direction by supervisor. In the extreme, intern considers giving up teaching.

   D. *Anxiety and planning*

1	2	3	4	5
	Flexible		Rigid	

Anxiety provides a spur to increase purposeful effort, e.g., concern for planning and a consideration of alternative ways to communicate content and/or relate to pupils. Can plan for the unexpected.

Anxiety inhibits cognitive process, e.g., has poor lesson plan and poor control of time, gets trapped in digressions, can't handle the unexpected.

Table 14.3 Teacher rating scale (cont.)

E. *Overall rating for intellectual process-manner and cognitive style in dealing with teaching*

1	2	3	4	5
	Flexible		Rigid	
	Optimal use of intellect. Plans, ideas, and language used are functional to pupil learning.		Overly theoretical approach in general. Intern overintellectualizes planning, teaching, and contacts with pupils.	

F. *Comments on intellectual process*

II. **Cognitive attitude toward the pupil**

A. *Responsiveness*

1	2	3	4	5
	Flexible		Rigid	
	Intern is responsive to the class; sees, listens and responds to discipline problems, inattention, learning difficulties, students' need for new knowledge and creativity.		Intern doesn't register "cues"; children's problems are tuned out. Calls on bright students too often and doesn't recognize when to call on the slow child.	

B. *Attitude*

1	2	3	4	5
	Flexible		Rigid	
	Intern views pupil as a partner in educational process.		Intern looks down on pupil; patronizes pupil intellectually.	

C. *Judgments*

1	2	3	4	5
	Flexible		Rigid	
	Intern withholds judgments about pupils' ability and performance until he/she has adequate evidence. Uses a balance of positive rewards and constructive criticism.		Intern makes quick judgments and is unlikely to look for contradictory evidence. May tend to employ negative criticism, i.e., pick the pupils' answers apart.	

D. *Overall rating for cognitive attitude toward the pupil as a person*

1	2	3	4	5
	Flexible		Rigid	
	Intern recognizes important signals from the class, sees pupil as having a substantive role, makes judgments carefully.		Intern is not sensitive to feedback, looks down on the pupil, and makes snap and categorical judgments.	

E. *Comments*

III. Cognitive attitude toward the communication of subject matter

A. Use of lesson plan

1	2	3	4	5
	Flexible		Rigid	

Lesson plan is seen as a vehicle; modification and elaborations are made when and where appropriate.

Literal adherence to lesson plan; sets up what class *must* do. Teaches a lesson plan rather than the pupils. Ignores pertinent related ideas of pupils.

B. Teaching method

1	2	3	4	5
	Flexible		Rigid	

Intern displays a variety of suitable teaching methods, e.g., inductive questioning, dramatization, role playing, projects, etc.

Intern relies on only one or two teaching methods.

C. Teaching goal

1	2	3	4	5
	Flexible		Rigid	

Teaching for inquiry; interested in means as well as ends; explores where the pupil got off the track. Can flexibly handle unfamiliar content.

Emphasis on ends; assumes a right answer that must be attained the teacher's way. Deals ineffectively with unfamiliar content.

D. Overall rating for cognitive attitude

1	2	3	4	5
	Flexible		Rigid	

Intern uses a variety of methods, uses flexibility in implementing plans, and employs inquiry for effective teaching.

Uses few teaching methods, adheres to one or two formats in planning lessons, and employs a prescriptive rather than problematic teaching approach.

E. Comments

teaching for careful review. If you find that your eye contact with pupils is highly sporadic, or that when you ask questions you look at the ceiling or your feet, etc., you could deliberately focus on that weakness in your teaching behavior. Try a brief lesson with more direct eye contact as you teach and review the video with that dimension in mind. If you then find you have gone to the other extreme and are staring at the students, you can once again readjust and try for more-moderate contact. The same would be true for voice tone, bodily movement, and facial expression. Thus both categories of effective teaching—pedagogical techniques as well as your affective or emotional expressiveness—can be examined through the microteaching process.

One final point: The learning of new and effective teaching procedures is not a process that must cease at the conclusion of student teaching. Self-evaluation on a continuous basis is an effective means of staying current with your own process; it is frighteningly easy even for experienced teachers to fall into traps and not recognize the dangers. We could all take a lesson from the many professional athletes who systematically and critically review their performances for any hints of "bad" habits creeping in. So, too, for professional dancers or, in fact, anyone who uses both verbal and nonverbal aspects of their behavior in difficult and complex tasks.

Summary

Teachers must first learn to differentiate between telling and teaching. The neophyte teacher often unconsciously proceeds to tell, order, direct, or manipulate pupils under the guise of teaching.

A second point concerns how the teacher perceives knowing and teaching. The teacher's epistemological view will directly affect role performance; his or her assumption about the nature of learning will to a great extent determine the teaching approach utilized. So-called "models" of teaching rest on a series of important assumptions. The most-common view of knowing is what we have called, metaphorically, the "Library of Congress approach." If teachers can see themselves as rummaging through the endless corridors of a huge library, reading, selecting, sorting, evaluating, and preparing lesson plans to impart the basic facts, they will gain a flavor of what this approach involves. Transmitting knowledge is but one aspect of the overall educational process.

The second model comes close to the Bruner approach, namely, discovery teaching and inductive inquiry. The teacher's role is to unveil the fundamental structure of a discipline. Excitement, intrinsic interest, and curiosity are all elements of this process. The discovery unfolds to the moment of insight—the so-called "aha!"—when the student suddenly sees new relations between ideas, facts, and theoretical explanations. A most-difficult aspect of this model, however, is helping students understand the concept of knowledge as structure.

In the third model, directly associated with Carl Rogers, the case is made for the importance of interpersonal learning. Lowering student anxiety and promoting risk taking and initiative are important goals of the humanistic approach.

No single model by itself is really adequate as a framework for teaching. Each has positive contributions as well as limitations that are important to consider.

The question of curriculum objectives is addressed in the form of an ancient debate found in a spoof, *The Saber-Tooth Curriculum*. Bloom's pioneering work provides educators with a way out of the paradox of educational "relevance" versus general education. His six-level taxonomy allows a teacher to specify an objective and to assess the degree of success in achieving those objectives.

In addition to Bloom, the work of William Perry and David Hunt adds further credence to the concept of a developmental taxonomy for intellectual objectives.

The relation between intellectual and ethical developmental objectives is presented as a means of combining those domains of growth. Curriculum materials and exam questions can be assessed as to ethical and intellectual level through a two-way analysis.

Effective teaching demands a combination of transmitting knowledge, teaching for the process of inquiry, and encouraging interpersonal relations. A promising approach to teaching, the Flanders system of indirect instruction, encourages teachers to ask open-ended questions that discourage rote response. Flanders's findings are similar to the concept of cognitive flexibility—i.e., adapting teaching objectives to changing classroom interaction, thinking on one's feet. Approaches such as micro-teaching (concentrating on one element at a time through mastery), the use of video feedback, small-group practice, etc., are seen as helpful means of *learning* to teach. Great teachers are not necessarily "naturals."

REFERENCES

1
J. Bruner, *Toward a Theory of Instruction* (Cambridge, Mass.: Belknap Press, Harvard University, 1966).

2
C. R. Rogers, *Freedom to Learn* (Columbus, Ohio: Merrill, 1969).

3
N. A. Flanders and G. Morine, "The Assessment of Proper Control and Suitable Learning Environment," in N. L. Gage, ed., *Mandated Evaluation of Educators* (Stanford: California Center for Research and Development in Teaching, 1973).

4
J. Abner Peddiwell, *The Saber-Tooth Curriculum* (New York: McGraw-Hill, 1939).

5
B. Bloom, ed., *Taxonomy of Educational Objectives, Handbook 1: Cognitive Domain* (New York: McKay, 1956).

6
D. Hunt and E. Sullivan, *Between Psychology and Education* (New York: Dryden, 1974).

7
William G. Perry, *Intellectual and Ethical Development* (New York: Holt, Rinehart and Winston, 1968).

8
N. A. Flanders, *Analyzing Teacher Behavior* (Reading, Mass.: Addison-Wesley, 1970), p. 401.

9
N. A. Sprinthall, J. M. Whiteley, and R. L. Mosher, "A Study of Teacher Effectiveness," *Journal of Teacher Education* 1 (1966):93–106.

10
D. Allen and K. Ryan, *Microteaching* (Reading, Mass.: Addison-Wesley, 1969).

15

Teaching: the personal dimension

We have characterized teaching and learning as difficult and complex processes. As we noted in the previous chapter, teaching encompasses an almost infinite number of components—from the makeup of each child, to the unique nature of a group of children, to the attitudes and values of the adult teacher. This chapter focuses on the teacher, who determines much of what happens or does not happen in the classroom. Without question, the teacher is the major influence on a class. Whether that influence is positive or negative is the question at hand. For years schooling has operated on the assumption that if children do not do well in school, it is their own fault. Teachers were either competent in everything or, at worst, could inflict no harm. Teaching problems were diagnosed as problems of pupil learning.

"They need to work harder, to pay closer attention to the teacher, and to stop talking so much." Such a statement certainly characterizes the usual assumption that once a teacher has mastered a few rudimentary skills, the rest is up to the pupils. We now realize that the teacher is the chief agent for success or failure in the classroom. Indeed, it has been distressing to find in so many recent studies of education that too often the teacher is an architect of educational failure. In other words, the failure of pupils to learn anything can be traced directly to the teacher.

THE TEACHER AS A PERSON: THE ELUSIVE QUESTION (OR, "THOU SHALL NOT")

One of the most elusive factors in education concerns the human qualities of the effective teacher. One of the long-standing myths of education is that teachers should manifest all the noble virtues and have no human frailties. The char-

The myth of the flawless teacher

395

acter of the teacher, like Caesar's wife, should be beyond reproach. For example, a teacher's contract in North Carolina in the 1930s specified the following personal requirements:

> *I promise to abstain from all dancing, immodest dressing, and any other conduct unbecoming a teacher and a lady.*
>
> *I promise not to go out with any young man except insofar as it may be necessary to stimulate Sunday School work.*
>
> *I promise not to fall in love, to become engaged or secretly married.*
>
> *I promise to remain in the dormitory or on the school grounds when not actively engaged in school or church work elsewhere.*[1]

Sounds a bit like an acceptance speech at the Republican national convention. The problem is that no human can possibly live up to the myth. Even worse, teachers soon realize the impossibility of such a goal, but have to keep busy preventing other people from finding out. A more realistic perception of the teacher would dispense with both the myth of human virtues (all teachers love all children all of the time) and the assumption that teachers are not responsible for children failing to learn.

TEACHING: WHAT IS IT REALLY LIKE?

A number of popular accounts have recently presented both the humorous and the tragic aspects of what it is really like to teach. Bel Kaufman's *Up the Down Staircase*,[2] Kozol's *Death at an Early Age*,[3] and Ryan's *Don't Smile 'til Christmas*[4] are some first-person accounts that reveal the disparity between the myth and the reality of school, depicting harried teachers trying to live up to some idealized version of patience, love, and total responsiveness, all of the time, every day. Such teachers are like overly permissive parents who try to fulfill the perfect-mother or father ideal by withholding all genuine feelings ("Don't smile 'til Christmas!"), and finally "boil over," screaming and hitting out at their children. Teachers are no better than parents at holding in their genuine feelings. Some incident inevitably opens the floodgate, and all the pent-up anger and personal disappointment break loose. The class learns just what it had suspected all along and may, in fact, have been testing: the teacher was putting on an act of always being "nice."

Trying to be "nice" all the time

Unfortunately, the teacher usually feels guilty about having lost control and therefore never realizes the true nature of the problem: it is the impossibility of living up to the myth that sets the entire process in motion. Instead of developing more realistic perceptions of teaching and learning, teachers who have tried and failed often adopt a set of attitudes that justify and rationalize their failures. "Pearls before swine" becomes their bitter motto.

TEACHER ATTITUDES AND TEACHING

The hidden agenda

One of the most important—and discouraging—findings from recent research is the extent to which teachers' true feelings about children (as opposed to their idealized version) affect their ability to be effective educators.

We need to realize that our attitudes are not always clearly known to us. Because we develop our attitudes slowly over a long period of time, we are often not conscious of what they are, nor of how our attitudes and expectations influence our behavior. This is why we can say one thing and do another. We may pay lip service to one set of goals, while a careful examination of how we act may reveal a completely different set. This discrepancy has been called the hidden agenda or the implicit curriculum of teaching.

Attitudes and the hidden agenda

The hidden agenda has special significance for the teacher. We have to be honest with ourselves in determining how much we act without consciousness.[5] As teachers, our own attitudes toward learning will determine the conditions we create for learning in the classroom. For example, if we feel that learning requires there be no ambiguity, that the "right" answers be presented, and that the pupils know exactly what to say, you can imagine what sort of classroom environment we would provide. Our attitude would affect the way the desks would be arranged, the books and readings we would use, and the way we would manage the discussion time. And this environment would have a very definite influence on the pupils' learning "set." In other words, we affect the attitudes the pupils themselves develop toward learning. There is truth to the old saying, "Actions speak louder than words"; our attitudes, motives, and perceptions influence the way we act and are transmitted to our pupils through our actions, thereby affecting their attitudinal development.

The medium and the message

Marshall McLuhan has suggested one of the ways our attitudes influence our communications.[6] McLuhan's famous phrase, "the medium is the message," expresses the idea that the verbal content of a message is interpreted, or given its true meaning, by the way it is delivered.

Teacher attitudes and values as a medium for the message

Our view is less extreme: content is important, yet we do wish to emphasize the importance of the way messages are transmitted. We have all had the experience of being put down by someone. It isn't so much what that other person says but the way it is said (the medium). The real message lies in the person's tone, inflection, facial expression, demeanor. It is the nonverbal, the visual and auditory, cues that deliver the real message. A bad medium in the classroom creates an atmosphere in which learning and growth cannot take place.

Important nonverbal cues

TEACHER ATTITUDES: TOWARD LEARNING, TOWARD PUPILS, AND TOWARD SELF

Teachers' attitudes can be grouped into three related categories: attitudes toward teaching and learning; attitudes toward pupils; and attitudes toward self.

"Oh, my teacher and I communicate,
all right . . . she looks at me a
certain way and I understand
what I'd better do!"

Attitudes toward teaching and learning

We have often mentioned that the way teachers perceive teaching and learning is crucial. Is "knowledge" a finite list of facts for students to memorize? Do we tend to encourage "correct answers" and focus on outcome, or do we consider the process of learning important? Do we consider teaching to be more like training, so that we "tell" pupils what to do? There are widely divergent assumptions about teaching and learning, and our own attitudes and the way we actually behave in class are molded by those assumptions.

Attitudes toward knowledge

If we had to single out one major attitude that pervades schools, it would be the cherished belief that knowledge equals the truth. Teachers and pupils tend to believe that there is an answer for every question, that the truth is known, and that the teacher's voice is like the voice of God. In Chapter 2 we discussed classroom trivia, a form of rapid-fire question-and-answer interaction. Obviously, this kind of teaching reinforces the concept of knowledge-as-truth and puts the teacher in charge of deciding whether the pupil is "right." The teacher is the center of the classroom, the decision-maker. "That's absolutely correct" means a bull's-eye. "That's almost right" means a near miss. A scowl ("teachers' dirty looks") means the student was completely and absolutely wrong.

This view of knowledge-as-truth also has unfortunate consequences from a developmental standpoint. During elementary school, children move into Piaget's stage of concrete operations (see Chapter 6) and are extremely literal-

The teacher should avoid the "knowledge-as-truth" syndrome, and should discourage black-and-white thinking.

minded. They also, at this age, tend to divide the world into two camps, the "good guys" and the "bad guys" (see Chapter 8). In other words, children already have a built-in personal and cognitive bias in favor of "truth." If we then consider the special influence of initial learning experiences—recall how strongly we are affected the first time we experience something (see Chapter 5) —we begin to realize how easy it is for the pupils to accept the notion that there is only one answer. The main problem for teachers is the temptation to exploit this situation. It's very easy for them to become the fountainhead of all knowledge, the master who knows the truth and then decides how close or far away the pupils' answers come. In fact, the pupils actually encourage such behavior by the teacher. And teachers may enjoy their presumed omniscience.

Pupils looking for the single correct answer

In this way the teacher's authority can easily become authoritarianism. The confusion of authority and authoritarianism is perhaps the basic dilemma teachers face. This is partly our own fault, especially if we are guilty of confirming the pupils' view of knowledge as fixed and unchanging. Many poignant examples come to mind. Think of the number of times students of all ages ask questions like, "What are you going to cover on the next exam?" "How much will this count toward the final grade?" "Do we have to read all the assigned pages?" If you listen closely, you will hear exactly what such students have learned: to please the teacher you only have to mouth the "right answer."

These attitudes have been learned for the most part in school. Don't blame the students if they are expert apple polishers. That is the behavior that has received the most positive reinforcement throughout their school life.

John Holt, an educational critic, has recently blamed children's failure in school on the teachers' belief that knowledge is fixed truth. In his provocative volume, *How Children Fail,* Holt claims simply that the teacher-centered classroom ensures that the pupils learn that the teacher has all the answers and they have none.[7] If they want to do well, they must tell the teacher the answers the teacher wants to hear. This means that children are so busy trying to figure out what the teacher wants, there is no time for them to puzzle over the problems themselves. Although Holt may overstate his case somewhat, he does remind us of the significance of teachers' attitudes, especially attitudes toward knowledge.

Some recent research by Professor O. J. Harvey also suggests that teachers' attitudes and belief systems strongly reinforce students' feelings that conformity and obedience is what learning is all about.[8] In a series of studies involving large numbers of teachers, Harvey found that their predominant attitude involved the desire for the "right answer"—what he would call System 1 or System 2 (see Table 15.1). Examples of System 1 or 2 statements are: "It's annoying to listen to a lecturer who cannot seem to make up his mind about what he really believes." "A group that tolerates extreme differences of opinion among its own members cannot exist for long." "I don't like to work on a problem unless there is a possibility of arriving at a clear-cut answer." "I don't like things to be uncertain and unpredictable."

The evidence from single critics like Holt and from large-scale research like the studies of Professor Harvey seems unequivocal—teachers' "belief" systems, their attitudes toward teaching and learning, significantly influence the classroom environment and, therefore, the attitudes students develop toward knowledge and learning.

Table 15.1   Harvey's analysis of teacher attitudes.

System 1

These teachers have a belief in divine fate or religious fundamentalism. This is assessed by such items as: "There are some things that God will never permit man to know"; "In the final analysis, events in the world will be in line with the master plan of God"; and "I believe that to attain my goals, it is only necessary for me to live as God would have me live."

System 2

These teachers have a need for certainty or simplicity, as expressed in such statements as: "I prefer a story that has two themes rather than one that has five or six themes going at once"; "People who seem unsure and uncertain about things make me feel uncomfortable"; and "The effective person is one who does not hold conflicting beliefs."

System 3

Tolerance of complexity and uncertainty is expressed in such statements as: "I have so much trouble finding out what is or is not true that I can't understand how some people can feel so certain that they know the truth"; "More often than not, I like some aspects of a person and do not like other aspects of him"; and "I find that I cannot help analyzing almost everything I see and hear."

System 4

Relativism of truth is expressed by such statements as: "There can be as many truths as there are individual points of view"; "Man is the judge of the truth or untruth of his thoughts and behavior"; and "Something is true or untrue depending on one's assumptions and the context."

Most teachers can be classified as System 1. Less than 8% of teachers can be classified as System 4.

Characteristics of System 1 Teachers: Compared to other teachers, these teachers are less resourceful in the classroom, significantly more dictatorial, more punitive, lower on encouraging pupil initiative, lower on creativity, and lower on allowing pupils' to express their feelings.[10]

Characteristics of System 4 Teachers: These teachers are perceptive of children's needs, and have flexible, relaxed, interpersonal relationships. They encourage pupil initiative, display great classroom ingenuity, and are less rule-oriented, less anxious, and less punitive than other teachers.

Attitudes toward pupils

Teachers' attitudes toward the pupil are also important in determining the classroom atmosphere. Learning climates are subjective, and we were all adept as children in determining whether a teacher "likes kids." The feeling is readily apparent. Does the teacher feel we are competent? Does he or she expect us to do well? Do we feel that the teacher really wants us to be successful?

The importance of teacher expectations, attitudes, and feelings about children has been demonstrated dramatically in a recent series of studies by Professor Robert Rosenthal, a social psychologist.[9] He has shown that the teacher's expectations determine to a considerable extent how much pupils, or for that matter almost any animals, will learn. His studies have shown, for example, that if experimental psychologists are told that the rats in their study are especially bred for intelligence, these rats will learn the mazes quicker than the "control" rats, even though no such special breeding was carried out. In other words, Rosenthal has shown that when experimenters expect their rats to do well, those rats outperform their rivals. If they expect a good performance, experimenters encourage their breed, handle them more carefully, pat them frequently, root for them—in short, they treat them with concern and great care because they expect them to do well. If so for rats, what about pupils?

In the now famous Oak-Hall School Experiment, Rosenthal and co-worker Lenore Jacobsen told a group of schoolteachers at the beginning of the school year that particular pupils would have a "growth spurt" during the coming term. In order to lend credence to this prophecy, the researchers said that a special test, "The Harvard Test of Inflicted Acquisition," had been administered to all of the children in the elementary school. The results of the test became the basis for their alleged prediction. They identified some pupils as "growth spurters" even though their selection had been random—the identified pupils as a group were not any "smarter" than the remaining pupils. At the end of the school term, the results showed that the pupils originally identified as in the growth-spurt group did much better on a series of tests than the other pupils. Their academic performances had improved and, especially in the early grades, their measured IQ's were significantly higher than the other pupils'. Also, all the designated children received glowing comments from their teachers. Thus a major research study has substantiated the effect of the self-fulfilling prophecy. When teachers expected some pupils to experience a growth spurt, they improved in academic performance and intelligence.

A second major finding of this study—and one that is rarely reported—concerns the teachers' attitudes toward the other children. Rosenthal selected a subgroup of pupils in his control group, a group of children who showed intellectual gains during the term but who hadn't been identified ahead of time to the teachers. He found that the teachers regarded these children as less well adjusted, less interesting, and less affectionate than the others. In other words, the pupils who made it on their own, who gained intellectually in spite of the prediction, were perceived negatively by the teacher.

Thus, we have almost a three-way effect: (1) pupils who are expected to do well tend to show gains; (2) pupils who are not expected to do well tend to do less well than the first group; and (3) pupils who make gains despite expectations to the contrary are regarded negatively by the teacher. What the effect of those negative expectations may be on such pupils the next time around has not been determined. We can guess, however, what negative expectations in general produce. Rosenthal quotes Eliza Doolittle from George Bernard Shaw's famous play *Pygmalion:*

Pygmalion in the classroom—the self-fulfilling prophecy

> *You see, really and truly, . . . the difference between a lady and a flower girl is not how she behaves, but how she's treated. I shall always be a flower girl to Professor Higgins, because he . . . treats me as a flower girl, . . . but I know I can be a lady to you, because you always treat me as a lady, and always will.*[10]

There have been serious criticisms of Rosenthal's work, the most comprehensive and readable account being John Jung's recent work, *The Experimenter's*

Robert Rosenthal

Born in 1933, Rosenthal dashed over the academic hurdles in record time. He received his B.A. at twenty years of age and his Ph.D. by the time he was twenty-three, both at the University of California at Los Angeles. He then spent brief periods at U.C.L.A., Ohio State, and the University of North Dakota. His work attracted increasing notice throughout the professional world. The idea of the self-fulfilling prophecy was not new to psychology. What was new, however, was Rosenthal's ability to demonstrate how often this phenomenon was affecting the work of the psychologists themselves. His findings were almost immediately controversial. And, as if to create more controversy among psychologists, since his early work had not then been replicated, the department of social relations at Harvard University reached halfway across the country to North Dakota and offered Rosenthal a Harvard professorship, all by the time he was twenty-nine years old.

With the move to the East and more time for research, Rosenthal shifted into high gear. He not only replicated his original findings but began to produce studies on his important concept in a wide variety of areas. As noted in the text, each time one of his studies is criticized he has been able to answer the critics not with rhetoric but rather with more research data to validate his position. The controversy itself, of course, continues. The major outcome has been to produce more evidence, more-sophisticated research designs, and thus more-comprehensive information for educational psychology.

Dilemma.[11] A series of major reservations have also been detailed by Barber and Silver in the same volume. The statistical procedures especially have been questioned. As Jung notes, these details are complicated and there is considerable disagreement among the experts themselves as to the correct procedures. A second level of criticism has suggested that Rosenthal himself may have unintentionally biased his own results. For example, Barber and Silver present evidence from their own studies which have failed to replicate Rosenthal's results. Of course, the difficulty is obvious: were the critics also guilty of unintentionally biasing their studies? As Jung suggests, there may be no way out of this dilemma. Each time the self-fulfilling prophecy has been criticized, Rosenthal enumerates additional studies, now numbering in the hundreds and conducted all over the world, the great majority of which provide strong support for his contention.

Perhaps we should recall that the whole question of the self-fulfilling prophecy first came to light some sixty years ago. A horse in Germany who came to be known as "Clever Hans" gained notoriety for his ability to add, subtract, multiply, and divide by tapping his foot. A psychologist named Pfungst, after long study, finally figured out that the questioners were unintentionally cueing the horse by lifting their heads up just before the horse reached the correct number of taps. He found that most humans who questioned Hans gave some cue, without meaning to—raising their heads, lifting an eyebrow, or even dilating their nostrils. Pfungst concluded that he had spent far too much time, "Looking for, in the horse, what should have been sought in the man."

Clever Hans, the horse

Attitudes and social-class differences.   The influence of teachers' attitudes toward their pupils is doubly significant if we examine social-class differences. Obviously, our social class influences our attitudes not only toward those in our own class, but to those in other socioeconomic classes as well. Howard Becker, a sociologist, has documented the differences in perception and attitude by social class. In a large urban school system, he found that most teachers could be grouped as lower-middle class on a socioeconomic scale. In general, these teachers valued conformity, obedience, neatness, cleanliness, punctuality, hard work—highly conventional values. He then interviewed over sixty such teachers to find out how they perceived their pupils. He found three sets of perceptions that closely followed class lines. These teachers perceived children from their own class (lower-middle class and blue-collar working class) as the "best" pupils. They were neat, orderly, clean, and followed directions. In the words of one teacher:

Teachers' lower-middle-class values

> Those children were much quieter, easier to work with. When we'd play our little games there was never any commotion. That was a very nice school to work in. Everything was quite nice about it. The children were easy to work with.[12]

Teachers felt that pupils from lower-class backgrounds (essentially poor blacks) were, in general, morally unacceptable. "They don't wash." "Never use a toothbrush." "Will steal anything movable." "One girl in my class now makes money as a prostitute." These teachers reported being shocked by the "awful" language and upset because "they" (the lower-class students) don't really value

Attitudes toward lower-class children

education or wish to improve themselves. It is not difficult to imagine how these attitudes affect the teachers' expectations regarding the pupils they describe in these terms.

Attitudes toward
upper-class children
Finally, the teachers had a third set of attitudes toward children from upper-class, well-to-do homes. They found these children to be very fine students, bright, clever, quick—but very difficult to teach. "They are too unruly—have no manners—interrupt me—are quick to correct my mistakes," noted one teacher. Another said, "They all have maids and servants at home. They won't pick things up that they drop. One student said to me 'If I picked that up, there wouldn't be any work for the janitor to do.' "

The teachers also tended to be fearful of reprisal from the parents of the third group. While the children from the ghetto could be dealt with severely if necessary (including the use of corporal punishment), the children from well-to-do backgrounds were immune from direct punishment. The teachers were obviously worried about "influential" parents calling the school board or going directly to the superintendent with complaints about the teachers' actions toward their children.

The influence of nega-
tive attitudes
It is obvious, then, that teachers' attitudes are directly related to their pupils' social class. The way these attitudes affect pupil achievement is, of course, a most significant problem. The Robert Rosenthal and Lenore Jacobsen study showed only the influence of positive expectations on pupil achievement. Howard Becker has shown the variety of negative attitudes teachers tend to manifest toward children from social classes other than their own—but not the effect on achievement. Professor Eleanor Leacock from New York conducted a study showing that both positive and negative expectations by teachers actually affect pupil achievement. Leacock's researchers, unlike Rosenthal, Jacobson, or Becker, actually went into the classroom. They observed the teacher's behavior and checked student achievement. As a result, they found a fairly systematic pattern of negative attitudes and expectations toward most lower-class ghetto blacks. Teachers universally expected less of those pupils, even in the very first years of elementary school, compared to children from the higher social classes. In addition, their expectations declined the longer the pupils were in school. Fifth graders were seen as less capable and less competent than second graders in the same school. Leacock found that the schools in the areas where poor blacks lived were neither in continual rebellion nor were they a "blackboard jungle." Rather, the schools were populated by "over-worked, ineffective, and frustrated teachers and bored, uninterested and withdrawn children." There were one or two "trouble-makers" in each class, but the majority of pupils were quiet, dull, and listless. Leacock also compared teacher-pupil interaction in the lower-class black school with that in middle-class schools (with both black and white children) and found less than half as much interaction in the lower-class school. This low rate of interaction means that the "poor" children are being ignored, that most of the time they spend in class is spent in quiet boredom, and that their teachers display a genuine lack of interest. Also, the interaction that did take place tended to be twice as negative as that in the middle-class schools; teachers tended to undermine the children, were very derogatory toward their work, and were supercritical of their attempts to read, do math problems, and blackboard work.[14]

Urban schools: bore-
dom and negative
criticism

On learning shame

Dick Gregory

I never learned hate at home, or shame. I had to go to school for that. I was about seven years old when I got my first big lesson. I was in love with a little girl named Helen Tucker, a light-complected little girl with pigtails and nice manners. She was always clean and she was smart in school. I think I went to school mostly to look at her. I brushed my hair and even got me a little old handkerchief. It was a lady's handkerchief, but I didn't want Helen to see me wipe my nose on my hand. The pipes were frozen again, there was no water in the house, but I washed my socks and shirt every night. I'd get a pot, and go over to Mister Ben's grocery store, and stick my pot down into his soda machine. Scoop out some chopped ice. By evening the ice melted to water for washing. I got sick a lot that winter because the fire would go out at night before the clothes were dry. In the morning I'd put them on, wet or dry, because they were the only clothes I had.

It was on a Thursday. I was sitting in the back of the room, in a seat with a chalk circle drawn around it. The idiot's seat, the troublemaker's seat.

The teacher thought I was stupid. Couldn't spell, couldn't read, couldn't do arithmetic. Just stupid. Teachers were never interested in finding out that you couldn't concentrate because you were so hungry, because you hadn't had any breakfast. All you could think about was noontime, would it ever come? Maybe you could sneak into the cloakroom and steal a bite of some kid's lunch out of a coat pocket. A bite of something. Paste. You can't really make a meal of paste, or put it on bread for a sandwich, but sometimes I'd scoop a few spoonfuls out of the paste jar in the back of the room. Pregnant people get strange tastes. I was pregnant with poverty. Pregnant with dirt and pregnant with smells that made people turn away, pregnant with cold and pregnant with shoes that were never bought for me, pregnant with five other people in my bed and no Daddy in the next room, and pregnant with hunger. Paste doesn't taste too bad when you're hungry.

The teacher thought I was a troublemaker. All she saw from the front of the room was a little black boy who squirmed in his idiot's seat and made noises and poked the kids around him. I guess she couldn't see a kid who made noises because he wanted someone to know he was there.

It was on a Thursday, the day before the Negro payday. The eagle always flew on Friday. The teacher was asking each student how much his father would give to the Community Chest. On Friday night, each kid would get the money from his father, and on Monday he would bring it to the school. I decided I was going to buy me a Daddy right then. I had money in my pocket from shining shoes and selling papers, and whatever Helen Tucker pledged for her Daddy I was going to top it. And I'd hand the money right in. I wasn't going to wait until Monday to buy me a Daddy.

I was shaking, scared to death. The teacher opened her book and started calling out names alphabetically.

"Helen Tucker?"

"My Daddy said he'd give two dollars and fifty cents."

"That's very nice, Helen. Very, very nice indeed."

That made me feel pretty good. It wouldn't take too much to top that. I had almost three dollars in dimes and quarters in my pocket and held onto the money, waiting for her to call my name. But the teacher closed her book after she called everybody else in the class.

I stood up and raised my hand.

"What is it now?'

"You forgot me."

She turned toward the blackboard. "I don't have time to be playing with you, Richard."

"What is it now?"

"My Daddy said he's . . ."

"Sit down, Richard, you're disturbing the class."

"My Daddy said he'd give . . . fifteen dollars."

She turned around and looked mad. "We are collecting this money for you and your kind, Richard Gregory. If your Daddy can give fifteen dollars you have no business being on relief."

"I got it right now, I got it right now, my Daddy gave it to me to turn in today, my Daddy said . . ."

"And furthermore," she said, looking right at me, her nostrils getting big and her lips getting thin and her eyes opening wide, "we know you don't have a Daddy."

Helen Tucker turned around, her eyes full of tears. She felt sorry for me. Then I couldn't see her too well because I was crying, too.

"Sit down, Richard."

And I always thought the teacher kind of liked me.[13]

The message is clear as far as lower-class children are concerned. They are either ignored, allowed to "be," or criticized and undermined in their attempts to learn. Leacock suggests that such teachers are teaching their children not to learn. It therefore comes as no surprise to find that pupil achievement in such schools is significantly lower than in middle-class schools. The teachers' unfortunate attitudes toward their pupils pervade the lower-class schools and doom these children to failure. Other research has indicated that such children end up not only with lowered academic achievement but also with a negative concept of themselves as learners. They have lower self-confidence in problem-solving situations. For such children, "formal" education in school may be worse than no education at all.

Teaching children not to learn

Self-confidence vs. self-doubt

The negative impact of teacher attitudes and expectations has also been documented in a recent study by Brophy and Good. By examining how teachers and students interact, the researchers uncovered a list of teacher behaviors that communicate low expectations. If teachers thought that some children were slow learners, the typical teacher responses included:

1
Waiting less time for the pupil to answer

2
Not following up when a pupil answered incorrectly

3
Rewarding inappropriate behavior

4
Not providing feedback to such pupils.

In other words, the study of Brophy and Good provides further confirmation to Rosenthal's self-fulfilling prophecy and the observational study of Leacock that some teachers are systematically shortchanging their pupils. They summarize their findings:

Thus to put it badly, in some school systems a student's career is somewhat determined as of the day he enters school simply on the basis of his clothing, appearance, and other factors related to the SES of his family but not necessarily to his ability or potential.[15]

A massive study carried out by James Coleman, a sociologist from Johns Hopkins, concluded that the single most important factor affecting pupil achievement is the social-class composition of the school. The famous "Coleman Report" surveyed literally thousands of schools and found that the quality of education the pupils received did not depend on teachers' salaries, per-pupil expenditures, the number of books in the library, equipment, buildings, or the teachers' educational backgrounds. Instead, the social-class composition of the student body had the greatest effect on academic success. If the children were all from upper- or middle-class backgrounds, their academic performances were high. If they were from lower-class backgrounds, their performances were low and tended to deteriorate the longer they stayed in school.[16] Here we have an instance of how schooling itself can inflict harm on children.

These studies demonstrate that pupil achievement depends to a great extent on social-class differences and on the teacher's attitudes toward pupils from different backgrounds. Unfortunately, we have pretended for too long that such problems do not really exist.

Attitudes toward self

We humans have known about the importance of self-knowledge for a long time. Socrates and the early Greek philosophers were the first to stress self-examination. Socrates said that the unexamined life was not worth living. It is obvious that the way teachers perceive and feel about themselves is a major determinant of classroom atmosphere and student performance. Self-confidence, poise, self-control, an eagerness to lead a class of children, will obviously set the tone for cooperation and learning in the class. Similarly, a superanxious, trembling, insecure teacher will set the opposite tone. We have all had the unfortunate experience of being in a class led by a petrified teacher. The scene might unfold as follows: The teacher shakily appears in class, filled with distress, and requests that the pupils be "nice." The effect is often electric. The pupils, using their private channels of communication, soon turn the class into a field trial. How long will it take to drive the teacher into hysteria? Usually, it doesn't take long. Loud talking, books dropping, desks banging, pupils walking in and out (aways stumbling over the wastepaper basket), erasers and chalk flying around, the din builds and the students finally succeed. The teacher runs from the class in full retreat. Unfortunately, the teacher usually never realizes that he or she is responsible for the chaos—the teacher's obvious lack of confidence and self-doubt were immediately communicated to the pupils and sparked the inevitable reaction. Pupils are expert at reading the hidden agenda; teachers must come equipped with some degree of self-assurance, no matter what other attitudes they have toward themselves.

Professor Herbert Thelen from the University of Chicago has catalogued some of the common views teachers have of themselves and of their roles as teachers.[17] He uses some interesting metaphors.

Model 1: Socrates.

This teacher sees himself or herself much like the wise old tutor of antiquity. Craggy and crusty, this reputation is based on love of argument, debate, and deliberately provocative statements. He or she often takes the role of devil's advocate, arguing for unpopular views. The self-image is of a person constantly searching, asking questions, and rarely, if ever, coming to a conclusion. Finality is rarely appropriate. Rather, the teacher strolls around the classroom asking new questions when the old ones have been fully debated. The style is highly individualistic and unsystematic.

Every once in a while, when professional agencies mention teacher certification, someone is bound to hold Socrates up as an example of an excellent teacher who would not meet the usual standards. His or her lesson plan consists of relentless questioning. Through constant confrontation, much like a cross-examination in a trial, pupils are forced to defend their own conclusions, or more likely, to end up agreeing with the cross-examiner.

The consensus seeker

Model 2: the town-meeting manager. This teacher is always seeking consensus and cooperation among members of the class. Educators who speak of the importance of community fall into this category: they view their classes as communities of interdependent and equal human beings. Thelen notes that the town-meeting manager is more of a moderator than an expert. As moderator, the teacher encourages members to participate and contribute to the group. Thus, he or she views the process of seeking this democratic consensus as more important than the specific outcome.

Educators have just begun to take a closer look at the idea of community as an educational force for the classroom. Should this idea continue to take hold, teachers may have to view themselves more and more as moderators seeking consensus and group participation.

This model should not be confused with the idea of direct involvement in the school by people who live in the community, by community residents as teachers and as policymakers in the school program. The classroom as a community does not include such "outsiders." Instead, it includes only the teacher and the pupils working together as a group. Direct participatory democracy is the major educational objective when the teacher perceives himself or herself as a town-meeting manager.

Model 3: the master/apprentice. This teacher perceives himself or herself as a genuine model for students (we are using the word model in its literal sense, as something to be emulated). The teacher is like an old-fashioned preceptor, and the pupil is the apprentice. This teacher is concerned with far more than academic performance; he or she is concerned with how the student learns to live. Consequently, the teacher plays multiple roles, as teacher, father, mother, friend, colleague, and boss. The pupil becomes a miniature version of the master. Perhaps we should rename this model the Father or Mother Goose image. The teacher gathers the flock around and the class becomes a "gaggle," waiting to be imprinted.

Model 4: the general.   This teacher adopts pretty much of an "old blood and guts image." He or she lays down the law and expects and demands obedience. There is no room for any sort of ambiguity, and the teacher has the power to reward or punish as he or she sees fit. Thelen reminds us that this teacher doesn't necessarily use severe punishment. In fact, the teacher can be kind and gentle as long as the pupils remain dependent and subordinate. The self-image obviously has to do with the teacher knowing best and the pupil following orders. Like an army recruit, the pupil's job is to do exactly what he or she is told. When you have a general for a teacher, it's true to say: "I'm free to do as I please as long as I do as I'm told." Thelen notes that this model is more prevalent than all the others combined.

The army model

Model 5: the business executive.   This teacher functions as a business executive, operating a company (the classroom) and working out business deals with the employees (the pupils). The pupils write contracts specifying what tasks they will take on during the contract period. The business executive then consults with each employee during the task, to exert a kind of quality control, and inspects the final product. An air of efficiency and crispness goes along with this image. Detailed "production charts" may line the walls of the classroom, and the chief executive can usually be identified by a very tidy desk. This corporate image has become "official" in some of the newest classrooms, where thick wall-to-wall carpeting is now standard equipment.

Contract learning

The corporate classroom

Model 6: the coach.   This teacher is worlds apart from the business executive. The atmosphere now resembles that of a locker room. Pupils are like members of a team; each one is insignificant as an individual, but as a group they can move mountains. The teacher views his or her role as inspirational—desire,

Locker room teaching

dedication, and devotion are the hallmark of team talks. "Go get this one for the Old Gipper," or words to that effect, echo down the corridors, and the pupils can be heard responding in unison precise phrases learned by heart. The coach is totally devoted to the task. The only measure of effectiveness is the outcome, the final score. "Nice guys" come in last when the name of the game is WIN. In the coaching metaphor, "Winning isn't everything, it's the only thing."

Model 7: the tour guide.   This teacher bears an unmistakable resemblance to a professional guide. He or she clearly knows the way around, all the facts, all the time—indeed, the teacher seems to be a walking encyclopedia. He or she also tends to be somewhat reserved, disinterested, and laconic. After all, the guide's been over this route many times before and has heard every possible question hundreds of times. The answers are comprehensive and soundly programed. Technically perfect, the guide shows only a hint of boredom. He or she could be conducting a tour of the Washington Monument, the Empire State Building, the Mayflower, Yosemite, Sutter's Creek—we've met the type before, we will meet again, and not only in class. It is, after all, a relatively safe, impersonal role.

The seven teacher self-images: a summary

It is important to remember that these models are all derived from the needs of the teachers, not from the requirements of the pupils. Each one is, at best, an extremely truncated version of what an educator should be. When critics speak of adult-centered rather than child-centered classrooms, it is with reference to these images. We must have an unusual self-image to be able to set aside our own needs and really serve those of the children in our charge. The model that is conspicuously absent from Thelen's catalogue is that of an educator of children.

At this point, you may be wondering whether there is any way out of this value dilemma. We know that attitudes, expectations, and images toward learning, pupils, and self are of critical importance in the classroom. We also realize that in many cases teachers become trapped in their own values. Recall the studies showing that teachers reward only those children whose background is similar to their own. Recall Thelen's observation about how teachers' self-images fill their own needs in the classroom. Are we doomed to teach only for our own benefit or only for those few children who are just like us? Isn't education supposed to be for all children? Sooner or later we must confront these questions head on.

Teacher images as adult-centered

VALUES AND TEACHING

Inculcation and brainwashing

The dilemma of values and indoctrination

A number of attempts have been made to resolve the above-mentioned dilemma. One very common approach has been to say that teaching is like indoctrination. "Face it, teaching is a form of brainwashing," or so this view proclaims. Since adults know more than kids, it is right and just for the adults to induct each new generation of children into the ways of the adult world. There is no need to be upset by this indoctrination; it's simply the way things are—a natural law. This is something like saying, "Well, so what's wrong with teaching middle-class values; after all, that's the majority view. And most everybody would like to be middle class anyway!" The fact that such rhetoric makes the shabby rationalizations seem palatable to some raises more questions than it answers.

Value-free teaching

Another, more elegant, solution to the value dilemma has been to suggest that teachers really should express no genuine personal values: they should present all sides of any question fairly and impartially. Like anthropologists studying another culture, teachers would be trained for neutrality. Their only values would be plurality and relativism: all views would have merit and receive equal treatment. Not only would there be freedom for all views, but teachers would also be expected to pursue and embody all views with equal vigor.

Value neutrality

Perhaps the most adequate means of conveying the impossibility of value neutrality in teaching is to offer a brief example. A social-studies teacher who was supervising a group of teacher trainees had become embroiled in this very controversy. His trainees insisted that the pupils were to be "free." They, as future teachers, had no right to impose their views on the children. The social-studies master teacher at this point gave up on the dialogue and invited the teachers-in-training to observe his next class. To make his point as dramatically as he knew how, he decided to teach his pupils about the disadvantages and the advantages of the concentration camps of World War II. After listing the obvious disadvantages, he proceeded "objectively" to list the advantages—the creation of jobs (guards, dog trainers, searchlight makers), the uncrowding of cities, the increase in availability of housing, and even the production of certain goods almost too grisly to mention. The horrified practice teachers immediately protested that the master teacher was being unfair. How was it possible to even consider a concentration camp as an advantage to anyone? The master teacher had reduced the idea of value-free teaching to an absurdity. To say that he was merely presenting evidence from a "different point of view" was simply a means of begging the question of values.*

An example of value-free teaching

We all inevitably reach the point where we must confront our own values, our own system of beliefs and attitudes. Our image of ourselves as people, our self-knowledge, will inevitably affect our every interaction, including those with our pupils. Whether formally in the classroom, or informally in the corridors and walkways of the school, each of us will communicate our values and priorities to those in our charge. We can arrange the school or the classroom to meet our own needs. We can differentiate among our pupils according to their social classes, making some our "pets" and some the object of our scorn. We can handle some children as if they are diseased and others as if they are prized humans. We can become personally close or remain distant and aloof. Our human qualities are out there for all to see in our every action with our children.

---

*

This case example was provided by Dr. Bernard Seiderman, currently Director of Curriculum for the Great Neck, Long Island, school system.

Summary

There is a need for a realistic perception of the teacher as a human being rather than as some standard of personal perfection, a paragon of virtue. Historically, communities have lumped teachers in the same category as clergymen and other guardians of public chastity.

To counteract this view we need to understand the "hidden agenda" in teaching. In the McLuhan sense, we see three sets of attitudes as forming important segments of the "medium as the message" in the classroom. The differences between what we say or pay lip service to and how we actually behave in class is another way of underscoring the same point—namely, the importance of our own attitudes.

Three important sets of attitudes should be considered. The first involves general attitudes toward learning, the most pervasive of which is "knowledge equals truth." In this view there is always a right answer and a wrong answer. Knowledge is fixed and static, to be memorized and repeated back. Thus, how a teacher understands the nature of knowledge or knowing is an important attitude.

A second attitudinal set concerns how a teacher views children. The Rosenthal self-fulfilling prophecy, along with other studies of classroom interaction, attest to the power of these concepts and their positive or negative impact on the pupils.

In the third category are teacher attitudes toward self. How a person views his or her self is usually transmitted clearly to the pupils. The seven self-images from Professor Thelen underscore the Socratic dictum of "know thy self."

Finally, should teachers inculcate values in their pupils or should they develop a value-free teaching approach? The value-free view is reduced to an absurdity with reference to the World War II Concentration Camp example. Teaching to stimulate growth and development is presented as an alternate view.

REFERENCES

1
M. B. Smiley and J. S. Diekhoff, *Prologue to Teaching* (New York: Oxford University Press, 1959), p. 32.

2
B. Kaufman, *Up the Down Staircase* (Englewood Cliffs, N.J.: Prentice-Hall, 1964).

3
J. Kozol, *Death at an Early Age* (Boston: Houghton Mifflin, 1967).

4
K. Ryan, *Don't Smile 'til Christmas* (Chicago: University of Chicago Press, 1970).

5
N. V. Overly, ed., *The Unstudied Curriculum* (Washington, D.C.: Association for Supervision and Curriculum Development, NEA, 1970).

6
H. M. McLuhan, *Understanding Media* (New York: McGraw-Hill, 1964).

7
J. Holt, *How Children Fail* (Boston: Pitman, 1964).

8
O. J. Harvey, *Experience, Structure and Adaptability* (New York: Springer, 1966). See also O. J. Harvey et al., "Teachers' Beliefs, Classroom Atmosphere and Student Behavior," *AERA Journal* 5, no. 2 (March 1968):151–166.

9
R. Rosenthal, "Teacher Expectation and Pupil Learning," in N. V. Overly, *The Unstudied Curriculum*, pp. 53–84.

10
R. Rosenthal and L. Jacobson, *Pygmalion in the Classroom* (New York: Holt, Rinehart and Winston, 1968).

11
J. Jung, *The Experimenter's Dilemma* (New York: Harper & Row, 1971).

12
H. Becker, "Social Class Variation in the Teacher-Pupil Relationship," in R. C. Sprinthall and N. A. Sprinthall, eds., *Educational Psychology* (New York: Van Nostrand Reinhold, 1969), pp. 300–308.

13
R. Gregory with Robert Lipsyte, *Nigger: An Autobiography* (New York: Pocket Books, 1964). Copyright © 1964 by Dick Gregory Enterprises, Inc. Reprinted by permission of the publishers, E. P. Dutton & Co., Inc.

14
E. Leacock, *Teaching and Learning in City Schools,* (New York: Basic Books, 1969).

15
J. E. Brophy and T. L. Good, *Teacher-Student Relationships: Causes and Consequences* (New York: Holt, Rinehart and Winston, 1974).

16
J. Coleman et al., *Equality of Educational Opportunity* (Washington, D.C.: U.S. Department of Health, Education, and Welfare, 1966).

17
H. Thelen, *Dynamics of Groups at Work* (Chicago: University of Chicago Press, 1954), pp. 36–41.

Before going on ...

So far in this volume we have been stressing a set of assumptions that represent a system of values, attitudes, and perceptions we prize. We feel, for example, that the idea of stages of growth and development allows us to view the problems of education from the point of view of our children's needs. When L. K. Frank (see Chapter 8) spoke of the fundamental psychological needs of children as opposed to those of adults, he provided us with a basic framework for examining our values as educators. If children grow and develop at different rates and proceed through different stages, we as educators have the opportunity to facilitate and nurture that growth. We noted in Chapters 3, 4, and 5 that certain sensitive periods provide us with an opportunity to nurture particular kinds of growth. In Chapters 6, 7, 8, 9, and 10 we outlined in greater detail the stages of cognitive, linguistic, personal, and moral development. Equipped with this understanding, the teacher's self-definition as an educator can include the objectives of promoting maximal growth and development within each stage and across all stages. In Chapters 11 through 15 we stressed the problems of intervention, both from a theoretical and from a practical point of view. These five chapters should allow you to put theory to practice.

When we noted the problems confronting educational psychology in Chapters 1 and 2, we emphasized the troublesome dichotomy between thinking about educational problems and doing something about these problems. The teacher's self-image is clearly a key element in resolving this separation. If the self-image is that of someone who arranges practice and creates the conditions for maximal learning matched to the pupils' developmental stages, then the dichotomy disappears. By valuing the growth and development of each child and by knowing what the effective teaching techniques are, the educator comes close to the original definition of an educator. To educate, in its root sense, means to draw out, to elicit, to develop. We need to clear away the psychological blind spots imposed by social-class distinction, our own stereotyped perceptions, and the narrow and confining sets of attitudes we have toward knowledge, children, and ourselves. By putting on a new set of personal "lenses" we may come to see both ourselves and children in significantly different ways.

In closing this section, one final, very significant point should be made. Developmentally oriented teachers and professors are generally so convinced of the basic value of growth and development that they at times become overly zealous and ideological. If we are convinced that it is important for children and

419

teenagers to learn to think more logically, systematically, divergently, and convergently, as well as to develop empathy, compassion, and their own humanness, then it is all too easy to become a single-minded "pusher" of our own pet goals. If we are convinced that growth is good, we may find ourselves constantly pulling, exhorting, cajoling, shoving, engendering perpetual dissonance, always "jamming," always saying to pupils in so many words, "Well, that's O.K., but not quite good enough. Let's move on!"

This creates a double bind for the pupil. If new growth requires constant agitation, we shall soon opt out. We all get sick of being constantly prodded, nagged, or exhorted to excel. Thus, the educator needs a special blend of competence to create a learning atmosphere that helps pupils grow *and* affirms the acceptability of their current status.

Robert White has used the metaphor of the horticulturist as a way to sum up the paradox of human teaching and human learning:

> *The nurturing of growth requires the patience of the gardener rather than the hasty intervention of the mechanic. It requires waiting for impulse to declare itself, for interest to appear, for initiative to come forth. . . . When the fast technological march of our civilization is encouraging us all to think like mechanics it is particularly important to preserve where it is still needed the long patience of the husbandman.**

William Perry presents the process and the paradox in more personal terms. He recently described an incident in his own life as an illustration. He was introducing his wife, Mary, to his aging father; only later did he learn his father was terminally ill at the time and this was to be the last meeting of Bill, his wife, and his father. At one point in the conversation, the father looked carefully at Mary and asked her if she was progressing. When she nodded in the affirmative, he then went on: "Well that's just fine, Mary, I'm glad that you're progressing. It's always important to grow, to improve yourself, to move ahead." At this point there was a moment of silence. Then the aging man leaned forward and, looking very directly at Mary, said: "But, remember, it's also important to be okay where you are right now!"

---

*
R. W. White, *Lives in Progress*, 2nd ed. (New York: Holt, Rinehart and Winston, 1966), pp. 409–510.

Individual differences

"There's An Art To Analyzing Statistics"

from *Herblock's State of the Union* (Simon & Schuster, 1972).

16

Measurement and individual differences

NO ONE IS EXACTLY LIKE ANYONE ELSE

As you look within yourself and at the people around you, you realize that you are a very special and unique being. Nobody else in the world is quite like you. Nobody else in the world has the same physiological equipment, the same genetic endowment (unless, of course, you are an identical twin), or has experienced the same sequence of life situations. Nobody else uses the identical blend of defense mechanisms that you use when encountering stress, and nobody else is guided by the exact mixture of motives, attitudes, and feelings. Thus, one of the basic themes of psychology is that of individual differences: No one is exactly like anyone else.

IN SOME WAYS ALL PEOPLE ARE EXACTLY ALIKE

It is, however, impossible to avoid drawing comparisons as you look at the people around you. Perhaps you notice many similarities. You have a friend who seems to enjoy the same things you do. You play chess with someone who beats you just about as often as you beat him. You and your best friend spend about the same amount of time studying for an exam, and you make similar grades on that exam. Perhaps you have been pleasantly surprised to discover, during a conversation with someone you have just met, how similar your abilities, goals, tastes, and feelings really are. In many ways you are surprisingly like many other people. In some ways you are just like all other people; that is, you eat, drink, breathe, sleep, exercise, and have the same physiological needs. Therefore, it can be said that in some ways all people are exactly alike.

At some schools, students are given the responsibility of recording their own progress in a subject area.

MEASUREMENT

In order to assess how much you resemble and how much you differ from other people, you must in some way be measured. Meaningful comparisons cannot be made without meaningful measurements. Measurement is the assignment of a number to an object or event according to rules. This may represent something physical, as when you step on the scales and note, with dismay or pleasure, the number that indicates your weight. Or it may be more subtle, as when you take a vocational aptitude test and receive your score in "mechanical aptitude." You have, in fact, been measured hundreds of times in hundreds of areas. In order to buy new clothes you must know your size. When you visit a physician, your temperature and blood pressure are taken. Before entering college, you probably took an aptitude test. Hundreds of numbers have been assigned to you, from shoe size to that first quiz grade you received in elementary school.

RELIABILITY AND VALIDITY

In order to draw meaningful comparisons, there must be meaningful measurements. In order to have meaning, all measurements must satisfy two basic criteria: they must be reliable and they must be valid.

Reliability

Reliability is an indication of the consistency of a measurement; that is, if we measure something which is not itself changing dramatically, we should assign roughly the same number to it over repeated measurements. If you stepped on the scales and read 140 pounds one day, 240 pounds the next day, and 40 pounds the day after that, your faith in the precision of the scale would be severely shaken. The numbers would be meaningless. The same is true of psychological tests. If you took an IQ test one day and received a score of 140, and then you took the same test the next day and received a score of 50, you would undoubtedly feel bewildered. In order to have any meaning, our measurements must be consistent over repeated measurements—that is, reliable.

Reliability indicates a measurement's consistency

On the other hand, a test cannot be so consistent as to be rigid and misleading. It was mentioned that a good test yields roughly the same scores over repeated measurements as long as that which is being measured does not change dramatically. Suppose, however, you went on a crash diet, and every day your friends commented on how much weight you had lost, and after a few weeks you found your clothes no longer fit. If, in this instance, you still found the scales were reading the same weight, it would be obvious that the measurements were too consistent to be an adequate reflection of reality.

Validity

While measurements must be reliable, they must also be valid. Validity is an indication of the extent to which a test measures what it is supposed to measure. When you step on the scales you want to know your weight, not your IQ, or mechanical aptitude, or some unknown quality. To assess validity we compare test scores against some separate or independent observation of the thing being measured. For example, if we were trying to establish whether or not a certain test of flying ability is valid, we might give the test to a large group of student pilots and then compare their test scores with the flight instructor's ratings of each person's actual ability to fly a plane. If those with the highest test scores also turn out to be the best pilots, the test is considered valid. The validity of such a test is important, because it allows us to predict on the basis of a person's test score whether or not that person will profit from flying lessons. Similarly, a valid test of college aptitude would predict whether an individual will be able to profit from the college experience. Thus, measurements must be an accurate reflection of what they are intended to measure—that is, valid.

A test should measure what it is intended to measure

CORRELATION: A TOOL FOR JUDGING RELIABILITY AND VALIDITY

In order to give precise statements about reliability and validity, a statistical technique called correlation is utilized. Although correlation does not allow for cause-and-effect statements, it does allow the scientist to make predictions.

Correlation is a statement about the strength of the association between two (or possibly more) variables. If the correlation between two variables is high, the variables will tend to vary together: that is, wherever one of the traits is

Correlation shows the strength of the association among variables found, chances are good that the other trait will also be found. If we observed that people with blonde hair usually have blue eyes, then we would say that there is a correlation between the variables hair color and eye color. This is not to say that having blonde hair causes one to have blue eyes, but it does allow us to predict, whenever we know that certain individuals have blonde hair, that they are also likely to have blue eyes.

Reliability can be established through the use of correlation

Correlation is one way to assess reliability. If a certain test is given to a large group of subjects on two separate occasions, and if those individuals who score high on the test the first time also score high the second time and those who score low the first time also score low the second time, the two sets of measurements are said to correlate and the test is considered reliable. A high correlation between the two sets of scores indicates reliability because it demonstrates that the test is yielding consistent scores. The two variables, that is, the scores on the first administration of the test and the scores on the second, are in fact occurring together, or correlating.

Correlation can also establish validity

Correlation can also establish validity. To establish validity we would give a test measuring some ability or trait to a group of individuals and then correlate their scores with actual performances by these same individuals on the ability or trait being measured. For example, we might compare scores on a sales aptitude test with actual performance in selling a certain product. If, in fact, there is a correlation between the two variables (the test scores and the number of sales achieved), the test has been shown to be valid—it is indeed measuring what it is intended to measure.

Reliability and validity are only two ways to apply this extremely useful technique. Later in this chapter we will cite other applications of correlation in educational psychology, and we will present a simple mathematical procedure for computing correlation.

DISTRIBUTIONS

To create meaning out of the apparent chaos of raw data, the researcher begins by putting his or her measurements into an order. The first step is to form a distribution of scores. "Distribution" simply means the arrangement of any set of scores in order of magnitude. Table 16.1 is a set of IQ scores.

Arranging these scores into a distribution means listing them sequentially from high to low. Table 16.2 is a distribution of the IQ scores from Table 16.1.

A distribution allows the observer to see general trends more readily than the unordered set of raw scores does. To further simplify our inspection of the data, they can be presented as a frequency distribution. A frequency distribution is a listing of each score achieved, together with the number of individuals receiving that score. Table 16.3 is a frequency distribution of our IQ scores.

The X at the top of the first column stands for raw scores (in this case, IQ) and the f over the second column stands for frequency of occurrence. As can be seen, of the fifteen people taking the test, two received scores of 115, two received 110, three scored 100, two scored 95, and everyone else made a unique score.

Table 16.1 Unordered IQ scores.
75
100
105
95
120
130
95
90
115
85
115
100
110
100
110

Table 16.2 Distribution of IQ scores.
130
120
115
115
110
110
105
100
100
100
95
95
90
85
75

Table 16.3 IQ scores presented in the form of a frequency distribution.

X (raw score)	f (frequency of occurrence)
130	1
120	1
115	2
110	2
105	1
100	3
95	2
90	1
85	1
75	1

GRAPHS

In addition to presenting frequency distributions in table form, statisticians often present their data in graph form. A graph has the advantage of being a kind of "picture" of the data. It is customary to indicate the raw scores, or actual values of the variable, on the horizontal, or X-axis, called the abscissa. The frequency of occurrence is presented on the vertical, or Y-axis, called the ordinate.

Figure 16.1 shows the data previously presented in tabular form arranged in a graphic form called a histogram, or bar graph. To construct a histogram, or bar graph, a rectangle is drawn over each raw score. The height of the rectangle indicates the frequency of occurrence for each score. Much of the data in educational psychology is presented in this way.

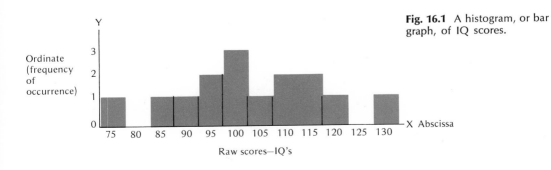

Fig. 16.1 A histogram, or bar graph, of IQ scores.

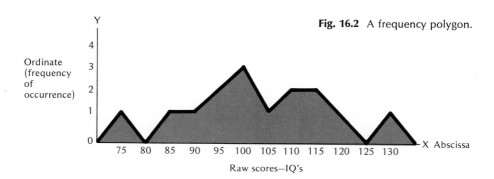

Fig. 16.2 A frequency polygon.

Figure 16.2 shows the same data arranged in another commonly used graphic form, called a frequency polygon. To construct a frequency polygon, the IQ scores are again shown on the X-axis and the frequency of occurrence on the Y-axis. However, instead of rectangles, we use a single point to designate the frequency of each score. These points are then connected by a series of straight lines.

In both the histogram and the frequency polygon it is essential that the base of the ordinate represent a frequency of zero—if not, the graph may tell a very misleading story. For example, suppose we are graphing data from a learning study which shows how increasing the number of learning trials increases the amount learned.

Let us plot the number of trials on the abscissa and the frequency of correct responses on the ordinate (Fig. 16.3). Our graph shows that by trial 4 the subject made eight correct responses and that by trial 10 the subject made twelve correct choices. These data are typical of the results obtained in learning studies;

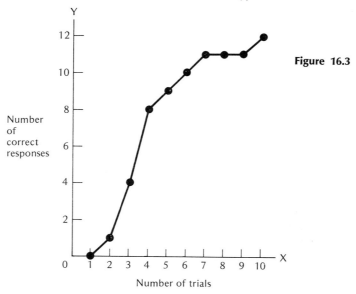

Figure 16.3

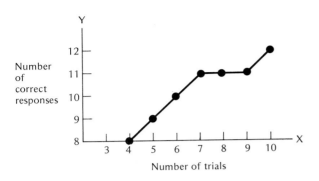

Fig. 16.4 Here, the base of the ordinate is not set at zero. Be wary of such graphs, since they can easily lead to a false interpretation of data.

that is, a great deal of learning usually occurs during the first few trials, but, as the number of trials increases, there is less and less further increase in learning.

Suppose, however, the statistician wished to give a false interpretation of the data. He or she could simply focus on one small area of the graph (see Fig. 16.4). Now the same data tell a very different story about how learning takes place. Now it looks like no learning took place before trial 4 and that the great bulk of learning took place between trials 4 and 10. We know from the previous graph that this is incorrect. In fact, the majority of the learning took place during the first four or five trials and, between trials 4 and 10, was actually beginning to top out or level off. This is one instance of how statistics can be used to distort data—if the audience is naive about statistical techniques. Whenever a graph is presented in which the base of the ordinate is not set at zero, be on the alert. The stage has been set for a possible sleight-of-hand trick.

Figures don't lie

But liars can figure

FIND THE "AVERAGE"

To help us understand how individuals differ and how they are alike, there are some useful techniques for finding the "average," or typical score, in a distribution. Knowing the average IQ for a certain class may help us plan the curriculum, decide how extensively certain topics should be covered in class, or choose books for the library. Information about the typical score in a distribution allows us to interpret more meaningfully all the scores in the distribution.

Central tendency: averageness, or typicality

Statisticians have three methods for obtaining the average, and each is designed, when used appropriately, to give us the most accurate possible picture of the distribution. The averages are called measures of central tendency, because they describe the typical, middle, or central score in a distribution; they tell us about our average or typical person's score. Choosing the appropriate method can be tricky, because the interpretation of the data may vary widely, depending on how the average has been obtained.

The mean

If you were given a set of IQ scores and asked to find the average score, you would most likely compute the mean. That is, you would add all the IQ scores together and divide by the total number of scores. The mean is thus the arithmetic average; it is certainly the most commonly used measure of central tendency.

Statisticians use the symbol $\overline{X}$ to denote the mean. The equation for computing the mean is

$$\overline{X} = \frac{\Sigma X}{N}$$

The Greek letter Σ (capital sigma) is a symbol that tells us to add; it is read as "summation of." N stands for the number of cases. Thus the equation tells us that the mean ($\overline{X}$) is equal to the summation (Σ) of the raw scores (X) divided by the number of cases (N). The mean of our distribution of IQ scores would be computed as in Table 16.4.

Use the mean when the distribution is balanced

As it happens, the mean is an appropriate measure of central tendency in the preceding example because the distribution is fairly well balanced; that is, there are no extreme scores in any one direction. Since the mean is computed by adding together all the scores in the distribution, it is not easily influenced by extreme scores, unless the extreme scores are all in one direction. The mean is typically a stable measure of central tendency.

Interpreting the mean can sometimes be very deceptive, especially in groups where the population itself or the size of the population changes. For example, the mean IQ of the typical freshman class in college is usually about five points lower than the mean of the same class when the students later become seniors. Does this indicate that students increase their IQ's as they proceed through college? No, because since the size of the senior class is almost always smaller than the size of the freshman class, the two populations are no longer the same. The lowest IQ's in the freshman class are apt to leave college and never become seniors.

The median

In some situations, however, the use of the mean can lead to an extremely distorted picture of the "average" in a distribution. For example, look at the distribution of annual incomes in Table 16.5.

In Table 16.5 one income score ($10,000,000.00) is so extremely far above the others that to use the mean income as a reflection of the average income would give a misleading picture of high prosperity for this distribution. A distribution that is unbalanced due to a few extreme scores in one direction is said to be skewed.

Use the median when the distribution is skewed

A much more accurate representation of central tendency for a skewed distribution is the median, or middlemost score in a distribution. Whereas the mean income in Table 16.5 was found to be $777,546.15, the median would be $9,400.00, a much more accurate reflection of the typical income for the distribution. Since income distributions are usually skewed, you should be on the alert for an inflated figure whenever the mean income is reported. The median is generally a more appropriate value when reporting incomes. To calculate the median, be sure the scores are in distribution form, that is, arranged in order of

Table 16.4 Calculation of the mean from a distribution of raw scores.

X	Calculation
130	
120	
115	
115	
110	
110	
105	
100	
100	
100	
95	
95	
90	
85	$\overline{X} = \dfrac{\Sigma X}{N} = \dfrac{1545}{15}$
75	
1545	$\overline{X} = 103$

Table 16.5 A distribution of income scores that is skewed to the right.

$10,000,000.00
10,000.00
10,000.00
9,500.00
9,400.00
9,400.00
9,400.00 — Median
9,300.00
9,000.00
8,500.00
8,000.00
8,000.00
7,600.00
$10,108,100.00
$\overline{X} = $777,546.15$

magnitude. Then count down through one-half of the scores. For example, in Table 16.5 there are thirteen income scores in the distribution. We therefore count down six scores, and the seventh score is the median (there will be the same number of scores above the seventh score as there are below it). If there are an even number of scores in a distribution (see Table 16.6), the median is found by determining the score that lies halfway between the two middle scores or, in this case, 114.5. Unlike the mean, the median is not affected by an extreme score in one direction. In Table 16.6, for example, the median would still be 114.5 even if the low score were 6 instead of 112, whereas the mean would be an unrepresentative 97.83 (see Table 16.7).

Table 16.6 Calculation of the median with an even number of scores.

120
118
115
114 —114.5 Median
114
112
693
$\overline{X} = 115.50$ Mean

Table 16.7 Calculation of the median with an even number of scores and a skewed distribution.

120
118
115
114 —114.5 Median
114
6
587
$\overline{X} = 97.83$ Mean

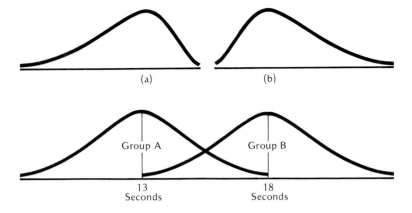

Fig. 16.5 A graphic presentation of skewed distributions: (a) negatively skewed; (b) positively skewed.

(a)   (b)

Fig. 16.6 Bimodal distribution.

Group A   Group B

13
Seconds

18
Seconds

Figure 16.5 shows what skewed distributions look like in graphic form. In the positively skewed distribution, most of the scores are found at the low end of the distribution, whereas in the negatively skewed distribution, most of the scores are at the high end. We label this according to the direction of the tail. When the tail goes to the right, we call the curve positively skewed; when it goes to the left, it is negatively skewed.

The mode

The third measure of central tendency is called the mode. The mode is the score that occurs most frequently in a distribution. In a frequency polygon the mode is located where the curve is at its highest point; in a histogram it is located at the tallest bar. Some distributions, called bimodal, have two modes (see Fig. 16.6). Distributions of this type occur where scores are clustered in two separate places, or where the group being measured probably breaks down into two subgroups.

Assume that the distribution in Fig. 16.6 represents the running speed (in seconds) in the seventy-yard dash for a large group of seventh graders. There are two modes: one at 13 seconds and the other at 18 seconds. Since there are two scores sharing the same high frequency, it is probable that two subgroups are being portrayed. For example, the running speeds for boys may be clustering around one mode while the speeds for girls are clustering around the other.

VARIABILITY: THE NAME OF THE GAME IN EDUCATIONAL PSYCHOLOGY

Just as the measures of central tendency give us information about the similarity among measurements, measures of variability give us information about how scores differ or vary. Measures of variability are crucial in education, since they give us vital information about one of psychology's basic themes—individual differences.

The range—*R*

One way to describe variability in any distribution of scores is to compute the range. The range is the difference between the highest and lowest scores, and it is a measure of the width of the total distribution. The range is given as a single value. For example, if the highest score in an IQ distribution is 140 and the lowest score is 60, the R would equal 80.

The standard deviation

Though the range is important in giving meaning to a set of scores, more important still is the standard deviation. The standard deviation (S.D.) tells us how widely the scores vary around the mean. The higher the S.D., the more the scores vary around the mean, or the more heterogeneous is the group of scores. Since there are individual differences, the S.D. tells us how much all the scores typically differ from the mean. This standard or typical deviation is then presented as a single value.

Variation around the mean

In calculating the S.D., the following steps are needed (see Table 16.8):

Calculating the standard deviation

1
Add the X's to obtain ΣX.

2
Divide by N to obtain $\overline{X}$.

3
Subtract the mean from each score to get $X - \overline{X}$.

4
Square each of these differences to get $(X - \overline{X})^2$.

5
Add the squares to get $\Sigma(X - \overline{X})^2$.

6
Divide this total by N.

7
Take the square root to obtain the S.D.

Table 16.8 Calculation of the standard deviation from a distribution of raw scores.

X	$(X - \overline{X})$	$(X - \overline{X})^2$	Calculations
130	27	729	
120	17	289	
115	12	144	
115	12	144	
110	7	49	
110	7	49	
105	2	4	
100	−3	9	$\overline{X} = \dfrac{\Sigma X}{N} = \dfrac{1545}{15}$
100	−3	9	
100	−3	9	
95	−8	64	$\overline{X} = 103$
95	−8	64	
90	−13	169	$\text{S.D.} = \sqrt{\dfrac{\Sigma(X - \overline{X})^2}{N}} = \sqrt{\dfrac{2840}{15}} = \sqrt{189.33}$
85	−18	324	
75	−28	784	
1545		2840	S.D. = 13.76

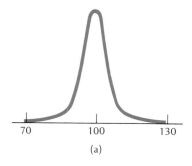

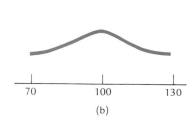

(a)   (b)

Fig. 16.7 Two IQ distributions with different standard deviations.

In Fig. 16.7 we see a representation of two IQ distributions, both of which have the same range (60) and the same mean (100). The distributions are different because they have different standard deviations. Distribution (b) has a relatively large standard deviation, indicating that the scores deviate widely from the mean. Distribution (a), with a smaller standard deviation, indicates that the variability is much less, that most of the scores are clustering rather tightly around the mean.

The normal curve

Many behavioral measures in educational psychology conform to what statisticians call the normal curve (see Fig. 16.8). The normal curve is actually a theoretical distribution, but so many measurements come so close to this ideal that it is of utmost importance. The normal curve is a frequency-distribution curve

Fig. 16.8 The normal curve is a frequency distribution curve with scores plotted on the x-axis and frequency of occurrence on the y-axis.

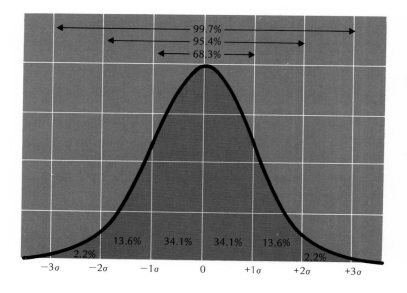

with scores plotted on the x-axis and frequency of occurrence on the y-axis. However, it has a number of interesting features that set it apart from other frequency-distribution curves. First, in a normal curve most of the scores cluster around the center of the distribution, and as we move away from the center in either direction, there are fewer and fewer scores. Second, it is symmetrical; that is, the two halves of the curve are identical. It is in perfect balance. Third, the mean, median, and mode all fall at the same point, the midpoint of the distribution. Finally, the normal curve has some constant characteristics with regard to the standard deviation.

The mean divides the normal curve into two equal halves, with 50 percent of the scores falling above the mean and 50 percent falling below it. (Note that the mean and mode are at exactly the same point as the median in the normal curve.) The area between the mean and a point one standard deviation above the mean includes 34 percent of the scores. Since the normal curve is symmetrical, 34 percent of the cases also fall between the mean and a point one standard deviation below the mean. Thus, between the two points which are one standard deviation away from the mean, that is, ±1 S.D., there are 68 percent (just twice 34 percent) of all the cases. As we go away from the mean another full standard deviation, 13.5 percent of the distribution is added to each side. Thus, approximately 95 percent of the cases fall between ±2 S.D. units. Similarly, since going out a third S.D. from the mean adds 2.5 percent in each side, 99 percent, or virtually all the cases, fall between ±3 S.D. units. Less than 1 percent of the scores lie beyond ±3 S.D. units.

These facts relating percentage of cases to units of the standard deviation are constants; that is, the facts are true regardless of the size of the standard deviation. These constants hold as long as the curve is normal.

The mean, median, and mode divide the normal curve in half

The normal curve and the standard deviation

STANDARD SCORES

It is difficult to compare scores on different tests without knowing the mean and the standard deviation for each test. For example, if you were to get a score of 72 on a certain math test and 64 on an English test, you wouldn't know on which test your performance was higher. The mean on the math test might have been 85, and the mean on the English test might have been 50, in which case you scored higher on the English test even though your raw score was lower. The point is that information about the distribution of scores must be obtained in order that raw scores can be interpreted. For this reason, we use standard scores, or z scores, which take the distribution into account. This allows us to understand an individual's test performance relative to others taking the same test. The z score is equal to the difference between the raw score and the mean, divided by the standard deviation.

The z score

$$z = \frac{X - \overline{X}}{\text{S.D.}}$$

The z score indicates, in units of standard deviation, how far above or below the mean a certain score lies. If the mean of the math distribution (85) were subtracted from your math score of 72 and divided by the S.D. (10), your z score would be −1.3.

$$z = \frac{72 - 85}{10} = \frac{-13}{10} = -1.3$$

Thus on the math test you fell 1.3 S.D. units below the mean. A negative z score always indicates the score is below the mean, while a positive z score shows the score is above the mean. A score of 64 on the English test minus the mean of 50, and divided by a standard deviation, again of 10, yields a z score of 1.4.

$$z = \frac{64 - 50}{10} = \frac{14}{10} = 1.4$$

Since the sign in this case is positive, your score on the English test falls 1.4 S.D. units above the mean. Though your raw score on the English test is lower than your raw score on the math test, your actual performance on the English test, compared to all other performances on the same test, is considerably higher. Thus, by converting raw scores into z scores, comparisons can be made between an individual's performance on different distributions, with different means and standard deviations.

Centiles

A raw score can be described very precisely by converting it into a centile or percentile. A centile is that point in a distribution at or below which a given percentage of scores fall. For example, a score at the 95th centile means that 95 percent of the scores in the distribution are at or below that point, whereas a score at the 5th centile means that only 5 percent of the scores fall at or below that point. By knowing the percentage of cases falling between various S.D. units on the normal curve, one's centile may be calculated. In the distribution for the normal curve (Fig. 16.8), for example, 34 percent of the cases fall between the mean and −1 S.D. Since 50 percent of the cases fall below the mean, and since 34 percent of these cases fall between the mean and −1 S.D., we can see that 16 percent of the cases must fall below −1 S.D. A z score of −1, meaning a raw score one full S.D. below the mean, would yield a centile score of 16. Or, a z score of +1, indicating a raw score of 1 full S.D. above the mean, would mean a centile score of 84 (the 34 percent falling between the mean and 1 S.D. plus the 50 percent falling below the mean).

The relationship between z scores and centiles Statisticians can determine the centile for any z score, not just those for whole numbers. For example, a z score of 1.52 shows that about 44 percent of the cases fall between the mean and 1.52 S.D. units. Thus the centile for that z score would be 94 (the 44 percent falling between the z score and the mean plus the 50 percent lying below the mean). Tables giving the percentage of cases between the mean and any z score can be found in all elementary statistics texts.

Assume that we are working with an IQ distribution whose mean is 100 and whose S.D. is 15. A student with an IQ of 122 would have a z score of 122 − 100, divided by the S.D. of 15, or 1.47. The student with an IQ of 122 would fall 1.47 S.D. units above the mean. A z score table indicates that 43 percent of the cases fall between a z of 1.47 and the mean. Adding that to the 50 percent below the mean, we now know that the student with an IQ of 122 is at the 93rd centile.

CORRELATION: A USEFUL TOOL FOR MAKING PREDICTIONS

Although correlation does not imply causation, it is a useful tool for making predictions. A correlation is a statement about the relationship between two variables; it tells us the extent to which the two variables are associated, or the extent to which they occur together. There is, for example, a correlation between College Board scores and college grades. This means that the two variables, College Board scores and college grades, tend to occur together: people with high College Board scores tend to have higher college grade-point averages than do people with low College Board scores.

The sign of the correlation

Correlations come in three general forms: positive, negative, and zero. Positive correlations are produced when individuals who score high on the first variable also score high on the second, and those who score low on the first variable also score low on the second. For example, a positive correlation between height and weight means that those individuals who are above average in height are also above average in weight, and those who are below average in height are correspondingly below average in weight. Negative correlations are produced when individuals who score high on the first variable tend to score low on the second, and those who score low on the first, score high on the second. A negative correlation between college grades and number of absences means that those who are above average in college grades tend to have fewer absences, whereas those who are below average in college grades tend to have more than the average number of absences. Finally, zero correlations are produced when individuals who score high on the first variable are as likely to score high on the second variable as they are to score low; or, when individuals who score low on the first variable are as likely to score low on the second variable as they are to score high.

A positive correlation

A negative correlation

A zero correlation

Correlation values

In order to express the degree to which two variables are associated, or correlated, a single number is used. This number may vary from plus 1 through 0 to minus 1. A value of +1 indicates a maximum positive correlation. A maximum relationship is obtained when two measures of a group of individuals, for example, height and weight, associate perfectly. There can be no exceptions when the correlation is +1. Thus, every single individual in the group who is higher than another in height is also higher in weight. A value of 0 indicates no relationship at all, or a zero correlation. A value of −1 indicates a maximum negative correlation. A correlation of −1 between college grades and number of absences would mean that every single individual in the group who is higher than

Correlations range from +1.00 to −1.00

ANNE ANASTASI

Anne Anastasi was born in 1909 and brought up in New York City. She attended Public School 33, where she was awarded a gold medal for general excellence. She then entered public high school, but after two frustrating months she dropped out. Although she had found her stay at P.S. 33 to be happy, productive years, she found high school to be a total waste of time. Her high school was overcrowded, and she resented both the fifteen-minute trolley-car ride and also the fact that her teachers were remote and impersonal.

During her drop-out phase, there were many family discussions about her academic future. Finally, a friend suggested that she should simply skip high school completely and go to college. Thus in 1924, at the precocious age of 15, Anne Anastasi became a freshman math major at Barnard College. As a freshman, she took an introductory psychology course, and although she found the course interesting, it was not until her sophomore year, when she took a course in developmental psychology with Hollingworth, that she decided psychology was to be her life work. Psychology gave her the opportunity to have the best of two worlds. She could satisfy her interest in mathematics through the study of psychological statistics and also her emerging interest in human development and behavior.

She graduated from Barnard at nineteen and immediately entered the Ph.D. program in psychology at Columbia University. She received her doctorate two years later. The high point of her short tenure as a graduate student came during the summer of 1929. She began that memorable summer as a research assistant to the famous American geneticist Charles B. Davenport. Next she took a six-week course with the illustrious learning theorist Clark Hull. Finally, as the summer ended, she enjoyed the "heady privilege" of attending the International Congress of Psychology at Yale University. There she saw and heard great psychologists from all over the world, including Pavlov, Spearman, and McDougall.

In 1930 Anastasi joined the faculty at Barnard College, where she remained until 1939. She then went to Queens College in New York as chairman of the psychology department, and in 1947 she joined the faculty at Fordham, where she still teaches and continues her research.

Anastasi considers herself to be a "generalist" in the field of psychology. Her interests range widely, and she has published in such diverse areas as the psychology of art, memory, personality, intelligence, emotion, statistics, language development, test construction, cultural differences, creativity, male and female differences, and the nature-nurture controversy. The bibliography of Anastasi's papers and books reads like a compendium of the whole field of psychology. There are few areas in psychol-

ogy to which this talented woman has not devoted some of her time and energy.

In 1971 Anastasi was honored by her professional colleagues by being chosen as the president of the American Psychological Association, a group of over 31,000 members.

Anastasi is a firm believer in the influence of early experience on intellectual growth and development. She urges a program of concentrated effort on improving environmental conditions at early life stages, especially for disadvantaged groups. She feels that early in life the cumulative effects of an impoverished environment can be minimized. She is also a firm believer in intelligence testing, when the tests are administered properly and evaluated fairly. She feels that IQ tests should not be discontinued just because some children receive lower scores than others. This would be like asking a physician to throw away his thermometer just because children who are ill register an undesirable deviation from the norm. Measuring instruments don't produce social discrimination, only people do.

In 1958, in her paper "Heredity, Environment and The Question 'How?'" Anastasi argues that people should stop asking the question about which component, heredity or environment, is more important in determining individual differences. A better question is "how" heredity and environment interact in the development of behavioral differences. The focus should be on the mechanism of the interaction, because behavior is the result of the interaction. Anne Anastasi, the generalist, specifically recommends here that we take a new look at one of psychology's oldest and most-often-debated problems.

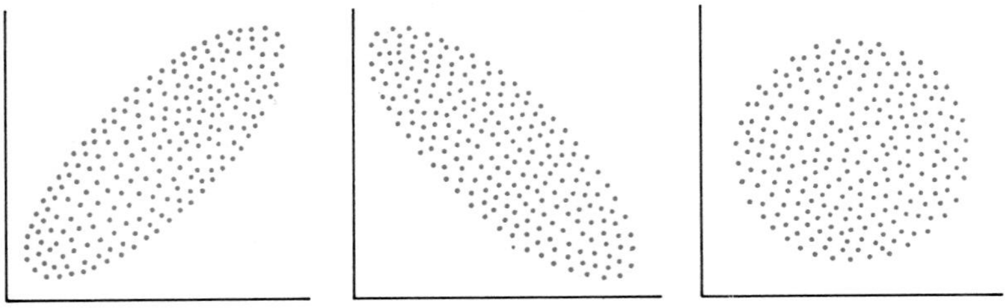

Fig. 16.9 Scatter plots showing three kinds of relationships existing between two variables.

another in college grades is also lower than that other in number of absences. Most correlations found in the literature fall somewhere between these perfect correlations of +1 and −1. The closer the correlation is to ±1, however, the more accurate the resulting prediction; and prediction, after all, is the major goal of correlation research. For example, if the correlation between height and weight were +.65, we could more accurately predict a given individual's weight, knowing his height, than if the correlation were only +.25.

The higher the correlation, the more accurate the prediction

Scatter plots

In order to get a visual representation of how two variables might correlate, statisticians use a graphic device known as a scatter plot. A scatter plot is a correlation graph in which each dot represents a pair of scores: one for the distribution of one set of scores and the other for the distribution of the other set of scores. Figure 16.9 shows the three kinds of relationships that can exist between two variables. The scatter plot on the left portrays a positive correlation: the array of dots goes from lower left to upper right, telling us that as one variable increases, so too does the other. The scatter plot in the middle portrays a negative correlation: the array of dots goes from upper left to lower right, telling us that as one variable increases, the other decreases. Finally, the scatter plot on the right portrays a zero correlation, or no relationship at all: as one variable changes, there is no related change in the other.

The Pearson *r*

One of the most frequently used correlation coefficients is called the Pearson Product Moment Correlation or, more simply, the Pearson *r*. This measure was developed by Karl Pearson, a student of Sir Francis Galton.

The Pearson *r* is the mean of the z-score products of the *X* and *Y* variables:

$$r = \frac{\Sigma z_x z_y}{N}$$

Calculating the Pearson r

To compute the Pearson *r* each raw score is converted into a z score. The z scores for each variable are then multiplied, and these products are added. The sum of the products is then divided by the number of products to get the mean product, which is the correlation coefficient. This is obviously a long and laborious process. Statisticians have therefore derived a simpler equation, one with fewer mathematical manipulations. If you have learned to calculate a standard deviation, computing a Pearson r will be fairly easy. Assume that we are interested in testing the hypothesis that there is some relationship or correlation between math ability and spelling ability among fifth-grade students. We administer a 12-item math quiz and a 12-item spelling quiz to a group of fifth graders. Let the math scores be represented on the X distribution and the spelling scores on the Y distribution. Then the Pearson r is calculated as follows:

1
Calculate the mean for each distribution. In Table 16.9, ΣX (or 65) divided by N (or 10) equals 6.5. Similarly, ΣY (or 70) divided by 10 equals 7.

2
Compute the standard deviation for each distribution. Subtract the mean from each raw score $(X - \bar{X})$ and square each of these differences. Thus for the X distribution, the first difference is −2.50, which when squared equals 6.25. Next, the difference of 5.50 is squared, yielding 30.25, and so on. These squared differences are added, yielding 104.50 for the X distribution. The Y distribution is treated exactly the same way: Subtract the mean from each raw score $(Y - \bar{Y})$. Square the differences and add the squares. Thus for the Y distribution, $\Sigma(Y - \bar{Y})^2$ is 86. Each of these values is then used to obtain the standard deviation for each distribution. For the X distribution, we divide 104.50 by 10 (thus obtaining 10.45) and then extract the square root (3.23) to obtain the standard deviation. For the Y distribution, we divide 86 by 10 (thus obtaining 8.60) and then extract the square root (2.93).

3
Multiply each raw score in the X distribution by its corresponding score in the Y distribution. Thus 4 times 6 equals 24; 12 times 10 equals 120; 2 times 3 equals 6, and so on. These XY values are then added, yielding a total ΣXY of 525.

4
Divide the ΣXY by N, and then subtract the product of the means. Thus 525/10 minus the product of 6.50 times 7 equals 7.

5
This value is then divided by the product of the standard deviations of X and Y. Thus 3.23 times 2.93 equals 9.46. Dividing 7 by 9.46 gives us a Pearson r of .739, which is rounded to .74.

Interpretation of r

Since the highest possible correlation is 1.00, which is a perfect positive correlation, the Pearson r of .74 indicates a fairly strong association between the two variables, math scores and spelling scores. Thus, our sample of fifth graders provides data that tell us that students who perform well on the math quiz are also likely to perform well on the spelling quiz. Since the correlation is not 1.00, we cannot say that every student who is high in math ability is also high in spelling ability. Our correlation of .74 indicates that there will be some exceptions, but

Karl Pearson, a student of Sir Francis Galton, devised the Pearson Product Moment Correlation, the Pearson r, which indicates the correlation between two variables.

Table 16.9 Calculation of the Pearson r.

Student No.	Mathematics			Spelling			
	X	$(X - \bar{X})$	$(X - \bar{X})^2$	Y	$(Y - \bar{Y})$	$(Y - \bar{Y})^2$	XY
1	4	−2.50	6.25	6	−1	1	24
2	12	5.50	30.25	10	3	9	120
3	2	−4.50	20.25	3	−4	16	6
4	5	−1.50	2.25	4	−3	9	20
5	9	2.50	6.25	5	−2	4	45
6	6	− .50	.25	10	3	9	60
7	2	−4.50	20.25	3	−4	16	6
8	10	3.50	12.25	10	3	9	100
9	6	− .50	.25	9	2	4	54
10	9	2.50	6.25	10	3	9	90
	65		104.50	70		86	525

$$\bar{X} = \frac{\Sigma X}{N} = \frac{65}{10} = 6.5 \qquad\qquad \bar{Y} = \frac{\Sigma Y}{N} = \frac{70}{10} = 7$$

$$S.D._x = \sqrt{\frac{\Sigma(X - \bar{X})^2}{N}} = \sqrt{\frac{104.50}{10}} = \sqrt{10.45} \qquad S.D._y = \sqrt{\frac{\Sigma(Y - \bar{Y})^2}{N}} = \sqrt{\frac{86}{10}} = \sqrt{8.60}$$

$$S.D._x = 3.23 \qquad\qquad S.D._y = 2.93$$

$$r = \frac{\Sigma XY/N - \bar{X} \times \bar{Y}}{(S.D._x)(S.D._y)} = \frac{525/10 - 6.5 \times 7}{3.23 \times 2.93} = \frac{52.50 - 45.50}{9.46}$$

$$r = \frac{7}{9.46}$$

$r = .739$, which is rounded to

$r = .74$

that in general the relationship will be dependable. Thus, knowing a student's math score allows us to predict his or her spelling score, and because the correlation is fairly strong, we will be right in our predictions far more often than we will be wrong. Athough correlation does not imply causation, it does allow for accurate predictions. We can't say that an individual is a good speller because he or she has high math ability, but we can say that, given information about the pupil's math ability, we can predict, with a fair degree of accuracy, how well he or she will spell.

SAMPLING: SOME FACTS ABOUT GENERALIZATION

Perhaps you have been told never to generalize, never to leap to conclusions on the basis of a few observations. An old proverb states that one swallow does not make a summer. Statisticians say, "Never generalize from an N of one." Someone once said that no generalization is absolutely true, even that one.

This is certainly all good advice. It prevents us from committing the inductive fallacy; that is, automatically assuming that all members of a class have a certain characteristic because one member of that class has it. It would be fallacious to say, "I once met a Mongolian who was a liar; therefore all Mongolians are liars."

However, under certain prescribed conditions, that is, using certain strategies or rules of the game, it can be appropriate to generalize on the basis of a limited number of observations. Certain statistical techniques exist that allow us to generalize to a whole group after observing some part of that group. The key to these techniques is that the small groups must be representative of the entire group; they must reflect the traits and characteristics of the entire group. If we want to predict political attitudes of Americans in general, we cannot interview just men, or just women, or just Democrats, or just people who are receiving social security. We must interview a group that represents all these traits and many more.

Good samples represent the population from which they are selected

The entire group, or the total number of people, things, or events having at least one trait in common is called a population. Any group selected from the population is called a sample. In order to ensure that the sample is representative of the population, statisticians usually use a technique called random sampling. Random sampling gives every single member of the entire population an equal chance of being selected for the sample. If you wanted to select a random sample of the population of students at your college, you could not do it by selecting every third person in the college cafeteria. Perhaps some students never eat in the cafeteria and they would not be represented in the sample. Nor could you choose a random sample by selecting every nth person who enters the library. Again, some students avoid the library and would not be represented in the sample. To be sure to have a random sample, to be sure that every student in the college has an equal chance of being chosen, you would take the names of every student enrolled in the college, drop the names in a barrel, and, blindfolded, select out, say, 50 or 100 names. In this way the group selected would be truly random, and because the group was selected on a chance basis, it would likely be representative of the entire population. Random sampling allows the statistician to legitimately generalize to the population.

Random sampling

TO THE PROSPECTIVE TEACHER
The material presented in this chapter has been aimed at giving you a general introduction to some of the techniques employed by statisticians and educational researchers. Though as a working teacher you may never have to compute the reliability or the validity of a measuring instrument, your understanding of these vital concepts will be greatly enhanced if you roll up your sleeves and "dirty your hands with the data." If you can calculate the standard deviation and Pearson r, you will not necessarily be a master statistician, but you will be better able to evaluate the statistical analyses of researchers in the field. In the next chapter you will see how researchers use some of these techniques to achieve a better understanding of the facts and theories of educational psychology. As a professional teacher you will be expected to read and understand the literature of the field. A basic introduction to statistical procedures will enhance your ability to understand this literature.

Summary

Measurement is the assigning of a number to a concept according to rules. To give meaning to these numbers, all measurements must satisfy two basic criteria. They must be reliable, and they must be valid. Reliability indicates the consistency of a measurement, while validity is the extent to which a test measures what it is intended to measure.

Correlation is a statement as to the strength of the association between two (or possibly more) variables. Though correlational statements do not imply causation, they can be used to make better-than-chance predictions.

Correlation may also be used in assessing reliability and validity. In the case of reliability, a test might be given to a group of subjects on separate occasions. If the two sets of measurements correlate, the test would be considered reliable, since the scores are consistent. For validity, the scores on a given test could be correlated with the actual later performance exhibited by the subjects on the ability or trait being measured.

To make meaning out of the chaos of the raw data from a study, the statistician arranges his or her scores in order of magnitude, called a distribution of scores. When the scores are listed beside another column giving the frequency of occurrence for each score, we have created a frequency distribution.

Statisticians also use graphs to present their data in more meaningful form. The actual scores are indicated on the horizontal axis, or the abscissa, and the frequency of occurrence is presented on the vertical axis, or the ordinate.

In order to aid in our understanding of both the ways in which individuals differ and also the ways in which they are alike, techniques are employed for finding the "average" or typical score in a distribution. These techniques are called measures of central tendency, and include the mean, which is the actual arithmetic average; the median, which is the middle-most score in a distribution; and the mode, which is the most frequently occurring score in a distribution.

Just as the measures of central tendency give us information with regard to similarity among measurements, measures of variability give us information regarding how scores differ or vary. Two measures of variability are the range, which is the difference between the highest and lowest scores in a distribution, and the standard deviation, which is a measure of how much each of the raw scores varies or deviates from the mean.

Many behavioral measures in psychology conform to what is called the normal curve. The normal curve is a theoretical distribution of scores which in general shows the majority of scores falling in the center of the distribution. As we move away from this center, in either direction, we find fewer and fewer scores.

A standard score, or z score, is a translation of a raw score into units of standard deviation. A centile or percentile is that point in the distribution at or below which a given percentage of cases fall.

Hypotheses may be tested either by the correlational method or the experimental method. The correlational method allows for predictions, and a common technique for computing correlation is the Pearson r. The experimental method allows for the possibility of isolating a causal factor, and two common techniques for handling the data from such studies are the t test and the F test.

By using proper sampling techniques, such as random sampling, the scientist can legitimately generalize the results of his or her measurements of a small group to an entire group. Thus, the scientist may measure only a sample, and yet generalize to a population. The key issue in this procedure is that the sample must be representative of the population.

17

Reading and understanding the research

Every teacher should have a basic understanding of research methods, since the findings of research studies are reported at teachers' meetings and conventions, and in educational journals. The results of these studies may often appear bewildering and at times can even be misleading if the teacher is unfamiliar with the general rules of science and statistical analysis. Benjamin Disraeli, Queen Victoria's prime minister, once said that there are three kinds of lies—lies, damned lies, and statistics. Disraeli was concerned over the fact that it often seems that one can prove anything with statistics.

FIGURES DON'T LIE, BUT LIARS CAN FIGURE

If it is true that one can prove anything with statistics, then of course there should be a real question regarding the value of statistical analysis. The fact is, however, that the only time one can "prove anything with statistics" is when the audience is totally naive about statistical procedures. To the uninitiated, liars can indeed figure, and these figures can seem plausible. But an audience that has even a little knowledge of statistical techniques will not easily be misled by the statistical artful dodger. Unscrupulous persons will probably always try to make points with faulty statistical interpretations, but by the time you finish this chapter they will not so easily be able to lie to you.

PASS-FAIL: A RESEARCH EXAMPLE

A recent controversy in education revolves around the issue of whether or not to adopt the pass-fail grading principle. Proponents of pass-fail claim that students will actually learn more, be more likely to explore different course areas,

447

and feel less anxiety when taking a course without the pressure of regular letter grades. The opponents, on the other hand, argue that students will be less motivated and therefore learn less if they are graded on the less-precise pass-fail basis. A large number of studies have been done at a wide variety of educational institutions, and the data are fairly consistent on the following point: when students who are taking a course for regular grades are compared with students who are taking the same course on a pass-fail basis, the graded students achieve higher grades.[1] The comparison is made possible by not telling the instructor which students are taking the course on the pass-fail basis and having him or her assign letter grades to all students. The registrar converts these to pass-fail for those students who had previously elected this option. This provision is included to protect the pass-fail students from possible instructor bias.

Some argue that pass-fail grading leads to more learning

Some argue that regular letter grading leads to more learning

The data clearly show that there is a difference in grades between the two groups of students in the same class, those electing to take the course for pass-fail and those taking the course for regular letter grades. The interpretations of this difference, however, vary widely. Some claim that this difference proves that pass-fail students simply don't work as hard or take the course as seriously as students taking the course for letter grades. Others claim that this difference proves that only the less-competent students elect the pass-fail option. Others claim that this difference proves that students only take their most difficult (for them) courses under the pass-fail option and therefore are exploring areas they might otherwise attempt to avoid. Others claim that this difference proves that students use the pass-fail option only in courses where the teacher is so personally uninspiring as to need the threat of letter grades in order to goad his students into studying. Others claim, etc., etc. What, in fact, do the data really prove? Nothing, other than that there is indeed a difference in grades between the two groups. All the previously mentioned explanations are only hypotheses; that is, guesses about the possible reason for the difference. This isn't to say that one or even several of these hypotheses might not eventually be proved valid, but the point is that at present none of the studies really prove any of the hypotheses. Yet, in the hands of a statistical charlatan, the data may seem to an unsophisticated audience to prove whatever he says they prove.

ISOLATING THE ELUSIVE CAUSAL FACTOR

The most common error in reading and interpreting research studies is assuming that a causal factor has been isolated when, in fact, it has not. As will be seen, most studies in the field of educational psychology do not allow for a cause-and-effect interpretation, and yet it is extremely tempting to interpret them as though they did. This is probably the major booby trap lying in wait for the unwary student. Just because two variables are associated doesn't necessarily mean that one is the cause of the other.

When two variables occur together, one is not necessarily the cause of the other

A study was done to show that there is a relationship between the amount of time teachers spend smiling and the achievement level of their students.[2] Observers noted the various lengths of time that a group of teachers spent smiling and compared this with the grades their respective students received. It was found that the more the teacher smiled, the higher were the students' grades. The reader of this study should not assume that smiling teachers cause students to achieve more. It is just as likely that the reverse is true; that is, that the high level of student achievement causes the teacher to smile, apparently basking in reflected glory. Or, it might be that the teacher who smiles a great deal is a happy optimist, who only sees the best in everyone and therefore likes to award higher grades. The point is that although all these explanations are possible, none of them were proven by the study.

When a cause-and-effect relationship is indeed discovered, it must be unidirectional; that is, there must be a one-way relationship between the variables. When you flip the light switch and the lamp goes on, you have established a unidirectional relationship, because the reverse relationship is not present in this case; although flipping the switch lights the bulb, unscrewing the bulb does not move the switch.

THE TWO BASIC TYPES OF RESEARCH

In general terms we can state that there are two basic types of research: S/R and R/R. In S/R research, which utilizes the experimental method, the researcher manipulates a stimulus, or input variable, to see if by doing so he or she causes a change in the responses of a group of subjects. The S/R method does allow for cause-and-effect statements. In R/R research, on the other hand, the researcher does not manipulate a stimulus. Rather, the responses of a group of subjects are measured on one variable and then compared with their measured responses on a second variable. R/R research does not allow for cause-and-effect inferences.

S/R RESEARCH: THE CASE OF CAUSE AND EFFECT

The S/R, or experimental, method requires careful controls on the part of the experimenter. It also requires the experimenter to actively manipulate the stimulus variable. This actively manipulated stimulus variable is called the independent variable. In educational psychology the independent variable is all of the following:

The independent variable

1
Some form of stimulus that is presented to the subjects

2
The causal half of the cause-and-effect relationship

3
Always under the full, active control of the experimenter.

After presenting the subjects with the stimulus variable, the experimenter seeks to determine whether any response changes in the subjects result. The measurement of the subject's response is called the dependent variable, for it depends on whether or not the stimulus was previously presented. The dependent variable is:

The dependent variable

1
A measure of the response made by the subject

2
The effect half of the cause-and-effect relationship.

A double-blind study. Neither the experimenter nor the subjects should be aware of which group is receiving the stimulus variable.

For example, suppose a researcher wishes to test the hypothesis that a certain drug will increase IQ scores. She selects two groups of subjects, groups that are as equivalent as it is humanly possible to make them. Once the two groups are formed, the experimenter treats them exactly alike, except that one group gets the drug and the other does not. The group that receives the drug is called the *experimental* group, and the group that does not is called the *control* group. The subjects should not know which group they are in, for it is possible that if subjects know they are in the experimental group, they might somehow be affected, perhaps more motivated. For this reason, when the members of the experimental group are given a capsule containing the drug, the subjects in the control group are given a placebo. In this case the placebo would be an identical-appearing capsule that contains a sugar substance. The experimenter should also not know which group is which. Otherwise, she might unconsciously help one group more than another. When neither the subjects nor the experimenter are aware of which group is which, the study is said to be a double blind. This procedure should be followed wherever possible in carrying out actual experimental research. Obviously, both groups must be given the same IQ test, with the same directions and time limits.

Experimental and control groups

Using a placebo

In this example, whether or not the subjects received the drug would be the independent variable and the IQ scores the dependent variable. If, all other things being equal, the subjects who received the drug scored significantly higher on the IQ test than those subjects who did not receive the drug, the claim can legitimately be made that the drug caused an increase in IQ. Notice that the drug was (1) a stimulus, (2) the causal half of the cause-and-effect relationship, and (3) actively manipulated by the experimenter. By active manipulation, we mean that the experimenter, not the subjects, decided which group would receive the drug and which group would not. Notice also that the IQ scores were (1) responses made by subjects on the test, and (2) the effect half of the cause-and-effect relationship.

Significance

In the previous example it was mentioned that in order to validate the hypothesis, the researcher had to show a significant difference in the way the two groups scored on the test. The term "significant" simply means nonchance; a significant difference is one that the researcher feels confident is due, not to chance variation, but to the manipulation of the independent variable. When reading the research in educational psychology, it is important that this be kept in mind. A significant difference is simply one in which chance has been ruled out, and it doesn't mean that the difference is necessarily important, profound, or even very meaningful. A significant difference can be trivial, but at least it is not due to chance. Significance should never be confused with importance, though, of course, important differences must first be significant.

Experimental designs: creating equivalent groups

There are three basic experimental designs: the after-only, the before-after, and the matched group. In each instance, the researcher is attempting to create that crucial S/R condition: equivalent groups.

After-only.   Here the researcher measures the dependent variable only after having manipulated the independent variable. The problem of equivalent groups is solved through random selection. Subjects are randomly selected and randomly assigned to the experimental or control groups. It is assumed that whatever differences might exist between the two groups will be cancelled through the random selection process. In the previous example—testing the effect of a certain drug on IQ—an after-only design would mean that the researcher would:

Subjects are randomly assigned to groups

1
Select the groups randomly

2
Administer the drug to the experimental group and a placebo to the control group

3
Give all subjects the IQ test.

The dependent variable (IQ) is measured only after the introduction of the independent variable (the drug).

Before-after.   The before-after design assumes that nobody could be more like you than you, so let's use you twice. The dependent variable is measured both before and after the introduction of the independent variable, and any change in the second measurement is assumed to result from the administration of the independent variable. There are hazards in this technique, however, simply because some amount of time must elapse between measurements. During this period of time the subjects are open to a myriad of possible influencing stimuli. It is essential, therefore, that a control group be used, a group that is given both the before and after tests but is not presented with the independent variable. For example, assume that we wish to test the hypothesis that a speed-reading course improves scores on an English achievement test. One group of subjects is given the achievement test, then the speed-reading course, and then the achievement test again. The control group is given the achievement test twice but is never given the speed-reading course. The researcher can then ferret out the pure effects of the speed-reading course, as opposed to an improvement on

Repeated measurements of same subjects

the test the second time around due to other factors, such as maturation, more schooling, or just simply having seen the test before. With a control group, the before-after design can be a powerful research tool. Without a control group, it often leads to ambiguous results.

Matched group. Another method of forming equivalent groups is to equate or match the subjects, subject for subject, on the basis of relevant variables. Thus the researcher interested in assessing the effects of a certain drug on IQ would probably want to equate his or her subjects on the basis of IQ, age, past schooling, and so on. If one group includes a ten-year-old boy with an IQ of 118 and five years of previous school experience, then the researcher must find another boy of similar characteristics for the other group. This method, though certainly effective, is sometimes difficult to follow. It might be very difficult to find subjects with the necessary characteristics. Often, too, it is not entirely obvious what the relevant matching variables should be.

Subjects are equated on some relevant variable

The hypothesis of difference in S/R
In all S/R research, the hypothesis of difference must be tested; that is, after equivalent groups are formed, they are exposed to different stimulus conditions and then measured to see if response differences can be observed. If these differences are significant (nonchance), then the researcher concludes that they are caused by the differential treatment the subjects received.

R/R RESEARCH: CAUSATION NEVER PROVED
The majority of research studies in the literature of educational psychology use the R/R method. The subjects are measured on one dimension, and these measurements are compared with measurements in other dimensions: that is, responses are compared with other responses. Since there is no active stimulus manipulation, however, R/R research never proves a cause-and-effect relationship. However, it does allow the researcher to make predictions, and this is the real goal of R/R research. The fact that the researcher can make predictions makes the R/R method an extremely valuable research tool. But the researcher who uses this method must be very careful not to be enticed into assuming that a causal factor has been isolated.

R/R research allows for predictions

An illustrative example
Suppose a researcher is interested in finding out whether teacher rejection of a student is related to student aggression. Assume further that the researcher has developed a reliable and valid scale for measuring teacher rejection; that is, the researcher has a tool for determining a given teacher's acceptance-rejection attitude toward each student. It can thus be shown that the teacher psychologically rejects student No. 20 more than student No. 12, student No. 8 more than student No. 16, and so on. The researcher then spends a week observing the students and counts the number of aggressive responses each student exhibits during that time. Lo and behold, the researcher finds that a relationship does

indeed exist; that is, the more the student is rejected by the teacher, the more aggressively he or she acts. Now, this would be a very interesting finding, since it would allow for predictions of future behavior. We could predict the amount of each student's aggressiveness on the basis of the teacher's rejection-acceptance attitudes toward them. But has a cause-and-effect relationship been established? In fact, it has not, for without active stimulus manipulation, we cannot determine the direction of the relationship. Let us use the letter A to symbolize teacher rejection, the letter B to symbolize student aggression, and an arrow to indicate cause. (Using letter symbols in analyzing research is usually a good idea, because symbols don't have the added literary overtones that are almost always carried by word descriptions of the variables.) The following hypotheses are then possible:

$$A \rightarrow B$$

It is possible, though not proven by this study, that A (teacher rejection) does cause B (student aggressiveness).

$$B \rightarrow A$$

It is also possible that B (student aggressiveness) caused A (teacher rejection). The teacher may not have warm feelings of acceptance toward a student who is constantly punching other children or throwing chalk at her.

$$X \rightarrow A + B$$

It is further possible that X (some unknown variable) is the real cause of both A (teacher rejection) and B (student aggressiveness).

Variable X could be a general atmosphere of frustration and despair that permeates a given school, leading both teacher and pupil to generate basic feelings of hostility.

All three of these situations are possible explanations, but the point is that with the R/R method we don't know which is the real explanation. We can ask, as on the TV show, *To Tell the Truth*, "Will the real causal variable please stand up." But with the R/R method, none of the contestants will rise.

Again, it must be emphasized that there is nothing inherently invalid about the use of the R/R technique. It is the misuse of R/R research that is at issue. As stated previously, R/R research is invaluable in allowing us to make predictions. The problem is that newspapers, magazines, and even a few journal articles have so blatantly ignored the rules of good R/R research that the student must be alerted to the dangers that lie in wait. For example, a newspaper headline states that our prison population has tripled since women in large numbers have invaded the field of politics, and the article advises women to stay at home. Or, a magazine compares the growth in the number of PTA room mothers to that of small business failures and finds that they tally. Again, women are advised to stay home. In both cases the cardinal sin was committed of implying a cause-and-effect relationship when indeed there is none.

A study attempting to determine whether participation in the Boy Scouts led to better community adjustment in later life provides an example from the pro-

Boy Scouts and community adjustment

fessional literature.[3] The researcher selected a group of adults, and then went back and checked the records to see how much Scout work each adult had once been involved in. He then measured the differences in community adjustment between those who had done several years of Scout work and those who had done little such work. This is definitely R/R research; and again, it is improper to imply a cause-and-effect relationship. Too many variables other than Boy Scout work could have caused an individual to have good community adjustment later in life. In order to isolate a causal factor, the researcher in this study would have had to select a random sample of young boys, randomly assign half of them to an experimental group and half to a control group. He would then assign all the boys in the experimental group to the Boy Scouts, and prevent any boys from the control group from ever joining the Scouts. Years later, the researcher would check all the subjects in terms of their community adjustment. This would then be an S/R study with active stimulus manipulation; and, if differences were noted, a cause-and-effect statement could be made.

An S/R study of this nature, however, raises some important ethical questions. Is it ethical to force some boys to join the Scouts and prevent others from joining? Was not the R/R study, in which the boys were free to join or not to join, a far better study from an ethical point of view? These questions indicate another reason for the importance of R/R research. Although the R/R method does not allow the researcher to isolate a causal factor, it does allow him or her to gather evidence in areas that might be too sensitive, and possibly harmful to subjects if the S/R method were employed. For example, suppose a researcher is interested in testing the possible negative relationship between a certain drug and school achievement. To do this as an S/R study, one would have to randomly select students who had never used the drug, divide them into two groups, and then force one group to take the drug and the control group to take a placebo. Then, if grade-average differences were found between the two groups, the researcher could legitimately claim that the drug was the cause of these differences. But in order to isolate the causal factor, the experimental subjects may have suffered in ways other than just receiving lower grades. Suppose just one of the experimental subjects developed a drug-induced psychosis and had to be hospitalized. Should the researcher be allowed to expose his subjects to possible long-term damage merely for the sake of nailing down the causal factor? Of course not; the S/R method should be used only when the risks to the subjects are minute compared to the potential benefit to mankind.

The previously mentioned study on drug effects might have been more ethically handled by the R/R method. For example, the researcher could compare the grades of those students who are already using the drug with the grades of those who aren't. In this case, the subjects themselves choose whether or not to use the drug, and the researcher simply finds out whether there is a relationship between this choice and grade averages. Of course, no cause-and-effect inference is possible, for even if a significant relationship is found, we don't know the direction of the relationship. Perhaps A (use of the drug) caused B (lower grades). Perhaps B (lower grades) caused A (drug use). Or, perhaps X caused both A and B. In this case X might be a depressed state of mind which caused the student to both use the drug and not be able to do the work necessary for academic achievement.

Hypotheses tested in R/R research
The R/R researcher may test two general hypotheses, the hypothesis of difference and/or the hypothesis of association.

The hypothesis of difference.   In this case, the researcher selects two groups that are clearly different in one measurement, and then seeks to find out whether they also differ on some other measurement. Unlike the S/R researcher who selects equivalent groups and then subjects them to differential treatment, the R/R researcher selects different groups and then subjects them to equivalent treatment. For example, a study was done to compare college grade-point averages of those students who had previously attended public schools and those who had attended private schools.[4] This study found significant differences between the two groups, differences consistently favoring the public-school graduates. (When the two groups were compared on the basis of aptitude and motivation, however, most of the differences disappeared.) This is a classic example of R/R research testing the hypothesis of difference. It is R/R research because the students themselves, not the researcher, decided which school to attend. It tests the hypothesis of difference because the researcher seeks to determine whether these groups differ on their college grade-point averages.

Public and private school graduates: a comparison

The hypothesis of association.   In this case, one group of subjects is selected and measured on two or more variables to determine whether there is any correlation between the variables. This is correlational research and, although no cause-and-effect assumptions can be made, valid predictions are possible. For example, a study was done to investigate whether there is a relationship between grade-point average and number of absences.[5] A group of almost 3000 students was selected and a correlation was computed between their grade-point averages and their number of absences. A significant negative correlation was obtained, showing that the more a student was absent, the lower that student's grades were. Although no cause-and-effect relationship could be (or was) implied, the results allow for a better-than-chance prediction of a student's grades on the basis of that student's attendance record. Another study was done in which length of time spent studying was correlated with grade-point average.[6] The researcher in this case compared the hours of study time reported by the students with the grades they later obtained. The positive correlation was significant, indicating that the more a student studies, the higher the grade point.

Number of absences and school achievement

Length of time spent studying and grade-point average

Thus, R/R research testing the hypothesis of association attempts to establish associations, or correlations, among various subject response measures. The goal is to seek significant correlations that will allow for better-than-chance predictions.

THE HALO EFFECT
It has long been known in psychology that people who are viewed positively on one trait tend also to be thought to have many other positive traits. If the public recognizes that certain athletes are extremely competent on the playing field, they often attribute to those athletes expertise in many nonathletic areas. This is called the halo effect, and it explains why advertisers pay huge fees to athletes

for endorsing their products. If a football player can score dozens of touchdowns, then "obviously" he is also an expert in the field of selecting razor blades, deodorants, and any number of other products.

The halo effect can be a hazard to both the researcher and the research consumer. The problem is especially apparent in R/R research testing the hypothesis of association. An investigator was interested in determining whether the grades a student receives from a teacher might be influenced by that student's personality.[7] The research was R/R; that is, the students' measurements on one trait were compared to their measurements on other traits. In this case, the researcher had the teacher make personality ratings for each pupil and compared these ratings with the grades the pupil had received from the same teacher. The correlation was high and positive; that is, the more favorable the personality rating, the higher the grades. What the study tells us is that teachers must guard against the halo effect in assigning grades. A poor grade in reading, for example, should reflect the student's poor level of reading achievement, not the teacher's unfavorable impression of the student's personality. If, on the other hand, the study had been designed to test the possibility of an independent relationship between personality and academic achievement, then the personality ratings should have been given by someone other than the person who was doing the grading.

THE HAWTHORNE EFFECT

Another pitfall awaiting the unwary reader of research is the Hawthorne effect. Many years ago, a research study was conducted at the Hawthorne plant of the Western Electric Company.[8] The object of the study was to determine whether increased illumination would increase worker productivity. The researchers went into one of the assembly rooms and measured the rate of worker productivity. Then they increased the illumination and measured productivity again. Just as they had suspected, under conditions of increased illumination productivity did indeed go up. This is an example of S/R research, before-after design, but with no control group. When the researchers later added a control group—that is, another group of workers whose illumination they only pretended to increase—they found to their dismay that productivity also went up. This again points up the importance of using a control group in the research situation, for it often happens that subjects will improve their behavior merely because someone is paying attention to them. If a control group isn't used, the researcher will never know whether the subject's response improved because of manipulation of the independent variable, or because the subject was flattered by the researcher's attention.

The Hawthorne effect has great significance in educational psychology. Researchers must especially be aware of the possible Hawthorne effect in all studies of student change. For example, a researcher may feel that she has discovered a new technique that helps students greatly increase their ability to solve math problems. She designs a study in which she first measures the math ability of a group of students. She then spends two weeks instructing them about how to use this new method, a magic formula she probably calls the "rich, meaningful method," and then she measures their math ability again. The researcher may find that great gains have occurred, that the students have significantly increased their ability to solve math problems. But, can the reseacher be certain that it was

Any change in a teacher's behavior may appear to produce student gains. Only by using a control group can we be sure.

the new teaching technique that caused the difference? Certainly not! The gain may have been the result of the Hawthorne effect. Perhaps any change in the math curriculum might have produced the gain. The gain might have occurred if the researcher had simply, yet enthusiastically, stood on her head and repeated the multiplication tables eight hours a day.

Ambiguous results due to the Hawthorne effect are most common when the researcher is using the before-after experimental design without an adequate control group. One researcher, in the field of learning disabilities, has complained that, "any idea or finding which is unacceptable to anyone today can be explained away on the basis of the Hawthorne effect."[9] In point of fact, the only time results can be "explained away" on the basis of the Hawthorne effect is when the researcher carelessly fails to use a control group. In one sense, the Hawthorne effect is important to the researcher in that it teaches extreme caution in assigning specific causes to observed changes in student behavior.

Appropriate control groups lessen the problem of the Hawthorne effect

LONGITUDINAL AND CROSS-SECTIONAL RESEARCH

Researchers often wish to obtain data on possible growth trends, or changes in population characteristics that might occur over the years. For example, we might like to know whether a person's IQ tends to decline after age sixty. One method of obtaining this information would be to measure a subject's IQ at age twenty and then again at age sixty-five. This obviously takes a very patient researcher (and a very young one) since it will take forty-five years to answer the question. This is, however, the way longitudinal research proceeds. Subjects are measured, followed through the years, and measured again. A study of intellectually gifted children that we cite in Chapter 18 is an example of longitudinal research.

Another method, a short-cut for gathering this type of data, is called cross-sectional research. Using this method, the researcher would select a sample (or cross section) of twenty-year-olds and compare their IQ's with those obtained from measuring a sample of sixty-five-year-olds. The trouble with this method is that although we may learn that the average sixty-five-year-old has a lower IQ than the average twenty-year-old, we don't know whether the older subjects have actually suffered an IQ decline. It might very well be that those sixty-five-year-old subjects have always been less bright than the present twenty-year-old subjects. Perhaps they had less schooling, or less-adequate diets, or a host of other variables which affected their generation's ability to score well on an IQ test compared to today's twenty-year-olds. The point is that in order to assess whether or not behavioral changes are due to the aging process, the cross-sectional method just won't do. Whenever we need research answers to problems of growth and development, the longitudinal method should be used.

STATISTICAL TESTS

A bewildering number of statistical tests are used in research studies today. The reader who is new to the literature of educational psychology may be hopelessly confused by the myriad of Greek and English symbols and letters which are woven into almost all research studies. The goal of all these statistical tests, however, is the same: to determine whether or not the findings are due to chance. The object is simply to determine whether the results of the study are significant, that is, not the result of chance or random factors. Assume that a researcher wishes to find out whether watching violence on TV causes aggressive behavior. He does an appropriate S/R study and finds that there are indeed more aggressive responses among the subjects in his experimental group (exposed to TV violence) than in his control group (not so exposed). Just to be certain, he replicates (repeats exactly) the experiment on another group of children. This time the results are reversed; that is, the control group now exhibits more aggressive behavior. The researcher replicates again, perhaps eight more times, only to find the original result occurring in half the studies and the reverse occurring in the other half. In this instance, it is obvious that the results are probably due only to chance. The probability of his original finding being due to chance, it now becomes apparent, is .50; that is, there are 50 chances out of 100 (or 1 out of 2) that his original finding was correct. As it turns out, instead of doing the study, he might just as well have flipped a coin, for his original finding was apparently a result of chance factors. Through the use of statistical tests, however, he could have determined, after the first study, what the probability was that his result was due to chance. This is not to say that the replication of studies is never needed. Replication is often necessary and is one of the great advantages of the scientific method. But statistical tests make it unnecessary to do a study over and over to estimate the probability that the result was due to chance.

Statistical tests to determine the probability that a result is due to chance

CHANCE IS NEVER COMPLETELY RULED OUT

Regardless of the power or elegance of the statistical analysis, chance can never be completely ruled out of any study. The statistical test, however, tells us what the probability is that the result is due to chance; if the probability is .05 (5

chances out of 100) or less, the researcher can be far more confident in his or her result than if the probability of chance had been .50. Research studies never provide ultimate truth, for that will not be known until the last fact is in on Judgment Day; but they do tell us how probable it is that the findings are accurate.

Statistical studies typically use two levels of significance: the .05 level and the .01 level. When a result is said to be significant at the .05 level, there are only 5 chances out of 100 that it is due to chance. Similarly, if the result is shown to be significant at the .01 level, there is only 1 chance in 100 that it is still a chance result. (Sometimes, differences are found to be so great, or associations so strong, that a significance level of .001, one chance in a thousand, is reported.) A .05 level of significance is usually considered acceptable by the majority of researchers in educational psychology.

THE FOUR MOST COMMON TESTS

Despite the tremendous number of statistical tests used in research studies today, four tests are used so often that they deserve special mention. With a little understanding of each of these four tests, you will be remarkably well equipped to pursue the literature in a more secure fashion.

The *t* test

The *t* test establishes the probability of a difference between two groups

The *t* test, or *t* ratio, is a method of testing the hypothesis of difference when only two groups are being used. It can be used in either S/R or R/R research and always answers the question as to whether there is a significant difference between *two* groups. In S/R research the *t* test is used when the independent variable is manipulated at two levels, one level for the experimental group and a different level (usually zero) for the control group. Thus, to test whether a certain drug increases IQ, the experimental group would receive one level of the drug (say, 25 cubic centimeters) and the control group would receive a placebo, or none of the drug. Both groups would take the IQ test, and the *t* test would be used to tell us whether the average IQ's for the two groups differed significantly. In R/R research, the *t* test can be used to establish whether two groups known to be different on one characteristic are also different on a second. For example, to determine whether people raised in the city have higher IQ's than people raised in the country, two groups would be selected that differ on the characteristic of where they had been reared. Both groups would then be given IQ tests, and the *t* test would tell us whether the average IQ of the two groups differed significantly.

The value of the *t* ratio needed to establish significance depends on the size of the two sample groups. For example, if the two groups were composed of 50 persons each, a *t* ratio of only 1.98 would be needed to indicate significance at the .05 level. If, however, the groups were composed of five persons each, the *t* value needed to indicate a .05 significance level would be 2.31. Statistical tables are used to indicate precisely what *t* values are needed for whatever size groups are being tested.

The F ratio

The F ratio is the statistic resulting from a procedure called analysis of variance. This is also referred to as ANOVA, from ANalysis Of VAriance. The F ratio, like the t ratio, is used to test the hypothesis of difference. Unlike the t ratio, however, the F ratio can establish differences among many groups simultaneously. Whereas we use "t for two," we use F when many groups are being compared.

The F ratio establishes the probability of differences among many groups

The F ratio tells us whether the differences that separate the groups are greater than the differences that exist within the groups. For example, an F ratio of 10.00 would tell us that the differences separating the groups are 10 times greater than the random differences existing within the groups.

Like the t ratio, the F ratio can test the hypothesis of difference in the context of either S/R or R/R research. In the previous example of S/R research, we could test the drug/academic-success hypothesis, but this time we could use more than two groups and test the effects of various amounts of the drug. For example, we could set up a four-group design; that is, three experimental groups and one control group. The control group would receive none of the stimulus variable (the placebo); the second group would receive 25 cubic centimeters of the drug; the third group, 50 cubic centimeters; and the fourth group, 75 cubic centimeters.

In R/R research, we could use the F ratio to test more precisely the relationship between IQ and the area in which the subject was raised. Rather than simply comparing city-raised and country-raised people, as we did with the t test, we could select people from various population-density areas. For example, Group I would contain people raised in communities of less than 5000 people; Group II, people raised in communities of 5000 to 25,000; Group III, people raised in communities of 25,000 to 50,000; and so on. Then we give all the groups IQ tests and use the F ratio to establish whether or not there are significant IQ differences among the groups.

The Pearson r

The Pearson r, or product-moment correlation, is a statistical test used to test the hypothesis of association. Used only in R/R research, it tells us whether or not there is a relationship between two sets of measurements. If there is a significant relationship, the Pearson r also tells us the strength of that relationship. The value of r ranges from +1.00, down through zero, to −1.00. The farther the r is from zero, whether in a positive or negative direction, the stronger the relationship. The Pearson r is used ultimately to make predictions, and can never be used to ferret out a causal factor. A researcher may wish to discover whether there is a relationship between reading speed and academic grades. He selects a large number of students and compares their reading-speed scores with their grade-average (R/R research). Assume he obtains a significant r of +.70, meaning that most of the subjects who scored high on the reading-speed test also had high grade averages, and those who scored low had low grade averages. From this, he can now make a better-than-chance prediction of a given student's grade average by knowing how that student performed on the reading-speed test. This research, however, offers no proof that taking a speed-reading course causes a student to have higher grades. It may be that A (reading speed) causes B (high

Pearson r establishes the strength of a relationship between two variables grades). Or, it may be that B (high grades) causes A (high reading speed). Or, it may be that some X (perhaps a high IQ) causes both A (high reading speed) and B (high grades).

χ^2 (chi square)

Chi square, symbolized χ^2, is the real workhorse test in educational psychology. It is used in virtually every type of research situation, S/R and R/R, and to test both the hypothesis of difference and the hypothesis of association. Chi square is useful whenever research data are in the form of classified frequencies; that is, whenever the researcher is interested in the actual number of cases that fall into two or more discrete categories. When results are recorded in this way, they are called *nominal data*. They reflect the frequency of occurrence within discrete categories, rather than the exact or relative performance of any individual. For example, subjects might be categorized according to their college major, and then compared with regard to whether or not they went on to graduate school. In both cases the data are in the form of frequencies of occurrence within categories: when we categorize our subjects on the basis of college major, we know exactly how many students majored in each subject. When we then compare these frequencies with the on-to-graduate-school variable, we again know exactly how many persons went to graduate school and how many did not. This is the kind of situation in which chi square is the ideal statistical test. With the t, F, and r statistical tests the actual measurements of the subjects are used. That is, with t, F, and r, we know exactly how each subject scored in a given area, such as IQ, grade-point average, height, weight, correct responses on a learning task, whatever. With chi square, we know only how many subjects fall into certain discrete categories: how many took a college-prep course as opposed to how many did not; how many subjects live on campus as opposed to how many do not; how many children in a given school district eat hot lunch as opposed to how many do not, and so on.

Chi square is extremely versatile, since even when the researcher has actual measurements of his or her subjects, these measurements can always be converted into frequency data. For example, if we know the actual IQ scores of our subjects we can, if we want to, categorize these measurements according to how many subjects scored above 100 and how many scored below. Or, if we know the actual grade-point averages of a group of students we can, if we want to, categorize them on a pass-fail basis.

A TEACHER'S OBLIGATION

A knowledge of the rudiments of research methodology is essential to any student or teacher who hopes to profit from the literature of the field of educational psychology. Although this chapter has only skimmed the surface of the subject, a thorough reading and analysis of the material it contains should pay rich dividends in future understanding. The student who is serious about becoming a professional teacher is urged to follow this up with at least a one-semester course in statistics and research design. The field of educational psychology is constantly changing. New theories are being offered and new supporting data are being introduced. The dedicated teacher, in whose hands the lives of our children are placed, has an obligation to stay on top of the research literature.

Summary

The most-common error in interpreting research studies is the assumption that a cause-and-effect relationship has been established when in fact it has not.

Two general types of research are used in educational psychology, S/R and R/R. S/R involves active stimulus manipulation on the part of the experimenter, and attempts to specify whether the manipulated stimulus *causes* a response difference. R/R research involves comparing measured responses on one dimension with different measured responses on another dimension. This method does not allow for cause-and-effect inferences.

The term *significance* as used in research simply means nonchance. A significant difference or a significant correlation indicates only that chance has been ruled out; it does not refer to the importance or even meaningfulness of the result.

There are three basic experimental designs, all aimed at creating equivalent groups when involved in S/R research.

1
After-only: where random selection and random assignment of subjects to two or more groups is used to create equivalence.

2
Before-after: where a group is measured before and after the introduction of the manipulated variable, and equivalence is maintained by the use of the same subjects in each condition.

3
Matched-group: where subjects are selected for the various groups on the basis of a matching process. The subjects are equated on some relevant variable, subject for subject, and then assigned to groups.

S/R research always tests the hypothesis of difference—that is, the hypothesis that the measured responses of the subjects are in some way different as a result of the previously manipulated stimulus.

R/R research may test either the hypothesis of difference (though not implying a cause-and-effect relationship) or the hypothesis of association. In the latter case, the researcher attempts to discover whether two or more response measures of the same subjects are significantly related.

Two major research errors are the halo effect and the Hawthorne effect. The halo effect occurs when a researcher measures a subject on one variable, and is then influenced by that measurement (either positively or negatively) when evaluating the subject in a different area. This problem can be eliminated by using independent observers when measuring subjects on more than one trait. The Hawthorne effect occurs when the researcher, using a before-after experimental design, assumes that a given response difference is the result of the stated stimulus variable, when in fact the result may be due to the flattery and attention paid by the researcher to the subjects. The judicious use of extra control groups can eliminate this problem.

The longitudinal research method, where the *same* subjects are measured at different ages throughout life, is preferred over the cross-sectional method, where different subjects of different ages are measured. This preference is especially apparent whenever the research is concerned with growth and development.

Though a bewildering number of statistical tests are used in research studies today, the prospective teacher can become reasonably adept at reading these studies if the four most-common tests are understood.

1

The t test: for testing the hypothesis of difference when no more than two groups are being compared.

2

The F ratio: for testing the hypothesis of difference when many groups are being compared.

3

The Pearson r: for testing the hypothesis of association.

4

The chi square: for use in research studies where frequencies of occurrence are compared within various categories. This is an important test when we don't have the subject's actual measured score.

REFERENCES

1
W. M. Stallings and H. R. Smock, "The Pass-Fail Grading Option at a State University," *Journal of Educational Measurement* 8 (1971):153–160.

2
G. M. Harrington, "Smiling as a Measure of Teacher Effectiveness," *Journal of Educational Research* 49 (1955):715–717.

3
F. S. Chapin, *Experimental Designs in Sociological Research* (New York: Harper, 1947).

4
J. A. Finger and G. E. Schlesser, "Academic Performance of Public and Private School Students," *Journal of Educational Psychology* 54 (1963):118–122.

5
A. M. Anikeef, "The Relationship between Class Absences and College Grades," *Journal of Educational Psychology* 45 (1954):244–249.

6
R. Carver, "A Test of an Hypothesized Relationship between Learning Time and Amount Learned in School Learning," *Journal of Educational Research* 64 (1970):57–58.

7
J. L. Russell and W. A. Thalman, "Personality: Does It Influence Teachers' Marks?" *Journal of Educational Research* 48 (1955):561–564.

8
F. J. Roethlisberger and W. J. Dickson, *Management and the Worker* (Cambridge, Mass.: Harvard University Press, 1939).

9
N. C. Kephart, "On the Value of Empirical Data in Learning Disability," *Journal of Learning Disabilities* 4, no. 7 (1971):393–395.

SUGGESTIONS FOR FURTHER READING

Anderson, B. F. *The Psychology Experiment.* Belmont, Calif.: Brooks/Cole, 1971.

Cook, D. R., and N. K. LaFleur. *A Guide to Educational Research.* 2d ed. Boston: Allyn and Bacon, 1975.

Hardyck, C., and L. F. Petrinovich. *Understanding Research in the Social Sciences.* Philadelphia: W. B. Saunders, 1975.

ANTHROPOMETRIC
LABORATORY

For the measurement in various ways of Human Form and Faculty.

Entered from the Science Collection of the S. Kensington Museum.

This laboratory is established by Mr. Francis Galton for the following purposes:—

1. For the use of those who desire to be accurately measured in many ways, either to obtain timely warning of remediable faults in development, or to learn their powers.

2. For keeping a methodical register of the principal measurements of each person, of which he may at any future time obtain a copy under reasonable restrictions. His initials and date of birth will be entered in the register, but not his name. The names are indexed in a separate book.

3. For supplying information on the methods, practice, and uses of human measurement.

4. For anthropometric experiment and research, and for obtaining data for statistical discussion.

Charges for making the principal measurements:
THREEPENCE each, to those who are already on the Register.
FOURPENCE each, to those who are not:— one page of the Register will thenceforward be assigned to them, and a few extra measurements will be made, chiefly for future identification.

The Superintendent is charged with the control of the laboratory and with determining in each case, which, if any, of the extra measurements may be made, and under what conditions.

H & W. Brown, Printers 20 Fulham Road. S.W.

18

Intelligence

THE MEANING OF INTELLIGENCE

What do psychologists mean when they use the term intelligence? In a famous statement, published in 1969, P. E. Vernon suggested three basic meanings of the concept of "intelligence."[1]

1

Intelligence as genetic capacity. This assumes that intelligence is completely inherited, that intelligence is simply part of one's genetic equipment. Hebb refers to this as Intelligence A, the genotypic form of intelligence.

2

Intelligence as observed behavior. This second meaning, referred to by Hebb as Intelligence B, is based on an observation of what the individual does. This is the phenotypic form of intelligence and is a result of the interaction of the genes and the environment. In this sense, intelligence becomes an adverb, and we define it on the basis of whether or not the individual acts *intelligently*.

3

Intelligence as a test score. The third meaning of intelligence, Intelligence C, is based on a strict operational definition of the concept. Intelligence is what the intelligence test measures. Though this seems to be a straightforward, no-frills definition, it creates a meaning of intelligence which can differ from what the majority of individuals would regard as intelligent behavior.

According to Jerome Sattler, an expert in the assessment of children's intelligence, there are a number of problems associated with Intelligence C.

> A number of extrinsic handicaps, especially found among disadvantaged children and among those from underdeveloped nations, can serve to lower test performance, including (a) the examinee's unfamiliarity with the test situation and his lack of motivation; (b) difficulties associated with the item format and testing conditions; (c) mistrust of the examiner, and anxiety and excitement; and (d) difficulties in understanding the instructions or in communicating the responses.[2]

Despite these problems, however, neither Sattler nor Vernon advocate the abandonment of intelligence tests. Vernon believes that since Intelligence B is based on observed behavior, a good IQ test is one way through which that behavior can be observed—i.e., both the Stanford-Binet and the WISC, in the hands of skilled examiners, thoroughly sample Intelligence B (at least among Western children). Sattler says that despite the limitations inherent in intelligence testing, the tests have made valuable contributions to the decision-making processes in schools and clinics.

Perhaps the most significant fact to emerge from Galton's study was the concept of individual differences. The concept allows for a comparison of unlike traits.

IN THE BEGINNING

Over a century ago an Englishman named Sir Francis Galton began speculating on a subject that has very recently become one of the most explosive in all of educational psychology. Galton, who was Charles Darwin's younger cousin, attempted to relate Darwin's theory of evolution to human intellect. Believing that intelligence was a result of one's sensory equipment, and that one's sensory equipment was a result of heredity (since keen sensory powers would seem to have survival value), Galton tried to measure these sensory powers, and thus, intelligence. In 1882 he set up a testing booth in a London museum and charged people a fee to have their hearing, vision, reaction time, and other sensory-motor equipment measured. It is certainly an indication of Galton's own genius that he could devise a way to turn a profit while collecting his data. Perhaps the most significant fact to emerge from his data was the concept of individual differences: Galton found that people varied widely in their abilities to perform on simple sensory-motor tests.

Galton's first "Intelligence Test"

Galton and individual differences

Galton firmly believed that intelligence was inherited. He may have felt this way partly because he had some extremely bright relatives, including Charles Darwin. But he also felt he had objective evidence. He collected data on assumed intellectual relationships between pairs of twins. As we will see, virtually all later studies of intelligence are based on Galton's idea of studying relationships in the context of individual differences. One of Galton's students, a mathematician named Karl Pearson, actually worked out the basic equation for the correlation coefficient, and thus furnished the statistical groundwork for the data analysis which has proved so useful in the study of intelligence.

INDIVIDUAL DIFFERENCES AND CORRELATION

Galton and Pearson were impressed by the fact that individuals varied so greatly in such characteristics as height, weight, and intellect. Because of this variety, the measurements of these characteristics would be more useful if they reflected the frequency with which they could be expected to occur in the population, on the basis of chance, rather than their own absolute units of measurement, such as feet or pounds. The idea of relative standing is of great importance in psychology. It is more important to know that a man's height places him in the relative position of exceeding 50 percent of the adult, male population than to know that he stands 5'8" tall.

The concept of individual differences also makes it possible to find a common ground of comparison between different kinds of measurements. Even though height and weight cannot be compared directly because different units of measurement are used, they can be compared in terms of how much they vary from their own average. In effect, this means that apples and oranges can be compared on the basis of whether, say, a given orange, and a given apple are both larger, or smaller, or juicier, or riper than the average orange and apple. Thus, the relationships between two measurements could be expressed in quantitative terms, and this value is called the correlation coefficient. As we saw in Chapter 16, correlations range in value from +1.00, through zero, to −1.00. The stronger the relationship, the greater the deviation from zero.

Sir Francis Galton

Francis Galton was born near Birmingham, England, in 1822. His family was wealthy and highly educated. Among his relatives were many of England's most-accomplished and gifted citizens, including Charles Darwin, who introduced the modern theory of evolution, and Arthur Hallam, the subject of Tennyson's "In Memoriam." Galton even published a list of his wife's "connections," indicating that her father had been headmaster of Harrow.

In 1838 Galton took up the study of medicine at Birmingham General Hospital and later at King's College in London. In 1840 he shifted his career plans and transferred to Trinity College, where he majored in mathematics.

Following college, Galton went on several trips to Africa, exploring some areas of that continent for the first time. For his African explorations, Galton received the Royal Geographical Society's gold medal in 1854. After his marriage in 1853, Galton turned to writing. His first book, *The Art of Travel*, was a practical guide for the explorer, and his second book, on meteorology, was one of the first attempts to set forth precise techniques for predicting the weather.

During the 1860s Galton became impressed with his cousin Charles Darwin's book on evolution, *On the Origin of Species*. He was fascinated with Darwin's notion of the survival of the fittest, and he attempted to apply this concept to human beings, thus founding the field of *eugenics*, or the study of how the principles of heredity could be used to improve the human race.

In 1869 Galton published his first major work, *Hereditary Genius*, in which he postulated the enormous importance of heredity in determining intellectual eminence. He felt that "genius" ran in families, and he was able to point to his own family as "exhibit A." He also became impressed with the wide range of individual differences which he found for virtually all human traits, physical as well as psychological. Assuming that intelligence was a function of man's sensory apparatus, he devised series of tests of reaction time and tests of sensory acuity to measure intellectual ability. He is considered, therefore, to be the father of intelligence testing. Although Galton's tests seem naive by modern standards, his emphasis on the relationship between sensory ability and intellect foreshadow much of today's research on the importance of sensory stimulation in determining cognitive growth. Galton also invented what he termed the "index of co-relation" in order to analyze the test data that he was collecting. It was left to one of his students, Karl Pearson, however, to work out the mathematical equation for this index, which is now called the Pearson r, or product-moment correlation.

Following the publication of *Hereditary Genius*, Galton wrote other major works, including *English Men of Science, Natural Inheritance,* and *Inquiries into Human Faculty*. His range of interests in psychology was extremely wide, delving into such topics as imagery, free and controlled associations, personality testing, and, of course, the assessment of intellect. Certainly Galton takes his place in history as being a hereditarian. He did not overlook environment completely, however. To gain understanding of the possible differential effects of heredity and environment, Galton performed psychology's first research studies on twins.

In 1909, just two years before his death, Galton was knighted. Galton's place in the history of psychology is ensured. More than any other person, he set psychology on the road to quantifying its data, and, of course, the whole testing movement in educational psychology owes a major debt to Galton's early work.

ALFRED BINET AND MENTAL AGE

In 1904 the Minister of Public Instruction in Paris, France appointed Alfred Binet to a special commission that was to study the problem of educating mentally retarded children. The commission concluded that separate schools should be established to educate those children who could not profit from the regular classroom situation. Binet and his colleague, Theodore Simon, developed the first real intelligence test for the express purpose of identifying these children. Binet discarded Galton's notion of measuring intelligence through the use of sensory-motor tasks, and assembled instead a series of intellectual tasks. It was Binet's belief that intelligence was the ability to make sound judgments. The various tasks were arranged in order of difficulty and presented to a group of French children. Binet later used the concept of mental age to score the test. He discovered, for example, how many of the tasks the average six-year-old could pass, and then any other children who passed the same number of tests were assigned a mental age of six years. Thus, Binet defined mental age in terms of the age at which a given number of test items are passed by an average child. This means that from the very beginning the measurement of intelligence has been a relative measure of mental growth. Binet's intelligence scores were not absolute, for they were based on how well a given child does compared to the average child of the same age.

Binet tried to define intelligence in terms of an individual's ability to make sound judgments. "To judge well, to comprehend well, to reason well, these are the essentials of intelligence. A person may be a moron or an imbecile if he lacks judgment, but with good judgments he could not be either."[3] But, unlike many of the theoreticians who followed, Binet spent little time fretting over the intricacies and possible embellishments of his definition. Binet's goal was to measure intelligence, not merely to talk about it. He understood intelligence by what it enabled children to do, the same way an electrician understands electricity. The point is, Binet's test worked. With it, he could predict reasonably well which children would do well in school and which ones would have difficulties. Of course, there were exceptions, but these were fewer and fewer as the test improved. Sometimes a bright but disobedient child would do worse in school than his intelligence-test score would predict, and sometimes a dull but docile child would do better. This, however, may have been due as much to faulty teacher evaluation as to inaccurate test scores. Binet's test was an individual test of intelligence; that is, the test was given to one child at a time, and administered by a trained examiner.

LATER INDIVIDUAL TESTS

The Stanford-Binet

Binet continued working on his 1905 scale, continually creating new items to improve the test. He revised the whole test twice, in 1908 and in 1911. In 1916 an American psychologist, Lewis M. Terman of Stanford University, published an American revision of the Binet test. Terman's test was standardized on American children and introduced so many new items that it was virtually a new test. He called it the Stanford-Binet, and this test soon became immensely popu-

Binet's first intelligence test

Mental age

Binet's concept of intelligence—the ability to make sound judgments

Binet's test predicted school success

Terman's revision of the Binet test

Binet defined mental age in terms of the age at which a given number of test items are passed by an average child. In 1916 Lewis Terman of Stanford University introduced the Stanford-Binet test. The latest version of the test, last revised in 1960, uses a different method of computing IQ. The method is particularly important in measuring IQ's of individuals.

Alfred Binet

Alfred Binet was born in Nice, France, in 1857. He later went to school in Paris and received a law degree in 1878. Practicing law did not appeal to Binet, and he soon decided to go back to school. In 1890 he received a degree in the natural sciences, and in 1894 he earned his Ph.D. in science. His doctoral thesis was on the nervous system of insects. During the time he was working on his doctorate, Binet became deeply interested in hypnosis, and in 1886 he published a book on the subject, showing the effect of different suggestions on subjects in both the hypnotic and waking states. He published another book in 1886 on the general topic of reasoning and intelligence. Later he would devote all his time to the pursuit of knowledge in this field.

In 1902 Binet wrote another book on intelligence, using as his basic data the thinking processes displayed by his two teen-age daughters. He would give a reasoning problem to his daughters and analyze the steps they took to reach a solution. Though he found that they attacked and solved some problems in the same way, he noted marked differences in their approach to other problems. In his own immediate family Binet thus observed the pervasiveness and importance of individual differences.

When in 1904 the French minister of public instruction announced his wish to identify and place in special schools those children who were mentally retarded, it was no wonder that Binet took on the challenge. This was a situation made to order for a student of individual differences. He asked for and was granted an appointment to the special committee being set up for this purpose. If children who could not seem to profit from regular schooling were to be placed in special classes, a device or technique had to be developed to identify these children. Binet argued that the diagnostic technique should be intellectual, not medical. It had been the practice in France to use physicians to diagnose mental retardation, since retardation was believed to be a physical condition. Binet pointed to the errors and inconsistencies which occurred in these medical diagnoses. If a child were seen by three different physicians on three successive days, three completely different medical diagnoses would result from these examinations.

Thus in 1905 Binet, with a collaborator named Theodore Simon, published the first real intelligence scale. For their test, Binet and Simon assembled a series of intellectual tasks, rather than the sensory-motor tasks that Galton had used. Binet felt that intelligence was displayed in one's ability to make sound judgments, rather than in one's ability to react quickly to a physical stimulus. Binet thus took intelligence out of the medical-physiological realm and placed it in the intellectual-psychological area.

In 1908 Binet revised his original test, retaining the best items from the 1905 scale and adding a number of new tasks. In scoring this 1908 test, Binet utilized a new term, *mental age*. The test would not be scored simply on the basis of the number of items a child passed, but rather in reference to age standards. Binet's scoring technique thus defined intelligence as a *developmental* rather than a *static* concept.

In 1911, shortly before Binet's untimely passing, a second and final revision of the Binet-Simon test was published. This test was a further refinement of the original scale, again substituting new items for previous items that had failed to predict which children would or would not profit from the school experience.

Binet's death in 1911 shortened a career just reaching full bloom. It is certain that many of the controversies that erupted in the field of intelligence would have been lessened had Binet lived long enough to complete his work. For example, Binet believed that intelligence was not just a fixed, immutable individual trait, but rather a developing, trainable, dynamic cluster of abilities that could be nourished or stifled as a result of environmental inputs.

Binet's contribution to educational psychology was enormous. If a man's work can be measured by the amount of research his work has generated, Binet must stand near the very top in psychology.

Terman measures intelligence in terms of IQ

ular in this country. In scoring the test, Terman introduced to America the concept of the intelligence quotient, or IQ.* IQ was determined by dividing mental age by chronological age and multiplying by 100 to get rid of the decimals. Thus, $IQ = MA/CA \times 100$. A six-year-old child scoring a mental age of 9 years would have an IQ of $9/6 \times 100$, or 1.5×100, or 150. On the other hand, a six-year-old child scoring a mental age of five years would have an IQ of $5/6 \times 100$, or .833 $\times 100$, or 83. Since the test was standardized in such a way that the mental age was determined by how well the average child in a given age group did on the test, the average IQ for each age group had to be 100. That is, a six-year-old child scoring a mental age of six years (as the average six-year-old had done), would have an IQ of $6/6 \times 100$, or 100. Since the IQ expresses a child's rate of mental growth, the child whose IQ is 100 is progressing at an average rate.

The Stanford-Binet test was revised in 1937 and again in 1960. The 1960 revision used a different method of computing IQ, a method previously used by David Wechsler and called the deviation IQ. The problem with the original method of calculating IQ was that by about age thirteen the ratio began to break down. Teenagers no longer continue to increase their mental age as they had when younger. Nor do adults add to their mental age from year to year. Thus, the ratio of mental-to-chronological age could be used only with fairly young

The deviation IQ

children, unless statistical corrections were added in. The deviation IQ avoids this problem by using the percentage of cases in each age group achieving a given score. Thus, a seventeen-year-old scoring at the 84th percentile for that age group (that is, equalling or exceeding 84 percent of all seventeen-year-olds taking the test), would have a Stanford-Binet IQ of 116. This is because the Stanford-Binet has a standard deviation (a statistical measure of the variation of scores from the average) of 16 IQ points. Statistical tables are used to find what percentages of cases fall below the various standard deviation unit points.

In 1972 the Stanford-Binet test was restandardized on a representative sample of 2100 children. The new norms again produced a mean IQ of 100 and a standard deviation of 16. The 1972 standardizing group, unlike the one used in 1960, did include some black children and other nonwhites with Spanish surnames. The test itself, however, is almost identical with the 1960 revision, both in content and in scoring procedures.

The Wechsler tests

David Wechsler has produced a number of individual intelligence tests. Like the Stanford-Binet, these tests are administered individually by trained examiners and take about an hour. Wechsler introduced his first test, then called the Wechsler-Bellevue, in 1939. This was an adult test, standardized on an adult sample group. In 1949 he published the Wechsler Intelligence Scale for Children (WISC), and in 1955 he revised his adult test, calling it the Wechsler Adult Intelligence Scale (WAIS). In 1963 Wechsler published the Wechsler Preschool

---

*

Terman borrowed the term IQ from a German psychologist, William Stern, who published a paper describing its use in 1913.

and Primary Scale of Intelligence (WPPSI), which was designed for children from four through six-and-one-half years old.

Recently Wechsler introduced a new version of the WISC, 1974, calling this test the WISC-R (the R standing for "revised"). The WISC-R was standardized on a group of 2200 children, and this sample included both whites and nonwhites (blacks, Puerto Ricans, Mexican-Americans, American Indians, and Orientals) in somewhat the same proportions as they are represented in the population. About 28 percent of the test items in the WISC-R did not appear in the original test. Also, the age range is slightly different in the revision, the WISC having covered ages five to fifteen whereas the WISC-R covers ages six to sixteen. Like its predecessor, the mean IQ on the WISC-R is still 100, and the standard deviation is 15. The IQ range on the WISC-R is 40 to 160. Anyone familiar with the WISC should read the WISC-R manual carefully before administering the new test. Administration of the WISC-R demands far more probing in order to determine whether or not the child really knows the answer.

The Wechsler tests mark a rather significant departure from the tradition of the Binet tests. Wechsler believed that the Binet tests were too heavily loaded with verbal items. According to Wechsler, "Intelligence . . . is the aggregate or global capacity of the individual to act purposefully, to think rationally, and to deal effectively with his environment."[4] Thus, not only is the poet with high verbal facility able to score well on the WAIS, but so too is the garage mechanic who can expertly reassemble a four-barrel carburetor, even if he cannot quote

Wechsler tests are a significant departure from verbally oriented Binet tests

The Wechsler tests—those for both children and adults—measure IQ as a function of verbal as well as performance abilities. Wechsler's tests also perform another valuable function, that of personality evaluation.

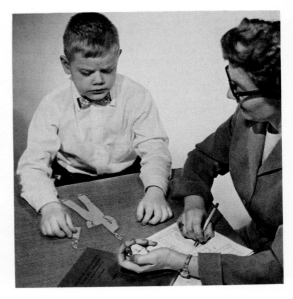

David Wechsler

Wechsler was born in Lespedi, Roumania, in 1896, one of seven children. His family moved to New York City when David was six years old. He attended the New York public schools and in 1916 graduated from the College of the City of New York. Following college, he immediately enrolled in the graduate psychology program at Columbia, doing his M.A. thesis under R. S. Woodworth in 1917. With America's entry into World War I, Wechsler was drafted into the army. While awaiting his induction he joined the great Harvard psychologist E. G. Boring at Camp Yaphank in Long Island and helped to administer and score the recently developed Army Alpha intelligence test. Because of his training in psychology, and especially because of his work with Boring on the Alpha test, Wechsler, after his own induction, was sent by the army for basic training at the School of Military Psychology at Camp Greenleaf in Georgia. He was then assigned to Fort Logan, Texas, where his duties included testing thousands of recruits on the Army Individual Performance Scales, the Yerkes Point Scale, and the Stanford-Binet IQ test.

During this time, Wechsler became increasingly impressed by the disparity often shown between a man's tested intelligence and the quality of his previous work record. Often a man would test at a very low level on the various assessment devices, yet his past history indicated that he had been quite successful on his civilian job. The same man often proved later to be extremely competent in performing his miliary duties. Wechsler began to question the validity of the tests, especially the Stanford-Binet with its high verbal content. Perhaps the Binet test did predict success or failure in school, but it was proving to be less effective in predicting performance in the military. Wechsler concluded that perhaps by emphasizing the intellectual component, the Stanford-Binet was missing other aspects of a person's makeup which may contribute to one's overall intelligent behavior. These ideas, however, were not fully solidified, nor did they result in public expression until 1939, with the publication of Wechsler's own intelligence test.

In 1919 the Army sent Wechsler to France and later to England, where, at the University of London, he had the rare opportunity of working with both Spearman and Pearson. From Spearman, Wechsler learned of the two-factor theory of intelligence, "g" and "s," and from Pearson he was schooled in statistical techniques, especially the techniques of correlation.

Wechsler was discharged from the army in August 1919 and then applied for and won a fellowship for study in France. From 1920 to 1922, he studied at the University of Paris and at the Laboratory of Psychology at the Sorbonne. During this time he met both Theodore Simon and Pierre Janet.

In 1922 Wechsler returned to the United States, where he became both a part-time graduate student in psychology at Columbia and a staff psychologist at the Bureau of Child Guidance. In 1925 he received his Ph.D. degree from Columbia.

From 1925 to 1932 Wechsler worked in private practice as a psychologist. During this period he also worked part-time for the Psychological Corporation, the company which was later to publish the tests that bear his name.

In 1932 he became chief psychologist at New York's Bellevue Psychiatric Hospital, and in 1933 he also joined the faculty at New York University's College of Medicine. From this point on, Wechsler devoted much of his energy to the creation of a new intelligence test, a test that would be suitable for adults (which the Stanford-Binet wasn't), and a test that would tap performance

as well as verbal factors. After trying out many items from previous tests, and also creating new items of his own, Wechsler produced in 1939 the now-famous Wechsler-Bellevue Intelligence Scale. Concurrently, he published *The Measurement of Adult Intelligence*, a book in which he brought together all his ideas on the question of intelligence and how it should be measured. He defined intelligence as "the global capacity of an individual to think rationally, to act purposefully, and to deal effectively with his environment." He saw intelligence, thus, not as a narrow capacity but as a global capacity that includes emotional and motivational as well as intellectual components. Wechsler did not separate intelligence from other personality factors.

In 1949 he developed the Wechsler Intelligence Scale for Children (WISC), and in 1955 he revised his adult test, calling it the Wechsler Adult Intelligence Scale (WAIS). In 1963 he introduced the Wechsler Preschool and Primary Scale of Intelligence (WPPSI), a test designed for children of ages four through six-and-a-half. Recently, Wechsler introduced a new version of the WISC, called the WISC-R. The WISC-R was standardized on a sample group of 2200 children, including whites and nonwhites in approximately the same proportions as they are represented in the population.

Wechsler's name has become synonymous with intelligence testing in America. He is truly one of the great psychologists of our time.

Wechsler tests pro-
duce three IQ scores

long passages from Shakespeare. The Wechsler tests, which use a deviation IQ, produce three IQ scores: a verbal IQ, a performance IQ, and a full-scale IQ score. Thus the garage mechanic may receive a verbal IQ of only 105, but with a performance IQ of 126, he would achieve a full-scale IQ of 115, which is at the 84th percentile.

The verbal subtests. On the WAIS the verbal IQ is calculated on the basis of six subtests:

1
Information. Twenty-nine items that test the subject's general storehouse of information about the world.

2
Comprehension. Fourteen questions that evaluate the individual's level of practical information and general ability to utilize past experience.

3
Arithmetic. Fourteen questions that test the individual's powers of arithmetical reasoning. The skills needed for this subtest don't go beyond those taught in grade school.

4
Digit span. A test of short-term memory in which the examiner reads a series of digits and asks the subject to repeat them.

5
Similarities. Thirteen items in which the subject attempts to discover in what way two things are alike. This test appears to measure an individual's ability to think in abstract terms.

6
Vocabulary. Forty words that attempt to predict the size of a person's vocabulary.

The performance subtests. The performance IQ is computed on the basis of five subtests:

1
Picture arrangement. Seven pictures which, when arranged properly, tell a logical story. This is an attempt to measure an individual's ability to size up and understand a total situation.

2
Picture completion. The subject is shown a set of incomplete pictures and is asked to name the missing part. This is a test of visual recognition.

3
Block design. The subject is given a number of small wooden blocks which must be put together to form a number of patterns. This is a test of perceptual analysis and visual-motor coordination.

4

Digit symbol.   The subject must associate certain symbols with certain digits and then be able to write the appropriate symbol in squares containing the associated digit. This is a test of speed of movement and memory.

5

Object assembly.   The subject must arrange various puzzle parts to form a certain object. This is a test of manual dexterity and powers of recognition.

In addition to being important instruments for measuring intelligence, the Wechsler tests have useful diagnostic capabilities that enable a skilled examiner to evaluate such personality characteristics as defense mechanisms, the ability to cope with stress, and the general mode of handling life's situations. Thus, a Wechsler test gives a three-dimensional picture of the subject, and can often tell us not only that a given child lacks motivation, but also why.

Group tests of intelligence

Though the Stanford-Binet and Wechsler tests have made an extremely important contribution to the field of intelligence testing, the fact that they are individual tests means that they are time consuming and therefore rather expensive to administer. During the First World War there was suddenly an urgent need to test huge groups of men quickly, and a new approach to testing was introduced. Two group tests of intelligence were devised in 1917, the Army Alpha Test for the men who could read, and the Army Beta Test, a nonverbal test for illiterates. Though the Beta test, the nonverbal test, proved to be less effective than the Alpha, the success of the Alpha led to the development of a great number of group tests. The most widely used group tests in the schools today are: the California Test of Mental Maturity (McGraw-Hill), the School and College Ability Tests (SCAT, Educational Testing Service), the Tests of General Ability (TOGA, Science Research Associates), the Otis-Lennon Mental Ability Tests (Harcourt Brace Jovanovich), the Kuhlmann-Anderson Intelligence Test (Personnel Press), and the Lorge-Thorndike Intelligence Test and the Henmon-Nelson Test of Mental Ability (Houghton-Mifflin). These group tests are also referred to as paper-and-pencil tests, and they usually consist of a series of multiple-choice items. They must be administered and timed precisely as stated in the directions.

The Army Alpha and Beta Tests

SEX DIFFERENCES IN IQ

The full-scale IQ's of males and females of a given age are almost identical. This is partly due to the averaging out of differences that do occur among the various subtest scores. Males typically score higher on spatial, mechanical, and numerical tests, whereas females score higher on verbal tests and tests involving quick, manual movements and attention to detail.

The development of IQ also reveals certain sex differences. The mean IQ of males increases slightly after age six, while the female mean tends to go down.[5] This may have a cultural explanation. If society demands more achievement from males than females, which apparently is the case, and if achievement motivation and IQ correlate at all, then perhaps society's emphasis on inculcating the achievement motive more in males accounts for this difference. As social psychologists continually remind us, people tend to behave as others around them expect them to behave.

WHAT DO IQ TESTS PREDICT?

Academic achievement

During our earlier discussion of Alfred Binet and the first intelligence test, we said that Binet's test was effective in predicting which children would do well in school. The evidence gained since then is generally consistent with Binet's early results. Over seventy years and hundreds of studies later it is now clear that IQ tests do predict scholastic success. The correlation between IQ and grades in school runs better than +.50. Since the highest possible correlation is 1.00, IQ scores are not infallible predictors in every case. There are children whose IQ scores are lower than other children's but whose grades are higher, for a number of nonintellectual factors also influence scholastic success. Physical illness, emotional upset, and lack of motivation, for example, all can interfere

IQ scores are not infallible predictors of school achievement

IQ scores are not infallible predictors of school achievement. Among other factors influencing academic success is ego strength, that is, how a student perceives himself or herself. Successful students possess strong egos.

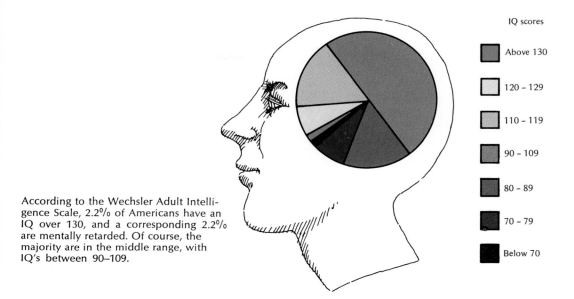

IQ scores

Above 130

120 – 129

110 – 119

90 – 109

80 – 89

70 – 79

Below 70

According to the Wechsler Adult Intelligence Scale, 2.2% of Americans have an IQ over 130, and a corresponding 2.2% are mentally retarded. Of course, the majority are in the middle range, with IQ's between 90–109.

with success. Recent research suggests that lack of ego strength is another related factor. Academic achievement has been shown to be largely a result of a student's reality orientation, or ego strength. That is, successful students possess strong egos, are willing to postpone pleasure, are not so easily distracted, and are generally more able to pursue tasks in an organized fashion. Underachievers, on the other hand, have low ego strength and are less able to control their impulses, and are especially unable to postpone gratification.[6]

Success in life

Although it is true that IQ tests do predict academic achievement with some degree of accuracy, this fact in and of itself may not seem all that important. After all, IQ is measured by means of tests, and grades are determined exactly the same way, by performances on tests. Perhaps all this proves is that children who do well on one test also do well on other tests. How well does an IQ score predict success or failure in other areas of one's life? Do children with high IQ's and high-school grades also succeed in later life, on the job, financially, in marriage, emotionally?

    To help answer these questions, Lewis M. Terman began a monumental study of hundreds of California school children in the 1920s.[7] All of the children had performed exceptionally well on IQ tests (they all had tested IQ's of 140 or more). Terman followed the lives of these subjects for the next twenty-five years in order to find out whether there were any significant adult correlates of a high IQ in childhood (and many of these subjects are still being followed today by some of Terman's later co-workers).

Terman study investigated correlation between IQ and success in later life

Terman's study of gifted children suggested that high-IQ children are healthier and stronger than average children, are better adjusted emotionally, and tend to be leaders among their peers.

First, Terman dispelled the myth that very bright children are physically fragile and undersized. Terman's subjects were above average on many physical characteristics, including height, weight, physical development, and general health. Also, the gifted children tended to be heavier at birth, cut their first tooth two months earlier than average, walked and talked two months earlier than average, and reached adolescence earlier than the average child.

While in school the gifted children received significantly higher marks than their classmates and were more likely to be skipped ahead to a higher grade. In fact, by the end of elementary school Terman's entire group of 1500 children had averaged a skip of one full grade. Perhaps this is how the myth of the undersized and puny genius originated. Since children with high IQ's do tend to skip frequently, they are likely to end up in classrooms with children who are larger because they are older.

On tests of emotional adjustment the gifted children were found to be better adjusted than the average child. They were also more socially adaptable, and more likely to be leaders among their peers.

As adults, Terman's group continued to be successful. They earned more money, had more managerial jobs, and made far more literary and scientific contributions than the average adult. When checked in 1959, the group had published over 2000 scientific papers and 33 novels and had taken out 230 patents. A great number of them were listed in Who's Who and in American Men of Science.

Finally, they had fewer divorces than the average adult, and criminal convictions and alcoholism were rare. Even the death rate was about 33 percent lower than that for the general population.

In a more-recent study it was found that IQ has a significant correlation with income. As a matter of fact, IQ predicted a person's income better than such other measures as parents' education or parents' income.[8]

It is obvious that the IQ test predicts more than just elementary-school grades. It must be pointed out, though, that not all of Terman's subjects attained the great success of the majority. It is also true that many highly successful people in this world do not have IQ's of 140 or more. High IQ's are associated with a wide range of achievement in a wide variety of areas, but high IQ's do not tell the whole story. Personality variables such as ego strength and motivation, and physical variables such as health or accidents, also play a vital role in determining one's ability to live effectively and achieve success.

Personality variables, as well as IQ, contribute to one's success in life

HEREDITY AND ENVIRONMENT
In earlier chapters of this book, especially in Chapter 5, we pointed out that all human behavior, including intelligent behavior, is a product of heredity interacting with environment interacting with time. This is one of psychology's basic axioms, and nowhere is the validity of this axiom more compelling than in the area of intelligence.

Hereditary factors
Heredity limits the extent to which intelligence can be influenced by environment and time. It is now fairly certain that intelligence has a genetic component. As long ago as 1937 it was demonstrated that the closer two people are genetically related, the more similar their IQ's will be.[9] This study showed that identical twins reared apart had IQ correlations of .79. In other words, even though these genetically identical individuals had been raised in different environments, they still had fairly similar IQ's. A fairly exhaustive review of the literature revealed the IQ correlations shown in Table 18.1.[10]

Identical twins have similar IQ's

These data make it clear that genetic factors are indeed involved in determining IQ. The closer the genetic relationship, the higher the reported IQ correlations.

Table 18.1 IQ correlations.

Relationship	Number of studies	Average correlation
Unrelated children reared apart	4	−.01
Foster parent and child	3	+.20
Unrelated children reared together	5	+.24
Siblings reared apart	33	+.47
Siblings reared together	36	+.55
Identical twins reared apart	4	+.75
Identical twins reared together	14	+.87
Grandparent and grandchild	3	+.27
Parent and child	13	+.50

Environmental factors

The IQ correlation chart also shows the importance of environmental factors. For example, when identical twins are reared together in the same environment, their IQ's are more similar than when they are raised apart. Note, too, that when unrelated children are reared together, there is a significant correlation between their IQ's. In this instance, where there is no genetic linkage at all, similar IQ's result from the identical environment. The correlation for unrelated children reared together is almost the same as the correlation for grandparent and grandchild. The correlation of +.20 between foster parents and children is also of great importance. Here again we have an example of genetically unrelated persons whose IQ's are too similar to be simply the result of chance.

In another very important study, a correlation of +.43 was obtained between the quality of the home environment and the child's IQ.[11] In this study the homes of 133 children (mostly white and mostly low socioeconomic status) were visited and scored on an instrument called the Home Environment Review. The significant correlation that was obtained indicates that the higher the quality of the home environment, the higher the IQ of the children. The most important of the home factors were:

1
The number of books and other learning materials in the home.

2
The amount of reward and recognition the children receive from their parents for academic achievement.

3
The parents' expectations regarding their children's academic achievement.

Specific environmental influences

It's not enough to talk in generalities about environmental influences. Just what are some of the specific environmental inputs that appear to affect intelligence?

Protein deficiency can damage intellectual development

Nutrition.   Gross deficiencies of diet can adversely affect IQ's and even produce mental retardation. Kwashiorkor, an illness resulting from a protein-deficient diet, has been found to be extremely damaging to intellectual development.[12] If nutritional deficiencies occur in early childhood, the damage to intelligence can be pronounced, even if the protein deficit is less than that needed to produce kwashiorkor. The exact physiological link between nutritional deficiencies and mental retardation is still unknown. However, recent studies have led to some speculation that inadequate protein intake prevents full development of the brain, especially those areas involved in memory storage.[13,14]

Further, as was pointed out in Chapter 4, Bonnie Kaplan's recent review of the relationship between inadequate dietary intake and mental deficiency presents rather convincing evidence that mental retardation can result from malnutrition. This is especially true if the malnutrition occurs during the nine months of gestation and the first two or three years of the baby's life.[15]

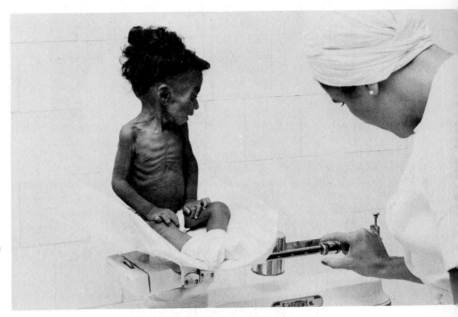

This child is a victim of protein malnutrition. Nutritional deficiencies occurring in early childhood can result in pronounced damage to intelligence.

Stimulus variety.   A second important environmental factor in intelligence is stimulus variety, especially in early childhood. As we saw in Chapter 5, important figures in the field of psychology, such as J. McVicker Hunt, Jerome Bruner, Benjamin S. Bloom, and David Krech, feel that stimulus variety is perhaps the most important ingredient in intellectual development. Hunt states that the more we see, hear, and touch in early childhood, the more we will want to see, hear, and touch later on. The key to cognitive growth, according to Hunt, is matching the child's present intellectual ability with just the right amount of stimulus variety to bring out the natural desire to continue learning. Bruner insists that infants must be exposed to a wide variety of stimulus inputs and a shifting environment if normal intellectual growth is to be maintained. Bloom says that an abundant early environment is the key to full development of intelligence. And David Krech has shown, at least in animals, that without stimulus heterogeneity, animals are less able to learn, and their brains never develop fully.

Past experience.   Another crucial environmental ingredient in intellectual development is past experience in learning situations. Children who learn to master one problem are able to transfer this knowledge to other problems they may encounter later. The knowledge gained from past experience may begin to snowball and provide the child with a solid base for future understanding. Harry Harlow has shown how this works with monkeys. Monkeys that were trained to solve a certain problem (the oddity problem) were far better at solving complex discrimination problems presented to them at a later time than monkeys that

Many psychologists believe that the importance of stimulus variety, especially in early childhood, cannot be overemphasized.

Learning how to learn

were not so trained. Through training, the monkeys had developed what Harlow called a learning set. They had, in effect, learned how to learn. As Harlow says, "Learning to learn is no doubt an essential feature of the intellectual development of monkeys, apes, and children growing up in their natural environments.[16]

Other environmental variables. Finally, Ben Bloom (1964) lists three environmental variables which he feels are important in developing a child's intellectual abilities:

1
The amount of stimulation children receive for verbal development.

2
The amount of affection and reward children receive for verbal reasoning accomplishments.

3
The amount of encouragement children receive for "active interaction with problems, exploration of the environment and the learning of new skills."[17]

We have seen the importance of hereditary and environmental interactions for intellectual development. It is also vital to understand the nature of this interaction from the point of view of time. Chapter 5 was devoted entirely to the importance of early experience on psychological development. Let us now look at some of the highlights.

Most psychologists today are convinced of the profound importance of early experience for proper cognitive growth. Ben Bloom states the case forcefully in saying that environmental effects on intelligence are most pronounced during a child's first few years of life.

The heavy line in Fig. 18.1 show's Bloom's famous negatively accelerated curve for intellectual growth. Notice that as age increases intellectual development increases less and less. By four years of age we have already achieved 50 percent of our adult intelligence, and by eight years of age we have achieved 80 percent. The shaded area surrounding the main curve indicates the potential for changes in intelligence. You will notice that as age increases, there is also less and less potential for changes in intelligence. Therefore, during the first few years, a beneficial environment is most effective in increasing intellectual development, but as time goes on this beneficial environment comes to have less effect. Similarly, a stultifying environment is most damaging during those early, critical years. Bloom feels that the difference between a beneficial and a stultifying environment during these early childhood years can produce IQ differences of 20 points or more. Bloom may be too conservative, however. Rick Heber's study, cited in detail in Chapter 5, found that massive educational intervention can increase IQ's by an average of 33 points. It must be remembered, however, that Heber's program begins when the child is only a few weeks old.

Wayne Dennis's study of a Teheran orphanage where the children were kept in a condition of extreme sensory deprivation also showed that stimulus variety at an early age is critical for cognitive growth (see Chapter 5). Almost all

As age increases, intellectual development increases less and less

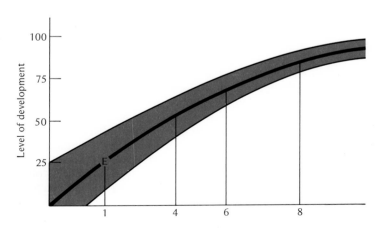

Fig. 18.1 Bloom's negatively accelerated curve for intellectual growth.

of these sensory-deprived children were intellectually retarded.[18] In another study, Dennis described a Lebanese orphanage where environmental conditions were so dismal that mental retardation was the rule.[19] The average IQ of the 133 children tested was only 53. This is probably the lowest average IQ ever reported for a group of children who were otherwise considered normal. Some of these children were later adopted by middle-class families, and in every case there was a fairly dramatic IQ increase. The more stimulating home environments provided an average gain of 28 IQ points. Despite the improvement, the mean IQ of the adopted children was still only 81, again showing that improved environmental conditions at a later age cannot compensate fully for a deprived environment during the first few years of life.

ARE THERE GENETIC DIFFERENCES IN INTELLIGENCE BETWEEN RACIAL GROUPS?

It has long been known that on standardized IQ tests (standardized primarily on white sample groups) the average IQ of white children and the average IQ of black children generally differ. It is also known that the difference favors the white children. The two IQ distributions do overlap, so that despite the difference between the averages, there are still many black children whose IQ's are higher than those of many white children.

A study of World War I Army Alpha IQ scores found that although the average IQ of black soldiers was lower than that of white soldiers, there were some fairly interesting reversals. For example, the average IQ of black soldiers from several Northern states was higher than the average IQ of white soldiers from certain Southern states.[20] It has also been found that the more money a state spends on education, the higher the IQ's of its schoolchildren, black and white.[21] The correlation between the amount of money a state spends on education and the IQ's of the state's children is +.70.

Jensen argues for the genetic basis of intelligence

Arthur Jensen of the University of California at Berkeley has recently interpreted this difference between the tested IQ's of blacks and whites as implying that white children are genetically superior to black children. This argument claims that IQ has an extremely high genetic factor (about 80 percent) and that there must therefore be racial differences in intelligence.[22] Jensen says that differences in intelligence are "predominantly attributable to genetic differences, with environmental factors contributing a minor portion of the variance among individuals in IQ."[23]

This claim must be closely examined. The rules of science demand that in order to establish a cause-and-effect relationship, all the possible input variables must be controlled. If, for example, you wished to determine whether increased noise in a classroom had a depressing effect on reading speed, you wouldn't put all the fast readers in the low-noise group and all the slow readers in the high-noise group. Nor would you have different conditions of illumination in the two groups. Nor would you test one group at 9:00 A.M. and the other at 3:00 A.M. Instead, you would want the two groups to be as equivalent as possible: same age, same average reading speed, same conditions of illumination, same time of testing. If, after controlling for all the variables, the group tested under high-noise conditions reads significantly more slowly than the group

Environmental effects on intelligence are most pronounced during a child's first few years of life. By four years of age, a child has already achieved 50% of his or her adult intelligence.

tested under low-noise conditions, you could say that noise does, indeed, lower reading speed. This is the cautious way science proceeds before assigning causal factors to observed differences. Perhaps Jensen is correct when he says that the assumption of a genetic difference in intelligence between the races is not an unreasonable hypothesis. But the point is, and this is an important point for the prospective teacher to remember, Jensen's hypothesis has not been proved, nor may it ever be a testable conclusion.

As we have seen, intelligence has three crucial inputs: heredity, environment, and time. In order to determine the extent to which any one of these variables affects intelligence, the other two must be controlled. Large numbers of children, black and white, would have to be raised in identical (or, at the very least, reliably measured) environments. Also, because of the time variable, stimulus variety would have to be increased at precisely the same developmental stage for each child. The enormity and complexity of such a study makes it appear improbable that Jensen's hypothesis could ever be adequately tested. All of Jensen's reported twin studies (which were all done on white children, incidentally), and all of his correlations (regardless of whether they're "corrected for unreliability"), cannot alter the fact that the average black child is not raised under the same, or under even remotely similar environmental conditions as the average white child. Does anyone seriously believe that if white children were to be raised in black homes in Harlem's ghettoes they would achieve the same scores on an IQ test as if they had been raised in Scarsdale's suburbs?

IQ comparisons between the races are made even more difficult to evaluate because of the possibility that IQ scores may reflect the race of the examiner. A number of studies have suggested that the IQ scores of black children are underestimated by white examiners, or perhaps overestimated by black examiners. In one experiment a single group of black children was tested by both black and white examiners. Using different forms, L. and M. of the the Stanford-Binet, the children were tested in a counterbalanced design, first by an examiner of one race and then by the other. The mean IQ score of these black children when tested by the black examiner was 105.7, but dropped to a mean of 101.9 when tested by a white. This difference was statistically significant.[24] Since both black and white examiners were equally trained and equally competent, the difference in IQ scores probably results from either differing expectations on the part of the examiner or differing motivational sets on the part of the children.

It is important to note that the high correlation obtained between the IQ's of parents and children overemphasizes the genetic explanation. An impoverished home environment has an adverse effect not only on the intellectual development of the children raised in it, but also on the way those children eventually raise their own children. The childhood experiences of the second generation are a function of the childhood experiences of the previous generation. "Such handicaps combine to sustain the very conditions from which they are derived, so the vicious circle tends to be repeated for generation after generation. Clearly the correlations between IQ's of parents and children are bound to be high, and give a superficial impression of genetic determination."[25]

High correlations between IQ's of parents and children overemphasize the genetic component

HERITABILITY

The concept of "heritability" does not apply to single individuals; it is a population concept

Jensen based his argument on the concept of heritability. Heritability is the proportion of the total variability in a population which is due to genetic, as opposed to environmental, factors. Thus, if all the variation in IQ scores in a given population is due to genetic factors, the heritability of IQ would be 1.00. If all the variability were due to environmental factors, then the heritability of IQ would be zero. Since, as we have seen over and over again, IQ is the result of heredity, environment, and time, the heritability value for IQ lies somewhere between 0 and 1.00. Jensen argues that the actual value is around .80. Regardless of Jensen's estimate, however, we must remember that heritability does not apply to any single individual. Behavior geneticist Jerry Hirsch has said that heritability only explains variation "in some particular population at a single generation under one set of conditions."[26] Thus, since heritability applies only to a specific environment, it really matters very little what the estimate of the actual heritability value is in the discussion of a given black child's IQ. "High or low heritability tells us absolutely nothing about how a given individual might have developed under conditions different from those in which he actually did develop."[27]

Jensen appears to accept this definition when he says that heritability is a population statistic that has "no sensible meaning with reference to a measurement or characteristic of an individual. . . . Estimates of H are specific to the population sampled, the point in time, how the measurements were made, and the particular test used to obtain the measurements."[28] Despite the clarity and precision of this definition, Jensen then presents a case that goes far beyond the bounds of his own careful restriction. Jensen's estimated H value of .80 is generated by a review of identical twin studies done exclusively on white American and English children, and yet he applies this value to both black and white children alike—hardly identical populations. As a matter of fact, in a study of over 1000 twins of differing economic and racial backgrounds conducted by Sandra Scarr-Salapatek, it was found that the heritability of IQ is always higher among economically advantaged than among lower-class children.[29] Thus, it is not an unreasonable hypothesis that the value of H increases as a function of an increase in the socioeconomic backgrounds of the populations being studied. As one reviewer stated it: "In other words, 'native talent' may manifest itself conspicuously in people who grow up in favorable environments and remain suppressed in adverse environments."[30]

Jensen also argues that compensatory education has been tried and has failed. He makes two main points on this subject. First, he feels that experiments with early education (such as Head Start), have not lived up to expectations; that, although the Head Start program does produce some short-term IQ gains, these gains are not sustained over the years. Second, he implies that since the IQ disadvantage of blacks is mostly inherited, it is useless to spend money for early-education programs that obviously cannot affect the genes.

With regard to the first point, Head Start admittedly did not live up to the hopes of many educators. But Head Start may have been a case of too little too late. The Head Start program typically involved teaching disadvantaged children how to get along in school six months before they got there. By the time Head Start enrolled these children, they had already gone through too many critical learning periods. Also, the fact that the immediate gains in IQ points were not maintained is not surprising. Just as there are cumulative positive effects on intellectual growth as a result of an improved environment, so, too, there are cumulative negative effects from an impoverished environment. A study of white children from the "hollows" of rural Virginia found the average IQ of six to eight year olds to be only 84, and the average for ten to twelve year olds to be only 53.[31] The point is that with children from impoverished environments, early educational intervention would be a marked success if all it accomplished was the prevention of IQ decline. Rick Heber's Milwaukee Project, described in detail in Chapter 5, may do far more than this, however. Heber's program, which begins when the infant is scarcely home from the hospital, may not only prevent intellectual deterioration, but may even give the children an IQ gain.

Studies of this type, while not refuting the importance of heredity on intelligence, make it clear that the time factor and the environmental factor are extremely important in determining later levels of intellectual functioning. "To overstress the genetic factor is inevitably to assert that the blame belongs on the shoulders of the victim. This whole method of diagnosis and treatment takes us into the theatre of the absurd."[32] Jensen's comment that compensatory education has been tried and has failed may be like that of an observer who, after watching Orville Wright's first flight at Kitty Hawk, said that air travel has been tried and failed.

Robert Carkhuff, an expert in the fields of counseling and human relations, makes the point that although the mean IQ of black children is about 86 when

Jensen sees no value in preschool programs such as Head Start they enter first grade, it drops even lower by the time the children reach fifth grade. Carkhuff attributes this drop to environmental forces working on the black child in the school setting. Since teachers and counselors often treat black children as if they were devoid of intellectual resources, the children begin to fulfill this expectation by achieving less and less as the school years go by. Says Carkhuff, "the teachers and counselors respond to black children as if Jensen and Garrett were correct."[33]

To compound the felony, Carkhuff argues, the least-competent teachers are assigned to ghetto and predominantly black schools. It can be no wonder then that black children often do not achieve beyond the eighth- or ninth-grade level, since it may be that the level of their teacher's own competence does not extend beyond this point. One study found that two-thirds of the teachers tested scored lower than junior-high-school level on tests of proficiency in the teacher's own specialty area.[34] Says Carkhuff of these teachers, "They could not pass their own exams."

THE CONFLUENCE MODEL

Recently, R. B. Zajonc has interpreted the relationship between family size and intelligence as a product of general environmental stimulation. The data are as follows: (1) first-born children tend to have higher IQ's than do their younger siblings; (2) the more children there are in a family the lower the IQ's of all the children; (3) twins have lower IQ's than do nontwins; (4) children in one-parent homes have lower IQ's than do children from homes where both parents are present (the younger the child at the time of parental loss, the more severe the resulting IQ deficit); (5) the only child has a lower IQ than does the first born in a two- or three-child family.[35]

In his interpretation of these facts, Zajonc uses what he calls the "confluence model," a model which predicts that the intellectual growth of each child is a function of the intellectual levels of all the other family members. A given child's intellectual environment is based on the average of the intellectual levels of all the family members, and since children contribute less than their parents to the absolute level of the family's intellectual environment, the more children there are, the lower the absolute level. However, the more spacing between children, the less the damage to the family's intellectual environment. The data on only children does reveal a discontinuity in this prediction, and Zajonc suggests that a child in some way benefits from having younger siblings. The only child has less opportunity to be a "teacher," to show his younger brother how to hold a pencil, or his younger sister how to grip a baseball bat, or tie her shoes.

Also based on his confluence model, Zajonc has provided an interesting and provocative explanation of the steady decline in SAT scores which has occurred over the past decade. The decline is simply a reflection of the fact that, following World War II, American parents decided to have large families, and to have these children close together. Further, since the size of American families began decreasing in the early 1960s, Zajonc predicts a dramatic upswing in SAT scores by 1980.

Finally, Zajonc explains racial IQ differences on the basis of his confluence model. Since black families generally have more children (and have them closer together) than do the average white families, that fact alone could explain the difference in average IQ scores between the two groups. Add to this the further fact that more black than white families are one-parent families.

Zajonc's conclusions are based on studies conducted on well over a million subjects from four different countries: the United States, France, The Netherlands, and Scotland. And, more importantly, his predictions have held up regardless of nationality, race, social status, or income level.

For this research, Zajonc and one of his colleagues, Gregory Markus, won the 1975 Social-Psychological Prize of the American Association for the Advancement of Science.

SHOULD IQ TESTS BE ABANDONED?

The controversy currently raging about whether or not intelligence is racially correlated is not just an esoteric scientific debate, for the lives and futures of our children are at stake. This is not like a group of physicists debating the theory of aperiodic crystals; this is a here-and-now issue. If government officials become convinced that Jensen is correct, funding for urgently needed preschool programs could be siphoned off into other areas. One recent result of this controversy is that some school systems are inclined to do away with IQ testing completely: they feel that if the results of such testing are going to reinforce racist attitudes, then perhaps the best solution is to stop giving the tests, especially to black children. This position certainly has some merit, for IQ testing has at times damaged the lives of some children. The Rosenthal and Jacobson study discussed in Chapter 15 showed that children's test scores can be affected by the teacher's belief about the child's intellectual potential.[36] This phenomenon of a self-fulfilling prophecy on test scores is now known in the literature as the Rosenthal Effect. Teachers must not be allowed to use low IQ scores as a "cop-out" for not doing their job.

Some school systems abandon IQ testing

Despite the dangers of misusing and misinterpreting the results of IQ testing, there is perhaps greater danger in simply abandoning IQ testing. In the first place, the IQ test, with all its limitations, is still the most reliable, the most valid test in all of psychology. It has had too long a history of success to be casually dismissed. The IQ test, for example, is a very effective instrument for identifying underachievers, students whose academic achievement falls far short of what their IQ scores predict. The case of the underachiever is often tragic, but without a means of testing children's intellectual potential we would have no way of identifying the underachiever and, thus, would be unable to intervene to try to correct the problem.

Abandoning IQ tests may create new problems

In the second place, abandoning IQ testing might have severe racial overtones. If we stop testing and are no longer able to identify those children who need help, we may begin to believe that there is no problem. This kind of Alice-in-Wonderland approach could halt any further efforts to erase the differences. It could doom a major segment of our society to never achieving much success in our competitive and technological society.

Summary

Psychologists have generally used three meanings of the concept "intelligence": intelligence as a genetic capacity, intelligence as observed behavior, and intelligence as a test score.

The history of intelligence testing begins with Sir Francis Galton. Galton believed that intelligence was largely an inherited characteristic and attempted to measure intelligence through the use of simple, sensory-motor tests. Galton's test results led him to emphasize what later became the theme of all measurement practitioners—individual differences.

Galton's student and colleague, Karl Pearson, analyzed the testing data and, in order to make more-meaningful comparisons, introduced a new statistical technique, called the correlation coefficient. Through the use of Karl Pearson's technique, what had been expressed only as rough qualitative relationships could now be stated as more-precise quantitative relationships. The stronger the relationship, the more the correlation coefficient deviates from zero.

Alfred Binet discarded Galton's idea of measuring intelligence through the use of sensory-motor tasks and adopted instead the approach of using intellectual tasks. Binet used the concept of mental age in order to assign a numerical value to performance on his test. Binet created his test in 1905 for the very practical purpose of identifying which children could or could not profit from the regular school experience. Binet's test was an individual test of intelligence, administered to one child at a time.

Later, in 1916, an American psychologist, Lewis M. Terman, published an American revision of the Binet test, introducing new items and standardizing the test on California school children. The scoring of this test, called the Stanford-Binet Test, was based on the concept of the intelligence quotient or IQ. IQ was determined by dividing a child's mental age by his or her chronological age and multiplying by 100.

In 1939 David Wechsler introduced the first of a series of new individual IQ tests. Wechsler felt that the Stanford-Binet test was too heavily laden with verbal items, and so he created a series of performance tasks to be presented along with the more-traditional verbal tests. Wechsler's tests were scored on the basis of the deviation IQ method, a statistical procedure based on how far an individual's score (in units of standard deviation) varies from the average for his or her age group.

During World War I, group tests of intelligence were introduced, allowing for the testing of large numbers of people in one sitting. Because of their ease of administration and lack of expense, group tests of intelligence quickly became popular throughout most school systems.

What do tests of intelligence tell us that we couldn't determine before? Studies have shown that IQ tests do predict how well a child will perform in school. These predictions, though not perfect, are considerably better than chance. Studies also indicate that high IQ scores correlate with success in later life, as measured by such things as physical health, emotional adjustment, financial income, and literary and scientific contributions.

Intelligence, like all human behavior, is a product of heredity interacting with environment interacting with time.

1

Heredity. Studies show that the closer the genetic similarity between people, the higher the resulting IQ correlation.

2

Environment. Similar environments also produce similar IQ's. The specific environmental parameters studied include home factors (such as number of books in home and parental attitudes toward schooling), nutrition, stimulus variety, past experience, and parental encouragement.

3

Time. The Bloom curve indicates that environmental influences on intelligence are most pronounced during a child's first few years of life.

The question of racial differences in intelligence was recently raised by Arthur Jensen. The evidence thus far fails to substantiate any claims of racial superiority or inferiority based on intelligence. Though the average IQ's of black and white children do differ, there is no reason to assume that this difference is due more to genetic than environmental factors.

A new theory by Zajonc, called the confluence model, predicts that the more children in a family, especially if the children are close together in age, the lower the IQ's of all the children. Birth order is also important since first borns have the highest IQ's, unless there is a wide age spacing between the children. Zajonc's findings have held up regardless of nationality, race, income level, or social status.

There has been some recent discussion as to whether IQ testing should be abandoned. Proponents urge abandonment of IQ testing, since the test results are often misinterpreted and/or used to reinforce racist attitudes. On the other hand, if we stop testing, we may begin to believe that there is no problem, that no differences exist. This could doom a segment of the population to failure in our competitive and technological society, for once we believe that no differences exist, efforts to erase the disparity in IQ scores would halt.

REFERENCES

1
P. E. Vernon, *Intelligence and Cultural Environment* (London: Methuen, 1969).

2
J. M. Sattler, *Assessment of Children's Intelligence* (Philadelphia: Saunders, rev. ed., 1974), pp. 8–9. Reprinted by permission of the publisher and author.

3
A. Binet and H. Simon, "Application des méthodes nouvelles au diagnostic du niveau intellectuel chez des enfants normaux et anormaux d'hospice et d'école primaire," *L'Année Psychologique* 11 (1905):245–266.

4
D. Wechsler, *The Measurement of Adult Intelligence* (Baltimore: Williams and Wilkins, 1944).

5
N. Haan, "Proposed Model of Ego Functioning: Coping and Defense Mechanisms in Relation to IQ Change," *Psychological Monographs* 11 (1963).

6
R. Hummel and N. A. Sprinthall, "Underachievement Related to Interests, Attitudes, and Values," *The Personnel and Guidance Journal* 44 (1965):388–395.

7
L. M. Terman, *Genetic Studies of Genius* (Stanford, California: Stanford University Press, 1925, 1926, 1930, 1947, 1959).

8
O. D. Duncan, D. L. Featherman, and B. Duncan, *Socioeconomic Background and Achievement* (New York: Seminar Press, 1972).

9
H. H. Newman, F. N. Freeman, and K. J. Holzinger, *Twins: A Study of Heredity and Environment* (Chicago: University of Chicago Press, 1937).

10
L. Erlenmeyer-Kimling and L. F. Jarvik, "Genetics and Intelligence: A Review." *Science* 142 (1963):1479.

11
M. Garber and W. B. Ware, "Relationships between Measures of Home Environment and Intelligence Scores," *American Psychological Association Proceedings* 5 (1970):647–648.

12
H. F. Eickenwald and P. C. Fry, "Nutrition and Learning," *Science* 163 (1969):644–648.

13
H. F. Harlow, J. L. McGaugh, and R. F. Thompson, *Psychology* (San Francisco: Albion, 1971), p. 354.

14
D. Krech, "The Chemistry of Learning," *Saturday Review,* 20 January 1968, pp. 48–50.

15
B. J. Kaplan, "Malnutrition and Mental Deficiency," *Psych. Bull.* 78 (1972):321–334.

16
H. F. Harlow, J. L. McGaugh, and R. F. Thompson, *Psychology* (San Francisco: Albion, 1971), p. 353.

17
B. S. Bloom, *Stability and Change in Human Characteristics* (New York: Wiley, 1964).

18
W. Dennis, "Causes of Retardation among Institutional Children: Iran," *Journal of Genetic Psychology* 96 (1960):47–59.

19
W. Dennis, "The Mental Growth of Certain Foundlings Before and After Adoption," paper delivered at American University of Beirut, Lebanon, 1969.

20
R. M. Yerkes, "Psychological Examining in the U. S. Army," *Memoirs of the National Academy of Sciences,* no. 15, 1921.

21
J. N. Spuhler and G. Lindzey, "Racial Differences in Behavior," in J. Hirsch, ed., *Behavior-Genetic Analysis* (New York: McGraw-Hill, 1967).

22
A. R. Jensen, "How Much Can We Boost IQ and Scholastic Achievement?" *Harvard Educational Review* 39 (1969):1–123.

23
Ibid., p. 4.

24
B. J. Forrester and R. A. Klaus, "The Effect of Race of the Examiner on Intelligence Test Scores of Negro Kindergarten Children," *Peabody Papers in Human Development* 2, no. 7 (1964):1–7.

25
S. Rose, "Environmental Effects on Brain and Behavior," in K. Richardson and D. Spears, *Race and Intelligence* (Baltimore: Penguin Books, 1972), p. 142.

26
J. Hirsch, "Race, Intelligence and IQ: A Debate," in N. Chalmer, R. Crawley, and S. P. R. Rose, eds., *The Biological Bases of Behavior* (London: The Open University Press by Harper & Row, 1971), pp. 244–245.

27
Ibid.

28
A. R. Jensen, "How Much Can We Boost IQ and Scholastic Achievement?" *Harvard Educational Review* 39 (1969):42–43.

29
S. Scarr-Salapatek, "Race, Social Class and IQ," *Science* 174 (1971):1285–1295.

30
G. Piel, "The New Hereditarians," *The Nation,* 19 April 1975, p. 457.

31
M. Sherman and C. B. Key, "The Intelligence of Isolated Mountain Children," *Child Development* 3 (1932):279–290.

32
D. Daniels and V. Houghton, "Jensen, Eysenck and the Eclipse of the Galton Paradigm," in Richardson and Spears, *Race and Intelligence,* p. 75.

33
R. R. Carkhuff, *The Development of Human Resources* (New York: Holt, Rinehart and Winston, 1971).

34
M. Brenton, *What's Happened to Teacher?* (New York: Coward, 1970).

35
R. B. Zajonc, "Family Configuration and Intelligence," *Science* 192 (April 1976), pp. 227–236.

36
R. Rosenthal and L. Jacobson, "Teacher's Expectations as Self-fulfilling Prophecies," in R. C. Sprinthall and N. A. Sprinthall, eds., *Educational Psychology: Selected Readings* (New York: Van Nostrand-Reinhold, 1969), pp. 295–300.

SUGGESTIONS FOR FURTHER READING

Loehlin, J. C., G. Lindzey, and J. N. Spuhler. *Race Differences in Intelligence.* San Francisco: W. H. Freeman, 1975.

Richardson, K., and D. Spears. *Race and Intelligence.* Baltimore: Penguin Books, 1972.

Sattler, J. M. *Assessment of Children's Intelligence.* Philadelphia: W. B. Saunders, 1974.

19.

Learning styles and creativity

This unit has focused on individual differences. In some ways this focus is almost the opposite of that of previous units. It may also seem contradictory to speak about stages of development on the one hand and individual differences on the other. As we have noted, especially in Unit II, virtually all children and adolescents go through certain stages of development in an invariant sequence. Each stage is qualitatively different from the preceding one and represents a major new reorganization, or "great leap forward," in some particular area (such as cognitive development).

From this point of view, then, it may seem that individual differences are relatively unimportant, and that it is more important for the educator to understand the stages of psychological development. Unfortunately, such is not the case. The framework for stages is essential, but we cannot ignore the individual differences that exist within the stages themselves. It is vital to remember that individuals go through stages at different rates, that within any particular stage there will be significant individual differences. Any teacher of junior-high teenagers, for example, can cite dramatic differences in pupils' abilities to use formal operations. Some students can grasp the symbolic significance of metaphors, similes, or other abstractions quickly, while the rest of the class sits with puzzled expressions on their faces, not having the slightest clue as to what it all means. So, too, at other stages.

We have already discussed individual differences in intelligence, personality, and physical growth. We now focus on another aspect of individual differences: creativity.

CREATIVITY AND LEARNING STYLES

Creativity is one of those concepts that is talked about more than it is under-stood. The word itself has been used in so many different ways that some would say it has no meaning at all. Every day we hear references to the need for crea-tive people, creative teachers, creative pupils, creative books, creative lesson plans . . . the list is endless. In practically every educator's speech there is a call for creativity, as if it were a coveted and revered American virtue. Yet, all too

The definitional problem

frequently, those who exhort us to be more creative are totally unable to define what they mean in operational terms. If we are to teach children to be creative we need a reasonable working definition. We can't keep falling back on the circular reasoning of such often-heard statements as, "Be creative and figure out how to teach children to be creative."

Recently a number of theorists have attempted to provide some working definitions of creativity. Although not wholly successful, these views do help resolve some of the ambiguity and contradictions.

GUILFORD'S THEORY: A FACTOR APPROACH

Perhaps the most-comprehensive view of creativity from a conceptual point of view is one that comes from the work of G. P. Guilford. Using a technique that allowed him to carefully and exhaustingly sort through many possible compo-nents of intelligence, Guilford concluded that intelligence was not one dimen-sional. What we have termed cognitive, or intellectual, activity is made up of a series of distinctly different modes of thought. After thoroughly examining and testing out many diverse positions, he arrived at a system that grouped similar modes together into appropriate categories. His famous phrase "the three faces of intellect" suggests that intellectual functioning can be separated into three different compartments: operation, content, and product. Each compartment it-self contains a series of dimensions. Figure 19.1 shows the "three faces" in the form of a cube (followed by the dimensions added).[1] The schema of Fig. 19.1 makes the complexity of the framework immediately apparent: it requires a

Traits of creative people

matrix of $5 \times 6 \times 4$ blocks, or a total of 120 different "traits," to comprehend the entire structure. Each block has its own operational definition in the form of a test, and each test has been subjected to the procedures of reliability and validity checking. Guilford has demonstrated the existence of some 70 traits al-ready and obviously has his life's work cut out for him in demonstrating the existence of the remaining traits. Each trait is defined as a "distinguishable, rela-tively enduring way of functioning." A group of traits makes up what he calls a factor. Thus a factor, a cluster of traits all interacting, is something like a supertrait.

Although it has been unwieldy to develop, the procedure yields a series of traits which Guilford sees as primarily responsible for what is usually called cre-ativity. The traits are fluency, flexibility, and originality, all of which involve divergent thinking and elaboration.

The creative triad: fluency, flexibility, originality

Fluency involves the process of association. Thus, in a word-association test, a person who can rapidly think up many synonyms or even antonyms would be

OPERATIONS

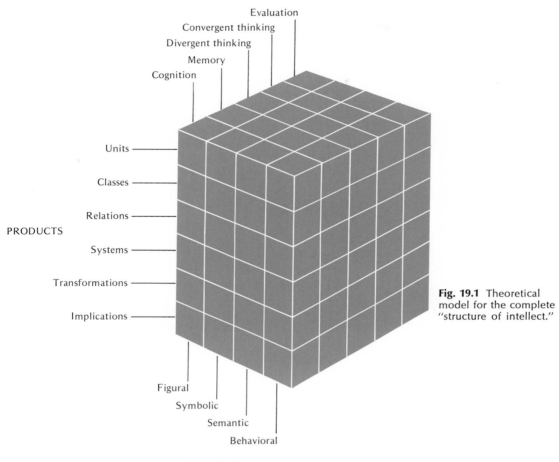

Fig. 19.1 Theoretical model for the complete "structure of intellect."

CONTENTS

employing this ability. A second aspect of fluency is called ideational fluency. Rather than coming up with synonyms for specific words, ideational fluency involves the production of many ideas and concepts. Thus a writer employs *word fluency* in finding a variety of words to express meaning, while he or she would employ *ideational fluency* to describe a series of different concepts, theories, or explanations.

Flexibility also involves two domains of thought: adaptive and spontaneous flexibility. Adaptive flexibility involves changing directions in problem solving as you confront new conditions. Take, for example, the often-heard puzzler of the farmer who must transport grain, a chicken, and a wolf across a river. He can't leave the chicken alone with the grain, or the grain will be eaten; he can't leave the wolf and chicken together for obvious reasons; and he can carry only one at

The creative triad: fluency, flexibility, and originality. All involve divergent thinking and elaboration.

a time in his boat. You may figure out that he should take the chicken across first, leaving the grain and wolf together, then bring the wolf across and take the chicken back. Next, he should leave the chicken on the original bank and bring the grain across, leaving the grain and wolf together. Finally, he should go back for the chicken. Now if the problem changes, your adaptive flexibility would be called on for a new solution—e.g., suppose while the farmer was transporting the chicken on the first trip, a second wolf appeared on the bank he was heading toward? Spontaneous flexibility, on the other hand, involves coming up with new ideas without a specific problem in mind.

Originality, the third process, involves the ability to think in uncommon modes with clever, unique, or even way-out concepts. Originality helps a person see remote and far-reaching consequences of what on the surface may appear to be small changes. Improvisation is closely related to originality, since it represents the ability to discover new and original relationships between objects and/or ideas.

As a result of Guilford's work, creativity is no longer viewed as a single process but as a series of processes in the service of divergent thinking. In fact, the concept of divergent thinking has become almost interchangeable with creativity itself. To be creative, then, means to think in divergent modes, to come up with numerous novel or unique meanings, new or original thoughts, to depart or diverge from usual or conventional ideas.

MACKINNON, BARRON, AND ROE: STUDIES OF "CREATIVE" PEOPLE

Theorists such as Donald Mackinnon,[2] Frank Barron,[3] and Anne Roe[4] have approached the study of creativity in a completely different way from Guilford. They studied actual people who were judged to be creative, such as well-known scientists, poets, artists, architects, writers, and mathematicians—people whose work was acclaimed by their colleagues and other experts as creative, original, and unique. These researchers tried to identify the processes that set the creative people apart from their colleagues.

Using a series of assessment procedures, including psychological personality tests, the researchers came to very much the same conclusions as Guilford did. Creative people were seen as "inventive and industrious" (Mackinnon), "independent in judgment" (Barron), and as possessing "autonomy in judgment" (Roe). Other researchers employing this approach use similar phrases to describe creative people. Persons judged high on creative performance show a "lack of preoccupation with what the group thinks," a "nonconformist" way of thinking, an ability to "see new relationships among ideas and theories." Thus, Guilford's factor approach and the study of creative persons themselves seem to bear one another out.

CREATIVITY IN CHILDREN: WALLACH AND KOGAN, GETZELS AND JACKSON

Two of the most-significant studies of creativity in school-age children were conducted by Michael Wallach and Nathan Kogan, who studied elementary-age children, and Jacob Getzels and Phillip Jackson, who studied teenagers. Both groups of researchers came to similar conclusions: creativity is not simply a function of intelligence. There has been a common assumption that creative thought was possible only above a threshold IQ; an IQ above 120 was thought to be a prerequisite to creativity. Instead, researchers have shown that creative thought is somewhat separate from general intelligence, which is a more independent process.

The relation between creativity and IQ

Wallach and Kogan administered a large battery of tests to their elementary-aged subjects, some as measures of intelligence and others as estimates of creativity.[5] Using correlation statistics, they found extremely low correlations between IQ and creativity. No correlation exceeded an r of $+.23$. They reported moderate correlations among the various measures of IQ and among the measures of creativity. It is particularly important to note their conclusion: divergent or creative thinking is not limited to children who have high IQ scores. However, the controversy over the relationship between IQ and creativity tests is by no means over. To some degree it makes a difference just which tests a researcher employs. The Wallach and Kogan creativity tests demonstrate low correlation to general IQ, as we have noted. The Torrance tests, however, show a closer relationship between IQ and creativity: with IQ's below 120, $r = +.50$, while above 120, $r = +.20$. This finding means creativity is more dependent on intelligence in the lower range than in the upper range. It is well to remember, however, that even in the lower range, the correlation of $+.50$ accounts for 25 percent of the variation between IQ and creativity. This leaves 75 percent of the variation between measured IQ and creativity unexplained or independent.

A second part of the controversy derives from the assessment question itself. If we attempt to assess creativity in the same way that we assess IQ (with timed tests, emphasizing correct answers and convergent thinking), we find a moderate relationship between such creativity test scores and IQ test scores. When Wallach and Kogan tested children under relaxed conditions in a "play context," they reported that the fluency, flexibility, and originality of the children's products were "quite independent of how bright or dull the child is in terms of general intelligence indicators."[6]

The Getzels and Jackson study

To further isolate the differences between intelligence and creativity, Getzels and Jackson studied two groups of teenagers: a highly intelligent group and a highly creative group.[7] They were able to conclude that highly intelligent students (with average IQ scores of 150) are not necessarily creative and that highly creative pupils do not necessarily have extraordinarily high IQ scores. Again, the point is that the mental processes that produce high IQ scores will not necessarily produce high scores on creativity tests. Another important finding of Getzels and Jackson was that the teachers in the study preferred the students with high IQ's to those with high creativity, despite the fact that the creative pupils produced significantly more imaginative and original writing samples. A further indication that teacher preference was determined by the mode or the learning style (convergent versus divergent), the researchers found no difference on outcome or amount learned by the two groups. Standard measures of academic achievement in various academic subjects revealed no differences between the two groups.

Teacher preference for noncreative pupils

It now seems apparent that intelligence tests do not measure the mental operations that are called for in creativity. Within their selective sample (the high-IQ's averaged 150 IQ points, the high-creatives averaged 127, a difference

IQ and creativity are not synonymous, and teachers seem to prefer students with high IQ's to those with high creativity.

of 23 points, or more than one and one-half standard deviations), Getzels and Jackson also found that teachers preferred the high-IQ groups even though there were no differences in academic performance.

We can conclude that the concept of creativity does have some genuine meaning for education. Factor analysis studies and investigations of creative adults, teenagers, and children yield a consistent pattern of ideas that help define the process as one of divergent thinking. Remember that IQ and creativity are not synonymous and that there appears to be a negative relationship between teacher preference and pupils scoring high on divergent thinking. Perhaps most noteworthy on this point was a comment Getzels and Jackson made to the effect that highly creative pupils had somehow "learned" to get along without the support and encouragement of their teachers. How many such pupils fell by the wayside remains an open question. Even though some highly creative pupils do survive, and indeed thrive, such negative teaching simply cannot be justified. Naturally we would hope that teachers themselves will develop a greater variety of learning tasks so that both convergent and divergent thinking can be rewarded in the classroom.

CREATIVITY: HOW IS IT MEASURED?

An increasing sophistication has been brought to the task of adequate procedures for assessing creativity—and we stress the word "adequate," because there are as yet no completely acceptable measurement systems. However, important work is going on, and although the answers are not yet all in, we can present some promising assessment methods. A few samples of the kind of question used in tests of creativity are given in Table 19.1.

Creative thinking assessment

Table 19.1 Sample tests of creativity and problem-solving ability.

Answers

1

Flanagan's Ingenuity Test:

As part of a manufacturing process, the inside lip of a deep, cup-shaped casting is machine threaded. The company found that metal chips produced by the threading operation were difficult to remove from the bottom of the casting without scratching the sides. A design engineer was able to solve this problem by using one of the following. Can you determine which solution he chose?

a) i—————p h——h
b) m—————n c——e
c) f—————r w——i
d) l—————d b——k
e) u—————e d——n

1

The correct answer is (e), upside down, or uʍop ǝpısdn.[8]

2

Guilford's Sample Insight Problem

A man went out to hunt a bear one day. He left and hiked due south for ten miles, then due west for ten miles. At this point, he killed a bear. He dragged the bear back to his camp, a distance of exactly ten miles. What was the color of the bear? Why?

2

Answer: "white." Only at the North Pole could these directions have been possible. Is it creativity or a good convergent knowledge of geometry and geography that one employs in finding the "correct" answer?[9]

3

Pattern Arrangement Test:

Arrange the glasses shown in the sketch to form an alternating pattern of one filled and one empty by moving just one glass. (The pattern may begin with either a filled or an empty glass.)

3

Pour the contents of glass #6 into glass #3.[10]

Table 19.1 Sample tests of creativity (cont.)   Answers (cont.)

4

Using only the objects shown in the drawing below, can you balance the wooden plank on the edge of the prism in such a way that after a few minutes one of the ends of the plank will tip down automatically, that is, without being touched, or blown upon, or the table shaken, and so on?[11]

4

Solution to the problem:

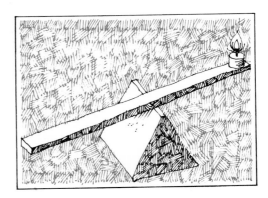

5

Using only the objects shown in the drawing below, the man must tie the two strings together. How can he do it?[12]

5

Answer: The man can tie the two strings together by swinging one string while pulling the other.

Torrance, working with a group of gifted elementary-age children, uses the Magic Net technique of storytelling and problem solving.

E. Paul Torrance, who spent many years at the University of Minnesota and is now at the University of Georgia, has devoted more time and effort to the assessment problem than any other psychologist in this country. The famous *Minnesota Tests of Creative Thinking* are the result. The early tests were primarily verbal in content. For example, pupils were asked to respond to items such as the following:

Select one title from the list below as a subject for a story. Do not be afraid to make it unusual.

The Man Who Cries
The Woman Who Can But Won't Talk
The Flying Monkey
The Lion That Won't Roar

Torrance considered the responses to be "creative" if they included fluency, flexibility, originality, and imagination. These are similar to Guilford's concepts. Ideas that might appear offbeat or "wild," nonstandard or uncommon, humorous and playful were rated as creative. These kinds of items or questions can be used in any classroom situation. Teachers could start with the above titles or make up some of their own as a means of promoting divergent thinking. The pupils, however, will probably need substantial encouragement to overcome the tendency to play it safe.

1. Complete this figure in such a way as to make an interesting picture. Add details to make it tell an interesting story.

2. Add to this sketch of a stuffed toy dog some improvement that you think will make it more interesting to play with.

Fig. 19.2 Choose one of these tasks.

Another example of an assessment item is the "unusual uses" approach. The researcher asks for unusual uses for everyday objects: "How many uses can you think of for a tin can or a brick?" Creative people tend to generate many original ideas for possible uses (fluency). An ability to "free associate" is obviously part of the creative process of coming up with ideas that are not commonplace. For example, common uses for a brick might be to pave a walk, to make bookshelves, to edge a walk. Can you think of uncommon or unusual uses for a brick, a tin can, or a cardboard box? Examples can be found in the Torrance studies.[13]

Unusual-uses approach

More recently Torrance has added some nonverbal assessment items, such as incomplete drawings. Figure 19.2 shows samples of the kind of question he is using.[14] One of the criticisms of the unusual-uses approach had been its heavy reliance on verbal ability. By using incomplete drawings the nonverbal aspects of creativity could be called into the assessment process. There is no single "correct" procedure for the assessment of divergent thinking.

Incomplete-drawings test

Sarnoff A. Mednick, another researcher in the assessment of creativity, has developed what he calls a test of "Remote Associates."[15] This procedure relies on the ability to produce remote (far-out) associations for concepts. For example:

Remote-associates test

What word is related to all three words in each example?

1) Railroad   Girl   Class
2) Wheel   Electric   High
3) Out   Dog   Cat

E. PAUL TORRANCE

Paul Torrance was born in 1915 and completed his undergraduate program in 1940 at Mercer College, a small liberal arts college with an excellent reputation in Macon, Georgia. He completed a master's degree in educational psychology at the University of Minnesota in 1944 and then moved to Michigan for his Ph.D. in 1951. All the while he was engaged in the actual practice of education, serving as a vocational teacher, school counselor, and even school principal in the late 1930s. While he was completing his Ph.D. at the University of Michigan, he returned to Minnesota and was a college counselor, instructor, and eventually an associate professor, all prior to completing the doctorate. After a six-year stint with the U.S. Air Force survival-research field unit from 1951–1957, he moved back to Minnesota as a full professor in educational psychology and became director of the bureau of research.

It was at this point that his research career began to focus on the problems of creativity. Questions on the nature of creative activity as a process or a product were explored. Also, he began to question whether it was enough simply to identify creativity. Could we go beyond the question of measurement and assessment? Here he was directly confronting a major tradition at the University of Minnesota—the tradition of empirical measurement as the definition of educational psychology itself. For Torrance this posed something of a dilemma. He was clearly interested in building effective and efficient procedures to measure the concept of creativity with sufficient precision; however, he was not content to stop there. If we could assess creativity, could we also develop methods to teach people to become more creative? If we knew what creativity was, could it become an educational objective? Most psychologists across the country were taking a conservative position, stressing, along with Torrance's Minnesota colleagues, the importance of assessment. Torrance, however, gradually became convinced that his intuition was correct and that the time had come to teach for creativity. He saw this as a logical next step. His early schoolwork certainly influenced the decision of this now-famous educational researcher to move into the classroom and build teaching strategies. As we have noted in the text, it may have been simply a logical extension to Torrance, but to the field it was more dramatic. The implications of his work have not yet been fully worked out. We can say, however, that if school programs do achieve his objectives and improve creative performance in all children, we shall owe a major educational tribute to Professor Torrance. At present his own work continues at a high level of creativity at the University of Georgia.

The answers are: (1) Working, (2) Wire, and (3) House. This serves as an example both of the idea behind the test and of its limitations. The major limitation is that the "Remote Associates" test of creative association produces items that have only one answer.

Problem solving or finding uncommon solutions to difficult problems has also been used as an assessment procedure. The difficulty here is usually that the solution may be more "tricky" than creative (see Table 19.1).

Wallach's and Kogan's assessment procedures for elementary-age children are probably the most comprehensive currently available. Using a whole battery of tests, they found that valid discriminations could be made with six- to twelve-year-old children. Their procedures include questions such as:

1) Name all the round things you can think of.
2) Name all the things that will make noise.
3) Name all the things that are square.
4) Name all the things that move on wheels.

These responses are scored for fluency (simply count how many answers the pupil can generate) and for uniqueness. For round things "Life Savers" is unique, whereas "tire" would be common. Here are some more examples:

Category	Unique	Common
Round	mouse hole	plate
	drops of water	doorknob
Noise	disposal	car horn
	cash register	airplane
	snoring	thunder
Wheels	tape recorder	wheelbarrow
	clothesline	trolley car

A second assessment procedure developed by Wallach and Kogan is much like the "unusual uses" item already noted.

How many different ways can you use

1) a newspaper?
2) a knife?
3) an auto tire?
4) a cork?
5) a shoe?

Wallach's and Kogan's most original procedures were probably those they derived from the work of Renato Tagiuri, in the now famous line and pattern meaning tests. These items are incomplete drawings that do not depict anything at all. The subject has to create a meaning by association, finding similarities, being willing to approximate. The process is similar to the classic test of personality, the Rorschach Ink Blot test. At the literal level each ink blot is merely a blob of ink. The line and pattern meaning tests, too, are meaningless in themselves (see Table 19.2); it is the subject's job to add the meaning.

Table 19.2 Nonverbal tests of creativity.

Pattern meanings. Tell what each card looks like to you.	**The line meaning test.** What does each incomplete drawing bring to your mind?

1.  3.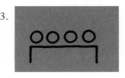

1. 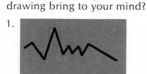 3.

5.   7.

9.

	Unique response	Common response		Unique response	Common response
1	"Lollipop bursting into pieces"	Flower	1	Squished paper	Mountain
3	Foot and toes	Table with things on it	3	Squeezing paint out of a tube	Piece of string
5	Five worms hanging	Raindrops	9	Fishing rod bending	Rising sun
7	Three mice eating a piece of cheese	Three people sitting around a table			

GETZELS AND JACKSON: HUMOR AND CREATIVITY

Getzels and Jackson used many similar procedures in their assessment system for adolescents. In addition to the types of items already noted, they used tests with a heavy emphasis on what is commonly called "humor." By presenting pupils with "situations," or open-ended stories, or even simply asking them to write a brief autobiography, they were able to differentiate between the commonplace and the unique. This makes sense if we remember that, especially for adolescents and adults, humor usually consists of a reversal of the obvious in a common situation.

For example, the authors report the following opening sentences to teenage autobiographies: "In 1943 I was born. I have been living without interruption ever since." And, "I was transferred from another world or 'hatched,' as you might call it, at a very young age (0 for a fact)." And, "My family is not extraordinary except that my brother has two heads . . . ." And, "When my father saw me he ran away screaming into the hills. We followed . . . ." In contrast to these, "I was born on November 10, 1942 in Chicago. I am the first of three children to be born to my mother and father."[16]

The playfulness, imagination, and uninhibited expressiveness are obvious when compared to the overtrained realism of the last example.

SUMMARY OF MEASUREMENT PROCEDURES

While the assessment procedures are by no means conclusive, we can use them to gain a more-comprehensive understanding of pupils. Even a rudimentary set of techniques allows us to examine the way pupils perform in class from a broader perspective than academic achievement tests. And, one of the advantages of creativity measures is that the procedures can be used directly with pupils in class: the assessment technique can become a teaching technique. By trying out a series of procedures, including some that you may think up yourself, you can help students begin to see firsthand the differences between the convergent and divergent responses.

CREATIVITY: IMPLICATIONS FOR TEACHING

For too long, in our view, researchers and theorists have considered the creative process to be inborn or innate. The world in general (they thought) should cherish those few creative artists, scientists, humorists; the rest of us were simply relegated to common humdrum lives, hopelessly devoid of talent. At best, all of us ordinary people might appreciate creativity from the sidelines, but there was little we could do to get in on the act, so to speak.

If we viewed creativity as inborn we would be in the same position as those who viewed intelligence as fixed at birth, or even personality as innate. All we could learn was what we missed out on, and what we couldn't become, possibly with some sense of regret.

However, the framework of developmental psychology allows us to take the position that the creative process can be taught. We can, through instruction, teach pupils to think in uncommon ways, to develop divergent solutions to problems, to associate flexibly, to elaborate fluently. Our major problem is to break the set, or in terms of the language of creativity, to break out of the "functional fixedness" which has led educators to believe that the creative process is born, not made.

Learning to become uncreative

William James, almost a century ago, suggested that the problem of creativity is a paradox. We all possess the ability or capacity to become creative, but we learn to be uncreative. In other words, the educational process most of us go through, our learning experiences at home and at school, teach us the "habit" of convergent thinking. James called this, in his own inimitable way, the problem of "old fogeyism."

> Educated as we already are, we never get an experience that remains for us completely nondescript: it always reminds us of something. . . . In admitting a new body of experience, we instinctively seek to disturb as little as possible our pre-existing stock of ideas. We always try to name a new experience in some way which will assimilate it to what we already know . . . .[17]

The process of becoming an old fogey is the process of convergent thinking, fitting the new to the old, seeing new things in terms of their similarity to the old. The difficulty, as James has noted, is that the process starts when we are still young ("there are young fogies"). James commented from observing his own

The teacher can teach the creative process and encourage pupils to think in uncommon ways, to develop divergent solutions to problems, to associate flexibility, to elaborate fluently.

Water-jar problems

Problem no.	Jar capacity (quarts)			Quarts of water needed
	A	B	C	
1	29	3	0	20
2	21	127	3	100
3	14	163	25	99
4	18	43	10	5
5	9	42	6	21
6	20	59	4	31
7	23	49	3	20

family: "My child of two played for a week with the first orange that was given him, calling it a 'ball'! He called the first whole eggs he saw 'potatoes'... a folding pocketscrew he unhesitatingly called 'bad-scissors'."[18] And if we take another look at the classroom we will find, all too often, that convergent thinking is rewarded and divergent, punished. Thus, the lesson starts early.

CLASSROOM PROCEDURES AND CREATIVITY

Most classroom instruction is organized to promote convergent thought. There is often a single correct answer to a history question, a single problem-solving approach to long division, a single correct spelling for a word, a single proper outline for book reports. We can list hundreds of ways in which teaching deliberately, or even accidentally, reinforces noncreativity. If we taught artists to paint by numbers, imagine the horrifying result of hundreds of standard paintings, all alike, none unique. Yet, in all too many schools, this approach is universal. Few schools have any room in their curriculum for programs to promote creative, divergent thought. The result is learning "by the numbers," a narrowing of our perceptions. The inability to change set means we are forever doomed to think of the same old solutions to new problems. For example, in the famous water-jar experiments,[19] pupils were given the chart above and asked to solve each problem. ("Using jars A, B, and C only, find a way to measure the amount of water in the right-hand column.")

ANNE ROE

Born in 1904, Anne Roe completed her undergraduate and master's degrees in psychology and education at the University of Denver. For her doctorate she moved to Columbia Teachers College and received a Ph.D. in 1933. At this point her career pattern appeared almost traditional for women in psychology. She moved to Worcester State Hospital to complete her clinical training. The expectation was that like most women she would head toward the "softer" areas of psychology, clinical practice. This view derived from the stereotyped assumption that being female usually meant being unable to think very clearly or do rigorous research in psychology. In general, it was felt that although they lacked these qualities, women would naturally be warm, feminine, and therapeutic.

Early in her career at Worcester, Anne Roe was able to confront both myths simultaneously. First, she was able to demonstrate such superb clinical skills that she eventually became a clinical training director. In addition, she soon started publishing hard, data-based research that was clearly rigorous. Her research interest in career development began at this time and remained as a major research theme throughout her professional life. It was, however, only one of a series of research interests that she successfully pursued. Thus her name became synonymous with a cluster of areas in psychology. These included: the psychology of career development, studies of creativity, parent-child relationships, and the personality development of eminent scientists and artists. In career development she created the famous two-way classification scheme for occupational choice. She also was able to provide a theoretical bridge for career development and personality. Her studies in creativity provided important evidence to demonstrate the negative as well as the positive aspects of personality. She found, for example, that many creative artists also had problems of alcoholism.

Her level of productivity remained high throughout her career. She moved from a series of clinical settings to New York University in 1957 and to Harvard in 1960. At Harvard she capped her own career by starting the Center for Research on Careers. There she was named a full professor and was the recipient of the Association of the Harvard Graduate School of Education Award. In 1973 she was voted a special award for distinguished service by the American Psychological Association Division of Clinical Psychology. In many ways her career stands as the best example of creativity itself. She was inventive, industrious, independent, and autonomous in judgment. Clearly, she was also not preoccupied by group conformity but was able to see new relationships among ideas and theories. She produced over ninety papers and monographs and five books demonstrating fluency, flexibility, and elaboration. Above all else, her own humanity has sparkled brightly throughout her long career. Her citation from the Division of Clinical Psychology puts it best: "Her deeply human concerns and her dedicated investment in the affairs of our profession have made her professional biography a mirror of the issues and problems our field has faced during the past twenty-five years."

The first problem can be solved by filling jar A and then pouring the water out of it into jar B three times. The amount of water remaining in A would be 20 quarts. If you work out problems two through six you will find the solution is always the same: fill the largest jar and then empty it into the smaller jars until the amount left meets the required number of quarts. Almost everyone tries to solve problem seven the same way. Some hang onto the old method even after a deliberate warning to the contrary, "Don't be blind!"

There are many examples in everyday life of how often we simply persist in old ways or old "habits" of perception. Jerome Kagan has noted that the first motor cars looked almost exactly like buggies.[20] In fact, they even had buggy whip holders. Nowadays the new, "all new" cars that roll out of Detroit each year look strangely similar to last year's models.

HOW TO TEACH FOR CREATIVE/DIVERGENT THINKING

The first thing to do to promote the creative process is to modify the expectations within a classroom, to create some time in the curriculum for alternative learning experiences. We cannot simply exhort children to be creative and then have an art teacher or poetry teacher come into class for one hour every two weeks and "teach for creativity." A significant portion of curriculum time is obviously necessary.

Assessment procedures as teaching methods

Given a reasonable amount of time, then, you might use some of the creativity assessment procedures as teaching techniques. For example, you might administer some of the Wallach and Kogan tests to elementary-age children and then discuss their responses with them. This intervention makes obvious the difference between using these items for assessment and using them for teaching. It is also a means of helping children realize that divergent, uncommon, or unique perceptions can be both valid and valuable. Finally, if you are teaching a class for the first time, you may find that some of the pupils who do not excel on the usual convergent learning tasks show hitherto unsuspected capacities. In other words, this kind of teaching may benefit you as a teacher as well as your students: it may change your own perceptions of them as well as their perceptions of what's "right." Considering the so-called Rosenthal effect of teacher expectations, this would be of more than small consequence.

Classroom environments and creative teaching

If we really want our pupils to understand how to be creative, divergent thinkers, we will also have to create a classroom environment that will help them break their mind-set. We cannot expect them to be active, divergent thinkers in an atmosphere they associate with passive and convergent problem solving. For example, we would accomplish very little if we tried to teach children to think up unusual solutions, humorous beginnings for stories, unique uses for common objects, while requiring them to sit up straight, raise their hands before answering, and sit in desks arranged in nice, neat rows. We cannot foster imaginative thinking if we keep pupils in a straitjacket.

Thus, there are two essential conditions to any program designed to teach for creativity:

1

We must abandon the assumption that creativity is inborn, that it is a special gift allotted to a chosen few.

2

We must alter the classroom atmosphere or environment so that the hidden agenda does not imply convergent solutions.

Robert Wilson, a colleague of Guilford, has suggested that classroom atmospheres are in fact essential first conditions to enhance creativity. Psychological safety precedes psychological freedom in the classroom. Thus, pupil-anxiety level must be relatively low. You can't expect pupils to brainstorm if they fear you'll adversely judge the quality of their products. In writing free associations, obviously your own productivity would decline if you started to worry about spelling, grammar, syntax. If you become highly self-conscious, you will find it difficult to listen to others. Thus Wilson recommends that in developing creativity lessons for pupils, you start with the classroom climate.[21] Recall that in Chapter 15 we noted the significance of Carl Rogers and the three conditions to enhance learning: unconditional regard, empathy, and genuineness. These conditions are particularly important when you are asking pupils to try new activities. The pupils' first responses to your creativity lesson may be similar to William James's two-year-old child when he insisted for a week that the orange was, in fact, a ball.

If Piaget's equation of intelligence with activity is a reasonably accurate description of the development of cognition in general, then it is possible to suggest a parallel in the growth of creativity. Certainly, one of the very early pioneers in psychology, Alfred Binet, was a strong advocate of such a view. Schools, he insisted, should not teach pupils to retain and reproduce. Torrance has said,

"Instead Binet thought the child should be taught to produce and test ideas on his own, to act spontaneously, to judge for himself, to participate in life about him . . . to plan, to imagine, to invent. . . ."[22]

A curriculum for creativity and divergent thinking cannot be a single classroom exercise. Instead, a series of connected experiences are necessary—if only to break the pupils' expectations that the teacher is still looking for *the* correct answer. Any such change will require substantial patience at the outset.

Torrance's recent book, *Encouraging Creativity in the Classroom,* is a comprehensive description of classroom teaching techniques, especially for the elementary-school level. The work also clearly marks a shift in assumptions about creativity. Instead of suggesting that creativity is only for a "gifted" few, Torrance demonstrates how all pupils, including those from poverty backgrounds, can be trained for creativity through a sequence of learning experiences.

A most-recent study has shown that teachers can not only help pupils become more creative in the classroom, but that it is also possible to teach pupils to teach themselves to become more original in thought process and product. In a really intriguing study (itself an example of creativity), researchers developed a strategy of self-instruction.[23] This included such techniques as having the students talk out loud to themselves. Statements were employed as advance organizers and reminders to guide the students toward divergent rather than convergent goals. Thus the students were taught to use a variety of phrases as they approached a problem-solving situation. Some examples follow:

Self statements about creativity:

Be unique.
Think of something no one else will.
Be free wheeling.
Quantity helps breed quality.
Break away from the obvious.

Let your mind wander.
Let ideas flow.
Feel like a bystander through whom ideas flow.
Let it happen.

You're in a rut—try something new.
Go slow—no hurry.
Good—you're getting it.
That was a pretty neat answer.

The results indicated that students who were taught to engage in such a dialogue with themselves did demonstrate a positive change in both their self-perception and their performance in creative problem solving. Self-instruction does *not* suggest that creative individuals actually emit such statements. There is no reason to believe that Einstein, Picasso, or Elizabeth Barrett Browning talked to themselves with comments like, "Good, Pablo, you're getting it." On the other hand, it does seem that learning to remind ourselves may be helpful. The researcher does suggest that each person may develop his or her own vocabulary for self-instruction. William James may have said to himself on occasion, "Don't be an old fogey."

Effective teaching requires more than a one-shot exposure. By participating in a series of units in divergent learning, the children can become comfortable enough to venture into the new areas. The researchers all agree that a key element in the growth of creativity is the ability to take a risk, to make a change, to give up the known and the familiar. This is beautifully illustrated by one of Ferlinghetti's poems.

Creativity and risk-taking

A Coney Island of the Mind

Constantly risking absurdity
                        and death
        whenever he performs
                    above the heads
                            of his audience
        the poet like an acrobat
                    climbs on rime
                            to a high wire of his own making
        and balancing on eyebeams
                        above the sea of faces
            paces his way
                        to the other side of the day
            performing entrechats
                        and sleight-of-foot tricks
            and other high theatrics
                        and all without mistaking
                anything
                        for what it may not be
    For he's the super realist
                        who must perforce perceive
            taut truth
                before the taking of each stance or step
        in his supposed advance
                        toward that still higher perch
            where Beauty stands and waits
                        with gravity
                            to start her death-defying leap
    and he
        a little charleychaplin man
                        who may or may not catch
            her fair eternal form
                    spreadeagled in the empty air
            of existence*

---

*
Lawrence Ferlinghetti, *A Coney Island of the Mind*. Copyright © 1958 by Lawrence Ferlinghetti. Reprinted by permission of New Directions Publishing Corporation.

Ferlinghetti clearly links the theme of risk-taking with that of creativity. The poet—a symbol of creativity—is one who ventures into the unknown and, like a high-wire acrobat, risks "absurdity and death whenever he performs above the heads of his audience." The poem serves as a dramatic reminder of how difficult it is for most of us to shed our usual thought patterns, our common approaches to problem-solving, and to move beyond the obvious. By teaching children to take such risks we could influence an increase in creative production. A recent survey evaluated some forty programs of deliberate attempts to improve fluency, flexibility, originality, and elaboration. The results indicated that approximately 90 percent of those programs significantly increased the levels of creative production of the students.[24] This seems to indicate that creative potential really is universal and only needs to be developed. Deliberate education for creativity appears to be a promising new direction for school programs.

It is the educator's decision, then, that is critical. Do we invent classroom activities and learning environments that will help stimulate such development? Torrance provides a starting point for some new directions. It is likely that in the coming decade we will see the systematic development of sequential learning activities for the development of creativity. The success of such activities will depend ultimately on the teacher's willingness to teach for these new objectives. Without that willingness and understanding we will end up with another curriculum designed to enhance convergent thought and dampen creativity.

Summary

Creativity has always been difficult to define because the concept has so many different meanings. The comprehensive work of Guilford presents a consistent framework to understand the concept. His work defines the creative process as a combination or a cluster of traits—fluency, flexibility and originality—all involving divergent and elaborated thinking.

Other advances in understanding creativity have been derived from studies by Mackinnon, Barron, and Ann Roe, with results similar to Guilford's findings.

Teaching for creativity in the classroom is a relatively new enterprise. Classroom assessments are possible with systems from Kogan and Wallach at the elementary level and Getzels and Jackson at the secondary level. Results tend to indicate that IQ and creativity are independent. Based on assessments, the work of Paul Torrance suggests that not only can children be classified on the dimension of creativity, but more importantly, deliberate instruction can be provided to stimulate creative development. In fact, Torrance reversed the emphasis completely by using assessment of creativity as a means of direct instruction.

Recent programmatic studies have confirmed Torrance's suggestions that divergent problem solving can be taught. Pupils can be aided in finding new solutions to problems, to take risks, and to develop originality. Some very recent research indicates that self-instruction and "cueing" aid in stimulating creative thought.

REFERENCES

1
J. P. Guilford, "Three Faces of Intellect," *American Psychologist* 14 (1959):469–479.

2
D. MacKinnon, "The Nature and Nurture of Creative Talent," *American Psychologist* 17 (1962):484–495.

3
F. Barron, *Creative Person and Creative Process* (New York: Holt, Rinehart and Winston, 1969).

4
A. Roe, *The Making of a Scientist* (New York: Dodd Mead, 1952).

5
M. A. Wallach and N. Kogan, *Modes of Thinking in Young Children* (New York: Holt, Rinehart and Winston, 1965).

6
M. A. Wallach, "Creativity and the Expression of Possibilities," in *Creativity and Learning,* ed. J. Kagan (Boston: Beacon Press, 1970), p. 52.

7
J. W. Getzels and P. Jackson, *Creativity and Intelligence* (New York: Wiley, 1962).

8
Barron, *Creative Person and Creative Process.*

9
W. S. Ray, *The Experimental Psychology of Original Thinking* (New York: Macmillan, 1967).

10
Eastern Airlines Magazine, November 1969.

11
Problem adapted from L. Székely, "Thinking and Acting," *Acta Psychologica* 7 (1950): 1–24. Drawing from W. J. McKeachie and C. L. Doyle, *Psychology,* 2nd. ed. (Reading, Mass.: Addison-Wesley, 1970), p. 333.

12
Problem from Székely, 1950. Drawing from McKeachie and Doyle, 1970, p. 336.

13
E. P. Torrance, *Guiding Creative Talent* (Englewood Cliffs, N.J.: Prentice-Hall, 1962).

14
E. P. Torrance, *Encouraging Creativity in the Classroom* (Dubuque, Iowa: W. C. Brown, 1970), p. 11. Reprinted by permission.

15
S. A. Mednick, "The Associative Basis of the Creative Process," *Psychological Review* 69 (1962):220–232.

16
J. W. Getzels and P. Jackson, *Creativity and Intelligence* (New York: Wiley, 1962), pp. 100, 101.

17
William James. *Talks with Teachers* (New York: Norton, 1958).

18
W. James, *Psychology* (New York: Macmillan, 1972; Collier ed.), pp. 323–333.

19
A. S. Luchins and E. H. Luchins, *Rigidity of Behavior* (Eugene, Oregon: University of Oregon Press, 1959).

20
J. Kagan and E. Haveman, *Psychology: An Introduction* (New York: Harcourt, Brace and World, 1968).

21
R. C. Wilson, "Creativity," in *Education for the Gifted, NSSE Yearbook,* 1958, Part II,
ed. N. B. Henry (Chicago: University of Chicago Press, 1958), pp. 108–126.

22
E. P. Torrance, *Encouraging Creativity in the Classroom,* p. 35.

23
D. Meichenbaum, "Enhancing Creativity by Modifying What Subjects Say to Themselves,"
AERA Journal 12, no. 2 (1975):129–145.

24
J. Freeman *et al., Creativity* (London: London Society for Research in Education, 1968).

Social psychology and mental health

20

The classroom as a social unit

Every classroom is a distinct social unit with its own set of norms, its own psychological atmosphere, its own set of role relationships, its own special blend of behavioral expectancies. Every classroom has a social climate unlike that of any other classroom. An observer walking from room to room in a typical elementary school finds one room charged with excitement and enthusiasm; another, withdrawn, tense, submissive, going through the motions; and still another, wildly boisterous, perhaps bordering on anarchy.

Nor does the psychology of the classroom operate in a vacuum, for every classroom is part of the larger social unit, the school itself. Again, the observer traveling from school to school can sense social-climate differences among the various schools. The differences among schools may not be as blatant as the differences among classrooms, but they are there, and they do have an effect.

What causes these differences among rooms, among schools, among any different number of groups? The quick and easy answer is the personality of the teacher or principal. This, however, is only part of the answer. Just as the principal's behavior helps shape the teachers', so the teachers' behavior shapes the principal's actions. And just as the teacher's behavior influences the pupils' behavior, so the pupils' behavior has a profound effect on the teacher. Teachers may firmly believe that their classrooms have the same social climate year in and year out, despite the shifting student population, but these same teachers will stare in shocked disbelief at a videotape showing one of their classes two or three years ago, or even last year. The shifting student population creates a shifting social climate. Sometimes the shift is subtle, but often it is dramatic. Many teachers freely confess that with one particular class they barely weathered

Each classroom has its own social climate

Teachers influence students and students influence teachers

529

The observer traveling from school to school can readily sense social-climate differences among the various schools.

the year; or the opposite—"for the first time in my life my class this year was an absolute dream." This chapter takes a look at some of the findings of social psychology, which will hopefully increase your understanding of the classroom as a social unit.

SOCIAL PSYCHOLOGY DEFINED

Social psychology attempts to understand human behavior in the context of the social situation. Social psychologists study the ways people affect and are affected by other people. As a subfield of psychology, social psychology still uses the behavior of the individual as its unit of analysis, the individual's behavior in the social context. The social psychologist would probably not be interested in the lonely figure of an Ebbinghaus going about the business of memorizing long lists of nonsense syllables, but would be very much interested in how Ebbinghaus's performance might have been affected by the presence of other people. The very first studies in the field of social psychology were concerned with the effect of a group situation on a person's behavior.

SOCIAL FACILITATION

Even before the turn of the century, studies were done which indicated that on certain tasks a person's performance would improve when others were around.[1] This phenomenon later became known as social facilitation. It was also found that this was not a universal phenomenon. Social facilitation was most pronounced in the case of fairly simple mechanical tasks. The more difficult and the more intellectual the task, the less the effect of social facilitation. Later studies have revealed the operation of social inhibition; that is, on some tasks, a person's performance suffers when there are others around. In one study students were given a word-learning task, either alone or in the company of other students. Some of the tasks were designed to be easy, while others were much more difficult. On the easy tasks the students did better when in the presence of others (social facilitation), but on the difficult tasks they did much worse when in the presence of others (social inhibition).[2] Still other studies have shown that when a person is first attempting to learn something new, the presence of other people is detrimental. Thus, in preparing for a final exam, when the material has already been learned well, reviewing the course in a small-group situation would probably be facilitative. When the material is new, however, spending the night before the final in absolute solitude would be more productive.

Social facilitation is most pronounced on simple motor tasks

Social inhibition

THE RISKY SHIFT

When people get together in group situations, one effect that has been demonstrated in several experiments is the *risky shift*.[3] The group situation apparently produces an environment in which individuals become far less cautious than they would be if they were alone; consequently, an attitude shift in the direction of "throwing caution to the wind" occurs. Individuals are suddenly willing to take greater risks regarding their attitudes and behavior. They become less conservative and more willing to gamble. One explanation of this phenomenon is that individuals who are basically risk takers to begin with also happen to be more persuasive and able to have their opinions prevail in the group setting. These high-risk people become opinion leaders when interacting in the group. Another explanation is that in our culture the daredevil is more revered than is the individual who prudently and cautiously weighs all the outcomes before acting. We are more apt to honor an Evil Knievel than a stodgy, trust-department banker. If so, many individuals would prefer to have the group see them as risk takers. They prefer the public image of being a "gutsy gambler" and, therefore, shift in the culturally approved risky direction when in a group situation.

Whatever the explanation, the risky shift is an empirical fact. The teacher who is aware of this is less apt to be overly concerned when some budding daredevil disrupts the class with an image-building display of bravado. Perhaps a short, "alone" session with the student will be sufficient to restore the equilibrium and integrity of the classroom.

BRAINSTORMING

The concept of social facilitation has also been used to promote a technique called "brainstorming," where individuals get together in an attempt to solve problems in new and creative ways. The idea is that because of the mutual

An experiment on brainstorming

stimulation of a brainstorming session, each participant will individually produce more creative solutions than when in isolation. Individuals in a brainstorming session are urged to interact freely, to call out any ideas no matter how bizarre, and to hold nothing back. The technique is used in many businesses, especially in areas where creativity is crucial, as in an advertising agency mapping out a new compaign. Actual research in this area, however, casts some doubt on the real benefits of this technique. The most-famous study on brainstorming had subjects assigned either to a five-person group situation or to an isolated situation.[4] In both situations, the subjects were given five problems to work on and a time limit of twelve minutes. One problem, for example, asked the subjects to suggest methods for increasing the number of European tourists visiting the United States. Subjects were told that they should come up with as many ideas as possible and that they should be as creative as possible. They were told:

1

Criticism is ruled out. Adverse judgment of ideas must be withheld until later.

2

Freewheeling is welcomed. The wilder an idea, the better. It is easier to tame down than to perk up.

3

Quantity is wanted. The more ideas there are, the more winners there are likely to be.

4

Combination and improvement are sought. In addition to contributing ideas of your own, you should suggest how others' ideas can be improved or how two or more ideas can be put together into an even better one.[5]

The results of this study startled many social psychologists. Subjects who were isolated produced almost twice as many different ideas as the subjects who were working in groups. Also, the subjects working alone produced twice as many ideas judged to be unique and creative.

DIFFERENTIAL EFFECTS ON BEHAVIOR

Research in the area of social facilitation thus suggests that people do behave differently when in the group situation. The seemingly contradictory results of the studies (groups sometimes enhance performance and sometimes inhibit it) show that the group has differential effects on behavior.

Group situations induce feelings of competition

Working in a group situation has two main effects: it increases feelings of competition and motivation on the one hand, and it increases feelings of anxiety and provides distractions on the other. The presence of other people explicitly or implicitly creates a competitive situation. In research, the subjects assume that the researcher will be making comparisons and/or they hope to impress other members of the group. If the subject's motivation is high to begin with, increasing it may have a damaging effect. However, if the subject's motivation is low, the competitive atmosphere of the group situation may enhance performance.

The group situation affects individual behavior, and social psychologists study the ways people affect and are affected by other people.

The nature of the task is also of great importance. When an individual in a group situation begins feeling both more competitive and more anxious, his or her performance on simple, nonintellectual tasks is enhanced. As the task becomes more difficult and more intellectual, the effect of working in a group becomes increasingly detrimental to performance. Before using any of the group techniques in a learning situation, the teacher should carefully take into account both the level of the students' motivation and the nature of the task.

The classroom by its very nature is always going to promote some competitive feelings. Students, like the subjects in the previously mentioned research studies, assume that performance comparisons will be made. They will also try to gain the attention of their teacher and peers by various methods of "trying to impress." Despite this, however, the teacher can choose to emphasize competition in certain areas and to deemphasize it in others. Highly motivated students working on difficult math problems would be better off working privately at their desks. Students with less motivation who are working on more-simple, rote tasks might do better if the work were done openly, as in using flash cards to drill the whole class in multiplication tables.

Competition can probably never be completely ruled out of a classroom situation. Social psychologists have shown over and over again that even in

Highly motivated students may work better alone than in the group

Competitive behavior among students will probably always be a factor in the classroom, but teachers can do much to promote cooperative behavior. One method is to assign group projects for which one grade is given to all group members.

situations where cooperation is the most-efficient route to success, competition continues to dominate. Studies have shown that even when subjects fully realize that the rewards will be greater for cooperative group interaction, they still prefer to compete with one another.[6]

Despite this powerful competitive tendency of American students, the teacher can still set up conditions that reduce competition, if not completely eliminate it. Preparing group projects where a single grade is assigned helps promote cooperation. Any situation in which the students are working toward a superordinate goal, a goal none of them can attain independently, will help to reduce competitive responses.

COHESIVENESS

One by-product of cooperation is an increase in the group's feeling of cohesiveness. The cohesive group tends to stick together more and have more of a sense of "we-ness" than "I-ness." Some teachers have been known to feel threatened by this turn of events.

Cohesiveness is one of the few truly group concepts in social psychology. It is the cement that binds the group together, or the attraction of the group for its members. Groups can range from collections of unrelated individuals (strangers waiting together at a bus station) to highly cohesive groups, in which norms are shared and status and role relationships are highly structured. When students and teachers meet in the classroom for the first time in September, they resemble a collection of individuals more than they do a cohesive group. As the weeks go by, however, the social situation may change dramatically as the loosely knit collection of individuals becomes more cohesive. Cohesiveness may be enhanced by:

A collection of individuals becomes a cohesive group

1
Friendly interaction. Interaction per se is not the crucial ingredient; a husband and wife fighting it out in divorce court are interacting. The interaction must be on friendly terms.

2
Cooperation. The more the group works together to achieve superordinate goals, the more cohesiveness is allowed to develop.

3
Group status. High-status groups tend to be more cohesive than low-status groups. If a classroom is broken down into various reading groups, for example, and if it is obvious to every child that the groups have been rank-ordered on the basis of ability, the top group will feel more cohesive than the bottom group. A teacher may also increase the status of the entire classroom by pointing out that they are in some way a special group and will have special privileges.

4
An outside threat. A group's cohesiveness may be dramatically increased by the presence of an outside threat. This is true of large and small groups. In wartime, when a country's very existence is threatened by an outside force, a country's morale and cohesiveness are often at their highest level. In a classroom this same kind of situation may inadvertently occur when a coercive teacher is perceived by the class as overly threatening. The class may band together and form a highly cohesive group—a group, incidentally, which does not include the teacher.

5
Style of leadership. We will look at this phenomenon in more detail in a later section. Suffice it to say here that groups in which the leadership is based on democratic factors are usually more likely to be cohesive than are groups in which more-authoritarian leadership techniques are employed.

Cohesiveness and productivity

Research indicates that there is no simple one-to-one relationship between cohesiveness and productivity. A cohesive group is one in which the members stick together, but this doesn't necessarily mean the group is more productive. For example, a highly cohesive labor union is more likely to be able to call a strike, where production on the job goes down to zero, than is a union whose members are not so attracted to one another. Highly cohesive groups may be

Cohesiveness may
lower productivity

more productive than less-cohesive groups when the motivation of the members is positive, yet when the motivation is negative, the more-cohesive group will be even less productive than the less-cohesive group.[7]

Cohesiveness and conformity

Group pressures re-
duce one's freedom
of action

Any group brings a certain amount of pressure to bear on its members to conform to the group's standards and norms. In a highly cohesive group the pressure to conform is greater than in a less-cohesive group. This helps explain the previously mentioned relationship between cohesiveness and productivity. When the group norm is for high productivity, the highly cohesive group conforms to that norm; likewise, when the group norm is for low productivity, the highly cohesive group conforms to that norm, especially in matters of consequence to the group (working conditions and salary, for example).

CONFORMITY

One of the most striking facts about life on this planet is that human beings form groups and live out their lives in group situations. Equally striking is the fact that, while in the group situation, people tend to behave in a uniform way. Conformity is a fact of life. Wherever we look we find groups of people, and within each group almost everyone is behaving alike. The behavior of an individual may change from group to group, and the norms of any particular group may shift from time to time, yet the phenomenon of conformity remains. We may like to feel as though we can act with some degree of independence, and yet in truth our freedom of action is severely limited by group pressure.

In a structured situation such as in church, conformity may be most obvious. People stand, sit, and kneel with the precision of a marching band. The pressure to conform, however, can be just as compelling in less-structured situations.

Within a group, great pressure exists for conformity, and group pressure to conform is highest when the group is highly cohesive.

"Well, heck! If all you smart cookies agree, who am I to dissent?"

Drawing by J. B. Handelsman;
© 1972 The New Yorker Magazine, Inc.

If, during the give and take of a dormitory "rap" session, someone suddenly stood up and started singing "Onward Christian Soldiers," that person might be referred to the counseling center.

The message from the group is always the same, "Be like us!" and the pressure to conform is virtually irresistible. The pressure may come in a variety of forms. It may be physical force, as in the case of a bouncer throwing a rowdy customer out of the local tavern, a customer who has exercised too much individuality. Or, it may be more subtle, as when the hostess at a formal dinner party raises her eyebrow when one of the guests chooses the wrong fork for the salad. Regardless of the form it takes, the pressure on the individual to conform makes itself known. Conformity has been demonstrated experimentally in many studies. The two most famous, however, are the classic studies by Sherif and Asch.

Sherif and the autokinetic effect

A stationary, pinpoint source of light in an otherwise darkened room will appear to move. You may have noticed this phenomenon yourself. You may have been looking up at a certain star, and out of the corner of your eye it appears that another star has suddenly moved. Or, you may have been driving on a turnpike when the rear light of the car in front of you suddenly starts to dance crazily before your eyes. Some plane crashes have even been caused by this autokinetic effect. The stationary runway lights suddenly appear to move just before the pilot lands the plane. The effect is even more dramatic if the subject doesn't know how far away the light really is.

Muzafer Sherif utilized the autokinetic effect to demonstrate conformity.[8] He put his subjects in a darkened room in groups of three, presented them with the pinpoint source of light, and asked them to call aloud their estimates of how far the light moved. The first subject might estimate that the light moved

A stationary pinpoint of light appears to move

16 inches; the second subject, 3 inches; and the third subject, 24 inches. After a few trials, however, all three subjects reported essentially the same distance—a group norm emerged. Repeating this procedure with other groups, Sherif found that conformity occurred in every case. The groups formed different norms, to be sure, but the point is, they all created some standard to which every member conformed.

Another interesting result of Sherif's study was that when he later tested many of the subjects individually, they still perceived the light on the basis of the norms created in the group situation. A member of a "7-inch" group, for example, when later tested alone, would continue to conform to this 7-inch standard. A member of a "22-inch" group would continue to see the light moving this distance, even when tested individually.

Group norms develop when individuals interact

Sherif's study shows us that in a relatively unstructured situation, group norms will be created and that individuals will follow these norms, not only while they are in the group, but even when they are alone.

Asch and group pressure

Sherif had shown that conformity occurs in a fairly unstructured situation (remember that, in fact, the light didn't move at all), and Asch wondered whether the same result would be obtained in a more-structured setting.[9] Asch presented his subjects with cards showing four lines: three comparison lines and a standard (see Fig. 20.1). The subject was asked to indicate which of the three comparison lines was closest in length to the standard line on the left of the card. As you look at the illustration you may feel that the task is too easy, that the solution to the problem is too obvious. Yet, when Asch conducted this study, his subjects were in error one out of three times. The difference is that as you look at the lines, you are not being exposed to group pressure, whereas Asch's subjects most certainly were. Asch's subjects sat in a room with what appeared to be eight other subjects. In fact, these other "subjects" were really stooges, told beforehand just what to say and how to respond. Each group contained one naive subject and eight previously rehearsed bogus subjects. The subject

Group pressure can change what a person "sees"

was thus in a situation where his eyes told him one thing, while all the other people in the room made a unanimous judgment that contradicted his own. The stooges were set up in advance so that every once in a while they would all agree on a certain line, even though that line could not possibly be the correct

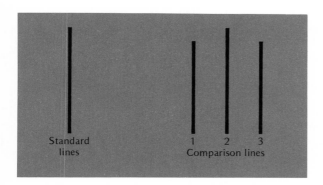

Fig. 20.1 Asch's study of group pressures for conformity.

one. It was in this setting that the subjects were incorrect one-third of the time; that is, 33 percent of their judgments were errors in the direction of the majority. As we have already said, group pressure is tremendous in its insistence on conformity.

As a matter of fact, the majority does not have to be so large. Asch's later studies revealed that a majority of three-to-one has just as much effect as a larger majority; that is, the naive subject made as many errors with three stooges as with eight. A two-to-one majority caused errors to drop to only about 12 percent, while the influence of only one stooge was negligible.

a)

b)

c)

d)

e)

In Asch's conformity study, some subjects are able to maintain independent judgment throughout. Most, however, are unable to do so and yield to group pressure on at least one trial. (a) The experimenter gives instructions. (b) The critical subject, number 6, listens to the instructions. (c) He makes his first judgment disagreeing with the consensus. (d) He leans forward as the next set of lines appears. (e) He feels conflict as he listens to new, incorrect peer judgments.

When the situation was reversed, when there was a naive majority of sixteen against one lone stooge, the errors of the stooge were met with uncontrolled laughter from the rest of the group.

Sherif and Asch have thus demonstrated experimentally the compelling power the group exerts on the individual to conform. Sherif has been able to produce norms in the laboratory and show how they govern individual behavior, and Asch, though artificially creating the norms, has shown us the force of the group's influence in a relatively structured situation.

CAN GROUP PRESSURE BE LIBERATING?

So far, conformity and group pressure have been shown to be repressive and limiting, generally robbing people of their individuality. Sherif has shown us how a group of people can come to believe that a stationary light is moving a certain distance; Asch has shown that our need to conform to group standards will cause us to distort our perceptions and judgment. In fact, virtually all of the studies done in the area of conformity follow this theme: the noble individual is robbed of human integrity by the insidious pressure of the group.

The experiment by Stanley Milgram which was discussed in Chapter 10 shows the reverse side of the coin.[10] Milgram, in a somewhat frightening experiment, shows us that group pressure can also have a liberating effect. We say "frightening" experiment because Milgram's study also points up man's destructive potential and shows what a thin veneer of socialization we have.

Human beings have a high potential for aggression

To establish a base line for our potential for hostility, Milgram asked subjects to deliver increasing amounts of electric shock to another person. Despite the "victim's" anguished cries and pleas for mercy, the experimenter urged the subject to keep increasing the voltage all the way up to 450 volts. The dial in front of the subject contained 30 voltage levels from 15 to 450 volts and was printed with such warnings as "Danger" and "Severe Shock." The subject had witnessed the "victim" being strapped into the electric chair and could clearly hear the "victim's" cries.

Milgram established his base line. Fully 65 percent of his subjects were willing to administer the maximum 450 volts; that is, almost two-thirds of the subjects were willing to risk killing a fellow subject.

Who were these subjects? Where and when was this experiment conducted? Were these Gestapo agents being trained in some sadistic Nazi laboratory during the 1930s? In fact, these subjects were ordinary American citizens, from twenty to fifty years of age, from all walks of life, and living in New Haven, Connecticut. The study was done at Yale University during the 1960s. Unknown to the subjects, of course, the "victims" did not really get shocked. The wires connecting the control panel to the electric chair did not really carry any electricity, and the victim was really an ally of the experimenter. But the subjects didn't know this, and were still willing to deliver the shock as the experimenter instructed.

The second phase of Milgram's study was to see what would happen in a group situation. How would subjects react if they were placed in the same situation with two other subjects who refused to follow the experimenter's commands? The results were dramatic. Under the condition of group pressure, only 10 percent of the subjects still pushed the lever all the way to 450 volts. The majority of the subjects refused to go beyond the half-way point. In this case, then, group pressure liberated the individual from the experimenter's authoritarian control and had a positive effect.

Conformity and group pressure may often be beneficial to the individual. Milgram's study suggests that they may help a person act in a more-humane and less-destructive manner.

Group pressure freed individuals from the yoke of authoritarian control

SOCIALIZATION

Conformity is a key issue in social psychology because it is a driving power of socialization. Socialization is the process of learning society's rules and customs and is accomplished through pressures to conform. The newborn infant—at best an innocent little hedonist and at worst a savage bundle of Freudian id—is slowly transformed into a conforming member of society. The individual slowly but surely gives up personal independence as socialization continues; learning how and when to eat, where and when to urinate and defecate, how to interact with other people, and so on. Finally, the mature adult emerges who has learned these lessons so well that he or she conforms with the instinctive precision of a homing pigeon.

Socialization, the process of learning society's rules and customs, is accomplished through pressures to conform. As we have seen, true nonconformists are rare.

Are there any nonconformists? There are only a few, and most of them are either in prison or in a psychiatric hospital. For example, you might think that members of a nudist colony are nonconformists, and yet they are all conforming to their own group norm. The only nonconformist in a nudist camp would be the person who is fully dressed. Or, you might assume that members of a hippie commune are nonconformists, and yet they are conforming as rigidly to their norms as middle-aged Rotarians are to theirs. There aren't many crewcuts in a hippie commune.

The so-called "generation gap" is essentially a difference in group norms. Both the under-thirty and the over-thirty groups are conforming to their own group norms. Each group is marching in unison, but to different drummers.

Who is the drummer in the classroom? Who sets the beat for the in-unison march of classroom members? To a large extent, it is the norms of society at large. After all, most students and teachers have been socialized in a common culture. The way they dress, the ideas they consider important, the way they interact, the way they express feelings, are all determined by the core culture. The fact that most students feel a sense of competition is in large part culturally determined and already part of their characters before they ever set foot in the classroom. The fact that they are in the classroom at all, pursuing an educational goal, is a cultural dictate. But this doesn't explain it all, for each classroom has its own distinct set of norms which exists within the larger context of society's norms. The teacher contributes much of the tone, but so does every single member of the class. The crucial ingredient in a norm formation, and thus conformity, is interaction among group members. Interactions produce group norms which then set the limits within which further interactions can take place. Status and role relationships begin to emerge, and further demands and expectancies are set for each individual's behavior. Who sets the beat? The classroom, within the context of the larger social situation, sets its own beat, and every single member of the class participates in the process.

COGNITIVE DISSONANCE

Another aspect of socialization has been described by Leon Festinger. According to Festinger, people strive to achieve a state of equilibrium among their various attitudes, beliefs, and behavior.[11] This is because we prefer consistency, or consonance, to inconsistency, or dissonance. Therefore, whenever we have a thought that is not consistent with our behavior, we are motivated to restore the equilibrium. To avoid self-contradiction, we can either change our thinking so that it conforms to our behavior, or change our behavior so that it conforms to our thought. For example, someone who enjoys smoking and who hears that smoking is a health hazard can either conclude that the evidence linking smoking with disease is flimsy, *or* stop smoking. One smoker, it has been said, became so nervous after reading the evidence linking smoking with cancer that he gave up reading.

The point is that whenever our thoughts and deeds conflict, we are driven to reduce the anxiety-provoking dissonance. Teachers should be alerted to the possible consequences of cognitive dissonance when it occurs in the classroom. The desire for consonance operates within the individual and within the group.

Inconsistent thoughts and actions produce cognitive dissonance

*"If those soak-the-rich birds get their way, I can tell you here's
one coolie who'll stop putting his shoulder to the goddam wheel."*

Drawing by Donald Reilly;
© 1972 The New Yorker Magazine, Inc.

The chances against finding a classroom where all thirty pupils and the teacher have totally compatible interests, attitudes, and values are so great that it is safe to say that dissonance is inevitable. The important thing is the way that dissonance is resolved. If the teacher decides to always "fight and never switch," if the pupils have to do all the changing, then the reduction of dissonance in the classroom will be more apparent than real. We have already noted in Chapter 9 that the way a teacher handles pupil discipline will help define the educational atmosphere of the class. The imposition of too strict a set of sanctions may reduce dissonance, but the resulting compliance is likely to be begrudging at best. Pupil discipline is just one instance of the general problem of the incongruity between the individual and the group.

Dissonance is inevitable in the classroom

AGGRESSION

Social psychologists have long been interested in the phenomenon of aggression. Human society is obviously fraught with violence. The United States has the dubious distinction of leading the world in rates of homicide, rape, assault, and robbery. In fact, the homicide rate in the United States is twice that of Finland, which is the second most-violent nation on the planet. Almost a thousand children are murdered every year in the United States, and even more common are the tiny broken bodies resulting from the "battered child syndrome." As every football, hockey, and boxing fan knows, violence also has crowd appeal. And "hit 'em again harder" apparently is not reserved for the sports arena, for on September 23, 1967, at a large southwestern university, when a depressed student crawled to the edge of a dormitory roof threatening suicide, thousands of students stood below and chanted in unison, "Jump! Jump! Jump!" As for major conflicts, the world has rarely seen a day since the beginning of recorded history when there wasn't a full-scale war some place on the globe. These facts seem to argue that aggression is an inevitable by-product of people getting together in groups.

Psychology has generated four basic positions regarding the issue of aggression: the Freudian, the ethological, the frustration-aggression, and the social-learning explanations.

1

The Freudian.   According to Freud, aggression is built into the organism and is as basic to human behavior as sexuality. The urge to violence is a result of pressure from our innate and irrational id instinct. The trouble with the Freudian hypothesis is that, by explaining so much, it may in fact not explain anything. To say that people are aggressive because they have an aggressive instinct built into their ids smacks of circular reasoning. This was referred to in Chapter 3 as the nominal fallacy.

2

The ethological.   Lorenz and other ethologists view aggression as a constant potential in virtually all organisms. If the proper releaser occurs, the potential for aggression will quickly be translated into action. For example, the male stickleback fish attacks whenever stimulated by the color red. As for humans, Lorenz feels that aggression actually has survival value for the species. Since population density often outruns available food supplies, aggression acts to both reduce the size of the population and also to spread out the remaining population over a larger area.[12] Another ethologist, Robert Ardrey, suggests that aggression results from a fundamental territorial need. Ardrey says that all organisms have an innate drive to own, defend, and gain territorial areas.[13] The ethological explanation runs the risk of possibly having ventured beyond the actual observed data. Since Lorenz has based his theory on observations of lower organisms, more research is needed before extrapolation to the human level becomes convincing.

3

Frustration-aggression.   Led by Miller and Dollard, a group of Yale psychologists in the late 1930s introduced the now-famous frustration-aggression hypothesis.[14] Aggression was explained as being the result of being frustrated, or of having one's goals blocked. Said Miller, "the occurrence of aggression always presupposes frustration."[15] In many instances the Miller-Dollard hypothesis is obviously valid. We have all seen people become angry, sometimes to the point of irrationality, over having a goal blocked: an individual, already late for an important appointment, becomes furious when the car won't start; a teenage boy gets in a fist fight on the way home from school after having been "cut" from the varsity basketball team.

The frustration-aggression hypothesis, however, does have some major drawbacks as an explanatory model. Some people react to frustration, not with overt aggression, but merely by sitting quietly and seething inwardly. Another person may respond to goal blockage by regressing, that is, acting in a less-mature fashion. Also, there are countless examples of aggressive behaviors that were not triggered by frustration. Being annoyed or attacked by another person often results in aggression aimed at the source of the annoyance. A student was playing poker in the dorm when, without provocation, another student moved quietly behind his chair and playfully poured beer on his head. Five seconds and two punches later the "playful pourer" was on his back and nursing a bruised eye and jaw.

4
Social learning or modeling. As noted in Chapter 12, Albert Bandura's social-learning theory has been used to explain aggressive behavior. Children who watched an adult model punch and kick a large "Bobo" doll also punched and kicked the doll when they later got the chance. In this instance, the children were imitating the adults' aggressive behavior. The children had not been provoked, annoyed, or frustrated, and yet because of modeling they exhibited aggressive responses. It has also been shown that if children watch a film of an aggressive adult model, they, too, will imitate the aggressive behavior.[16]

Aggression and the mass media

One question that has recently become of great concern to social psychologists is whether the portrayal of violence in movies and TV encourages aggressive acts on the part of the viewer. This is an especially important question with regard to TV, since most children are avid television viewers. One survey report indicates that the average sixteen-year-old has spent more hours of his or her young life watching TV than in the classroom.[17] Some of the studies done in this area have shown a relationship, especially among boys, between watching violence on television and the acting out of aggression. In the typical study, a group of boys are asked to indicate which TV shows they watch, and these results are then correlated with the peer group's evaluation of each boy's overt aggressiveness. Significant relationships have been discovered. That is, boys who report watching the most TV violence are also the ones rated most aggressive by their peers.[18] As was pointed out in Chapter 16, studies such as these are difficult to evaluate in terms of the direction of the possible cause-and-effect relationship. Does the violence on TV cause the boys to be aggressive, or does aggressiveness in boys cause them to select violent TV shows? Or, are some boys characterologically aggressive, and because of this they both act out their aggression more and also choose to watch more aggressive TV shows? With R/R research studies such as these, the direction of the relationship is virtually impossible to interpret.

Stanley Milgram has recently attempted an experimental evaluation of this problem using a large portion of the United States as his laboratory. Milgram talked CBS into creating two versions of their popular program *Medical Center,* one version having far more aggressive cues than the other. Milgram was unable to detect any difference in the rates of violence among the cities receiving the aggressive versus nonaggressive programs, even though they were equated for prior levels of violent crimes.[19]

Finally, in an attempt to subject this problem to a controlled, experimental analysis, a study was conducted in which the TV fare was actually manipulated (as an independent variable) by the experimenter.[20] The subjects, again all boys, were enrolled in private boarding schools or state residential schools. By random assignment, the boys were either required to watch violent shows (*The FBI,*

Does violence in movies and on TV encourage aggressive acts?

Gunsmoke and *The Untouchables*) or nonviolent shows (*Bachelor Father* and *Ed Sullivan*). Both before and after six weeks of this controlled viewing regimen, the boys were measured for both overt and covert aggressiveness. Overt aggressiveness was determined by a supervisor's daily tally of each boy's aggressive incidents. Covert aggressiveness was measured by projective personality testing.

The results showed that the boys who watched the violent TV shows expressed more covert or fantasy aggression as measured by the Thematic Apperception Test. The boys who watched the nonviolent shows, however, exhibited twice as many fist fights and far more overt, verbal aggression. The results suggest that TV violence has a possibly cathartic effect on boys, rechanneling their hostility so as to inhibit overt aggression. The authors of the study caution, however, that watching real-life violence on newscasts may increase rather than decrease the expression of aggressive responses on the part of the viewer. They say that "violence presented in the form of fiction is much less likely to reinforce, stimulate, or elicit aggressive responses than violence in the form of a news event."[21] Thus, whereas TV's coverage of a violent news story may increase viewer aggression, fictitious violence may even inhibit overt viewer aggression.

TV violence possibly has a cathartic effect on boys

Aggression: nature or nurture?

Like the great intelligence debate, the question of whether aggression is primarily innate or learned has also stirred controversy among psychologists. The nature theorists see humans as instinctively violent, destined by their genes to be aggressive. The nurture position is that humans, being a product of environmental stimulation, can be shaped into peaceful and loving beings. Indeed, the four positions on aggression just outlined can be categorized according to this issue. Both the Freudian and ethological positions rest on the assumption that aggression is largely inherited. Both the frustration-aggression and social-learning explanations, however, view aggression as basically a product of the environment.

The genetic argument.

As pointed out in Chapter 4, white mice have been selectively bred for aggressiveness. In one study, a large group of mice was separated on the basis of the amount of aggressiveness displayed. The most- and least-aggressive mice were then selectively bred, and after seven generations two nonoverlapping groups were identified. That is, the least aggressive of the aggressive strain were more aggressive than the most aggressive of the nonaggressive strain.[22]

At the human level a number of studies have been done comparing MZ (identical) twins with DZ (fraternal) twins on the criterion of aggression. Regarding crimes of violence, it has been found that the concordance rate (the percentage of co-twins having the trait) was significantly higher for MZ than DZ twins.[23] Since MZ twins result from a single fertilized egg, they have identical genetic endowments. DZ twins derive from separate eggs fertilized at the same time, and are, thus, no more alike genetically than siblings in general.

The environmental argument.   Psychologists holding the environmental view see aggression resulting from the way society reinforces and punishes its member's attitudes and behavior. The environmentalists state that the attitudes of the majority of people in each society determine whether or not violence will be tolerated. Cultures are cited where aggression is apparently almost nonexistent, and other cultures have been found where hostility is a major characteristic. In short, the environmentalists argue that aggression is determined by group norms and the frustrations of day-to-day living.

Is there an answer?   As is the case with so many areas in psychology, all the answers are not yet in on the issue of human aggression. It is known, however, that behavior is multiply caused, and perhaps the safest prediction is that aggression will be found to result from heredity interacting with environment interacting with time. The fact that there is a genetic component in aggression seems to be fairly well established. Also, the built-in aggressive tendencies emerge at different times through maturation, depending on individual differences, sex, and species. Just as certainly, since aggression can be expressed in so many ways and in so many different situations, there is obviously a very large learning component.

Aggression has both a genetic component and a learning component

Harry Harlow comments:

> There is little disagreement among comparative psychologists that aggression is part of the biological heritage of primates. However, some social psychologists who limit their studies to the human animal still believe that aggression is basically a learned behavior, and that the differences which occur between the sexes or among individuals within their sex group are accountable solely on the basis of experience. No doubt the late appearance of aggression in the developmental sequence has led some observers to underestimate its biological basis.[24]

STATUS AND ROLE

If you met someone for the first time and he suddenly put his hand into your mouth, you might be pretty startled. Or, suppose a perfect stranger told you to take off all your clothes. Your reaction might be hard to predict. Yet all of us have been in situations like these and have hardly blinked our eyes. When the individual putting his hand into your mouth is a dentist, or the stranger telling you to undress is a physician, the situation has a context in which the behavior is expected.

Social psychologists use the terms status and role to describe expected behavior of this type. Status is the position we occupy in society's prestige hierarchy. Role is the behavior that is expected of us because of the particular status we have. Conformity is essential to status and role because status gives us an obligation to behave (act out the role) the way society expects us to (to conform to society's expectations). For example, our society expects far different behavior from

Status—the position

Role—the behavior

"This will teach you not to hit people."

a used-car salesman than from a college president. People might smile if the used-car salesman created a drunken scene in public, but would be severely disapproving if the college president did the very same thing. Our behavior is expected to conform to society's norms for our position in life. If it does not conform to these expectations, society has ways of exerting great pressure to bring us back into line.

Because of the complicated nature of our society today, most people find themselves occupying different status positions at the same time. A man may have a job as a clerk in a shop and spend each day quietly taking orders, while at night he issues directives with an authoritative flourish in his capacity as Boy Scout executive. In each case his role conforms to his status. A given status often has multiple roles. A woman may have a number of status positions and roles, as mother, clubwoman, wife, and corporation executive. The variety of roles may create conflict and a feeling of frustration and despair if she feels she cannot carry out all her roles, that she can't continue to work and also fulfill the role of a good mother. Yet if she doesn't work, she may feel frustrated and perhaps even guilty over the fact that she isn't living up to her full potential as a woman.

People respond on the basis of how they are treated

It is crucial to understand role behavior in order to understand human behavior. People tend to behave the way society (as embodied by the people around them) treats them. One of the contributing factors in adolescent rebellion is the lack of consistency with which society treats this nonchild-nonadult.*

---
*

See Chapter 8 for a more complete description.

When adolescents are treated like children, they will tend to respond like children, no matter how many speeches they hear about their failure to assume responsibility or act maturely. The parents' words are often drowned out by the volume of their own contradictory behavior.

EXPECTATIONS AND "LOOKS": NEVER JUDGE A BOOK BY ITS COVER

It has long been suggested that some individuals tend to "get by" on their looks. That is, the individual's appearance, his or her own physical stimulus value, seems to influence the kinds of expectations and treatment provided by other people. Recent evidence suggests that this is indeed the case. In one study, attractive individuals were judged to possess more positive personality traits, more prestigious occupations, and more potential for future success than were unattractive people.[25] This physical-attractiveness stereotype apparently begins early in life, at least by the time the child reaches kindergarten.[26] What this means to the teacher is obvious. The attractive and docile child should not be overrewarded with grades and praise—"looks" should not be confused with achievement.

LEADERSHIP

The highest position in the status hierarchy of any group is that of leader. The leader has the most influence in shaping the group's norms and expectations. Before relating styles of leadership with group functioning, we must first get some understanding of the concept of leadership itself.

Is leadership something we either have or don't have? Are there people who, regardless of the group, the social setting, the cultural norms, will always rise to the top? Or, is leadership strictly a function of the group norms, the task being performed, or the social context? In other words, is leadership a quality of the individual or a quality of the group? The two positions are called the great-leader theory and the group theory.

The great-leader theory

The great-leader theory sees leadership as a quality of the individual. In its boldest form the theory states that certain individuals possess just the right blend of looks, personality traits, and intelligence to be almost automatically thrust into leadership positions. These individuals—who are said to have charisma—will always become leaders in any situation or in any group. Charisma is a kind of personal magnetism and hypnotic appeal. When a charismatic person walks into a room, the room is suddenly charged with excitement, and the others in it become submissive and willing to follow the individual anywhere. Some of history's charismatic leaders include Mahatma Gandhi, Joan of Arc, Winston Churchill, Cleopatra, Adolf Hitler, Charles De Gaulle, John F. Kennedy, Martin Luther King, and Golda Meir. Each had or has a personal appeal that is spellbinding, almost mystical. People such as these, says the theory, have to become leaders regardless of the times in which they live.

Leadership and charisma

The group theory

According to the group theory, almost anyone who fulfills some basic need of the group can be a leader. And, since the needs of the group shift, so too does leadership. For example, a group on a camping trip would see leadership constantly changing according to the dictates of the situation. If the group became lost, the individual with the compass would become the leader. If someone became injured, the person with first-aid knowledge and supplies would become the leader

Even history's great leaders are explained on this basis. Winston Churchill became a leader late in his career, when the times called for someone with his special talents. Hitler would have found no followers and would have probably had to spend his entire life painting portraits in Austria had Germany not been rocked by runaway inflation and crushing depression. The group theory suggests that the unfolding of history is like the opening of a combination lock—only when a certain sequence of events occurs will a certain individual be called upon to lead.

A blending of the two theories

The actual evidence regarding leadership now suggests that the best explanation lies somewhere between these two theories. Both theories are needed to account for the data. Certain individual qualities do seem to be more common in leaders than in other group members. For example, leaders do tend to be taller but not too much taller, and more intelligent but not too much more intelligent, than other members of the group. Leaders also seem to possess more social skills than do followers. For example, leaders are apt to give more information, ask for more information, and make more interpretations about a situation.[27] But it has also become increasingly evident that the demands of the situation are crucial in determining the group's choice of a leader. In one study of school children it was found that the boy who could spit the farthest was the leader in first grade. By fourth grade it was the child who "sassed" the teacher the most. In high school the girl who had always stayed in the background in grade school suddenly blossomed into leadership because of her "dating power."[28] Thus, the demands and values of the group are just as important in determining leadership as are many of the personal qualities listed above. Leadership results when the individual's qualities match the group's demands.

Leaders have some traits in common

Leadership changes as the situational demands change

STYLES OF LEADERSHIP

Most of you have been members of many different groups, scout troops, athletic teams, school clubs, whatever. You have thus been exposed to various styles of leadership, and you may have noticed that the efficiency of the group's performance and the satisfaction of the group's members were due in large measure to the style of the group's leadership. You may recall a coach who was so lenient that the team failed to perform to expectations. Or, perhaps you remember a scout leader who was so rigid and domineering that most of the members quit and the troop had to fold.

Many years ago Kurt Lewin, who had once been a student of Max Wertheimer, conducted an experiment to assess the ways in which groups respond to different kinds of leadership.[29] One aspect of the study was to compare the effects of authoritarian and democratic styles of leadership on group activity. The subjects were young boys who were placed in "club" groups under the direction of adult leaders. The authoritarian leader was domineering, never asking for suggestions about group activities and controlling every aspect of the group situation. The democratic leader, on the other hand, guided the group gently, constantly asking for suggestions and allowing the group to make decisions. The results of the study indicated that completely different atmospheres were generated in the two groups. The "democratic" group's members were more satisfied, more cooperative, less hostile, and better able to carry on group activities when the leader was not present. Though the "authoritarian" group did have a higher rate of production (building model planes), the work of the democratic group was of a higher quality.

In interpreting this study, it is important to recall the discussion of social norms and conformity. This study was done in the United States, where child-rearing practices are not as authoritarian as in some other cultures. One of the boys in the study was the son of an Army officer and had been raised in a highly rigid and disciplined home. This subject actually responded better in the authoritarian group; he enjoyed that group more and felt less anxiety in the highly structured situation.

Democratic and authoritarian leaders create different group atmospheres

Changing the role of one individual in the group may change the whole group, since the classroom is a collection of interdependent individuals and the dynamics of their interrelationship depend on roles established through interaction.

CLASSROOM LEADERSHIP

Although the teacher is handed the main leadership role in the classroom, other leaders are also present. The broad base of influence from which the teacher operates in large measure shapes the social climate in the classroom. The degree to which the teacher is authoritarian, or submissive, or coercive, or democratic, sets the tone for norm formation in the classroom. But, once school has been in session for a few weeks, student leaders begin to emerge. Again, it is the teacher who, to a large extent, may determine which students attain leadership positions. The teacher may encourage and reinforce leadership behavior from one child and withhold reinforcement when the same behavior is exhibited by another child. Yet the teacher can also succumb to reinforcement. One prominent sociologist has said that "influence over others is purchased at the price of allowing one's self to be influenced by others."[30] He feels that an influential leader must have the esteem of everyone in the group. This means that students can exert considerable pressure on a teacher by giving or withholding their esteem and that they can, by this means, shape their teacher's behavior. It also explains why a given teacher might be a successful leader with one group of students and not so successful with a different group.

Students may shape the behavior of the teacher

Social psychology assumes that leadership ability is a set of behavioral skills that most people can learn. David Johnson, an expert in the social psychology of education, says that effective leadership depends on:

Leadership skills can be learned

1
Flexible behavior.

2
The ability to know what behaviors are needed at a particular time in order for the group to function most efficiently.

3
The ability to behave as required or to get other members of the group to do so.

An effective leader must learn to spot what the group needs in a given situation and then be flexible enough "to provide diverse types of behaviors that are required under different conditions."[31] The effective leader must also get the cooperation of various members of the group so that they will help perform the necessary group functions.

GROUP DYNAMICS OF THE CLASSROOM

The classroom is a collection of interdependent individuals. The dynamics of their interrelationships depend on the roles that have been established through interaction. Whenever there is a change in the expected behavior of any group member, the dynamic interrelationships of the entire group must necessarily change. The pressure on role behavior is so great that if a group has certain expectations about an individual's behavior, that individual usually responds in a way consistent with those expectations. The group's expectations become a self-fulfilling prophecy. For example, in a two-person group, or dyad, the expectations of the superordinate member clearly determine the behavior of the sub-ordinate member. Suppose a mother is convinced that red hair causes a child to have a quick temper. She will then tolerate the temper tantrums of her red-haired child, while at the same time extinguishing these same responses in her blonde or brunette children. Or, suppose a high-school student complains that his mother treats him as if he were a child; an objective analysis of the student's behavior may reveal that he indeed doesn't let his mother down—he acts like a child. Or, imagine a husband who complains that his wife is domineering. During the conversation he mentions that he recently dropped one of his wife's plant pots and was thereupon banished to the cellar, where his son later brought him his supper. In each case, the dynamic relationship between the people involved could exist only if both members played their expected roles. If the student who was being treated like a child stopped acting like a child, his mother would have to change her expectations and, thus, her behavior toward him. The man with the domineering wife must have played the role of a dominated husband to the hilt. Why else would he meekly allow himself to be served dinner in the cellar? In the words of a once-popular song, "It takes two to tango." There can be no tango, or any other consistent form of interaction, unless both partners play their expected roles.

Change your own behavior to change behavior of others

The same phenomenon can also be observed in larger groups. In an educational-psychology course taught by one of the authors, the power of role behavior was demonstrated in the following way:

Two students, selected at random, were chosen as subjects and asked to leave the room and wait in the corridor. During their absence, roles were assigned to them: one student was given the high-status position of a world-famous cultural anthropologist, and the other student was given a low-status position of a college dropout who could not find a job. The class was instructed to discuss a certain topic, keeping firmly in mind the roles that had been assigned to the two naive subjects. The two subjects, unaware of their roles, then rejoined the group. The group consistently treated the high-status student with dignity and respect, and the low-status subject with derision and inattention. Within fifteen or twenty minutes the group's expectations began affecting the subjects' behavior. The high-status subject began dominating the discussions, even pontificating grandly for minutes at a time. He later explained that he had thoroughly enjoyed himself and would like to take part in more group discussions. The low-status subject, especially during the early stages of the discussion, made repeated attempts to become involved, but as time went by these became more infrequent. His behavior showed general signs of regression; the pitch of his voice even rose perceptibly until it bordered on a preadolescent squeak. During the final five minutes of the discussion he withdrew totally and sat stiffly in tight-lipped silence!

This demonstration of the influence of a group's expectations on individual behavior has been tried a number of times. In each case the results have been generally similar, though not always as dramatic as the case just described: personality differences cause differences in the ways subjects respond to the group's

Group expectations influence an individual's behavior

pressure. The point, however, is that consistent and predictable behavioral effects occur despite the personality differences.

In a classic case reported by the famous learning theorist, Edwin R. Guthrie, a group of male college students decided to make an all-out effort to cater extravagantly to a shy, socially inept coed. They made sure she was invited to all the social functions, constantly flattered her with gifts and attention, and in general saw that she was the "belle of the ball." By the end of the college year she had developed an easy, confident manner and had become a popular campus favorite even among those not aware of the original plot. Says Guthrie, "What her college career would have been if the experiment had not been made is impossible to say, but it is fairly certain that she would have resigned all social ambitions and would have found interests compatible with her social ineptitude.[32]

Teachers may inadvertently implant prejudice

The influence of group expectations on individual behavior can also be seen in the area of racial prejudice. Though prejudice is primarily learned in the home, teachers may also implant prejudice, especially during the first few grades. They may not directly teach hatred, but the message still comes through loud and clear. The teacher's differential treatment of minority races and religions sets the stage for differential student responses. Black children, for example, can hardly be expected to act maturely in the classroom when they are not treated with dignity and respect. The mass media have also helped communicate this social distortion. Until the last few years movies typically cast blacks in subservient roles, as maids and servants. They also played up stereotypes, often characterizing a black as a wide-eyed, frightened fool. This sort of thing could hardly lend dignity to the black race.

Group expectations can be so powerful that the minority-group members may learn to hold the prejudices and stereotyped attitudes toward their own group that the majority group holds. This can be very destructive to the minority-group member's self-image.[33]

The classroom teacher is obviously a potent reinforcer and through the judicious use of social approval can shape the behavior of the entire class. The teacher must realize, however, that the classroom is a social unit with a dynamically balanced set of role relationships. Any shift in the role of one student necessarily results in a change in the social balance of the entire group. If the teacher clamps down on the class jokester, for example, the social climate could shift in a negative direction. The jokester may be fulfilling the important role of relieving group tensions in moments of social stress. Removing that function could lead to a far more anxious social climate where the conditions for learning could deteriorate. By the same token, shutting off the antics of a loud-mouth who is motivated more by compulsive attention seeking than by reducing class tensions could produce better learning conditions for the rest of the class. Some tinkering and adjusting can be attempted, but remember that changing the role of any individual in the group produces changes in the whole group.

SEX ROLES IN THE SCHOOL

Just as the school often acts to transmit the traditional values of the larger culture in general, it also transmits society's version of the sex role. Boys are encouraged to be more "masculine" and girls to be "ladylike." One recent analysis indicated that this is done, often inadvertently, in three ways:[34]

1

Schools encourage sex typing by separating male and female activities and interest areas. Young boys are more apt to be sent to the "block corner," whereas girls are placed in the "housekeeping" and art areas.

2

Teachers project sex-typed expectations and the children live up to these expectations—exactly the kind of situation that role theory would predict. If teachers expect little boys to be less manageable than little girls, the boys pick up these cues and don't let the teachers down.

3

Schools have typically created an ideal "pupil role." The ideal pupil is conforming, docile, dependent, and manageable—that is, the pupil exhibits the very traits that have traditionally defined the female role. By more easily adopting this role, girls learn to be more receptive than active. Boys, on the other hand, have more difficulty conforming to this ideal-pupil image and thus often find school to be a stressful and alienating experience.

ROLE AND PERSONALITY

Finally, we would like to point out that, although the pressure of group expectancies is a powerful influence on our behavior, our basic personality will determine the way our role in the group is interpreted and carried out. The fact that individual behavior is consistent across different roles in different groups shows that we each bring an integrated and coherent behavioral unity to our groups. The way role and personality interrelate is reciprocal. The role we play in a group also has a definite impact on our personality. For example, an actor who for years plays the "tough guy" in the movies slowly incorporates this image into his personality and begins to believe and act as if he *is* that tough guy.

The therapy technique called psychodrama is based on this notion. Neurotic patients are put on the stage and given roles that they typically find uncomfortable to act out. With encouragement, and in the context of a nonthreatening situation, they learn the behavior required for certain roles and experience a concomitant personality change. The relationship between role and personality also works the other way. We will consciously or unconsciously select roles that are consistent with our underlying personality. Extroverted personalities usually assume roles that allow them to stay in the limelight, while introverts adopt roles that keep them away from stage-front.

Studies have shown that the majority of college seniors majoring in education prefer to work with people rather than things, and describe themselves as "conventional in opinions and values."[35] Teachers also tend to score above average in such personality areas as friendliness, sociability, and personal relations.[36] A summary of the research on teacher personality profiles as determined by the Minnesota Multiphasic Personality Inventory (MMPI) describes teachers as:

1

Responsible, conscientious, conforming, and friendly;

2

Likely to emphasize control of self and adaptation to the needs and demands of others.[37]

The way role and personality interrelate is reciprocal

Evidence indicates that the personalities of teachers are fairly consistent with the role demands of their job. However, the research in this area is correlational, meaning that the interpretations can go either way. In other words, teachers may have a modal personality style which causes them to select the role of teacher, or the role demands of the teaching position may shape the personalities of those involved in the teaching profession. The best guess is that both selection and shaping are involved.

Personality profiles of teachers

OTHER VARIABLES AFFECTING SOCIAL CLIMATE

We have discussed the importance of status-role relationships, leadership, conformity, and cohesiveness in influencing the school's social climate, but these variables do not tell the whole story. We would like to mention briefly three other factors.

1

Socioeconomic status of the school.   The average socioeconomic status of a high school affects the competitive climate of the school. Working-class students are more likely to go on to college when they attend predominantly middle-class high schools than when they attend working-class high schools. Similarly, middle-class students are less likely to go on to college when they attend predominantly working-class high schools.[38]

Socioeconomic status of a school affects subsequent education

2

School facilities.   Another study found that school facilities, such as the size and quality of the library, the number of science laboratories, the amount of laboratory equipment, have no significant effect on student achievement.[39] This study shows that academic achievement is influenced far more by socioeconomic background than by school facilities.

3

Size of the school.   In comparing high schools of various sizes, it has been found that students participate in extracurricular activities more and assume more leadership roles when they attend smaller high schools.[40] It has also been found that the size of the school has no significant influence on academic achievement.[41]

All the variables mentioned in this chapter will be operative at one time or another in almost any classroom. The question is, What kind of a group will the classroom become? The teacher as leader can clearly exert a major influence on the definition of the group. We have noted that classes can run the entire gamut from a collection of egocentric individuals "doing their own thing" to a smoothly functioning machine where each individual may be defined only as a group member. If the teacher does not know about the social variables or chooses not to exert definitional leadership, the students will impose their own definition. This is likely to create a very awkward situation: the teacher's role would be totally defined by the group. The opposite extreme, where the teacher sets the classroom atmosphere and educational objectives solely in terms of his or her own needs and values, is equally undesirable. Thus, the way a teacher uses concepts like social facilitation, conformity, competitiveness, cohesiveness, and group pressure is part of the teaching problem. An equally significant question involves the whole area of social goals and objectives. A knowledge of social psychology can truly help the teacher promote human development through education.

Summary

Social psychology is the study of human behavior in the context of the group situation. It is the study of how people affect and are affected by other people. Each classroom is a social unit with its own unique set of norms, role relationships, and behavioral expectations. Though the social atmosphere of the classroom is in large part shaped by the teacher, it is also a function of each student's behavior. A change in the behavior of anyone in the classroom changes the dynamic relationship within the classroom, and thus changes the existing social atmosphere. Sometimes the influence of the group acts to increase an individual's performance (social facilitation), and sometimes the group's influence decreases an individual's performance (social inhibition). Working in a group situation has two main effects: (1) it increases feelings of competition, and (2) it increases feelings of anxiety. Thus, a student's performance will be facilitated by the group's influence when (a) the student's motivation level is on the low side, and (b) when the task is neither overly difficult nor overly intellectual. Cohesiveness is defined as the amount of attraction the group has for its members. Cohesiveness can be increased in a group as a result of (a) an increase in the amount of friendly interaction, (b) an increase in the amount of cooperation, (c) an increase in the group's feeling of status, (d) an outside threat, or (e) a change in the style of leadership.

One result of group life is the overwhelming desire of individuals to conform to the norms of their group. Two major studies indicate the compelling nature of conformity: Sherif and the autokinetic effect, and Asch's study of group pressure. In each case, the behavior of individuals conformed to the group norm; the virtually irresistible message from the group is "be like us."

Though most conformity studies tend to show the power of the group as being repressive to the individual, a study by Milgram showed that the influence of the group may actually allow an individual to act in a more-humane and less-aggressive fashion. Milgram's study also pointed out the basic aggressiveness within the human species. Psychologists continue to debate the nature-nurture argument with respect to aggression. The Freudian and the ethological positions assume that a major portion of aggressiveness is innately determined; the frustration-aggression hypothesis and the social-learning theory view aggression as a product of the environment. Studies on the effect of violence in the mass media on aggression have had equivocal results: some indicate that violence on TV has increased aggressive behavior on the part of the viewer, while other studies suggest that violence on TV may have the cathartic effect of reducing the viewer's overt aggression.

The behavior of the individual also conforms to the expectations society forms on the basis of one's status and role. Status is one's position or niche in society's prestige hierarchy and role is the behavior expected of a person having a particular status.

Leadership in a group is focused on the individual or individuals with the highest niche in the status hierarchy and the most influence over the other group members. Leaders seem to be chosen on the basis of both personal characteristics and the demands of the group.

In a study comparing styles of leadership, democratic versus authoritarian, it was shown that democratic leaders (those who gently guided the group, asked for suggestions, allowed for group decisions, etc.) were apt to have groups in which the members were more satisfied, more cooperative, less hostile, and better able to follow through on group projects even when the leader was absent.

Because of the preset status and role requirements of the classroom, the teacher automatically holds the leadership position. He or she is not the only leader, however, for student leaders inevitably arise and can influence the behavior of both the teacher and the other students.

The group dynamics of the classroom, or of any group situation, are based on interdependent status and role relationships. When a group has a certain expectation regarding an individual's behavior, the individual usually responds in a way consistent with that expectation. For the individual, the group's expectation becomes a self-fulfilling prophecy. This can be especially damaging to the minority-group youngster when the group's expectation is based on prejudice and stereotyping.

Although the pressure of the group is a powerful force on individual behavior, people do not respond in the same ways. The individual's personality helps determine how group pressures will be interpreted. An individual with an extroverted personality, for example, is apt to seek group roles that are attention getting. On the other hand, the fact that the individual has an extroverted personality is due partly to past experiences in group situations.

Studies have shown that certain common personality types are found among groups of teachers. Perhaps an individual's personality causes him or her to select a teaching career, or perhaps the role demands on teachers help shape their personalities in a common direction. It is likely that both selection and shaping are involved.

The social atmosphere of the classroom is influenced also by pressures outside the school. Among those variables affecting group dynamics are: (1) socioeconomic status of the school, (2) school facilities, and (3) the size of the school.

A basic understanding of the principles of social psychology will better enable a teacher to attain the major goal of promoting human development through education.

REFERENCES

1
N. Triplett, "The Dynamogenic Factors in Pacemaking and Competition," *American Journal of Psychology* **9** (1897):507–533.

2
N. B. Cottrell, R. H. Rittle, and D. L. Wack, "Presence of an Audience and List Type as Joint Determinants of Performance in Paired-Associates Learning," *Journal of Personality* 35 (1967):217–226.

3
D. G. Pruitt, "Choice Shift in Group Discussion, An Introductory Review." *Journal of Personality and Social Psychology* 20 (1971):339–360.

4
D. S. Taylor, P. C. Berry, and C. H. Block, "Does Group Participation when Using Brainstorming Facilitate or Inhibit Creative Thinking?" *Administrative Science Quarterly* 2 (1958):23–47.

5
J. L. Freedman, J. M. Carlsmith, and D. O. Sears, *Social Psychology* (Englewood Cliffs, N.J.: Prentice-Hall, 1970, p. 188).

6
J. S. Minas, A. Scodel, D. Marlowe, and H. Rawson, "Some Descriptive Aspects of Two-Person Non-Zero-Sum Games," *Journal of Conflict Resolution* 4 (1960):193–197.

7
S. Schachter, N. Ellertson, D. McBride, and D. Gregory, "An Experimental Study of Cohesiveness and Productivity," *Human Relations* 4 (1951):229–238.

8
M. Sherif, *The Psychology of Group Norms* (New York: Harper & Row, 1936).

9
S. E. Asch, *Social Psychology* (Englewood Cliffs, N.J.: Prentice-Hall, 1952).

10
S. Milgram, "Liberating Effect of Group Pressures," *Journal of Personality and Social Psychology* 1 (1965):127–134.

11
L. Festinger, *A Theory of Cognitive Dissonance* (Stanford, California: Stanford University Press, 1957).

12
K. Lorenz, *On Aggression* (New York: Harcourt, Brace and World, 1966).

13
R. Ardrey, *The Territorial Imperative* (New York: Atheneum, 1966).

14
J. M. Dollard, L. W. Doob, N. E. Miller, O. H. Mourer, and R. R. Sears, *Frustration and Aggression* (New Haven: Yale University Press, 1939).

15
N. E. Miller, "The Frustration-Aggression Hypothesis," *Psychological Review* 48 (1941): 337–342.

16
A. Bandura, D. Ross, and S. Ross, "Imitation of Film-Mediated Aggressive Models," *Journal of Abnormal and Social Psychology* 66 (1963):3–11.

17
A. E. Siegel, "Mass Media and Violence: Effects on Children," *Stanford M.D.* 8 (1969): 11–14.

18
L. D. Eron, "Relationship of TV Viewing Habits and Aggressive Behavior in Children," *Journal of Abnormal and Social Psychology* 67 (1963):193–196.

19
S. Milgram and R. L. Shotland, *Television and Antisocial Behavior* (New York: Academic Press, 1973).

20
S. Feshback and R. D. Singer, *Television and Aggression* (San Francisco: Jossey-Bass, 1970).

21
S. Feshback, "Film Violence and Its Effect on Children: Some Comments on the Implication of Research for Public Policy," A.P.A. address, Washington, D.C., 1969, p. 5.

22
K. Lagerspetz, *Studies on the Aggressive Behavior of Mice* (Helsinki: Soumalainen Tiedeakatemia, 1964).

23
D. Rosenthal, *Genetic Theory and Abnormal Behavior* (New York: McGraw-Hill, 1970).

24
H. F. Harlow, J. L. McGaugh, and R. F. Thompson, *Psychology* (San Francisco: Albion, 1971), p. 114. Reprinted by permission of the publisher.

25
K. Dion, E. Bercheid, and E. Walster, "What Is Beautiful Is Good?" *J. of Personality and Social Psychology* 24 (1972):285–290.

26
E. Bercheid and E. Walster, "Beauty and the Best." *Psychology Today* 5, no. 10 (1972): 42–46, 74.

27
D. Cartwright and A. Zander, *Group Dynamics* (Evanston, Ill.: Row, Peterson, 1953), p. 536.

28
R. Cunningham, "Leadership and the Group," in *Group Dynamics and Education* (Washington, D.C., National Education Association, Division of Adult Education, 1948).

29
K. Lewin, R. Lippitt, and R. K. White, "Patterns of Aggressive Behavior in Experimentally Created Social Climates," *Journal of Social Psychology* 10 (1939):271–299.

30
G. C. Homans, *Social Behavior: Its Elementary Forms* (New York: Harcourt, Brace & World, 1961).

31
D. W. Johnson, *The Social Psychology of Education* (New York: Holt, Rinehart and Winston, 1970), p. 128.

32
E. R. Guthrie, *The Psychology of Human Conflict* (New York: Harper & Row, 1938).

33
R. C. Sprinthall, M. Lambert, and M. Sturm, "Anti-Semitism: Some Perceptual Correlates among Jews and Non-Jews," *Journal of Social Psychology* 84 (1971):57–63.

34
P. C. Lee and N. B. Gropper, "A Cultural Analysis of Sex Role in the School," *Journal of Teacher Education* 26, no. 4 (1975):335–339.

35
J. A. Davis, *Great Aspirations* (London: Aldine, 1964).

36
M. S. McLean, M. S. Gowan, and J. C. Gowan, "A Teacher Selection and Counseling Service," *Journal of Educational Research* 48 (1955):669–677.

37
Johnson, *The Social Psychology of Education,* p. 57.

38
R. P. Boyle, "The Effect of the High School on Students' Aspirations," *American Journal of Sociology* 71 (1965):628–639.

39
J. S. Coleman et al., *Equality of Educational Opportunity* (Washington, D.C.: U. S. Office of Health, Education, and Welfare, 1966).

40
R. G. Barker and P. V. Gump, *Big School, Small School: High School Size and Student Behavior* (Stanford, California: Stanford University Press, 1964).

41
R. R. Altman, "The Effect of Rank in Class and Size of High School on Academic Achievement," *Journal of Educational Research* 52 (1959):307–309.

SUGGESTIONS FOR FURTHER READING

Bandura, A. *Aggression: A Social Learning Analysis.* Englewood Cliffs, N.J.: Prentice-Hall, 1973.

Cartwright, D. O., and A. Zander. *Group Dynamics,* 3rd ed. New York: Harper & Row, 1968.

Freedman, J. L., J. M. Carlsmith, and D. O. Sears. *Social Psychology.* Englewood Cliffs, N.J.: Prentice-Hall, 1970.

Johnson, D. W. *The Social Psychology of Education.* New York: Holt, Rinehart and Winston, 1970.

Lindzey, Gardner, and Elliot Aronson. *Handbook of Social Psychology.* 2d ed. Reading, Mass.: Addison-Wesley, 1971.

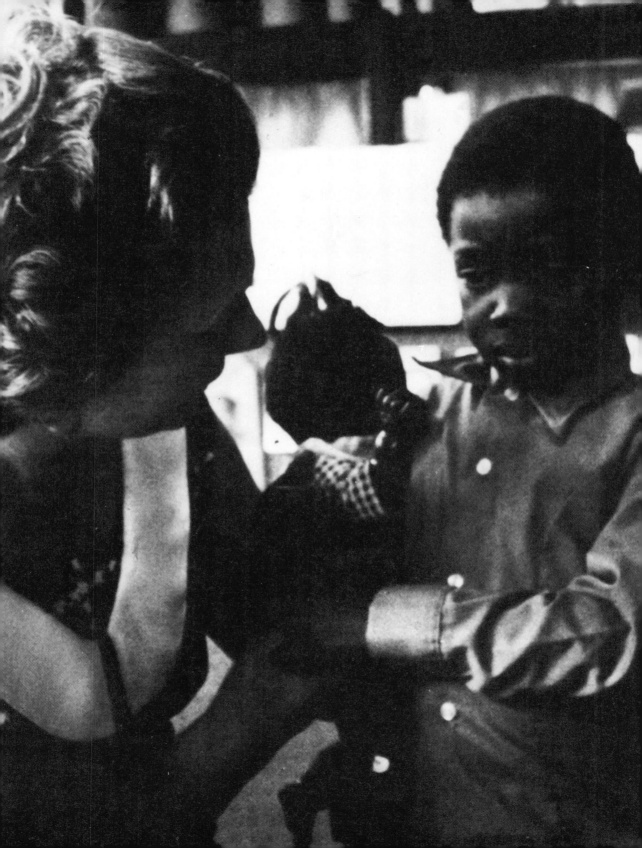

21

Affective education and mental health in the classroom

There has been growing concern in the past five years about the psychological impact of schooling on children. We feel, as we have already said, that it is time to question the assumption that schooling doesn't really harm children. Recent studies suggest that schooling actually inhibits and prevents growth. This chapter examines the way schools limit personal development and describes some of the new educational programs designed to reverse this negative trend.

THE HIDDEN AGENDA: HOW PUPILS PERCEIVE SCHOOL

We have already noted that there is often a great discrepancy between what teachers say about their roles and what they actually do in the classroom. We have called this phenomenon the hidden agenda, or the implicit curriculum. The danger of the hidden agenda is that it (the teacher's expectations, feelings, innuendos, and hidden messages) is as much a part of the students' education as the curriculum itself. Therefore, it seems logical to continue our examination of educational problems by looking at the impact of school from the pupils' point of view.

"Voices from the back of the classroom"

A recent three-year study of students' perceptions of the impact of school used extensive individual interviews, questionnaires, attitude and value indices, and some psychological projective techniques to get as close as possible to teenagers' actual experience of secondary school. One of the projective techniques used

Schooling: the pupils' view

involved showing students a series of photographs and asking them to make up a story describing what they saw in the pictures. Those pictures that showed students in class with a teacher produced stories that were almost always about achievement or homework and always expressed either very negative or very positive feelings about studying and learning. However, those pictures that showed students alone—whether in class, in the library, in study halls, or in laboratories—produced stories about social situations (cheating, arranging for dates, or planning nonacademic activities). It seems obvious from these studies that students do not admit the possibility that their interactions with other students might be an academic activity. Learning, in their view, is strictly a process managed by a teacher.

Learning to do as you are told

This is, of course, a very discouraging finding. After eleven or twelve years in school, students seem to "learn" that academic or intellectual activity apparently depends on the presence of a teacher. Self-directed learning, independent study, intellectual discussion with other students—all such desirable educational objectives are not perceived by the student. They see the teacher as the hub of intellectual activity in the classroom; without a teacher they will socialize, try to sabotage the school, in fact will do everything except what they are there to do.

This is an example of what we mean by the impact of schooling and the discrepancy between what students learn and the avowed educational objectives.[1]

ATTITUDES, VALUES, PERCEPTIONS, AND SOCIAL-CLASS DIFFERENCES

Class-linked educational values

In addition to the general view just described, the three-year study found two very different sets of attitudes toward learning and school. These different attitudes follow socioeconomic-class lines.

Some educational values are class-linked. Students from working-class schools see learning as quietly following orders.

Urban schools

Students from a working-class, or blue-collar (lower-middle-class) school district generally perceived school as a place where passivity and conformity are the order of the day. Learning means quietly following orders. The teacher is supposed to present facts and the students are supposed to accept the facts without question. The teacher has all the "right" answers, and no dialogue is expected between teacher and pupil, no exchange of ideas. When asked why they were in school, most if not all of the students said, "I have to stay in school to graduate, to get a good job." The boys felt that if they didn't graduate, their only future was a physically demanding job, "where you end up breaking your back." The girls thought that if they didn't graduate their only future was menial work.

The view from the working-class school is negative and depressing. If this education has any impact it is only to perpetuate certain conventional assumptions and stereotyped values. The major assumption is that memorization (or rote learning) is the same thing as thinking. The stereotyped values are those that promote obedience and conformity.

A theorist, Joe Grannis from Teachers College, has recently suggested that such working-class schools are, in fact, an accurate reflection of the larger working-class community.[2] He suggests that the schools socialize and educate children to take their places on the assembly lines, in the offices, and in the stores of the country. If performing routine work assignments, following orders, and never asking questions are the qualities these working environments require, then the working-class schools are educating their students for just those jobs. The study reported above indicated that the students themselves transmitted and accepted these values; they saw school as an acceptable and necessary waste of time.

Suburban schools

Suburban students' attitudes differed significantly from those of working-class students. The suburban school building, the teachers, and the setting were all dramatically different. Indirect lighting and carpeted floors, well-trained and competent teachers, green grass and well-groomed surroundings provided a sharp contrast to the battered buildings, the minimally trained teachers, and the tenement houses of the working-class district. You would expect these advantages, plus well-stocked libraries, low teacher-pupil ratios, and modular scheduling, to produce significantly different student attitudes. You might not expect the differences the study found, however.

The suburban students were significantly more negative toward schooling than the urban students. In spite of the apparent advantages in the suburban schools, the students found school to be boring, oppressive, filled with busy-work. Their major motives for studying (and these students did an average of two to three hours of homework each night) were almost totally extrinsic or functional: "You have to study, to get good grades, to go to college," was their frequent explanation. The pressure for academic achievement was enormous, yet the reasons for study were strictly vocational. In fact, the students were aware of this discrepancy: "I know we are supposed to say we want to go to a liberal arts college for general learning, but for me it's to take pre-law." We could just as appropriately substitute pre-medicine, pre-dentistry, pre-engineer-

Significantly, suburban students are more negative toward schooling than are urban students. In spite of the apparent advantages, they consider school boring, oppressive, and full of busy-work.

ing, pre-business administration—pre-anything! Little intrinsic interest in learning, ideas, or any kind of independent thinking was ever expressed.

In the suburban high school, then, the students seemed almost trapped between two contradictory forces. They disliked school, found little academic stimulation, perceived learning as vocational preparation and yet did not drop out. Instead, they worked and studied very hard to get good grades—"to get into a good college, to get a good job, to earn enough money, to buy a house in the suburbs and put my kids through the same thing," as one boy put it.

SILBERMAN: THE MINDLESS SCHOOL

Many separate studies have come up with results similar to those described above. Probably the most widely distributed is Charles Silberman's *Crisis in the Classroom*. Silberman wanted, initially, to study the problems of teacher training, but eventually expanded his focus to include the general effects of schooling. He found that it was meaningless to create a new model or a new system for training teachers and to then put these teachers back into the same old school system. It would be like teaching people to ride unicycles and then asking them to perform on tricycles. Thus what began as a small study of teacher training turned into a much more comprehensive study of schooling.[3]

Silberman concluded his study by questioning the basic purpose and structure of schooling. He found very little evidence that schools were educating children and teenagers in positive and psychologically healthy ways. Instead, he discovered a mindless institution characterized by passive learning, memorization, and conformity. While many so-called romantic critics in the 1950s and early 1960s had issued similar pronouncements (Paul Goodman in this country and A. S. Neill at Summerhill in England), the public generally dismissed such criticisms as too extreme. Silberman, on the other hand, could not be so easily ignored. His careful work has commanded respect for its searching examination of a difficult and complex problem, and he has provided a context in which we can acknowledge some of the basic problems of schooling. That, in itself, is a first step toward positive change.

School characterized by passive learning, memorization, and conformity

SCHOOLING AND PERSONAL GROWTH

The school curriculum, at least in the last ten to twenty years, has tended to become too narrow, too exclusively subject-matter, or content oriented. A series of major curriculum projects—the "new" math, "new" social studies, chemistry, and physics—have all tried to make the subject so interesting and exciting that students would be more than willing to cooperate. And the subject was made interesting by approaching it through its structure. Passive, resistant students were expected to be transformed into eager learners, clamoring to know more about the "new" math, or social studies, or science. Of course, no such transformation took place—the students were simply not interested. The new approach may have appealed to the graduate students and professors who constructed the curricula, but to the students it was the same old thing.

ARE SCHOOLS PRISONS?

The most startling suggestion recently has been that schools are more like prisons than educational institutions. Although this may be a slight exaggeration, a
case can be made. The formal and informal curricula compare rather easily to
the prison's. While both claim their objective is to educate for life outside the
walls (prisons call it rehabilitation), outcome studies indicate just the opposite.
Students leave school after twelve years with less intrinsic interest in learning,
lowered self-concepts, more hostility toward learning, and more prejudiced
thinking than when they entered.* Inmates leave prison better prepared for a
life of crime than to go "straight" (most ex-cons soon return to prison). Thus
the similar negative outcomes of total institutions such as schools and prisons
invite comparison.†

> The similarity of
> schools and prisons

> Control and "total"
> institutions

The parallel between schools and prisons is also apparent in their daily routines. Sociologists have noted the tendency of institutions to socialize/train/
brainwash their members to fit the system.[4] Regimentation and routine serve not
only to maintain order but also to mold and shape their members' behavior. It
is virtually impossible for a single individual (pupil, teacher, prisoner, or guard)
to remain independent for long. It is readily apparent, especially with young children, how schools wipe out individuality and rebuild the "self" into a school
pupil. The requisite pupil behaviors—"Sit quietly, wait your turn, raise your
hand, leave 1/2 inch margins on your papers, use the proper headings, copy the
assignments in order, . . ."—are too familiar to require comment.‡ We have already noted (Chapter 8) that young children have such a strong desire to please
adults that they are virtual sitting ducks, easily amenable to manipulation and
brainwashing.

Regulated activity performed in unison is another characteristic of total institutions. Members have little control over the choice of activities but are ex-

---

*
References to the negative effects of schooling can be found in J. S. Coleman, *The Ado-
lescent Society* (New York: Free Press, 1961); P. Minuchin et al., *The Psychological Im-
pact of School Experience* (New York: Basic Books, 1969); J. R. Seeley et al., *Crestwood
Heights* (New York: Basic Books, 1956); R. Ojemann, "Incorporating Psychological Con-
cepts in the School Curriculum," *Journal of School Psychology* 5, no. 3 (1967):195–204;
C. Nordstrom, E. Friedenberg, and H. Gold, *Society's Children* (New York: Random
House, 1967); W. Cody Wilson, "The Development of Ethnic Attitudes in Adolescence,"
Child Development, March 1963, p. 34.

†
A "total" institution is one to which members have not chosen to belong, but have been
sent or admitted.

‡
An excellent example of such routines can be found in P. Jackson, *Life in Classrooms*
(New York: Holt, Rinehart and Winston, 1968). Jackson shows how much teacher activity
involves traffic management, control, and regimentation at the expense of teaching and
learning. A recent empirical investigation has confirmed Jackson's findings on the low
amount of actual teaching time in classes. See P. V. Gump, "Education as an Environmental Enterprise," in R. A. Weinberg and F. H. Wood, *Observation* (Minneapolis, Minnesota: Leadership Training Institute, College of Education, University of Minnesota, 1975),
pp. 109–121.

pected to move through them in a uniform sequence. It is ironic that schools ignore individual differences in pupils. It is tragic in prisons.

Although we don't wish to belabor this comparison, it is important to realize that we often forget to consider the effect these institutional structures produce, especially when educational reform is considered. If the present structure of school, the organization of classroom activity and the curriculum routines, is having a negative effect on education, it is the structure that should be the target for reform. A recent review of proposals for reform in secondary education comes to a series of conclusions that all suggest we need to examine most closely the structure of schooling.[5] Otherwise, we will miss the mark; we will chase the shadow instead of the fox, as Piaget might say.

THE SCHOOLS: TO SOCIALIZE OR TO EDUCATE?

Part of the problem with our schools is that the system of socialization has apparently interfered with the educational process. Teachers felt that socializing children, teaching them to become pupils, was a prerequisite for learning. Children had to learn to sit still and pay attention (or "banish every other object from their minds," as William James would say) before they would be ready to learn. But we now know that at least some of these socialization/control routines misfire. Instead of helping, such procedures may deter learning. In remaking or rebuilding children the school too frequently closes out creativity, inhibits individuality, and has a negative effect on personal competence.

Socialization as negative education

We have been too eager to accept the dictum that it's easier to change the child than the institution.* Outcome studies indicate that, in fact, it is easier, as long as we ignore what it does to the child.

It is remarkably easy after reviewing these negative studies to seek a single culprit and to heap the blame on any convenient target. In fact, it is quite popular to find such a scapegoat in the teacher, the principal, the community, the curriculum materials, the colleges of education, the parents, etc. Soon everyone involved in education may be pointing their collective fingers at each other. There is obviously no single agent; it probably is more accurate to say that too many in the educational enterprise have been working for too long with too many erroneous assumptions. If we derive practice from an inadequate set of assumptions, then no matter how hard we work, how earnestly we try, and how committed we are as educators, we cannot succeed.

SCHOOLING: THE EFFECTS OF COMPETITION

A series of recent studies has also demonstrated the negative impact of individualistic competition on classroom learning atmospheres, self-concepts, and academic achievement. Unfortunately, too often the hidden agenda of a classroom conveys the message to pupils that only a few will succeed academically, and

---

*An example of this can be found in D. McClelland et al., *Talent and Society* (Princeton, N.J.: Van Nostrand, 1958).

frequently pupils view schooling as essentially a negatively competitive experience. The extensive research in social psychology, some 300 studies at last count, demonstrates the harmful effects of these climates. Yet for some reason schools persist in promoting such atmospheres, usually unwittingly. While it has been shown that competitive teaching may be superior to cooperative when the task is a simple rote-like drill, as the learning tasks become more complex, competitive classroom atmospheres negatively affect learning achievement and self-concepts. Such climates act to defeat all of the higher and more-complex levels of human functioning in developmental terms.[6]

THE NEED FOR AFFECTIVE EDUCATION

Another assumption we have too easily accepted is that healthy psychological growth occurs as a result of the standard curriculum. If we teach pupils about the human condition through literature, the arts, and social studies, healthy functioning human beings will magically result. The school's standard curriculum was justified as a training ground for humanism and citizenship. However, if we look at the attempts to actually "grow" healthy future citizens through the standard curriculum, we see the rhetoric but little reality.

A taxonomy for affective education

After producing their framework for the assessment of objectives, Benjamin Bloom and his associates tried to create a parallel system for personal growth, or as it is sometimes called, affective/emotional education. It would be overly simplistic to separate cognitive knowledge and affective learning; people do not fall into two neat categories, "thinkers" and "feelers." In fact the two areas interact constantly. It is clear that Bloom and his associates found the distinction between cognition and feelings continually troublesome.[7] More importantly, they found it difficult to come up with any examples of personal, psychological, or affective educational programs. They found instead that school after school and college after college claimed to educate pupils as persons, or as citizens, or as autonomous, liberally educated, and mature adults. They could find no evidence to support these claims. In fact, the authors concluded that there was, in all the programs they examined in the 1950s and 1960s, a "constant erosion of affective objectives." The standard curricula of those eras focused more and more on the transmission of knowledge about a formal discipline.

The difficulties of classifying affective-education objectives

In less-weighty terms, this meant that the interdisciplinary, cross-disciplinary, contract-learning, project method, and team teaching procedures of that time—procedures that were thought to enhance personal education—were being replaced by a subject-matter focus. Educators apparently still hoped that a close look at *Macbeth*, or *The Iliad*, or *Death of a Salesman*, or *The Red Badge of Courage* would promote healthy psychological and personal growth. Unfortunately, this is something like teaching children to become "cultured" by taking them to the symphony, opera, ballet, or to a museum. We may feel we have done our duty for civilization, but such learning experiences may remain well beyond the reach of most pupils.

The standard curriculum: safe but innocuous

Schooling as playing
it too safe

Bloom and his associates correctly diagnosed the reason affective education had failed. Educators have been confused for a long time on the question of objectives. Schools, teachers, and, increasingly, communities have been content to play it safe and to say their objectives are to teach skills (the three R's) whose by-products would be good citizenship, laudable values, good decision making, and clean thinking. It was unthinkable to approach personal development directly. "We must preserve pupil privacy. . . ." "The integrity of each student must be respected. . . ." Thus, the paradox. The goal of schooling was to produce good citizens, on the one hand, but the programs to accomplish those goals were not to be personal or "emotional," on the other hand. The school was supposed to promote growth, but through an antiseptic curriculum, guaranteed safe. We now realize that the overemphasis on safety has backfired. Because of their neglect and abdication of responsibility, the schools have done more harm than good: their influence, the psychological education they give, is negative. The problems of personal education will simply not go away. They are admittedly "sticky," but that's no reason to turn our backs and pretend they do not exist.

A CURRICULUM FOR PERSONAL GROWTH

The separation of psy-
chological services
from classroom in-
struction

Given the scope and complexity of the problem, some promising attempts to come to grips with educating for personal development have recently occurred. These new attempts are unique in that they aim at directly modifying what we have called the standard curriculum.* Previous attempts to humanize the school or to provide special psychological help to children through individual counseling have not been successful. Most schoolchildren remain untouched by the special guidance and psychology services. Guidance has too often been a minor administrative service—the team of clinically trained psychology personnel never resolved the dilemma inherent in being a "little white clinic" in "a little red school."[8] The metaphor suggests that psychological services became clinical medical treatment and remained outside of the classroom door. As a result, educators now realize that, if significant change is to take place, the structural curriculum must be modified, changed, and revitalized. So, when we speak of new forms and new instructional techniques for psychological growth, we are talking about curriculum development and teacher training, not the creation or addition of a few more special services.

---

*
In this volume we will not discuss all the issues involved with psychological counseling in schools. There have been two major attempts in the last twenty years to establish special psychological services in school to help children grow and develop: the guidance-counselor movement and the school psychological specialist. In neither case did these efforts directly affect the mainstream of the school or its curriculum. The school counselors attending to 300 or 400 or 500 pupil case-loads were faced with an impossible task at the outset. The school psychologist, on the other hand, generally worked with a very few and very special cases.

Humans have a natural drive to learn to function competently. James Coleman's study underscored the significant relationship between personal competence and school performance.

ASSUMPTIONS ABOUT PERSONAL GROWTH

We noted earlier that our assumptions about the nature of children and adolescents vitally affect any scheme for educational intervention. Nowhere is this more important than in programs for personal or affective education. Obviously, the way we understand the process of development will govern our choice of educational experiences. If we believed, as we have said many people do, that "the child is only a midget-sized adult," our teaching would reward only adultlike behavior and would punish childlike activities. We would try to remake our children into little ladies and gentlemen. Recall that this assumption was so common in the 18th and 19th centuries that painters who were in full command of their technique persisted in painting children with faces that looked like old men and women. There may be no clearer example of the way our assumptions affect what we actually see—these artists reorganized their perception of children to fit the assumption that children are miniature grownups. Thus, in spite of growing evidence, it has been difficult for adults, including adult psychologists, to revise assumptions and to change their mind-set concerning personal growth during childhood and adolescence.

One crucial assumption for affective education is the theory of competence motivation developed by Robert White at Harvard almost twenty-five years ago (see p. 203). We have discussed the importance of this concept to an understanding of the process of growth. In the area of personal/psychological or af-

Competence, motivation, and personal growth

fective education, the concept is even more significant. White has shown that humans have an almost inborn drive to learn to function competently. This drive is further proof that we are neither inert, empty organisms, nor bundles of reactions, responding only when provoked. Instead, we feel compelled to develop personal competence, to be in control of our environment. In everyday language, it's like being in charge of yourself rather than being someone else's robot.

Personal competence takes many different forms at different life stages. College students making major life decisions are exercising a different form of personal competence than the two-year-olds who push mommy away and work laboriously to tie their own shoes. White maintains that the extent and degree of adult competence is determined largely by early experiences at home and in school which may either promote or deter such growth.

The relationship between personal competence and school performance was recently demonstrated as part of a massive study directed by James Coleman, already noted in Chapter 15. Coleman found that pupils who felt they were in control of their own fate (self-directed competence) were successful in school. An even more-significant finding was that the feeling of personal efficacy was more important to achievement than any of the other factors in the study, including social-class differences, race, pupil-teacher ratios, the number of books in the school library, and the educational background of the teachers.

Coleman's fate control

> *Despite the very large achievement differences between whites and Negroes at the 9th and 12th grades, those Negroes who gave responses indicating a sense of control of their own fate achieved higher on the tests than those whites who gave the opposite responses. This attitude was more highly related to achievement than any other factor in the student's background or school.*[9]

PERSONAL EFFICACY: CULTURE BOUND?

Thus we can say that a sense of competency is not necessarily limited by social and cultural differences. Each pupil has a need to function, to master, and to gain control of the environment. One of the main reasons few pupils manifest self-direction and independence in learning and personal maturity may simply be that the home and school environments do not actively teach for competence. Eli Bower, a leader in the field of mental health, maintains that adults (teachers, psychologists, and even psychiatrists) have failed to recognize this basic need to function effectively. He has suggested that the basic "business" of a society and its institutions is to foster the conditions that will produce competent adults out of growing children. During the child's formative years the school should be the primary agent for promoting competence. As a result, Bower urges the schools to broaden their educational focus to include personal and social competence as well as intellectual mastery. As he puts it, "The object of learning or living is to make further learning and living more possible."[10]

Schooling for personal independence

This concept becomes even more important when we realize the long-term implications for growth and development. The treatment of emotional disturbances in childhood (child psychotherapy, child analysis) has recently been shown to have little or no effect on the emotional adjustments called for later in life. Childhood predictors of adult mental health were not derived from clinical treatment of emotional problems. Instead, "the best predictors of the absence of mental illness and maladjustment are the *presence* of various forms of *competence* and ego maturity rather than the absence of problems and symptoms as such."[11] Thus, instead of treating children and adolescents for emotional problems, it is strongly suggested that the schools develop educational programs that would promote the development of personal competence and efficacy.

There is an old expression about an ounce of prevention being worth a pound of cure. Certainly, the prevention of mental and emotional maladjustment would be far more effective than treatment after the fact. Building a sense of personal competence and ego maturity should become a basic objective of what we have called affective education. While studies have shown the importance of personal efficacy to school performance and indeed to the healthy functioning of adults, we must remember that psychological maturity and ego strength do not unfold automatically. We have already emphasized that the development of intelligence depends on an active and responsive environment. The same abundant, facilitating interactions that promote cognitive/intellectual growth are also required for personal mastery. We cannot simply hope that children and teenagers will develop in psychologically healthy directions, to higher levels of personal competence and moral maturity. Deliberate educational experiences are essential.

The need for preventive programs

Psychological growth and cognitive development: not really separate

NEW DIRECTIONS: SCHOOL PROGRAMS AND PERSONAL DEVELOPMENT

As a result of the growing concern over these issues of personal development, some educators have recently devised appropriate new teaching and learning programs. There is a genuine need for new programs to reverse the current effect of schooling; "business as usual" will simply not do. If the standard curriculum does not positively encourage personal/ethical development, then we need to revise the standard curriculum and possibly enlarge or alter the nature of learning experiences. Programs that are responsive to students' psychological needs—most notable for personal competence—could form the framework for a new approach to curriculum activities.

The need for achievement: McClelland and Alschuler

Professors David McClelland and Alan Alschuler have been experimenting for the past four or five years on a system for the deliberate teaching of psychological control to teenagers. Their program is a specially designed sequence of educational interactions aimed at helping teenagers develop greater control over themselves and their environment.

A unique set of classroom simulations allow students to experience the consequences of their own decision making. Problem-solving and personal decision-making activities help students learn the extent to which they are in control of

Table 21.1 Ring toss payoff table.

Distance from peg	Points
Less than 5 feet	10
5 feet	30
6 feet	50
7 feet	65
8 feet	85
9 feet	110
10 feet	150
11 feet	300
12 feet	500
13 feet	1000

their environment. The emphasis is on showing them how they presently make decisions and suggesting new ways to approach problems that will place them in more-effective control of themselves and their environment. There is an obvious and direct connection between these learning activities and the objective of personal competence.

One of the McClelland/Alschuler techniques makes use of a ring toss game. The players may vary their distance from the peg on the floor. The scoring system is set so that a successful toss from a great distance is worth many points, whereas a toss from just a few feet away is worth only a few points (see Table 21.1).

Obviously, the amount of risk and the individual skill of the players determine who the successful scorers are. A sure route to score would be to stand less than five feet away (perhaps even directly over the peg) and place the ring on the peg for ten points each time. A riskier approach, but one that could yield greater rewards, would be to stand thirteen feet away and "go for broke" every time. The game is thus a means of simulating real-life decision making and risk taking. "But life is not a ring toss game," you might object at this point. The teacher using this approach must have the skills to help students see the relationships between the way they play the game and the way they approach more important decisions in life. It may surprise you to know that there are often very striking relationships between behavior in such a game and behavior in other situations. McClelland and Alschuler have shown that those who play it excessively safe in the game tend to approach all problem solving the same way. The same is true for the person who always plays the long shots.

Based on a long series of studies, McClelland and Alschuler have concluded that successful decision makers share certain characteristics: they compete with a standard of excellence in mind; they take moderate risks; and they make good use of concrete feedback. These three characteristics form what the authors term the "achievement syndrome." People who excel in a variety of fields demonstrate these motivational characteristics. The most-interesting aspect of McClelland's and Alschuler's work, however, is not that their research has uncovered a group of psychological traits that lead to general achievement, but that a system of intervention has evolved from their research. In other words, they can teach

Simulating risk-taking

The McClelland-Alschuler ring toss game. The most interesting aspect of their work is the system of intervention which evolved. In short, they can teach pupils to become successful achievers.

pupils (or for that matter, business executives, teachers, salespersons, or anyone at all) to become successful achievers. They can shape motivational patterns through a series of games and produce the achievement syndrome. These techniques can put students more in control of their environment by helping them abandon excessive caution or excessive risk taking. These experiences help children learn that success is not just a matter of "fate," but is well within their own reach.[12]

Affective education: Newberg and Borton

A somewhat different approach—one that uses highly imaginative role playing and improvisational drama techniques—is currently under development. Norman Newberg and Terry Borton, working on the Philadelphia Project on Affective Education, have tried out a wide assortment of techniques aimed at active student involvement. A series of deliberately novel situations teach pupils more about themselves as human beings—how they perceive the world; how they feel and react in general; how they "experience" their present life situation. The

Experiences for personal growth

approach is heavily experiential (based on direct experience), nonverbal in many instances, and nonacademic. For example, the authors will have pupils walk blindfolded around a classroom and down the school halls with a nonblindfolded student "guide." This gives both students the opportunity to feel and sense the world from a substantially new perspective. The way the "blind" students react to this novel experience of helplessness and dependency can be used as a starting point for examining certain affective issues. Likewise, the way the student "guides" react to helping someone else also raises important affective issues: Were they overly protective and smothering? Harsh and mechanical? So fearful that their "blind" friend became anxious? These are only a few of the human-relationship questions that such an experience poses.

One of Newberg's and Borton's improvisations is called "mirroring." Students are paired up and one member of each pair is designated leader; the other is told to mirror every movement the leader makes. The authors indicate that a shy child learning to lead a classmate in such an exercise often develops greater self-confidence. Similar effects have been noted in role-playing situations.

The Newberg-Borton system has two main objectives: to help students learn positive aspects about themselves as human beings while in their regular classrooms and to train (or retrain) regular classroom teachers to use the curriculum units in affective education. The published results of the study indicate that both objectives are being reached. Teachers can learn to use a wide variety of affective learning techniques.

Teaching techniques and classroom atmosphere.   One notable finding that came out of the project is that when teachers use these techniques, the classroom atmosphere shifts from a negative learning environment to a positive one (see Tables 21.2 and 21.3). These techniques apparently modify the hidden agenda, or the implicit curriculum. The classroom atmosphere invited student participation, initiative, and positive interpersonal relations.

The effects on classroom atmosphere

The Newberg-Bolton learning tasks were not unilaterally imposed on the pupils. The teachers became less authoritarian and more democratic in classroom management.

Table 21.2 Teaching techniques employed by teachers (1970–1971 comments from pupil interviews).

Affective-education classes	Regular classes
Discussions	Tests
Readings	Discussion
Games	Reading
Field trips	Writing
Writing	Reviewing test
Role-playing	Chapters
Fantasy	Answering teachers' questions

Table 21.3 Classroom climate survey comments.

Affective classes	Regular classes
Students can challenge the teachers opinion ($\chi^2 = 45.4$)	Teacher does a lot of talking ($\chi^2 = 30.6$)
Teacher seems to understand the students —work well together ($\chi^2 = 45.3$)	Teacher is too strict ($\chi^2 = 38.6$)
People in class care about one another ($\chi^2 = 33.3$)	It's the student against the teacher ($\chi^2 = 22.5$)
Students learn from one another ($\chi^2 = 67.2$)	Kids cut class ($\chi^2 = 27.2$)

(The chi square statistics are all reported with $p < .005$, so that the differences noted could occur by chance only 5 times in 1000.)

Students' attitudes and self-concepts. The project also assessed the students' self-concepts. If they perceived the affective-education classes as more open, livelier, more concerned with their personal growth, and demanding greater initiative, then what was the effect on their self-concepts? Does affective experience in the classroom produce individual affective growth? Questionnaires, interviews, classroom-attendance patterns, and referrals for student discipline all indicate that students in the affective classes did experience a shift to more-positive attitudes about themselves. They had greater feelings of self-control and self-direction, a more-positive perception of their teachers, fewer class absences (50 percent fewer in one school), and they were seldom referred for serious discipline problems (only one of eighty-eight pupils in affective classes was referred).

Increasing positive attitudes

Students in the affective classes showed gains in the areas of personal and interpersonal competence and self-understanding, and in problem-solving skills (see Table 21.4). Pupils in regular classes showed gains in the more-traditional learning areas of literature and language skills. Thus, the affective-education

Increasing self-understanding

Table 21.4 Reported types of learning.

Affective classes	Regular classes
Problem-solving skills ($\chi^2 = 24.3$)	Appreciation of literature ($\chi^2 = 7.5$)
Self-understanding skills ($\chi^2 = 29.8$)	Language skills ($\chi^2 = 41.4$)
Personal competence ($\chi^2 = 25.5$)	
Interpersonal competence ($\chi^2 = 78.6$)	

classes seem to be reaching objectives similar to Eli Bower's, namely, the promotion of personal competence and ego maturity.

The project investigated one further question: Did participation in the affective education have an effect on academic achievement or reading skills? If such techniques made pupils "feel better" or more in control of their own lives and yet reduced their academic performance or acquisition of skills, the benefits would be questionable. The results, presented in Table 21.5, indicate that there was no difference in achievement test scores or in reading comprehension.* In the words of the project evaluator:

> It attests to the value of the affective program that affective students learn as much as controls in reading comprehension and history knowledge and also gain more positive attitudes towards themselves and teachers and a knowledge and use of various personal and interpersonal processes.[13]

Although it is far too early to assume that this evidence proves that affective education works, we can say that the program results are very promising. The Newberg-Borton program for affective education is one new system of instruction that seems to achieve personal-growth objectives and does not hinder the more-traditional academic achievement learning.

Experience-based learning: Sprinthall-Mosher

In addition to the McClelland-Alschuler and Newberg-Borton projects, a third approach is currently being developed by one of the authors of this book and a group of colleagues. The project, which was begun at Harvard and is continuing at the University of Minnesota and Boston University, seeks to promote healthy personal growth as part of the regular learning activity of secondary-school classrooms. Like the other two projects, the objective is to design curriculum experiences that will have direct psychological impact on all pupils. In other words, all three projects seek to reverse the negative effects of schooling by revising the content and the experience of the classroom.

---

*

George Brown's *Human Teaching for Human Learning* (New York: Viking, 1971) indicates that academic achievement improves in affective-education classes when compared to regular classes.

Table 21.5 Academic achievement and reading comprehension.

Affective classes (N = 325)	Regular classes (N = 325)
Test:	American History Knowledge Survey
	Comprehensive Test of Basic Skills
Results:	No difference between pretest and posttest achievement scores or on reading-comprehension test scores.

Sprinthall, Mosher, and colleagues use educational techniques different from the other projects. Rather than approximate real experience through role playing or games, the Sprinthall-Mosher approach incorporates direct experience into the learning situation: students learn first by doing and then by examining the experience in terms of their self-concepts.

Students in adult roles. High-school students in the project are enrolled in psychology classes. However, rather than learning about psychology indirectly, they directly assume certain adult roles that allow them to experience firsthand some of the areas psychology touches on. They can elect one of several courses, including cross-age teaching, counseling peers, or nursery-school work. Each course involves the teenage pupils in the appropriate adult role of teacher, counselor, or nursery-school worker. They are not volunteers or aides but actually assume some major responsibility for educating others. In fact, the key element in this approach is the direct experience of responsibility. As we have already stressed, a major problem of most educational programs is the passivity the standard curriculum imposes on pupils, even though we now realize that it is better to learn by active involvement.

> Deliberate psychological education
>
> Real experience for personal learning

The Sprinthall-Mosher project is based on the idea of active student involvement. It allows pupils to put psychology into action, in that they learn how to teach other pupils, counsel other pupils, or apply principles of child development in a nursery-school setting. To help students also examine the meaning of their new experiences, each course includes a seminar. The process and the content of the course are not artificially separated but are allowed to reinforce one another. For example, in the cross-age teaching class teenage "teachers" learn how elementary-age children grow and develop through classroom observation, readings, and discussions. They also learn much about themselves, about the way they confront the task of managing instruction—e.g., Are they excessively authoritarian, punitive, wishy-washy, inconsistent, confused, or ambiguous?

> Active involvement

The old saying "experience is a good teacher" summarizes this experimental curriculum in psychological education. If we have to put into practice what we learn and if we are held responsible for such learning, then our psychological maturation may naturally increase. When pilots first started flying after World War I, there were many incidents of parachutes failing to open. The packers were not always careful to follow the complicated and exacting directions. Instead of setting up more formal schooling in parachute packing a remarkably more-effective solution was developed. The pilots themselves were taught how

Teenagers can assume adult roles and responsibility for educating others and, in the process, learn much about themselves.

Responsibility a key element

to pack their own chutes. The problems of classroom inattention, lack of motivation, lack of interest, in fact all the usual difficulties with classroom learning, were solved. By joining learning with responsibility, the passive "pupil" role was eliminated.

EFFECTS OF PSYCHOLOGICAL EDUCATION

Learning skills

Learning psychology by doing psychology

Since the Sprinthall-Mosher program of psychological education involved two outcomes, the results were divided into separate categories. At one level the students were expected to learn particular adult skills such as elementary-school teaching, high-school counseling, or early-childhood teaching. At the skill level the question was simple: Can teenagers learn the skills that are usually taught only to upper-division undergraduate or graduate students? The evaluations indicated that the high-school student in each of the three classes did learn the skills. For example, in the seminar and practicum in peer counseling, the pupils learned to perform counseling responses effectively. In fact, their ratings on dimensions of effective communication (accurate empathy, genuineness, positive regard) at the end of one semester were higher than scores achieved by graduate students. In the classes in cross-age and nursery-school teaching similar results developed. The high-school students learned classroom-management procedures as well as how to respond effectively to young children in a variety of trying experiences. For example, they learned how to rechannel nursery-school fighting and block throwing into more constructive areas and to provide warmth and security in moments of stress. Thus, there can be no doubt that teenagers can learn to perform significant adult roles. The teenagers in the project showed that in addition to benefitting personally from these experiences, they were also an important educational resource.

Teenagers can set aside their well-known preoccupation with themselves and become an effective agent for others. In this area the most encouraging results emerged.[14]

Personal growth

The project stressed the importance of helping teenagers assess their experiences in adult roles. Without this opportunity, they might miss the point of the experience itself. This is something we have stressed throughout this text. Our innermost needs, values, and interests can be brought to the surface only by examining our performance in action. So, too, with the teenagers in the seminar.

Although the classes in psychological education all had somewhat different content (teaching, counseling, and nursery-school work), all had similar effects on the teenage participants. A series of measures of personal and psychological growth and change was used to rate the experimental and the control groups. The pupils in the psychological-education curriculum (the experimental group) were rated at higher levels of psychological maturity than comparable pupils in regular classes (the control groups). The experimental pupils were less stereotyped in their thinking after the experience; that is, they did not see complicated situations in simple black and white terms. The experimental classes were also rated higher on measured levels of moral maturity than the control classes (the Kohlberg scales were used). Finally, based on participant observation and pretest and posttest interviews, the pupils themselves indicated that they felt more mature, more at ease with adults, better able to communicate, and more self-confident than they had felt prior to the program.

> The impact of adult roles

At present, seven specific studies have employed the Deliberate Psychological Education model with positive results on measures of psychological maturity.[15] Even though the content varied from class to class, the process was similar. In a child-development class, for example, the readings would focus on information about the nature of children between three and five years; in a course in counseling, the readings and films would examine theories of counseling and communication; and in a cross-age teaching class, the readings and films would feature theories of teaching. In spite of the differences in academic content, however, all the classes involved *applying* the ideas and principles gleaned from the readings. Also, all the courses involved the careful reexamination of these attempts at application. This is an important point, for it probably accounted in large part for the success of the program. A close inspection of the many so-called "action learning" projects in the country would probably reveal that very little attempt is made to help the pupils really learn the skills, read systematically on the topic, carefully try out the skills, and then reanalyze the experience. The DPE program strives to achieve a careful balance between action and reflection.

Experiential learning plus intellectual analysis on a regular basis are the two key factors in the learning-by-doing approach. It is not sufficient simply to send pupils out of the school building so they can "get" experience, nor is it sufficient to keep them in class as preparation. Educational programs have tended to become caught in this dichotomy—namely, that learning should be exclusively experiential (soft, warm, subjective, humanistic) *or* that it should be intellectual (hard, cold, objective, scientific).

Perhaps the best way of reminding you that neither approach by itself is sufficient is to consider Ogden Nash's comment on the futility of learning by experience. In the last few lines of his "Experience To Let" he notes:

> *Life's little suckers chirp like crickets*
> *While spending their all on losing tickets*
> *People whose instinct instructs them naught*
> *But must by experience be taught*
> *Will never learn by suffering once,*
> *But ever and ever play the dunce*
> *Experience, Wise men do not need it!*
> *Experience, Idiots do not heed it;*
> *I'd trade my lake of experience*
> *for just one drop of common sense.*[16]

William James, on the other hand, has also noted the futility of memorizing ideas without reference to experience or comprehension with his memorable recollection of the classroom in science, all students repeating in robotlike fashion, "The center of the earth is in the condition of igneous fusion."

The promising findings of the Sprinthall-Mosher program in psychological education suggest that an experience in learning under conditions of responsibility produce change and growth. If we remember that so much of a teenager's life in school and at home is passive, and includes almost no chance for initiative, direction, and control; if we also remember that teenagers are expected to stay in school and off the job market for longer and longer periods; and, finally, if we take note of the fact that the time lag between adolescence and adulthood has been lengthened to inordinate proportions, we can perhaps begin to understand the apathy and boredom of teenagers. This apathy is only a hallmark of the marginal status of adolescence as a stage between childhood and adulthood. The psychological-education curriculum seeks to reverse this very process; instead of delaying adult responsibility, the program encourages active participation in adult roles. The need to do and to examine the doing apparently combine to broaden the teenager's experience. The teenager is less egocentric or self-centered as a result, and maturity seems to increase.

Recently, other research projects have indicated similar outcomes to those reported in the Deliberate Psychological Education Program. Dr. Barbara Varenhorst working in the Palo Alto School system has developed and assessed a peer counseling program with high-school teenagers. Teenagers learn and employ counseling techniques with younger high-school and junior-high pupils. The results are positive and impressive.[17]

"Exploring Childhood," a curriculum project of the Educational Development Corporation, incorporates both action and learning and examination as a means of promoting cognitive and personal growth by teenagers. The preliminary findings from that project are encouraging and represent further confirmation of the same general principles.[18]

Finally, the National Commission on Resources for Youth under the unusually dynamic leadership of Judge Mary Conway Kohler has been developing a series of cross-age and peer teaching programs. In *Children Teach Children,* Kohler and her colleagues show that the children who are tutored by teenage tutors do improve in reading skills and self-concept. The greatest gains, however, are registered by the teenage tutors themselves. Their reading scores improved the most, as did their sense of personal competence. A dramatic illustration of such impacts is the film, "Time to Share," available from the Commission.[19]

THE FUTURE OF AFFECTIVE EDUCATION

There has been increasing evidence that the schools are not doing their job: not only are they apparently failing to produce academic competence, they also seem to have negative psychological impacts on pupils. One result has been the recent shift in curricula focus toward affective education or courses in deliberate psychological education. In these courses, the student's personal development becomes the primary educational objective rather than a hoped-for by-product, as in the traditional curriculum. These new programs have also emphasized classroom experiences that create personal involvement and raise issues of personal effectiveness. Students then have the opportunity to examine the meaning and the personal impact of those experiences. However, since all these programs are relatively new, it would be premature to draw definitive conclusions. We hope that the tentative results will prompt further development and experimentation with new methods that breathe new life into the day-to-day school experience.

Summary

Recent studies have shown that the impact of schooling on the pupils is often negative. The longer pupils remain in schools, the greater the negative effects. A major three-year study indicated that schools were teaching social-class-specific values. In suburban schools, pupil motivation was extrinsic and materialistic; in working-class schools, pupils were learning "to follow orders."

The need for general curriculum reform to promote healthy psychological growth as well as intellectual development is outlined, based on Eli Bower's concept of ego competence as an objective of schooling. One of the major reasons few pupils manifest self-direction in learning may simply be that the home and school environments do not actively teach for competence.

The Coleman study indicated that key ingredients for success in school include a strong sense of self-direction, a low concern for "fate" control, and a feeling of personal effectiveness or efficacy.

A series of new affective-education programs for schools are promising trends in school reform. The McClelland-Alschuler approach involves procedures designed to teach pupils how to take moderate risks, use feedback, and assess their own progress on a standard of excellence. The Borton-Newberg technique employs wholistic—or "gestalt"—learning: imaginative role plays, drama, and high levels of personal experiencing as a means of stimulating personal growth. The Sprinthall-Mosher procedure involves action learning, "real world" application of psychological principles, and careful systematic reflection on the meaning of such experience as a plan for deliberate psychological education.

Assessments of all three procedures indicate modest but consistently positive outcomes in improving the psychological maturity of pupils. Other new programs in cross-age and peer teaching and cross-age and peer counseling have achieved similarly positive outcomes.

In summation, the traditional curriculum of schools can be expanded to include programs that promote healthy psychological growth as a deliberate instructional goal.

REFERENCES

1
N. A. Sprinthall and R. L. Mosher, "Voices from the Back of the Classroom," *Journal of Teacher Education* 197, no. 22:166–175. Also see *Studies of Adolescents in the Secondary School,* Report #6, Center for Research and Development on Educational Differences, Harvard Graduate School of Education, Cambridge, Mass., 1969.

2
J. Grannis, "The School as a Model of Society," *Harvard Graduate School of Education Bulletin* 12, no. 2 (1967):15–27.

3
C. Silberman, *Crisis in the Classroom* (New York: Random House, 1970).

4
J. Henry, "American Schoolrooms; Learning the Nightmare," Columbia University Forum, 1963, 24–30; E. Goffman, *Asylums* (New York: Doubleday Anchor, 1961); E. G. Friedenberg, *The Vanishing Adolescent* (Boston: Beacon Press, 1959).

5
R. E. Bruce et al., "A review of Recent Proposals for Reform in Secondary Education," *Educational Forum* 40, no. 2 (1976):145–156.

6
These studies are all summarized in D. W. Johnson and R. T. Johnson, *Learning Together and Alone* (Englewood Cliffs, New Jersey: Prentice-Hall, 1975).

7
D. Krathwohl, B. Bloom, and D. Masia, *Handbook II: The Affective Domain* (New York: McKay, 1964).

8
M. A. White, "Little Red Schoolhouse and Little White Clinic," *Teachers College Record* 67 (1965):188–200.

9
J. S. Coleman et al., *Equality of Educational Opportunity* (Washington, D.C.: U.S. Department of Health, Education, and Welfare, 1966).

10
E. M. Bower, "Primary Prevention in a School Setting," in G. Caplan, ed., *Prevention of Mental Disorders in Children* (New York: Basic Books, 1961).

11
L. Kohlberg, J. LaCrosse, and D. Ricks, "The Predictability of Adult Mental Health from Childhood Behavior," in B. Wolman, ed., *Handbook of Child Psychopathology* (New York: McGraw-Hill, 1970).

12
See D. C. McClelland, "Toward a Theory of Motive Acquisition," *American Psychologist* 20, no. 2 (1965):321–333; and A. S. Alschuler et al., *Teaching Achievement Motivation* (Middletown, Conn.: Education Ventures, 1970).

13
W. Gollub, *Affective Educational Development Program Research Report* (Philadelphia: Philadelphia School District, 1971).

14
R. L. Mosher and N. A. Sprinthall, "Deliberate Psychological Education," *The Counseling Psychologist* 2, no. 4 (1971):3–82. (Box 1116, Washington University, St. Louis, Missouri 63130).

15
N. A. Sprinthall, "Moral and Psychological Development: A curriculum for Secondary Schools, in T. J. Hennessey, ed., *Values and Moral Development* (New York: Paulist Press, 1976), chap. 2.

16
O. Nash, *I'm a Stranger Here Myself* (Boston: Little, Brown, 1935), pp. 51–52. Excerpted from "Experience to Let." Copyright © 1935 by Ogden Nash.

17
B. B. Varenhorst, "Training Adolescents as Peer Counselors," *Personnel and Guidance Journal* 53, no. 4 (1974):271–275.

18
Exploring Childhood: A Curriculum for Child Development, Educational Development Corporation, 55 Chapel Street W., Newton, Massachusetts.

19
A. Gartner, M. Kohler, F. Riessman, *Children Teach Children* (New York: Harper & Row, 1971.) National Commission on Resources for Youth, 36 W. 44th Street, New York, New York 10036.

Educational psychology and public policy

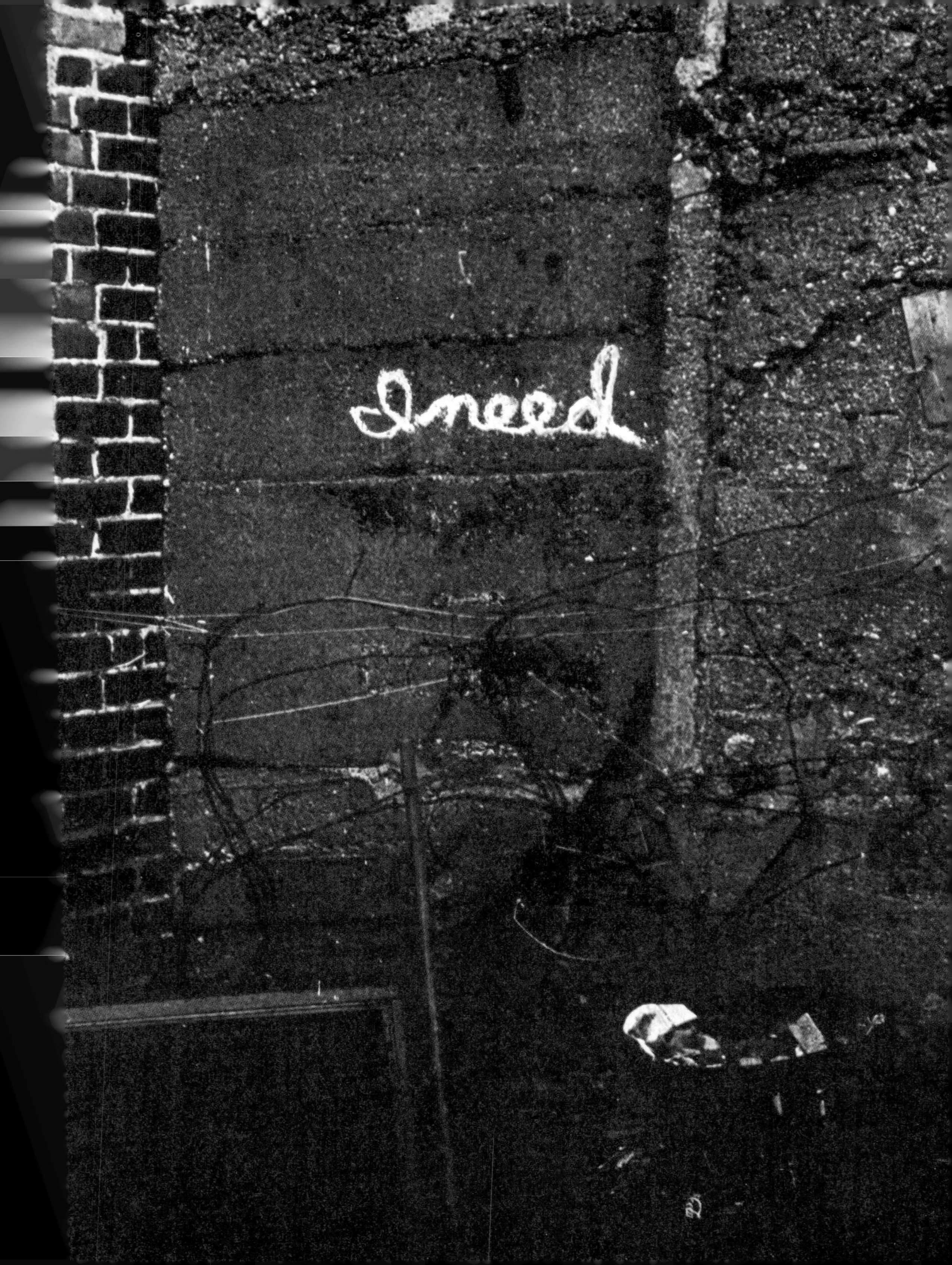
I need

22

Special education: retarded children in regular classrooms

As a result of both a gradual revision of educational theory and a series of milestone legal decisions, special education for so-called atypical and exceptional children is undergoing a period of major formulation. Traditionally, societies have followed one of three policies with regard to children and teenagers labelled handicapped or difficult: (1) remolding, (2) exclusion, or (3) deviate-status placement. Different civilizations, and the same societies at different times, have naturally used a variety of methods to achieve each policy goal. In this chapter, we describe these methods and discuss their shortcomings in view of both our current psychological understanding of such children and the emergence of a series of new "Right to Education" laws. We follow this with a discussion of current classification schemes in special education, the movement toward "mainstreaming," and implications for classroom teachers.

CLASSIFICATION METHODS: REMOLDING, EXCLUSION, SEGREGATION

As noted in Chapter 8, practically all societies have practiced remolding and reshaping their children during the early formative years, utilizing methods that vary from the somewhat benign to the most grotesque. For example, one old wives' tale suggests that it is important to play soft music to very young children to soothe the beast within their breast; at the other extreme might be the medieval practice of exorcism, popularized in a recent movie.

Remolding

The objective of all remolding methods was essentially to fit the child to the society. This means that, at least to some degree, the process of socialization was and is designed to eliminate individual variation or difference. Remolding can be in the form of physically reshaping a child (binding the feet, elongating the neck, etc.), alteration of the physiological characteristics (such as conditioning feeding patterns—recall the old debate of demand versus scheduled eating), or psychological reshaping (for example, brainwashing). Thus societies have attempted through physical, physiological, and psychological means to remake children.

Of course not all societies seek to rebuild each child completely in its own adult image. It is clear, however, that a major goal of the policy is toward eliminating some real or imagined negative attributes in children. Thus, in general, we should take a careful look at some of the procedures in early education to insure that the programs are in the child's best interests and reflect effective methods toward promoting individual development. We have certainly stressed this view throughout the entire volume: children are not miniature adults. For our purpose here, however, the critical question is, What happens when children do not fit, when the procedures for remolding and reshaping do not work? What policies have societies followed when some children remain different? One policy is obvious: simply exclude such children from the rest of society.

(margin note) Early education should promote individual development

Exclusion

The implementation of exclusion policies can vary from an extreme—e.g., murder—to psychological avoidance and exile. Ancient Sparta placed physically handicapped children on a mountainside; in seventeenth-century Salem, Massachusetts, teenage girls were burned to death because they were thought to be witches. David Bakan has recently provided a detailed account of such blood-curdling procedures in his appropriately titled work, *The Slaughter of the Innocents*. Such gruesome episodes in history as the "Children's Crusade" or Adolf Hitler's last public appearance reviewing a contingent of ten- and eleven-year-old boys before sending them into the field against Russian tanks all remind us that the causes, ideologies, or rationalizations may vary, but the effects on the children are the same.

Of course not all exclusion policies necessarily result in physical death. In some instances a society simply pretends that the atypical or different child doesn't really exist. Thus it is not unusual to find children labeled as retarded living a marginal existence, hidden from view most of the time or, even if they do appear in public, generally not acknowledged. Such "different" children are spoken of only in hushed voices, in the hope that they will soon return to attic rooms, cellars, or garages. Every so often newspaper stories announce the "discovery" of such children in a headline story; the famous case of the "wild boy" of Aveyron is only the most well-known instance of this exclusion.* It goes without saying that such children have literally no chance to grow and develop, suffering either actual physical or, perhaps even worse, a psychological death at an early age.

(margin note) Exclusion leads to physical or psychological death at an early age

---

* An eleven-year-old boy was found living in the woods as an animal in Southern France in 1799. He was subsequently cared for and educated by a famous French special educator, Jean Marc Gaspard Itard.

Segregation: deviate-status placement

A more common policy, at least recently, has been the system of categorizing some children as deviant and placing children so designated in segregated environments. Various societies employ literally hundreds of different methods of classification—e.g., physical handicaps, racial characteristics, ancestry, intelligence testing, degrees of skin color, and so on. Naturally, a critical question here is the validity of the assessment procedures so employed, and we will discuss this issue more fully in a later section. At this point, we wish to emphasize that the effect of the overall policy is to exclude, separate out, and segregate such children from the mainstream of society.

Sometimes the segregation policy is referred to as "warehousing": states and nations build human warehouses, usually in remote areas, and place designated children within those walls for safekeeping. This policy is, of course, almost the same as deportation. So-called undesirables are literally shipped out, and thus are effectively removed from citizenship roles in a manner similar to sending the French Emperor Napoleon to the Island of Helena. The obvious natural tendency is for a society then to feel it has solved the problem; the education and growth of such children are now taken care of and we can all turn our attention toward other concerns. The exclusion policy eliminates designated children from society while the deviate-status-placement procedures segregate them—"out of sight, out of mind" is the hoped-for result.

Segregating children by "warehousing"

Segregation policies: a mockingbird

In the Pulitzer Prize winning novel *To Kill a Mockingbird,* the following dialogue appears. The scene is the first day of school for a new second-grade teacher, Miss Caroline Fisher, in a small rural Southern community. In the middle of a lesson a small "cootie" jumps out of Burris Ewell's hair, scaring Miss Caroline half to death. In the process of examing the youngster more closely, Miss Caroline concludes that he should be sent home to wash his hair with lye soap and the rest of himself with soap and water. As the novel's little-girl heroine "Scout" remarks, Burris "was the filthiest human I had ever seen. His neck was dark grey, the back of his hands were rusty and his fingernails were black deep into the quick. He peered at Miss Caroline from a fist-sized clean space on his face."

Miss Caroline emphatically comments that Burris is to go home immediately and return "tomorrow" for the second day of school, clean as a whistle and ready to learn.

> The boy laughed rudely. "You ain't sendin' me home, Missus. I was on the verge of leaving. I done done my time for this year."
>
> Miss Caroline looked puzzled. "What do you mean by that?"
>
> The boy did not answer. He gave a short contemptuous snort.
>
> One of the elderly members of the class answered her. "He's one of the Ewells, Ma'am—Whole school's full of 'em. They come the first day every year and then leave. The truant lady gets 'em here cause she threatens 'em with the sheriff, but she gives up trying to hold 'em. She reckons she's carried out the law just gettin' their names on the roll and running 'em here the first day. You're supposed to mark 'em absent the rest of the year."[2]

The Ewell children, then, were deviates and segregated from the other pupils. The letter of the law in this case was honored but the educational future of the children was ignored. The school itself could then avoid having to cope with the special problems of the Ewell children, cooties and all. In a less-humorous vein, unfortunately, much of the segregated special-class placements for children have had the same effect. For the past forty years or so the common educational policy has been to place children classified as mild to moderately educationally handicapped (IQ scores roughly in the 50 to 70 range) in special classes, separated from the other school children. This practice has continued until recently, even though a long series of studies beginning in the 1930s has consistently indicated that such special-class placements are not superior to regular-class placements. In fact, no research evidence supports such special-class placements for "mild to moderately" retarded children; there are no academic gains for children placed in these classes and equivocal social gains.[3] A recent review suggests that the pupils placed in segregated classes suffer negative psychological consequences—namely, a lowered self-concept—as a result of separation.[4]

MAINSTREAMING

An alternative policy for children and teenagers classified as exceptional and/or mentally retarded is so-called "mainstreaming." Essentially the goal here is to expand the boundaries and reduce the barriers that have segregated such children from the mainstream of society. For many centuries this country legally sanctioned a segregated public-school system that prevented black children from attending our society's mainstream "white" schools. The famous *Brown* v. *The Board of Education* Supreme Court decision of 1954 ruled that separate facilities were inherently *not* equal. Thus, even if black children attended schools in new buildings filled with books, new carpets, and well-trained teachers, their schooling experience would still not be equal to that of mainstream white children. Segregation equals second-class citizenship was the dictum of the court. At a philosophic and psychological level equal educational opportunity means that each child should have access to the same educational experience. To rule otherwise is a logical absurdity. A public school is for the public's children.* Segregation is inherently separate and *not* equal.

In a manner similar to the 1954 *Brown* decision, a number of recent legal rulings have struck down the segregation of so-called retarded children. Following the same reasoning as the Supreme Court decision of 1954, decisions such as the Pennsylvania Right to Education Law (1971) clearly commit educational policy to a goal of integrated education. The schools in Pennsylvania as well as other states are to provide public education for all children, regardless of the "label," "condition," "potential," or any other characteristic of the child.

Marginal note: Segregating is inherently separate and not equal

---

* We are emphasizing the legal grounds on which the segregation laws were changed. This still doesn't touch the issue of so-called defacto segregation—a system of housing patterns, redrawing school-district lines, etc.—which produces a separate, segregated educational system in spite of the legal sanctions.

For many centuries this country legally sanctioned a segregated public-school system that prevented black children from attending our society's mainstream "white" schools.

Such legal decisions clearly lower the barriers and expand the boundaries so that more children hitherto excluded from regular classes and regular schools will be entering the mainstream. New sets of issues, especially involving the question of classification, now arise. At what point do we draw the line between regular classes and separate "special" classes? In other words, even if such legal decisions really open up the public school system by sanction, will there be some children for whom some type of separate education would still be the most humane experience? This is really a two-part question that combines the problem of diagnosis with the problem of educational programming. How do we legitimately classify and/or label a child and how do we alter the educational environment? It is clear that we cannot simply close up all the existing "human warehouses," shut the doors on all the existing special classes, and dump all children in the mainstream. To examine that question we will discuss the diagnostic problem first, and then turn to the question of the educational intervention. It is important to realize that these are two sides of the same coin: we need more-accurate means of classifying so-called retarded children, as well as a broadened educational program to promote their development. It makes little sense to misjudge a child's potential to learn on one hand, or, on the other, simply to place children in regular classes for the sake of appearances. We wouldn't expect young fish to survive if we dumped them into a mainstream, especially if the stream was polluted and couldn't support life in the first place.

A two-part question: diagnosis and educational programming

THE DIAGNOSTIC PROBLEM: "ONCE A DEVIANT, ALWAYS A DEVIANT"

The traditional system of classifying children or teenagers as retarded or deviant has been criticized on at least two grounds: (1) the system of assessment is too narrowly based, and (2) the labels become permanent. The traditional method was based on an attempt to group children by degree of retardation, using an IQ test as the major assessment procedure. This resulted in three major categories.

Three categories of retardation

1

Educable Mentally Retarded (EMR). IQ scores are generally between 50 and 80 on standard tests. Usually classed as a slow learner and a "concrete" thinker. Can be successfully employed.

2

Trainable Mentally Retarded (TMR). IQ scores generally between 25 and 50 on standard tests. Considered not capable of "ordinary" academic learning, but can learn self-care and safety rules. "Sheltered" workshops can provide an employment environment. Can learn social adjustments.

3

Profoundly Retarded. IQ scores between 0 and 25. Require constant supervision. Many are bedridden.

As you can immediately see, the IQ score becomes extraordinarily important in deciding on the assignment of children to the EMR, TMR, or Profoundly Retarded groupings.* Also you may notice that these three labels can easily become euphemisms or "softer" words replacing the older categories of "moron," "idiot," and "imbecile." The primary difficulty, of course, is the effect of such a global classification based on a somewhat singular method of assessment. The major criticism is that we are overgeneralizing from a limited evaluation system. Professor Maynard Reynolds has provided an incisive critique of this issue. He notes:

1

There is no sharp discontinuity in mental ability between people with IQ's of 79 and 81 nor between 49 and 51 yet the tests can lend themselves to such absurd assumptions.

2

The test scores are also subject to the limitations of examiner influence and culture bias. Examiners either consciously or unconsciously do influence the scores achieved by their pupils. Also, there are few if any tests that claim to be completely culturally fair.

IQ tests do not test child's complete range of functioning

3

The test themselves are not assessing the complete range of the child's functioning. For example, a "blind" child is usually not completely blind, nor is

---

*
The American Association for Mental Deficiency has recently reclassified this system to four categories—Mild (69–55), Moderate (54–40), Severe (39–25), Profound (24–0)—in an attempt to provide for more-accurate differential diagnosis. It is problematic that creating a distinction between Severe and Profound based on IQ will be an educational advance.

he or she necessarily incapable of functioning well in other areas. In the same way a low-tested-IQ child is not necessarily without school achievement potential, nor is he or she necessarily incapable of functioning well in other areas.

4

The tests themselves are virtually useless for making educational decisions with regard to placement. Educational classifications for special education only make sense when the classification is related to programs.

IQ tests are useless for making educational placement decisions

5

We should spend far less time predicting how children with special needs may perform in "traditional" classrooms as a result of an IQ score. Instead, we should develop more-effective instructional procedures that will reach more children—e.g., increase the educational potential of each classroom to teach almost all children.

6

Special education should talk less about dysfunction, low IQ's, deficits, impairments, and disabilities. Instead, absolutely no child should be omitted from a commitment to differentiate school offerings sufficiently so that all children receive the help they need to develop maximally.[5]

HOW SOCIETY TREATS "RETARDED" HUMANS

In the popular novel, *Flowers for Algernon,* the leading character is a young "mentally retarded" man, Charlie Gordon. He had participated in a scientific experiment that temporarily made him a genius, but at the end of the story he has returned to his previous mental condition. This entire experiment was, of course, fictional, but the human insight provided by Charlie is pertinent to our discussion. In the novel, Charlie is describing what it was like to be classified as a slow learner and to be taught to read by a punitive teacher (his mother) who constantly emphasized his errors. Her voice commanded him to read. He tried his best.

"*See Jack. See Jack run. See Jack see.*"

"No! Not *See* Jack *see!* It's *Run* Jack *run!*" Pointing with her rough-scrubbed finger.

"*See Jack. See Jack run. Run Jack see.*"

"No! You're not trying. Do it again!"

Do it again . . . do it again . . . do it again . . .

"Leave the boy alone. You've got him terrified."

"He's got to learn. He's too lazy to concentrate."

Run Jack run . . . run Jack run . . . run Jack run . . . run Jack run . . .

"He's slower than the other children. Give him time."

"He's normal. There's nothing wrong with him. Just lazy. I'll beat it into him until he learns."

Run Jack run . . . run Jack run . . . run Jack run . . . run Jack run . . .

And then looking up from the table, it seems to me I saw myself, through Charlie's eyes, holding *Paradise Lost,* and I realized I was breaking the binding with the pressure of both hands as if I wanted to tear the book in half. I broke the back of it, ripped out a handful of pages, and flung them and the book across the room to the corner where the broken records were. I let it lay there and its torn white tongues were laughing because I couldn't understand what they were saying.[6]

The classification system itself is inadequate and its effects may often be damaging. The negative consequences can be summarized statistically. For example, the label "retarded" has been so overused by school systems that children from low socioeconomic backgrounds are fifteen times more likely to be "diagnosed" as retarded than are children from higher-income families. Dr. Burton Blatt, an expert in special education and assessment, has shown that, especially in poor neighborhoods, the label "mentally retarded" has been applied to up to 16 percent of a school's population. He notes that careful reassessment studies have shown that, in fact, only about 2 percent of the children are accurately classified.[7]

The damaging effects of a misdiagnosis

Perhaps these figures are too impersonal or too "objective" as a means of understanding the negative effect of such a misdiagnosis. Yet imagine if it happened to you as an individual: What if your teachers, the principal, your friends, and family all believed you were retarded and possessed little learning potential? You would soon find your world substantially different. Expectations would change. You might either be excessively cuddled and demeaned—e.g., "Now Dick or Jane, you just sit quietly and gaze out the window while the rest of us learn to read . . . and here is a lollipop that's your favorite color!" Or you might find that in addition to feeling underchallenged, you eventually begin to suspect that "they" are correct: you are not only economically poor, but "dumb" as well. Certainly the social and personal stigma from the label would be enormous. And remember that the label tends to remain and even to generalize. Thus even if you were slower or behind other children in one specific learning area, the label would pronounce you as slow in all areas and probably for the balance of your life. Facetiously this process has been called "hardening of the categories"; seriously its effect is to permanently label some children as deviant and atypical, a process of carving the designation in stone—and in public. What that does to the person's own view of himself or herself may be even more indelible, a personal self-concept etched in shame and self-contempt.

Dibs: a case of misdiagnosis

Virginia Axline, a gifted child psychotherapist and author as well, has provided a dramatic case study of a little boy, *Dibs.* From parental description and nursery-school behavior it appeared as if Dibs was grossly mentally defective. His parents reported that from birth on he was always remote, untouchable, slow to talk and walk, unable to play and, "striking out at people like a little wild animal."

The nursery-school teachers were baffled by him. The school psychologist had been unable to test him. The pediatrician had concluded he was "strange," or mentally retarded, psychotic, or brain-damaged. No one was apparently able to get close enough to Dibs to find out the causes of his difficulties.

The parents themselves were both brilliant and successful, yet terribly ashamed, fearful, and anxiety ridden over their "problem" child. Deep down they believed the awful truth was that Dibs was an "idiot."

As the mother related an incident at home to Dr. Axline, she described a terrible fight between Dibs and her husband. The four-year-old had apparently hurled a chair at his father, kicking and screaming all the while, "I hate you." This was in response to the husband's direct comment to Dibs that he was babbling like an idiot. The mother reported to the therapist that she had said to her husband, "Dibs wasn't babbling like an idiot now. He said he hated you!" Then, my husband sat down in a chair and actually wept! It was terrible, I had never seen a man cry before. I had never thought anything could cause my husband to shed a tear. I was afraid, suddenly terrified, because he seemed to be just as scared as I was. I think we were closer to each other than we have ever been. Suddenly, we were just two frightened, lonely, unhappy people with our defenses crumpled and deserted. It was terrible—and yet a relief to know that we could be human, and could fail and admit that we had failed! Finally, we pulled ourselves together and he said that maybe we had been wrong about Dibs. I said I would come and ask what you thought about Dibs. She looked at me with an expression of fear and panic in her eyes. "Tell me," she said. "Do you think that Dibs is mentally defective?"[8]

Dibs was "defective" only in the sense that he had suffered enormous emotional deprivation. For whatever reason, neither parent had been capable of forming a warm, supportive, nurturing early environment for him. In the language of a psychiatrist who interviewed the family, Dibs was "the most rejected and emotionally deprived child" he had ever seen.

Dibs's "defect" was emotional deprivation

In the case study itself Dr. Axline describes the emotional reeducation she provided for Dibs, as well as the assistance to the parents so they could maintain the gains. Dibs gradually yet dramatically emerged from his shell into the world of human relationships and in the author's words, "was able to be a child." The work stands both as a moment of high drama and as a reminder of our basic human needs for supportive relationships to encourage healthy psychological development—an essential first step to becoming a person. The word "Dibs" is a common expression in England for "self."

AN ALTERNATIVE CLASSIFICATION PROCEDURE: "THE CASCADE"

As we noted earlier, test interpretation is a critical process, for it indicates how we make meaning and judgments. We certainly need a more-comprehensive system of educational diagnosis for all children and particularly for those currently being classed as "special." Evelyn Deno, as eminent theorist-practitioner in this field, has developed a system that respects both the complexity of the problem and the need to employ careful assessment in the service of the children.[9] Rather than viewing the problem from society's perspective first, she suggests we start with the fundamental needs and rights of children. In this way we can keep our educational priorities in mind. The system is also based on a positive assessment concept designed to uncover the areas of positive educational

The need for a more-comprehensive system of educational diagnosis

potential. Thus, rather than generalizing from one negative aspect of a child's functioning, the system seeks to differentiate general functioning into a series of elements. This acts as a means of preventing "globalizing" children into negative categories. Instead the children can be grouped into one of seven levels of educational environments from regular classes to "total" care. The critical point, however, is the dynamic commitment in the plan to always move children upward in the system as far and as fast as possible. Thus assignments are at first functional to the level of activity the child brings to the environment. The educational goal of any particular level then is to provide preparation for the next level up, so to speak; none of the levels, two through seven, is regarded as a permanent placement.

ALTERNATIVE EDUCATIONAL ENVIRONMENTS: PROMOTING DEVELOPMENT

Evelyn Deno's "Cascade" clearly implies the need for differential diagnosis as well as differential service. The diagnosis problem, as we indicated, involves broad assessment procedures in all areas of functioning. The critical assumption, however, is not the initial prescription—instead it's the developmental program. From this point of view, the variety of categories of retardation are, at best, only the immediate and temporary station for the child. Growth is determined by interaction. The labels are dangerous since it's so easy to assume that the problems are safely locked up inside the child. Recalling the framework from Piaget, Bruner, J. McV. Hunt, and Robert White suggests the following educational assumptions:

1
Retarded children develop through the same sequence of stages as "normal" children but at slower rates.

2
The growth of retarded children thus depends on the same set of principles applicable to "regular" children, namely: (a) a rich, stimulating, abundant

Several studies conducted during the last twenty-five years all clearly indicate that intellectual functioning and general development can be positively influenced by a rich, stimulating early environment.

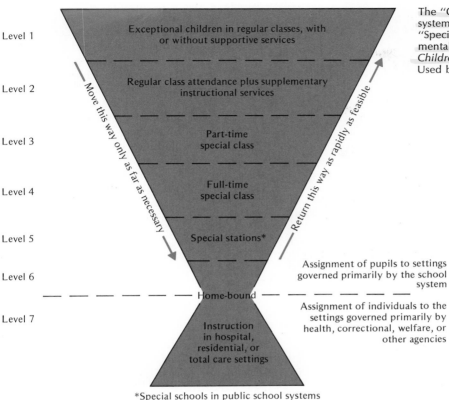

Level 1 — Exceptional children in regular classes, with or without supportive services

Level 2 — Regular class attendance plus supplementary instructional services

Level 3 — Part-time special class

Level 4 — Full-time special class

Level 5 — Special stations*

Level 6 — Home-bound

Level 7 — Instruction in hospital, residential, or total care settings

Move this way only as far as necessary

Return this way as rapidly as feasible

The "Cascade" classification system. From Evelyn Deno, "Special Education as Developmental Capital," *Exceptional Children* 37 (1970):229–237. Used by permission.

Assignment of pupils to settings governed primarily by the school system

Assignment of individuals to the settings governed primarily by health, correctional, welfare, or other agencies

*Special schools in public school systems

early environment (Hunt); (b) an active versus passive learning environment, including a heavy emphasis on practice and participation from the early years onward (Piaget and Bruner).

3
Careful educational preparation is needed for stage growth and transition to the next stage "up." This includes the process of "equilibration," Piaget's term for a constructive match between the child's functioning stage and the learning environment—for example, a rich stimulating sensory environment during the very early years. Developmental growth, as we have noted, depends on interaction between the child and the environment. The isomorphic view is just the opposite of this developmental assumption, namely, that the learning problem is a deficit locked up inside the body of the designated child.

A series of studies including the classic Skodak and Skeels study (1949),[10] the Heber Milwaukee Project (see Chapter 5), and the most recent Scarr-Salapatek and Weinberg study,[11] all indicate rather clearly that intellectual functioning and general development can be positively influenced by a rich, stimulating

Maria Montessori

Maria Montessori was on the forefront of change and innovation throughout her entire life. Born in 1870, she was raised in a conservative European atmosphere in the small Italian town of Chiaravelle. Her aspirations, however, led her, upon the completion of the equivalent of a secondary-school education, to seek admission to the prestigious University of Rome for the study of medicine. It was literally unheard of at the time for a female to pursue a medical career—there were simply no female physicians in the entire Italian nation. Such barriers, however, could not deter Madame Montessori. Her brilliance of intellect, combined with personal drive and dedication, soon won the respect of the all-male college. At the age of twenty-four she became the first woman physician in the country.

Her interest in practicing general medicine, which at that time consisted largely of treating symptoms, soon waned. She began to ask larger questions and shifted more toward the problems and needs of retarded children. The streets of Rome were inhabited by urchins, many of whom were regarded as insane. Maria's clinical intuition, however, suggested that the difficulty might not be medical insanity. Careful observation of these children gradually created in her a conviction that the problems experienced by these waifs were not medical but rather pedagogical. The children, many from the most economically depressed areas of the city, were growing up under the worst possible conditions. Grinding poverty created devastating learning atmospheres during their early formative years. In a sense, Montessori's children were similar to the slum children described by Eleanor Pavenstedt in *The Drifters*, mentioned in the text.

She continued to challenge the existing views of her day by establishing a special school for the so-called insane children. At the age of twenty-nine she became the school's director, created new learning materials, and applied her theories to the classroom, while studying the techniques of Seguin (who had emigrated to this country) and Itard. She soon revolutionized the entire educational approach for such children; many were able to learn to read and write, using her highly structured materials and multisensory procedures. Montessori's children became the first generation to be what we now call "mainstreamed," in that they were placed in regular classes with normal children. This demonstrated rather dramatically that previously designated insane or retarded children were capable of learning under appropriate conditions.

Her work continued to expand in scope as she became increasingly interested in the general learning problems of all children, not just emotionally disturbed or "slum kids." She began to realize that learning was dependent on the interaction between the child and the environment. David Elkind, a contemporary American expert in cognitive-developmental theory, has noted that this concept of Montessori's was highly similar to some of Piaget's later theories.* She viewed development as occurring in a sequence of stages or "sensitive periods" as she called them, and that such development proceeded by leaps and bounds followed by periods of integration. She used the term growth "explosions" to denote the qualitative shifts to new cognitive stages. Of course, Montessori's other obvious similarity to Piaget was what Elkind termed her genius for empathy with children. Without doubt, this sensitivity, which enabled her to understand both the thoughts and feelings of young children, was the central ingredient, the *sine qua non* of her educational leadership.

Above all else, Maria Montessori throughout her entire life was committed to educational practice. Whereas Piaget focused mostly on discovering how children learn as an interesting theoretical question, Montessori always viewed every problem with an eye to practical application. She was a bridge between theory and practice; she both *described* how children learn and *prescribed* teaching methods to accomplish developmental goals.

---
*

D. Elkind, *Children and Adolescents* (New York: Oxford Press, 1970), p. 104.

Thus, she attempted to synthesize a theory of learning and a theory of instruction. From her naturalistic observations of how young children learn she developed her now famous "prepared environment." She wished not to accelerate growth or force children to grow up over night, but rather to maximally develop their own competencies within each stage of development. The environment, if carefully matched to the child, is seen as providing the nourishment for such growth. Naturally, as seems to be the case with all major innovators, some of Montessori's "disciples" have misunderstood her intentions and have created some lock-step environments that do not serve children well. For Montessori, development involved the matched environment of repetitive learning, multisensory materials, as well as spontaneity and empathy. Children do not learn in prescriptive educational straitjackets.

Her long life was devoted to increasing our theoretical and practical knowledge of child development, for both the normal and atypical child. In her lifetime she addressed many audiences: the teacher, the educational researcher, the curriculum-materials developer, and the parent. By the time of her death at age 82, Maria Montessori had become a powerful voice for children, and her pioneering efforts had opened the way for continuing explorations in the field of educational practice.

early environment. Skodak and Skeels demonstrated that cognitive functioning could be dramatically increased for young children by modifying an extremely barren, orphanage environment. Heber has shown the positive effects of a stimulating preschool environment, while Scarr-Salapatek and Weinberg have shown the positive effects of modifying early-home-care environments. Whether the actual environment was an orphanage, a nursery school, or a home, the principles were the same—namely, that significant increases were found in cognitive functioning as a result of "active" learning, positive interaction, and developmental-stage equilibration. This is simply a means of placing the explanations for positive growth in developmental language. In all these studies, many preschool children were initially classified, on the basis of an IQ test, as retarded or slow learners.

Cognitive functioning and early home care

The Drifters: a case study

Perhaps the most-striking example of this general point is the monumental study of poor, white, "retarded" children in Boston entitled *The Drifters*, by Eleanor Pavenstedt. These children, by the time they were three- or four-years-old and starting a special nursery-school program, were distinctly "retarded." From families categorized as poor, multiple problem, skid-row area, and disorganized, the children had been allowed to grow up without parental guidance or attention (raised on the streets) and simultaneously were expected by their families to assume adultlike responsibilities at unbelievably young ages. Three-year-old children were often expected to do the family shopping, care for younger children, cross busy streets, clothe and bathe themselves, stall the bill collectors at the door—in other words, jump from infancy and childhood directly into adulthood.

Eleanor Pavenstedt's study demonstrated the critical importance of positive teacher-child interactions in promoting intellectual growth.

The effects of such a stressful environment on these young (and by definition) very-impressionable children was enormously negative. The descriptions of their behavior during the first months in the special nursery school are compelling, poignant, and tragic. Having been forced to grow up so fast, the children

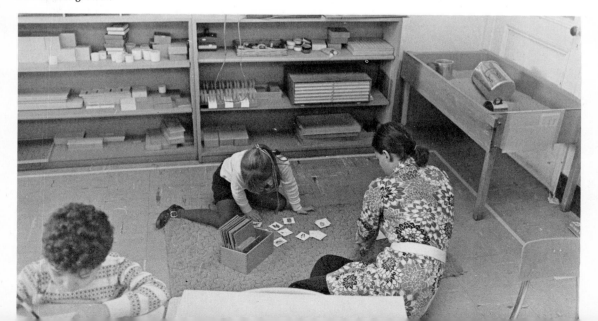

exhibited a massive "danger orientation"—constantly fearful, expecting calamity, with cringing bodies and worried brows reflecting their general outlook. In one deeply ironic sense the children had obviously learned a great deal; they were quick, agile, and capable of advanced motor skills. Yet the psychological cost was more than apparent. It was almost impossible for them to learn even the most rudimentary intellectual skills, such as counting, letter recognition, attending to stories, etc. Their psychological and intellectual activity was all placed in the service of basic survival—they had overlearned an important lesson. They could trust no one, depend on no one, and relate to no one. Such excessive premature personal autonomy did allow them to survive, yet also acted as a massive learning barrier. Curiosity, exploration, trying new things and materials were virtually nonexistent during the initial phase of the nursery-school experience. Most of the time the children appeared to sit docilely, while underneath they were preparing themselves for the next calamity. Any casual observer would quickly class all these children as moderately to severely retarded based on performance at schoollike tasks.

The educational program: success-failure

After an average of two years in the school, conducted by a superb and loving early education teacher, Ilse Mattick, the children clearly demonstrated remarkable gains in almost all areas of functioning. The program represented a high-quality learning environment and the humane atmosphere was a major contributing factor. The children were gradually helped to experience learning without fear of annihilation. Their curiosity, risk taking, verbal skills, attending behavior, use of materials, etc. all improved to the point where their cognitive functioning would be considered within the normal range. In analyzing these successful changes, the research team was convinced that the marked improvement in intellectual functioning resulted from the substantial improvement in the children's capacities for interpersonal relationships. In other words, the positive human interactions between the nursery-school teachers and the children were viewed as the key to unlocking their development. Thus the abundant, stimulating environment of humane teaching and appropriate materials formed the necessary and sufficient conditions to promote growth—almost. The massive early intervention appeared to repair the early damage inflicted by their "danger orientation."

Improved intellectual functioning resulted from improved capacities for interpersonal relationships

The children themselves happily expected to leave the nursery school and enter the first grade in the nearby public school. In fact, the children all impressed their first-grade teachers initially as capable and well balanced. Unfortunately, however, the regular first grades were not particularly responsive to the needs of these children. The school experiences were highly routine, the teacher behaviors were generally rigid, the rule structure of the schools was carefully enforced. If a child was late, even by five minutes, he or she would find all doors locked and was forced to ring a loud bell and undergo questioning prior to admission. Many simply roamed the streets instead. Gradually the accrual of a series of similar minor events—a yelling teacher, errors in desk work, excessive recopying of assignments—all contributed to a reemergence of fearfulness. A few children found an understanding and supportive teacher and "as long as this person was available they achieved remarkably well."

In a most ironic epilogue, the author notes:

As time went on, their newly found and still shaky self-esteem was lost again, the lively spark left their eyes, and their dealings became guarded and manipulative.

Teachers became "annoyed" or "disappointed," blaming the parents or accusing the children of "not trying hard enough." The children felt themselves disliked by teachers; some of them began to dread going to school, others expressed disappointment and anger.[12]

The danger orientation reemerged accompanied by signs of mental retardation.

INTERVENTION PROGRAMS: INCREASE THE ACCOMMODATIVE CAPACITY OF CLASSROOMS

As mainstream programs increase, it is obvious that the educational environments will need careful preparation, including attention to teacher attitudes and the use of imaginative materials and methods. Certainly a critical factor in the failure reported in *The Drifters* was the inability to help regular teachers become more responsive to the needs of the "danger orientation" children. Other studies have shown similar patterns of teacher behavior—namely, the discomfort, anxiety, and stress that teachers experience when dealing with children who are different. We noted earlier that in some urban classrooms white teachers were not responsive to the needs of black children—less eye contact, more negative statements, more punitive behavior than toward white children. Whether mainstreaming succeeds, then, will depend on the ability to teach teachers to become more responsive to the fundamental needs of all children. In the special-education literature this is referred to as the need to increase the accommodative capacity of regular classrooms—to broaden the learning environment in order genuinely to include all pupils in positive learning activities. For example, it does little good to legalize racial integration in a school only to have the school operate as a segregated institution with students eating separately, occupying different spaces in the same building, participating in separate activities, being treated separately by school rules and teachers. In the same way, if previously separated special-education pupils are mainstreamed only to be resegregated once again, changing the form but not substance will produce a perpetuation of the status quo.

Teachers must broaden learning environment to include all pupils

Professor Jack Birch at the University of Pittsburgh has summarized a series of studies in mainstreamed school districts. The positive attitudes of regular teachers was stated as, "the most effective force for excellent special education." He summarized the cluster of attitudes as follows:

1
Belief in the right to education for all children.

2
Readiness of special-education and regular-class teachers to cooperate with each other.

Teachers don't want to be labeled

Harry W. Forgan*

When teaching a course on tests and measurement at Kent State University recently, I decided to administer an adult group intelligence test to the class. I wanted the students to "feel" what it was like to take such a test and realize what items we use to measure intelligence. I also thought they might be more aware of the short time it takes to obtain a number which is regarded as very important by many educators.

The students were told not to write their names on the test papers, but rather to use a code such as their house number, physical measurements, or any less obvious symbol. I explained that I really didn't have faith in IQ scores; therefore, I didn't want to know their IQs.

The administration of the test required only 50 minutes. The students seemed to enjoy taking it and chuckled at some of the tasks they were expected to perform. I had to laugh myself when I saw some of them looking at their hands and feet when responding to items concerning right and left.

Upon scoring the test I found that the lowest IQ was 87 and the highest 143. The mean IQ for the 48 students was 117. I was not astonished by the 87, even though all of the students had successfully completed the general education courses and student teaching at Kent State and were ready to graduate by the end of the term. After all, IQ tests have many limitations.

Then I got an idea. I decided to prepare a report for each student, writing his code on the outside and "IQ 87" on the inside of each. I folded and stapled each paper—after all, an IQ is confidential information!

At the next class period I arranged all of the folded papers on a table at the front of the room. I wrote the range and the average IQ on the chalkboard. Many students snickered at the thought of somebody getting an 87. The students were eager and afraid as I began by explaining the procedures for picking up their papers. I made a point of telling them not to tell others their IQ score, because this would make the other person feel as if he too had to divulge this "total endowment." The students were then directed to come up to the table, row by row, to find their coded paper. I stood sheepishly—ready to laugh out loud as I watched the students carefully open their papers and see "IQ 87." Many opened their mouths with astonishment and then smiled at their friends to indicate they were extremely happy with their scores.

There was dead silence when I began to discuss the implications of the IQ scores. I explained that in some states a person who scores below 90 on an

Phi Delta Kappan, September 1973. Reprinted by permission.

IQ test is classified as a slow learner. The fact that group intelligence tests should not be used to make such a classification was stressed. I also emphasized the fact that *someone* in this class could have been classified as a slow learner and placed in a special class on the basis of this test.

I told how many guidance counselors would discourage a child with an 87 IQ from attending college. Again I emphasized the fact that one person in this room was ready to graduate from college having passed several courses in history, biology, English, and many other areas.

I then went on to explain that the majority of elementary and secondary school teachers believe in ability grouping. This is usually done on the basis of intelligence tests, so I explained that I would like to try ability grouping with this class—again to see "how it feels." Some students objected right away, saying that "I did not want to know their IQ scores." I calmed them by saying it would be a worthwhile learning experience and assured them that I really didn't believe in IQ scores.

I told the students not to move at this time, but I would like all of those with an IQ below 90 to come to the front so they could sit nearer to me for individual help. I told the students who had an average IQ (between 90–109) to go to the back of the room and then take the seats in the middle of the class. The students with an above average IQ were asked to go to the side of the room and take the seats in the back because they really didn't need much extra help.

"O.K., all those who got an IQ below 90 some to the front of the room." The students looked around to find those who scored below 90. I said that I knew there was an 87 and maybe a couple of 89's. Again, there was dead silence.

"O.K., all those students whose IQ is between 90–109 go to the back of the room." Immediately, to my amazement, 8 or 10 students picked up their books and headed for the back of the room. Before they could get there I said, "Wait a minute! Sitdown! I don't want to embarrass you, but you would lie and cheat—the same way we make our students lie and cheat—because you don't want to be classified as 'slow.' I wrote 'IQ 87' on every paper!"

The class erupted. It was in an uproar for about five minutes. Some of the women cried. Some indicated that they needed to use the restroom. All agreed it was a horrifying and yet valuable experience.

I asked them to do one thing for me: Please don't label kids. Because we are all "gifted," "average," and "slow," depending on the task at hand. They promised.

3
Willingness to share competencies as a team in behalf of pupils.

4
Openness to include parents as well as other professional colleagues in planning for and working with children.

5
Flexibility with respect to class size and teaching assignments.

6
Recognition that social and personal development can be taught, and that they are equally as important as academic achievement.

He also noted that in the school districts that successfully "mainstreamed," including elementary and secondary levels, and across disciplines, three factors stood out:

1
There was genuine appreciation of the team work with the special-education teachers, particularly the help the regular-classroom teachers received with the children already in their rooms.

2
Regular classroom teachers found that EMR pupils were usually no more difficult to include in their classes than some children already there.

3
The spirit that "all the children are in the same school system" was expressed time after time.[13]

Individualization of instruction requires that all educational activities be easily available to all children.

The reasons and attitudes for supporting mainstream education have been classified into three general domains: (1) philosophical-social, (2) educational, and (3) economic. As you examine the listings you might try rank-ordering the positions. What appears to you to be the most-important arguments or reasons for mainstreaming? Which reasons seem least important to you? By examining your own ratings you will have some idea of your method of thinking through these issues and will be able to pinpoint your own key assumptions. This will give you an idea of where you stand on the special-education issue of mainstreaming.

Reasons for mainstreaming (Stanley Deno scale)

A. Socio-philosophical positions

1

If our society is to be free and open for all then it is the right of every child to share in the experiences available to his or her peers—therefore, each child regardless of his or her difference has a right to participate in regular educational programs.

2

The "richness" of a society depends in large measure on its heterogeneity rather than its homogeneity—therefore, the regular classroom should be rich in human difference as well as material stimulation.

3

If we are ever going to learn to live with the differences among us we are going to have to live with those differences—therefore, children who are physically and psychologically different from the modal population should be included in mainstream education, as well as children who are culturally different.

4

Segregation for whatever reasons requires labelling and results in stigmatization and lowering of self-esteem among the segregated—therefore, placing handicapped children in special classes must be avoided.

5

The very existence of special classes results in inappropriate labelling and misplacement of children, particularly children from minority groups—thus, special classes should be disestablished wherever they exist.

6

Special class arrangements inappropriately place the responsibility for failure on children rather than schools and teachers—therefore, we must encourage the schools to accept responsibility for failing to teach rather than give them "handicap" as a scapegoat.

B. Educational concepts

1

Ability grouping with normal and handicapped children is an educational practice that has not made the teacher's job easier nor resulted in increased achievement by the children in ability groups—therefore, the practice as a basis for improving instruction for handicapped children makes no sense.

2

Individualization of instruction requires that all educational activities be easily available to all children—therefore, the regular classroom must be an available option for each individual as it is deemed appropriate.

3

Children learn through observing other children (and adults)—therefore, we can provide handicapped children with appropriate models by allowing them to participate in the "normal" classroom.

4

Peer and cross-age tutors are a highly effective resource for individual teaching—therefore, able children should be in the same rooms as the less able to assist in their instruction.

5

Skilled teachers as resource to the regular classroom can provide assistance to teachers in the classroom, as well as to handicapped children—therefore, we must move special educational assistance out of the special class and into regular classrooms.

6

The methods and materials used successfully with handicapped children should be equally available to all children having difficulty learning—therefore, we must develop organizational arrangements that permit the flexible use of these materials.

7

Teachers learn to teach more effectively when working with "high challenge" youngsters—therefore, including handicapped children in regular classrooms will result in benefits to regular class children as well.

C. Economic views

1

Handicapped children in special classes generally do less well than handicapped children in regular classes—therefore, since special education costs more and is no more effective, we would do well to disestablish special classes and reintegrate handicapped children.

2

Less than one-half the handicapped children in the nation are receiving special-education services—therefore, we can develop new and cost-efficient ways to increase the proportion of handicapped children being served by bringing special education to the regular classroom.

3

Maintaining resources (human and material) for separate (educational) systems results in duplication and is unnecessarily costly—therefore, it is administratively and economically sensible to combine special- and regular-education-program resources.

4
The availability of special classes and extra financial support seduces school administrators into establishing procedures for increasing the number of children identified as handicapped, thereby increasing educational costs—therefore, eliminating the option will result in decreased costs.[14]

INCREASING THE ACCOMMODATIVE CAPACITY: ATTITUDES PLUS SKILLS

In addition to the obvious importance of teacher attitudes, we also need to consider the other side of the coin, new teaching skills for the classroom itself. It would do the teacher little good to have the most positive attitudes in the universe toward so-called retarded children, but not have the requisite teaching skills to help them. We noted earlier that the critical developmental assumptions are: (1) retarded children can develop through the same Piagetian stages (especially sensori-motor, preoperational, and concrete) in a manner similar to regular children, yet at slower rates; and (2) interaction with a rich, stimulating environment and active learning will promote growth.

Educational researcher David Hunt has shown repeatedly in a key series of studies that it is important to match the educational environment with the stage of development of the child.[15] Pupils who are functioning at relatively low levels of conceptual thinking tend to learn most adequately in a highly structured teaching environment. Thus in elementary schools, as pupils are attempting to master the initial stages of concrete thinking, Hunt's work would definitely support carefully structured teaching. The educational tasks assigned should be:

Hunt: match educational environment with child's stage of development

1
Carefully explained

2
Relatively brief

3
Monitored quickly

4
Systematically varied

5
Involve learning through multiple senses.

At first, this may strike you as overmanaging the child, shutting out the possibility of creativity and being too preplanned or programmed. If you view it from the child's position, however, it may not seem as negative. Children starting school at low conceptual levels can be confused easily by ambiguity. Also, they may be afraid to ask for clarification, especially if they see that other children apparently understand the directions. Under such conditions children may revert to lower-stage thinking. If you were just on the threshold of learning to think concretely and became confused, anxious, and unsure of an educational task, it would be understandable to fall back into an earlier mode of thought—namely, preoperational thinking.

From an educational standpoint the careful use of a structured approach to teaching is legitimate as a means of helping so-called slower, or lower-conceptual, children to master some initial tasks. We wish to avoid, however, suggesting that all problems of retardation can be "cured" through high-structured learning. Although there may be some individual cases of dramatic improvement within a group of children previously segregated in special classes, those will remain the exception. In the nineteenth century in this country an early pioneer in special education, Edourard Seguin, unfortunately suggested that slow learning and retardation could be stamped out. With training and responsive environments all children could be normalized. Such overly optimistic hopes, of course, created a backlash of disappointment when reality indicated that improvement was slow and limited. However, we need not expect that retarded or slow-learning children are capable of becoming geniuses. Instead, the goal of the educator is to stimulate development. Small gains, in the long run, may in fact be the most significant and long lasting.

PRECISE TEACHING

Substantial work has been done in a method called "precise teaching" as a means of providing high structure for children newly mainstreamed. Essentially the method is derived almost directly from learning theory and so-called Skinnerian principles. The specific advantages of the system are that it allows the learner to focus on a structured task, proceed at his or her own pace, receive positive reinforcement for accomplishments, and build up feelings of being a successful learner. The overall process, then, represents a method of tailoring educational tasks to fit each child, or as it's sometimes called, "individualizing instruction." A discussion of the key elements involved in setting up this process follows.

High structure for children newly mainstreamed

Select a manageable task

The task to be learned by the child needs to be very specifically defined. Thus, the educational objective should not be too cosmic. To say you want the child to become more human, to appreciate American civilization, to be spontaneous, etc. are too ambiguous as manageable tasks for precise teaching (see Chapter 13). Instead, and this may sound hopelessly pedestrian to you, it is important to identify a highly specific task: learning to count from one to ten, to recognize vowels, to read ten single words without an error, or similar highly structured learning activities. We should also note that this approach is useful not only for special-education children, but can be helpful in almost any new learning situation, especially where the ambiguity of a task may generate anxiety. Thus the first problem is to pinpoint the specific area. Examples are:

Identify a highly specific task

> *Subject areas.* Multiple mistakes in oral reading, faulty knowledge of the multiplication table, erratic completion of homework assignments, not enough divergent products in art work, etc. (These must be described in behavior terms—i.e., in terms of something you can see and count with a very low level of inferences.)
>
> *Deportment areas.* Hitting others, "out of seat behavior," shouting out, not talking, never volunteering, excessive profanity, poor attendance, too much

staring out of the window, etc. (Be careful in picking out topics here. We don't want to turn all pupils into "goody two shoes.")

Personal areas. Negative feelings toward self, putting self down, overly apologetic, hostile feelings, not speaking up for self, trying a new activity, etc.

Set up a contract with the pupil

The contract should specify who will keep track of the counting, how the chart is to be set up, and how the count is to be kept. Contracts can be developed in almost any area and can even employ words or pictures to describe the activities for nonverbal pupils. For example, in the contracts depicted in Fig. 22.2 the positive behavior and desired reinforcements are described pictorially.

Feedback is essential to the contract system

Other more-sophisticated contracts naturally are possible and may specify more-complex behaviors. Also, other methods of keeping track of the counting are available. The important point is that the record be visible to the pupil so he or she can see on a cumulative basis how the score is mounting. This feedback is essential to the system. You could have pupils keep paper charts and graphs, use a plastic grocery-store counter, or have them make a leather bracelet containing small movable beads on strings of pipe cleaners. The one thing to avoid is asking them to keep track of the behaviors in their head.*

Negotiate a significant "award"

There is a debate among behavior theorists as to whether just seeing a line on a chart "improve" is sufficient. In general, the younger the pupil, the more concrete the reinforcer the better. There are thousands of funny stories about erroneous choices of reinforcers—e.g., have kids collect red chips for not speaking out of turn, then exchange five reds for one blue, collect two blues and exchange for one gray, and exchange one gray for extra recess time. The children wouldn't exchange blue for gray. They don't like the color.

It is certainly permissible to discuss the choice reinforcers with the children. Also realize that you don't have to select conventional reinforcers, like a candy bar, gold stars, or extra recess time. Other possibilities might include open discussion time with you—setting aside a few moments of "special time" between an adult and a child can be an unusually powerful reinforcement. Remember that the quality of time, not quantity, is the crucial aspect. A few moments of focused individual attention can be most meaningful for a child, and for that matter, an adult too!

A final point on the reinforcement schedule is to make sure that the reinforcement itself follows close on the heels of the desired contracted behavior. Long delays between accomplishment and reinforcement are ineffective, in spite of what we may think about building character through self-denial and disci-

---

* The classic research of George Miller has shown that humans in general can keep about five to seven discrete pieces of "knowledge" in their consciousness at one time. After that point, unless we associate the thinking, we become easily confused.

Contract		
What I Do	My Count	What Happens
	1 2 3 4 5 6 7 8 9 10 11 12 13 14 15 16 17 18	5 = ☆ ☆☆☆ =

Teacher: ______

Student: ______

Dates: ______

Contract		
What I Do	My Count	What Happens
	1 2 3 4 5 6 7 8 9 10 11 12 13 14 15 16 17 18 19 20	Each day = get 00000 Lose 0 for each talk out. End of day (L) 00 = help teacher

Teacher: ______

Student: ______

Dates: ______

Behavior-development-center contracts.[16]

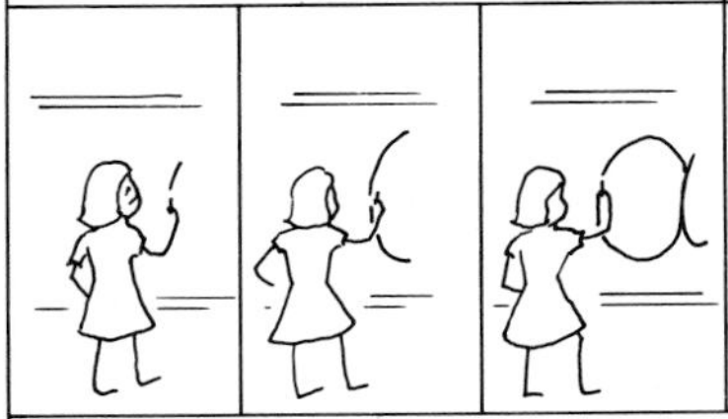

pline. B. F. Skinner has commented that a person would never learn to play a piano if the person had to wait a week to hear the note played. In baseball parks, electric scoreboards literally explode the very moment a home-run ball lands in the seats. The opera audience does not wait a month to reward an outstanding aria. A doctor is congratulated on the spot after a successful surgical operation.

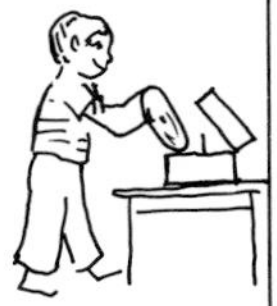

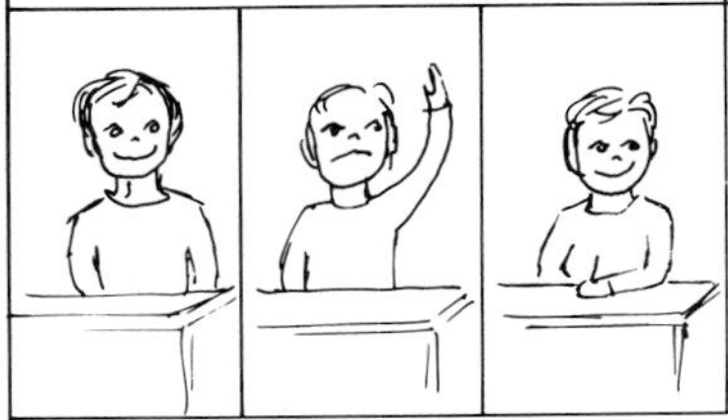

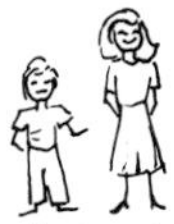

Don't employ the system too broadly

Try the system in single areas for relatively brief periods of time. It would be an obvious mistake to bombard a child with an endless series of contracts—there can be too much of a good thing, so to speak. Thus, if we have children "chart-

Contract

Date:_____

I will earn checks ✓ each day for

     ✓ *raising* hand to speak . . .

     ✓✓✓ *helping* others . . .

     ✓✓ *working* at each center . . .

I will lose checks ✓ each day for

     ✓ talking out . . .

     ✓✓ fighting . . .

     ✓✓ not working . . .

At the end of the week . . . I may . . .

✓✓✓✓✓✓ = 1. extra recess time
✓✓✓✓✓✓   2. "good" note home
             3. extra art time
             4. Hershey bar

Teacher:_____

Student:_____

M   T   W   TH   F   M   T   W   TH   F

ing" in all their subject areas, in a series of personal-management domains, and in extracurricular activities, the entire system of contracting may soon become aversive. The pupils will feel trapped, hemmed in, and rebellious. And that is not an invitation to ask them to keep track of that too!

Contract system helpful in mastering a variety of tasks

Naturally, the point of the contract system is to help pupils become successful in mastering a variety of tasks. It can provide positive motivation to help children focus their energies, receive positive feedback, and develop a sense of personal mastery in learning. The chart obviously should be used to help a child see how he or she is improving. Each child compares present performance only with his or her past performance—it would be destructive to have them compare their charts with each other, since the whole point of individualizing instruction would be lost amidst a flurry of competition. If I initially don't know how to read and then learn to recognize "cat," "hat," "bat," and "sat," that achievement should be regarded as significant in its own right. I should not be asked to compare my progress with that of another pupil who's learning to parse the ablative case in Latin.

THE CASE FOR MAINSTREAMING

Recently Nicholas Hobbes, an eminent educational psychologist and clinician, headed a national commission charged with the responsibility of examining the problems of special-education classification systems. In a work significantly titled *The Futures of Children*,[17] Hobbes advances the thesis that a comprehensive educational plan is required to classify children according to the services they need rather than the capabilities they lack. Special education and "regular" education essentially need the same point of view—namely, to create and emphasize educational programs that start where the learner is and then stimulate and nurture positive development. Both new skills and positive attitudes are needed for educational success in this area. For too long we have been satisfied to follow policies too-often designed to exclude or segregate significant numbers of children from not only the mainstream of schooling, but from life as well. When so-called retarded children are placed in regular classrooms containing effective accommodative capacities, the pupils make as much or more educational progress than they would if they remained in separate classes. In addition to "academic" learning, such pupils all gained socially: their self-concepts became more positive, less stigmatized, and less characterized by self-hatred and self-contempt.

A key factor in the entire concept of mainstreaming is the phrase *"increasing the accommodative capacity of all classrooms to respond to a broad range of individual differences."* A responsive humane environment with positive regard to all children and sets of manageable learning tasks represents an appropriate learning atmosphere for *all* children. In other words, we can either say that special education becomes less "special" or that all education becomes more special and significant for each child.

Summary

As a result of new legislation, a major policy shift has been implemented concerning special-education classes. Instead of separate or segregated classrooms for so-called "Educable Mentally Retarded" (EMR), these pupils are to be mainstreamed.

The process of mainstreaming involves placing EMR children in regular classes for virtually the entire day. The policy shift occurred for numerous reasons: (1) research studies indicated special-class pupils showed no significant academic gains in separate schools and a definite decline in self-concept; (2) the Supreme Court had declared segregated classes separate and not equal in previous decisions; and (3) the public school is for all children.

Assessment for special-education placement has most often been based on far too narrow evaluation procedures. The limitations of IQ testing, for example, make this an inadequate method. A more-dynamic assessment system based on Evelyn Deno's "Cascade" is suggested. Special placements should always be considered temporary. The child should be shifted to constantly less-restrictive environments on a gradual basis.

Studies are reviewed indicating the powerful effects of stimulating, facilitating environments on positive cognitive growth. Particular mention is made of Skodak and Skeels, Heber, Scarr-Salapatek, and Weinberg. In all these studies, many preschool children were initially classified, on the basis of IQ, as retarded or slow learners.

A developmental approach, "precise teaching," is noted as an educational program for so-called EMR children. Based on Piaget, Hunt, Robert White, and Skinnerian principles, the program would involve the use of high-structured learning environments, concrete tasks, immediate feedback, and visible and significant positive reinforcement at the outset. Through such individualization, newly mainstreamed children can develop and progress at their own speed. Gradually, the amount of structure can be reduced and extrinsic reinforcers lessened.

REFERENCES

1
D. Bakan, *The Slaughter of the Innocents* (San Francisco: Jossey-Bass, 1971).

2
Harper Lee, *To Kill a Mockingbird* (New York: Popular Library, 1962), pp. 31–32. Copyright © 1960 by Harper Lee. Reprinted by permission of J. B. Lippincott Company.

3
B. Blatt, "The Physical, Personality and Academic Status of Children Who Are Mentally Retarded Attending Special Classes as Compared with Children Who Are Mentally Retarded Attending Regular Classes," *American Journal of Mental Deficiency* 62 (1958): 810–818.

4
G. S. Baroff, *Mental Retardation: Nature, Cause, and Management* (New York: Wiley, 1974).

5
M. Reynolds, *Exceptional Children in Regular Classrooms* (Minneapolis: University of Minnesota, Department of Audio-Visual Extension, 1972).

6
Danial Keyes, *Flowers for Algernon* (New York: Bantam, 1967), p. 202. Reprinted by permission of Harcourt Brace Jovanovich, Inc.

7
B. Blatt, *Exodus from Pandemonium: Human Abuse and a Reformation of Public Policy* (Boston: Allyn and Bacon, 1970).

8
Virginia Axline, *Dibs* (New York: Ballantine, 1967), p. 90. Reprinted by permission.

9
Evelyn Deno, "Special Education as Developmental Capital," *Exceptional Children* 37 (1970): 229–237.

10
M. Skodak and H. M. Skeels, "A Final Follow-up Study on One Hundred Adopted Children," *J. Genetic Psychology* 75 (1949):85–125.

11
S. Scarr-Salapatek and R. Weinberg, "The War Over Race and IQ," *Psychology Today* 9, no. 7 (1975):80–82.

12
Eleanor Pavenstedt, *The Drifters* (Boston: Little, Brown, 1967), p. 219.

13
W. Jack Birch, *Mainstreaming* (Reston, Virginia: Council for Exceptional Children, 1974), p. 94.

14
Stanley Deno, "Attitudes toward Mainstreaming Scale," Pattee Hall, University of Minnesota, Minneapolis.

15
D. Hunt and E. Sullivan, *Between Psychology and Education* (New York: Dryden, 1974).

16
B. Dollar, Leadership Training Institute, Burton Hall, Univ. of Minnesota, Minneapolis.

17
Nicholas Hobbs, *The Future of Children* (San Francisco: Jossey-Bass, 1975).

SUGGESTIONS FOR FURTHER READING

Edgerton, Robert B. *The Cloak of Competence: Stigma in the Lives of the Mentally Retarded.* Berkeley and Los Angeles: University of California Press, 1967. (219 pages, bibliography and index; foreword by Walter Goldschmidt.) A research study presented as a series of portraits describing the lives of adult "retardates" living outside an institution.

Hewett, F. M., and S. R. Forness. *Education of Exceptional Learners.* Boston: Allyn and Bacon, 1974.

Smith, R. M., and J. T. Neisworth. *The Exceptional Child.* New York: McGraw-Hill, 1975.

Both are highly recommended as basic comprehensive introductions to the complete range of special education concerns—retardation, physical handicaps, and a wide variety of different educational interventions.

23

Contemporary issues

As the demand for quality education increases, there will be a corresponding increase in the public awareness of and concern for educational policy issues. The school will not remain apart from the rest of the community; the public will increasingly question, criticize, and even oppose educational programs. This criticism and opposition will range from public debate at school-board meetings to individual teacher-parent conferences. The increased costs of education and a generally increased educational level combine to make a more-informed, more-interested, and less-compliant public than ever before. This means that program changes, curriculum innovations, and new policies will stimulate public questioning.

This chapter reviews briefly some of the major policy questions currently confronting educators, in order to acquaint you with the issues you yourselves will have to confront. We hope to expand your awareness of the necessity for educational psychology to relate to the real world of school, children, teenagers, and the community. In Chapter 1 we noted that the field is now moving from an exclusive focus on laboratory experimentation to observation and experimentation in the natural setting of the classroom. We called this recent trend an ecological focus because it involves studying educational problems in a broad context that includes the psychological variables of each individual child and the teacher, and the learning atmosphere of the classroom. Those who implement educational policies, who put theory into practice, are the hope of the future. If they fail to reverse the trends of the past, maintaining the separation of research, theory, and practice, the field in the future will be exactly as it is now, and future generations of children will be as "turned off" as they presently are. Fifty years from now another educational psychology text will start a Chapter 2 just the way we did in this volume, showing that teaching and learning remain separate from and almost unaffected by theory and research.

LEARNING TO READ

Almost all schoolchildren learn to read. Reading is a central part of the curriculum in every school district in the country. Yet, there seems to be no consensus about the best way to teach this very important subject. Instead, there is a great diversity of techniques, each claiming superiority over its rivals. What is the best way to teach Dick and Jane to read? Fifty years of research have been devoted to the question in this country alone. Surely there must be some documented answers.

Learning to read: the unending debate

Jeanne Chall, an eminent authority on reading, reviewed practically the entire body of research conducted from 1912 through 1965 and concluded that "some of the most fundamental questions have yet to be asked." Not only did she find much of the reading research to be of little consequence, she also noted that the way beginning reading was being taught was almost always inconsistent with the few substantial research findings. For example, the studies

After reviewing the major reading research of 1912 through 1965, Jeanne Chall concluded that "some of the most fundamental questions have yet to be asked."

demonstrated that the best way to teach beginning reading (first through third grade) was by teaching phonics—separate letter sounds—first. This code-breaking approach begins by systematically teaching children what each letter sounds like. Even though this method has been demonstrated to help children learn to read faster than do other approaches, most children have been taught by other procedures.

Although Professor Chall has observed that the code approach produces literacy and comprehension rates, and possibly even reading speed more efficiently than do other methods, she does not speculate on the reasons for the almost universal use of an inferior method, the so-called meaning-emphasis approach. She does note that there has been a long-standing fear that if children learn the code first, they will not learn what the words they decode actually mean. This fear has apparently prompted us to ignore the research findings and continue to teach children the meanings of words before they know what the alphabet is all about. In addition, Professor Chall found that it does not matter which code system is used. The ITA (Initial Teaching Alphabet) with "cum" for "come" and the Rebus Vocabulary with "C" for "see" achieve similar results. She notes, "I cannot emphasize too strongly that the evidence does not endorse any one code-emphasis method over another."[1]

Furthermore, Professor Chall emphasizes that a code method is appropriate only to teach beginning reading. As soon as children can recognize in print the words they know, it is a sheer waste of time to continue decoding. It may be significant that she concludes her work with the remark that authors and publishers of readers are already misinterpreting her. "They are developing decoding exercises for upper elementary and high school pupils, erroneously assuming that if this approach is good at the beginning, it is also good later on."[2]

For some reason the field of reading progresses only with difficulty. Professor Chall wryly documents the fact that in the 1920s silent reading was found to be good for older pupils and that it was immediately assumed that silent reading must therefore be good for beginners, too, even though the beginners could have little idea of what all those printed characters were supposed to represent. So, too, today. If our schools adopt decoding methods for older elementary and junior-high nonreaders, they will be making the same kind of mistake—generalizing beyond the evidence.

In addition to her major recommendation, Professor Chall also suggests that we take the following steps:

1

Reexamine current ideas about content. Too many people are making serious recommendations about content on the basis of no evidence at all. Questions for reexamination include: "Should all the stories be familiar?" "Should folktales and fairy tales be used?" The real problem here seems to be that many people are pinning their hopes of helping inner-city children on changing content alone. It is hard to imagine that rewriting Dick and Jane in terms of, say, the black experience will in itself produce results.

2

Reevaluate grade levels. Research evidence does not justify the restricted vocabulary of most beginning reading books now being used. Such vocabularies are understimulating our children. "Schools should take the ceilings off the levels of readers from which children now receive instruction."[3]

3
Develop new tests.   The present standardized reading tests seem a poor compromise. They often "mask" the effects of reading instruction. Tests should be devised to assess progress in specific areas, such as word recognition, letter sounds, comprehension, critical readings, and appreciation. The present standardized tests tend to measure a "conglomerate of skills and abilities at the same time."[4]

Professor Chall concludes that although much is already known about effective reading instruction, much remains to be learned. Her minute examination of the research, a sifting and sorting process that required enormous skill and patience, indicated that the major problem is still that of translating research findings into classroom practice. In fact, it is discouraging to note how easily present practice distorts and defeats important educational ideas. In our view, teachers, counselors, and administrators must understand the practical implications of educational programs and policies. Without such understanding, their practice will remain uninformed, and they will continue to repeat past errors.

EQUALITY OR INEQUALITY OF EDUCATIONAL OPPORTUNITY

Coleman sets out to document the effects of racial segregation

In 1964, when the United States Congress commissioned the eminent social scientist James Coleman to study the impact of schooling, one of the findings everyone anticipated was that children in all-black schools were being denied equal access to educational opportunity. The U.S. Office of Education apparently wished to document the gross differences in school facilities between predominantly white and predominantly black schools. Coleman set to work, and from 1964 to 1966 conducted a massive survey of almost 600,000 pupils, 60,000 teachers, and 4000 schools—by far the largest social-science investigation of the general effect of schooling ever attempted.[5] And, while engaged in the study, Coleman was quoted as saying in an interview, "The study will show the difference in the quality of schools that the average Negro child and the average white child are exposed to. You know yourself that the difference is going to be striking."[6]

In fact, the original Coleman report, published in 1966, shocked educators and the general public because its findings were in direct opposition to expectations. The report did indicate that the country was maintaining essentially two separate school systems, one white and one black. Eighty percent of all white pupils (K–12) attended schools that were 90 to 100 percent all white, and sixty-five percent of all black pupils (K–12) attended virtually all-black schools. But:

1
There were no large differences in school facilities (buildings, libraries, laboratories) between white schools and black schools.

2
Differences in the academic achievement of pupils were not significantly related to the physical facilities (bricks and mortar) or to the characteristics of the teachers (background and training).

Thus, the bombshell: the amount a student learns in school bears little relation to the usual educational "inputs"—i.e., the facilities and the characteristics of the teachers. The variables that affect student learning are far more complicated.

Coleman finds social-class effects stronger than racial

The two variables that were found to be most directly related to pupil achievement were the socioeconomic level of the family and the socioeconomic background of the other pupils in the particular school. In other words, the socioeconomic level of the community had a much greater effect on achievement than the teachers' characteristics, the school facilities, or the curriculum. The social-class backgrounds comprehend interests, values, and attitudes toward learning, economic variables such as unemployment or underemployment, and attitudes toward community involvement and participation in school policies that inevitably determine the school's viability as an educational institution. (The socioeconomic correlations are reported in Table 23.1) The report then pointed out that the initial differences, primarily those of social class, continue to be the important differences throughout the years of formal public education (the study examined children in grades 1, 3, 6, 9, and 12).

Thus, instead of reaching the expected conclusion that the way to provide equal educational opportunity for all children would be to eliminate segregated schools, the report suggested that the problem was too complex and difficult for easy solutions. It basically documented the class-linked nature of the supposedly free public-school system of the country. If we close the all-white schools and the all-black schools while retaining lower-class, working-class, middle-class, and upper-class schools, we will have changed nothing in terms of the inequality of educational opportunity. If we mix white and black children from the same social class, we may change some racial attitudes, but there will be no significant change in the achievements of either group.

Individual initiative and socioeconomic forces

One of our most-cherished myths has received a challenge from the Coleman Report. We have always believed that every individual can pull himself up by his own boot straps. We even point to the few exceptions that seem to prove the rule: If Abraham Lincoln could teach himself by firelight with a broken slate ... If A. Phillip Randolph could rise from being a pullman car porter ... If Shir-

Table 23.1 Academic achievement: grade nine.*

	Correlations			
	r Black North	r Black South	r White North	r White South
Family background (socioeconomic levels)	+.23	+.22	+.34	+.34
Student-body characteristics (socioeconomic levels)	+.23	+.23	+.09	+.11
Teacher educational training	+.13	+.12	+.09	+.07
Physical facilities	+.13	+.07	+.10	+.07

*
The correlations for grades six and twelve are essentially the same as those reported for grade nine.

ley Chisholm could make it through the urban ghetto to run for president . . . If Daniel Patrick Moynihan could rise from "Hells Kitchen" in the Bronx and become ambassador to the UN . . . , and on and on. In fact, however, these outstanding exceptions are just that. The implication is that the future, for most children, is entirely predictable, as long as schools continue to serve homogeneous socioeconomic populations.

At the beginning of this volume we warned against the danger of simple cause-and-effect thinking. The Coleman Report exploded the myth that educational problems and inequality of educational opportunity could be eradicated by eliminating the country's dual school system. Given the magnitude of the problem, a quick and easy solution is obviously a fantasy, but it would be just as wrong to conclude that the problem is too enormous to solve. Educational policy and practice, however, can change if some small but important steps are taken. Recognizing class-linked schools and understanding the effect of teachers' attitudes toward children of different social classes are a beginning. Informed educators can begin the process of reducing the effects of social-status variables and of increasing the importance and power of the learning experiences for children and teenagers.

In the decade of the 1960s billions of dollars were spent on educational innovations that yielded few positive results. Hopefully we have learned from that experience that fast change never really scratches more than the surface of educational reform. It will take a sustained effort of effective leadership from the superintendent to the classroom teacher, and from the national to the local level. Effective schooling may not be able to achieve a goal such as complete equality of intellectual and technological skills. The idea that each person is infinitely educable is surely a romantic illusion. At the same time it is clear that schooling can be improved so that the level of human development, both the cognitive and the personal, can be facilitated.

DYSLEXIA—WORD BLINDNESS

In addition to the fifty-year controversy about learning to read, an equally long debate has been waged over the question of word blindness in children and teenagers. Although given various labels, such as dyslexia (word disability), strephosymbolia (twisting symbols), and minimal brain dysfunction, the symptoms of the syndrome are all the same. Essentially, children and teenagers afflicted with this disability reverse words and numbers, have enormous difficulty spelling, remembering telephone numbers, looking up words in a dictionary, keeping number columns straight, and learning a foreign language—to name just a few

Dyslexia: problems in symbolic processing

of the most-common symbolic processing areas. One of the great advances in the evolution of Homo sapiens was the development of symbolic communication. For all the obvious reasons, it was a great leap forward for humans over animals to invent language, writing, and a wide variety of symbols. Thus, for any human to experience difficulty in this most-basic area of functioning creates substantial barriers to growth, particularly with respect to school learning. Since many of the objectives of schooling are related to symbolic manipulation—the three R's are exclusively symbolic—any fundamental deficiency in intellectual processing necessarily has a broad impact.

Dyslexia has afflicted many famous and successful people. Public figures such as Nelson Rockefeller, General Patton, Thomas Edison, and Woodrow Wilson have all described the frustrations they suffered during their difficult school days.

The syndrome has a long history and has afflicted many famous people. Public figures such as Einstein, General Patton, Woodrow Wilson, and Nelson Rockefeller have all described in the most poignant way what it was really like during these most difficult school days. They were being asked to perform activities that they literally could not understand. In math, for example, a child might be asked to add 783 and 227, but might actually read these numbers as 873 and 272 without realizing the reversal. Thus, when his answer was marked wrong, the reason for his failure would remain a mystery. Similarly, in writing, "no" might become "on," "god" might be seen as "dog," and so on (or so no!). Again, and this is hard for nondyslexic people to realize, the child is almost totally unaware of the reversals in letters. Nelson Rockefeller's diary, written at age twelve, contained the following phrases: "picknick lunc, Uncil Harold, engen repar schop, parak" (for park) and three tries at writing the childhood diseases of sister Abby and brother Lawrence as "mealess, measless, mislees."* The feeling is similar to being asked to play a game without knowing the rules. It's worse, however, because you wouldn't be able to understand the rules even after having been told and would have to try madly to figure out what cues other people seemed to be following. You'd find yourself pretending, copying, feigning, and perhaps even learning to put on a pretty good act. Underneath, of course, that awful gnawing feeling would remain: "at any moment I may be unmasked, revealed as an imposter and fake." In a game it would be troublesome; in real school learning situations it may be tragic.

In spite of the long history of personal accounts, systematic research studies, and a wide variety of documentation, there continues to be substantial opposition to acknowledging the existence of the disability within educational circles. Estimates run as high as one of seven pupils afflicted, with a large preponderance of males over females. There remains, however, on the part of too many teachers, a substantial resistance to admitting that some pupils actually suffer from the disability. At an intuitive level the common view is that it is just a question of willfulness and motivation; somehow the dyslexic child isn't really working hard enough: "All it takes is an act of will"; "Let's not coddle our pupils"; "It's important to treat all children equally without exceptions"; "If the child recopies the assignment enough times..."; "We can't accept such messy papers..."; and so on. Thus one myth is that word blindness is really just a crutch masking a failure of will.

A second common misperception is that, if dyslexia isn't a fancy psychological label for laziness, it's just a cover-up for mental retardation. The reason that Johnny can't read, or add, or spell, is simple—he's stupid. Even though studies have shown that individually administered IQ scores do not correlate with dyslexia, this second myth continues. The ability to think at an abstract level is not impaired by dyslexia, even though the written product may be filled with a myriad of technical flaws, misspellings, poor paragraph construction, scratched-out words, and the like. The real error is to assume that technical performance

Too many teachers refuse to acknowledge the problem

---

*
Quoted in an article by Warren R. Young, *Minneapolis Tribune*, 28 September 1975. This prompted one of the authors to recall that he had been secretary of a junior-high-school "Raido" club, a fact recalled when perusing a recently discovered juvenile "dairy."

—like keeping numbers in neat columns, accuracy in spelling, and correct punctuation—are indices of intellectual functioning.

If teachers have experienced difficulty in accepting the reality of dyslexia, psychologists and researchers have had difficulty in documenting the causes. In fact, for too long researchers have attempted to discover the single crucial factor. Much of the work in this area for the past fifty years can be characterized in this manner, the hunt for the one variable that explains it all. The so-called rosetta stone search for a single key has proved to be disappointing. Also, it has resulted in a bewildering array of single prescriptions. Each single variable has its proponents; from each single "cause" springs a single solution. Some feel the problem is basically a physical-coordination deficiency. Others suggest a chemical basis from artificial food coloring or a hyperactivity due to a drug imbalance, or a psychoanalytic problem from anal fixation, or a lack of training during the formative preschool years, or a problem of birth order, or of parental neglect, or fatherless homes. The physical-coordination school suggests solutions ranging from reliance on exercises, such as bouncing on trampolines, jumping rope, walking balance beams, and bouncing basketballs, to the extreme of surgical correction, such as removal of adenoids or altering eye muscles. The chemical-view proponents suggest measures such as the careful supervision of diet, food without preservatives, and massive doses of vitamins, tranquilizers, and sea-sickness pills. Theorists who attribute dyslexia to an intrapsychic problem suggest solutions ranging from individual counseling and play therapy to family analysis.

As we have been emphasizing throughout, human behavior cannot be reduced to a single cause, yet when a problem like dyslexia comes along researchers tend to forget that dictum and grab for a single explanation and cure. It is disheartening indeed to find parents, teachers, and educators first resisting that dyslexia exists at all, and then, reversing field almost 180 degrees, not only accepting the problem but seeking a single magical cure. Recently a somewhat cynical educational psychologist commented that, in the last decade, all the people who sold used cars, bait-and-switch real estate in Florida, and bust-development machines have moved into the dyslexia business. In fact as a teacher you may be questioned in depth by anxious parents or school boards as to which single remedy is best—the "talking" typewriter, the sensory-deprivation booth, the color-coded alphabet, underwater swimming, behavior modification, organized crawling, or wall-to-wall trampolines?

Both theory and research evidence, of course, strongly suggest that no singular technique will produce cures. In fact, the remedies are something less than spectacular, consisting of multisensory tutoring and massive amounts of human support. If some pupils cannot use the usual channels for processing symbols, then an educational program needs to include a broader array of techniques and experiences. Multisensory programs allow the child quite obviously to use all the senses—see the letter, trace it in sand, cut it out of cardboard, say it out loud, pick it out of magazine ads and street signs, and touch it in block form. Thus the techniques really come down to "good" instruction— namely, an array of alternatives to help children learn the code. The same "solutions" apply to helping pupils learn to produce symbols. Since regular writing is difficult and at times torturous, other channels can be employed. In addition to paper and pencil, fat crayons, and chalk and blackboard, pupils can

The rosetta stone search for a single cause

No single technique will produce a cure

also be "allowed" to tape-record reports, give oral reports in class, or use a typewriter.

Employing multiple techniques is, of course, not enough. In learning new and difficult tasks, any pupil will need extra human support and encouragement—and this support is especially crucial for the dyslexic child. Signs of impatience, despair, and discouragement by a teacher are quickly transmitted to a child afflicted with word blindness, and such a child will be hyperalert to teacher feelings. Positive human support is necessary to create a low-anxiety atmosphere that will help the pupil take risks and not feel it necessary to cover up his or her difficulty. Some dyslexic children learn magnificent social skills to prevent a teacher from finding out that they can't read or write. Probably the best tutoring in this instance would be from older children and adults who themselves have struggled with the problem. Given support, encouragement, and a multi-sensory approach, the word-blind children do learn to read. They also learn that they are worthy and useful citizens. There simply are no shortcuts; it takes long effort, consistent positive support, and patience.

THE OPEN CLASSROOM

In the last decade there has been an increasing interest in the concept of the open classroom. As with most new educational concepts, substantial confusion exists as to the exact meaning of the idea, resulting in great diversity in practice.

Open classrooms and free schools—a difference

One important distinction to make is that the open classroom is not the same as the so-called "free school." The free school is what could be termed laissez-faire education or spontaneous schooling. The adults who run free schools impose no conditions, no sanctions, and no structure on learning. The pupils are free to come and go, partake in learning activities if they want, or simply sit and wool-gather if that be their bent. The open classroom, however, is basically a structured learning environment in which students are encouraged to initiate and participate in learning activities. Carefully planned learning centers or stations are constructed. Options, alternatives, and a variety of approaches are deliberately presented to engage the pupils' attention.

In many ways the concept of the open classroom relates directly to Piaget's developmental concepts. The open classroom deliberately builds in a series of options. Children are not expected to study the same subject at the same time and in the same way. Whereas the teacher-dominated, static atmosphere of the regular classroom teaches passivity and lowers student initiative, Piaget has shown that the key to cognitive development is just the opposite. A pupil needs to act on material and actively confront ideas. In everyday language, when we speak of "hitting the books," "tackling theories," "attacking problems," we are referring to active learning. When we say that students learn best with a "hands on" experience, we are talking about the open classroom. The open classroom

Active learning

involves both active learning and as much direct experience as possible. The teachers design the environment and create the conditions that will, if all goes well, facilitate the growth of each pupil.

The flexibility and individual initiative of the open classroom does not mean that children can avoid learning to read, write, and do numbers. The open classroom is merely designed to break out of the lock-step approach to learning and to individualize instruction. Piaget has indicated that development is uneven and characterized by individual differences. Students in the open classroom can pursue topics the very moment they discover an interest in them. A student may be extremely interested in reading at one time during the school year, in scientific experimentation at another, in art and sculpture in yet another. The classroom is designed so that the students don't have to drop what they may be actively engaged in simply because the time period usually allocated to that learning activity has expired.

Breaking the lock-step approach

It is obviously fine to say that the open classroom is based on individualized learning. We all like the sound of that idea: it connotes respect for the individual pupil. The idea of the open classroom is also appealing because it sounds easy. Probably the most-important single point to underscore is that teaching in an open classroom is more demanding and more tiring than teaching in a regular classroom. And this is because the classroom is geared to individual differences. In this sense, the teacher in the open classroom, or as it is sometimes called, the "integrated day," is in charge of individual lesson plans for every child. The teacher may be guiding twenty or twenty-five instructional units simultaneously —no easy task, and yet essential to the idea of learning monitored and paced by the pupil.

The "integrated day"

Some of the major assumptions inherent in the open classroom are the following.

Assumptions concerning children

1
Children are innately curious and display exploratory behavior without being prompted by adults.

2
Exploratory behavior is self-reinforcing under conditions with low levels of anxiety.

3
Self-confidence comes with decision making and self-direction.

4
Play and work are not necessarily separate activities for young children.

Intellectual development

1
Concept formation occurs slowly.

2
Active learning and active manipulation facilitate cognitive growth.

3
Children go through similar stages of cognitive growth, but each in his or her own way and own time.

4
Experience should precede verbal explanations, action followed by reflection or examination.

Kenneth B. Clark

Kenneth B. Clark, noted black educator and psychologist, was born in the Panama Canal Zone in 1914. Clark's father, Arthur B. Clark, was a passenger agent for the United Fruit Company in Panama. When young Clark was five years old, his mother left Panama for the United States, bringing her children with her. To support the children, Mrs. Clark worked as a seamstress in a New York garment factory where she also helped organize a union. Clark says his first contact with social issues was listening to his mother tell of her problems in trying to organize a union in her shop.

Clark's education began at Public School 5 in Harlem. Later he attended P.S. 139 and then graduated from George Washington High School. The following year he enrolled at Howard University in Washington, D.C. He received his B.A. degree from Howard in 1935 and his M.A. in 1936, when he was twenty-two years of age. For the next two years Clark taught psychology at Howard, but the following year he enrolled as a Ph.D. candidate in experimental psychology at Columbia University. He was awarded his degree in 1940, and during the academic year 1940–1941 he became an assistant professor of psychology at the Hampton Institute in Virginia. The following year, Clark worked as a social science analyst for the Office of War Information, traveling throughout the country in his study of morale problems in black population centers. In 1942 he joined the psychology department of the College of the City of New York, where he has been ever since. He became a full professor in 1960.

In 1946 Clark and his wife, Dr. Mamie Clark, established the non-profit Northside Center for Child Development in New York City. The center is devoted to treating children with emotional problems. In 1950 Clark worked on a report which showed that segregation in the schools is detrimental to the growth and development of white as well as black children. The United States Supreme Court relied on Clark's study when, in 1954, it made its important decision that segregation in public schools is unconstitutional.

Clark has devoted his life to improving school conditions for all children. He has found racial prejudice to be a two-edged sword that harms both the prejudiced as well as the objects of the prejudice. In 1970 Clark received his colleagues' highest honor when he was named president of the American Psychological Association. His many articles and books include: *Desegregation: An Appraisal of the Evidence* (1953), *Prejudice and Your Child* (1955), *Dark Ghetto* (1965), and *A Relevant War against Poverty* (1968).

As an educator and psychologist, Kenneth Clark ranks at the top of his profession. Although a brilliant theorist, he has not sought refuge in an ivory tower, but prefers to remain on the front lines, working, doing, and making things happen.

Examination

1

Errors are an important part of the learning process and should be expected and desired.

2

Learning can be assessed intuitively by direct observation.

3

The most-accurate evaluation occurs by careful observation over long periods of time.

4

Children can learn what kind of questions they can ask and answer for themselves and what kind require help from an external authority.[7]

The interest in open education increased substantially when the so-called Plowden Report was published in England. The study team, headed by Lady Bridget Plowden, advocated the creation of the open-classroom model as a kind of master plan for elementary education. Whether or not such a plan succeeds, of course, ultimately depends on a corps of trained teachers who can put the ideas into practice. With some rather precise British phraseology the report notes:

> *What is immediately needed is that teachers should bring to bear . . .*
> *astringent intellectual scrutiny. Yet, all good teachers must work intuitively*
> *and be sensitive to the emotive and imaginative needs of their children.*[8]

There has recently been an attempt to examine actual classrooms for evidence about the comparative nature of the open and the traditional class by trained participant-observers (see Table 23.2 for socioeconomic classification). More than sixty classrooms in the United States and Great Britain were examined.

The classes were visited at least three times. The observational scales were then scored and coded. The results yielded the five major characteristics of open classrooms described on the following page.

Table 23.2 Classrooms studied by Walberg and Thomas.

	Nos. of classrooms		
	United States		Britain
Socioeconomic status	Traditional	Open	Open
Higher	12	11	11
Lower	9	10	9
Total	21	21	20

1

Provisioning for learning. Manipulative materials are supplied in great diversity and range with little replication, i.e., not class sets. Children move freely about the room without asking permission. Talking among children is encouraged. The teacher does not group children by ability according to test or norms. Children generally group and regroup themselves through their own choices.

2

Humaneness, respect, openess, and warmth. Children use "books" written by their classmates as part of their reading and reference materials. The environment includes materials developed or supplied by the children. Teacher takes care of dealing with conflicts and disruptive behavior without involving the group. Children's activities, products, and ideas are reflected abundantly about the classroom.

3

Diagnosis of learning events. Teacher does not use test results to group children for reading and/or math. Children do not expect the teacher to correct all their work. Teacher gives children tests to find out what they know. To obtain diagnostic information, the teacher closely observes the specific work or concern of a child and asks immediate, experience-based questions.

4

Instruction, guidance, and extension of learning. Teacher bases instruction on each individual child and his or her interaction with materials and equipment. The work children do is not divided into subject-matter areas. The teacher's lessons and assignments are not given to the class as a whole. Teacher does not base instruction on curriculum guides or text books for the grade level he or she teaches. Before suggesting any extension or redirection of activity, teacher gives diagnostic attention to the particular child and his or her particular activity.

5

Evaluation of diagnostic information. Teacher keeps notes and writes individual histories of each child's intellectual, emotional, physical development. Teacher may have children for more than just one year. Teacher does not use tests to evaluate children and rate them in comparison to their peers. Teacher keeps a collection of each child's work for use in evaluating development. Teacher views evaluation as information to guide instruction and provisioning for the classroom.[9]

Five major characteristics of the open classroom

As you read these actual observations of teachers in open-classroom work with pupils, you will note how well they fit the assumptions outlined above. The open-classroom teachers were rated high on all these activities, whereas the traditional classroom teachers were rated low. The authors of this important study acknowledge that their work is, in effect, just beginning. Now that they have established that genuine differences exist between what really happens in open and in traditional classes, "seeing if these processes are related to valued educational outcomes is an obvious next step for those who wish to evaluate Open Education."[10]

COMPETENCY-BASED TEACHER EDUCATION

An important new issue in education and public policy is the so-called performance or competency base for teaching. The logic seems clear and the reasoning faultless. To make teaching accountable, school boards, colleges of education and the like should specify in observable terms a list of positive teacher competencies. Once the list is identified, then we merely hold up the catalogue of such competent behaviors and see if a teacher measures up. The recent upsurge of interest across the nation has been no doubt partly due to the clear and simple logic of such an appeal. It sounds reasonable and is certainly much more appealing than viewing teaching and learning as an enigma.

The creation of the Multi-State Consortium on Performance-Based Teacher Education and the 1974 National Conference on Competency, Assessment, Research and Evaluation attest to the growing institutionalization of the concept. State departments of education, teachers unions, and educational administrators are becoming heavily involved in the process of analyzing teaching from a competency base. There is even the possibility that many states may require a series of behaviorally described teacher competencies for pre-service and in-service teacher certification. In other words, instead of requiring the accumulation of undergraduate and/or graduate course credits for a teaching certificate, states

Certification based on teacher behaviors

may move toward certification based on teacher behaviors in the form of a competency checklist. Whether a teacher can actually perform in a classroom with children becomes the criterion, rather than course grades as such.

The difficulties with the competency framework are almost as great as the promise. It is hard to quarrel with the basic objective that in the long run it is how well a teacher actually performs that counts. If a surgeon could write "A" papers on theories of medicine yet couldn't handle a scalpel, we probably wouldn't line up outside his or her operating room for appendectomies. A lawyer who could write brilliant briefs yet couldn't conduct a cross-examination would hardly be our choice for an important trial. A dentist who doesn't know the difference between a drill and the novocaine needle. . . . You can readily see that in any profession the performance question sooner or later becomes the significant outcome focus. We have stressed that view continually throughout this volume—teaching is both thinking and doing. The problem, of course, is

The problem: creating and specifying teacher competencies

creating and specifying the exact nature of teaching competencies. It is on this point that all the controversy about PBTE (Performance-Based Teacher Education) comes to a head in the form of the following questions:

1
Who decides what competencies are placed on the "approved" list?

2
How specific can the behaviors be defined to avoid erring in the direction of the overly microscopic or the absurdly broad?

3
How can the behaviors be classified or grouped into larger categories?

These three questions are really subsets of the larger questions: Is there an adequate theory for teacher education and do we need a theory at all?

Bruce Joyce has recently commented, with regard to the first question, that the difficulty in determining who decides on the approved competencies involves the question of present skills versus the skills required of future teachers. If we examine today's teaching skills, "They will look more like the skills of a country postmaster than those of a creative artist or behavioral technician."[11] Thus, it might be a substantial mistake to draw up a long list of country postmaster skills if we are really seeking creative teaching artists.

Similarly, the second question raises a series of problems as to the definition of the competency. We noted earlier that educational objectives have suffered from this same definitional problem—i.e., they tend to be overly cosmic or too mundane and trivial. Thus a teacher competency might be defined behaviorally as, "maintains at least one-second eye contact with each pupil during questioning"; or, at the other extreme, as, "humanely self-actualizes all pupils." If we move toward specificity, as in the first case, we would need a list as long as the shopping list for the Man from St. Ives (with Seven Wives, and Seven Cats, and Seven Kits, etc.). Indeed, one of the major criticisms of PBTE is that it may produce an almost infinite "laundry list" of highly specific teacher behaviors. On the other hand, if we move too far in the other direction, we may end up defining teaching competence with a series of glittering generalities.

The third problem is also noteworthy since it suggests the necessity of ordering, grouping, or categorizing competencies, again similar to the problem of educational objectives and Bloom's taxonomy. He and his colleagues were able to suggest different levels of objectives based on degrees of complexity.

These three problems clearly suggest the need for an overall framework or theory for teacher education. Such a teaching "model" will help answer the country-postmaster-versus-creative-artist question and the length-of-the-laundry-list question, and will provide a means of ordering and grouping the competencies by variation in educational objectives. Throughout this text we have been suggesting the need for both practice and theory. Without theory, practice really becomes bits and pieces of conventional wisdom, folklore, and a new fad or two, permitting teaching practice to wander more or less aimlessly, constantly subject to the latest bit of educational wisdom. We see, then, that PBTE potentially can offer a significant breath of fresh air to teaching, by forcing us to look both at teaching as practice and at educational objectives. Naturally our own view is that a developmental framework provides needed guidelines for teachers and pupils both in theory and practice for competence.

The need for an overall framework for teacher education

SESAME STREET: CHILDREN AND TELEVISION

Although it has been estimated that children and teenagers watch television an astounding number of hours, there have been surprisingly few systematic attempts to use the medium for a deliberate educational purpose. The few attempts that have occurred in the past decade were for the most part sporadic and at best scratched the surface. For example, public television networks were established for educational objectives, yet the formats for these network shows were anything but imaginative. Most commonly the instructional use was limited to a series of televised lectures, seminar discussions, play productions,

In the late 1960s, the trend toward dullness in public television was dramatically reversed through the efforts of the Children's Television Workshop under the dynamic leadership of Professor Gerald Lesser.

and/or news commentary. By comparison with commercial TV, the low-budget public television seemed dull, pedantic, and unimaginative—and was largely ignored. Thus the 18,000 hours or so that children spend in front of a TV between birth and adulthood have largely been for entertainment.

In the late 1960s this trend was drastically reversed through the efforts of the Children's Television Workshop under the leadership and direction of the dynamic and imaginative Professor Gerald Lesser. Professor Lesser gathered professional educators and experts in the art of television programming, two groups that are not generally considered to have the most compatible working relationship. Educators tend to view TV "types" as excessively crass, commercial exploiters, too concerned with the packaging rather than the quality of the message itself. On the other hand, professionals in television production were often horrified by the seemingly boring word games of academic types. Lesser's work was thus cut out for him right from the start. He needed both groups, but more importantly he needed a synthesis of the two worlds of TV production and legitimate educational instruction. That he was able to walk this tightrope is a tribute to both his leadership skills and the importance of the task itself. In the fall of 1969, the first episode of *Sesame Street* appeared. Soon Big Bird, Bert and Ernie, Oscar the Grouch, and the Cookie Monster were household words among the ten or so million preschool-age children who began to avidly follow the series.

Big Bird and the Cookie Monster reach millions of children via television

Of course the main point of *Sesame Street* was not simply entertainment or to draw big audiences from the short-pants set. Instead, the object was to take some of educational psychology's most important findings and translate those principles into educational lessons for young children. As we noted in Chapters 3 through 6, initial learning experiences prior to grade one are important precursors to success in the regular school years. The developmental framework derived from Piaget, Erik Erikson, Robert White, J. McV. Hunt and others, combined with the research findings of "Bud" White, Rick Heber, Eleanor Pavenstedt, Sandra Scarr-Salapatek, Rich Weinberg, and others, all point to the importance of positive educational experiences during the preschool years. Thus Lesser's educational objectives were solidly based in theory and research evidence. Also, his instructional techniques represented a great leap forward for educational television programming. As a result, he was able to launch the first large-scale attempt to enlist TV technology in the service of highly important educational objectives.

Firmly believing that evaluation was as essential to the workshop as the actual programming, Lesser also set up a careful framework for assessment. Dr. Edward L. Palmer, a psychologist with experience in measuring children's attention to television, was hired to direct the research group making extensive observations of children watching *Sesame Street*. The collaboration between Dr. Palmer's research group and the creative staff of *Sesame Street* was a key ingredient in the program's success. In addition, the Educational Testing Service of Princeton, New Jersey, contracted for an independent, longitudinal study of effects. Obviously, in any new venture such as *Sesame Street*, there were bound to be numerous skeptics, along with many who honestly doubted the legitimacy of such an enterprise. After all, it is not difficult for a concerned parent or teacher to worry over the *1984* overtones of a "Big Brother" television teacher, or to see TV as increasing passivity in children, or as an interference with family cohesion. Concern was also expressed, especially by psychoanalytic theorists, that *Sesame Street* would not only teach convergent rather than divergent thinking, but also would impinge on the rich and important fantasy life of young children. In a sense this view held that *Sesame Street* would become a premature introduction of young children to reality testing—some extremists even suggested that such exposure would inflict irrevocable damage on young, impressionable minds. Thus many segments of the educational community anxiously awaited the outcome studies.

It is almost anticlimactic to report that the very careful ETS study dispelled the concerns and worry. *Sesame Street* was clearly not destroying young minds, children were not being turned against their families or peers, their fantasy life was as lively as ever, "Big Bird" was not related to "Big Brother." Instead, the results indicated impressive educational outcomes among all the experimental groups studied. Children clearly make academic gains as a result of exposure to the program. Areas such as prereading skills, number concepts and manipulation, visual discrimination, and reasoning and problem-solving all demonstrated improvement, regardless of differences by age, sex, socioeconomic status (SES), geographical location, IQ score, and whether or not the children watched at home or in school.

Naturally any such project is not without its critics even today. However, it does seem as if *Sesame Street* is almost a unique success. More complete details of the work can be found in *Children and Television: Lessons from Sesame Street*.[12] In a real sense the project may mark a turning point for both television and educational psychology. There is even hope that the *Sesame Street* experience may yet influence public policy with regard to commercial

Enlisting TV technology in the service of educational objectives

Children make academic gains as a result of watching Sesame Street

programming for young children. Certainly children deserve something better than Saturday-morning cartoons, day-time soap operas, reruns of *The Three Stooges,* or the latest "sit-com" or "shoot-em-up" western.

In the words of Professor Robert M. Liebert, an authority on both the positive and negative effects of television on children:

> *The advent of Sesame Street was a true milestone in both broadcast television and, perhaps, in psychology's contribution to matters of deep concern throughout our entire society.*[13]

EDUCATION AND WOMEN'S DEVELOPMENT*

One of the most controversial areas confronting educational psychology and schooling is the issue of women's development. Traditionally, both educational psychology and psychology have ignored the question. Most of the educational-psychology laboratory studies have been conducted either with animals or with male subjects; much of the research in social psychology has been based on all-male samples; and, as you may have guessed, almost all of the researchers themselves have been men. Psychology has traditionally channeled women graduate students into the more clinical, practical, applied, and/or "soft" areas. Research investigations were almost always headed by men who tended to investigate problems using male subjects.

A negative self-fulfilling prophecy?

One question we must ask is whether the lack of research information concerning women and the predominance of men in research point to the inferiority of women or whether it is simply another example of the self-fulfilling prophecy. If the male establishment in education and psychology determines who receives research training; who is admitted and trained as educational policymakers and school superintendents; and who "runs" the American Psychological Association, the American Educational Research Association, the Association for School Superintendents—to name a few of the major professional associations—then it looks like the absence of female representation may indeed be a social invention.

We noted earlier that for years educators and psychologists have claimed that intelligence was fixed at birth, yet it turns out that in fact cognitive growth depends on the interaction of heredity and environment. Some light can be shed on this interaction process by examining scores on the same measures at different age levels.

For instance, research indicates that young male and female adolescents show no significant differences in such areas as academic achievement and achievement motivation, career aspirations, self-concept, and moral judgment. Yet, by late adolescence and early adulthood it appears that females' scores in these areas prematurely plateau, while males' scores continue to increase. It is as though a "functional" sellout occurs in the lives of young women. Given the

---

*

This section was written for this volume by Dr. V. Lois Erickson, Assistant Professor, College of Education, University of Minnesota. Portions of the research summary occur in her curriculum article in *The Counseling Psychologist* 6, no. 4 (1977).

**"I've thought of joining the women's liberation front —
demonstrating, learning karate, manning the barricades
against the male chauvinist pigs — but it just
isn't ladylike!"**

pressures to accept stereotyped role assignments at this life period, it is not surprising that many women compromise their competence when a choice is before them. "Everyone knows a guy wants a gal a few shades simpler than himself." Let's briefly overview relevant findings in the above areas.

In the area of achievement, reports from Project TALENT (Flanagan, 1973) using nationally representative samples indicate that girls performed as well as, or slightly better than, boys when tested on measures of abstract reasoning, arithmetic reasoning, reading comprehension, and creativity near the end of the ninth grade. However, when a sample was retested near the end of the twelfth grade it was found that on all the measures the boys had gained more than the girls. The author concludes the boys' gains were notably larger than those of the girls on tests of arithmetic reasoning and creativity, and that most of the girls forgot more than they learned with respect to both mathematics and science during their high-school years.[14] The recent findings on the decline of SAT scores of high-school students (*Newsweek,* 8 March 1976)[15] also merit concern. Perhaps the most-poignant revelation in these data is that the sharpest overall drop in the achievement-test scores has been among females. Even on the verbal SAT's, on which women have consistently scored above men since they were first administered in 1948, the women's scores now fall below the men's.

There is some evidence to link the decline in achievement performance to a shift in motivation and the development of a negative self-concept. One recent study conducted by Martina Horner, a female psychologist, on achievement motivation indicated that college-age females actually desired to avoid achievement success and that their real achievement motivation was contaminated by such a desire. This was not the case for men in the study. The women showed substantial fear of social rejection associated with achievement. They had

Achievement of college-age females contaminated by a desire to avoid achievement

Matina S. Horner

Born in 1939, Matina Horner has had a career little short of meteoric. After receiving her B.A. degree in 1961 from Bryn Mawr, Ms. Horner received her master's degree in 1963 and her doctorate in 1968 from the University of Michigan. With honors in psychology and an election to Phi Beta Kappa, she demonstrated substantial early promise. She was appointed a lecturer and then assistant professor at Harvard in 1968–1969 with the department of social relations.

Her research focus gained almost immediate attention, not because of the topical nature of her investigation but due to the careful examination she performed and the significance of the findings themselves. Her work provided a breakthrough in understanding the paradox and the dilemma of female development. For educators, of course, the implications of her work are most far-reaching. Her theory, which indicates how societal expectations shape and mold the motivational systems for females, forces educators to revise practically all their assumptions concerning male and female differences. She has been able to show that such differences in motivational patterns are a result of social conditioning or social inventions. This means that educa-

tors need to revise their ideas, practices, and policies concerning young women in schools and colleges. The need is to promote full development for all, regardless of gender. Professor Horner's work forms the important basis for these needed changes.

As if to indicate her own versatility and her willingness

to meet the major educational challenges of the '70s, Dr. Horner moved in 1972 from an assistant professorship at Harvard to the presidency of Radcliffe College—at the age of thirty-four. A model of achievement motivation, scholarship, and administrative talent, she sets a high standard for others to follow.

doubts about the "femininity" of achievement and actually denied that women could achieve success. Sixty-five percent of the women subjects ($N = 90$) and less than 10 percent of the men subjects ($N = 88$) denied that they could achieve success.[16]

Perhaps research in the areas of career aspirations can further enlarge the above perspective. In a major study on vocational orientation by Matthews and Tiedeman (1964) with a sample of 1,237 girls and women aged eleven to twenty-six, it was found that a definite change in girls' vocational orientation occurred between junior high and high school. The shift was from a strong vocational orientation in the seventh grade to a strong marriage orientation in the twelfth grade. Of additional importance, the most predominant of the five major themes emerging at every level was the perception that men view the women's use of their intelligence negatively.[17] This conflict, between being competent and being desirable to the opposite sex, is now being recognized as a double-bind position that has contributed heavily to the "lid" placed on women's growth in our society.

Let us examine this in relation to self-esteem. Maccoby and Jacklin (1974) indicate that on most measures of self-esteem girls and women show at least as much satisfaction with themselves as do boys and men. However, during the college years sex differentiation emerges: women have less confidence than men in their ability to perform well on a variety of tasks assigned to them; they have less sense of being able to control the events that affect them; and they tend to define themselves more in social terms than do men. Again, the authors note that it is during this age period when many young adults are marrying or

During the college-age years, when individuals are defining themselves in terms of their "masculinity" and "femininity," a critical branching occurs—a focus on agency can be noted in the lives of males, and a focus on communion in the lives of females.

forming some kind of committed sexual liaison.[18] Perhaps it is during this period more than any other, when individuals are defining themselves in terms of their "masculinity" and "femininity," that the critical branching becomes most evident between the focus on agency in the lives of males and the focus on communion in the lives of females (Block, 1973).[19] Although we do not clearly understand the dynamics involved in this branching process, we do know that females' achievement in spheres other than the domestic one drop off sharply in the years after they have finished their schooling.

The cognitive-developmental position presented by Lawrence Kohlberg would not posit sex differences in moral orientation. A structural view of moral development implies that the same stages appear in the thinking process of both girls and boys. However, studies using the Kohlberg moral-judgment scales indicate trends showing parallel gains in moral development between males and females until the adolescent period, after which time adolescent males are more advanced than adolescent females. Turiel (Kohlberg and Turiel, 1974) concluded

Males and females differ in rate of moral development

that while boys and girls pass through the same stages of moral reasoning, there appear to be differences in the rate of development through the stages. In his study of 104 boys and 106 girls, on the average at ages ten and thirteen the girls are more advanced than the boys. By age sixteen, the boys are more advanced than the girls. The age by sex interaction is statistically significant, indicating that sex role and stage of development are significantly related.

In samples of college students, Haan (Kohlberg and Turiel, 1974) found that more men than women attain moral-judgment stages 4, 5, and 6, while twice as many college women as men stay at moral-judgment stage 3, the stage of social conformity.[20] Holstein (1973), from a sample of upper-middle-class parents, found four times as many women at stage 3 as men. Moral-judgment stage 3 appears to be a stable adult stage of moral development for most women. More men than women are likely to attain stages 4, 5, and 6.[21] Kohlberg hypothesizes this is due to the limitations imposed on women's growth in our society. He indicates that men fill roles requiring more social participation and responsibility, which stimulate their maturity. When these factors are equalized between the sexes, so are the indices of moral growth. In support of this position, the results of the Turiel study cited above can be examined by types of school ("progressive," "traditional," parochial). It becomes evident that environmental differences in treatment and expectations for males and females may be important variables for determining rate of stage attainment. Overall, subjects from the "progressive" school were more advanced than those from the "traditional" school, who in turn were more advanced than those in the parochial school. Turiel asserts that in environments in which males and females have experiences of similar nature, as in the "progressive" school, no sex differences in moral judgment are apparent. In support of this position, Weisbrodt (1970)[22] found that professional women or those attending graduate school attain the higher stages with the same frequency as men with similar backgrounds, lending some additional evidence to the notion that the "problem" isn't in the genes.

Surely, early success and self-confidence in school should serve as a strong basis for later success. To find that the growth process is literally turned inside out indicates that the socialization process combined with the educational experience is having a negative impact. Starting on an equal footing in almost all

The educational system can teach girls that they are competent
or that they are inferior. The movement toward equal rights
and responsibilities finds no more important thrust than
through equal educational and personal-development programs.

known psychological areas, girls move forward for a while and then either start
a slow decline or stabilize at levels well below males. There are, of course,
exceptions; many outstanding women have survived this process. Unfortunately,
they are exceptions. Today, still only 7 percent of United States lawyers are
women, only 9 percent of United States physicians are women, only eighteen
women served in the 94th Congress, and the Catholic church has yet to recognize women as priests.[23]

A host of social factors account for the underrepresentation of women in
leadership positions. The dumb-blonde image may be a caricature, but, although
it has no research validity, it plays a distinct role in shaping society's attitudes toward women. We noted in Chapter 5, for example, that early-maturing girls are
perceived negatively by adults. So the educational problem becomes clear, if
complex: it is one of teaching for more choice, greater options, and more paths
for self-fulfillment. Under the present system—and it is unfortunate that administrators, teachers, and counselors all play an important part in this sequence—
women tend to be relegated to second-class citizenship in education as well as
in other aspects of life. When counselors suggest nursing rather than doctoring,

The dumb-blonde
caricature

There is no region, no country, no school, and no household that will not be affected in some major way by the move toward equal rights and equal educational opportunities for women. Our choice as a society is whether or not we have the will and the wisdom to promote effective development for all human beings.

Discrimination closes off women's options

when teachers suggest majoring in home economics rather than economics, when administrators channel far more funds into men's athletics than into women's, the invidious pattern is reinforced. This discrimination closes off options and reduces alternatives. The educational support system and adult expectations can teach girls that they are competent or that they are inferior. The movement toward equal rights and equal responsibilities finds no more important thrust than through equal educational and personal-development programs. Title IX of the U.S. Education Act demands that institutions evaluate their practices to ensure the elimination of practices that discriminate by sex. This is a necessary legal step, but surely it needs to be accompanied by preventive and developmental action.

A high-school curriculum to promote psychological growth for adolescent girls has recently been developed. Employing an active learning format similar to programs described in Chapter 21, the curriculum has resulted in significant changes in ego maturity and moral maturity. Women's development thus can be promoted through educational programs.[24]

In some ways, the so-called "problem" of women's growth is simply another aspect of the overall problem of human development. Failure to grow toward psychological maturity, both cognitive and personal, has traditionally been blamed on a series of convenient but nevertheless wrong-headed views. In the fifties and sixties, during the initial phases of the struggle for black liberation, the mainstream of white society tended to believe that the entire nation of black people in this country was genetically inferior. The same was said for Mexican-Americans, Indians, and Puerto Ricans, each in their turn. Ironically, the mainstream of the country, those who held such views, were themselves the offspring of immigrants. The only discernible difference was that their immigrant ancestors arrived long enough ago that their status had been overlooked. Women are the newest, and possibly the largest, of all the groups relegated to a second-class status to make their voices heard. There is no region, no county, no school, and no household that will not be affected in some major way by the move toward equal rights and equal educational opportunities for women. Our choice as a society is whether or not we have the will and the wisdom to promote effective development for all human beings.

Summary

The objective of this chapter is to provide the reader with information on current controversial educational-policy questions.

First, issues in the continuing "Great Debate" on reading are identified, and a series of significant recommendations by Professor Jeanne Chall are reviewed. In addition to her major recommendation, that beginning reading be taught via a phonics "code-breaking" approach, Professor Chall also suggests that educators: (1) reexamine ideas about content; (2) reevaluate grade levels; and (3) develop new tests.

The question of equality and inequality of educational opportunity in our public-school system remains a pressing issue. The survey research study by Professor James Coleman indicates that there is a close relationship between social class and school achievement. Children in lower-class (SES) districts achieve at lower levels than their middle-class counterparts. The effect of SES appears to be stronger than the effects of race or ethnic background.

The issue of dyslexia (word blindness) is both new and old. The syndrome has a long history and continues to be a topic of heated debate. Dyslexic pupils need careful tutoring, and a teaching strategy that utilizes a multisensory approach along with strong emotional support. There are no magical cures, no sure-fire panaceas.

The concept of the open classroom—as opposed to the "free school"—has generated increasing interest over the last decade. Some observational procedures have been developed by Professor Walberg to more accurately compare the characteristics of open versus traditional classrooms. These procedures allow for accurate on-site evaluation of dimensions of the open classroom.

The issue of competency-based teacher education (CBTE) is reviewed, especially as it affects the goals and practices in teaching and in teacher education. The idea of a competency base for teaching is clearly appealing. On the other hand, the many difficulties inherent in defining and evaluating an unending laundry list of teacher behaviors also must be addressed.

The potential for positive educational impact by children's television has been demonstrated by the program *Sesame Street*. The problems of developing an entertaining yet educationally sound method of instruction are discussed, with attention to the solutions developed by Professor Gerald Lesser.

The chapter's final issue concerns the general question of women's development. A careful review of extensive research indicates that major differences between males and females in learning, self-concept, and achievement result from environmental rather than genetic variables. The role of schools and teachers as sources for encouraging positive psychological growth for girls and women is detailed. The chapter, and the book itself, ends on a note calling for positive growth and development for all humans.

REFERENCES

1
J. Chall, *Learning to Read: The Great Debate* (New York: McGraw-Hill, 1970), p. 307.

2
Ibid.

3
Ibid., p. 312.

4
Ibid.

5
See F. Mosteller and D. P. Moynihan, *On Equality of Educational Opportunity* (New York: Vintage Press, 1972).

6
An interview reported in *The Southern Education Report,* December 1965.

7
These issues are presented in more detail in R. Barth, "Assumptions about Children's Learning," in C. H. Rathbone, ed., *Open Education* (New York: Citation Press, 1971), pp. 116–136.

8
Children and Their Primary Schools: A Report to the Central Advisory Council for Education, vol. 1 (London: Her Majesty's Stationery Office, 1966), p. 548.

9
H. J. Walberg and S. C. Thomas, "Open Education: An Operational Definition and Validation in Great Britain and United States," *American Educational Research Journal* 9, no. 2 (1972):200–201.

10
Ibid., p. 207

11
B. R. Joyce, "Listening to Different Drummers," *PBTE* 3, no. 6 (1974):7, 8.

12
G. S. Lesser, *Children and Television: Lessons from Sesame Street* (New York: Random House, 1974).

13
R. M. Liebert, "Sesame Street: Anatomy of a Success," *Contemporary Psychology* 20, no. 9 (1975):717–718.

14
John C. Flanagan, "Education: How Far and For What," *American Psychologist,* July 1973, pp. 551–556.

15
Newsweek, 8 March 1976, p. 58.

16
M. Horner, "Women's Will to Fail," *Psychology Today* 3, no. 6 (1968):36–38.

17
E. Matthews, and D. Tiedeman, "Attitudes toward Careers and Marriage and the Development of Life Style in Young Women," *Journal of Counseling Psychology* 11 (1964): 375–384.

18
E. Maccoby and C. Jacklin, *The Psychology of Sex Differences* (Stanford: Stanford University Press, 1974).

19
J. H. Block, "Conceptions of Sex Role: Some Cross-Cultural and Longitudinal Perspectives," *American Psychologist,* June 1973, pp. 512–526.

20
L. Kohlberg and E. Turiel, *Moralization: The Cognitive Developmental Approach* (New York: Holt, Rinehart and Winston, 1974).

21
C. Holstein, "Moral Judgment in Early Adolescence and Middle Age: A Longitudinal Study," paper presented at the biennial meeting of the Society for Research in Child Development, March 29–April 1, 1973, Philadelphia, Pennsylvania.

22
S. Weisbrodt, "Moral Judgment, Sex, and Parental Identification in Adults," *Developmental Psychology* 2 (1970):396–402.

23
Time, 5 January 1976, pp. 6–16.

24
V. L. Erickson, "Deliberate Psychological Education for Women: From Iphigenia to Antigone," *Counselor Education and Supervision,* June 1975, pp. 297–309. Also, V. L. Erickson, "Deliberate Psychological Education for Women: A Curriculum Follow-Up Study (or 'Disturbers of Mankind's Sleep')," *The Counseling Psychologist* 6, no. 4 (1977)

Glossary

Jerome Bruner has said that the student must have a background of facts, the "stuff of learning," before discovery-learning can take place. The glossary that follows helps provide the "stuff" for creative thinking in educational psychology.

Listening to lectures or reading text material, the student new to the field often becomes dismayed over the number of technical terms and seemingly endless jargon. But the forbidding jargon is an attempt to be precise. In order to understand the more-global concepts in educational psychology, the student must master the tools of the trade, the methods and terms used by educational psychologists in communication with each other.

The glossary entries define specific terms, outline broad theoretical positions, or provide a brief biography of some of the significant persons in educational psychology. Every entry is a self-contained unit, giving complete information. Though there is some cross-referencing, this has been kept deliberately to a minimum. Where essential, you are directed to one or two additional entries in order to develop a complete thought.

NAMES

Anastasi, Anne (1909–)

A past president (1971) of the American Psychological Association, Anne Anastasi has written on a wide variety of subjects in the field, ranging from the psychology of art to the nature-nurture controversy. She is best known, however, for her work in statistics and test construction. A firm believer in IQ tests, she feels that discontinuing the IQ test would be like asking a physician to throw away his thermometer just because children who are ill register an undesirable deviation from the norm. In her 1958 paper, "Heredity, Environment and the Question 'How?'", Anastasi puts the nature-nurture controversy in perspective. Instead of asking which component, heredity or environment, contributes more to the child's development, the better question is *how* heredity and environment interact in the development of behavioral differences. She also cites the importance of early experience on intellectual growth and development.

Bayley, Nancy (1899–)

Developmental psychologist and author of the famous Berkeley Growth Study, Bayley was the first woman ever to win the American Psychological Association's

"Distinguished Scientific Contribution" award. Bayley's major findings have been that:

1) IQ's are not constant
2) IQ variability is greatest during the first few years of life
3) intellectual growth may continue throughout life
4) the components of intellect change with age level.

Binet, Alfred (1857–1911)

Originator of psychology's first, modern intelligence test (1905). In assembling his test, this French psychologist set up a series of intellectual tasks, as opposed to the sensorimotor tasks previously used by Galton. Binet also introduced the concept of *mental age* as the basis for scoring his later tests (1908). The original Binet test items were later used as the basis for the famous Stanford–Binet intelligence test (1916), published in the United States by Lewis M. Terman. This test was scored on the basis of a ratio between one's mental age and one's chronological age. This ratio multiplied by 100 is known as the Intelligence Quotient, or IQ. (See also *Intelligence quotient*.)

Bloom, Benjamin S. (1913–   )

American educational psychologist and professor at the University of Chicago. He is most widely known for his work in two important areas in educational psychology.

1) Bloom sought to describe systematically the classroom teacher's educational goals, and methods for achieving those goals. This work is called his *taxonomy for educational objectives*.
2) Bloom also published the now-classic *Stability and Change in Human Characteristics* (1964), which outlined an early-experience position regarding intellectual growth. Bloom maintained that there is a decreasing positive effect from a beneficial environment on intellectual growth as the child gets older. Three-year-old children profit far more from enriching experiences than do seven- or eight-year-old children.

Bruner, Jerome S. (1915–   )

Jerome Bruner spent most of his professional life at Harvard University, where he has researched such varied subjects as propaganda techniques and the effect of need on perception. His most significant contributions, however, have resulted from his studies in cognitive psychology, or the study of how people obtain knowledge and how they develop intellectually. In 1960, he founded Harvard's Center for Cognitive Studies, and although he didn't invent cognitive psychology, he went a long way toward making it systematic and consistent with the rules of science. Perhaps Bruner's most famous statement is that any subject can be taught effectively in some intellectually honest form to any child at any stage of development. He stresses "discovery learning" and communication at three levels: enactive, iconic, and symbolic.

Cattell, James McKeen (1860–1944)

A pioneer in the field of intelligence testing, Cattell, an American, studied both in Germany under Wundt and in England under Galton. Cattell brought the message of European psychology back to America, and in 1888 was appointed to the first professorship in psychology anywhere in the world. As Galton had done previously, Cattell devised a series of sensorimotor tests (auditory range, visual range, reaction time, etc.), designed to measure man's intellectual potential by testing his sensorimotor equipment. Cattell taught for many years at Columbia University, and on his illustrious list of students are the names E. L. Thorndike, R. S. Woodworth, and E. K. Strong.

Cattell is credited with fathering the mental-testing movement in the U.S., and in fact it was Cattell, in 1890, who first used the term "mental test."

Chomsky, Noam (1928–   )

American psychologist interested in cognitive growth through language development. Chomsky has severely criticized the typical American learning-theory explanation of language being the result of straight conditioning. Chomsky insists that the conditioning model of language development simply doesn't fit with the facts. Children learn the use of language far more quickly than the conditioning theory can explain. Chomsky explains this rapid rate of language development on the basis of a built-in capacity for language acquisition. That is, the baby enters the world genetically prewired, or born with biological "givens" that direct the course of language development.

Clark, Kenneth B. (1914–   )

Noted black educator, psychologist, and professor at City College of New York. Clark's 1950 report on the effects of segregation in the schools was used extensively by the Supreme Court justices in making their historic 1954 decision declaring that segregation in public schools is unconstitutional. Clark has worked and written in a wide variety of areas within the fields of educational and social psychology. He was elected president of the American Psychological Association in 1970.

Dewey, John (1859–1952)

Philosopher and psychologist, John Dewey is probably best known for his educational philosophy of "learning by doing." At the time of this pronouncement by Dewey, American education was still in the grip of the formal discipline theorists, educators who were convinced that children should sit quietly in a classroom and "strengthen their minds" through the study of a classical curriculum. Dewey attempted to change this traditional method of education by creating learning environments in which children were to engage actively in learning. To some extent, Dewey was anticipating the ideas of Piaget and the open classroom. Dewey's curriculum came to be known as "progressive education," and was incorrectly translated by many into meaning totally unguided education.

Before moving to Columbia, where he spent most of his professional career, Dewey was involved with the functionalist school of psychology at the University of Chicago.

Ebbinghaus, Hermann (1850–1909)

The father of the experimental study of learning, this German psychologist spent long hours memorizing long lists of nonsense syllables (CAV, PAM, DEK). Later he would relearn the lists, and he measured his retention capacity on the basis of how much more quickly he could learn the lists the second time. This technique is known as the *Method of Savings*. He drew two major conclusions from this work:

1) forgetting occurs at an uneven rate, most of what is forgotten being lost very quickly
2) in learning new material it is more efficient to space the practice sessions rather than mass them together.

Erikson, Erik H. (1902–   )

German-born personality theorist, Erikson studied under Sigmund Freud at the Psychoanalytic Institute in Vienna. Erikson has been in the United States since 1936, and since 1960 has been a professor of human development at Harvard University. Although his theory of personality development has its obvious roots in psychoanalytic theory, it is definitely not just "warmed-over" Freud. His theory of the stages of personality development extends throughout life, though there is special emphasis on childhood. The focus is always on the normal and healthy personality, and Erikson sees development progressing through eight stages, each typifying a particular crisis. Through the attempt to resolve these crises the healthy personality emerges. (The stages are sequential, and when a healthy adjustment to a particular crisis does not oc-

cur, it is even more difficult to resolve a similar crisis at a later stage.) The mature personality should have a sense of identity, and although the climax of this search occurs during adolescence (identity crisis), residues of the conflict can emerge throughout life.

Festinger, Leon (1919–   )

American social psychologist, and part of the research wing of the group-dynamics movement at the University of Michigan in the 1950s. He defined the concept of "cohesiveness" as part of his general attraction theory. Originator of the term "cognitive dissonance," Festinger researched in detail the dimensions of this important cognitive conflict. Festinger has taught at Stanford and at the New School for Social Research.

Flanders, Ned (1918–   )

American educational psychologist, Flanders is known primarily for his work on defining teacher effectiveness. Using the concepts of direct and indirect teaching, Flanders has found that despite various subject matters, different grade levels, and different school settings, teachers using "indirect" teaching styles were producing higher levels of student learning than were "direct" teachers.

Freud, Sigmund (1856–1939)

Perhaps psychology's single most famous figure, Freud originated the school of thought called psychoanalysis. A physician in Vienna, Freud treated patients with "nervous disorders" during the day and wrote down his thoughts and observations at night. From these observations and his own genius for speculating came the theory of psychoanalysis. It stated that all behavior is motivated, and that the motives are usually hidden from the individual, thus causing much behavior to appear to be irrational. The basic source of energy for these motives is the libido, or pleasure-seeking drive. Freud described the personality as being composed of three structural components: id, ego, and superego. Most human anxiety results from inner conflict among these three components. Adult personality disorders can always be traced to and found to be directly caused by childhood trauma and anxiety. (See *Psychoanalytic theory*.)

Galton, Sir Francis (1822–1911)

Considered to be the "father of intelligence testing," Galton put together the first series of tests designed to measure intellectual ability. Although his tests seem somewhat naive by modern standards, his emphasis on the relationship between sensory ability and intellect foreshadows much of today's research on the importance of sensory stimulation in determining cognitive growth. Galton assumed that intelligence was dependent on the quality of man's sensory apparatus, and so his tests measured such abilities as reaction time, visual and auditory range, and sensory acuity. Galton firmly believed that one's sensory apparatus was largely inherited. Thus the testing movement, from its very inception, sided with nature in the nature-nurture debate. Galton emphasized *individual differences,* and more than any other man, set psychology on the road to quantifying its data.

Gesell, Arnold L. (1880–1961)
American child psychologist, Gesell spent his professional lifetime working first as the director of the Yale Clinic of Child Development and later at his own Gesell Institute of Child Development in New Haven, Connecticut. Throughout the 1920s and 30s Gesell was considered to be "Mr. Child Psychology" in the U.S., that is, America's leading authority in the field. Despite American psychology's largely environmental stance, Gesell stressed the importance of maturational factors in growth and development. He said that growth stages occurred in a fixed sequence and that each stage was a major period of change. Each child goes through these periods of major reorganization followed by periods of integration when a new stage is reached and the changes are assimilated.

Guilford, J. P. (1897–   )
A specialist in the area of statistics and measurement theory, Guilford has constructed, through the use of factor analysis, a model of "the structure of intellect." Guilford concluded that intelligence is not just a single trait, but is made up of a series of distinctly different modes of thought. He has grouped similar modes together into appropriate categories, and his famous phrase, "the three faces of intellect," suggests that intelligence can be separated into three categories: operation, content, and product. Each of these three categories contains a further series of dimensions. So far, he has identified a total of 70 separate traits of intelligence (out of a possible 120 traits provided for by his model). Among the traits identified so far are those responsible for what is usually called *creativity.* They are fluency, flexibility, and originality, all three of which involve *divergent thinking.*

Harlow, Harry F. (1905–   )
An American psychologist, Harlow has spent most of his professional career at the primate lab of the University of Wisconsin. Harlow's research, usually on rhesus monkeys, has shed light on many important topics in psychology. Perhaps his three most famous studies were on: (1) surrogate mothers—in which frightened young monkeys preferred cloth-covered, cuddly surrogates rather than wire-framed surrogates which delivered food; (2) learning sets—in which monkeys solved oddity problems by developing solution-rules or strategies, rather than on the basis of either insight or the slow accumulation of stimulus-response associations; (3) curiosity drive—in which monkeys exhibited a motive to manipulate novel items in their environment, despite the fact that no primary reinforcement was presented.

Hebb, Donald O. (1904–   )
Canadian physiological psychologist, Hebb is now president of McGill University in Montreal. His most famous publication, *Organization of Behavior* (1949), revolutionized psychological thought, especially in the United States. In this work Hebb dared to infer the existence of some possible physiological correlates of behavior. He stated that there was a relationship between intelligence and the way brain cells are organized. This organization occurs first at the level of cell assemblies, then as phase sequences, and finally in the total organization of the brain cells. Hebb also proposed a distinction between Intelligence A and Intelligence B, the former being one's innate potential, and the latter, one's present ability level on the intellectual growth continuum. (See also *A/S ratio* and *Cell assembly.*)

Horner, Matina (1939–   )
Professor at Harvard University and, since 1972, President of Radcliffe College, Horner achieved almost instant recognition in the area of the psychology of women's attitudes and motives. Horner contends that society often conditions women to both expect and want to fail. Since motivational differences between the sexes are a result of social pressures, then educators must revise their ideas, practices, and policies concerning young women in schools and colleges. Horner's own career is a model of academic achievement.

Hull, Clark L. (1884–1952)
American psychologist (Yale University) and learning theorist in the tradition of behaviorism, Hull developed a rigorous set of learning principles. Hull's principles of learning, based on an intricate series of postulates and theorems, outlined the most-elaborate theory of learning yet produced. Hull's central position was that learning, or, as he called it, habit strength, was increased when stimulus-response con-

nections were followed by reinforcement. He explained reinforcement on the basis of "drive reduction." It was probably Hull's grand design to become the "Newton of psychology," and certainly no psychologist, before or since, ever constructed a more-comprehensive theory of learning.

James, William (1842–1910)

America's first, and probably most revered, psychologist, James spent his entire academic lifetime at Harvard University, first as a student and later as a professor. Though he received an M.D. degree, James carved out his career in academe, being a professor of both psychology and philosophy. In 1876 he created and taught the first psychology course ever offered in the United States. In 1890 he published *Principles of Psychology,* a book that still provides today's reader with a relatively modern version of psychology, so great was his vision. Later, in his famous "Talks with Teachers," James turned his attention to the classroom teacher and pointed out that the entire enterprise of education is determined by the performance of the teacher in the classroom. James is credited with originating the school of *functionalism* in psychology, a school of thought interested not so much in what the elements of consciousness are, but more in what they are for.

Jensen, Arthur R. (1923–   )

Jensen received his Ph.D. from Columbia University in 1956, and is now a professor of educational psychology at the University of California at Berkeley. Jensen's 1969 article "How Much Can We Boost IQ and Scholastic Achievement?" created a big stir in educational psychology due to its pronounced emphasis on genetic factors in the development of intellect. Jensen has been especially criticized for one of the implications of his article: that the difference between the tested IQ's of black and white children is a result of the genetic inferiority of the black children.

Kallikak Family

Case name (taken from the Greek words for "good" and "bad") for a family that was studied in great detail by Henry Goddard during the early years of this century. Goddard traced back two branches of the Kallikak family, both branches having originally been created by the Revolutionary War soldier, Martin Kallikak. One branch, "good Kallikaks," resulted from Martin Kallikak's marriage, while the "bad Kallikak's" were a result of Martin's affair with a barmaid. Goddard found that the two branches were significantly different in virtually every way, and especially in regard to intelligence—most good Kallikaks being superior and most bad Kallikaks retarded. This "good seed–bad seed" account is regarded as totally fanciful by today's students of genetics.

Kohlberg, Lawrence (1927–   )

Kohlberg is one of those rare scholars whose Ph.D. thesis turned out to be a definitive statement in an important area of psychological research. Now a professor at Harvard, Kohlberg's Ph.D. thesis at the University of Chicago outlined a theory of how moral reasoning develops in children. His theory of moral development states that children proceed through a series of development stages, preconventional (ages 0–9), conventional (ages 9–15), and postconventional (ages 16 and up). Like Piaget's theory of cognitive development, Kohlberg sees moral development occurring in an invariant sequence, with each stage qualitatively different from the preceding stage. (See also *Moral development.*)

Kohler, Wolfgang (1887–1967)

Kohler was one of the founders of Gestalt psychology, having been a student of Max Wertheimer's at the University of Frankfurt, just before World War I. Kohler spent the war years on Tenerife Island, one of the Canary Islands, where he performed Gestalt psychology's most famous animal-learning study. Kohler discovered, while studying an ape named Sultan, that some learning occurs on the basis of *insight,* rather than solely on the basis of the slow accumulation of specific associations. Insight, or the "Aha!" phenomenon, is learning that occurs suddenly as a new relationship among perceptions is discovered. Kohler's most-important publications were *The Mentality of Apes* (1925) and *Gestalt Psychology* (1929). (See also *Insight.*)

Lewin, Kurt (1890–1947)

German-born psychologist who worked with the founder of Gestalt psychology, Max Wertheimer, when both were on the faculty at the University of Berlin (1916). Profoundly influenced by Wertheimer, Lewin helped develop the principles of Gestalt psychology and apply them in the areas of personality theory and social psychology. Lewin came to the U.S. to stay in 1933 and spent the rest of his life in this country, first as a full professor at the University of Iowa, and later (1945) at M.I.T. where he set up and headed the famous Research Center for Group Dynamics. Lewin's system, sometimes called *Field Theory,* is concerned with the forces, barriers and valences operating within the individual's life space (the person's situation as he or she sees it). Lewin was an excellent teacher and prolific writer.

Lorenz, Konrad (1903–   )

Austrian ethologist and winner of the Nobel Prize in medicine in 1973, Lorenz has long insisted that to understand animal behavior one must study the animal in its natural habitat, not in the artificial confines of the laboratory. In 1937, Lorenz first described the phenomenon of *imprinting,* a form of learning which dramatically illustrates the interaction of heredity, environment, and time in the determination of behavioral characteristics. Lorenz was able to revive the long-discredited instinct theory, and, by carefully analyzing the biological mechanisms involved, make the theory scientifically respectable. He is currently the director of the Max Planck Institute in Germany. (See also *Imprinting.*)

McClelland, David (1917–   )

Harvard psychologist interested in achievement motivation, McClelland has studied the problems of underachievement, both from the point of view of the individual and also an entire society. McClelland's studies indicate that the achievement motive or "achievement syndrome" is composed of three major factors:

1) the ability to compete with some standard of excellence in mind,
2) the ability to take moderate risks, and
3) the ability to make use of concrete feedback.

Milgram, Stanley (1933–   )

Milgram became an overnight success in the 1960s because of his studies on human aggression and conformity. Milgram asked subjects to deliver increasing amounts of electric shock to another person. He found that almost two-thirds of those tested were willing to risk killing someone they perceived to be a fellow subject. When tested in groups, however, only about 10 percent of the subjects pushed the shock lever all the way. Milgram interprets this on the basis of the liberating effects of conformity and group pressure on individual behavior. Milgram is currently a professor of social psychology at the City University in New York.

Montessori, Maria (1870–1952)

Italian educator, psychologist, and physician, Montessori was one of the first theorists to stress the developmental nature of humans in an evolutionary setting. Her approach to education was based on her work first with mentally retarded children and later with the culturally deprived children living in the slums of Rome. Her educational technique, now called the Montessori Method, stressed sensory training in a prepared environment. She insisted on the importance of early experience on cognitive development, and although her approach was rejected by most American behaviorists, it is now receiving renewed attention by serious educational psychologists.

Pavlov, Ivan (1849–1936)

Russian physiologist, Pavlov won the Nobel Prize in medicine in 1904 for his work on digestive activity in dogs. His lasting fame, however, resulted from his observation that dogs salivated, not only when meat powder was placed in their mouths, but also to stimuli which occurred well before that (for example, when they heard Pavlov's footsteps coming down the stairs to the laboratory). Pavlov coined the term "conditioned reflex" to describe this phenomenon. Pavlov attempted to relate these behavioral observations with the neural activity in the brain; for example, he introduced the concept of "cortical inhibition," which he believed important in producing sleep. Though most modern psychologists consider his theory of neurological activity as something of a historical curio, his laboratory findings on conditioning are still of great importance. Pavlov's system of conditioning is now generally referred to as "classical conditioning."

Piaget, Jean (1896–   )

Swiss psychologist who has spent most of his adult life studying cognitive development. Through carefully detailed, hour-by-hour observations of the developing child, Piaget has formulated a theory of how children go about the business of learning to know, learning the methods of concept formation. Piaget states that children learn concepts only as they go through a series of developmental stages which are sequential in nature and biologically based. Thinking processes are a biological extension of inborn motor processes. Piaget's developmental stages are: (1) sensorimotor (0–2 years), (2) preoperational or intuitive (2–7 years), (3) concrete operations (7–11 years), and (4) formal operations (11–16 years).

Roe, Anne (1904–   )

Eminent clinical psychologist and researcher, Anne Roe is best known for her work on career choice. She set up the Center for Research on Careers at Harvard University, and developed the now-famous, two-way classification scheme for occupational choice. Her system established a relationship between career development and personality factors. She has also done extensive work in the area of creativity, in which she was able to show that creative people possess a trait called "autonomy in judgment."

Rogers, Carl (1902–   )

Founder of the client-centered, or nondirective, approach to personality, Rogers challenged the orthodox psychiatric and psychological treatment techniques then in vogue. Rogers felt that psychiatrists often harmed their patients more than they helped them. Rogers insisted that all persons have a natural tendency to grow in healthy directions, and that the role of the therapist is to provide conditions whereby the patient (or client) can fulfill his or her destiny of self-actualization. The famous Rogerian triad of unconditional positive regard, empathy, and congruence became the crucial ingredients in the helping process. Good teaching, like good counseling, is based on this same triad. Classroom interaction should be based on the development of equal and genuine relationships.

Skinner, B. F. (1904–   )

Psychology's most important and honored behaviorist, Skinner is the originator of the system of operant conditioning. Using Thorndike's Law of Effect as a starting point, Skinner has shown that conditioning can take place when responses are allowed to occur and are then followed by reinforcing stimuli. Reinforcement is thus contingent on the fact that the response (operant) has been emitted. Skinner's emphasis is on response analysis. He is not concerned with what goes on inside the organism, but is concerned with specifying the environmental conditions associating with and affecting the organism's response repertoire. Skinner's most notable contributions to education are the techniques of programmed instruction and behavior modification.

Terman, Lewis M. (1877–1956)

Professor of psychology at Stanford University for thirty-two years (1910–1942), Terman is best known for his construction of the Stanford–Binet IQ test and his longitudinal study of gifted children. In 1916 Terman published an American revision of the original Binet intelligence test. He standardized the test on American school children, and introduced so many new items that it was virtually a new test. He scored the test on the basis of IQ (Intelligence Quotient), rather than mental age as Binet had done. His long-term study of intellectually gifted children (IQ's of 140 or higher) proved that a high IQ does correlate with many traditional measures of success, both in school and in later life.

Thorndike, Edward L. (1874–1949)

One of America's most renowned educational psychologists, Thorndike studied at Harvard under William James and later taught at Columbia Teacher's College for 41 years. Early in his career Thorndike did important laboratory studies of learning, using animals as subjects. From the results of these studies he constructed the first internally consistent learning theory. He created three major laws of learning (the Law of Readiness, the Law of Exercise, and the Law of Effect) and many subordinate laws. Thorndike considered learning to occur in a trial-and-error fashion, and thought of learning itself as the result of a buildup of connections between stimuli and responses. Thorndike insisted that educational psychology must utilize the scientific method in establishing its "book of knowledge."

Tolman, E. C. (1886–1959)

Calling his system "Purposive Behaviorism," Tolman attempted to bridge the gap between rigid Behaviorism and doctrinaire Gestaltism. Tolman was a Behaviorist to the extent that he accepted observable responses as psychology's basic data, but he insisted that, far from being random or based on trial-and-error, learning was purposive, or goal directed. Tolman agreed with the Gestaltists that persons learn by forming cognitive maps of their environment. People can form hypotheses, see relationships, and then respond on the basis of these cognitive maps, rather than respond solely on the basis of a conditioned stimulus-response connection. Tolman's system is called an S–S (sign–significate) theory, rather than an S–R psychology.

Torrance, E. Paul (1915–   )

Professor of educational psychology at the University of Georgia, Torrance is most noted for his work in the area of creativity. Torrance has devised methods whereby creativity can be measured, but he has also gone beyond this. He reasoned that if creativity can be assessed, perhaps it can also be taught. Working with children in the classroom, Torrance has demonstrated strategies for teaching children to think more creatively.

Watson, John B. (1878–1958)

Founder of Behaviorism, Watson became psychology's most vocal critic of subjectivism, mentalism, and especially the technique of introspection. Watson was a strong believer in the importance of environment (as opposed to heredity) in shaping virtually all human behavior. He also believed that learning resulted from a buildup of stimulus-response connections, or what he called "habits." He was a strong advocate of Pavlov's concept of classical conditioning, and utilized this method in his study of the acquisition of fear in the baby, Albert. Watson taught psychology at Johns Hopkins, and later spent many years working for an advertising agency in New York. (See also *Behaviorism*.)

Wechsler, David (1896–   )

America's premier psychologist in the area of intelligence testing and test construction. Beginning in 1939 with the publication of the Wechsler–Bellevue test, Wechsler has introduced a series of individual IQ tests—the WAIS (Wechsler Adult Intelligence Scale), the WISC (Wechsler Intelligence Scale for Children), and the WPPSI (Wechsler Preschool and Primary Scale of Intelligence). Wechsler defined intelligence as "the global capacity of an individual to think rationally, to act purposefully, and to deal effectively with his environment." All the Wechsler tests report three separate scores, a verbal IQ, a performance IQ and a full-scale IQ. (See also *WAIS*.)

Wertheimer, Max (1880–1943)

Founder of the Gestalt school of psychology (early 1900s), Wertheimer had criticized the Structuralists and their insistence that all psychological phenomena should be analyzed into the smallest possible parts. Wertheimer felt that the whole was more than just the sum of its parts. In order to understand psychological phenomena, one had to study all the parts together in their particular "Gestalt," a German word which means whole, or totality of configuration. Wertheimer's first studies were in the area of perception, especially the perception of apparent movement (phi phenomenon). Later he became interested in education and the principles of learning. He insisted that educators should teach for "understanding," rather than relying on repetition and rote memorization. (See also *Gestalt psychology*.)

Wundt, Wilhelm (1832–1920)

German psychologist and founder of the Structuralist school of thought, Wundt created the world's first laboratory of psychology at the University of Leipzig in 1879. Wundt believed that psychology should devote itself to the study of the basic elements that make up conscious experience. To ferret out these individual elements, Wundt used trained subjects who looked within themselves and reported all their most

fleeting and minute thoughts, feelings, and sensations. This technique of looking within the self is called introspection. Wundt's goal was to take psychology out of the field of philosophy and give it a sense of scientific respectability.

TERMS

Accommodation

Concept used by Piaget in his discussion of cognitive development. Accommodation is the adjustment the individual makes when incorporating external reality. Piaget uses this concept in conjunction with *assimilation*, which is the individual's ability to internalize and conceptualize his or her environmental experiences. Accommodation is the individual's response to the immediate and compelling environmental demands that have been and are being assimilated.

Anal stage

Second of Freud's psychosexual stages of development. During this stage the child's libido is focused in the anal area, and the child takes great pleasure, first in the act of defecating, and later in the act of withholding the feces. This stage usually takes place between the ages of 18 months and three years. The first part of this stage is called the anal expulsive stage, and later develops into the anal retentive stage. Freud says that the way in which the child is treated during this stage (toilet training, etc.) makes a permanent imprint on the later adult personality.

Analysis of variance

Statistical test of significance developed by Sir Ronald Fisher. It is also called the F ratio, or ANOVA, for ANalysis Of VAriance. The test is designed to establish whether or not a significant (or nonchance) difference exists among several sample means. Statistically, it is the ratio of the variance occurring between the sample means to the variance of the scores occurring within the sample groups. A large F ratio, that is, when the variance between is larger than the variance within, usually indicates a nonchance or significant difference.

A/S Ratio

The A/S ratio is a concept developed by D. O. Hebb, the Canadian physiological psychologist. Hebb developed the ratio by comparing the amount of brain space devoted to association areas to the amount devoted to sensory areas. As he went up the phylogenetic ladder, from rat to monkey to man, Hebb found an ever-increasing A/S ratio. Rats, with their lower A/S ratio, are more sensory bound, whereas humans, with a higher A/S ratio, are capable of far more-varied and greater amounts of learning.

Assimilation
Concept used by Piaget in his theory of cognitive development. Assimilation is the process of taking within, or internalizing, one's environmental experience. Assimilation is used by Piaget in conjunction with the concept of accommodation. Piaget believes that assimilation is a spontaneous process on the part of the child. (See also *Accommodation*.)

Attitudes
An attitude is a *learned* predisposition to respond either positively or negatively to persons, situations or things. Attitudes carry a strong emotional component, and therefore can never be neutral. When a negative attitude is generalized to include an entire group of people, it is called a *stereotype*. This can be destructive to the holder of the stereotype as well as to the group about which it is held. It can be especially destructive to the minority-group member's self-image.

Autokinetic effect
A visual effect produced when a small but stationary pinpoint of light in an otherwise darkened room *appears* to move. Since the light remains physically stationary, and since the perceived movement is only apparent, the autokinetic effect has been used to further our understanding of how group norms emerge. Experiments using the autokinetic effect have been performed by the social psychologist, Muzafer Sherif.

Behavior genetics
A fairly new discipline within the field of animal psychology, behavior genetics is concerned with the effects of genotype on behavior. Specifically, the behavior geneticist studies the effect of genetic differences on behavioral differences *within a population*. The method of study typically used is that of selective breeding and/or the use of inbred animal strains. An example would be the Tryon study (1940) where maze-bright and maze-dull rats were selectively bred and then compared over several generations according to their ability to run a maze. It must be pointed out that behavior genetics *is not* allied with the now-discredited instinct theory.

Behavior modification
A system for changing behavior based on the principles of conditioning. The term behavior modification, or "behavior mod," is usually applied either to the classroom or to a patient undergoing therapy. When desirable behavior is exhibited it is followed by a reinforcing stimulus, and when undesirable behavior is emitted it is followed either by no reinforcement (extinction) or, less commonly, by punishment. It is important when using this system that:
1) goals be defined precisely *and in behavioral terms,* and
2) the conditioning schedule be followed with absolute consistency.

Behaviorism
A school of thought in psychology usually considered to have originated in the work and writings of John B. Watson. In 1913, Watson outlined the Behaviorist position in his paper "Psychology as the Behaviorist Views It." Briefly stated, Watson argued against the use of introspection in gathering psychological data. He considered observable behavior the only valid data in psychology. According to Watson, any concepts, like mind or consciousness, which have mentalistic overtones must be purged from the field of psychology. The most famous current spokesman for this tradition is Harvard University's B. F. Skinner.

Brainstorming
A technique for generating new ideas where individuals get together in a group and are urged to interact freely and call out any idea, no matter how seemingly bizarre. Brainstorming is used in many businesses, especially in areas where creativity is important, as in an advertising agency mapping out a new campaign. The actual research on brainstorming, however, casts some doubt as to its effectiveness, with regard to both the number of new ideas and the quality of the ideas produced by the group.

C.A.I.–Computer-assisted instruction
A space-age form of programmed instruction, C.A.I. is an extremely sophisticated "teaching machine." It involves a series of computers, TV screens, and automatic typewriters to instruct students, not just in specific facts, but in complex skills as well. Through the C.A.I. system, hundreds of students can be involved at one time, and each student *can proceed at his or her own pace.* C.A.I. uses the principle of reinforcement in order to enhance learning.

Cell assembly
Concept used by D. O. Hebb in describing cognitive growth. The cell assembly defines the action of a group of brain cells, organized into a coherent unit, and enabling the young child to learn at an ever-

increasing rate. The child learns slowly and ploddingly when operating at the single-cell level, but after cell assemblies are formed in the brain, the child's learning speed increases dramatically.

Central tendency

A statistical term used for describing the typical, middle, or central score in a distribution of scores. Measures of central tendency are used when the researcher wants to describe a group as a whole with a view toward characterizing that group on the basis of its most-common measurement. The researcher wishes to know what score best represents a group of differing scores. The three measures of central tendency are the mean (or arithmetic average), the median (or the mid-point of the distribution), and the mode (the most frequently occurring score in the distribution).

Charisma

Term used in describing a leader, or a leadership trait or quality, as in a charismatic leader. An individual who has charisma is thought to possess a kind of "animal magnetism" or "hypnotic appeal." The power of a charismatic leader is seen by some as being almost mystical in its spellbinding appeal. When a charismatic person enters a room, the room is supposed to be suddenly charged with excitement.

Chi square, or χ^2

A statistical test of significance used to determine whether or not frequency differences have occurred on the basis of chance. Whenever the researcher is interested in the actual number of cases (frequency of occurrence) which fall into two or more discrete categories, chi square becomes the appropriate statistical test. It is considered to be a nonparametric test since no population assumptions are required for its use. The basic equation is:

$\chi^2 = \dfrac{\Sigma(f_o - f_e)^2}{f_e}$, where f_o denotes the frequencies actually observed and f_e the frequencies expected on the basis of chance.

Classical conditioning

Term used to describe conditioning techniques introduced by Ivan P. Pavlov. It is the pairing of a conditioned stimulus with an unconditioned stimulus over long numbers of trials until the conditioned stimulus alone has the power to elicit the conditioned response. During the conditioning trials, the conditioned stimulus acts as a *signal* that the unconditioned stimulus will follow, and the organism thus eventually learns to respond to the conditioned stimulus

alone. In Pavlov's basic experiment, a dog was conditioned to salivate to the sound of a tone. The tone was presented (conditioned stimulus), followed by meat powder (unconditioned stimulus), until the dog began salivating just to the tone. Skinner calls this technique *respondent conditioning.*

Cognitive conceit

Term used by Piaget to describe the adolescent's preoccupation with his or her appearance and behavior. Cognitive conceit is based on *egocentrism,* a thought process that focuses almost completely on the self. The adolescent also assumes that he or she can create ideas and theories, never before known to mankind, which will restructure the entire world and make it a better place in which to live. The adolescent also assumes, incorrectly, that just thinking and talking about these solutions will make them effective instruments of change.

Cognitive dissonance

Concept introduced by the social psychologist, Leon Festinger. Individuals prefer to maintain a state of equilibrium among their various attitudes, beliefs, and behavior. Inconsistency between thoughts and actions sets up within the individual a state of cognitive dissonance, an uncomfortable state which the individual attempts to resolve by changing either his or her actions or beliefs. It is far more comfortable, and thus desirable from the individual's point of view, to attain *cognitive consonance* over cognitive dissonance.

Cognitive learning

The view that learning is based on a restructuring of perceptions and thoughts occurring within the organism. This restructuring allows the learner to perceive new relationships, solve new problems, and gain "understanding" of a subject area. Cognitive learning theorists stress the reorganization of one's perceptions in order to achieve understanding, as opposed to the conditioning theorists who stress the importance of associations formed between stimuli and responses. Gestalt psychology has been oriented toward the cognitive view of learning.

Cohesiveness

A concept introduced by the social psychologist, Leon Festinger. Cohesiveness describes those positive forces which hold a group together and prevent its deterioration. Cohesiveness is one of the few truly group concepts in social psychology. It can be thought of as the "cement" that binds the group together, or the attraction of the group for its members. Group cohesiveness can be increased by (1) friendly interaction,

(2) cooperation, (3) increased group status, (4) an outside threat, or (5) democratic rather than authoritarian leadership.

Coleman Report
A massive study carried out by the sociologist James Coleman, now of the University of Chicago, which disclosed, among other things, that the single most important factor in determining the scholastic achievement level within a given school is the social-class backgrounds of the students. The academic achievement in schools where the student backgrounds were middle or upper-middle class was consistently higher than the achievement level in schools where the student backgrounds were lower class. This held true regardless of teacher salaries, per-pupil expenditures, number of books in the library, or even the teacher's educational background.

Competence drive
Part of the theory of competence motivation developed by the personality theorist Robert White. White feels that all humans, and even some animals, have a basic drive to achieve competence as a way of developing control over their environments. People have a need to be competent in some area. Of course, as competence increases, so too does enjoyment. Competence is a key concept for many educators, and is viewed as being synonymous with personal mastery and self-direction.

Concordance rate
Term used in behavior genetics. The concordance rate is the percentage of co-twins exhibiting a specific phenotypic trait.

Concrete thought
A mode of thinking, according to Piaget, which is characteristic of the period of concrete operations (ages 7–11 years). Also called *operational thinking*, concrete thought describes a thinking process which is based on specifics and literal mindedness. The child using this mode of thought is objective and logical, but almost too literal minded. The child wants facts and wants the facts to be specific, but he or she cannot separate facts from hypotheses during this stage.

Conditioned reinforcement
Sometimes called secondary reinforcement, it describes the situation where a previously neutral stimulus acquires reinforcing power by being repeatedly associated with a primary reinforcer. The sequence of events for establishing conditioned reinforcement is as follows: (1) response; (2) neutral stimulus, such as a light or buzzer; (3) the primary reinforcer, such as a pellet of food. In the classroom, conditioned reinforcers might be good grades, prizes, promotions, and generalized social approval. The use of "tokens" by behavior-modification proponents is another example of conditioned reinforcement at work in the classroom.

Conditioned response
Term used both in classical (respondent) conditioning and in operant conditioning. In classical conditioning the conditioned response is the response being elicited by the conditioned stimulus. The stronger the conditioning, the greater the magnitude of the conditioned response and the shorter its latency. In Pavlov's experiment, the conditioned response was the dog's salivation to the tone.

In operant conditioning, since the response must precede the reinforcer, the conditioned response is defined not in terms of magnitude or latency, but in terms of either the rate of the response or its resistance to extinction. For example, a strongly conditioned operant will occur far more rapidly than one which has been only weakly conditioned. Also, a strongly conditioned operant will be far more difficult to extinguish.

Conditioned stimulus
In classical (respondent) conditioning, the previously neutral stimulus takes on the power to elicit the response through association with an unconditioned stimulus. For this to occur, the conditioned stimulus must precede the unconditioned stimulus on enough occasions that it will come to serve as a *signal* that the unconditioned stimulus will follow. In Pavlov's experiment on conditioning the dog, the tone was used as the conditioned stimulus. The tone was consistently followed by the meat powder, until the dog began salivating to the tone alone.

Conditioning
Process of learning where stimuli and responses become associated through training. There are two general types of conditioning, classical (respondent) and operant. In classical conditioning, a conditioned stimulus is presented, followed by an unconditioned stimulus. Conditioning is exhibited when the organism learns to respond to the conditioned stimulus alone. In operant conditioning, the operant is allowed to occur, and then is followed by a reinforcing stimulus. Operant conditioning is exhibited when the rate of responding increases over the original, preconditioned rate.

Conformity

Term used in social psychology to describe the fact that individuals in group situations tend to behave in a uniform way. Group pressure acts on the individual to force him or her into acting in accord with the rules and norms of the group. Important studies in this area include: (1) Sherif study, in which individuals formed a common estimate of how far (autokinetic effect) a light appeared to move; (2) Asch study, in which a naive subject's estimate of the length of a line conformed to the group's estimate, even though the group was obviously wrong; (3) Milgram study, in which subjects who believed they were severely shocking their lab partner were less apt to deliver high voltages when acting in a group situation than when acting alone.

Congruence

One of the three necessary and sufficient conditions for the promotion of learning, according to Carl Rogers (the other being empathy and unconditional positive regard). By congruence, Rogers means total and complete honesty. To promote learning the teacher must be "real" and honest in dealing with the students. Teachers can't go through the motions of liking students. A teacher without congruence should probably try a different line of work.

Conservation

Term used by Piaget in his theory of cognitive growth, and illustrated by the idea that water from a tall, thin glass can be poured into a short, wide glass *without changing the amount of water involved*. According to Piaget, the concept of conservation is typically acquired by a child reaching the stage of concrete operations or operational thinking (at about the age of seven).

Control group

In experimental or S/R research, the control group is the comparison group, or the group that ideally receives zero magnitude of the independent variable. The use of a control group is critical in evaluating the pure effects of the independent variable on the measured responses of the subjects.

Convergent thinking

A type of thinking which is rigid, conforming, and inflexible. It is the opposite of *divergent* or *creative thinking*. (See *Creativity* and *Divergent thinking*.)

Correlation (coefficient)

A numerical statement as to the relationship among two or more variables. A correlation is said to be positive when high scores on one variable associate with high scores on another variable, and low scores on the first variable associate with low scores on the second. A correlation is said to be negative when high scores on the first variable associate with low scores on the second, and vice versa. Correlation coefficients range in value from $+1.00$ to -1.00. Correlation coefficients which fall around the zero point indicate no consistent relationship among the measured variables. In psychological research, the correlation coefficient is usually based on taking several response measures of *one group of subjects*.

Creativity

Also called *divergent* thinking, creativity defines a thinking process by which original and innovative thoughts and solutions are exhibited, as opposed to usual or conventional thinking. Most of the research in this area has been conducted by Wallach and Kogan, Getzels and Jackson, and E. Paul Torrance. Though all the researchers seem to agree on what is or isn't to be defined as a creative response, there is still some lack of agreement regarding the question of the degree of relationship between creativity and basic intelligence. (See also *Torrance, E. Paul*.)

Critical periods

Concepts used by Lorenz and other ethologists to define certain age periods in the organism's life in which learning can occur more easily than in any other age period. For example, Lorenz found that goslings imprint on moving stimuli only between hatching and an age of about thirty hours.

The concept of critical periods was also used in describing human growth and development by Myrtle McGraw in her study of the twins, Johnny and Jimmie.

The critical period hypothesis is usually used by those psychologists who favor an *early experience* position on growth and development. (See also *Imprinting*.)

Cross-sectional research

Type of nonexperimental research, sometimes used to obtain data on possible growth trends in a population. The researcher selects a sample (cross section) at one age level, say twenty-year-olds, and compares these measurements with those taken on a sample of older subjects, say sixty-five-year-olds. Comparisons of this type are often misleading in today's twenty-year-olds may have had very different environmental backgrounds (educational experience, for example) than would the sixty-five-year-olds. (See also *Longitudinal research*).

Curiosity drive

An inborn motive that is satisfied not by food, drink, or praise, but simply by getting the answer. Harlow feels the curiosity drive is fundamental and primary in monkeys and man. (Why else would a child take apart the watch just to find out what makes it tick?) Berlyne, another theorist who posits the existence of a curiosity drive, believes that there is an optimum level of curiosity arousal which is a function of brain excitation.

Developmental stage

A growth and/or behavior organization category which satisfies the following four criteria:
1) It is qualitatively different from the preceding stage.
2) It represents a new and more-comprehensive system of organization.
3) It occurs in a maturationally fixed sequence.
4) It is age-related within general confines.

Deviate-status placement

A system, sometimes called "warehousing," whereby certain individuals are categorized as deviant (on the basis of IQ, physical or emotional handicaps, etc.) and then placed in segregated environments, usually in remote areas. Persons categorized as being deviant are thus segregated from the mainstream of society. (See also *Mainstreaming*.)

Discovery learning

Term used by Jerome Bruner to describe a form of learning which results not from rote memorization or conditioning, but from the active exploration of alternatives on the part of the learner. Bruner maintains that the learning attained through discovery is more meaningful and long lasting than that from memorization.

Discrimination

A term used by learning theorists to describe the ability of an organism to respond to one stimulus and not to respond to another, similar stimulus. Pavlov first demonstrated this phenomenon by conditioning dogs to salivate to a given conditioned stimulus, say a 500 cycle tone, while not salivating to a similar stimulus, say a 400 cycle tone. This was accomplished by continuing to reinforce (with the unconditioned stimulus) the presentation of the 500 cycle tone, while withholding reinforcement of responses following presentation of the 400 cycle tone.

Skinner has identified essentially the same phenomenon in the area of operant conditioning. Skinner reinforces a response which occurs in the presence of a given stimulus (S^D), while extinguishing the response when it occurs in the presence of the similar stimulus (S^Δ).

Distribution

A statistical term defined as the arrangement of measured scores in order of magnitude. Listing scores in distribution form allows the researcher to notice general trends more readily than the unordered set of raw scores would allow. A *frequency distribution* is a listing of each score achieved, together with the number of individuals receiving each score. When graphing frequency distributions, it is usual procedure to indicate the scores on the horizontal axis (abscissa) and the frequency of occurrence on the vertical axis (ordinate).

Divergent thinking

Thinking that displays characteristics of originality and creativity, as opposed to thinking that is conventional, rigid, or convergent. (See also *Creativity*.)

Dizygotic (DZ) twins

DZ or fraternal twins are the result of eggs that are fertilized at the same time but are not identical. Thus, DZ twins are no more alike genetically than any set of brothers and sisters.

DNA (deoxyribonucleic acid)

Rather large organic molecules located in the chromosomes (which lie in the nucleus of every one of the body's cells) and act toward directing the body's growth and development. DNA has been called the building block of genetic organization, and along with RNA makes up the chemical composition of the gene. Geneticists say that DNA acts as a blueprint, or template, for the formation of certain enzymes that guide the development of the organism. The coded information stored in the DNA molecule is transmitted to other parts of the cell by the RNA molecules.

Double-blind study

A method used by researchers to eliminate experimental error. In a double-blind study neither the individual conducting the study nor the subjects are aware of which group is the experimental group and which is the control. This prevents any unconscious bias on the part of the experimenter, or any contaminating motivational sets on the part of the subjects. If a subject knows he's in the experimental group, he may simply try harder.

Early-experience school of thought

A position taken by those researchers and theorists who stress the crucial importance of an individual's early environmental experiences in determining later adult characteristics. The early-experience proponents typically argue that the child goes through various time periods when certain cognitive and other skills can best be learned. Attempting to develop these skills either too early or too late can result in wasted effort on the part of the teacher and possible permanent damage to the student.

Educable mentally retarded (EMR)
IQ scores range from 50 to 80 on standard tests. EMR individuals are considered to be slow learners and concrete thinkers, though they can often be successfully employed.

Ego
Part of Freud's theory of the structure of personality. Freud saw personality as structured on the basis of the id, ego, and superego. The ego is the second of the structural components of personality to emerge, and is that part of personality which is essentially in contact with reality. Freud felt that if an individual were to pass through the first six or seven years of life without having suffered any crippling psychic trauma, the individual would probably have a strong and healthy ego. Such an individual can perceive reality accurately, delay gratification, and focus attention on significant tasks.

Empathy
The ability to realize, understand, and appreciate another person's feelings. The ability to experience and "feel" the world through another person's eyes. Also, one of the three necessary and sufficient conditions for the promotion of learning, according to Carl Rogers. The other two are unconditional positive regard and congruence.

Enactive representation
Stage of cognitive development and method of communication introduced by Jerome Bruner. During this, Bruner's first stage of development, the child thinks and communicates with "wordless messages." Young children understand things best at the action level: a chair is to sit on, a spoon is to eat with, etc. Even adults may, and perhaps should, revert to this level of thinking when learning a new skill, especially a motor skill. An adept ski or tennis instructor often will ask the student (child or adult) to imitate his or her actions physically, rather than just teaching at the verbal level.

Equilibration
Term used by Piaget to describe the motivational force for arriving at an adjustment between the twin con-

cepts of assimilation and accommodation. Equilibration makes its possible for the child to go on to new, higher-level assimilations.

Ethology
The study of the behavior of organisms in the *organism's natural habitat*. Unlike experimental psychologists who often study animal behavior in artificial, laboratory situations, the ethologists (like Konrad Lorenz) study behavior in the animal's natural environment. Ethologists have introduced such terms as *I.R.M.* (innate releasing mechanism) and *imprinting* into the working vocabulary of psychologists. (See also *Lorenz, Konrad.*)

Experimental design
Technique used in experimental, or S/R research, for creating equivalent groups of subjects. There are three basic experimental designs: (1) After-only—where subjects are randomly assigned to control and experimental groups, and the dependent variable is measured only after the introduction of the independent variable; (2) Before–after—where a group of subjects is used as its own control, and the dependent variable is measured both before and after the introduction of the independent variable; (3) Matched–group—where subjects are matched or equated, person for person, on some relevant variable.

Extinction
Term used by conditioning theorists to describe a forgetting process in which the stimulus–response associations are eroded. In classical conditioning, extinction occurs when the conditioned stimulus is presented without being followed by the unconditioned stimulus. Extinction is then defined when the magnitude of the conditioned response returns to zero. In operant conditioning, extinction occurs when the conditioned operant is allowed to occur without being followed by a reinforcing stimulus. Extinction is defined when the rate of responding returns to its preconditioned level (operant level).

Formal discipline (theory)
Early educational theory which stressed a curriculum designed to discipline the mind. The theory rested on the assumption that the mind was like a muscle and must be systematically exercised until it becomes so strong it can learn and understand almost any new material. Subjects such as logic, Latin, and Greek were included in the curriculum, not because they were thought to have any immediate practical use, but because they would strengthen the mind. The theory of formal discipline originated in ancient Greece, and remained in vogue until the early twentieth century.

The theory was finally challenged by three psychologists, William James, E. L. Thorndike, and Charles Judd, whose independent studies in the area of positive transfer refuted the formal discipline position. (See *Transfer.*)

Formal operations
Concept used by Jean Piaget to describe a stage of cognitive development occurring during early adolescence. The period of formal operations (11 to 16 years) is the last of Piaget's stages and is characterized by the youth's ability to develop full, formal patterns of thinking based on *abstract symbolism*. The youth is able to reason things out logically at the abstract level, develop symbolic meanings and generalize to other situations. This is the highest level of thinking, and according to Piaget, must await the maturation of certain cerebral structures in the brain for its full development.

Frustration-aggression hypothesis
An attempt to explain the reason for aggressive behavior, this hypothesis, produced by Yale psychologists Neil Miller and John Dollard in the late 1930s, states that aggression results from environmental causes. When a person is frustrated, or experiences goal blockage, aggressive behavior results.

Functional fixedness
A term used in the study of creativity. Functional fixedness causes a person to think in convergent ways. In order to develop creative and divergent thinking in a person, the person must be led out of the pattern of functional fixedness. The pattern must become unfixed or unfrozen in order that the person may break out from this rigid mode of thought.

Genetics
The study of the rules and lawful relationships of heredity. Geneticists are interested in how inherited characteristics are transmitted from generation to generation. They study both the *continuity* and the *variation* of traits across generations. The first studies in genetics were those of Gregor Mendel (1860s), who determined that the color of flowers could be predicted from one generation to the next. Thomas Hunt Morgan (1910s) studied the fruit fly, and suggested that genes are arranged in the chromosomes in an ordered sequence. Watson and Crick won the Nobel Prize in 1962 for their pioneering work on genetic composition. A subfield in genetics, called *behavior genetics,* is of special interest to psychologists since it studies the effects of genotype on behavior. (See *Behavior genetics.*)

Gestalt psychology
A school of thought which insists that the organized whole, configuration, or totality of psychological experience be the proper object of study. Founded in Germany by Max Wertheimer in the early 1900s, Gestalt psychology's first interest was in the field of perception. Later, under Kohler's direction, studies were done in the area of learning, and, under Lewin's direction, in the area of motivation. Gestalt psychologists tend to emphasize cognitive processes in the study of learning. They stress that true understanding occurs only through the reorganization of ideas and perceptions, not through memorization or conditioning. (See also *Wertheimer, Max.*)

Group dynamics
A subfield of social psychology which studies the processes that create and maintain group life. Group dynamics has as its goal the systematic understanding of group functioning, the discovery of general laws concerning group properties, and the application of these laws to enhance group life. Generally there are two broad positions within the field of Group dynamics, the basic research wing and the applied wing.

Halo effect
The fact that people who are viewed positively on one trait tend also to be thought to have many other positive traits. Advertisers depend on this effect when they use famous personalities to endorse various products—anyone who can throw touchdown passes *must* be an expert in evaluating razor blades. Teachers must guard against the halo effect in assigning grades. A poor grade in reading, for example, should reflect the student's poor level of reading achievement, and not the teacher's unfavorable impression of the student's personality.

Hawthorne effect
A major research error which is due to response differences resulting not from the action of the independent variable, but from the flattery or attention paid to the subjects by the experimenter. Typically the potential for this error is inherent in any study using the before–after experimental design without an adequate control group. Any research, for example, where subjects are measured, then subjected to some form of training, then measured again, should be viewed with suspicion unless an appropriate control group is used—that is, an equivalent group which is measured, then *not subjected to the training,* and then measured again. Only then can the researcher be reasonably confident that the response differences are due to the pure effects of the independent variable.

Heritability

The proportion of the total variability of a given trait in a population which is due to genetic as opposed to environmental factors. Heritability is expressed as a value, running between 1.00 and zero. Thus, regarding measured intelligence, if all the variation in IQ scores in a given population was due to genetic factors, the heritability of IQ would be 1.00. If all the variability was due to environmental factors, the heritability would be zero. The concept of heritability only applies to a particular population of a single generation under one set of environmental conditions.

Iconic representation

Bruner's second stage of cognitive growth and mode of communication, the first stage being the enactive level. At the iconic level, objects become conceivable without resorting to muscular action. The child can now visualize an object or concept. The child possesses an image which no longer depends on action. The use of pictures and diagrams illustrates the iconic mode of communication.

Id

Term used by Freud to describe one component of personality, the other two being the ego and superego. Freud saw the id as the unconscious storehouse of man's basic, instinctive pleasure needs. The id seeks the immediate gratification of these pleasure urges without regard to objective reality. Freud felt that the majority of neurotic disorders result from internal conflicts involving the id, ego, and superego.

Imprinting

A special form of learning which is acquired early in life, usually during a very specific time interval, is triggered by a releasing stimulus, and is not reversible. Lorenz demonstrated this phenomenon by presenting himself as a moving stimulus to a group of newly hatched goslings. The goslings then imprinted on Lorenz himself and followed him around as though he were the mother goose. (See also *Critical periods* and *Lorenz, Konrad*.)

Inductive fallacy

An error in logic resulting from overgeneralizing on the basis of too few observations. The inductive fallacy results when one assumes that all members of a class have a certain characteristic because one member of that class has it. It would be fallacious to assume that all Mongolians are liars on the basis of having met one Mongolian who was a liar.

Insight

A suddenly realized solution to a problem, sometimes called the "Aha!" phenomenon. Introduced by Kohler, the concept of insight is used to explain the sudden solution to problems which appears to occur spontaneously. Insight results from the reorganization of ideas and perceptions, rather than from simple, trial-and-error behavior. The concept of insight is used typically by Gestalt psychologists.

Instinct theory

A now-discredited theory which attempted to explain behavior by simply describing it and then calling it "instinctive." For example, humans were seen as going to war because of an "aggressive instinct," or forming groups because of a "gregarious instinct," or even twiddling thumbs because of a "thumb-twiddling instinct." Instinct theorists committed a logical error called the "nominal fallacy." (See *Nominal fallacy*.)

Integrated day

A term sometimes used to describe the concept of the open classroom. (See *Open classroom*.)

Intelligence

Definitions of intelligence vary widely—from Wechsler's "global capacity of the individual to act purposefully, to think rationally, and to deal effectively with his environment" to E. G. Boring's positivistic definition of intelligence as simply that which an intelligence test measures. The problem with intelligence as a concept is that it cannot be directly observed. It must be inferred from behavior. Rather than *being intelligent*, one can be viewed as acting intelligently.

Intelligence as a hypothetical construct has come to mean higher-level thought processes, or intellectual abilities, as opposed to Galton's original notion of acute sensory powers. Statistical studies of intelligence utilize the concept of *measured intelligence*, which is the score received on a standardized intelligence test. (See *Intelligence quotient*.)

Intelligence quotient (IQ)

The intelligence quotient, or IQ, was originally a measure of intelligence calculated by dividing a subject's mental age by the chronological age and multiplying by 100. That is, $IQ = MA/CA \times 100$. This is called the ratio method of obtaining IQ.

More recently, IQ has been computed by the deviation method. An individual's deviation IQ is defined by his relative standing among his peers. The deviation IQ is computed on the basis of how far an individual's score deviates from the mean score obtained for the entire group of individuals of the same chronological age. This technique is based on the standard or z-score concept and assumes a normal distribution for each age group.

Introspection
A technique used for ferreting out psychology's data by having a subject look within himself or herself and then report all feelings, sensations, and images. This technique was the basic method for obtaining data in the days of Wundt, Titchener, and the Structuralist School of psychology. J. B. Watson, the founder of Behaviorism, attacked the use of introspection as being too subjective for an objective, scientific discipline like psychology. The technique is rarely used in psychology today.

Language competence
The underlying knowledge of the structure and rules of language. Language competence must be distinguished from language performance, or the overt language responses.

Law of effect
Basic law of learning set down by E. L. Thorndike. When an association between a stimulus and response is followed by a satisfying state of affairs, the association (or connection) will be strengthened. When the association is followed by an annoying state of affairs, it will be weakened. In brief, reward strengthens and punishment weakens any connection between stimuli and responses. In a later version of the law, Thorndike soft-pedaled the importance of punishment as a weakening agent. Thorndike's Law of Effect is considered by many psychologists to be the cornerstone on which Skinner built his system of operant conditioning. (See also *Thorndike, Edward L.*)

Learning
A very general term which refers to a process that results in a relatively permanent change in behavior resulting from past experience. Thus such activities as acquiring physical skills, memorizing poems, acquiring attitudes and prejudices, or even tics and mannerisms are examples of learning. Learning may be conscious or unconscious, adaptive or nonadaptive, overt or covert. Although the learning process is typically measured on the basis of a change in performance, most psychologists agree that an accompanying change occurs within the nervous system. Though there are a great many theories and explanations concerning the "whys" and interpretations of learning, there is general agreement regarding its definition.

Learning curve
A graphic presentation of learning performance, with the measure of learning being plotted on the vertical axis and the amount of practice on the horizontal axis. Though learning curves take many shapes, depending on what is being learned and under what conditions, the classical or ideal curve is negatively accelerated. That is, acceleration (improved performance) becomes less and less as the amount of practice increases. When there is no further increase in performance, the curve levels off into what is called a plateau.

Learning sets
Concept developed by Harlow and used as a modern explanation for the Gestalt-psychology term "insight." Harlow insists that what the Gestaltists had viewed as insight does not come about as a sudden reorganization of perceptions, but rather on the basis of learning how to learn, or the learning of general rules. The learning set does not occur "in a flash," but takes many trials and much experience in which to develop. The concept of learning sets is also in opposition to the straight, stimulus-response learning model, in that the learning set involves developing a learning strategy rather than the slow accumulation of stimulus-response associations. A learning set is a form of non-specific transfer.

LM (logico-mathematical) learning
Concept developed by Jean Piaget to describe a form of learning which results not from the physical environment acting on the learner but from the actions of the learner on the environment. LM, or logico-mathematical, learning is the result of an individual's continuous experience of organizing and reorganizing actions which lead to the goal of understanding. Piaget says that LM learning is internally motivated. The discovery of a new relationship is self-rewarding. (See also *P learning.*)

Longitudinal research
A type of R/R research where subjects are measured repeatedly throughout their lives in order to obtain data on possible age trends in growth and development. Terman's massive study of growth trends among intellectually gifted children is an example of this research technique. The study, begun in the early 1920s, is still in progress today and is still providing psychology with new data. Longitudinal research requires great patience on the part of the investigator, but the obtained data is considered to be more valid than that obtained via the cross-sectional approach. (See *Cross-sectional research.*)

Mainstreaming
Opposite of deviate-status placement, mainstreaming places persons who might be classified as deviant within the "mainstream" of society. Exceptional and/or retarded children are not placed in special classes, but

are kept in regular classrooms. (See also *Deviate-status placement.*)

Massed learning

Learning that occurs in massive doses, without a break, as opposed to spaced learning. Studies show that for many activities, especially motoric activities, massed learning is less efficient than spaced learning.

Milwaukee Project

Directed by Rick Heber, the Milwaukee Project was aimed at increasing the intellectual abilities of slum-raised children, born of low-IQ parents. Working with the children almost from the day of birth, Heber's staff at the Infant Education Center was able to increase the IQ's of these culturally deprived children by what appear to be significant amounts. More research is needed, however, to determine how permanent the gains might be.

Mnemonic devices

Memory aids used to increase retention powers. Mnemonic devices typically utilize one of the following learning strategies (1) visual imagery, (2) rhyming, and (3) associations with past learning. Using the word "HOMES" for recalling the names of the Great Lakes (Huron, Ontario, Michigan, Erie, and Superior) is an example of a mnemonic device based on association with past learning.

Modeling

Concept used in Bandura's social-learning theory. Learning can occur not only through response conditioning, but also through modeling, which is the imitation of the behavior of others. Learning by modeling can occur even when the imitative responses are not themselves being directly reinforced. (See also *Social-learning theory.*)

Monozygotic (MZ) twins

MZ or identical twins have identical genetic backgrounds. They result from the fertilization of a single egg which then divides. This provides for two individuals having precisely the same genetic make-up.

Moral development

The process whereby children come to adopt guiding principles of right and wrong, and achieve the ability to resist the temptations of unacceptable conduct. The view that morality develops in a series of growth-stages originated in the work of Jean Piaget, who believed the development of moral stages was similar to cognitive development. One of the leading current spokesmen for this view is Kohlberg, who sees moral development occurring in a series of stages: precon-

ventional (ages 0–9), conventional (ages 9–15), and postconventional (ages 16 and up). Like Piaget, Kohlberg describes moral development as occurring in an invariant sequence, with each stage qualitatively different from the preceding stage. (See also *Kohlberg, Lawrence.*)

Morphemes

The basic units of meaning in any language. Morphemes may be root words, prefixes, or suffixes. Morphemes consist of one or more phonemes. When a morpheme can stand alone, as in a root word, it is called a "free morpheme." Prefixes and suffixes, however, are called "bound morphemes," since they cannot stand alone and still convey meaning. (See also *Phonemes.*)

Motivation

A general psychological term used to explain behavior initiated by needs and directed toward a goal. Motives may be biogenic, stemming from tissue needs within the organism, or acquired, learned through interaction with the environment, especially the social environment. Almost all personality theorists have developed their own lists of important human motives, and great debates have occurred over which motives are of greatest importance, or which can rightfully be called universal. Among learning theorists, Bruner makes much of the principle of motivation, assuming that almost all children have a built-in "will to learn."

Nature-nurture controversy

Debate over which component, nature (heredity) or nurture (environment), is more influential in determining behavior. In psychology, the behaviorists consistently argued in behalf of nurture, and the intelligence testers favored nature. Educational psychology has long been the battleground on which this issue has been fought, since the psychologists primarily concerned with the issue were the learning theorists (largely behaviorists) and measurement practitioners.

Negative reinforcement

Any stimulus, the *removal* of which increases the rate of responding. If a rat is in a cage with an electrified floor grid and the electricity is turned off only after the rat presses a lever, the rate of the lever-pressing responses will tend to increase dramatically. Unlike punishment, which reduces response rates, negative reinforcement often increases response rates even more quickly than would positive reinforcement.

Nominal fallacy

A logical error resulting from the attempt to explain an event on the basis of a redescription of that same event. Saying that sleeping pills work because they have dormative power, or that men fight because they have aggressive instincts are examples of the nominal fallacy. The instinct theorists of the early 1900s built an entire system on the soft sands of the nominal fallacy.

Normal curve

A frequency distribution curve where scores are plotted on the horizontal axis (x) and frequency of occurrence is plotted on the vertical axis (y). The normal curve is a theoretical curve shaped like a bell, where (1) most of the scores cluster around the center, and as we move away from the center in either direction there are fewer and fewer scores; (2) the scores fall into a symmetrical shape, each half of the curve is a mirror image of the other; (3) the mean, median, and mode all fall at precisely the same point, the center; and (4) there are constant area characteristics regarding the standard deviation.

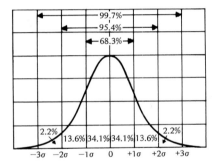

Open classroom

A structured learning environment in which students are encouraged to participate *actively* in the learning experiences of their choice. Learning stations are set up covering a variety of learning activities, and the student selects both the activity and the amount of time to be spent on a chosen activity. The learning stations are deliberately designed to be attention arousing and self-reinforcing. The open classroom is based on the individualized-learning concept, where children are not expected to study the same subject at the same time and in the same way.

Operant

A response, according to Skinner, for which the original stimulus is either unidentified or nonexistent. The consequences of operant behavior can be observed, even though the stimulus is not known. For example, if a rat presses the lever in a Skinner Box and this results in reinforcement, an increase in operant rate will

be observed despite the fact that no stimulus could be identified as initiating the original bar press. In operant conditioning, reinforcement is contingent upon the operant first being emitted. The organism must in some way "operate" on the environment in order that the reinforcement will follow. Operant responding at one time was called *instrumental* responding by some psychologists.

Operant conditioning

Form of conditioning described by B. F. Skinner in which the free operant is allowed to occur and is followed by a reinforcing stimulus which is, in turn, followed by an increased likelihood of the operant occurring again. For optimum conditioning, the reinforcing stimulus should follow the operant immediately. The rate of responding for a conditioned operant may jump dramatically over the preconditioned rate (operant level).

Operant level

The original, or preconditioned, rate of operant responding before any reinforcing stimuli have been introduced. If a rat happens to press the lever in a Skinner Box four times an hour (without being reinforced), the operant level for that response is established at four per hour. The operant level is, thus, the rate with which the free operant is typically emitted prior to conditioning.

Oral stage

First of Freud's psychosexual stages of development. During this stage libido is focused in the child's mouth. The baby lives through and loves through its mouth. This stage occurs between birth and about age eighteen months, and permanently affects the child's later feelings of independence and trust.

P (physical) learning

Form of learning described by Jean Piaget which results from the action of the physical environment on the child, rather than the actions of the child on the environment. Piaget's P learning (physical event acting on the learner) is very similar to Skinner's concept of operant conditioning.

Paired-associate learning

A method used in the study of verbal learning and memory. A subject is presented with a list of word pairs (blue–moon, red–dog, play–toy, etc.), and then tested by being asked to repeat the second word of the pair (response) each time the first word (stimulus) is introduced. This is by far the most common technique employed in the study of verbal learning, since many psychologists believe the learning of item pairs is a fundamental process in thinking and memory.

Pearson r

Statistical test introduced by Karl Pearson for showing the degree of relationship between two variables. Also called the product–moment correlation, it is used to test the hypothesis of association, that is, whether or not there is a relationship between two sets of measurements. The Pearson r can be calculated as follows:

$$r = \frac{\Sigma XY/N - (\overline{X})\,(\overline{Y})}{\sigma_x\,\sigma_y}$$

Computed correlations range from +1.00 (perfect positive correlation) through zero to −1.00 (perfect negative correlation). The further the Pearson r is from zero, whether in a positive or negative direction, the stronger the relationship. The Pearson r may be used for making better-than-chance predictions, but may not be used for isolating causal factors.

Percentile (or centile)

The percentage of cases falling at or below a given score. Thus, if an individual were to score at the 95th percentile, that individual would exceed 95 percent of all persons taking that particular test. If test scores are normally distributed, and if the standard deviation of the distribution is known, percentile scores can easily be converted from the resulting z scores.

Performance IQ

Term used by David Wechsler to describe the non-verbal component of intelligence. Wechsler believed that the Stanford–Binet test was too heavily loaded with verbal items, and thus when constructing his own test, Wechsler included a section designed to tap visual–motor abilities. The Wechsler IQ tests are scored on the basis of verbal IQ, performance IQ, and full-scale IQ. Scores in each of the three categories are computed.

Phallic stage

Third stage of personality development in Freud's theory of psychosexual development. During the phallic stage (ages three to seven years) libido is located in the child's genital area. Conflict results during this stage as the child focuses these sexual desires on the opposite-sexed parent and feels the fear of retaliation from the like-sexed parent. The conflict (Oedipal in boys and Electra in girls) is resolved at about age seven years when the child identifies with the like-sexed parent. The major crisis for the child during this stage is over the struggle for sexual identification.

Phonemes

The basic sound units of speech. Phonemes are the sounds produced by infants while babbling. The number of phonemes used in the world's languages varies from under twenty to over eighty. There are approximately forty-five phonemes in the English language. (See also *Morphemes*.)

Positive reinforcement

Any stimulus which, when added to the situation, increases the likelihood of the response recurring. A pellet of food may be a positive reinforcer to a hungry rat only if it can be observed that the rat emits the same response (pressing the lever in the Skinner Box) in order to get another pellet. In the classroom, positive reinforcement may be provided by primary reinforcers such as milk, cereal or candy, or by conditioned reinforcers such as gold stars, high grades, social approval.

Precise teaching

Teaching technique used on newly mainstreamed children. Precise teaching provides maximum structure in the learning environment and utilizes the behavior-modification approach in order to aid students in mastering a variety of educational tasks.

Premack principle

A principle of behavior modification introduced by D. Premack. Premack states that behavior that occurs at a naturally high rate of frequency may be used to reinforce behavior that occurs at a naturally low rate. The establishment of high- and low-frequency responses must be done through careful observation.

Profoundly retarded (PR)

IQ scores between 0 and 25 on standard tests. Most persons in this category are bed-ridden and require supervision.

Programmed instruction

An arrangement of instructional material in a step-by-step sequence designed to lead the student to a specified goal. The material being presented is broken down into small units called frames. There are two general approaches to programming: (1) linear programs—in which all students go through the entire program, and the frames gradually increase in difficulty; (2) branched programs—in which the student skips forward or backward in the program (the order of the frame presentation varies) as a result of the success or failure experienced in responding.

Programmed instruction can be in book form, or it can be presented through the use of a teaching machine. The concept of programmed instruction is credited to B. F. Skinner.

Psychoanalytic theory
Theory of human behavior and method of treating mental illness presented by Sigmund Freud at the turn of the century. The theory attempts to give a rational explanation for man's irrational thoughts and responses. Psychoanalytic theory states: (1) that all behavior is determined by specific motives, (2) that most human motives lie at the unconscious level and, therefore, people are unaware of the reasons for most of their own behavior, (3) that neurotic symptoms result from an individual's inner conflicts, and (4) inner conflicts are a product of childhood trauma and anxiety. The therapeutic technique is based on the therapist revealing to the patient the source of his or her anxiety, and helping the patient to thus achieve insight and emotional release. (See also *Freud, Sigmund*.)

Psycholinguistics
A branch of psychology in which the main focus is on the acquisition and function of language. There are three basic theories of language development: (1) conditioning theories, which see language as being acquired through the external reinforcement of randomly emitted verbal responses; (2) cognitive theories, which view language development as resulting from the learning of rules, strategies, or hypotheses regarding words and syntax; and (3) genetic theories, which assume that the child comes into the world genetically "prewired," or born with biological givens that direct the course of language development. (See also *Chomsky, Noam*.)

Punishment
A method for controlling behavior through the use of aversive stimulation. Punishment, though not itself causing the extinction of a conditioned response, does severely reduce the rate of responding *while the punishment is in force*. Punishment should not be confused with negative reinforcement. (See *Negative reinforcement*.)

Random sampling
A technique for obtaining research subjects in which everyone in the population has an equal chance of being selected. This helps to ensure that the sample will be representative of the population from which it was selected.

Reinforcement
Any stimulus that increases the likelihood of a response recurring. Reinforcement, as a Skinnerian concept, should not be confused with reward, feelings of pleasure, or any other concept with subjective or mentalistic overtones. Reinforcement may be used in either classical (respondent) or operant conditioning. In respondent conditioning the unconditioned stimulus serves as the reinforcement. In operant conditioning the presentation of any stimulus following the emitted response can be considered a reinforcement *if it results in a higher response rate*. (See *Positive reinforcement* and *Negative reinforcement* for distinction between these terms.)

Respondents
Name given by B. F. Skinner to that class of responses that are sometimes called reflexes. Respondents are those responses that may be automatically elicited by a specific unconditioned or unlearned stimulus. Respondents are also called unconditioned responses. (See *Unconditioned response*.)

Retroactive inhibition
A special form of negative transfer in which the learning of new material works backward to inhibit the memory of past material. An important factor in forgetting, retroactive inhibition produces a harmful effect on the retention of previous learning.

Risky shift
Concept from social psychology which suggests that persons in a group situation are less cautious and more prone to risk taking than are persons who are alone. The group situation apparently allows individuals to become less conservative and more willing to take chances regarding both attitudes and behavior.

Role
Term used by social psychologists to denote the dynamic aspect of status. Role is the behavioral repertoire associated with an individual's status—the bundle of responses available to a person as a result of his or her niche in society's prestige heirarchy. Society expects individuals of a given status to act in certain ways, and the individual feels *obliged* to act according to society's expectations. (See also *Status*).

Rosenthal effect
Concept introduced by Robert Rosenthal, who found that teachers often evaluate the performance of students, and the students then respond on the basis of a self-fulfilling prophecy. If a teacher assumes a child to be intellectually inferior, the teacher treats the child in such a way as to reinforce inferiority. The child thus begins to act in accord with the teacher's expectations.

R/R (response–response) research

A type of research which, though not allowing for cause-and-effect conclusions, does allow the researcher to make better-than-chance *predictions*. In R/R research, subjects are measured on one response dimension and these measurements are compared with response measures of another mode. Responses are compared with responses, as in comparing the S.A.T. scores with grade–point averages for a group of students. Since the experimenter does not treat the subjects differently—there is no manipulation of an independent variable—cause-and-effect conclusions may not be drawn from R/R research.

Schedules of reinforcement

According to Skinner, the arrangement of reinforcers on the basis of either time elapsed or number of responses emitted. Responses that are reinforced periodically, rather than each time they are emitted, tend to be conditioned more strongly and are thus more resistant to extinction. The major schedules of reinforcement are: (1) continuous, (2) fixed ratio, (3) fixed interval, (4) variable ratio, and (5) variable interval.

Sensorimotor stage

First stage of cognitive development, according to Piaget, in which the child learns to distinguish himself or herself from the external environment, begins to notice and follow objects in the environment, and develops the rudiments of trial-and-error learning. This stage lasts from birth to age two years, and the child operates at the level of raw, immediate stimulation as experienced through the senses. An important milestone during this stage is the development of the concept of *object permanence,* the thought that objects still exist even though they are not, at the moment, being seen. Piaget insists that mental processes are developed directly from inborn motor processes. The child's ability at birth to make certain motor responses forms the basis for the cognitive processes that come later.

Significance

A statistical term indicating that the results of the study are not simply a matter of chance. Researchers talk about significant differences and significant correlations, the assumption being that chance has been ruled out (on a probability basis) as the explanation.

Social facilitation

A concept from the field of social psychology, social facilitation is used to explain the fact that in some circumstances individuals perform more quickly in a group situation than when alone. Social facilitation is most pronounced in the case of fairly simple mechanical tasks. The more difficult and the more intellectual the task, the less the effect of social facilitation.

Social-learning theory

Theory proposed by Albert Bandura, which suggests that a large part of what a person learns occurs through imitation or modeling. Bandura's major concern is with learning that takes place in the context of a social situation where individuals learn to modify behavior as a result of how others in the group respond. Social learning *does not* require primary reinforcement.

Social psychology

The study of individual behavior in the context of the social situation. Social psychology analyzes the ways in which people affect and are affected by other people. Major topics in the field include conformity, cohesiveness, status and role, attitudes and attitude change, social perception, and group structure and leadership.

Spiral curriculum

Educational system designed to teach children the same concepts, though with increasing sophistication, throughout their entire (K through 12) schooling. The spiral curriculum assumes that cognitive growth, rather than occurring in qualitatively different stages, progresses quantitatively. That is, rather than assuming that twelve-year-olds think *differently* from six-year-olds, proponents of the spiral curriculum assume that twelve-year-olds simply have more of the same.

Spontaneous recovery

The fact that a conditioned response that has been extinguished will, after a brief length of time, tend to recur on its own. The conditioned response returns, despite having been extinguished, with no additional conditioning trials.

S/R research

Research conducted via the experimental method, where an independent variable is manipulated (stimulus) in order to bring about a change in the dependent variable (response). Using this method the researcher is allowed to make cause-and-effect inferences. S/R research requires careful controls in order to establish the pure effects of the independent variable. Equivalent groups of subjects are formed, then exposed to different stimulus conditions, and then measured to see if differences can be observed.

Status

Term used in social psychology to define an individual's niche in society's prestige hierarchy, or the individual's standing in a social system. The behavior expected of an individual of a given status is called his or her role. (See also *Role*.)

Stimulus–response theory

A theory that stresses the importance of the buildup of stimulus–response *associations* in defining learning. Most behaviorists adhere to stimulus–response learning theories, the major exception being E. C. Tolman. The leading stimulus–response theorists are Thorndike, Pavlov, Watson, Guthrie, Hull, and Skinner. Stimulus–response theorists stress the importance of environment in the heredity–environment debate. Most theories of learning during the first half of the 20th century, especially in the United States, were stimulus–response theories. The cognitive–Gestalt position, however, was *not* based on a stimulus–response theory.

Stimulus variety

Variation, at all sensory modes, of stimulus inputs. Seen by many early-experience theorists as the *crucial ingredient* in intellectual development. J. McV. Hunt states that the more the child hears, sees, and touches, the more the child will want to hear, see, and touch, and the more intellectual growth will occur.

Structure

Part of Bruner's theory of instruction, which states that any given subject area can be organized in an optimal fashion (structured), so that it can be transmitted to and understood by almost any student. Bruner feels that if a subject area is properly structured, then "any idea or problem or body of knowledge can be presented in a form simple enough so that any particular learner can understand it in a recognizable form."

Superego

Third of the structural personality components to emerge in the developing child, according to Freudian theory, the first two being the id and the ego. The superego is that part of personality concerned with moral standards and is the source of feelings of guilt. The superego is internalized at an early age, during the anal stage of psychosexual development, and reflects the value system of the society as perceived and transmitted by the parents. Individuals experience guilt and anxiety as a result of internal conflicts between the moral demands of the superego and the pleasure urges of the id.

Symbolic representation

Third stage of cognitive development and method of communication introduced by Jerome Bruner, the first two being the enactive and iconic levels. At the symbolic level the child is able to translate experience into language. Words can then be used for communication and for representing ideas. Symbolic representation allows children to make logical connections between ideas and to think more compactly.

t Ratio

Statistical test used to establish whether or not a significant (nonchance) difference exists between two sample means. It is the ratio of the difference between two sample means to an estimate of the standard deviation of the distribution of differences. That is, the t ratio is equal to $\bar{x}_1 - \bar{x}_2$, divided by the standard error of difference.

Teaching machine

A device used to present an instructional program one step (or frame) at a time. The student either writes in answers, or presses a button corresponding to the correct alternative. Advantages of the teaching machine are: (1) the student can proceed at his or her own pace, (2) the student receives immediate feedback, (3) for many students the machines are intrinsically motivating. (See also *Programmed instruction*.)

Terminal behavior

Concept used by experts in the field of behavior modification. Terminal behavior defines the educational goals for the class as a whole or for individual students, and defines these goals in objective, behavioral terms. Rather than using what they consider to be vaguely stated goals, like "understanding," the behaviorists insist that the goals describe specific behaviors that will result when the objective is attained. For example, students can be said to have learned how to multiply when they can recite the multiplication table with no errors.

Token system

A system of reinforcement used by proponents of behavior modification, in which tokens of varying point values are awarded to students for fulfilling specific behavioral objectives. The tokens (conditioned reinforcers) may be different colored pieces of cardboard or poker chips which the student may earn in order to achieve some desired prize or privilege. The system is said to have two main advantages: (1) it maintains a high daily rate of desirable responses, and (2) it teaches delayed gratification.

Trainable mentally retarded (TMR)

IQ scores range from 25 to 50 on standard tests. Considered not capable of profiting from normal classroom exposure. Persons so classified can often learn self-care and safety rules and are capable of some degree of social adjustment. Employment is usually in sheltered workshops.

Transfer

Transfer occurs when the learning of one activity influences the learning of a second ability. If the learning of A facilitates the learning of B, it is called positive transfer. If the learning of A inhibits the learning of B, it is called negative transfer.

Transformational grammar

The rules by which people change their own ideas into spoken language, and by which they come to understand the meaning of other people's spoken or written communication.

Unconditional positive regard

Concept used by Carl Rogers in dealing both with clients in therapy and with students in the classroom. Unconditional positive regard means accepting persons for what they are, without passing judgment, and without exacting any condition for full acceptance. According to Rogers this is one of the three necessary and sufficient conditions for the promotion of learning, the other two being empathy and congruence.

Unconditioned response

A reflex response, or in Skinnerian terms, a respondent. Any response that can be automatically elicited by the presentation of a certain stimulus, without any training or learning. The term is used in classical conditioning, and in Pavlov's original experiment the unconditioned response was salivation to the stimulus of meat powder being placed in the dog's mouth.

Unconditioned stimulus

Any stimulus that will automatically elicit a given response, without any training or learning. The term is used in classical conditioning, and in the case of Pavlov's own experiment, the unconditioned stimulus was meat powder placed in the dog's mouth.

Underachiever

Student whose academic achievement falls short of what his or her measured intelligence (IQ) would predict. Implicit in the concept of underachievement is the assumption that personality and emotional variables play a crucial role in academic success.

Variability measures

Measures that give information regarding individual differences, or how persons vary in their measured scores. The three most-important measures of variability are the range, the standard deviation, and the variance (which is the standard deviation squared).

Variable

Anything that varies *and can be measured.* In S/R research the two most-important variables to be identified are the independent variable and the dependent variable. The independent variable is a stimulus, is actively manipulated by the experimenter, and is the causal half of the cause-and-effect relationship. The dependent variable is a measure of the subject's response and is the effect half of the cause-and-effect relationship.

Visual cliff

The perceived drop-off at the edge of any steep place. Research has shown that the newborn of many species, including human babies, will avoid the "deep" side of a specially built platform. This seems to show that depth perception is innate rather than the result of learning.

WAIS

Wechsler Adult Intelligence Scale—individual IQ test developed by David Wechsler (along with the WISC—Wechsler Intelligence Scale for Children and the WPPSI—Wechsler Preschool and Primary Scale of Intelligence). All the Wechsler tests are administered by a trained examiner to one person at a time. All the tests yield three scores, a verbal IQ, a performance IQ, and a full-scale IQ. Wechsler believed that many of the intelligence tests of the day were too heavily laden with verbal items, and, to correct for that, the Wechsler tests all include a Performance section that tests an individual's visual–motor abilities. Wechsler uses the *deviation IQ* method of scoring his tests. In the hands of a skilled examiner the WAIS can be used as a projective test for ferreting out a subject's personality traits. (See also *Intelligence quotient.*)

z score (standard score)

The translation of a raw score into units of standard deviation. The z score specifies how far above or below the mean a given score is in the standard deviation units. Any score above the mean will convert into a positive z score, while scores below the mean will convert as negative z scores. The z score is also referred to as a *standard score.*

$$z = \frac{X - \bar{X}}{S.D.}$$

Photo credits

Index